EXPLORING ALTERITY IN A GLOBALIZED WORLD

This volume develops a unique framework to understand India through indigenous and European perspectives and examines how it copes with the larger challenges of a globalized world. Through a discussion of religious and philosophical traditions, cultural developments as well as contemporary theatre, films and media, it explores the manner in which India negotiates the trials of globalization. It also focuses upon India's school and education system, its limitations and successes and how it prepares to achieve social inclusion. The work further shows how contemporary societies in both India and Europe deal with cultural diversity and engage with the tensions between tendencies towards homogenization and diversity.

This eclectic collection on what it is to be a part of global network will be of interest to scholars and researchers of South Asian studies, philosophy, sociology, culture studies and religion.

Christoph Wulf is Professor of Anthropology and Education and a member of the Interdisciplinary Centre for Historical Anthropology and the Graduate School 'InterArts' at Freie Universität Berlin. Widely published, his books have been translated in more than 15 languages. He is Vice-President of the German Commission for UNESCO. His major research areas include historical and cultural anthropology, educational anthropology, rituals, gestures, emotions, intercultural communication, mimesis and aesthetics.

EXPLORING ALTERITY IN A GLOBALIZED WORLD

Edited by Christoph Wulf

In collaboration with Iris Clemens,
Padma Sarangapani and Sundar Sarukkai

LONDON AND NEW YORK

First published 2016
by Routledge
2 Park Square, Milton Park, Abingdon, Oxon OX14 4RN

and by Routledge
711 Third Avenue, New York, NY 10017

First issued in paperback 2017

Routledge is an imprint of the Taylor & Francis Group, an informa business

© 2016 Christoph Wulf

The right of Christoph Wulf to be identified as the author of the editorial material, and of the authors for their individual chapters, has been asserted in accordance with sections 77 and 78 of the Copyright, Designs and Patents Act 1988.

All rights reserved. No part of this book may be reprinted or reproduced or utilised in any form or by any electronic, mechanical, or other means, now known or hereafter invented, including photocopying and recording, or in any information storage or retrieval system, without permission in writing from the publishers.

Trademark notice: Product or corporate names may be trademarks or registered trademarks, and are used only for identification and explanation without intent to infringe.

British Library Cataloguing-in-Publication Data
A catalogue record for this book is available from the British Library

Library of Congress Cataloging-in-Publication Data
A catalog record has been requested for this book.

ISBN 13: 978-1-138-48835-9 (pbk)
ISBN 13: 978-1-138-99898-8 (hbk)

Typeset in Goudy
by Apex CoVantage, LLC

CONTENTS

List of figures ix
List of contributors xii
Preface xvii

Introduction: exploring alterity in a globalized world 1
CHRISTOPH WULF

PART I
Religion, philosophy and culture 35

1 Kali's daughters: the tantric conception of the divine feminine as an emancipatory role model for Hindu women 37
ARCHITA VAJPAYEE AND MATTHIAS SEMMLER

2 The sacred cow and the ideal of *ahiṃsā* 59
KRISTINA SCHMITZ-VALKENBERG

3 Re-reading Gandhi for a reformed knowing: where to put that *Little Inner Voice?* 79
BHAKTI PATIL

4 Education for a better world? Gandhi's ideas on education and their relevance in modern India 94
THERESA VOLLMER

CONTENTS

5 Asceticism in ancient and modern India   115
   FRANZISKA ROGGENBUCK

6 Cultivating simplicity as a way of life: insights from a
   study about everyday lives of Tibetan-Buddhist child
   monks in Ladakh   133
   TANU BISWAS

7 The legends of St. Thomas and the extensions of the
   magic/miracle dichotomy in the stories about
   Kadamattath Kattanar   147
   SUSAN VISVANATHAN

8 In-between places: the natural zoo as a cultural place   170
   MEERA BAINDUR

PART II
Dance, theatre and media   185

9 Cutting into history: the 'Hindu dancer' Nyota
   Inyoka's photomontages   187
   TESSA JAHN

10 The commune-ist air: living the everyday in times
   of struggle – the case of the Indian People's
   Theatre Association's Central Squad   197
   SHARMISTHA SAHA

11 Finding a path: notes on political forms between
   locality and globality in India's contemporary 'art world'   216
   SARAH RALFS

12 The message of their pictures: an essay on photographs
   taken by Indian auto-rickshaw drivers   226
   JULIA THIBAUT

13 Transmitting culture within linguistic alterity   251
   NIKA DARYAN

PART III
Education, self-education and human development   261

14   In line: a photo essay on entering a school in Bangalore   263
CHRISTOS VARVANTAKIS

15   Going to school in India: an ethnographical research
at two schools in Bangalore   277
URS KÜBLER

16   'The treasure of life lies in hard work': insights into
the discursive practices of becoming educated and
developed in schools in South India   300
MARTIN BITTNER

17   The impact of school environment on future
aspirations of high school students in India   317
BEATRICE LANGE

18   Sugarcane migration and the impact on education:
a perspective on seasonal migration in Maharashtra
and the linkage to children's education   330
SANDY HALLMANN

19   Educational experiences of students with disabilities
in higher education: a case study of a German university   347
NAGESWARA RAO AMBATI

20   A fresh perspective on indigenous tools
for inclusive education   368
MALLIKA SWAMINATHAN

21   Perception and inference   379
FRIEDERIKE SCHMIDT

22   When the solution becomes part of the problem:
the role of education in social conflicts – observations
in the Indian context   389
IRIS CLEMENS

PART IV
Homogenization versus diversity   401

23 Socialisation in the context of globalisation: how adolescents in India deal with global processes   403
BENJAMIN WAGENER

24 Power to the people: a long road to conscientization   418
MARIA SCHNEIDER

25 The new and young Indian middleclass: life between traditions and Western values   434
CHRISTIANE MÜLLER

26 Risk-taking and entrepreneurship in India: implications of social and cultural norms for poverty alleviation policies   441
ALEXANDER J. WULF

27 Thinking about climate change: young people from Ladakh responding to global warming – an explorative study   454
SOFIA GETZIN

28 Health promotion and diversity: theoretical reflections and personal experiences in everyday India   468
MARKUS WIENCKE

29 Absence of a presence: text, pedagogy and social anthropology in Northeast India   480
WILLIAM N. SINGH

30 Dispositions as properties: irrelevance of functional characterization   491
S. K. ARUN MURTHI

Index   507

FIGURES

6.1	Distribution of daily activities	141
12.1	Family made of stone, Jayaprakash Narayan Park, Bangalore, Mathikere	228
12.2	Man with newspaper and radio, Hanging Gardens, Mumbai	229
12.3	Hedge animals, Botanical Gardens Lal Bagh, Bangalore (preferred version)	230
12.4	Hedge animals, Botanical Gardens Lal Bagh, Bangalore (not preferred version)	231
12.5	Approximate composition of Figure 12.3	232
12.6	Approximate composition of Figure 12.4	233
12.7	Vaishno Devi Temple, Ahmedabad (preferred version)	234
12.8	Vaishno Devi Temple, Ahmedabad (not preferred version)	234
12.9	Approximate composition of Figure 12.7	235
12.10	Approximate composition of Figure 12.8	236
12.11	Garden, Malabar Hill, Mumbai (preferred version)	237
12.12	Approximate composition of Figure 12.11	237
12.13	Garden, Malabar Hill, Mumbai (not preferred version)	238
12.14	Approximate composition of Figure 12.13	238
12.15	Botanical Gardens Lal Bagh, Bangalore	241
12.16	Glass-house, Botanical Gardens Lal Bagh, Bangalore	242
12.17	Lake, Botanical Gardens Lal Bagh, Bangalore	242
12.18	Cows made of stone, Jayaprakash Narayan Park, Bangalore, Mathikere	243
12.19	Children made of stone, Jayaprakash Narayan Park, Bangalore, Mathikere	243
12.20	Children's playground, Garden, Malabar Hill, Mumbai	244
12.21	Garden, Malabar Hill, Mumbai	244

FIGURES

12.22	Beach, Mumbai	245
12.23	Hanging Gardens, Mumbai	245
12.24	Hanging Gardens, Mumbai	246
12.25	The car of a participant, street in front of the beach, Mumbai	246
12.26	Dinosaur made of stone, Science City, Ahmedabad, Gujarat	247
12.27	Space Shuttle, Science City, Ahmedabad, Gujarat	247
12.28	Traffic island on the way to Vaishno Devi Temple, Ahmedabad	248
12.29	Bir Hindu Temple, Delhi	248
12.30	Red Fort, New Delhi	249
12.31	Akshardham Temple, Delhi	249
13.1	Advertising on the occasion of the Hindu deity Krishna's Birthday – Varanasi, August 2010	253
13.2	Canvassing and movie advertisement – Mumbai, November 2010	255
13.3	Children and the Samarthak in the schoolyard of the primary public school in Phagi	258
14.1	Pupils play during break	264
14.2	Arriving at school	266
14.3	Entering the school in a line	267
14.4	Entering the school in a line	267
14.5	Latecomers at the inner gate of the schoolyard	268
14.6	A pair of leaders writing down the (noteworthy) news of the day	269
14.7	Pupil waiting for the morning prayers to begin	270
14.8	Details of the school building	270
14.9	Details of the school building	271
14.10	Details of the school building	271
14.11	Details of the school building	272
14.12	Morning prayers	273
14.13	Morning prayers	273
14.14	Morning prayers	274
14.15	Morning prayers	274
14.16	Leaving the schoolyard for the classroom	275
16.1	Morning prayers at the schoolyard	310
20.1	Children present at Seemantonnayana are helping to pound the herbs for the health of the pregnant lady	372

FIGURES

20.2	Various members of the society participating in celebrating motherhood, of which adorning the mother-to-be with glass bangles is one	372
20.3	Meal at the end of the prenatal celebration	373
24.1	Longwe based on Sharma (2000: 22)	423
28.1	Shared experience of sense	470

(All figures and images are courtesy of the authors of the respective chapters)

CONTRIBUTORS

Meera Baindur is Assistant Professor at the Manipal Centre for Philosophy and Humanities, Manipal University, India. Her research interests cover nature, ecological ethics and conservation in environmental humanities. She is currently working on place studies and Indian philosophical thought.

Tanu Biswas is a doctoral candidate at the University of Bayreuth, Germany. She took a degree in philosophy at the University of Pune and a degree in childhood studies from the Norwegian University of Science and Technology. Her project is to explore the scope of doing philosophy with children for the development of a world society.

Martin Bittner obtained his doctorate at Freie Universität; he is researcher at the Research Library for the History of Education at the German Institute for International Educational Research (DIPF), Berlin, Germany. His main focus of theory and research are ethnography, research on school pedagogic and teachings, progressive education, reconstructive methods as well as questions concerning the interrelation between practice and discourse.

Iris Clemens is Professor for Educational Science at the University of Bayreuth, Germany. She works mainly on globalisation, urbanisation and the world society. She has been researching for many years in the areas of systems theory, network theory, cultural theoretical perspectives on educational science and issues related to India.

Nika Daryan is Lecturer at the Department of Anthropology and Education, Faculty of Education and Psychology at Freie Universität Berlin, and Research Assistant at the Institute for Educational Science, University of Lüneburg. Her research focuses on historical and educational anthropology, theories of imagination and mediology.

CONTRIBUTORS

Sofia Getzin is a doctoral candidate at Leuphana Universität Lüneburg and previously studied educational sciences at Freie Universität Berlin. She works in the field of sustainability transitions, international attitudes towards sustainability and education for sustainable development.

Sandy Hallmann has a master's degree in Educational Sciences from Freie Universität Berlin. Her key areas of interest are education for sustainable development, landscapes of education and learning organisations. She is also a consultant in the field of renewable energies.

Tessa Jahn is a doctoral candidate at Freie Universität Berlin. She studies dance history of the twentieth century, exoticism in dance and the relationship between visual culture(s) and dance.

Urs Kübler has a master's degree in the course Education, Culture and Forms of Knowledge from the Freie Universität Berlin. His focus areas are pedagogical anthropology, corporeality of social interaction and theatre education.

Beatrice Lange is a master's student at the Department of Education and Psychology at Freie Universität Berlin. She focuses on institutionalised education and on the area of research and development.

Christiane Müller studied Science of Education and European Ethnology at the Humboldt Universität zu Berlin. Her Master's degree is in Education, Culture and Forms of Knowledge at Freie Universität Berlin. She is also a freelancer in non-formal, political education.

S. K. Arun Murthi is Assistant Professor at Indian Institute for Science Education and Research and is an alumnus of the National Institute of Advanced Studies, Bangalore. His areas of research include philosophy of science and Indian philosophy in the analytic perspective.

Bhakti Patil is a doctoral candidate at Jawaharlal Nehru University. Her doctoral research focuses on the categories of knowledge and selfhood in Gandhian thought and the limits and possibilities of their epistemic convictions.

Sarah Ralfs is a doctoral student at the International Graduate School 'Interart' of Freie Universität Berlin. Her research interests cover the works of German artist Christoph Schlingensief, and focuses on contemporary aesthetics in theatre and theories of contemporary art.

CONTRIBUTORS

Nageswara Rao Ambati is Assistant Professor of Sociology at Gujarat National Law University, Gujarat, India. His research interests are disability studies, education and social entrepreneurship.

Franziska Roggenbuck is a graduate in Educational and Social Sciences from Humboldt Universität zu Berlin and has a Master's degree in Educational Science from Freie Universität Berlin. Her focus of work is in philosophy of education, education in the family and in the context of theatre.

Sharmistha Saha has obtained her doctorate at the Internationales Graduiertenkolleg InterArt at Freie Universität Berlin. Her research interests are performance theory, aesthetics and politics, theatre, cinema, colonial India, critical theory and political philosophy.

Padma Sarangapani is Associate Professor and Head, Centre for Health Research and Development (CHRD), Institute for Social and Economic Change (ISEC), Bangalore, an All-India Institute of Interdisciplinary Research and Training in Social Sciences. She holds a BSc and MSc in Physics and a PhD in Education from the University of Delhi. Her areas of specialisation are in quality and education, teachers, teaching and teacher education, curriculum studies, indigenous knowledge and knowledge transmission in non-school settings, elementary education.

Sundar Sarukkai is Professor and Director of the Manipal Centre for Philosophy and Humanities, Manipal University, India. He is the author of *Translating the World: Science and Language* (2002); *Philosophy of Symmetry* (2004); *Indian Philosophy and Philosophy of Science* (2005); *What is Science?* (2012), and *The Cracked Mirror: An Indian Debate on Experience and Theory* (2012, with Gopal Guru). He is an Editorial Advisory Board member of the *Leonardo Book Series* and the Series Editor for *Science and Technology Studies* (Routledge).

Friederike Schmidt is Lecturer at the University of Bielefeld. She works on theories and concepts of (pedagogical) perception; historical-pedagogical anthropology; diversity; and qualitative social research.

Kristina Schmitz-Valkenberg is a student of the master's programme Education at Freie Universität Berlin. She studies intercultural education, gender studies and education for women in India.

Maria Schneider is a graduate from Erfurt Universität in self-determination and intellectual disability. She has worked at Red Cross Nordic United

World College and has a master's degree in educational sciences from Freie Universität Berlin.

Matthias Semmler is a doctoral candidate in the Department of Science of Religion at Freie Universität Berlin. His research interests are in the area of esotericism, occultism, New Religious Movements and the interactions between Indian spirituality and the Theosophy of H. P. Blavatsky, with a focus on the transformations of the *philosophia perennis* narrative in nineteenth-century occultism.

William N. Singh has a doctorate and teaches Sociology at Pachhunga University College, Mizoram. He researches on India's northeast in various fields: civil society, church, tribes and ethnic minorities. He is currently writing a biography on Laldenga.

Mallika Swaminathan has obtained her doctorate at Freie Universität Berlin. She has worked with children with learning and developmental disabilities for over 25 years. She studied History of Fine Arts, Public Administration, Education and Psychology and is currently a practising psychotherapist in Reykjavik.

Julia Thibaut has a master's degree in comparative education from Freie Universität Berlin and specialises in childhood development, culture and forms of knowledge. Her master's thesis was on the construction of meaning in photography.

Archita Vajpayee is an Erasmus Mundus scholarship holder and a doctoral candidate at Freie Universität Berlin. Her research interests lie in the area of social anthropology of education. In her PhD dissertation she explores the differential impact of mimetic learning on the transformation of identities by studying the rituals of Indian classroom.

Christos Varvantakis is an anthropologist, studying forms of cultural and transcultural visual communication. He obtained his doctorate at Freie Universität Berlin and is currently working as a Coordinator for the DIGITMED Project (Marie-Curie IRSES).

Susan Visvanathan is Professor of Sociology and the author of *The Christians of Kerala* (1993) and *The Children of Nature: The Life and Legacy of Ramana Maharshi* (2010) among her many other works.

Theresa Vollmer is a student of the master's programme in Education at Freie Universität Berlin. She studies moral education, learning in museums and education in modern India.

CONTRIBUTORS

Benjamin Wagener is a master's student at Freie Universität Berlin. He studies educational science with a special focus on comparative educational research and qualitative methods in social research.

Markus Wiencke is a psychologist and anthropologist and has a doctoral degree from Freie Universität Berlin. He has been conducting research concerning health at work at the Innovation Incubator/Leuphana University Lüneburg with his qualification in systemic therapy and consulting. He previously worked as therapeutic head of ward at a psychiatric and psychotherapeutic clinic and as organisational consultant. He has widely conducted fieldwork in Germany, Brazil, Chile, India and Tanzania.

Alexander J. Wulf works as professor at the SRH University of Applied Sciences, Berlin and has a doctorate from the Bucerius Law School. He studied business administration, economics and law at the WHU, the Bucerius Law School and the London School of Economics.

Christoph Wulf is Professor of Anthropology and Education and a member of the Interdisciplinary Centre for Historical Anthropology and the Graduate School 'InterArts' at Freie Universität Berlin. Widely published, his books have been translated in more than 15 languages. He is Vice-President of the German Commission for UNESCO. His major research areas include historical and cultural anthropology, educational anthropology, rituals, gestures, emotions, intercultural communication, mimesis and aesthetics.

PREFACE

This book is the result of several years of cooperation between Indian and German colleagues of different institutions. It involved about 40 graduate and doctoral students from India and Germany. The project was supported by the German Academic Exchange Service (DAAD). After a meeting between Prof. Sundar Sarukkai (philosophy) and Prof. Christoph Wulf (anthropology) in Bangalore 2008, initiated and arranged by Dr. Petra Vogler and Prof. Suresh Babu, the project started on the basis of a proposal to the DAAD in 2009. Ten postgraduate students from Freie Universität Berlin (FUB) and the National Institute of Advanced Studies (NISA) in Bangalore took part in the exchange. Partners of cooperation were Sundar Sarukkai and Christoph Wulf, supported by Iris Clemens. Accompanied by Sundar Sarukkai in 2010 and 2011, the exchange was organized by Prof. Padma Sarangapani, sociology of education, Tata Institute of Social Sciences in Mumbai, Christoph Wulf and Iris Clemens, Freie Universität Berlin. During these exchanges, the German students participated in a summer school, organized by Sundar Sarukkai in Manipal. Here they got important insights into Indian philosophy and culture. In 2012, two additional institutions took part in the project: Delhi University (DU) and Jawaharlal Nehru University (JNU). In these institutions, Prof. Anita Rampal, faculty of education (DU), and Prof. Susan Visvanathan together with Prof. Surindar S. Jodhka, both of the Centre for the Study of Social Systems, co-organized the exchange.

I would like to express my gratitude to these colleagues and to the DAAD for their support in realising this innovative project of exchange and cooperation. I also would like to thank my secretary, Gabriele Di Vincenzo, and the administers in the DAAD, Miriam Condé, Susanne Assmann, Anke Siemens, and Heike Martin, for their continuous support.

I also would like to express my gratitude to Dr. Michael Sonntag, who took care of the time-consuming editing process of this book.

The project was supported by the German Academic Exchange Service (DAAD) with funds of the Federal Ministry of Education and Research.

Christoph Wulf
Berlin, January 2015

INTRODUCTION
Exploring alterity in a globalized world

Christoph Wulf

'Exploring Alterity in a Globalized World' highlights one of the most important dimensions of societal development today. Globalization has led to an intensification of our encounters and confrontation with alterity which is constitutive of our relationship to the world. This applies to many areas of societal and cultural life, including politics, economics, culture and childrearing and education. Today these areas are more than ever determined by relations with other societies and cultures. The quality of life in our globalized world depends on the success of these relations.

First, we must investigate the dynamics of globalization. To start with, the focus is on the relationship between culture and interculturality. This is followed by an analysis of the relationship between the 'one-world mentality' that defines globalization and cultural diversity, and also of that between culture and cultural diversity. This relationship is strongly influenced by the acceleration of time and the shrinking of space. The focus then shifts to the dynamics of alterity and the association between alterity and heterological thinking and the roles played by differentiation, transgression and hybridity.

Second, it is evident how important these conditions are for the maintenance of peace and the sustainability of human development. We cannot achieve either peace or sustainability of human development if we fail to handle alterity successfully. This is clearly evidenced by the Sustainable Development Goals (SDGs) defined by the UN for the world community in the next few decades. If we are to handle alterity, peace and sustainable development successfully we need to take decisive measures in many domains of society. The fields of education, learning and human development are particularly important. A few structural elements are of central significance. The importance of multimodality for the organization of learning must be grasped and taken into consideration. The relevance of mimetic learning with its basis in creative imitation must be recognized, and in particular its relevance for the development of practical knowledge. For creative learning and development processes we also need to add the performative dimension of learning, inquiry learning and the ritualization of learning.

The third part of this introduction is devoted to the fascinating reports of young Indians about their experiences in Germany and of young Germans about their experiences in India.

Encounters with foreignness take place and help to better understand the familiar. Young academics from Germany do research in India and young Indian academics do research in Germany or in India, incorporating the new ideas they have gleaned during their time in Germany. In these encounters, attention revolves around the gaze of the foreigner, which 'defamiliarizes' familiar things and makes them appear in a new light. In this process, the young researchers are fascinated, disconcerted and skeptical in turn. Spontaneous ideas and experiences and explorative thinking and research create new cultural and social phenomena. In every encounter with the alien, different experiences overlap with each other. Which India and which Germany is it that we are experiencing? How do the young academics experience the many forms of the alien and how do they try to understand and investigate them? In this process, they adjust the ideas and concepts, methods and instruments they have learned at home to the new context in which they find themselves. Surprising images, ideas and constructs develop which expand their horizons. Investigative encounters with foreign cultures alter their horizons and perspectives and their experiences of themselves and others.

In this book, we pursue three aims. To start with, we want to develop and describe the understandings we have gained about India, Germany and Europe from research we have done ourselves. First, this includes findings not only about religious and philosophical traditions and cultural developments, but also about contemporary theatre, films and media. Here many of the studies apply ethnographic methods to produce a methodologically well based knowledge of alterity. Second, we focus on describing and investigating the Indian school and education system. Finally, the book concludes with empirical studies on how India and Germany deal with the challenges of globalization. Young academics from Germany and India gain a deeper understanding of foreign phenomena and arrive at some striking insights. In these explorations, many of them reveal a surprising creativity in dealing with cultural diversity and alterity. They cope with the challenges of globalization autonomously and competently. In so doing, they are confronted with the tensions between the tendencies towards homogenization and diversity and their effects on the current societal and cultural situations in India and Germany.

INTRODUCTION

Some basic information about India and Germany

While Germany with its roughly 80 million inhabitants lies in the heart of the European Union with almost 500 million people, India, with its population of roughly 1.3 thousand millions, is a continent with many faces. Whereas India is characterized by an overwhelming diversity, Germany is more homogenous. Unlike Germany, whose contemporary culture has developed against the background of Greek, Roman and Christian influences, the culture of India has been enduringly marked by the Vedic period (roughly 1500–500 BC) and the centuries-long Mogul period. To be added to this are the influences of British colonialism and the independence movements, with the partition of the British colony into Hindu India and Islamic Pakistan.

In the densely populated continent of India, the average age is 25 years and the average life expectancy 65 years, both figures being substantially lower than those for Germany. Unlike Germany, India is a country whose population includes many different peoples, 72 per cent of whom are Indo-Aryans and 25 per cent Dravidians, most of whom live in Southern India. In addition, there are 600 indigenous tribes. Whereas in Germany the majority religion is monotheistic Christianity and there are increasing numbers of Muslims and persons with no religious affiliation, in India 80 per cent of the population are polytheistic Hindus, 13.5 per cent monotheistic Muslims and 2.5 per cent Christians. It is only possible to understand India if one is willing to get to grips with its multifarious religions and the caste system that is associated with Hinduism.

While Germany is one of the richest countries in the world, in India over 40 per cent of the population live on less than one dollar a day. Hunger, malnutrition, child labour, debt bondage, unemployment, the disadvantages to which many women are subject and numerous social conflicts are the result. Like Germany, India is a democracy with a sophisticated legal system. Although the right to education and compulsory schooling for all are provided for in the constitution, in 2011 the national average literacy rate was only 74 per cent. For wealthy Indians, the health system is privately organized, while for the great majority of the population, particularly in rural areas, it is organized mainly by the state. Although there is also a similar dichotomy in Germany, the gap between the two systems is not as wide as that in India. In many regions of the country, the conditions are unhygienic and thus many people's lives are burdened by pandemic diseases.

In contrast to the social market economy which is still characteristic of Germany, India has a controlled economy, which has been increasingly deregulated and privatized since the early nineties and is now growing fast.

In 2005, the gross national product was approx. 760 thousand million US dollars, however, incomes were very unevenly distributed and thus 700 US dollars per individual is merely the arithmetic mean of the annual income. India is thus among those developing countries with the lowest per capita incomes. Despite its large population, India accounted for only 2 per cent of the production of the world economy. Despite the fact that its economy is constantly growing, much of India's infrastructure is outdated and it is burdened by widespread corruption, both of which are substantial obstacles to development. In contrast, Germany has a small population, but is the fourth largest economy in the world. Among the motors that drive its social affluence are machine engineering and the chemical industry. In India it is mainly the service sector (software and IT services) in which the country plays a leading role internationally.

Indian culture is one of the oldest and most fascinating in the world. This is true of the large number of different religions, languages and literatures and the broad diversity in architecture, music, painting and dance. Festivals, films, mealtime rituals and forms of meditation are also part of India's wealth, which can only be compared with the widely varying cultures and disparities of European culture as a whole.

Dynamics of globalization

In order to be able to arrive at a commensurate assessment of the following studies it is also necessary to delineate some of the central aspects of globalization (Wulf and Merkel 2002; Wulf 2006, 2013). These include: the relationship between a national culture and a world culture that transcends it, the acceleration of time and the shrinking of space and distances, the new demands on our handling of alterity and the evolution of mixed cultural forms.

India and Germany are part of the extensive globalization dynamics. The social transformation that goes along with this is a multidimensional process that has economic, political, social and cultural effects and alters the relationships between local, regional, national and global elements. In this process, there are commonalities but also substantial differences between the two countries. In this situation, there is talk of a synchronicity of the asynchronous. It is manifested in many points in the relationship between India and Germany and also within India itself. Here we find, for example, IT domains that are among the world leaders. At the same time we find numerous tribes whose members are dependent on financial support. Destitution exists alongside affluence and wealth. Similar but overall less pronounced differences are also evident between the wealthy and the precariat.

INTRODUCTION

National culture and interculturality

One of the major tasks of societal development in India consists in developing a national consciousness that contributes towards keeping a check on the heterogeneity in the country. In Germany the situation is different. Since the Second World War and its nationalist excesses, the task has been to develop a national culture within the framework of a European culture that is shared with other countries. The co-operative relationship between Germany and France is an illustration of the fact that today in both countries the guiding principle is one of identification with a common European culture over and above the identification with one's own culture. Although national cultures are losing significance, dominant cultures are still mainly national ones and as such tied to a territory, a language, common traditions and memories, symbols and rituals. In institutions such as schools, there is usually only awareness of other cultures if they are linked to the development of one's own national culture. Here, other cultures serve as a backdrop against which the uniqueness of a person's own culture and nation stands out in relief. As the regions within the European Union have gained in importance, more attention has gradually been turned to supranational elements in teaching in schools. This applies equally to the teaching of languages, knowledge about regional cultures and collective memories. The focus on national culture has been further diminished by the need, prompted by globalization, to include new content from other regions of the world. Thus, for example, today in Europe schools can no longer afford not to take cognizance of Indian and Chinese history and of how these countries see themselves.

One-world mentality versus cultural diversity

Today, globalization can no longer be understood as a process involving the creation of a one-world mentality on the basis of the European-American model of globalization. Rather, globalization must be understood as a process in which two global developmental tendencies that define the present are advancing reciprocally in a manner that is not without conflict. One tendency is towards universal standardization of the world; the other tendency is towards provision of room for cultural diversity in the process. Both tendencies also create new forms of globalization. In order to comprehend the complexity of these processes, I will first outline the central structural characteristics of the first tendency, i.e. the standardizing influence of globalization. After that, I will present in detail several central characteristics of cultural diversity that cause differences in globalization in the various regions of the world. This becomes clear in the differences between the Chinese and Indian forms of globalization. No matter how these processes occur in particular, they lead to people from different cultures communicating and interacting with each other intensively. As a result, they must learn to handle cultural diversity with caution and in a productive manner.

Let us now envision several characteristics of a globalization process that is oriented towards standardization, characteristics that have a profound influence on the lifestyles and self-concepts of many people. Globalization is now all-pervasive in many areas of life, with the result that the effects of crisis situations such as the current crisis of the financial markets and banks are exerted not only nationally but worldwide. Among many other aspects, the following six characteristics are of constitutive importance for a globalization process with standardization as its objective (Wulf and Merkel 2002):

- international financial and capital markets, the mobility of capital and the increasing influence of neoliberal economic theory;
- company strategies and markets with global strategies of production, distribution and cost minimization by means of outsourcing;
- transnational political bodies and the declining influence of the nation state;
- patterns of consumption, lifestyles and cultural styles and their tendency towards uniformity;
- the new media and tourism;
- research, development and technology;
- the one-world mentality.

To these characteristics we must also add the globalization of poverty, suffering, war, terror, exploitation and destruction of nature, which are related to colonialism and capitalism and have long been ignored. These developments are leading to a separation of the political from the economic spheres, to a globalization of lifestyles and to a rise in the importance of new communication media. These are no linear processes. They are disrupted in many places and produce contradictory results. They have different objectives and decision-making structures and are organized in networks, like rhizomes. They do not run parallel in space or time and they are subject to a wide variety of different dynamic forces. They are multi-dimensional and multi-regional and deeply rooted in the centres of neoliberal capitalism. The dominance of a globalized economy over political life and the globalization of lifestyles by means of the increasing presentation of experience as images in the new media help to bring about changes in the way we work.

All this has been accompanied by a decline in the influence of the individual nation states, while cultures have become increasingly permeable and heterogeneous, resulting in the development of new ways and spheres of life.

Directed against this tendency is another tendency that attempts to improve the regional appropriateness of the globalization processes and that points out that these processes cannot be successful without the integration of cultural diversity. Those taking this position proceed on the assumption that cultural diversity is a universal condition of humanity and that allowance for it must therefore be an integral part of globalization. The diversity of human cultures is created by the uniqueness and plurality of forms of expression of people and societies. It enables exchange between members of the various cultures that have long been impossible to clearly distinguish from each other, ensuring the vitality of the cultures. Cultural diversity protects creativity and requires respect for differences and alterity. However, the right to cultural diversity can only claim validity insofar as other human rights are not violated.

The challenges of globalization have made it necessary to conduct a thorough investigation into the conditions of human life as they stand today. This is the task of a contemporary anthropology that can no longer be reduced to ethnology, philosophical anthropology or anthropological issues in history, but must be reformulated as historical and cultural anthropology (Wulf and Kamper 2002; Wulf 2009, 2010, 2013, 2014). Thus defined, anthropology must set itself the task of elaborating a body of knowledge that makes a contribution to improving human beings' understanding of themselves and the world and takes cultural diversity into account. This anthropological knowledge must include a reflection of its historicity and culturality, thus providing a frame of reference for human development and identity in such a way that the anthropological perspective is included. If we are to grasp the situation of human beings today adequately, we also need, for example, to understand the historical and cultural coordinates of globalization (Wulf 2002, 2003).

Culture and cultural diversity

In many countries, human learning and development has been related to nation building. It has contributed to the building of national identity, national consciousness and the development of a nation state. Human development has meant and still means learning for national identity within the European context. This orientation was predominant in the nineteenth and twentieth centuries. Since the Second World War and above all since the fall of the Berlin Wall, education and human development in the European Union has also included a consideration of European and global cultural diversity. If it is now the case that culture, including the culture of the other, is viewed alongside the nation as a central point of reference for human development, then the understanding of culture that underlays my observations must first be defined. I would like to distinguish between two definitions of culture. The first sees culture as including art, music, literature, the performing arts and architecture. The second is broader and thus embraces 'the practices, representations, expressions, knowledge, skills – as well as instruments, objects, artifacts and cultural spaces associated therewith – that communities, groups and, in some cases, individuals recognize as part of their cultural heritage' (Art. 2.1 of the UNESCO Convention on Intangible Cultural Heritage 2003). When speaking of education in the sense of intercultural education in European civic societies, the basis for this understanding is formed by a broader concept of culture that includes the narrower concept of culture denoting aesthetic education (Imai and Wulf 2007).

This broader concept of culture also forms the basis for the UNESCO 'Convention on the Protection and Promotion of the Diversity of Cultural Expressions', which was adopted by the overwhelming majority of all countries and to date has been ratified by more than 150 countries. This convention emphasizes the ineluctability of cultural diversity in the face of the demands of globalization, which has a standardizing influence. It also makes clear that culture can no longer be equated with national culture, but must instead be understood in the sense of the definition quoted above. This definition places the focus of the convention on cultural identity rather than national identity. The right to cultural identity is understood as a human right whose realization must be protected and promoted by the international community of countries. All people should have the possibility to develop in dialogue with the members of other cultures in a spirit of mutual respect and recognition. In a paragraph of the convention that is extremely important for education and human development, it is stated that one of the convention's objectives is 'to foster interculturality in order to develop cultural interaction in the spirit of building bridges among peoples' (Art. 1d). Since cultural activities, products and objects are of central importance for the development of cultural identity, we must avoid reducing them to their character as commodities, which occupies centre stage within the World Trade Organization (WTO) and its agreements. Like India, the countries of the European Union and many other countries ratified the convention. With this action, India and the European Union committed themselves to respecting and promoting cultural diversity in the relationships to their states and to other countries.

Culture does not designate a self-contained, uniquely definable ensemble of practices, values, symbolizations and imaginations. The borders between cultures are dynamic and change according to context. They are permeable. They allow themselves to be crossed by many cultural phenomena and prevent other phenomena from crossing. Cultural phenomena overlap, intermix and change within and between cultures. They flow back and forth between the cultures. An exchange occurs in which asymmetries determine the cultural flow. The processes of exchange are the result of many constructive and destructive energies. Mimetic assimilations and translations of the cultural phenomena into new contexts occur in many of these processes of exchange. Economic, political and social processes as well as electronic media play an important role. An overlapping of the global and the local occurs, leading to the creation of 'glocal' phenomena whose origins are often difficult to trace.

It is now also no longer considered correct, as it was in the nineteenth century, to view a 'culture' as isolated or as a 'container' that is placed over a territory rendering it impermeable to outside influence. Nor can intercultural learning be viewed as one culture learning from another as a separate entity. Rather the different origins, approaches and focuses of culture overlap in such a way that the global, regional and local levels interpenetrate each other. This intermingling of the global and local, universal and particular through which new autonomous forms of cultural and social complexity evolve is aptly expressed by the term 'glocalization', coined by Roland Robertson. The overlapping and interdependence of different cultural elements do not lead to clearly defined cultural units but to a profound cultural diversity of conditions of life (Krüger-Potratz 2005). Despite the globalization, regionalization and localization of culture and education, cultural differences between the European countries remain, linked as they are to the diversity of languages and the associated imaginaries. The more we seek commonalities, the more clearly we see diversity; the commonalities tend to be more noticeable than if we attempt to ignore the differences. It would therefore seem natural to expect the diversity to be reduced, but not lost. It would seem neither possible nor desirable to have a unified world culture without any differences.

The acceleration of time and the shrinking of space

As time becomes accelerated, globalization is leading to a shrinking of geographical distances, allowing us to become more familiar with new, far-away cultural and social spheres. These spheres no longer coincide with the territories of the nation states that are closed off from each other by borders and border controls. Enormous distances are overcome at almost the speed of light with the aid of the new media (telephones, television and computers) (Bilstein et al. 1999). Distances are shrinking (Liebau et al. 1999). The costs of covering them are low in terms of time and expense. Images, discourses and mass tourism bring closer what is far away. The traditional order of space and time, distance and proximity, foreign and familiar is dissolving. New mixtures and 'contaminations' are coming into being. The slowly growing transnational world society is characterized not by uniformity and simplicity but by diversity, difference and complexity. While images of the 'planet earth' which have only been visible to us for the last few decades and portray Earth as the 'home' of human beings in the universe are already deeply rooted in our imaginaries, it does not mean that the Earth is culturally, economically or politically homogenous or is in the process of becoming so. Ideas about the Americanization (McDonaldization) of the world fail to capture the full picture. Neither America nor Europe is the centre of the world. The world has many cultural, economic and political centres that are transnational and in which different global technology, finance, media, image and discourse scenarios are evolving.

Dynamics of alterity

Although it seemed for a while as if the Other were gradually being unveiled and demystified, this has not proved to be true. Things, situations and people, right in the centre of our everyday well-known familiar world, are becoming increasingly foreign and unknown. Standards of living that one expected to remain secure and familiar are being called into question. Admittedly, the strategy that consisted in demystifying the unknown Other through increasing understanding has succeeded in making many foreign things seem more familiar and replaced people's insecurity and fear with confidence and trust. Yet this sense of security is often only superficial; underneath it (and at its margins), feelings of fear and danger are still strong. The gesture of 'making-the-world-familiar' has not fulfilled our expectations. Instead, increasing the realm of the familiar has meant expanding the sphere of the unknown. Knowing more about it does not make the world any less complex. In fact, the more we know about phenomena and connections, the more there is we do not know. Time and again, ignorance exposes the limits of knowledge as well as the limits of human action based upon that knowledge. Though attempts are often made to reduce the Other to a concept of 'sameness' it cannot as such be overcome. The Other expresses itself in the centre and at the boundaries of the familiar and demands to be considered.

INTRODUCTION

Dealing competently with cultural diversity necessitates experience with the Other, with alterity. Neither people nor cultures can develop competently if they cannot mirror themselves in others, if they do not engage and influence each other. Both cultures and people only form by way of exchange with others. Reciprocal exchange processes allow relationships to develop between people and their alterities and broaden the realm of life and experience in the process. Such exchange processes encompass the giving, receiving and returning of objects, donations and symbolic goods. The one and the other are not fixed quantities. What the one and the other exactly are only becomes apparent in cultural contact, that is, in the meeting of people who determine what exactly is their own and what is the Other according to both the cultural context of the meeting and their own singular predispositions. Both the own and the Other have to be dynamically imagined; only processes of cultural encounter determine what exactly is experienced as the own or as the Other.

In many areas, such processes of contact, encounter and exchange are determined by the circulation of capital, products, workforce and symbolic goods. Their dynamic leads to the meeting of people and cultures and causes material and immaterial relationships to develop. These processes occur within the framework of global power structures and are intrinsically unequal; they are determined by consolidated power relationships that have their roots in history. Despite the fact that many such processes are influenced by capitalist market movements and therefore foment inequality, they also promote encounters with the alterity of other people and cultures. Societies and cultures are constituted through contact with alterity. The experiences of other people and cultures are central to the development of children and youths. Only in the mirror and through the reactions of human beings and cultures can people understand themselves. This implies that self-knowledge presupposes an understanding of the incomprehension of alterity (Waldenfels 1990; Hüppauf and Wulf 2009; Wulf 2014).

Alterity and heterological thinking

In a globalization process that not only accepts cultural diversity as a condition of globalization but also promotes it, the focus is on the question of how dealing with the other of a foreign culture can be shaped and how the skills required for this can be transmitted. Two points of view must be taken into account here. Cultures are not self-containing entities that are clearly differentiated from each other and precisely defined. It is rather the case that most contain influences from other cultures, from which several elements have been assimilated in one form or another. Hence, we must understand cultures as dynamic and continuously changing. On the basis of migratory movements that are strong throughout the world, many people no longer belong to just one but instead to two cultures or even more, so that it is no longer possible to speak of an unambiguous cultural identity. Accordingly, the other is also not a self-containing static entity. The way in which it is perceived depends on context and the relationship that exists between the perceiver and the perceived. The perception of the other is relational and is subject to contextual changes. The importance of the relational character of our relationships to the foreign and the other cannot be overemphasized. What we experience as alterity always depends on us and is relational for this reason.

In the light of the one-world mentality which still dominates large parts of the discussion on globalization, it is imperative to highlight historical and cultural differences, even where appearances may be deceptively similar. It is this that makes it possible to communicate with the other. If human beings were aware of the otherness in themselves and their own cultures, this would open up new possibilities for understanding the otherness of other people and other cultures and of developing a way of thinking from the point of view of the other. With the increasing awareness of differences and alterity and the recognition of cultural diversity, it is increasingly becoming possible to identify common aspects of different cultures and to break down barriers between them. The ability to perceive and accept differences is essential and can even help to prevent violent conflict. However, even acceptance of cultural diversity has its limits; it has to be related to issues of human rights and global ethics. It must be accepted that disagreements will arise with members of other cultures in this context. Wherever possible, such disputes must be conducted without recourse to the use of force.

Living conditions in the twenty-first century are strongly influenced by the struggle between the uniformity of globalization and movements which emphasize cultural difference and diversity. These include the conflicts between the global and the local, the universal and the singular, tradition and modernity, the spiritual and the material, necessary competition and equal opportunities, short-term and long-term reflections, the rapid spread of knowledge and the limitations of our human capacity to cope with this (Delors 1996; VENRO 2009).

In order to be able to deal competently with cultural diversity, we need to experience the other. Neither people nor cultures can develop satisfactorily if they cannot mirror themselves in others, if they do not engage and influence each other. Both cultures and individuals are formed through exchange with others. Reciprocal exchange processes allow relationships to develop between people and broaden the horizons of their lives and experience in the process.

INTRODUCTION

In education, it is important to create an awareness of the fact that European cultures have developed three strategies to reduce alterity to the known and trusted. One of these is European rationality – logocentrism – which has led to foreign cultures and people being judged according to their adherence to logocentric norms. Whenever other cultures fail to live up to this expectation, they are degraded and not regarded as being of equal value. The second strategy centres on European individuality and the egocentrism that goes with it. This egocentrism led to the development of a high esteem for the individual and an increase in individualist self-assertion at the cost of community. The third strategy employed to reduce alterity to European standards is ethnocentrism which has also led to an overvaluation of European culture and a corresponding undervaluation of other cultures. The effects of these strategies are still apparent in the dynamics of globalization today and constitute an obstacle to dealing with cultural diversity productively (Wulf and Merkel 2002; Wulf 2006). If students become aware of these mechanisms, they might gain the ability to reduce their impact on the perception of the other.

In learning and human development from an intercultural perspective, people have to become aware that in many areas processes of contact, encounter and exchange are determined by the circulation of capital, products, the workforce and symbolic goods. The dynamics of these processes lead to meetings between people and cultures and engender both material and immaterial relationships. They occur within the framework of global power structures and are intrinsically unequal, being determined by consolidated power relationships that have their roots in history. Despite the fact that many such processes are influenced by capitalist market movements and therefore fuel inequality, they also promote encounters with the alterity of other people and cultures.

Societies and cultures are constituted by contact with alterity. To experience other people and cultures is central to the development of children and adolescents. People can only understand themselves as reflected by and through the reactions of other human beings and cultures. This implies that knowing ourselves means that we must be aware that there are limits to our understanding of alterity. How is it possible to accept one's experiences of other people without triggering mechanisms that reduce them to the known and trusted? There are several answers to this question that differ depending on context. One way to bear the alterity of strangers is based on the experience of one's own foreignness, i.e. feeling surprised by one's own feelings and actions. Such events can promote flexibility and curiosity about the alterity of other people and cultures.

Thus, in order to be able to understand and engage with alterity, we need to experience our own foreignness. This experience constitutes a basis for developing the ability to think and feel from the perspective of the other, in the context of which the engagement with the non-identical is of central importance. Such experiences can be expected to increase sensitivity and the readiness to be open to what is new and unknown. In turn, this results in a better ability to bear complex situations emotionally and mentally without acting out stereotypes. Obviously, these options for human development can also be subverted into their opposites. In such cases, the encounter with cultural variation is met by violent action aimed at reducing difference to sameness. Because such efforts mostly fail, a vicious circle of constantly escalating violent action ensues, which results from mimetic processes of mutual imitation (Wulf 2005).

To avoid encounters with cultural diversity and alterity ending in rivalry and violence, we need normative rules. These have been formulated in the Charter of Human Rights, which has come to command authority far beyond the boundaries of the European culture from which it emerged.

A consciousness of the non-identity of the subject constitutes an important prerequisite for openness towards the other. In the confrontation with foreign cultures, with the other in one's own culture and with the foreign in oneself, the capability is to be developed to perceive and think from the perspective of the other. This change in perspective makes it imperative to avoid the reduction of the foreign to the own. An attempt is to be made at suspending the own and experiencing it from the perspective of the other. The objective is the development of heterological thinking. Its focus is on the relationship of the familiar and the foreign, of knowing and not knowing and of certainty and uncertainty. As a consequence of de-traditionalization and individualization as well as of differentiation and globalization, many things taken for granted in daily life are called into question and require individual reflection and judgement. Nevertheless, the liberty accrued to the individual as a consequence of these developments does not represent a real gain in freedom. The individual often only has decision-making leeway in situations in which he or she has no control over the preconditions of the situation in which the decision is made. In the realm of the environment, for example, the individual is able to make environmentally conscious decisions, but he or she has little influence on the societal macrostructures that really determine the quality of the environment.

The increase in the inscrutability of the world leads to an increase in the uncertainty of the individual, who must tolerate the difference between him- or herself and the other. In this situation, uncertainty and insecurity become central characteristics of life in society. On the one hand, they have their origin in the world that is exterior to the person; on the other hand, their origin lies in the interior of the person and ultimately in the interrelationship between the interior and exterior. In the face of this situation, there is no lack of attempts to make this uncertainty bearable through ostensive certainties. However, these certainties do not help to regain the lost security. Their validity is relative and arises primarily from the exclusion of alternatives. What is excluded is determined on the one hand by the psychological and social constitution of the individual, and on the other hand, by the societal power structures and processes of setting and excluding values, norms, ideologies and discourses. These processes often lead to the otherness of the other not being perceived and the closing of the mind to the possibilities of perceiving and thinking from the perspective of the other.

Differentiation, transgression and hybridity

In this context, the concept of difference is important for creating boundaries and making a contribution to rendering them dynamic. It is not possible to form a national, cultural or European identity without differences. Thus, for example, in the processes of inclusion and exclusion that take place in rituals, differences are created which are crucial for the performative character of the rituals (Wulf et al. 2010a). The category of difference also takes on a special importance for understanding alterity. The ways in which heterogeneity and alterity are dealt with are crucial to this cultural diversity which is created by acts of differentiation (Wulf 2006).

For the analysis of social and cultural developments it is important to understand processes of transgression. Transgression consists of overstepping the limits set by rules, norms and laws on the one hand, and overstepping historically created boundaries on the other. These acts of transgression can be non-violent, but they frequently also involve manifest structural or symbolic violence. In dealing with cultural diversity, boundaries are often transgressed, leading to the creation of something new. Transgressions change norms and rules, ways of life and practices. They change and shift borders and create new cultural relations and constellations in the process. In order to understand these processes, we need to make a thorough analysis of their contexts, focusing on the origin of the change or innovation in question.

To understand our own time, the analysis of new hybrid cultural forms by means of difference and transgression is a crucial issue. As communication and interaction between different countries become ever closer and faster and economical, the political, social and cultural exchange becomes more intensive, and more and more hybrid cultural forms come into being. Homi Bhabha (2004) first used the term hybridization to define cultural contacts in a non-dualistic and non-essentialist way by describing them in terms of their function of creating identity by means of a 'third space'. The third space is liminal; it is a space in-between which emphasizes its own in-betweenness. In this liminal space, borders are subject to subversion and restructuring and hierarchies and power relationships are changed. The crucial questions are to what extent these processes result from performative practices and how these new forms of hybridization are created. They are mixed forms in which elements belonging to different systems and contexts change their character in a mimetic process, leading to a new cultural identity. This identity is no longer constituted by distinguishing oneself from another, but in mimetically assimilating oneself to the other.

These thoughts make it clear: only if the handling of cultural diversity is successful it will be possible to prevent wars and reduce violence between people. Avoiding war and violent conflicts, i.e. the creation and maintenance of living conditions that are relatively free of violence, is the decisive prerequisite for successful human life.

Education and human development

In an era of globalization, whether violence and war can be avoided and sustainability can be achieved as a political objective depends in no small part on how cultural diversity is handled. The mission of learning is contact with the other and with alterity in a manner that is free of violence. Sensibility for the alterity of nature and its resources includes the integration of sustainability into the cultural exchange and the associated reduction in violent treatment of nature. From the perspective of UNESCO, in order to promote better handling of cultural diversity (Wulf 2006) education and human development must be supplemented to include peace (Wulf 1973, 1974, 2008; Frieters-Reermann 2009) and sustainable development (Wulf and Newton 2006). If this is successful, learning, education and human development will have made an indispensable contribution to meeting the great challenges of humankind. In Germany, this perspective has gained greater acceptance in recent years. Hence, education for handling cultural differences and learning for sustainability have made their way into the recommendations of the Conference of the Ministers of Education and Cultural Affairs and the framework plans for education in schools (curricula), where they supplement the objectives and implementations of education for peace that have long existed (Stevenson 2003; Krüger-Potratz 2005; Nohl 2006; Georgi 2008).

Learning for peace

Violence between people of different societies and cultures is unavoidable if images of the other which help communicate perspectives of historical and cultural diversity as conditions of globalization do not become an integral part of the social imaginary. This was shown in the violent history of the twentieth century. The critical examination of the different forms of violence and the possibilities for peace are therefore a central task of education and human development in a society. Due to the existence of modern weapons of mass destruction, human beings still face an unprecedented threat of war and violence. Peace has become the prime condition for human life. Its production and preservation is key not only to the survival of individuals, generations and nations, but also to the survival of humanity as a whole. In the context of education, it is therefore imperative that curricula both cover the conditions that lead to war, violence and destruction and search for ways of rendering them less harmful or even overcoming them.

Learning for peace is a contribution to overcoming these conditions. It recognizes that they are often due to systemic problems rooted in the macrostructure and can only be reduced in part by learning. Learning concerning peace is based on the idea that a constructive manner of dealing with the major problems currently facing humanity must be part of a lifelong learning process that begins in childhood and continues throughout adult life. In the early 1970s, peace research elaborated on the fact that peace could not be brought about by a change in consciousness alone. The experiences of the peace movement have confirmed these analyses. The absence of peace and the presence of violence are too deeply rooted in social structures to be overcome by human striving for peace alone. Peace requires additional political action directed at reducing the violent structures inherent to the international system and to society at large.

Learning for peace must draw on central guiding ideas such as 'organized lack of peace', 'structural violence' and 'social justice'. These ideas emphasize the social character of peace and guard us from fantasies of omnipotence and naïve problem reductions. According to Galtung's differentiation, which is still valid today, peace not only denotes the absence of war and direct violence (a negative definition of peace), but also needs to be understood as the reduction of structural violence and the production of social justice (a positive definition of peace). According to this understanding of peace, learning must not only tackle war and direct violence between nations and ethnic groups, but also address the violent conditions at the base of society (Galtung 1973; Wulf 1973, 1974, 2008; Senghaas 1995, 2000; Frieters-Reermann 2009).

Learning towards peace condemns both organized open violence and structural violence. As an alternative, it promotes processes of non-violent conflict resolution, the realization of social justice and the improvement of co- and self-determination. It is conscious of the fact that this is a process rather than a state and that, despite its apparent unattainability, peace must remain its unconditional objective. Overcoming both apathy and experiences of powerlessness is the precondition for any peace-related learning process that can pave the way for a disposition to act. One way to learn consists of linking one's own experiences of deficiency with major global problems. The insight that certain macro-structural conflict formations determine and even endanger one's own life leads to a motivation to champion peace. Thus, beyond imparting relevant insights, learning can bring about changes in attitude and promote political commitment, both of which lead to changes in political action.

Learning for peace requires the establishment of certain standards if it is to further non-violent learning processes. It will also develop forms of participatory and autonomous learning. These learning processes place great responsibility for initiative in the hands of the teachers. They are encouraged to develop their visions of peace and a consciousness of the historical causes and the general changeability of conflict formations; this contributes to the conception and development of blueprints for changing the world. At the same time, it ensures that education and people's perception of problems are oriented towards the future.

The unrestrained consumption of non-renewable energy is also an expression of violence towards future generations. Hence, learning for sustainable development is also among the great tasks of global learning. What is meant by learning for sustainable development is – as is also the case for learning for peace – a task that is to be specified on a regional basis and that will differ significantly in accordance with the state of development of the region.

Learning for sustainable development

The analysis of violence and organizational lack of peace with the objective of developing a commitment to forms of conflict resolution that are free of violence must be directed not only at other people, societies and cultures. A task that is no less important for the survival of humankind consists of analysing violence exercised against nature and future generations through the consumption of non-renewable resources. Reducing this consumption through learning for sustainable development is the second part of this task. The aim of sustainable development is to realize a continuous process of all-encompassing social change which is to sustain the quality of life of the current generation while securing the options of future generations to create their own lives. Sustainable development has come to be recognized as a way of improving individual life chances and of promoting social prosperity, economic growth and ecological safety.

Agenda 21, ratified in 1992, led to the implementation of the 'world decade for sustainable development' by UNESCO (2005–2014). The aims that were pursued in this decade differed according to world region. In Europe, working towards sustainability means first and foremost effecting an ecologically motivated change in the economic system. In less developed countries, the term is used mainly with reference to efforts to ensure the provision of basic services and education with the aim of catching up with the more developed countries. The goal of learning for sustainability is to enable people to actively design an ecologically sane, economically productive and socially just environment, taking global aspects into consideration (Wulf and Newton 2006, Open Working Group on Sustainable Development 2015).

Sustainability is a regulative idea. Like peace, it can never be fully realized. Sustainable learning is an important prerequisite for the gradual realization of sustainability/sustainable development. As such, the teaching of history for learning for sustainability is directed at the individuals whose sensitivity and responsibility it seeks to promote. To this end, it needs to start with existing structures, and always bearing in mind individual and social conditions, to develop the creative abilities of young people. By this I mean the ability to shape their own lives and their own lifeworlds (Lebenswelt) in accordance with the premises of sustainable development. To do so, they need to be able to learn from concrete problems, study their contexts and prepare reflective action. Learning for sustainability implies a reflective and critical understanding of the society and a readiness to participate in relevant individual and social learning processes. To this end, minimal standards for studies of sustainable development need to be developed that do justice to the multiple perspectives of sustainability.

Learning for sustainable development should contribute to the establishment of social justice between nations, cultures, world religions and generations. Alongside the promotion and refashioning of the environment and economic conditions, the central principles of sustainability also include global responsibility and political participation. With these goals, which go far beyond protection of the environment and resources, the learning for sustainability takes up ideas that were prepared in the 1970s (Wulf 1973, 1974). However, at that time there was little recognition of a need for social justice between generations and of the growing importance of the task of conserving non-renewable resources.

Multimodality of learning

Learning, which is oriented towards a better understanding of the other and towards a reduction in violence towards other people and future generations, will also have to develop innovative forms of learning. In a radical perspective, a learning for sustainability oriented towards peace and social justice leads to a far-reaching reform of the educational system. If one wants to at least partially realize these objectives which, due to their general and comprehensive nature, cannot be fully achieved, then this goal must also include changes in the methods of learning. In curricular areas that are important for these questions and for the interdisciplinary integration of these perspectives into the human development of the coming generation, it is not just a matter of mere conveyance of new content and knowledge. The objective is the empowerment of children through a fundamental shift in the perspective of learning. This shift should not be limited to formal school-based learning. A learning for sustainability oriented towards peace and social justice is a continuous lifelong task that is part of the formal educational system, professional learning and continuing education as well as informal education.

Learning is multimodal (Kress 2010) and takes into account the following dimensions of learning (Delors 1996): learning to know, learning to do, learning to live with others, learning to be. The concept of multimodality makes it clear that learning takes place in many modes that must be taken into account. Only when this is successful does learning have lasting effects. Learning is synesthetic, meaning that it occurs not just through one sense, but through several senses. Images, sounds and touch play a central role. When development of language and imagination is at the centre of learning, its foundation in the senses takes on great significance. When this occurs, concepts are filled with perceptions and imagination can deal with material from the senses in a creative manner (Hüppauf and Wulf 2009).

In conjunction with the realization of a complex multimodal learning process, four perspectives play an important role: mimetic learning, performativity of learning, inquiry learning and rituals of learning and communication.

INTRODUCTION

Mimetic learning

Mimetic learning is a basic form of cultural and intercultural learning that is multimodal. Mimetic learning involves the body and the senses. In intercultural learning, mimetic processes are directed at people, objects and facts of foreign cultures. In these processes, a 'similarization' to the alterity of these non-self-containing cultures takes place. It occurs due to the fact that children take an impression, so to speak, from the representations of foreign cultures and integrate it into their imaginary. Through mimetic processes, both an individual and a collective imaginary are created. Without mimetic representations, learning remains inanimate and does not enrich children's imaginaries (Gebauer and Wulf 1995; Wulf 2007, 2013, 2014). The students' mimetic learning relates to a foreign culture and to a teacher whose method for examining, analysing and interpreting foreign objects is imitated. In this process, these students do not just copy the teacher's interest and the way that he or she deals with representations of a foreign culture. When children relate to the teacher mimetically, they develop their own approach to foreign cultures, to the other and to alterity using the teacher's behaviour as a guide. The teacher's model of behaviour is of major significance for the initiation and facilitation of the children's mimetic learning processes. Mimetic learning processes are not merely processes of copying; rather, they are creative processes of imitation in which an expansion of the everyday environment takes place by having children relate to foreign people and the foreign world or other cultures in an autonomous manner. Mimetic processes refer to other people not only in face-to-face situations, but also in imaginary actions, scenes and themes. Without reference to the other and to foreign cultures, children would not be able to develop adequately, neither into social beings nor into individuals.

The fact that humankind differs from all other forms of life through its distinct mimetic abilities was already recognized by Plato and Aristotle. This fact was studied in an extensive anthropological study on the conception and history of mimesis (Gebauer and Wulf 1995) and on the significance of mimetic processes in the acquisition of culture (Gebauer and Wulf 1998; Wulf 2013). More recent studies in primate research have shown that infants of eight months already command mimetic competencies that are more developed than those that can ever be attained by primates (Tomasello 1999). Other recent studies on 'mirror neurons' have shown that the cognition of situations related to action displays the same processes that can be observed during action itself (Rizzolatti and Craighero 2004; Iacoboni 2008). Last but not least, the 'Berlin Study on Rituals' was able to show for all of the four central fields of socialization studied that mimetic processes are of central significance for pedagogy, education and learning (Wulf et al. 2004, 2007, 2010a, 2010b; Wulf 2005).

Intercultural learning as a performative process

When one speaks about the performativity of intercultural learning processes, the emphasis is on their enactment, their performance and their reality-constituting character. The relationship between physical and symbolic action is investigated. Research has focused on education and learning as processes of dramatic interaction, in which bodily and vocal action overlap, and where social scenarios and mimetic processes of circulation are of prime importance; these can be investigated by way of ethnographic methods. The focus on the performative nature of these processes implies an understanding of pedagogy as knowledge of action, and therefore an interest in generating practical knowledge as a condition of pedagogic action.

Teaching and learning are not merely cognitive processes; they are also social processes in which interactions between students play an important role. In learning, bodily processes play a larger role than is generally perceived. An analysis of gestures in the context of interaction during instruction makes clear the extent to which learning and education are managed through facial expressions, gestures and posture (Wulf et al. 2010a). To render knowledge embodied, the staging of the body plays an important role. Three aspects of performativity are central. First, learning is a historical and cultural performance. This means that depending on the historical and cultural context and the associated traditions of school culture, education differs in different societies and cultures. To a large degree, these traditions determine which performative options exist for intercultural learning. Second, in learning, language is often performative and a mode of action. John Austin (1979) made this clear when he showed how important the performative character of speech is for communication and interaction. Hence, it is important to pay attention to this dimension in learning. And third, the performativity of learning has a sensuous or aesthetic dimension that needs to be considered (Suzuki and Wulf 2007; Wulf and Zirfas 2007).

Inquiry learning

A modern understanding of learning that is open towards the other does not only mean learning facts but also learning how to learn, how to live together, how to act and how to be (Delors 1996). Learning can make an important contribution to the implementation of an interdisciplinary mission that does not just convey subject-specific interrelationships of knowledge. For example, social life and the associated extracurricular experiences play an important role in the human development of young people. In these processes, young people can learn to be independent and operate in a self-reliant manner with others in the community. Using the rituals of cooperative learning, students learn to rely on themselves to manage their learning processes. Ritual arrangements help here in the acquisition of practical knowledge regarding how to learn independently. Inquiry learning is of particular importance here. This form of learning strives to learn how one learns. Inquiry learning requires time and a thorough examination of material that needs to be discovered, structured and interpreted. This means integrating mimetic, performative and poietic modes of learning in order to create intensive learning experiences (Wulf 2003; Wulf et al. 2004, 2007, 2010a, 2010b; Werler and Wulf 2006; Suzuki and Wulf 2007).

Rituals of learning and communication

To a great extent, schools are ritually organized institutions. School rituals, therefore, also play an important role in learning. They range from singular celebrations to repetitive school macro rituals such as annual enrollment, graduation ceremonies and pre-Christmas events, to the numerous rituals in class that mark the passage between breaks and lessons and to the design, structure and sequence of the various learning cultures in class. Rituals constitute social structures and functions and create communities in which children have their place. Apart from the symbolic content of their interaction and communication, the creation of community works by way of performative ritual practices that perform and enact community. Power relationships play an important role in the emergence of the order that these practices create. Through regularity and repetition, the relationships between children and between children and adults are confirmed as well as modified. Rituals and ritualizations have a beginning and an end. They are characterized by their dynamics which cause adaptations and changes in child behaviour. Their corporal practices create forms of action, images and schemata which children identify with, which they remember and whose performance and enactment bring forth new forms of actions.

For the development of multimodal learning cultures in schools, rituals and ritualization play a central role. Learning as well as intercultural learning is understood as ritual action and accomplished as a collective task. With the aid of ritual arrangements, poietic and performative learning processes are initiated and support is provided for students' independence and self-control. Learning in school is understood as a social activity whose intercultural and gender-specific dimension receives particular attention. Ritual increases in flexibility can serve to transition from mere transfer of knowledge to poietic learning. In the open work situation of project teaching and in standardized situations of group conversations and lecture, the teaching and learning forms of traditional school rituals can be made more flexible. Methodologically, instruction can shift its main concern in this way from knowledge transfer to active learning. Softer and more flexible ritualizations that increase individual territorial, temporal, content-related and methodological latitude appear to make sense for this form of learning culture. Ritualizations of this kind support the socially oriented individual and advance the social semiotic approach to learning.

Explorations in alterity

Grand tours – educational journeys – passages

Starting in the Renaissance, young noblemen began to undertake journeys or 'Grand Tours' across Europe and particularly Italy, in the course of which they would educate themselves. The Grand Tours of John Milton (1538), Michel de Montaigne (1580–1581) and Johann Wolfgang von Goethe (1786–1788) have become famous. While these journeys were originally the reserve of the nobility, later an increasing number of members of the wealthy middle class also undertook such travels. Forerunners of the 'Grand Tour' were the ascetic pilgrimages of the Middle Ages through which the pilgrims hoped to earn forgiveness for their sins and eternal life in paradise. The nobility and bourgeoisie were no longer pursuing religious salvation but seeking to educate themselves and perfect their minds and senses. The journeys were a ritual through which young people could become educated and grow. They used them to take leave of their previous lifeworlds and become transformed by their experiences. This was the intermediate or liminal phase of the ritual. There are many reports of the formative power of these journeys not only in Europe, but also in India. Young Indians and Germans are now continuing these traditions and seeking formative experiences in each other's cultures.

In the globalized world, such experiences that bring about a profound transformation in young people are of great importance. Young Indians experience Germany and Europe and young Germans experience India. They encounter the other country, its culture and its people. There is room for more in such encounters than in dialogue alone. This is revealed in many of the research results of these young Indians and Germans. The young people have physical, sensory and emotional experiences of alterity that are reflected in what they choose to focus on in their research and the perspectives that they take. It is our assumption that the body, the senses and social enactments and performances play an important role in these encounters with otherness. Previous research has shown how differently the body, the senses, the emotions and rituals are understood in India and Germany/Europe and how strongly these differences influence worldviews and people and how they understand themselves (Michaels and Wulf 2011, 2012, 2014).

Ethnographic methods for exploring alterity

Many of the young researchers have used ethnographic methods which allow them to find answers to the questions that have guided their exploring studies in alterity. Moreover, reconstructing and evaluating the empirical material allows many of them to expand some key questions of alterity further. Grounded Theory with its propositions regarding 'theory as practice' remains an important source of inspiration (Glaser and Strauss 1969; cf. Strauss and Corbin 1990, 1994; Borneman and Hammoudi 2009). Throughout this process, their methodological reflections have often been challenged by situations that have led them to change their assumptions. It has been important to constantly check how they reconstructed the material, how they interpreted it and related it to the theoretical questions of their investigation. The constructive elements of their research play an important role throughout their studies, so that they are led to confirm the conclusion that the notion of 'one' social reality or 'one' fixed alterity is replaced by various realities as versions of the world and of alterity. Protocols are revealed as methodically constructed texts. The idea of latent structures of meaning as objective, given reality which can be objectively proven therefore becomes highly questionable (Flick 1995). This epistemological view has also evolved from insights into the historical and cultural nature of knowledge which is currently of great interest in historical cultural anthropology (Wulf 2013).

Ethnographic methods of research are best suited to the purpose of many explorative studies. Since the staging and performance of social life is the focus of many of them, participatory observation and video-supported observation played a central role. The methodological problems inherent to participatory observation are well known. The ever-increasing importance of images and the iconic turn in cultural studies and the social sciences made some of the researchers develop an iconology of alterity (Hüppauf and Wulf 2009; Wulf 2013, 2014).

Considering the limitations inherent in any method of research and the well-known advantages and disadvantages of the various approaches to participatory observation, the most appropriate procedure is clearly to analyse a particular social phenomenon using overlapping methods, that is, through triangulation (Flick 1995). Thus, some young researchers have used recordings of conversations, group discussions and interviews too. In the various areas of their investigation, these methods are exploited in different ways, according to the different kinds of questions in each area and the varying conditions of study. As a result, the multiplicity of methodological approaches opens up new ways of exploring alterity.

In the following sections, I will shortly describe how young Germans and Indians make use of their stay during their visit to India and visit to Germany and Europe to investigate a broad range of topics mostly related to their theses.

Religion, philosophy and culture

Although India is a secular democracy, religion plays a role that to Europeans seems surprisingly important. Social and cultural phenomena are seen in the context of religion, and this shapes the Indians' worldview. Gender relations too are fundamentally influenced by views that have their origins in religious contexts which contain models for human coexistence. Thus, for example, images of the divine feminine determine how women are seen and how they see themselves and their possibilities for self-development (Vajpayee/Semmler). Also, sacred cows serve as an example of the influence of Hindu religious concepts on daily life in India. Thus, it becomes clear how vegetarianism is bound up with *ahimsa*, *karman* and *dharma* and how these concepts can be understood as an expression of the importance of the Vedas which continue to determine the Indian attitude towards cows and other creatures to the present day (Schmitz-Valkenberg). In his search for changed forms of knowledge and cognition, Gandhi continues this tradition in several respects. His evaluation of *swaraj* and *swadeshi*, self-knowledge and self-reform, is the expression of his search for a true knowledge which overcomes the splits of modern man as the basis for moral action. Gandhi's criticism of separateness, alienation and routinization of *himsa* and his striving for *swaraj*, *swadeshi* and the practice of *ahimsa*, of self-knowledge and self-reform, is a criticism of modernism and its lack of a moral basis (Patil). For many Indians, these thoughts form a moral foundation for education which is quite different from Western traditions.

INTRODUCTION

Sarvodaya, 'the uplift of all', is the foundation of social and spiritual education upon which considerations and plans for school reform and national education are based, considerations which continue to have a substantial influence on the education system (Vollmer). It is not only for Gandhi but also in India's religious and philosophical traditions that asceticism plays an important role. Asceticism can be broken down into four central aspects – the Sanskrit concepts of *tapas*, *vayragya*, *samnyasa* and *yoga* which are still important in India today. *Tapas* denotes forms of self control; *vayragya* signifies a state of detachment and desirelessness; *samnyasa* means 'renunciation of the world'. *Yoga* goes back to the time of the *Upanishads* and denotes the striving for *jnana*, for a higher form of illuminative wisdom by using exercises of the body (Roggenbuck). This leads on to a study on cultivating simplicity in which the everyday life and education of Tibetan child Buddhist monks in Ladakh is analysed. In contrast with the values of the consumer society, here Buddhist values are held in high esteem. Simplicity is understood to be an important spiritual aim of social development and education (Biswas). Belief in magical practices and miracles still plays an important part in many spheres of religious life in India. This is clearly to be seen in the legend of St. Thomas which is important for Syriac Orthodox Christian communities; at the centre is an analysis of the magical dichotomy in the stories of Kadamattath Kattanar (Visvanathan). These chapters conclude with an Indian perspective on Berlin Zoo as a place between nature and culture. It aims to show that this popular spot is an 'in-between-place', oscillating between putting the animals and our relationship to the animals on show and a place of scientific research (Baindur).

Dance, theatre and media

Whereas the previous section was mainly concerned with different discussions of traditional Indian culture, in this section the focus is on the artistic cultures in modern day India. Within the context of images and conceptions of India in which sections of the avant-garde of European dance took an interest at the beginning of the twentieth century, we begin with an analysis of the photo montages of the Hindu dancer, Nyota Inyoka, who lived in Paris from 1917 to 1933. In one photo montage, Nyota Inyoka's own image appears to merge with Indian dancers who are depicted in a picture. The result of this is a photo montage which has a special aesthetic expression (Jahn). The influence of Indian dance culture in Europe was evident in these photo montages. The next article concerns the work of the Indian People's Theatre Association's Central Squad. This ballet, dance and theatre work drew on the ideas of Gandhi and was active in Mumbai between 1942 and 1947. Its aim was to stage and perform India Immortal in order to pass on cultural norms and values from one generation to the next, and in the process to develop a community based on communist values. Considerable tensions arose between universal and regional or local goals (Saha). The tensions between 'locality' and 'globality' which were already beginning to arise at that time are still making themselves felt in the contemporary art world in India. Three examples from the Indian art world show us how these tensions between globality and diversity manifest themselves (Ralfs). In everyday life people's imaginary is filled by many images of their surroundings and the arts. It would be interesting to know what influence these images have on their perception of the world and of other people. In order to answer this question, several auto-rickshaw drivers were given a camera and asked to take pictures of objects that they found important. This resulted in several pictorial essays which can be compared with each other and give an enlightening insight into the imaginary of auto-rickshaw drivers and the way they perceive things (Thibaut). The section concludes with a study that examines how alterity is experienced both in and with the help of language and how these experiences affect people's relationships with the social sphere in India. It is shown how cultural learning takes place by means of mimetic processes and how a habitus is formed (Daryan).

Education, self-education and human development

How do lessons proceed in Indian schools? We can only answer this question by means of examples, since the Indian education and school system has so many shapes and forms. A pictorial essay on going into school before lessons begin gives the reader an impression of how different the Indian school system is (Varvantakis). This is followed by an ethnological analysis, supported by a wealth of data, of what it means to go to school in India. This study examines two schools, one in and the other in the area of Bangalore. One of the schools is a 'normal' mainstream school and the other a far better equipped alternative school. In both schools the study focuses on one school day and uses description and analysis to identify commonalities and differences in the everyday processes of instruction, learning and the teaching of life skills (Kübler). A further study shows the extent of the influence of colonialism on Indian schools and also how ethnographic methods can be used in research on schools. The study focuses on 'multilingualism', self-education and the teaching of life skills through discipline and 'social pride' (Bittner). What influence does the school environment have on pupils' expectations of the future? The documentary method, developed by Ralf Bohnsack, is used to identify key aspects of this issue in the presentation and interpretations of two group discussions with pupils (Lange). Using data from the National Census and the National Sample Survey, a case study examines how in Maharashtra parents' seasonal sugar cane migration affects their children's education. In this study, it is clear that seasonal migration and its effects on the children's education is a big problem that is addressed very differently in each region. The study includes a description of the Sakhar Shala, which was developed by the NGO Janarth, as one example of how this problem is addressed (Hallmann). Another important problem in every education system is how disabled children are treated. A study about the experiences of disabled students in Germany describes the rights of disabled people and the measures that are taken to support them in their daily lives. It also looks at how a group of disabled students at the Freie Universität in Berlin feel about their experience of studying there (Rao Ambati). Inclusive education, its historical origins and more recent initiatives developed in India are the subject of a further study that gives an overview of the current position with regard to inclusivity in schools (Swaminathan). Next comes an important analysis of the link between perception and knowledge that is acquired through perception in the area of education and educational theory. An example from Indian culture demonstrates the importance of this issue in politics and social contexts. The analysis demonstrates that this link has to do with tacit knowledge. This is an integral part of the professional knowledge that is so important for educational practice, knowledge that is largely learnt through mimetic processes and should be paid greater attention in our considerations (Schmidt). The section ends with a study which concludes that educational improvements often have the undesired side effect of leading to new social conflicts. This is demonstrated through an empirical investigation by the author (Clemens).

Homogenization versus diversity

It has repeatedly become clear that in our globalized world there is a constant tension between tendencies towards homogenization on the one hand and diversity on the other that runs through science and culture, the arts and the media, schooling and education. This leads us to ask what form the relationship between a 'one-world' mentality and cultural diversity can take and also to look at the importance of taking an intercultural perspective. A study follows how Indian youths come to terms with the processes of globalization. Using the documentary method, two discussion groups – one containing five youths from a town school in

Delhi and the other five from an international school in Rajasthan – are set up, presented and compared. Commonalities and differences between the two groups emerge which show clearly that the teaching in schools affects students' approach to the problems of globalization (Wagener). The next chapter looks at what can be done to help women become politically and socially empowered. Several Indian approaches are presented and discussed. The Tata Institute for Social Sciences project Stree Mukti Sanghatana is presented as an important project in women's struggle for empowerment (Schneider). These are also important issues for the Indian middle class, where there are heated arguments about the relationship between Indian traditions and Western values (Müller). The next case study about the risk behaviour of two entrepreneurs focuses on the way members of the middle class deal with risk and how middle-class entrepreneurship develops. This shows clearly how differences in the risk behaviour of the entrepreneurs are influenced by their backgrounds and environments, and it also demonstrates the extent to which the development of a risk culture is an important aspect of entrepreneurial success (A. Wulf). This is followed by an analysis of how the complex process of climate change is understood in India, how Indians respond to the associated risk and what emotions play a part in these processes. Using the documentary method, two group discussions with secondary school pupils from Ladakh are carried out and are evaluated, compared and interpreted. Here commonalities are observed but it is chiefly differences in the attitude to climate change that are identified (Getzin). The extent to which cultural differences affect attitudes to climate change becomes apparent. Cultural diversity is of similar importance when it comes to the treating of mental problems. It emerges that there is a performative potential for healing in the way mentally ill people view themselves. We gain new insights through observations of how people treat the mentally ill in India. These also help us to better understand Latin American and English case studies which focus on the cultural aspects of schizophrenia and methods of treating it (Wiencke). There then follow two chapters on epistemology. The first one develops theoretical considerations on the subject of 'parochial knowledge' and its importance for the development and the understanding of society in North East India. This knowledge has local or regional limits and constitutes a potential for resistance to the universalization of knowledge (Singh). The second of these two final chapters examines the status of dispositions in logical philosophy. It concludes that dispositions can be understood as forms of appropriation or ownership reflecting the irrelevance of functional characterization (Murthi).

INTRODUCTION

Outlook

Today, education and human development can no longer be understood as national education only. Being part of different cultures, it makes a contribution to the development of cultural identity. In view of the diversity of cultures, this is a complex task. As a result of the standardizing tendency of globalization, recognition of cultural diversity and its competent handling are increasing in significance. Hence, members of coming generations are encouraged to develop heterological thinking and an intercultural competence in an explorative dealing with the other. In this way, learning becomes intercultural learning. For the creation and maintenance of living conditions free of violence and for an orientation of education towards the values of peace and sustainability, this is indispensable. Intercultural learning is multimodal learning in the context of which mimetic convergence on the other plays a central role. Intercultural learning is performative, attempts to promote forms of inquiry learning and uses school rituals for the development of practical intercultural knowledge. For the future of humankind, it is imperative to introduce into the educational system perspectives of intercultural learning for sustainability that is oriented towards the values of peace and social justice.

References

Austin, J. L. (1979): Zur Theorie der Sprechakte. Stuttgart: Reclam (2nd ed.).
Bhabha, H. K. (2004): The Location of Culture. London, New York: Routledge.
Bilstein, J., Miller-Kipp, G., and Wulf, C. (eds) (1999): Transformationen der Zeit. Erziehungswissenschaftliche Forschungen zur Chronotopologie. Weinheim: Beltz.
Borneman, J., and Hammoudi, A. (eds) (2009): Being There. The Fieldwork Encounter and the Making of Truth. Berkeley: University of California Press.
Delors, J. (ed.) (1996): Learning – The Treasure within. Paris: UNESCO.
Flick, U. (1995): Triangulation in der qualitativen Forschung. In: Flick, U., von Kardorff, E., and Steinke, I. (eds): Qualitative Forschung: Ein Handbuch. Reinbek: Rowohlt, 309–318.
Frieters-Reermann, N. (2009): Friedens- und Konfliktpädagogik aus systemisch-konstruktivistischer Perspektive. Duisburg, Köln: WiKo-Verlag.
Galtung, J. (1973): Gewalt, Frieden und Friedensforschung. In: Senghaas, D. (ed.): Kritische Friedensforschung. Frankfurt, M.: Suhrkamp, 55–104.
Gebauer, G., and Wulf, C. (1995): Mimesis. Culture, Art, Society. Berkeley: University of California Press (German orig. 1992).
Gebauer, G., and Wulf, C. (1998): Spiel – Ritual – Geste. Mimetisches Handeln in der sozialen Welt. Reinbek: Rowohlt.

Georgi, V. B. (ed.) (2008): The Making of Citizens in Europe: New Perspectives on Citizenship Education. Bonn: Bundeszentrale für Politische Bildung, Schriftenreihe Band 666.

Glaser, B. G., and Strauss, A. (1969): The Discovery of Grounded Theory. Chicago: Chicago University Press.

Hüppauf, B., and Wulf, C. (eds) (2009): Dynamics and Performativity of Imagination. The Image between the Visible and the Invisible. New York: Routledge (German version 2006).

Iacoboni, M. (2008): Mirroring People: The New Science of How We Connect with Others. New York: Farrar, Straus and Giroux.

Imai, Y., and Wulf, C. (eds) (2007): Concepts of Aesthetic Education. Münster, New York: Waxmann.

Kress, G. (2010): Multimodality. A Social Semiotic Approach to Contemporary Communication. New York: Routledge.

Krüger-Potratz, M. (2005): Interkulturelle Bildung. Eine Einführung (Lernen für Europa, vol. 10). Münster: Waxmann.

Liebau, E., Miller-Kipp, G., and Wulf, C. (eds) (1999): Metamorphosen des Raumes. Erziehungswissenschaftliche Forschungen zur Chronotopologie. Weinheim: Beltz.

Michaels, A., and Wulf, C. (eds) (2011): Images of the Body in India. London, New York, New Delhi: Routledge.

Michaels, A., and Wulf, C. (eds) (2012): Emotions in Rituals and Performances. London, New York, New Delhi: Routledge.

Michaels, A., and Wulf, C. (eds) (2014): Exploring the Senses. Emotions, Performativity, and Ritual. London, New York, New Delhi: Routledge.

Nohl, A.-M. (2006): Konzepte interkultureller Pädagogik. Eine systemische Einführung. Bad Heilbrunn: Klinkhardt.

Rizzolatti, G., and Craighero, L. (2004): The mirror-neuron system. *Annual Review of Neuroscience*, vol. 27: 169–192.

Senghaas, D. (ed.) (1995): Den Frieden denken. Si vis pacem, para pacem. Frankfurt, M.: Suhrkamp.

Senghaas, D. (ed.) (2000): Frieden machen. Frankfurt, M.: Suhrkamp.

Stevenson, N. (2003): Cultural Citizenship. Cosmopolitan Questions. Issues in Cultural and Media Studies. Berkshire: Open University Press.

Strauss, A., and Corbin, J. (1990): Basics of Qualitative Research. London: Sage.

Strauss, A., and Corbin, J. (1994): Grounded Theory: an Overview. In: Denzin and Lincoln (eds): Handbook of Qualitative Research. Thousand Oaks: Sage.

Suzuki, S., and Wulf, C. (eds) (2007): Mimesis, Poiesis, Performativity in Education. Münster, New York: Waxmann.

Tomasello, M. (1999): The Cultural Origins of Human Cognition. Cambridge, MA: Harvard University Press.

UNESCO (2003): Convention on Intangible Cultural Heritage. Paris: UNESCO.

UNESCO (2005): Convention on the Protection and Promotion of the Diversity of Cultural Expressions. Paris: UNESCO.

INTRODUCTION

VENRO (Verband Entwicklungspolitik deutscher Nichtregierungsorganisationen e.V.) (2009): Global Learning, Weltwärts and Beyond. Global Perspectives on Education for Sustainable Development. Conference Report and Collection of Essays. Bonn: VENRO.

Waldenfels, B. (1990): Der Stachel des Fremden. Frankfurt, M.: Suhrkamp.

Werler, Th., and Wulf, C. (eds) (2006): Hidden Dimensions of Education. Münster, New York: Waxmann.

Wulf, C. (ed.) (1973): Kritische Friedenserziehung. Frankfurt, M.: Suhrkamp.

Wulf, C. (ed.) (1974): Handbook on Peace Education. Oslo, Frankfurt, M.: International Peace Research Association, Education Committee.

Wulf, C. (2002): Anthropology of Education. Münster, New York: Lit.

Wulf, C. (2003): Educational Science: Hermeneutics, Empirical Research, Critical Theory. Münster, New York: Waxmann.

Wulf, C. (2005): Zur Genese des Sozialen. Mimesis, Performativität, Ritual. Bielefeld: Transcript.

Wulf, C. (2006): Anthropologie kultureller Vielfalt. Bielefeld: Transcript.

Wulf, C. (2007): Une anthropologie historique et culturelle. Rituels, mimésis sociale, performativité. Paris: Téraèdre.

Wulf, C. (2008): Friedenskultur/Erziehung zum Frieden. In: Grasse, R., Gruber, B., and Gugel, G. (eds), Friedenspädagogik. Grundlagen, Praxisansätze, Perspektiven. Reinbek: Rowohlt, 35–60.

Wulf, C. (2009): Anthropologie. Geschichte, Kultur, Philosophie. Köln: Anaconda.

Wulf, C. (ed.) (2010): Der Mensch und seine Kultur. Menschliches Leben in Gegenwart, Vergangenheit und Zukunft. Köln: Anaconda.

Wulf, C. (2013): Anthropology. A Continental Perspective. Chicago: University of Chicago Press.

Wulf, C. (2014): Bilder des Menschen. Imaginäre und performative Grundlagen der Kultur. Bielefeld: Transcript.

Wulf, C., and Kamper, D. (eds) (2002): Logik und Leidenschaft. Berlin: Reimer.

Wulf, C., and Merkel, C. (eds) (2002): Globalisierung als Herausforderung der Erziehung. Theorien, Grundlagen, Fallstudien. Münster, New York: Waxmann.

Wulf, C., and Newton, B. (eds) (2006): Desarollo Sostenibile. Münster, New York: Waxmann.

Wulf, C., and Zirfas, J. (eds) (2007): Die Pädagogik des Performativen. Theorien, Methoden, Perspektiven. Weinheim, Basel: Beltz.

Wulf, C. et al. (2004): Bildung im Ritual. Schule, Familie, Jugend, Medien. Wiesbaden: Verlag für Sozialwissenschaften.

Wulf, C. et al. (2007): Lernkulturen im Umbruch. Rituelle Praktiken in Schule, Familie, Medien und Jugend. Wiesbaden: Verlag für Sozialwissenschaften.

Wulf, C. et al. (2010a): Ritual and Identity. London: Tufnell.

Wulf, C. et al. (2010b): Die Geste in Erziehung, Bildung und Sozialisation. Wiesbaden: Verlag für Sozialwissenschaften.

Part I

RELIGION, PHILOSOPHY AND CULTURE

1

KALI'S DAUGHTERS

The tantric conception of the divine feminine as an emancipatory role model for Hindu women

Archita Vajpayee and Matthias Semmler

> *All the daughters are no longer brought low*
> *They are araised*
> *In bright fire god given they rejoice*
> *And those who deny this world*
> *Is the soul of the unbroken one Lie*
> (David Tibet, *This Shining*
> *Shining World*)[1]

Introduction

The current chapter attempts to present an explorative analysis of the role of the Divine Feminine in Hinduism, focusing particularly on the Tantric goddesses. It deals with the sensitive issue of gender emancipation from the perspective of *Religionswissenschaft* ('Religious studies') and sociocultural anthropology. By applying a transdisciplinary perspective in the sense of Geertz's postmodern notion of 'blurred genres',[2] we discuss the idea of gender-inclusive *dharma*[3] in creative and emancipatory ways by evoking the Tantric goddesses as possible role models for Hindu women in contemporary India.

India is a land of diversities ranging from geographic planes to religious beliefs, ethnic origins to linguistic diversity. This kaleidoscope of coexisting religions and heterogeneous practices demonstrates the diverse nature of social reality in India. In this chapter we particularly focus on studying the expression of Hindu Tantra in the context of this diverse social matrix. Classical Hinduism has already been accused of betraying women on various occasions by feminist critiques.[4] However, our study does not emphasize drawing definite conclusions. Rather it offers alternative ways of interpreting Hindu myths of the Divine Feminine that question existing narratives of male-authored texts. These depictions often purport an orthodox ideological framework for women's religious and social roles legitimized by men. They are founded upon a 'Theology of Subordination',[5] which asserts that the female is inferior to the male. The Vedic scriptures give several examples for the exclusion of women from exercising power by stating that women cannot become priestesses, lead religious institutions, or have direct access to spiritual liberation.[6] This is further amplified by critical feminists, who reveal the gaps between the idealized image of the Goddess in Hindu religious texts and the actual inferior status of women on the social level. In this chapter, we explore the various images of the goddesses found in Brahmanic Hinduism with its implications of given role-models for women, and oppose them to the heterodox tradition of Tantra, which contains archetypes of the Divine Feminine that have the potential to transform the perspective on the role of women in the religious domain as well as in contemporary Indian society.[7] An important point in this endeavour is that these seeds of transformation are deeply rooted in the rich and fertile soil of the Hindu tradition itself. This means that a modern feminist interpretation of the Tantric myths does not neglect *dharma*, but is an inherent, albeit often ignored, part of it. As Madhu Khanna points out:

> It must be stressed here that in the Hindu context there is no such category as an absolute *dharma*. Even the views of the dominant tradition, which appear as absolute, are displaced or transformed by an endless series of expropriations and reappropriations of meaning. It is in the context of this very flexible interpretation of gender *dharma* that we frame our discourse. Moreover, given the diverse and culturally pluralistic environment of India, different interpretations can be applied to interpret images of women.[8]

We place our study in exactly this frame of discourse Khanna has put forward. Further, Derret's remark that '[t]he theoretical standards of the unseen world are not expected to be reproduced in the "seen" world uniformally',[9] is of paramount importance here. Arguing on the ground that in Indian Hindu tradition there is no single *dharma*, there are rather distinct schools that support a certain interpretation of *dharma* according to the region's sociopolitical context, which consequently leads to varied religious customs and beliefs, we explicate the use of the Tantric vision of the Divine Feminine for gender emancipation. 'The task of tracing issues of feminism within the Hindu tradition is compounded by structural differences due to historical and political contexts, geographic and linguistic boundaries, and community distinctions.'[10] These challenges notwithstanding, we are uncovering feminist aspects in the Hindu myths and present them in a way that makes them intelligible to the contemporary cultural setting of India.

Benign goddesses as social role models: taming the free-floating chaos

Dhol, gawar, shudra aur nari, sakal tadna k adhikari.
'Cattle, illiterate, lower castes and women should be humiliated and punished.'
Goswami Tulsidas (1532–1623), Hindu poet-saint and philosopher

Yatra naryastu pujvante, ramante tatra devta.
'Gods reside in the place where women are worshipped.'
Sanskrit *shloka*[11]

Despite the constitutional commitment to secularism, religion plays a very dominant role in the social and cultural life of India. It gets manifested in the presence and popularity of Hindu myths, day to day rituals, and salient symbol systems. Religious rituals usually affirm and reinforce the myths of a culture[12] in symbolic gestures and translate them into emotional impulses that charge the belief system with transrational meaning. They not only embody performative acts for the sustenance of a social group, but are also instrumental in the subjective appropriation of the social semiotics and cultural meanings by the members of the group.[13] As pointed out by Wulf,[14] individuals acquire the ways of social functioning and their roles mimetically[15] by listening to myths, participating in rituals and so on. This section analyses the myths about the divine archetypes of femininity found in popular Hindu mythology and the implied social role models they convey to girls and young women. In a second step[16] these 'mainstream practices' and orthodox views are contrasted by the Hindu myths of the Fierce Goddesses and the gender-inclusive *dharma* of Tantric philosophy.

Since the very inception of the *stridharma*, the normative *dharma* describing the duties of women, dual standards about the status of women crept into Hindu tradition that led to a gap and split in the perception of womanhood, which became an essential feature of Indian mentality, as the two traditional verses quoted above clearly explicate. The supposed divine status of femininity is not reflected in the social reality of India. The above mentioned phrase by Tulsidas shows in an exemplary manner the implicit contempt for women. He not only compares women to cattle, but also legitimizes humiliation and punishment. In India, this suppression remains often a subtle, hidden reality, which consequently manifests in the form of an accelerating number of cases of social violence against females.[17] This is not a mere accident, so we may be inclined to ask: what kind of female ideals and behavioural limits are promoted in the traditional views of Hinduism? A closer look shows that the popular versions of the goddesses display an ideal of womanhood which is submissive, chaste, pious and completely devotional to the dominant male. Brahmanic Hinduism dictates in smallest detail the behaviour of women, restrains women's rights, and thus limits their freedom of thought and action. The orthodox view of women in Indian mythology clearly promotes self-effacing virtues for women that are depicted in Hindu epics for heroines like Sita, Sati and Parvati. Traditionally, young girls are brought up to emulate the behaviour of these goddesses.[18] Beside these mythical role models a whole body of literature is concerned with the normative *dharma* that outlines the conduct and postures to be followed by Hindu women. These texts, explicated in the *dharmasastra* and *smrti* literature,[19] laid the foundation for socially acceptable behaviour in daily life. Sacred texts like Manusmrti, or the 'Laws of Manu', compiled from the second century AD, have specified the norms to be adhered to by the members of the community and hence function as a socioreligious code of conduct. It brought several innovations concerning women that debilitated the position of women in Indian society.

> The code eulogized the eternal nature of *dharmic* marriage and introduced a husband-deifying ideology according to which the spouse must be worshipped as a god by the faithful wife. Manusmrti was also instrumental in abolishing female property rights and prohibiting widow remarriage. [. . .] Martial restrictions placed on women decreased their authority considerably and introduced an era of sexual double standards that perpetuated the 'Theology of Subordination' and weakened the autonomy of women.[20]

These ideas articulated in the *smartized*[21] systems established phallocentric discourses, in which women became subjected to patriarchal models and social structures dominated by males.[22] But the popular Hindu Goddesses in their role as devotional wives offered the mythical, archetypal blueprints for the 'virtuous female' that were instrumental in the emergence of male control over women and hierarchy that led to a precarious relationship between *dharma* and gender. The social function of these myths is to set an ideal for the 'mainstream practice'. Therefore, studying the social role models represented by the Hindu heroines and analysing the moral imperatives transported in their myths provides us with insights about the cultural expectations for women in Hindu society.

The ancient Sanskrit epic about Lord Rama in the *Ramayana*, written by Tulsidas, is one of the most fundamental and popular religious texts for Hindus. Sita, the heroine of this epic, the daughter of king Janaka and wife of Lord Rama, is the embodiment of the ideal Hindu wife. She decides to go to the forests with her husband, when he had to go there for a 14-year exile, explaining that it is her *dharma* to serve her *patideva* (husband). Another mythical instance describes the widely used concept of *Lakshman Rekha*. During their exile in the forests, Sita prompts Rama to hunt a golden deer for her. Rama asks Lakshman to stay at the cottage for her protection. Sita compels her brother-in-law Lakshman to go to Rama's assistance. Lakshman draws a line, or *Rekha*, around their dwelling and tells Sita that she will be safe as long as she does not cross the line implying the behavioural limits for her. But the evil Ravana, who came to the cottage disguised as a saint convinces Sita on the grounds of morality to cross the *Lakshman Rekha* and thus succeeds in kidnapping her. After she was kidnapped by the demon king Ravana, she keeps on worshipping her husband, waiting to be rescued by him. Finally, after Rama frees her from captivity by killing Ravana, she has to undergo an ordeal by fire, *agni-pariksa*, in front of everyone to prove her fidelity. Even then, Rama leaves his pregnant wife. Since she cannot go back to her father as daughters are considered *paraya dhan*,[23] she goes to an *ashram* where she spends the rest of her life, taking care of her two sons. Another myth tells of the Goddess called Sati,[24] the first wife of Lord *Shiva*, who goes to her father's place against the will of her husband, where her father insulted him. Consequently, she realizes her sin and burns herself in the fire of the *yajna*.[25] Sati reincarnates in the form of Parvati, to correct her mistake. She worships Lord Shiva since her only aim in life is to marry him. To this end she keeps hard fasts and performs severe austerities for 60,000 years. After these heroic acts of self-denial she is able to marry him, gives birth to sons and spends a life of self-sacrifice devoted to her husband. The greatest epic *Mahabharata*, attributed to (Veda) Vyasa, narrates an instance about Draupadi, married to Arjuna, who shares her with his four brothers. Thus, Draupadi is married to the Pandavas, who were said to be the most righteous ones. The myth tells how the brothers lose all their riches as well as Draupadi in a game of dice. Moreover, Draupadi was stripped in front of the entire court and the Pandavas could not do anything about it, since she now was the property of the other party.

Since Sita, Sati and Parvati are worshipped in many Hindu homes, their behaviour is not to be questioned but to be idealized. Therefore, women have to follow *patni-dharma* and worship their husbands like Sita. They have to strictly adhere to the code of conduct as specified in the *stridharma*, otherwise they face dire consequences just as explicated in the myths, where Sita was kidnapped after she crossed the *Lakshman Rekha*. She has no right to question her husband when he leaves her pregnant and alone. Thus, the Brahmanic version of *dharma* for women only specifies duties, but does not leave any scope for the existence of rights. Women are *paraya dhan*, treated like objects and property just like Draupadi was lost in gambling. They have to obey every order be it *agni-pariksha* or *Lakshman Rekha* without questioning, otherwise they are punished according to 'divine law', *dharma*, manifesting in tragic consequences of a supernatural order. Hence, to the minds of orthodox Hindu men girls and women have to be protected, as they are unable to exist independently. The blueprints for this mode of thinking are laid down in the myths of Brahmanic Hinduism, like in the *Ramayana*, where the *Lakshman Rekha* myth demonstrates that women can be fooled easily like Sita, who was duped and kidnapped by Ravana. According to these myths women should always stay within their limits and be controlled, otherwise everyone along with them has to pay the consequences. Thus male control over women becomes justified. Another pattern that features widely in Hindu myths is that of the self-denying, devotional wife. The divine archetypes are placed in the matrix of role relationships. They are mothers, daughters, sisters and most importantly wives. They do not and cannot assume an independent existence. Young girls are to-be-wives and all their socialization is following this perspective, which perceives a girl-child as a burden, because her parents must train her from babyhood to live with and serve her spouse's family. These wives are expected to be selfless and to have no desires of their own. The Divine Feminine encoded in these archetypes promotes self-denial, willingness to suffer and complete devotion as desirable features. These are celebrated as the female virtues to be emulated by girls and young women. The Benign Goddesses exemplify soft, gentle and submissive values, which are supposed to contribute to the maintenance of the social structure and are conceptualized as an expression of *dharma*.

But in the Hindu tradition there is another paradigm of the Divine Feminine represented by the Fierce Goddesses. It is here that the ambiguous nature of the female becomes most evident, invoking feelings of ambivalence and fear. This ambivalent attitude towards the feminine is reflected in the attitudes towards women in the social domain as they are supposed to be kept under control. The aspects of the female expressed in the Fierce Goddesses are associated with uncontrolled chaos, disorder, destruction, temptation and transgressivity. The myth of Kali exemplifies that portion of the female power in an exemplary manner.[26] In the myths, the fierce manifestation of the Divine Feminine is shown as Kali, the Black Goddess, who destroys the forces of anarchy with her power, and in her rage loses her self-control. Everybody requests Lord Shiva, her husband, to control her. So, he lies down before her and she steps on him, and calms down. Though not documented in the *Puranas*, we can see, however, in the popular legends the attempt to tame this power. Here it is interpreted that Kali calms down, because she realizes her guilt of stepping on her husband.[27] In this sense, the power unleashed in the female, manifested in Kali, is described as potentially dangerous to the divine order (*dharma*). This popular interpretation of the Kali myth clearly explicates the image of women as perceived through the lenses of the Brahmanic paradigm: 'She is sensuous, a temptress, given to falsehood, folly, greed, trickery, impurity, and thoughtless action.'[28]

It is in this context that the feminine is perceived in the Brahmanic tradition as the root of all evil. Because of the woman's supposedly inconsistent character, she is an object of danger that needs to be kept under strict control by men, as shown in the popular legend of Kali.[29] These malicious characteristics thus demand for a strict control which is exercised by the male-dominated society. Women's sensuality and sexuality, movement and contact, and resources are strategically controlled by expecting their conduct to approach the virtues of the Benign Goddesses like Sita, Sati, Parvati, Lakshmi, etc.[30] A woman is expected to be *pati vrata*.[31] She is respected in Indian society only when she abides by these socioreligious boundaries. The transgression of these restrictions causes infamy and affects the family honour. The role centric myths governed by the premises of virtues and morals of *stridharma* thus become instrumental in the subtle maintenance of the patriarchal structure of traditional Hindu society. It is of paramount importance in this context to notice that the Fierce Goddesses, who are characterized by qualities like independence, rebellion and power, are – contrary to the Benign Goddesses – conceived of as cosmic processes by orthodox Hindus. Contrary to some Tantric interpretations, they are explicitly not understood as exemplifying social role models. Kinsley identifies them as 'antimodels, especially for women'.[32] Womanhood, according to males, needs to be controlled. For this purpose, the Benign Goddesses are interpreted in a web of familial relationships and corresponding roles. These roles evoke feelings of obligation, and if transgressed, evoke feelings of guilt, self-doubt and shame. Hence the supposedly female virtues like self-sacrifice, subordination and submission are instrumental for the male dominance as women's independence and strength are feared, as exemplified in Kali's myth. 'One reason behind such distinctions may be that *a strong, independent female is still thought to possess a free-floating chaotic potential*, whereas a married female who is controlled by her husband is far less likely to be able to give expression to such a potential.'[33]

In Tantra, the manifestation of the divine power is conceptualized and celebrated in feminine form. The Goddess is also worshipped in orthodox Hinduism, but it is only in the Tantric traditions that she is given such an exalted status, often being thought of as being superior to her masculine counterpart, Shiva. Tantric ideology thus stands in opposition to the patriarchic social reality of India, where Brahmanic interpretations of the Vedic scriptures are used as proof of male superiority over women and thus as a tool to maintain the existing power relations in the social structure. Feminine power is controlled in the name of tradition by religious authorities. But the Hindu tradition is far more diverse and open to other interpretations than this monolithic exegesis of Brahmanic priests. Tantric mythical models present ideals of womanhood, which are contradictory to the expectations of the hierarchical society. The discovery of such pro-women traces within Hinduism, however, is faced with difficulties. But before going on to discuss the concept of the Divine Feminine in Tantra and its antinomian implications for the social role of women in traditional Hindu society, it is necessary to define the term Tantra itself.

'At the left hand of the Goddess'[34]: *Shakti* and the *Vama Marga*

Vairagya-sadhana mukti, se mar nay, asamkyha bandhan mayhe mahanandamay labhiva mktir svad.
Liberation through renunciation is not for me.
                    Rabindranath Tagore (1861–1941)

The term Tantra refers to a huge array of diverse traditions in South and East Asia from about the fourth or fifth century CE onward.[35] In our study we examine exclusively Hindu Tantra, from where all the other forms of Tantric thought and ritual have spread. Tantra has been a controversial topic within academia and beyond since the nineteenth century. The first accounts of Tantra came to the West in the form of highly scandalized reports by Christian missionaries and administrators, who painted a picture of shocking images and wild orgies, where every taboo was broken and abominable acts of perversion and superstition were conducted. Over the last 200 years, there have prevailed three sorts of reactions to these distorted images. The first one was in India, where colonial and post-colonial Indians rejected or vilified Tantra, or simply neglected its existence or denied any connection to Hinduism.[36] The second reaction came from academics and scholars, both Asian and Western, who tried to counter the negative image of Tantra by stressing its philosophical speculations and metaphysical doctrinal systems. In this fashion, they largely ignored and downplayed the transgressive nature of Tantra and thus denied the fundamental importance of transgressivity or sexuality in the Tantric traditions. The third kind of reception of Tantra is a Western phenomenon[37] linked to the so-called New Age spirituality, where Tantra is more or less reduced to 'sacred sexuality',[38] mixing Eastern mysticism with modern, Reichian[39] psychotherapeutic ideas in an eclectic fashion. Many scholars specialized in the field of Tantra, like White and Feuerstein, dismiss those forms of Neo-Tantra completely,[40] whereas others, e.g. Urban, acknowledge those forms of 'New Age Tantra' as postmodern transformations of Tantra in the West.[41] These diverse approaches show that academics have changed their reception and understanding of Tantra over the last decades. The problem of understanding the heterogeneous phenomenon of Tantra has been even increased by Western scholars of the nineteenth century, who invented the term *Tantrism* first.[42] The term *Tantrism* suggests a homogenous, unalterable and timeless body of knowledge, which stands in contradiction to the heterogeneous, trans-religious unfolding of Tantric practices and ideas since its historical inception and subsequent development. Hence Tantra is not a unified religious system, but instead represents a rich and diverse body of scriptures, traditions, beliefs and practices.[43]

> As most scholars agree, the term *Tantra*, or *Tantrism*, does not refer to a singular, monolithic, or neatly defined entity; instead, it is a rather messy and ambiguous term that is used to refer to a huge array of diverse texts, traditions, sects, and ritual practices that spread throughout Hindu, Buddhist and Jain communities of South and East Asia from roughly the fourth or fifth century CE onward. As André Padoux and others have argued, the abstract category Tantrism – as a singular, unified 'ism' – is itself a relatively recent invention, and in large part the creation of Western Orientalist[44] scholars writing in the nineteenth century. And surely the identification of Tantrism with sex and sexual magic is a very recent idea.[45]

Tantra basically is the name for a category of texts and practices belonging to Tantric traditions, and its root *tan* can be translated as 'to spread or expand'. Despite the diversity of the practices there are identifiable threads common to most forms of Tantra. The most fundamental trait, on which we will focus here, is also the one that delineates Tantric belief from non-Tantric religions. It is the Tantric emphasis on *Shakti*,[46] the Divine Feminine energy that is the source of birth, death and liberation, and is identified in Hindu-Tantra with the body of the universe itself.[47] This awe-inspiring divine power is to be acknowledged, worshipped and practically applied by the Tantric adept. The Divine Feminine stands in a complementary relationship with its masculine counterpart, *Shiva*.

> An important aspect of *Tantric* belief is that the Absolute is conceived of as bipolar in nature having both masculine and feminine aspects, denoted by the term *Shiva-Shakti*. The masculine aspect is understood as the transcendent, unmanifest and unchanging aspect of divine consciousness, whilst the feminine aspect is understood as being immanent, active, dynamic, and the manifesting power of the Absolute.[48]

The task of the Tantric adept lies in the ability to tap into this power, to use, channel and manipulate it in ways that will finally lead to liberation in this life (*jivanmukti*). The adept achieves this by putting *kama*, desire in every sense of the word, into the service of liberation. Contrary to world-denying Indian systems, like Vedanta, he or she does not sacrifice this world for liberation's sake, but reinstates it, in varying ways, within the perspective of liberation.[49] The Tantric attitude towards cosmos is founded upon the idea of micro-macrocosmic correlations, which assumes that everything in the universe corresponds to other things on higher or lower levels of being. This is represented in the use of the Yantra, where the adept would locate himself in the lower levels of the grid, whilst the godhead is thought of as being the centre.[50] By various complex procedures, ritual techniques and meditative exercises the Tantric adept attempts to achieve union with the centre of the Yantra, and thus achieving union with the godhead: *moksha* or liberation. Despite the fact that there is no single definition of Tantra accepted by all scholars, the definition of David Gordon White explains in a clear way the essence of the Tantric *Weltanschauung*: 'Tantra is an Asian body of beliefs and practices which, working from the principle that the universe we experience is nothing other than *the concrete manifestation of the divine energy of the godhead that creates and maintains the universe*, are seeking to ritually appropriate and channel that energy, within the human microcosm, *in creative and emancipatory ways*.'[51]

As a heterodox phenomenon, Tantra, as a means to liberation, is open to all regardless of class, caste and gender. It is an essentially dynamic system that allows the devotee to achieve liberation in one life-time.[52] One important distinction within Tantra itself is that of the 'right' (*daksina*) and 'left' (*vama*) handed paths. In India the terms 'right handed' and 'left handed' convey culturally significant implications, as the right hand is used only for eating and 'pure' tasks, whilst the left hand is reserved for polluted and 'impure' functions.[53] Basically, the right-hand path is congruent with the rituals found in Brahmanic Hinduism. In contrast, the left-hand path challenges, sometimes in drastic ways, the moral codes found in Brahmanic Hinduism.

> [T]he 'left-handed' path employs techniques and practices that directly challenge the orthodox moral codes that are central to Brahmanical Hinduism, such as imbibing forbidden substances, engaging in sexual practices and flouting caste and purity rules through use of the infamous *pancamakara* or 5 Ms, five impure substances of power (meat, fish, alcohol, grain,[54] and sexual intercourse). The more extreme 'left-handed' path uses the actual 5 Ms, giving them both practical and symbolic importance.[55] Forms of left handed *Tantra* [. . .] believe that the correct use of the *pancamakara* will bestow transcendent powers on the partaking in such rituals.[56]

Henceforth it is quite obvious that it is the left-hand path, or *vama marga*, which is heavily misunderstood and frowned upon by outsiders. The antinomian implications of left handed Tantra are crucial for understanding the importance of the fierce goddesses and their subverting power, which allow the questioning of traditional role models for women in Hindu culture. In Tantric cosmology *Shakti* is conceptualized as the fundamental power of Ultimate Reality, she is triple-natured, the principle of creation, maintenance and destruction, penetrating the whole universe and being its foundation. Hindu Tantra conceives *Shakti* as a divine energy that can take on manifold forms. Hence the omnipotent Goddess manifests in a rich and diverse pantheon of goddesses. The Tantric practitioner strives to transform his ordinary consciousness by meditating on the body[57] as a manifestation of this divine *Shakti*. By continuously purifying the mind she/he eventually realizes the fundamental unity of her or his individual consciousness with the divine consciousness, the Absolute. In the same way the external world is seen as an expression of *Shakti*, and therefore imbued with transformative, magical powers. Based on this assumption certain objects and substances, like the Yantra or the 5 Ms, can obtain transformative powers. It is in this fashion that Tantric philosophy conceptualizes the body and the universe as the manifestation of the Divine Feminine.

ARCHITA VAJPAYEE AND MATTHIAS SEMMLER

Kali's gifts and paradigm shifts: invoking the fierce goddesses for empowering women

Woman is the creator of the universe, the universe is her form: Woman is the foundation of the world, she is the true form of the body, Whatever form she takes [. . .] is the superior form. In woman is the form of all things, of all that lives and moves in the world. There is no jewel rarer than woman; there is not, nor has been, nor will be; There is no kingdom, no wealth, to be compared to a woman;

There is not, nor has been, nor will be any holy place like unto a woman. There is not, nor has been, nor will be any holy Yoga to compare with woman, No mystical formula nor asceticism to match a woman. There is not, nor has been, nor will be any riches more valuable than her.
Saktisamgama Tantra[58]

The Great Goddess, *Mahadevi*, is three-natured. She is the creator and sustainer in the form of an affectionate mother – the cause and the embodiment of the universe – and the destroyer, manifesting in the shapes of the Fierce Goddesses conquering *kama, krodha, moha, mada* and *lobha*.[59] In Brahmanic Hinduism these qualities are seen as the five enemies on the path towards *moksha*. All these five characteristics are manifestations of *maya*, usually thought of as illusion. But in the Hindu Tantric context *maya* is another mask and guise of the power of *Shakti*.[60] What is an enemy in orthodox view becomes an ally for the Tantric initiate. For the *tantrika* these obstacles become tools to be used for spiritual liberation (*moksha*). In Hindu Tantric thought the world is 'embraced', not rejected for spiritual aims. As the world is conceived of as an emanation of the Goddess – immanent and transcendent simultaneously – the material world and humans are partaking in the outflow of divinity that permeates the whole universe. Humans and the world represent hypostases of the godhead. In Hindu Tantric perspective this means that the world is real, which is an important departure from the *maya* conception in mainstream Hinduism.[61] *Maya*, though dream-like and hence deceiving in nature, is perceived as a magical substance that can be used and wielded by the skilful Tantric adept. What appears as mere illusion to the uninitiated is 'powerful stuff' to the *tantrika*, a force that can be shaped by the initiate according to his will. The experience of life then turns into *lila*, the divine play or 'sports' of Shiva and Shakti. The Fierce Goddesses, as exemplified in the *Mahavidyas*, must be understood in relation to this philosophical superstructure. Each of the individual goddesses is an embodiment of the Great Goddess (*Mahadevi*), who is identified as the highest reality of the cosmos, identical with certain philosophical absolutes such as *brahman*.[62] Kali, for example, as a slayer of demons, conquers mighty demons that were even too powerful for the great male gods like Brahma, Vishnu and Shiva. In this respect she is said to transcend or empower the male gods.[63] 'One of the most distinctive features of the Shakta goddess is that she is no longer idealized as merely a wife of the male god, but is conceived of as his creator. She is the transforming power of creation and in that cosmic role appropriates the powers and attributes of the holy trinity who are visualized as no more than her mounts.'[64]

Still, the Fierce Goddesses[65] are often depicted as the consorts of Shiva and in this they also represent role models.[66] But these role models must be regarded far more as 'antimodels', since they violate all traditional expectations as represented in the *pati vrata* ideals of Sita, Sati and Parvati.

> By antimodels I mean that their roles violate approved social values, customs, norms, or paradigms. [. . . T]he most powerful approved model for Hindu women for centuries has been the goddess Sita, who is the ideal *pati vrata* (a wife devoted to her husband). Hindu women for generations have been socialized to view Sita as an ideal to imitate in their own lives. Sita's husband is the be-all and end-all of her existence. Her thoughts and actions, wishes and dreams, all focus on him; her life only has meaning in relation to him. Most of the Mahavidyas, however, either are independent from males or dominate (sometimes humiliate) them in one way or another. *Many of the Mahavidyas seem to mock the pati vrata ideal and to present an alternative social role that is almost its exact opposite.*[67]

In several myths the *Mahavidyas* originate when a goddess[68] exerts independence from her husband, namely from Shiva. It is exactly in this sense that the *Mahavidyas* are role models of female independence. Among them Kali is the most prominent one, who symbolizes fully awakened consciousness and female independence simultaneously. She is not the subservient wife of Shiva, but the embodiment of destructive frenzy, who dominates Shiva by standing on him. To mark her superiority over the male god, Kali assumes the upper position, 'the man's position', in sexual intercourse. In these myths she violates the ideal of a *pati vrata* in a very drastic way! Also her appearance is rather shocking, if compared to the ideal wife. Her hair is not tightly bound, she is not inhibited and modest. Kali displays her naked body, her hair is unbound, she is smeared with blood and her ornaments are made of skulls, often depicting chopped off heads of men. She is sexually aggressive, always described as having sex with Shiva.[69]

In her *sahasranama stotra* (thousand name hymn) many names emphasize her vigorous sexual appetite or her sexual attractiveness. She is called She Whose Essential Form Is Sexual Desire, Whose Form Is the Yoni, [. . .] Who Loves the Lingam, Who Dwells in the Lingam, Who Is Worshiped With Semen, [. . .] Who Is Always Filled With Semen, and many other such names. In this respect, Kali also violates the idea of the controlled woman who is sexually satisfied by marriage. Kali is sexually voracious, and dangerous because of this. Kali denotes freedom particularly from social norms. She [. . .] is totally unrestrained, totally free from social and ethical roles and expectations. [. . .] *And she is powerful,* [. . .] *a breaker of boundaries and social models.*[70]

It becomes evident then that Tantra contains keys for the promotion of the autonomy of women. As Tantra, especially in its *Vama Marga* manifestation, advocates a direct confrontation with the accepted social values through transgression, it follows that women following this path would emulate the behaviour of the goddesses they worship. The emphasis should not be laid, however, on sexuality as such, but on the social transgressions and the gender-inclusive *dharma* of Tantra that is a unique manifestation in the history of Hinduism. Khanna shows that in the history of Tantra, there existed exceptional women, who gained prominence in Tantric traditions. Some of them were even praised in Tantric scriptures and worshipped as goddesses.[71] White, though not denying this fact, objects that despite the prominence of the Goddess and *Shakti* in Tantric thought, women have never dominated in sociopolitical matters in Tantric communities.[72] It is commonly held that despite the Tantric emphasis on women and goddesses, female consorts actually remained as instrumental requirements of male initiates for transformation in ritual activities.[73] Khanna argues that women have more than just an instrumental role. She complains that scholars of Tantra have hitherto concentrated too exclusively on the yogic-sexual practices in their analysis of the role of women and their power relationship to men in Tantric circles. In Tantra, women have the right to be gurus and priestesses, and being initiated by a woman is considered as more efficacious than by a man.[74] This is a dramatic paradigm shift in Hindu culture as the Vedic scriptures and *dharmasastra* prohibit such positions for women. The social and ritual roles of women thus need to be reconsidered in terms of the Tantric scriptures like the *Shaktacara*.[75] Also certain forms of worship, like the *suvasini-puja*, transform the ritual role of women by worshipping them as living incarnations of the Goddess Tripurasundari or Lalita. Beside women worship there is also the significant attempt to develop a code of conduct in favour of women. Male devotees of *Shakti* are told to bow down if they stand in front of a group of women or if a man's gaze falls by chance on a woman, to imagine in his contemplation that he performs her worship. Furthermore, Tantra attempted to take strict stand against wife-beating and sexual abuse of women. Men are urged not to hurt, hate or anger women, rather they should honour them in special ways. Even widows, low-caste women and prostitutes are to be respected.[76]

All these ideas and practices present dramatic paradigm shifts in the Hindu context. This is due to the unique Tantric perspective that all women are manifestation of *Shakti*, the divine energy of the Goddess. Women are bearers of a divine flame by virtue of their own Shaktihood, the spark of the Goddess in them. Their physical bodies are expressions of the metaphysical 'body' of *Shakti*. The female body is not degraded and put down, but revered and worshiped. It is a vehicle to *moksha*, spiritual liberation, a mirror image of the Divine Feminine in terms of the micro-macrocosmic correlations, which underlies the magico-mystical worldview of Tantra. The body and the senses of the woman are manifestations of the spiritual energy of *Shakti*. Thus, even the secretions of the physical processes, including blood and other bodily substances, are considered to be pure and energy-bestowing.[77] This is truly astonishing considering the Brahmanic views on purity and impurity.[78] The Tantric perspective removes feelings of guilt and fear and subverts the logic of purity versus impurity. Tantra in this regard has the power to decentre hierarchies and to shift the balance towards a gender-inclusive *dharma*. Beyond its spiritual dimension, Tantra can provide a liberating and gender-inclusive perspective on the cultural front. Taking the Tantric view of womanhood one step further, namely by projecting it on the social fabric of modern India, the question arises if the Tantric conception of the Divine Feminine may be used as an emancipatory role model for Hindu women in general. 'Why not recast this paradigm in favor of a new one that is more radical and empowering for women? Why not, for example, invoke Kali not as a metaphor but as a kind of role model? As a goddess associated with transformative processes, Kali could well serve as a symbol of women's desire to transform and empower both their own lives and Hindu culture in general.'[79]

The more liberal attitudes towards women found in Tantric texts could be interpreted by Indian feminists in a postmodern fashion for emancipatory aims. In this way the divine archetypes of the Tantric goddesses may be seen as exemplary role models for women in contemporary India. Politically utilizing the myths deeply rooted in the Hindu tradition may show a way to reinterpret the role of women for their self-empowerment. Instead of leaving the monopoly of interpretation in the hands of male authorities, they may comb through the rich mythology of Hinduism for new ways of imagining the role of women in modern India. The Tantric archetypes have the potential not only to alter our perception of male-female relationships on the spiritual and cosmic scale, but also on social and physical/erotic levels.[80] Kali as well as other Tantric manifestations of *Shakti* may be invoked as goddesses symbolizing the transformative processes and liberating role models to serve women as ways of empowering themselves. The inclusive, holistic, body- and world-affirming vision of Tantra appears to make it very suitable in a globalized, postmodern setting of India, which is going through multiple processes of cultural, social and economic transformations. The undogmatic spirit of Tantra shifts the whole perspective on women, both in the religious and the social domain. Brooks already stated that Tantra should be considered as an essential aspect of Hinduism. Not taking Tantra into account, he argued, would not only impoverish our understanding of Hindu religiousness intellectually, but was historically negligent.[81] Instead of denying Tantra, it should be considered as enriching our understanding of Hinduism. Including Tantric notions into the academic and political discourses could not only empower women and their rights, but also energize Hindu culture in general.

Notes

1 From the album *Of Ruine or Some Blazing Starre – The Broken Heart of Man* (1994), Current 93 (David Tibet).
2 Cp. Geertz (1983).
3 *Dharma*, a Sanskrit term that is literally translated as 'that which upholds, supports or maintains (the regulatory order of the universe)'. It generally refers to the idea of 'Divine Law', 'Natural Law' or 'Divine Order', which is a key concept in Hindu philosophy. It forms the basis for various other important ideas in ancient Indian philosophy like reincarnation, karma, the caste system, *moksha*, etc. The notion of *dharma* is central for understanding the Indian concept of religion, which differs widely from Eurocentric conceptions of religion. *Dharma* implies duties and obligations for the individual members of a community, imposing certain behaviours considered necessary for the maintenance of the divine order. The understanding of this concept is key for the context of our study of the relationship of *dharma* and gender as the archetypal role models discussed in this essay are based on this very notion deeply rooted in traditional Hindu thinking.
4 Cp. Kakar (1988); Wadely (1988).
5 Khanna (2002: 36).
6 Ibid.: 35.
7 Khanna (2002); cp. Pinchman (1994).
8 Khanna (2002): 36f.
9 Ibid.: 56, fn 5.
10 Sharma and Young (1999): 28.

11 Skr.: *Shloka* is literally translated as 'song'. A category of verse line used in classical Vedic poetry, like in the ancient Sanskrit epic *Ramayana*.
12 Cp. Roberts and Yamane (2011): 87.
13 Cp. Wulf (2013); Michaels and Wulf (2012); Wulf et al. (2001).
14 Cp. Wulf (2005); Gebauer and Wulf (1996); Wulf (2009).
15 'Mimetic learning, learning by imitation, constitutes one of the most important forms of learning. Mimetic learning does not, however, just denote mere imitation or copying. Rather, it is a process by which the act of relating to other persons and worlds in a mimetic way leads to an enhancement of one's own world view, action, and behaviour. Mimetic learning is productive; it is related to the body, and it establishes a connection between the individual and the world as well as other persons; it creates practical knowledge, which is what makes it constitutive of social, artistic, and practical action. Mimetic learning is cultural learning, and as such it is crucial to teaching and education' (Wulf 2008: 56).
16 See below, *Kali's Gifts and Paradigm Shifts* . . .
17 Social violence includes cases of female feticide, infanticide, dowry, domestic verbal and physical abuse, sexual harassment, etc. 'General crimes against women have risen over the last five years, both in absolute numbers and as a percentage of all crimes, according to the National Crimes Record Bureau' ('The death of Kali', in: *Hindustan Times*, July 19th, 2012, p. 12).
18 Cp. Khanna (2002: 36).
19 The *dharmasastra* and *smrti* literature are codified Hindu religious texts describing *dharma*, law, customs, and codes of conduct according to the Brahmanical tradition.
20 Khanna (2002: 36).
21 *smartized* is the term for texts that come from the *smrti* literature, cp. fn. 19.
22 Cp. Khanna (2002).
23 Skr.: paraya 'not one's own', dhan: 'property, wealth, asset'. A term describing the concept that married daughters are considered the 'property' or 'asset' of someone else, namely her husband and his family.
24 The practice of Satipratha, self-immolation of a recently widowed woman, which existed in the past and was abolished by the British, follows this mythical idol.
25 Skr.: sacrifice.
26 It is noteworthy that Kali appears in several mythical tales as the alter ego of Parvati, when manifesting as her anger in the *Linga-purana*, etc. Kali also manifests as Sati's embodied anger or Durga's personified wrath (cp. Kinsley 1997: 71f.). In that sense we may say that Kali can be seen as the 'dark side' of the Divine Feminine, which is acknowledged in Hindu mythology, but as something that needs to be kept under control.
27 The esoteric interpretation in the Tantras is very different from this popular version. The Tantric perspective is that Kali represents the principle of divine energy whilst Shiva, lying motionless on the ground, symbolizes divine consciousness. By stepping on Shiva, the motionless, all-seeing consciousness becomes energized by the divine power of Shakti. For the bi-polar relationship of Shiva-Shakti, see below, '*At the left hand of the Goddess*'.
28 Dube (2004: 106).
29 For the Tantric view of Kali, see below, *Kali's Gifts* . . .
30 Cp. Dube (2004: 107).

31 A Sanskrit term literally meaning the one who takes a vow, *vrata*, to be completely devoted to her husband, *pati*.
32 Kinsley (1997: 6). For further implications see below, *Kali's Gifts* . . ..
33 Pinchman (1994: 212).
34 This term is inspired by Svoboda's (1986) Tantric book.
35 Cp. Urban (2003, 2006); White (2000); Kinsley (1988).
36 Another problematic term that defies categorization. It was introduced by the British colonials to describe a whole variety of different religious practices and beliefs scattered all over India.
37 Urban (2003, 2006) points out very convincingly the East-West divisions become blurred in a globalized world as 'New Age gurus', as Osho (former Bhagwan Rajneesh) proves, who was born in India and created a popular movement of *Neo-Sannyasins* in the West by eclectically mixing traditional Indian spirituality with ideas from modern philosophy and psychotherapeutic techniques.
38 Feuerstein demonstrates convincingly that the misunderstanding of Western New Age protagonists promoting those forms of Neo-Tantra is due to the confusion of mistaking ordinary orgasmic pleasure with the Tantric concept of bliss (*ananda, maha-sukha*). Reducing Tantra to sexuality is a gross misinterpretation and misrepresentation of the Tantric traditions (cp. Feuerstein 1998: xiv).
39 Wilhelm Reich was a psychotherapist of a rather radical psychoanalytic brand. He introduced the concept of the 'body armour' into modern psychology, which spurred a new branch of psychotherapeutic schools, such as 'body psychotherapy', Perls's 'Gestalt therapy', Lowen's school of 'bioenergy', or Pierrakos's 'Core Energetics'. Reich assumed that blocked sexual energy was stored in the 'body armour'. This, he believed, led to neurosis. By experiencing a full-blown, uninhibited orgasm the blocked emotions stored in the 'body armour', caused by sexual repression, could be released and thus heal the neurotic patient.
40 Cp. White (2000) and Feuerstein (1998).
41 Cp. Urban (2006).
42 Cp. Urban (2006).
43 Cp. Foulston and Abbott (2009): 98f.
44 *Orientalism* refers in this context to a term coined by Edward Said describing Western feelings of superiority over Asian cultures. It was developed in the field of postcolonial studies. Said basically analysed that many scholars in the West were purporting false assumptions about Asian, especially Middle Eastern and Muslim cultures, that were implicitly rooted in their Eurocentric prejudices. Further he implied in his critique of Eurocentrism that this Western attitude served as an underlying theoretical superstructure to justify Western colonial and imperial ambitions (cp. Said 1979). Said's concept of Orientalism has remained 'a hermeneutical tool for interrogating and uncovering hidden assumptions about the Other' (Sugirtharajah 2008: 76). This critique certainly also applies to many British scholars and/or missionaries in India of the nineteenth century, who were writing about Tantra and Hinduism in general. Cp. Urban (2003).
45 Urban (2006: 82). Sexual magic, *magia sexualis* or 'sex magick' has emerged as a practice in the nineteenth century in the West and was popularized by occultists like Pascal Beverly Randolph (1825–1875) and Aleister Crowley (1875–1947). This, however, has hardly to do with Tantra. In early Hindu Tantra, sexual intercourse was probably only the means for creating the sexual fluids that were conceived of as magical substances used for initiatory

purposes. It was believed that the female sexual fluids embodied the power of Shakti, containing the germ plasm of the godhead. It was only later that more sophisticated eroto-mystical practices would be developed, where the Tantric notion of sexual union was associated with the expansion of consciousness and blissful ecstasy *(ananda)*. Cp. White (2000, 2006); Urban (2003, 2006).

46 The belief in *shakti* as universe can also be found in non-Tantric Hindu traditions, but it is only 'within the Tantric traditions that we find fully developed, systematic philosophical theologies conveying eloquently this position' (Foulston and Abbott 2009: 99).

47 Cp. White (2000); Kinsley (1997); Foulston and Abbott (2009).

48 Foulston and Abbott (2009: 99).

49 Padoux (1986).

50 Cp. White (2000).

51 White (2000: 9), emphasis added.

52 Cp. Foulston and Abbott (2009: 99).

53 For the cultural implications of the concept of *purity*, cp. Douglas (2002).

54 May be a psychedelic drug of some sort, cp. Kinsley (1997: 78).

55 By undertaking the ritual of the *panca tattva* she/he 'tastes the forbidden', the 'five (forbidden) things'. The esoteric meaning behind this is that the *sadhaka* is affirming in a radical way the unity of the phenomenal world *(maya)* with the highest principle of ultimate reality *(brahman)*, the Absolute (for the implications of this, see below). As the phenomenal world, or matter, is an expression and emanation of *Shakti* (expressed in the concept of *prakriti*, see fn 60), all dualities perceived by the mind must be illusory in nature. Hence by the antinomian act of 'tasting the forbidden' the *tantrika* transcends the limitations of dualistic identity. By this method she/he transforms mundane consciousness into a state of enlightenment. Thus, it is assumed, the tantrika is freed from the delusion of separateness and embraces all existence, including 'the forbidden' or 'polluted'. She/He heroically triumphs over all limited concepts of clean and unclean, sacred and profane, and breaks her/his bondage to false conceptions of duality. The power of the forbidden is disarmed by changing the feared, the polluted, and the forbidden into spiritually transformative energy, *Shakti*. Cp. Kinsley (1997: 78).

56 Foulston and Abbott (2009: 100).

57 In Tantric view the body is conceived in terms of micro-macro correlations as discussed above. It is in this context that the notion of the divinity of the body is articulated, conceptualized as an emanation of the divine energy of *Shakti*. 'The human body is conceived as a miniature cosmos. Behind the corporeal frame there exists an "etheric" double which manifests in subtle form as pulsations of cosmic energy, technically referred to as the *kundalini-Shakti*. This *Shakti* resides in the divine body *(suksma-sarira)*, which symbolically mirrors all the elements and astral planes of the outer universe. Whatever forces govern the outer cosmos govern also the inner planes of the body cosmos. It is held in the Tantras that we do not experience our consciousness as external to our body. The subtle aspects of consciousness of the unity of creation, manifests in, and through, the subtle channels of the body cosmos. Tantra has evolved a very elaborate symbolic code of chakras, energy vortices and subtle channels, together with yoga to unfold the mysteries of creation' (Khanna 2002: 47). Cp. also White (1997); and White (2012).

58 Bhattacharyya and Dvivdei (1978): Part 2, ch. 13, verses 43–49.

59 Lust or sexual desire, anger, affection or infatuation, pride and greed.

55

60 Cp. Tuck (1986); Pinchman (1994). Pinchman demonstrates that the Great Goddess (*Mahadevi*) manifests as *Shakti* (creative energy), *maya* (objective illusion), and *prakriti* (materiality or the unfolding force of nature) simultaneously. The interrelationships between the concepts of *Shakti, maya, and prakriti* are especially expressed in Tantric theological ideas. Though firmly rooted in the ancient Vedic traditions, these concepts of the Great Goddess developed over centuries from Vedic times to the late Puranic period.
61 Cp. White (2000).
62 The Absolute or Universal Spirit. It is the Hindu conception of the highest or ultimate reality as an impersonal principle.
63 Cp. Kinsley (1997: 5).
64 Khanna (2002: 42).
65 Khanna focuses basically on all features of *Shakti* in the Hindu Tantric tradition. We emphasize especially her fierce, wild features, as especially manifested in the *Ten Mahavidyas*.
66 Cp. Kinsley (1997: 5).
67 Kinsley (1997: 6), emphasis added.
68 This goddess might have even the name of Sati or Parvati as these also represent the *Mahadevi*, the Great Goddess, albeit in her benign form. This might appear confusing to the outsider. But in the Tantric context it becomes even more evident that the paradigm of *pati vrata* is smashed, when the *Mahavidyas* receive their autonomy from Sati or Parvati, who normally symbolize the ideal wife. However, most drastically Kali is representing the role model of female independence.
69 Cp. Kinsley (1997: 79f.).
70 Cp. Kinsley (1997: 80), emphasis added.
71 However, Khanna (2002: 55) makes no exclusive claim that female *tantrika* have not been at all under the influence of the patriarchal structures of orthodox Hinduism.
72 Cp. White (2000).
73 Cp. White (2000).
74 Cp. Khanna (2002: 53f.).
75 Roles of conduct followed by the Shaktas, a Tantric sect devoted to the worship of *Shakti*.
76 Cp. Khanna (2002: 45f.).
77 Cp. ibid.: 47.
78 Traditionally, women are prohibited to perform spiritual services when they menstruate. The menstrual cycle is regarded as highly polluting and shameful and is associated with sin and feelings of guilt.
79 Pinchman (1994: 213).
80 Cp. Khanna (2002: 55).
81 Cp. Brooks (1990: ix).

References

Bhattacharyya, B., and Dvivdei, Vrajavallabha (1978): Saktisamgama Tantra. Barodia (India): Gaekwod Oriental Series.

Brooks, Douglas Renfrew (1990): The Secret of the Three Cities: An Introduction to Hindu Sakta Tantrism. Chicago: University of Chicago Press.

Douglas, Mary (2002 [1966]): Purity and Danger: An Analysis of Concepts of Pollution and Taboo. Oxford: Taylor & Francis.

Dube, Saurabh (2004): Stitches on Time: Colonial Textures and Postcolonial Tangles. Durham: Duke University Press.

Feuerstein, George (1998): Tantra – The Path of Ecstasy. Princeton: Princeton University Press.

Foulston, Lynn, and Abbott, Stuart (2009): Hindu Goddesses: Beliefs and Practice. Eastbourne: Sussex Academic Press.

Gebauer, Gunter, and Wulf, Christoph (1996): Mimesis: Culture – Art – Society. Berkeley, Los Angeles: University of California Press.

Geertz, Clifford (1983): Local Knowledge: Further Essays in Interpretative Anthropology. London: Collins.

Kakar, Sudhir (1988): Feminine Identity in India. In: Ghadially, Rehana (ed.): Women in Indian Society, 44–68. New Delhi: Sage.

Kinsley, David (1997): Tantric Visions of the Divine Feminine: The Ten Mahavidyas. Berkeley, Los Angeles: University of California Press.

Kinsley, David (1998 [1986]): Hindu Goddesses: Visions of the Divine Feminine in the Hindu Religious Tradition. Berkeley, Los Angeles: University of California Press.

Khanna, Madhu (2002): The Goddess-Woman Equation in Sakta Tantras. In: Ahmed, Durre S. (ed.): Gendering the Spirit – Women, Religion & the Post-Colonial Response, 35–59. London, New York: Zed Books.

Michaels, Axel, and Wulf, Christoph (eds.) (2012): Emotions in Rituals and Performances. London, New York, New Delhi: Routledge.

Padoux, André (1986): Tantrism. In: Eliade, Mircea (ed.): Encyclopedia of Religion, vol. 14, 272–276. New York: Macmillan.

Pinchman, Tracy (1994): The Rise of the Goddess in the Hindu Tradition. New York: State University of New York Press.

Roberts, Keith, and Yamane, David (2011): Religion in Sociological Perspective. California: Pine Forge Press.

Said, Edward (1979 [1878]): Orientalism. New York: Random House.

Sharma, Arvind, and Young, Katherine (1999): Feminism and World Religions. New York: State University of New York Press.

Sugirtharajah, Sharada (2008): Colonialism. In: Mittal, Sushil, Thursby, Gene (eds.): Studying Hinduism – Key Concepts and Methods. New York: Routledge.

Svaboda, Robert (1986): Aghora – At the Left Hand of God. Albuquerque: Brotherhood of Life Books.

Tuck, Donald (1986): The Concept of Maya in Samkara and Radhakrishnan. New Delhi: Chanakya Publications.

Urban, Hugh B. (2003): Tantra: Sex, Secrecy, Politics and Power in the Study of Religion. Berkeley, Los Angeles: University of California Press.

Urban, Hugh B. (2006): Magia Sexualis: Sex, Magic, and Liberation in Modern Western Esotericism. Berkeley, Los Angeles: University of California Press.

Wadely, Susan (1988): Women and the Hindu Tradition. In: Ghadially, Rehana (ed.): Women in Indian Society, 23–43. New Delhi: Sage.

White, David Gordon (1997): The Alchemical Body: Siddha Traditions in Medieval India. Chicago: University of Chicago Press.

White, David Gordon (ed.) (2000): Tantra in Practice. Princeton: Princeton University Press.

White, David Gordon (2006): Kiss of the Yogini: 'Tantric Sex' in its South Asian Contexts. Chicago: University of Chicago Press.

White, David Gordon (2012): Yogic Rays: The Self-Externalization of the Yogi in Ritual, Narrative and Philosophy. In: Michaels, Axel, Wulf, Christoph (eds.): Emotions in Rituals and Performances, 56–69. London, New York, New Delhi: Routledge.

Wulf, Christoph (2005): Zur Genese des Sozialen. Mimesis, Performativität, Ritual. Bielefeld: Transcript.

Wulf, Christoph (2008): Designs for Learning, vol. 1, no. 1 (March 2008). Source on 1.9.2012: http://www.designsforlearning.nu/archive_no1_08.htm.

Wulf, Christoph (2013): Anthropology. A Continental Perspective. Chicago: The University of Chicago Press.

Wulf, Christoph, Althans, Birgit, Audehm, Kathrin, Bausch, Constanze, Göhlich, Michael, Sting, Stephan, Tervooren, Anja, Wagner-Willi, Monika, and Zirfas, Jörg (2001): Das Soziale als Ritual. Zur performativen Bildung von Gemeinschaften. Opladen: Leske + Budrich.

2

THE SACRED COW AND THE IDEAL OF *AHIMSĀ*

Kristina Schmitz-Valkenberg

Meeting the sacred cow in India

While visiting India, I encountered animals in different areas and surroundings.[1] In the countryside, I saw bulls ploughing fields and it seemed that especially in rural areas people rely on the strength of their cattle. But also in the big cities like Udaipur[2] and Varanasi[3] cows and bulls harnessed to carriages could be observed. Sometimes cows and bulls stood, seemingly without a human owner, in the streets unimpressed by the surrounding traffic and the busy life of the city. Calmness and a feeling of freedom surrounded them.

Travellers can experience that diets in India vary. I observed that different states and regions offer different dishes and food. Fish and meat like chicken and mutton can be eaten in selected restaurants. Nevertheless, I learned that beef is never part of the menu of traditional Hindu restaurants and that vegetarian restaurants indeed are quite common in India. While studying and travelling through India, questions concerning the relationship between humans and animals and the aspects of nourishment and vegetarianism in Hinduism arose and started to interest me.

In India, 700 million people belong to Hinduism (Malinar 2009). Also in South Africa and Nepal Hinduism is widespread. Hinduism is categorized as a world religion. Diversity in traditions and communities occur and there is not only 'one' Hinduism. In my opinion these facts make it more interesting but also more difficult to grasp religious concepts which influence humans' diets and their relationship with animals in Hinduism. The sacred cow,[4] non-beef eating, *ahimsā*[5] and vegetarianism are aspects which are deeply connected with the treatment of animals and diets in Hinduism. The phenomenon of the sacred cow in Hinduism expresses itself through different practices. 'Cow protection' (Gandhi 1954: 3), 'festivals [. . .] ceremonies' (Sharpes 2006: 216f.) are only some ways to honour the sacred cow. *Ahiṃsā* or 'not to hurt any living thing' (Gandhi as cited in Walli 1974: xxii) is basic to Hinduism as well. Well known is Mohandas Karamchand Gandhi's positive stance on the importance of cow protection and the sacred cow in Hinduism. The special tie between humans and animals and all living beings is illustrated.

The goal of this explorative paper is to give a theoretical overview of selected historical and cultural aspects of the sacred cow and *ahiṃsā* in connection to nourishment in Hinduism. The extraordinary relationship between humans and animals will be looked at. The religious scriptures of the *Vedas*[6] and the legislative text of the *Manusmṛti*[7] are quoted. Which guidelines for cow protection and nourishment are mentioned there?

Gandhi was one of the most outstanding and active public figures in India and the British Empire in the first half of the twentieth century (Brown 2011). He is probably best known for his concept of non-violence[8] to protest against political injustice under the British occupation in India. Gandhi adjusted the concept of *ahiṃsā* and continued the tradition of *ahiṃsā* in Hinduism and Indian thought through the concept of non-violence. He wrote and published articles on various topics concerning India and Hinduism. While reading about Gandhi, I got the impression that Gandhi was a man who tried to represent his ideals through his whole personality and body. He was a devoted Hindu and vegetarian. In connection to the phenomena of the sacred cow and *ahiṃsā* in Hinduism this article will discuss Gandhi's view on the concepts of cow protection, *ahiṃsā* and vegetarianism.

Guiding questions for this paper are: which influences on the relationship between humans and animals do cow protection and *ahiṃsā* have? How can these concepts be defined? How are these concepts related and how do they have to be arranged in the context of Hinduism? Not preventable is the European perspective of the author. Questions are verbalized from a European perspective. Different aspects of the concepts of the sacred cow and *ahiṃsā* are highlighted and a historical and religious angle is applied. Historical-cultural anthropology looks at time, context and changes in culture (Wulf 2013). The constant change of human nature and culture leads to complexity and diversity in anthropology. In this paper the attempt to connect historical aspects of the sacred cow, *ahiṃsā* and nourishment to the present time is made. Today the phenomena of the sacred cow and *ahiṃsā* are unique and basic to Hinduism. The connection of religion and nourishment make these topics fascinating. It is inspiring to look at cultural factors which influence diets in globalized and fast changing cultures.

THE SACRED COW AND THE IDEAL OF AHIMSĀ

The paper starts with an overview on the historical and current use of cattle in India. The relationship between humans and cattle in Hinduism is analysed. A differentiation between the concepts of the sacred cow in connection to non-beef eating and *ahiṃsā* in connection to vegetarianism in Hinduism follows. The Hindu concepts of rebirth and *karman*[9] are presented in connection to *ahiṃsā* and vegetarianism. The scriptures of the *Vedas* and the *Manusmṛti* are looked at afterwards. Gandhi's view on the sacred cow and vegetarianism follows. A conclusion with a summary of the findings and ongoing aspects and questions concerning the sacred cow and vegetarianism in India complete this paper.

The historical and current use of cattle in India and the relationship with cattle in Hinduism

Sharpes (2006) states that prior to 2,200 BCE, Neolithic[10] people and their herds of Bos Indicus, the humped Indian cattle, entered central India from Iran. This is confirmed by ash mounds built by burned cow dung. Estimated by the size of the mounds the herds which accompanied people in these times consisted of about 500–800 animals. The burning of cow dung may not only have been practiced for making fire but also have been integrated in early religious ceremonies. In addition, terra cotta bulls and paintings on rock walls exist from this period.

Amazingly, today India has 3 per cent of the earth's land mass but 33 per cent of the earth's cattle population (Sharpes 2006). Travelling through India, one can see various kinds of cows. The zebu and the water buffalo are only two of the long list. Half of the water buffalo population lives in India. About 85 per cent of cows and 90 per cent of water buffalo are kept for their milk. The rest are kept as draught animals. These numbers show the importance of cattle in India. In addition, the fact that two-thirds of India's population lives in villages and depend on cattle as work animals and as source for dairy products underlines this importance.

The tradition of animal homes has a long history in India (Sharpes 2006). Already three thousand years ago there were sheds and land for weak and sick cattle. More elaborate places were attached to temples. Today these homes mostly shelter cattle but also other animals like horses, sheep, goats and deer. The animal homes connected to temples use the cattle's products like milk and dung for their services and also for sale. Sharpes states that these places are important especially during droughts. Farmers can bring their cattle to these homes and they are taken care of. Later the cows or other animals are released to people who are in need of them. These homes take care of animals out of ethical and religious reasons. Economically, they rely on donations and state aid.

Today, the cow plays a significant role in Hinduism. Lord *Kṛṣṇa*[11] is the most popular deity and the incarnation manifestation of god *Viṣṇu*[12] (Sharpes 2006). *Kṛṣṇa* symbolizes the cowherd and love. The cowherd and *Kṛṣṇa* have become inseparable with the Hindu belief. Additionally, *Nandi* as *Śiva's*[13] bull represents *Śiva's* strength and can give his power to humanity. Jansen (2002) mentions that in earlier times *Nandi*[14] was called *Nandikeshvara*[15] and an independent god of joy and represented as man with a bull's head. In my opinion the popularity of *Kṛṣṇa* and *Nandi* represents the importance of the cow in Hindu belief. The cow is a sacred animal in Hinduism (Sharpes 2006). Gandhi (1954) mentions the concern about the wellbeing of the cow and the bull which belong to Hinduism and a Hindu's everyday life. Cow statues are found in temples and feasts for the celebration of the cow and the bull are held (Sharpes 2006).

Sharpes (2006) also remarks that the feast of Gocharan in the Indian city of Nathdwara[16] is one example for how the cow is celebrated. Some selected cows are washed, decorated and coloured. They are fed with special food like molasses and sweet mash. These cows are paraded through the city's streets and later worshipped in the temple. People from every milieu attend this special celebration.

But today also the economical aspect of cattle in connection to the sacred cow is of great importance. Gandhi (1954) mentions the monetary price which has to be paid by protecting cows. In his opinion the religious belief and the concept of *ahiṃsā* or non-violence have to have a stronger significance than economical aspects.

The phenomena of the sacred cow and *ahiṃsā* and their role in the context of Hinduism

In the following, the notions of the sacred cow and *ahiṃsā* are differentiated and presented in detail. A connection between vegetarianism, *ahiṃsā*, rebirth, *karman* and *dharma* is made.

The differentiation and connection of the phenomena of the sacred cow and ahiṃsā

Alsdorf (1962) presents the two phenomena of the sacred cow and *ahiṃsā* as two basic guidelines in Hinduism. The important fact is that these two phenomena and their facets have to be seen and analysed separately. The sacred cow is connected to cow protection and non-beef eating in

Hinduism. Millions of Hindus do eat fish, chicken or goat,[17] but no beef. The consequence of *ahiṃsā* is the complete abstinence of meat, fish and often also of eggs. This results in a vegetarian diet. The religious reason for a strict vegetarian diet in Hinduism is unique and includes a huge part of the Hindu population in India.

The phenomenon of *ahiṃsā*

Alsdorf (1962) states that vegetarianism in India originates in *ahiṃsā*, the concept of respect and non-violence against fellow humans and other living beings. This includes the absence of the consumption of meat. The logical reason for this is 'no meat without animal killing, therefore no *ahiṃsā* without the abstinence of the consumption of meat' (Alsdorf 1962: 561, translation Kristina Schmitz-Valkenberg).[18] *Ahiṃsā* does not refer to a Western understanding of ethics but to a magical and ritual understanding of life leading to a prohibition of the destruction of life (Alsdorf 1962). The prohibition of eating meat in Hinduism is rooted in the belief that all living things are sacred (Sharpes 2006). Gosh (1988) states that *ahiṃsā* is more than non-killing. It is sacrifice and kindness of the highest order.

> The Ancient Vedic culture is the cradle of the concept of [*ahiṃsā*]. [. . .] The concept of [*ahiṃsā*] seeped through all the religions of India [. . .] The pervasive strain of vegetarianism forming the bed-rock of Hinduism was inspired primarily from the practice of [*ahiṃsā*]. In short, [*ahiṃsā*] has thus been held in high esteem in India in different times.
>
> Gosh (1988: 33)

The sacred cow in Hinduism

The cow probably already played an important role in the life and culture of the *ārya*[19] before they immigrated from the north to India (Alsdorf 1962). These immigrants brought their 'Indus culture' (Lipner 2007: 11) to India (Alsdorf 1962). These tribes are sometimes also called Vedic tribes and brought the *Vedas* and so-called Vedic culture with them, and so this marked the start of the Vedic time[20] (Malinar 2009). Scriptures written prior to the immigration of the *ārya* to India state that the washing of feet, hands and face with cow urine is mandatory (Alsdorf 1962). In this pre-Vedic practice, the special role of the cow is already visible.

The connection between the sacred cow and ahiṃsā

It is interesting that the special role of the cow in the āryan culture in pre-Vedic times did not exclude the consumption of beef (Alsdorf 1962). The special position of an animal was accompanied by its killing and meat consumption. Cow protection was not part of the pre-Vedic culture. The protection and sacredness of the cow presumably was an independent development in Hinduism which accumulated throughout the centuries until the sacred cow as a unique phenomenon presents itself today. It has to be separated from the phenomenon of *ahiṃsā* and vegetarianism in Hinduism. *Ahiṃsā* started its development later in the Vedic period (Malinar 2009). Nevertheless, Alsdorf (1962) proposes that in later times the ideal of *ahiṃsā* associated with the sacredness of the cow and influenced the development of the taboos[21] and the unique stance of cattle in Hinduism today.

Ahiṃsā and Vegetarianism in connection to rebirth, karman and dharma in Hinduism

Walli (1974) states that the concept of *ahiṃsā* is based on the understanding that the love and affection a human being feels for oneself and his family or relatives should be extended to the rest of the world. It is comparable to the Christian understanding of 'love thy neighbor as thyself' (Walli 1974: 14). Walli's definition of *ahiṃsā* is the following:

> Ahiṃsā means absence of hiṃsā. Hiṃsā means hurting or injuring (others). Ahiṃsā would mean not hurting nor injuring (others) in thought [,] word or deed. In other words it is of three types (1) Mānasika, i.e. ahiṃsā in thought, (2) Vācika, i.e. ahiṃsā in word, (3) Kāyika, i.e. ahiṃsā in deed. (ibid.: 15)

This definition reveals the wide spectrum of *ahiṃsā*. *Ahiṃsā* is part of *sattva*,[22] a pure and salvific way of living (Malinar 2009). *Sattva* includes ascetic values like vegetarianism, religious qualification and moderation. The absence of desire in act and thought is the aspiration. These moral and religious rules should be considered in a Hindu's everyday life. Additionally, '*ahiṃsā* is connected to the doctrine of *karman*, whereupon violence leads to an extraordinary negative charge for the next life; as well as the doctrine that all creatures – also animals and plants – an "immortal self" indwells' (Malinar 2009: 244, translation K. S.-V.).[23] This principle leads to the notion that you should not inflict pain on other creatures (Malinar 2009). Vegetarianism is a way to consider this. The concept of *karman* was probably developed during the time of the *Upaniṣads*[24] and *karman* describes the connection of the actor with the act (Tull 2007).

In detail, *karman* and rebirth regard the notion that everybody contains an 'immortal self'. This 'immortal self' is part of *saṃsāra*,[25] the cycle of birth and death, until it recognizes its own identity and is freed from its worldly body (Malinar 2009). The presence of a body itself means that the person or being has not recognized the true self yet. *Karman* describes the concept that every being brings deeds from the last life into a new life after rebirth. This means that every creature has to try and make the most out of the baggage it carries and has to improve itself. 'Thus the true cause of the birth of a being, together with its character and destiny, goes back to the Karma-volitions produced in former birth' (Mahathera 1964). This shows the importance and the far reaching consequences of *ahiṃsā* in Hinduism.

> In later texts of Buddhism meat-eating has been completely prohibited. The arguments put forth are numerous. In the cycle of rebirth each one is related to the other in different lives, and birds and animals of present birth might have been of nobler or higher birth in the former lives. Who knows with whom one was related in former lives or will be in future lives, so to eat the flesh of any living creature may be to eat flesh of our own kith and kin.
>
> Walli (1974: 152)

For Gupta (1968), cow protection in Hinduism is also a matter of *dharma*.[26] The lives of humans are closely connected with the lives of cattle. This makes cow protection inseparable from human religious life and is a duty. 'Service of Cow has become a Dharma in India on account of her being symbol and mother of physical, mental and spiritual prosperity. It should always be kept in mind that amelioration of cattle depends upon the growth of the man and vice-versa' (Gupta 1968: 2). *Dharma* describes a concrete regulating principle for sexual experience, aesthetic experience and economic and political wellbeing (Holdrege 2007). The influence of these different concepts in Hinduism is apparent and underlines the important role of *ahiṃsā* and vegetarianism in Hinduism.

The relationship between humans and animals and different guidelines in Indian history

In the following, the *Vedas* and the *Manusmṛti* as guidelines concerning nourishment in Hinduism are considered. Gandhi's view of the notions of the sacred cow, vegetarianism and nourishment follows.

The religious scriptures of the Vedas in connection to the sacred cow, non-beef eating, ahiṃsā and vegetarianism in Hinduism

The Vedas are a collection of religious writings in Sanskrit (Günther 1997). They were collected and written over centuries and had been orally transferred before. The Vedas consist of four chronological parts: The Samhitās,[27] including the ṛgvedas,[28] the Brāhmaṇas,[29] the Āraṇyakas[30] and the Upaniṣads. The oldest hymns of the ṛgveda originated around 1,500–1,200 BCE The Upaniṣads were probably formed from 750 BCE well into the last millennium.

The idea of a strictly non-violent and vegetarian base of the Vedic and later Hindu belief is promoted by several authors. Rosen (2004: 21) mentions that the older tradition of animal sacrifices found in the Vedas was soon replaced by 'an animal made of dough'. 'Vedic texts are clear that meat-eating is the result of both passion (i.e. killing) and ignorance (i.e. death). Hence, a true Brahmin would never eat meat' (ibid.). Rosen states that 'unlike other world scriptures that temporized in regard to meat-eating, the Vedic literature was quite clear that animal sacrifice was an inferior form of worship' (ibid.: 23f.). This shows an early attachment to the non-killing of animals for sacrifices. Rosen additionally proposes that early on the Brahmins[31] absorbed the concept of 'harmlessness' and a vegetarian diet.

On the other hand, Malinar (2009) states that the animal sacrifice including the sacrifice of domesticated animals like sheep and goats for special occasions like lifecycle rituals were part of the Vedic belief. The sacred cow did not exist yet and the ṛgveda is source of sacral cattle sacrifice (Alsdorf 1962). Nevertheless, cattle had a special stance in late Vedic times even though its killing for sacrifice and the consumption of sacrificial beef were still allowed. Alsdorf proposes that the consumption of meat and beef were part of the daily life of the aryā. He assumes that during the change of the old aryā-religion to Hinduism animal sacrifices were pushed aside by ahiṃsā. The conflict between the Vedic animal sacrifice and ahiṃsā widened and animal sacrifice was substituted by inanimate sacrifice.

The two reform religions Buddhism and Jainism dating from the sixth century BCE, which had a big influence on Hinduism as well, had a focus on the concept of ahiṃsā (Alsdorf 1962). Hence Jainism and Buddhism had developed an aversion against the killing of animals. The killing of animals was strictly prohibited, but not necessarily the consumption of meat. This lead to the rule that the killing of animals was strictly prohibited but not the consumption of meat from animals which were killed by other people. Buddha was not a vegetarian and didn't forbid monks the consumption of meat. He states that 'fish and meat are pure under three conditions: when (the monk) hasn't seen, hasn't heard and has no suspicion (that the animal was killed for him)' (Alsdorf 1962: 563, translation K. S.-V.).[32] In Jainism, *ahiṃsā* is the most valued notion today, but in earlier days monks were allowed to eat meat under similar circumstances (Alsdorf 1962). Two of the oldest canonical texts state that handouts which had no or not too much bones were allowed to be eaten by Jain monks. Jainism includes the notion of animism and therefore everything, even elements like water, has a soul.

The Manusmṛti *as an example for legislative texts about guidelines for nourishment in historical India*

Dharma as a connective concept in Hinduism describes the idea of place and function of beings in the world (Malinar 2009). This order is called *dharma*. Humans themselves are part of this order. Through special duties they have to fulfill and rules they have to follow they are protectors of this order. The *Dharmaśāstras*[33] describe these duties and rules. The Laws of Manu or the *Manusmṛti* is one of these early legislative texts. The *Manusmṛti* was written by Manu and mostly depicts rules and routines for daily life. It was written between the second century BCE and the second century CE 'The Laws of Manu [. . .] consist of 2,685 verses on topics as apparently varied – but actually intimately interrelated in Hindu thought – as social obligations and duties of the various castes and of individuals in different stages of life' (Doniger and Smith 1991: xvi).

As Alsdorf states, in Chapter 5, verse 48 the *Manusmṛti* says that 'Meat can never be obtained without injury to living creatures, and injury to sentient beings is detrimental to (the attainment of) heavenly bliss; let him therefore shun (the use of) meat' (Alsdorf 1962: 561).[34] Additionally in verses 44–55 the consumption of meat is illustrated as immoral and vegetarianism on the basis of *ahiṃsā* is highly praised. To emphasize this the *Manusmṛti* states in verse 51 that 'He who permits (the slaughter of an animal), he who cuts it up, he who kills it, he who buys or sells (meat), he who cooks it, he who serves it up, and he who eats it (must all be considered as) the slayers (of the animal) (Alsdorf 1962: 577).[35]

But Alsdorf also identifies contradictions in the Laws of Manu. There are verses in the *Manusmṛti* which completely object the concept of *ahiṃsā* and vegetarianism. In Chapter 5, verses 5 to 25, different rules for permitted and not permitted food are given. Amongst other things we find a list of animals which are not allowed to be eaten. This indicates that there where animals which presumably were allowed to be eaten. Certain limitations are given here but no necessity for a vegetarian diet is indicated.

Animal sacrifices are justified in the Manusmṛti. In later passages (Chapter 5, verses 27–44), the text discusses the killing and consumption of animals amongst other things in connection to animal sacrifices. The text argues that 'Svayambhū has created animals as sacrifice; the sacrifice serves the prosperity of the whole world; therefore the killing of a sacrifice is no killing' (Alsdorf 1962: 575, translation K. S.-V.).[36] The religious offering still plays an important role in Hinduism today. Even the refusal of the consumption of ritual meat on the basis of *ahiṃsā* was punished by the declaration that the person would be reborn as a sacrificial animal for 21 times. Probably as a reassurance the promise that the sacrificial animal and the sacrificer later will be reborn into a high status is made. The Manusmṛti expresses a positive stance on the consumption of meat by the phrase 'meat consumption in sacrifices for gods and Manes is no sin'[37] (Alsdorf 1962: 576f., translation K. S.-V.).

There are also paragraphs in the Manusmṛti which relativize the former commandments. In Chapter 5, verse 56 it is stated that 'There is no sin in eating meat, in (drinking) spirituous liquor, and in carnal intercourse, for that is the natural way of created beings, but abstention brings great rewards' (Alsdorf 1962: 577).[38]

Alsdorf supposes that the contradictions in the Manusmr.ti concerning beef-eating and vegetarianism express changes in traditions and old traditions are presented next to new ones. On one hand the consumption of meat is shunned, on the other hand animal sacrifices and the consumption of certain kinds of meats, at least sacrificial meat and beef, seemed to be allowed. The stricter rules are relativized and the new concept of *ahiṃsā* is still weak and animal sacrifices are still promoted. This changed gradually throughout the centuries until today the concept of the sacred cow and inanimate sacrifices are the rule.

The development and changes of the concepts of the sacred cow and ahiṃsā throughout the centuries

The origin of the sacred cow is hard to trace back. But it is safe to say that in pre-Vedic and early Vedic times it did not yet exist. Different law books state different commandments about beef-eating. Some do not give clear guidelines or leave the topic of beef-eating out. Alsdorf proposes that the special role of cattle in pre-Vedic and Vedic times associated with *ahiṃsā* in later times might have led to the holiness of the cow today. Alsdorf states that the special role of the cow and the bull in Vedic times becomes apparent amongst other things through the prohibition to eat non-sacrificial beef. This was common but had nothing to do with *ahiṃsā* or non-violence today. Even through the tenth century CE, physicians wrote about the healing effect of beef. These are indications for cattle-killing and beef-eating as part of Indian history until medieval times. The consumption of holy animals in general is nothing unusual, but the strict restriction of killing and consumption of cattle in Hinduism is a special phenomenon. Nevertheless, there never was an indication for the sprouting of vegetarianism from the worship of the cow and non-beef eating in India. It seems that the sacred cow is an Indian phenomenon which developed throughout centuries. Concerning vegetarianism, the vegetarian diet was a phenomenon which mostly occurred in the *Brahmanic* class. ' [. . .] while *the Laws of Manu*, for example, prohibit the eating of meat for Brahmins (intellectuals, philosophers, priests), these *Laws* merely discourage meat-eating for the remaining classes of society' (Rosen 2004: 24). Alsdorf (1962) states that it is hard to get an exact picture of vegetarianism in India. There is no data, and literary evidences do not always represent the practical execution. Alsdorf states that in medieval and modern times most *Brahmans* avoided meat and eventually more and more Indians adopted a vegetarian diet. The orientation towards these *Brahmanic* standards led to a vegetarian diet in Hinduism.

Mohandas Karamchand Gandhi on ahiṃsā *and its modern adjustment through non-violence including vegetarianism and the protection of cattle*

Gandhi was brought up and lived in the Victorian age of Imperialism in India (Brown 2011). He was a devoted Hindu and interested in the Christian religion as well. During his time in London he joined the Vegetarian Society. Some of his experiences in the Vegetarian Society are presented in his book *The Moral Basis of Vegetarianism* published in 1959. Gandhi had entirely embodied and represented his values and ideas. '[Gandhi] emerges as a serious but self-taught thinker; someone who wrote and spoke prolifically, about many political, economic, social, and religious issues. However, his thinking was never divorced from his life of action' (Brown and Parel 2011: 259). Gandhi tried to act on his religious beliefs. 'Gandhi made some relaxations in his concept of [ahiṃsā] for making its use in one's daily life. Gandhi was downright a very practical person in his principles [. . .] he transformed the prevailing concept of [ahiṃsā] into a very practical weapon' (Gosh 1988: 114f.). Bilgrami (2011) states that Gandhi was a devoted Hindu and a very religious man. Therefore, *ahiṃsā* and the sacred cow in connection to cow protection as basic concepts in Hinduism were part of his life (Gandhi 1954). This included a vegetarian diet.

> Cow slaughter and man slaughter are in my opinion the two sides of the same coin. And the remedy for both is identical i.e. that

we develop the *ahimsa* principle and endeavour to win over our opponents by love.

Gandhi (1954: 16)

Gandhi's book *How to Serve the Cow* first published in 1954 discusses the topic of cow protection and the worship of the cow in Hinduism. The quotation above demonstrates Gandhi's devotion to *ahiṃsā* and some of his motivations for the protection of the cow. For him, the cow represents innocence and by protecting the cow a human being protects all beings and also the weak. In Gandhi's eyes Hindus and other religious people should believe in *ahiṃsā* or non-violence and should not stop there but try to protect every animal. This results in the non-killing of animals and in vegetarianism. The cow is merely a symbol for the animal kingdom. To reach *moksha*[39] or enlightenment a Hindu must, among other things, protect the cow and everything that feels. Gandhi states that the sacredness of the cow and vegetarianism are unique to Hinduism. But the philosophy of non-violence and acceptance should also be part of other religions. In Gandhi's opinion especially Islam, which is an essential part of Indian culture as well, should not be judged on its non-vegetarian and beef-eating tradition. But the appreciation for the cow and Hinduism should be promoted. The prohibition of cow slaughter is not a goal Gandhi had in mind and supported. Gandhi had specific ideas about cow protection:

> HOW TO SAVE THE COW? Cow protection societies must turn their attention to the feeding of cattle, prevention of cruelty, preservation of the fast disappearing pasture land, improving the breed of cattle, buying from poor shepherds and turning pinjrapols [home for old and weak cattle] into model self-supporting dairies.
>
> Gandhi (1954: 29)

The influence of cow protection on economical aspects is mentioned by Gandhi as well, even though a monetary solution or specific economical plan is not given by him. Gandhi mentions the problem of poverty in India. The supply of people with the adequate amount of nutrition must be achieved. He states that there is a high number of starving people in India. For Gandhi, the life of humans and the life of cattle are connected. 'Most of our villagers live with their animals, often under the same roof. Both live together, both starve together. [. . .] But if we reform our ways, we can both be saved. Otherwise we sink together' (Gandhi 1954: 12).

Gosh (1988) emphasizes that for Gandhi the killing of animals and meat-eating were strictly prohibited. In addition, Gandhi was also, maybe even more so, concerned with the far-reaching economical, political and

THE SACRED COW AND THE IDEAL OF AHIMSĀ

social exploitation and suffering of human beings than with direct physical pain or injury. For him, the huge amount of human suffering is the result of this exploitation. Nevertheless, he tried to avoid fatalism and held on to practical concepts for daily life. In consequence, vegetarianism and the protection of animals are only one aspect of Gandhi's *ahiṃsā*.

The importance of cow protection for Gandhi especially in connection to Hinduism is underlined by the following quotation: 'And Hinduism will live so long as there are Hindus to protect the cow' (Gandhi 1954: 4). In conclusion, the uniqueness of the sacred cow and *ahiṃsā* including vegetarianism in Hinduism for Gandhi leads to a need of preservation and special meaningfulness of these two aspects.

Mohandas Karamchand Gandhi on vegetarianism and nourishment

Table 2.1 is taken from Gandhi's book *The Moral Basis of Vegetarianism* first published in 1959. The table shows his suggestion for a daily diet for a healthy average male and female. There is no differentiation of gender, age or the daily demand depending on the occupation and the daily training. How should the reader deal with these numbers and suggestions?

In the book Gandhi comments on his view on vegetarianism. For him a vegetarian diet has more to do with the spirit than the body. A moral basis and a deliberate decision for a vegetarian diet on this moral basis are important and necessary. The statement 'One should eat not in order to please the palate but just to keep the body going' (Gandhi 1959: 19) seems to be a little bleak but it shows Gandhi's practical approach to this topic. He has an all-out approach to a person's diet. Strict amounts and rules

Table 2.1 Gandhi's recommendations for food and amounts for a healthy average men and women

Cow's milk	2 lbs[40]
Cereals (wheat, rice, bajri,[41] in all)	6 oz.[42]
Vegetables leafy	3 oz.
others	5 oz.
raw	1 oz.
Ghee[43]	1$^{1/2}$ oz.
or Butter	2 oz.
Gur[44] or white sugar	1$^{1/2}$ oz.

Gandhi (1959: 12).

concerning what and how much to eat are part of his book. In this book, the religious background of vegetarianism is not discussed thoroughly but a moral ground is emphasized. Some personal experiences with a vegetarian diet during Gandhi's time in London and his experiences with food, nutrition and health are presented. Gandhi mentions a connection of local food and balanced diet briefly, but stays on the surface of this matter.

Today his book seems to be a little naive and the issues in India concerning the supply of the population with the adequate amount of food are more problematic than ever. Newsworthy articles about the problems of the warehousing of grains can be read for example in the popular weekly German *SPIEGEL* magazine.[45] It seems that today the worldwide matter of malnutrition is more pressing than ever.

Mohandas Karamchand Gandhi and his non-political view on the sacred cow

The phenomenon of the sacred cow cannot be seen as a religious concept only; it also is a political issue. Gandhi wanted more than just a political implementation of a legislation against cow slaughter: 'People seem to think that when a law is passed against any evil, it will die without any further effort. There never was a grosser self-deception' (Gandhi 1954: 23). Gandhi sees a lot of possibilities for injustice in power (Terchek 2011). He points out that these inequalities in power were a big allurement for injustice. Gandhi states that cow protection must prevent cow neglect out of economical reasons: 'We have allowed it to go into the butcher's hands because of our gross neglect, and we are wholly responsible for its slaughter. It is for us to make it economically unnecessary and so impossible to sell the cow to the butcher' (Gandhi 1954: 25).

Nevertheless, the political issues of the sacred cow and cow protection were secondary to their religious significance for Gandhi. 'Gandhi wants nonviolence to be much more than a political tactic but a way of life that rests on an understanding about the inherent worth and dignity of all life' (Terchek 2011: 117). Terchek also states that 'Gandhi has frequently been portrayed as an idealist, one far removed from the harsh realities of the world politics. Yet there is a compelling realism in much that he writes and does. He is acutely aware of power, the many forms it takes, and the excuses it offers for what it does' (ibid.: 128).

In conclusion, even though cow protection in Gandhi's eyes should be a political issue as well, it should be more than a political implement and it seems that Gandhi kept away from political engagement with this issue. Political interventions concerning cow protection seemed to be only secondary for him. The religious significance of *ahiṃsā* and cow protection was more important to him.

Conclusion and ongoing aspects of the sacred cow, *ahiṃsā* and vegetarianism in Hinduism and India

This paper gave an overview on different aspects of the sacred cow and *ahiṃsā* in Hinduism. An access to different historical and cultural occurrences in context of the sacred cow and *ahiṃsā* amongst other things in connection to nourishment was given.

The concepts of the sacred cow and *ahiṃsā* have to be differentiated. The phenomenon of the sacred cow developed independently and includes cow protection and non-beef-eating. *Ahiṃsā* or non-violence developed later and led to a vegetarian diet. Possibly these two notions united in later times. This could explain the taboos and the unique stance of cattle in India today. Presumably, the special role of cattle in pre-Vedic times in connection to *ahiṃsā* in later times has influenced the phenomenon of the sacred cow strongly. The bond between *ahiṃsā*, *karman* and rebirth illustrates a profound reason for a vegetarian diet in Hinduism. *Ahiṃsā* leads to a positive *karman* and hence to a positive influence on the next life after rebirth. The Vedic belief included animal sacrifice and the consumption of sacral meat and beef. But the influence of *ahiṃsā* changed this aspect and led to the substitution of the animal sacrifice by inanimate offerings. The tradition of sacrifice still exists in Hinduism and is an important religious act. Manu mentions animals qualified for sacrifice and consumption and this could have included cattle as well. Even though, a vegetarian diet and a life respecting animals through non-killing are expressed as a higher goal in the *Manusmṛti*. Especially the *Brahmanic* class as a special religious role model always favoured a vegetarian diet. Even though there are some contradictions in the *Manusmṛti* the concept of *ahiṃsā* slowly pushed away the tradition of animal sacrifices. The contradicting declarations concerning animal sacrifices and the consumption of meat in the *Manusmṛti* express the fact that old guidelines and rules are standing next to new ones and are hard to differentiate. Changes were fluent and a specific timeline cannot be given. There has never been an indication for the connection of vegetarianism and the sacred cow and non-beef-eating in India. The connection of *ahiṃsā* and vegetarianism though is evident. The prevention of pain and suffering ultimately leads to a vegetarian diet. The phenomenon of the sacred cow in Hinduism developed throughout centuries, until the sacred cow and the unique role of cattle represent themselves in Hinduism today. Impressively, the extraordinary stance of cattle in India can be traced back to Neolithic times. Ceremonies and special treatment of cattle for example through the custom of animal homes express this unique stance.

Gandhi as a promoter of non-violence as an adjustment of *ahiṃsā* was a strict vegetarian. His view on vegetarianism can be seen as a logical deduction of *ahiṃsā*. Gandhi lived his principles. He tried to give practical advices for daily life which included a vegetarian diet. The political aspect of cow protection never was an issue for Gandhi. The religious meaningfulness of the sacred cow and *ahiṃsā* was his main interest. The economical impact of the sacred cow and cow protection and its issues in Gandhi's eyes had to be overcome. Economical security of the Indian people would lead to a protected position of cattle.

The influence of the concepts of *ahiṃsā* and the sacred cow on the relationship between humans and animals is apparent in everyday life. Diets and religious customs and deeds are influenced by these concepts. *Ahiṃsā* and the sacred cow are two concepts basic to Hinduism and deeply positioned in the Hindu belief. The connection of these two concepts grew closer throughout the centuries and they influenced each other.

Conclusively, the insight emerges that humans can only in reference to animals find their own position and identity. This position constantly has to be redefined. The question 'What makes us human?' is tried to be answered through the distinction against animals. In connection to *ahiṃsā* animal protection and animal rights come to mind. Which rights do we give animals after we have defined the positions of humans and animals?

To widen the perception of this topic it would be interesting to look at other religions and their guidelines for nourishment. Is there also a basis for vegetarianism in the Christian faith? Kaplan (1988) indicates that altruism could be a motivation for a vegetarian diet. In my opinion there are more current questions which could be part of further research in connection to vegetarianism in Hinduism. How do diets in India change today? How will nourishment in India look like in the future? Rosen (2004) points out while the number of vegetarians in Western societies increases the opposite is the case in India. Globalization and the influence of Western cultures have the effect that the number of vegetarians in India declines. The question arises if this change will influence the relationship between humans and farm animals in India as well.

It was enlightening for me to see the existing diversity in guidelines for nourishment in Hinduism. It is astonishing which influences old relationships like the relationship between humans and cattle can still have on our culture today. In the case of the sacred cow old traditions seem to have changed throughout the centuries but never disappeared completely. The examples of the sacred cow and *ahiṃsā* show the influence of cultural concepts on each other and the ongoing changes in culture. Sometimes old and new concepts stand next to each other and it is hard to differentiate them. At the end of this paper there are still questions left unanswered and a full pattern of the concepts of the sacred cow and *ahiṃsā* cannot be given. Maybe this shows us, as Alsdorf (1962) states, that there are limits of research and definite answers. For me the influence of religious reasons on diets like vegetarianism can be described but remains manifold. There are always changes happening and the influences on everyday life make this topic versatile.

Notes

1 I thank Prof. Dr. Christoph Wulf for enabling my study visit to India and Dr. Iris Clemens for her guidance in India. I also thank the TISS Mumbai, the TISS Tuljapur and the Manipal Centre for Philosophy and Humanities for their excellent academic input. The study visit has been funded by a scholarship from the DAAD in the context of the exchange programme 'A New Passage to India'.
2 Udaipur is a city in Rajasthan, a state in the northwest of India.
3 Varanasi is a city in Uttar Pradesh, a state in the northeast of India.
4 Alsdorf (1962) points out that the phenomenon of the sacred cow includes the male bull as well. The terms 'sacred cow' and 'cow protection' include the male bull. In this paper the female term cow also includes the male bull and therefore indicates the plural term cattle.
5 Ahiṃsā: transcription taken from Malinar (2009).
6 The *Vedas* were written down in Sanskrit, after a process of oral transfer, starting around 1500 BCE (Malinar 2009). The *Vedas* are connected to the *āryan* culture and the Vedic time. They consist of four major parts. The *Vedas* will be presented and discussed in point 4.1. *Vedas*: transcription taken from Malinar (2009).
7 The *Manusmṛti* or Laws of Manu is a legislative text which presents social obligations and duties of castes and individuals (Doniger and Smith 1991). The text will be presented and discussed in point 4.2. *Manusmṛti*: transcription taken from Malinar (2009).
8 Terchek (2011: 117) states that Gandhi wanted non-violence to be a way to solve conflicts in political contexts but also to be a religious way of living. Gandhi 'tells us that he strives to live by the Truth, that Truth is God, and that nonviolence serves the Truth'.
9 ' [. . .] concepts of ritual purity, the alternating dependence of living beings or the link of acts to a result (*karman*)' (Malinar 2009: 37, translation K. S.-V.). German orig.: ' [. . .] Konzepte von ritueller Reinheit, die wechselseitige Abhängigkeit der Lebewesen oder die Bindung der Handlung an ein Resultat (*karman*).' Souls have to live in different bodies depending on their deeds in their former lives (Malinar 2009). These deeds have a special kind of quality which is called karman. Only when the soul is free from a body there is no new karman and deliverance or moksa can be reached. *Karman*: transcription taken from Malinar (2009).
10 'The Neolithic period or New Stone Age in human development is characterized by the domestication of cereals and animals, the beginning of settlements and

the origin of crafts like pottery and weaving. It roughly dates from 8000–5500 [BC]' (Sharpes 2006: 208).
11 Kṛṣṇa was already mentioned in the Upaniṣad and born from one of Viṣṇu's hairs. He grew up amongst cowherds (Jansen 2002). The Upaniṣad as part of the Vedas will be presented and discussed in point 4.1. Kṛṣṇa: transcription taken from Malinar (2009).
12 Viṣṇu was created with his opposite Śiva by a higher being in order to maintain what it had created when it wanted to create the world (Jansen 2002). Viṣṇu: transcription taken from Malinar (2009).
13 Śiva is one of the oldest gods in India. He is called 'the friendly one' (Jansen 2002: 107). Śiva: transcription taken from Malinar (2009).
14 Nandi: transcription taken from Jansen (2002).
15 Nandikeshvara: transcription taken from Jansen (2002).
16 Nathdwara is a city in Rajasthan, a state in the northwest of India.
17 Alsdorf (1962) states that so-called mutton in British-led hotels actually is goat.
18 German orig.: 'Kein Fleisch ohne Tiertötung, darum keine Ahimsā ohne Verzicht auf Fleischgenuss.'
19 'The Vedic religion was practiced by tribal communities which probably immigrated to Northwest India around 1500 B.C. [. . .] The Vedic tribes called themselves a͞rya' (Malinar 2009: 30f., translation K. S.-V.). German orig.: 'Die vedische Religion wurde von Stammesverbänden praktiziert, die wahrscheinlich ab ca. 1500 v. Ch. in Nordwestindien einwanderten [. . .] Die vedischen Stämme bezeichneten sich selbst als ārya'. The Vedas originated in this Vedic culture (Malinar 2009). Ārya: transcription taken from Malinar (2009).
20 The Vedas developed orally parallel to the migration processes of the ārya starting around 1500 BCE The Vedic period was followed by the Hindu period which lasts until today (Zysk 1990).
21 For example, the killing of cattle and beef-eating.
22 Sattva: transcription taken from Malinar (2009).
23 German orig.: 'Die ahiṃsā ist zum einen auf die Lehre vom karman bezogen, wonach Gewalt zu besonders negativen Belastungen im nächsten Leben führt; zum anderen mit der Lehre, dass allen Lebewesen – auch Tieren und Pflanzen – ein "unsterbliches Selbst" innewohnt'.
24 The Upaniṣads are part of the Vedas. Upaniṣads: transcription taken from Malinar (2009).
25 Saṃsāra: transcription taken from Malinar (2009).
26 The concept of dharma will be presented and discussed in point 4.2. Dharma: transcription taken from Malinar (2009).
27 Samhitās: transcription taken from Günther (1997).
28 r̥gvedas: transcription taken from Malinar (2009).
29 Brāhmaṇas: transcription taken from Malinar (2009).
30 Āraṇyaka: transcription taken from Malinar (2009).
31 The term Brahmin origins in the caste system. Brahmin is the highest caste of priests and scholars (Malinar 2009).
32 German orig.: 'Fisch und Fleisch sind rein unter drei Bedingungen; wenn (der Mönch) nicht gesehen hat, nicht gehört hat und keinen Verdacht hegt (daß das Tier eigens für ihn getötet worden ist)'.
33 Dharmaśāstras: transcription taken from Malinar (2009).

34 English translation according to Bühler (n. d.): 'Kein Fleisch bekommt man, ohne Lebewesen zu verletzen; die Tötung von Lebewesen aber führt nicht in den Himmel, darum soll man das Fleisch meiden.'
35 English translation according to Bühler (n. d.): 'Der (die Tötung) Billigende, der Zerschneider, Schlächter, Käufer, Verkäufer, Koch, Servierer und Verzehrer – sie alle sind Töter'.
36 German orig.: 'Svayambhū selbst hat die Tiere zum Opfer geschaffen; das Opfer dient dem Gedeihen der ganzen Welt; deshalb ist Tötung beim Opfer keine Tötung.'
37 German orig.: 'Fleischgenuß bei Götter- und Manenopfer ist keine Sünde [...].'
38 English translation according to Bühler (n. d.). German orig.: 'Keine Sünde ist bei Fleischgenuß, Rauschtrank und Geschlechtsverkehr; so ist (nun einmal) das (natürliche) Verhalten der Lebewesen – Enthaltung aber bringt großen Lohn.'
39 Liberation of the body and deliverance (Malinar 2009).
40 'lbs' is the abbreviation for pound (467 grams).
41 Type of millet.
42 'oz.' is the abbreviation for ounce (28.35 grams).
43 Clarified butter.
44 Unrefined cane sugar.
45 SPIEGEL Online *Lebensmittel-Verschwendung: Indien lässt millionen Tonnen Getreide verrotten*. Retrieved from http://www.spiegel.de/wissenschaft/mensch/indien-laesst-millionen-tonnen-getreide-verrotten-a-832714.html, 11 May 2012.

References

Alsdorf, L. (1962). Beiträge zur Geschichte von Vegetarismus und Rinderverehrung in Indien. In Akademie der Wissenschaften und der Literatur, *Abhandlungen der Geistes- und Sozialwissenschaftlichen Klasse*: Jahrgang 1961, Nr. 6: 557–625. Wiesbaden, Germany: Verlag der Akademie der Wissenschaften und der Literatur in Mainz.

Bilgrami, A. (2011). Gandhi's religion and its relation to his politics. In J.M. Brown, and A. Patel (eds), *The Cambridge Companion to Gandhi*, 93–116. New York: Cambridge University Press.

Brown, J.M. (2011). Introduction. In J.M. Brown, and A. Patel (eds), *The Cambridge Companion to Gandhi*, 1–8. New York: Cambridge University Press.

Brown, J.M., and Parel, A. (2011). Conclusion. In J.M. Brown, and A. Patel (eds), *The Cambridge Companion to Gandhi*, 258–261. New York: Cambridge University Press.

Bühler, G. (n.d.): The laws of Manu chapter 5. Retrieved from http://www.sacred-texts.com/hin/manu/manu05.htm, August 2012.

Doniger, W., and Smith, K. (1991). *The Laws of Manu*. London: Penguin.

Gandhi, M.K. (1954). *How to Serve the Cow*. Ahmedabad: Navajivan Publishing House.

Gandhi, M.K. (1959). *The Moral Basis of Vegetarianism*. Ahmedabad: Navajivan Publishing House.

Gosh, I.M. (1988). *Ahimsa: Buddhist and Gandhian*. Delhi: Fountain.

Günther, M. (1997). *Upanishaden: Die Geheimlehre der Inder*. 13th ed. München: Eugen Dietrichs Verlag.
Gupta, S.P.P. (1968). *A Case for Cow Protection [Food, Fodder and Stoppage of Cow Slaughter Are No Problem]*. Rajghat, Varanasi: Sarva Seva Sangh Prakashan.
Holdrege, B.A. (2007). Dharma. In S. Mittal, and G. Thursby (eds), *The Hindu World*, 213–248. Abingdon: Routledge.
Jansen, E.R. (2002). *The Book of Hindu Imagery: Gods, Manifestations and Their Meaning*. New Delhi: New Age Books.
Kaplan, H.F. (1988). *Philosophie des Vegetarismus*. Frankfurt am Main: Peter Lang.
Lipner, J. (2007). On Hinduism and Hinduisms: The way of the Banyan. In S. Mittal, and G. Thursby (eds), *The Hindu World*, 9–34. Abingdon: Routledge.
Mahathera, N. (1964). *Karma and Rebirth*. Kandy: Buddhist Publication Society.
Malinar, A. (2009). *Hinduismus: Studium Religionen*. Göttingen: Vandenhoeck & Ruprecht.
Rosen, S.J. (2004). *Holy Cow: The Hare Krishna Contribution to Vegetarianism & Animal Rights*. New York: Lantern books.
Sharpes, D.K. (2006). *Sacred Bull, Holy Cow: A Cultural Study of Civilization's Most Important Animal*. New York: Peter Lang.
Spiegel Online. *Lebensmittel-Verschwendung: Indien lässt millionen Tonnen Getreide verrotten*. Retrieved from http://www.spiegel.de/wissenschaft/mensch/indien-laesst-millionen-tonnen-getreide-verrotten-a-832714.html, 11 May 2012.
Terchek, R.J. (2011). Conflict and nonviolence. In J.M. Brown, and A. Patel (eds), *The Cambridge Companion to Gandhi*, 117–134. New York: Cambridge University Press.
Tull, H.W. (2007). Karma. In Mittal, S., and Thursby, G. (eds), *The Hindu World*, 309–331. Abingdon: Routledge.
Walli, K. (1974). *The Conception of Ahimsa in Indian Thought (According to Sanskrit Sources)*. Pande Haveli, Varanasi: Bharata Manisha.
Wulf, C. (2013). *Anthropology. A Continental Perspective*. Chicago: The University of Chicago Press.
Zysk, K. (ed.) (1990). *A.L. Bashram; The Sacred Cow: The Evolution of Classical Hinduism*. London: Rider.

3

RE-READING GANDHI FOR A REFORMED KNOWING

Where to put that *Little Inner Voice*?

Bhakti Patil

> To forswear all utopias because of the pathological nature of ideological utopianism is to renounce the possibility of a commonly shared horizon of history which never reaches its end but perpetually motivates moral agents to bring it nearer. Without this utopian function of imagination it is difficult to provide a historical motivation for moral solidarity.
>
> Kearney (1998: 227)

'A man labouring under the bane of civilization', Gandhi had said, was 'like a dreaming man': 'A man whilst he is dreaming believes in his dream, he is undeceived only when he is awakened from his sleep' (Gandhi 1938: 30). A critique of the modern, the quest for ways of knowing and being devoid of the violence of modernity as such, for Gandhi, ought to have remained necessarily outside of an inexorable completeness: outside of a definite comprehensiveness, of the logic of a perverse *separateness*, a permanent falsehood. 'The "soulless system" of modern civilization', for Gandhi, had to be 'destroyed without our becoming soulless ourselves' (Iyer 2000: 34), in a faculty that must remain in its definite radicalism, necessarily outside of the limits of reason, outside of a terse instrumentality, of an apathetic rationality.

The imagining of a reformed knowing then must necessarily presume a radical subversion: a fundamental unmaking of the most essential states of the modern, of the obdurate completeness of its history, the facticity of its persistent project. The possibility of critique, of contestation, must remain realized itself, in the effecting of a true self-knowledge, a realization and knowing of the self and the possibilities of its perpetual reform, of perpetual transcendence.

In the completeness of reform, in the comprehensiveness of such critique must be contained inevitably the possibility of imagination; the possibility of a reformed knowing, of a re-imagined *scientificity*. While the imagining of a new knowing must also necessarily presume a remaking of *being*, the rethinking of *method* must also contain a reformed *selfhood*. As such, it must presume both *swaraj* and *swadeshi*, self-knowledge and self-reform, for an authentic reflexivity. It is in the latter where the doctrine of *ahimsa* must be realized, of *swadeshi* that must necessarily contain the convictions of moral praxis, the epistemic pre-eminence then, of Gandhi's universal ethic: the reinstatement of the moral, of the conscience as a faculty of knowing, of *being*.

For ahimsa remains primarily, it is argued, a doctrine of moral praxis, *dharma* in its pristine calling. It remains both, the means and the end, *swadeshi* and *swaraj*. For Gandhi, it remains in itself the eternal Truth. Thus, for him it also contains the possibility of true knowledge, of a knowing realized in the promise of an irrevocable *ahimsa*: the possibility, that is, of a quintessentially moral science.

It is in the pursuit of the latter, of the possibility of a reformed knowing that this chapter argues for a radical rethinking – a re-imagining of both, the epistemic and the ontological, a comprehensive radicalism that inevitably must sustain the possibility of an emancipatory knowing, of a science devoid of a debilitating *separateness*, of a pervasive *himsa*. The recognition of the *conscience*, of Gandhi's 'still small voice within' (1939, in Iyer 2007: 214), it argues, makes for a definite epistemic rethinking, for a moral reflexivity realized in the convictions of a fundamental normativeness. For what it presumes is the praxis of true *ahimsa*, of non-violence as both *creed* and *policy*, thus effecting a comprehensive *swadeshi*: a knowing that must also contain a conviction of moral reform, of an emancipatory politics necessarily realized in a radical re-imagining of both, knowing and being, of *method* and its unassailable subject.

The problem of the ensuing study then remains a problem of the latter – for it remains undeniably intimate, sacrilegious nearly, in the intimacy of its conception, in its conviction and yearning. In it remains contained, both biography and history, the precariousness of my own being, its eternal faith. In that it remains in itself an act of transcendence, of a defiant method – a work of inescapable oneness, an act then of subject and object. Imagined then, as a project of the academy, an *object* of reason and critique, of a methodical rendering that ought to have been unmade for Truth, the authenticity of my being, it remains also persistently rebellious – obstinate in its immense familiarity, in both its sincere candour and irredeemable failings.

It is an inescapable biographic truth that the study also contains the many experiences of communion and difference: the realization of a quintessential hermeneutic possibility made conceivable in a terrifying and rapturous newness – of places, of people, a gratifying unfamiliarity of smells and sights, of language, of colour. The DAAD 'Passage to India' research exchange programme made a new learning possible, one that remained both familiar and immensely different, one that has remained pertinent, cherished so truly for the spontaneous realizations of a wondrous oneness, for the reminders also of a dogged difference.

In these and many other experiences, the strange identity of a definitive newness, the primal calling of the ensuing study emerged – a quest in an authentic knowing, one that must necessarily contain the specificity of being, the material facticity of the *knower* so cautiously unmade in the realizations of a fundamental incompleteness, in the realizations of a necessary oneness. Like Gandhi's 'still small voice within', the experiences have affirmed the incorrigible facticity of our tremendous histories, but also always the possibility of dialogue, of a fugitive humanness.

The sin of separateness: re-visiting Gandhi's condemnation(s)

Earth and Heaven are in us. We know the earth, we are strangers to the Heaven within us.

Gandhi (1961: 27)

What emerges as the central problem of modernity – the essential crisis of the modern, for Gandhi, is the fact of a persistent extrovertedness. For Gandhi, modernity remains fundamentally extroverted – affirmed necessarily in a callous preoccupation with the without, in an unhindered rapacity then that remained for him the inexorable consequence of an order of pervasive violence, of the sustenance of a relentless artifice.[1] Fundamental to the modern as such, for Gandhi, was a schema of systematized severance, a persistent separateness that made in its comprehensiveness, he argued, for both, the inevitable unmaking of the without, the remaking, more precisely, of the latter in a precarious *otherness* and the critical redefinition of the subject self.

Modern civilization, Gandhi argued, took note 'neither of morality nor of religion' (1938: 32); it effected, in the profanity of its materialism, an ethic of ordered avarice, the triumph of a mechanistic imagination that ousted for conquest the sacred and the divine, that unmade in its utilitarian ethic the primal command of the eternal spirit. Modernity remained premised then on a mindless pursuit of 'bodily welfare' (ibid.: 31), a persistent gratification of the flesh, of bodily pleasures – the savage cravings of what, for Gandhi, was a necessarily brute physicality. Modernity, he argued, remained premised on a fundamental misrecognition, an erroneous pursuit of an elusive without, of the material excesses of what he regarded as a necessarily terse instrumentality. 'But one thing was certain, and that was that, so long as this mad rush lasted, with its glorification of the body, the soul within which was imperishable, must languish' (1909, in Iyer 2007: 88).

For modernity, he said, was 'en-souled' by 'selfishness and materialism', it was 'vain and purposeless' (1909, in Gandhi 1961: 201) for it had, in the 'glorification' of the corporeal, in the celebration of the profane, ruthlessly annihilated the fundamental sentience of the human subject. The modern self as such remained necessarily a self devoid of spirit, fragmented systematically in the regimentation of callous order. Modern civilization necessitated a comprehensive fragmentation, the ordered dismemberment of both, the ontological wholeness of man and her essential relatedness. Modernity, for Gandhi, made inevitable both the fundamental severance of *being*, the ousting of sentience, of spirit and conscience, and the sustenance of what may be termed a thorough individuation – a pervasive *separateness*, a permanent estrangement of man in the certitude of an arrogant egotism. 'Packed like sardines in boxes', the modern crowds found themselves 'in the midst of utter strangers' (1961, in Ramana Murti 1970: 296), for the modern subject remained, for Gandhi, most fundamentally estranged – alienated irrevocably in the apathetic order of industrial modernity, in the obscene materialism of an atrophying ethic.

It is this severance, the dual diremption of the subject, on which remained premised the fundamental completeness of the modern order, the systematic ordering of both method and being in a permanent impairment of a primal human impulse: compassion and communion, in the inevitable purging of affect. The modern man as such, Gandhi argued, remained necessarily 'emasculated' (1938: 38), unmade persistently for the effecting of the modern logic, for the sustenance of its apathy, of the absurdity of its materialistic ethic. The latter had 'all but stifled' for him man's 'best instincts', impulses of primal authenticity that had formed the quintessential 'heritage of the human family' (1909, in *Collected Works* 10: 244). Thus, for Gandhi, modernity secured the fundamental estrangement of man, its alienating severance from the most authentic states of itself: from morality and affect, from the transcendental calling of an authentic conscience.

What modernism effected consequently was the epistemic expulsion of the normative, the expurgation of morality from the faculties of knowing and the making of an a priori sovereign – the Cartesian subject that remained, for Gandhi, the essential imperative of the modern order. Modernism, for Gandhi, then remained a vulgar fraud, a comprehensive artifice that celebrated in the triumphs of materialism, the deceptiveness of its own constitution: 'Behind all the splendour and behind all the glittering appearances there is something very real which is missed altogether' (1903, in Iyer 2007: 85).

It was this severance, the fact of a preliminary separateness that made, for Gandhi, the fundamental dogma of modernity, the essential problematics of its mechanistic order. It contained, for Gandhi, the condition of a pervasive dehumanization, thorough *objectification* in the cultivation of disciplined apathy, in the cultivation of an irrevocable extroversion. In that, it contained both the fundamental failing of the modern order and the fact of its obstinate persistence. It contained then the persistence of a relentless *himsa*, an ethic of ordered violence.

Alienation as knowing: science and the routinization of *himsa*

It is this separateness that remains then, also, the fundamental logic of the scientific – the epistemic necessity of modernism that must presume also a definite ontological facticity. Essential to the methodological constitution of *modern science*[2] remains the obstinate dualism that it institutes – a critical fragmentation that remains both the necessary condition of its primary legitimacy and the fundamental measure of its arrogant scientificity. What modern science makes imperative is a critical *separateness*, a dismembering of all essentialities in and for the colonization that it must effect. Fragmentation as such remains not merely a precondition of scientific knowledge, its preliminary requisite, but also its necessary method.

Essential to this *scientistic* dogmatism remains the fundamental segregation of matter from spirit, the mind from the body and hence of emotionality from all rational pursuit. It is this disjuncture that makes explicit the critical privileging of reason over conscience – more precisely, the institution of the obliteration of the moral as the critical condition of scientificity. What the latter makes fundamental instead is the 'dangerous human ability to separate ideas from feelings [. . .] to pursue ideas without being burdened by feelings' (Nandy 2005: 5), a condition that necessitates the *splitting* of the cognitive and the affective,[3] to institute uncritically the regime of reason, a hegemony of the rational as the exclusive apparatus of a *scientistic* order.

It is this universality of reason and the uncritical exaltation of the rational that also necessitates a radical distancing of the subject from its fundamental object, a methodological *rupture* that must make the scientist researcher systematically segregated from his/her thus objectified other. What emerges then is a process of *dual fragmentation*, where the primary segregation of the researcher from the researched, the distancing of the methodological subject and object, also necessitates a thorough disruption of their essential *selves*. What science presumes, makes inevitable then, is Gandhi's 'emasculated' man, the 'dreamer' who must remain inevitably estranged also from the conditions of his own fraudulence. *Objectivity*, it is argued, presupposes *objectification*.[4] The rationalization of the human subject also makes imperative its ruthless containment – the obliteration of all wholeness, the expulsion of sentience.

Objectification thus remains essentially neither a necessary prerequisite securing scientificity nor its effective legitimacy – what it secures instead is the effective fragmentation of the subject researcher, the act of objectification being a fundamental defense against the sentience – the blasphemous *humanness* of the researching self. It is hence that objectification, as effected in the pursuit of *modern scientificity*, remains in itself of a necessarily *dual* ordering – it implies the necessary dehumanization of both the subject and the object, the ruthless fragmentation of not merely the researched but also of the objectifying subject. The methods of modern science fragment to objectify not only the known, the essential object, but also the subject, 'the first as an object that can be known and handled through technical routines and the second as an agent who performs these routines impersonally and unemotionally – that is, "professionally"' (Segal 1988: 17). For it is this dual objectification that secures objectivity, that sustains, more precisely, the sovereignty of the rational.

What remains is an order of determinate *self-referentiality*, a logic of thorough 'obsolescence' (Visvanathan 1988) that must effect in itself a structured schema of systematic erasure, of persistent and violent expurgation. It is in the completeness of this self-referentiality, in the epistemic arrogance of modernism that the project of *critique* must remain effected, the pre-eminence of *reflexivity*,[5] the resurgence of the *subjective* and the reinstatement of the *self* in research, that is, must sustain in its methodological contestations, in the convictions of a pronounced radicalism, an inevitable orthodoxy.

What persists is an essential 'alienative dichotomy' (Roszak 1972: 183). What remains is not only the hegemony of the scientific, of *science* as the definite measure of Truth(s), but also the regime of *scientistic* pre-eminence. Of that 'single vision' (ibid.: 184) that must remain realized only in the fact of a fundamental estrangement. It is this estrangement, structured severance that, for Gandhi, constitutes the fundamental *himsa*. An order of routinized *himsa* not only makes for the fact of a persistent artifice, of a comprehensive inauthenticity, but sustains in its completeness the condition of a preliminary unfreedom. It is this separateness that precludes necessarily, for him, the realization of *swaraj*, of Truth in the authenticity of moral being.

Swaraj, swadeshi and the praxis of *ahiṃsā*: self-knowledge and self-reform in Gandhi's method

One of the most crucial departures of Gandhi from what may be regarded the fundamental traditions of Western modernity remains articulated in his engagement with the idea of freedom. Gandhi's freedom thus remains an essential category, of critical import in his engagements with modernism, in his condemnation, more precisely, of the elementary premises of modernity and its mechanistic order. For, for him, true freedom contains in itself a necessary denunciation of what were the inevitable disjunctures of modern selfhood, the inevitable estrangement of the self from both, the inner authenticity of its own being and the essential sameness of the other.

True freedom or *swaraj* presumes most pertinently an inevitable oneness, a unity of the self and other, of the individual and the social. Gandhi's freedom sustains as such, what must remain a perpetual paradox to the modernist epistemology, a transcendental communion in authentic *ahimsa*, the fact of permanent restraint – the authenticity of universal moral obligation. The affirmation of individual freedom(s) thus, for Gandhi, ought also to presume a recognition of an essential obligation: for individual freedom to be meaningful it has to be realized in the facticity of social restraint, of communal obligation. The autonomy of the individual as such must also contain her inevitable sociality: 'The word Swaraj is a sacred word [. . .] meaning self-rule and self-restraint, and not freedom from all restraint which "independence" often means' (1962: 3).

Swaraj, Gandhi claimed, was a category radically distinct from the modernistic 'independence'. *Swaraj*, even where it implied minimally an assertion of national self-determination, where it implied exclusively political independence, the right, more specifically, of India or any nation to be free of external command, remained fully realized only in a sincere recognition of its substantive significance. *Swaraj*, he argued, was not to be conceived as a 'goal in response to something offensive that some Englishmen had done' merely 'to oblige people or to resent their actions'. True *swaraj*, he asserted, had to be 'declared and pursued irrespective of the acts or threats of others' (ibid.: 352), as an end in and of itself. Outside of such valuations, *swaraj*, for Gandhi, was necessarily meaningless, undoubtedly ineffectual. An arrogant order that for him ought to implode eventually in the vanity of its self-pursuit.

Political independence as such, Gandhi asserted, had meaning only when conceptualized within the requisites of self-governance. Political *swaraj*, the independence from foreign rule or an external authority, was to be necessarily situated in the authenticity of self-discipline, as self-regulation, without which, it would remain for him both fraudulent and necessarily ephemeral. True *swaraj*, for Gandhi, thus was to be realized only in true restraint, in the conscious disciplining of the self which remained a fundamental prerequisite for him for both the authenticity of political independence and the true realization of individual freedom, for communal self-determination and its essential correlate, individual autonomy[6]: 'It is Swaraj when we learn to rule ourselves' (1938: 56).

Swaraj thus implied most essentially the thorough disciplining of the self, radical self-reform in perpetual self-transcendence. What it called for was a definite epistemic and ontological unmaking, a thorough reformation that necessitated the cultivation of the truest *ahiṃsā*. 'Individual freedom', Gandhi argued, could 'have the fullest play only under a regime of unadulterated Ahimsa' (1962: 7), of an authentic non-violence that ought to have as its only end the realization of an eternal Satya. *Swaraj* then presupposed both *ahimsa* and *satya*. In that, for Gandhi, *swaraj* presupposed an essential *swadeshi*.

Swaraj in Gandhi's schema remains linked inextricably to the praxis of *swadeshi*. While the former remains for him the ultimate end, a 'state of being', of authentic realization, of *satya* in its pristine calling, the realization of *swaraj* itself remains contained also in its principal means. *Swaraj* then becomes an inevitable ideal,[7] realizable necessarily in true effort, in a sincere yearning for its absolute achievement. *Swadeshi* as such remains both, the means and the end; it remains in itself the true *swaraj*. *Swadeshi*, he asserts, thus remains 'coeval with *Swaraj*' (1967: 47).

Swadeshi then remains, for Gandhi, necessarily comprehensive. Like *swaraj*, it remains an essentially substantive category, a positive notion implying not merely an economic exclusivity, 'the use of what is produced in one's country' or the refusal to use foreign products and products manufactured outside of one's immediate/nation's limits, but sustains in itself 'another meaning which is far greater and much more important' (1909, in Iyer 2007: 362). While it does contain then a definite affirmation of restraint, of a meticulously cultivated self-denial, the proscriptive import of *swadeshi* remains, for Gandhi, of a definitively affirmative order. While *swadeshi* 'was that spirit in us which restricts us to the use and service of our immediate surroundings to the exclusion of the more remote' (1967: 1), it necessarily transcended the condition of exclusivity, of plain proscription. *Swadeshi* thus remains, for Gandhi, a fundamentally affirmative doctrine, a moral law that contains in itself most essentially, as previously mentioned, the praxis of 'the purest *ahiṃsā*, i.e. love' (1931, in Iyer 2007: 374). It remains a comprehensive 'religious discipline' (1967: 7), man's eternal aspiration, the singular true *dharma*.

For Gandhi, it is this comprehensiveness that makes for the fundamental import of *swadeshi*, of the latter, more precisely, as the truest *ahimsa*. For it was *ahimsa* that, for Gandhi, made for the principal precondition of *satya*, the eternal Truth that made also for true knowledge[8]: for a knowing that presupposed inevitably the praxis of *swadeshi*, of *ahimsa* as *creed* and *policy*.[9] *Ahimsa*, for Gandhi, then remains not merely of a negative order, a doctrine that compelled most essentially non-killing, the containment of manifest violence, but sustained in its comprehensiveness what may be regarded as an eternal transcendentalism, a completeness in being that Gandhi regarded as the elementary human *creed*. 'Ahimsa is not the crude thing it has been made to appear. Not to hurt any living thing is no doubt a part of ahimsa. But it is its least expression' (Gandhi 1961: 42).

What Gandhi made fundamental was a necessarily affirmative articulation of non-violence: 'in spite of the negative particle "non"', *ahimsa* 'was no negative force'; it was 'more positive than electricity',[10] 'more powerful than even ether'; it meant for him an untainted love (1936, in Johnson 2006: 124), pristine affection that sought in its innocence the *realization* of an essential fraternity. For Gandhi, *ahimsa* was *identity*, a doctrine of universal oneness. *Ahimsa* presumed a recognition of 'living kinship with all life', a *realization* of the *Supreme* fact of an inclusive 'brotherhood' – a condition that for him ought to have been not merely an 'intellectual belief' but what he termed a 'heart realization' (1932, in ibid.: 123). The creed of *non-violence* demonstrated in effect a fundamental dissolution, the transcendence of an essential disjuncture – the severance of the self, the estrangement of the latter from the essential harmony of the *other*.

Swadeshi in essence was, for Gandhi, an eternal doctrine of universal identification. It contained the elementary recognition of the supreme *satya*, a realization of the divine, of God[11] in a definite awareness of both, the transcendentalism of the self and the artificiality of its separateness. A true votary of *swadeshi* consequently was to strive tirelessly to 'identify himself with the entire creation' (1931, in Iyer 2007: 371), to cultivate a true humility, devoid of which, for Gandhi, the former ought to have remained necessarily unrealizable. It was only in the annihilation of egotism, in the 'reduction of the self to zero', as Gandhi asserted, that it was possible to realize a universal fraternity, to effect a praxis of *swadeshi* in its absolute completeness, in the realization of an authentic *ahimsa*. 'If one has pride and egoism, there can be no non-violence', he asserted, for 'non-violence' was 'impossible without humility' (1927: 89) – *humility* for him was a critical requisite of the cultivation of true *ahimsa*, that necessarily implied the obliteration of the ego, the destruction of arrogance in the recognition of the permanence of *identity*, in the *oneness* of the blessed creation.

The realization of one's nothingness, of the authenticity of universal oneness, for Gandhi, also implied an essential interlinkage, the contingency of the *knowledge* of the *other* – the non-recognition, the impossibility of an *other*, that is, what he regarded as an *authentic knowing* of the self. The identity of the *other* remained premised, for Gandhi, on a realization, an intimate recognition of the self, a *reflexive realization*; it may be said, of the infinity of the *spirit*, the comprehensiveness of the self that sought in its vastness the recognition of a fundamental *identity*. What *swadeshi* presupposed as such, was the effecting of an essential *reflexivity*, an *authentic* turning-in that remained contingent itself on a substantive reform, the perpetual unmaking of the self in the pursuit of what ought to become then the supreme *satya*.

What such a knowing presumed was not merely a perpetual turning-in, but, necessitated in itself, an order of rigorous regimentation – arduous disciplining – for it was the latter, the thorough purification of the self that made possible an *authentic knowing*, that made permissible the praxis of *ahimsa*: 'Identification with everything that lives is impossible without self-purification; without self-purification the observance of the law of Ahimsa must remain an empty dream' (Gandhi 1927: 463).

For Gandhi, *ahimsa* thus inevitably presumed a persistent self-transformation, a perpetual transcendence of oneself in a sincere quest for the absolute *satya*. Implicit in it was a ceaseless practice of self-examination, a vehement criticality that took as its principal object the essential subject self. It is in this regard that *swadeshi* became, for Gandhi, the fundamental condition of a true *swaraj*, a realization in itself of the truest freedom. For, in the latter, Gandhi had asserted, was also presumed permanent self-restraint, the authenticity of both obligation and self-effacement. *Swadeshi* implied in itself a thorough disciplining of the self, 'self-restraint and self-denial' (ibid.: 41) in an ardent conquest of the corporeal, of the passions of an arrogant physicality.

True detachment or selflessness, Gandhi argued, meant the disciplined cultivation of an utter disregard for one's body, for pleasures and passions,[12] for the wants of the flesh that remained for him both impermanent and artificial, illusive in their temporality, in their eternal transience. 'Selflessness', he asserted, meant 'complete freedom from regard to one's body' (ibid.: 49), a thorough abandonment of all preoccupations with the corporeal, an absolute command of the ephemeral passions of what he regarded a necessarily brute physicality. For it was the body that remained, for Gandhi, the essential cause of all *attachment*, that made the fundamental condition of both fear and estrangement, vulnerability and egotism.

And yet, for Gandhi, it was the body that also sustained an essential prospect, that permitted in itself an *authentic realization*, for in it remained manifest also the essential spirit, the soul that sustained in its pervasiveness a critical identity with the corporeal, a oneness of *purpose* that, for Gandhi, made for the fundamental human *possibility*. The *body* thus became an essential *apparatus* – a *means* of its own transcendence. For it was only through the body that *true renunciation* was effected. It was only through the body that renunciation remained possible, since true detachment, for Gandhi, remained not in the abandonment of all action, a retirement from activity, but necessitated in itself the effecting of authentic service – what Gandhi regarded as the essential *swadharma* – service in the spirit of a true *selflessness*: 'The purpose of life is undoubtedly to know oneself. We cannot do it unless we learn to identify ourselves with all that lives. The instrument of this knowledge is boundless selfless service' (1932, in Iyer 2007: 175).

For a reformed knowing: where to put that *Little Inner Voice*?

A man of Truth must also be a man of care.
Gandhi (1927: 15)

The imagining of *ahimsa* in *method*, of non-violence as a fundamental epistemic category, then, must remain nothing short of a realization of an authentic *knowledge swaraj*: of a *swadeshi* science that must presume in its *particularism*, in the relativistic immediacy of its making, also the universalism of its moral praxis. For the pursuit of *swaraj*, of the absolute *satya*, of true knowing, must presume in itself the praxis of *swadeshi*. Knowing must presume not only self-knowledge but also self-reform. It is in the quest for the latter, for a thorough unmaking of the self that the scientific must remain not without a true *reflexivity*, without the possibility of both self-realization and self-reform, without the perpetual yearnings of self-transcendence.

A knowing imagined in the moral convictions of *ahimsa* calls for a thorough subversion, a radical rethinking of both the epistemic and the ontological: the effecting of a moral reflexivity in the substantive remaking of *method* and *self*, of science and being.

For a *method* imagined in the logic of *ahimsa*, in an ethic of communion, has also to presume the permanent incompleteness of the subject self, an essential humility in critical reform. *Self-knowledge*, for true *ahimsa* as aforementioned, ought to translate inevitably into thorough self-transformation, ceaseless reform of the *researcher* and the *researched* in the praxis of a moral order. Such a knowing ought to presume not only an authentic knowledge of the self and the process of knowledge production[13]: an ontological and epistemic reflexivity, but also its perpetual unmaking. In that, it ought to be necessarily normative, *moral* in instructs of both knowing and being. An authentic *ahimsa*, a method imagined in the conviction of non-violence, must presume, as Gouldner asserts, a critical link between 'being a sociologist and being a person' (1970: 493) such that it 'may come to yield not only information but perhaps even a modest measure of wisdom' (ibid.: 490). *Ahimsa* in method must address for the subject not merely 'how to work' but necessarily also 'how to live' (ibid.: 489).

In that the individual conscience must be reinstated, that 'inner voice' (1932, in Iyer 2007: 213), for Gandhi, was the ultimate arbitrator, the *truest* knowledge and the greatest *satya*. For it is the primacy of the conscience that must make for the normativeness of a *reflexive science*, must unmake the essential disjunctures of the modernist order: the severance of fact and value, of theory and practice, of the scientific and the political. The conscience, Gandhi had elucidated, was also a 'faculty distinguishing between right and wrong' (ibid.: 212), an outcome itself of 'strictest discipline' (1924, in CWMG 29: 25): the conscience, that is, was fundamentally *moral*, realized in a meticulously cultivated self, in the praxis then of an authentic *ahimsa*. It was the conscience that thus contained the possibility of both self-knowledge and self-reform, that necessarily implied a permanent transformation of the self, its inevitable dissolution in a moral praxis, in true service.

It is in this realization where our collective possibility remains: in a recognition of *communion* as the truest *ahimsa*; in a recognition of science as an act of selfless giving, of universal moral obligation; and in a recognition of *science* as true *service*. In this, our collective *dharma* remains: the quintessential ethic of our communal being.

Notes

1 'The modern organized artificiality of so-called civilized life', for Gandhi, remained radically distanced from what he regarded a 'true simplicity of the heart'. It remained for him a system of sustained inauthenticity, an order that remained both a 'gross self-deception' and 'hypocrisy' (1928, in Iyer 2000: 108).
2 *Modern Science* here relates specifically to the emergence of what may be termed the *new knowledge* – a system of knowing (and being) that presumed the systematic desacralization of man and nature, the decline of the *symbol* (see Roszak 1972; Uberoi 1978), facilitated by the theological legitimacy of the new

fragmented ethos, the moral legitimacy, more specifically, of the segregation of spirit from matter, mind from the body, the self from the other, by the delusive normalcy, that is, of a tremendously alienated order. It is the epistemic privileging of alienation, of what Roszak terms 'the act of objectification' (1972: 184) that makes for the distinction of modern science: a methodological consistency that must persist, the paper argues, in the many contemporary contestations of objectivism. Implicit then is the idea that what remains is the epistemic primacy of alienation: a fundamental *separateness* that must persist also in the many convictions of both, a resurgent subjectivism and nihilistic relativism.

3 The 'splitting of cognition and affect' here relates specifically to what may be regarded as the Freudian (as elucidated in Nandy 2005) conception of *isolation* – the act of *isolation* as an *ego defense*, a psychological mechanism wherein, as Nandy argues, 'the individual sometimes isolated an event, idea or an act by cauterizing it emotionally' (ibid.: 5). *Modern science*, he asserts, represents a *structured isolation*, its values of 'objectivity, rationality, value-neutrality and inter-subjectivity' drawing heavily from 'the human capacity to isolate' (ibid.: 8). It is also this *isolation*, it is evident, that makes for Uberoi's *Positivist Man, the Scientist* (Uberoi 1978).

4 As Nandy and Visvanathan (1990: 152) argue, the 'suppression and decomposition' of the 'person' in the *researched* remains imposed by 'a form of expertise which bases itself on the dualist worldview of modern science, a view which involves the necessary transition from objectivity to objectification'. It is the act of *objectification* as such that remains for them the fundamental requisite of *scientific objectivity*. See also Roszak (1972).

5 For the many sociological notions of reflexivity see, among others, Clifford and Marcus (1990); Giddens (1990, 1991); Bourdieu and Wacquant (1992); Beck et al. (1994); Alvesson and Sköldberg (2001); Bourdieu (2004).

6 For Iyer, while the freedom from external authority remains a fundamental precondition of *swaraj*, it does not translate in itself to the possibility of individual self-determination. 'The freedom from external intervention,' he asserts, 'is a necessary but not a sufficient condition for the effective and full realization of our liberty', which remains for Gandhi, according to Iyer, 'the product of self-rule' (2000: 354).

7 For Ghandi, fundamental to the recognition of an *ideal* was the fact of its remoteness, the idea that an *ideal* to be acknowledged as such must remain necessarily unrealizable, a permanent *utopia* that must sustain a moral adjudication of its appropriate *means*. The *inaccessibility* of the *ideal* did not imply an ineffectuality of transcendence that remained perpetually unmade in an incessant moral governance – in the intimate relevance of the *ideal*, more precisely in the normative regulation and direction of ethical action. Thus the pursuit, the means and the earnestness of the seeker's quest remained of critical relevance for Gandhi. The *ideal* remained necessarily unrealized, he asserted, and hence true 'satisfaction' lay 'in the effort, not in the attainment'. For him, 'full effort' was 'full victory' (1922, in CWMG 26: 293).

8 'Where there is Truth', Gandhi wrote, 'there is also knowledge which is true. Where there is no Truth, there can be no true knowledge' (1930, in CWMG 49: 383).

9 Gandhi made a definite distinction between what he thought were the two orders of operationality in the conceptualization of the doctrine of *ahimsa*. The latter, he argued, could be imagined as a creed as well as a policy – a strategy

to be deployed in an intelligent consideration of expediency. While the former made inevitable a commitment to the pragmatic implications of *ahimsa*, an efficacy, that is, of *ahimsa* as a practical apparatus, a recognition of *ahimsa* in policy, for Gandhi did not necessarily presuppose a commitment to the creed of *non-violence*, the inculcation of *ahimsa* in the fullness of one's being. When it was merely a matter of policy, *ahimsa* inevitably betrayed for him an essential futility, a vanity of sorts that made inevitable its consequent failure. 'Non-violence of the strong cannot be a mere policy', he asserted, it ought 'to be a creed, or a passion' (1940, in Iyer 2007: 250).

10 Gandhi made a distinction between what he regarded as the negative and the positive aspects of *ahimsa*. While in its negative form *ahimsa* meant merely non-injury – the fact that 'I may not hurt the person of any wrong-doer or bear any ill-will to him', and in its positive aspect it necessarily implied, he stated, 'the largest love, the greatest charity' – positive *ahimsa* for Gandhi included both 'truth and fearlessness', universal love and 'greatest courage' (Gandhi 1962: 36).

11 For Gandhi on the identity of Truth and God, see Gandhi (1955).

12 For Gandhi on *Brahmacharya*, see Gandhi (1928); see also Alter (1996); Lal (2000).

13 It is in such epistemic reflexivity that Gandhi situates the primacy of justice – of fairness as a critical measure of authenticity, of *swadeshi*. Where Gandhi asserts the pertinence of *intent* in the valuations of *swadeshi* (or, alternately, in the definition of *himsa*), it is a definite awareness of both purpose and process that becomes essential to the realization of true *swadeshi*. A *swadeshi* science thus necessarily remains participatory, devoid of an obstinate expert-lay dichotomy, and fundamentally just: egalitarian in production and consequence.

References

Alter, J. (1996): Gandhi's Body, Gandhi's Truth: Nonviolence and the Biomoral Imperative of Public Health. *The Journal of Asian Studies* 55 (2): 301–322.

Alvesson, M., and Sköldberg, K. (2001): *Reflexive Methodology: New Vistas for Qualitative Research*. New Delhi.

Beck, U., Giddens, A., and Lash, S. (1994): *Reflexive Modernization: Politics, Tradition and Aesthetics in the Modern Social Order*. Cambridge.

Bourdieu, P. (2004): *Science of Science and Reflexivity*. Trans. by Richard Nice. Cambridge.

Bourdieu, P., and Wacquant, L. (1992): *An Invitation to Reflexive Sociology*. Cambridge.

Clifford, J., and Marcus, G. (eds) (1990): *Writing Culture: The Poetics and Politics of Ethnography*. New Delhi.

Gandhi, M. K. (1909a): Preface to Leo Tolstoy's 'Letter to A Hindoo'. In: *The Collected Works of Mahatma Gandhi*. Vol. 10. http://www.gandhiserve.org/cwmg/VOL010.PDF [accessed 2 December 2012].

Gandhi, M. K. (1909b): Letter to Lord Ampthill. In: *The Collected Works of Mahatma Gandhi*. Vol. 10. http://www.gandhiserve.org/cwmg/VOL010.PDF [accessed 19 January 2012].

Gandhi, M. K. (1922): Non-Violence. In: *The Collected Works of Mahatma Gandhi*. Vol. 10. http://www.gandhiserve.org/cwmg/VOL010.PDF [accessed 19 January 2012].

Gandhi, M. K. (1924): Under Conscience's Cover. In: *The Collected Works of Mahatma Gandhi*. Vol. 29. http://www.gandhiserve.org/cwmg/VOL029.PDF [accessed 2 December 2012].

Gandhi, M. K. (1927): *The Story of My Experiments with Truth*. Trans. by Mahadev Desai. Ahmedabad.

Gandhi, M. K. (1928): *Self-Restraint V. Self-Indulgence*. Ahmedabad.

Gandhi, M. K. (1930): Letter to Narandas Gandhi. In: *The Collected Works of Mahatma Gandhi*. Vol. 49. http://www.gandhiserve.org/cwmg/VOL051.PDF [accessed 23 May 2010].

Gandhi, M. K. (1938): *Hind Swaraj or Indian Home Rule*. Ahmedabad.

Gandhi, M. K. (1955): *Truth Is God*. Compiled by Anand T. Hingorani. Bombay.

Gandhi, M. K. (1961): *My Philosophy of Life*. Compiled by Anand T. Hingorani. Bombay.

Gandhi, M. K. (1962): *Village Swaraj*. Compiled by H. M. Vyas. Ahmedabad.

Gandhi, M. K. (1967): *The Gospel of Swadeshi*. Compiled and ed. by Anand T. Hingorani. Bombay.

Giddens, A. (1990): *The Consequences of Modernity*. Cambridge.

Giddens, A. (1991): *Modernity and Self-Identity: Self and Society in the Late Modern Age*. Cambridge.

Gouldner, A. (1970): *The Coming Crisis of Western Sociology*. New York.

Iyer, R. (2000): *The Moral and Political Thought of Mahatma Gandhi*. New Delhi.

Iyer, R. (2007): *The Essential Writings of Mahatma Gandhi*. New Delhi.

Johnson, R. (ed.) (2006): *Gandhi's Experiments with Truth: Essential Writings by and about Mahatma Gandhi*. Lanham.

Kearney, Richard (1998): *Poetics of Imagining: Modern to Post-Modern*. New York.

Lal, V. (2000): Nakedness, Nonviolence and Brahmacharya: Gandhi's Experiments in Celibate Sexuality. *Journal of the History of Sexuality* 9 (1/2): 105–136.

Nandy, A. (2005): Science, Authoritarianism and Culture: On the Scope and Limits of Isolation Outside the Clinic. *The Radical Humanist* 69 (1): 5–10.

Nandy, A., and Visvanathan, S. (1990): Modern Medicine and Its Non-Modern Critics: A Study in Discourse. In: Marglin, F. A., and Marglin, S. A. (eds): *Dominating Knowledges*. Oxford, 145–184.

Ramana Murti, V. V. (ed.) (1970): *Gandhi: Essential Writings*. New Delhi.

Roszak, T. (1972): *Where the Wasteland Ends: Politics and Transcendence in Postindustrial Society*. New York.

Segal, D. (1988): A Patient So Dead: American Students and Their Cadavers. In: *Anthropological Quarterly* 61 (1): 17–25.

Uberoi, J. P. S. (1978): *Science and Culture*. New Delhi.

Visvanathan, S. (1988): On the Annals of the Laboratory State. In: Nandy, A. (ed.): *Science, Hegemony and Violence: A Requiem for Modernity*. New Delhi, 257–290.

4

EDUCATION FOR A BETTER WORLD?

Gandhi's ideas on education and their relevance in modern India

Theresa Vollmer

> The future for India lies in you. I have no doubt that you will become useful citizens of this society [...]. Let me close with another Sanskrit sloka that is at the heart of what I said and believe. [...] (Non-violence, controlling the desires, kindness to all, forgiveness, peace, meditation, charity and truth are the eight flowers that please the Lord.) Indeed, these attributes characterize the ideal Indian of the twenty-first century.
>
> N.R. Narayana Murthy

N.R. Narayana Murthy, Founder-Chairman of Infosys Technologies Limited, concluded a convocation address to students at the Indian Institute of Technology, New Delhi in 2001 by using these words. Murthy (2010) motivates the students to take responsibility for their society. They should develop a 'twenty-first-century mindset' (ibid.: 12) and become 'useful citizens' (ibid.: 16). Although India took a lot of development, it is far from reaching the vision propounded at the period of independence. Reading Murthy's speech one considers that Gandhi's vision of a more socially just society is kept in mind in modern India. Gandhi as a historical person and as Gardner (1997: 2) proposes one of four 'principal exemplars of Extraordinary Minds' provided an ethic of non-violence and a conception of non-violent resistance that is still relevant to many people at the present time.

At the beginning of the study visit my field of interest was non-formal education in modern India.[1] Attending the 'Philosophy of Education' course at the Tata Institute of Social Sciences (TISS) in Mumbai,[2]

I noticed that there was a vivid discussion on western and eastern educational concepts in the twentieth century and their relevance in modern India. Gandhi's *Nai Talim*[3] was discussed as the first policy for basic education in India. It was mentioned that even if Gandhi spoke for free and compulsory primary education his ideas on education were soon rejected. I defined my field of interest more precisely during a visit to the Vidya Bhawan Society,[4] an organization that provides education along the principles of progressive education in Udaipur.[5] During the visit I talked to professionals and experienced different forms of learning activities. Inspired by the educational practice of Vidya Bhawan Society I wanted to know more about their mission statement which is 'Commitment to Social Responsibility through Education' (Vidya Bhawan Society, retrieved from www.vidyabhawan.org on 29 August 2012). In an informal talk with Dr H. K. Dewan, Educational Advisor of Vidya Bhawan Society, the aim to ameliorate the situation of the weaker groups of the society was mentioned. For example, children who were dropouts from school shall experience a joyful learning environment and by that gain new motivation to learn. Moreover Vidya Bhawan Society emphasizes the importance of social learning. Education should enable children to become responsible citizens, to develop life-related abilities and also a community spirit. In addition, different approaches to the individual and the society were discussed. Among others, Gandhi and his notion of the relationship between the child and the community were named (Dr H. K. Dewan, personal communication, 18 June 2011). Again curious, I developed my research questions. What are the basics of Gandhi's educational concept and how does he describe the idea of man? To what extent are Gandhi's thoughts on education relevant in modern India?

The aim of this article is to first give an overview on Gandhi's educational ideas and then to evaluate their relevance in modern India. As Gandhi's ideas on education can be examined from different perspectives, authors from western and eastern contexts were chosen. Cenkner (1976), for example, regards Gandhi's concept of education as spiritual and creative. Cenkner's basic thesis is that to read Gandhi's ideas on education his philosophy has to be taken into account. Although there is plentiful research on Gandhi, his educational ideas are lesser-known. The fact that Gandhi wrote a lot makes it difficult to do research on Gandhi. Kumar (1999) focuses on Gandhi's critique of the Western civilization, in particular on his critical view on industrialization. Hence Kumar accentuates the creative aspect of Gandhi's concept of education. Lang-Wojtasik (2002) points out that there are similarities between Gandhi's ideas on education and the tenets of progressive education. Lang-Wojtasik examines Gandhi's *Nai Talim* from a European perspective.

To understand Gandhi's ideas on education I will first show some of their biographical and contextual origins. In a next step his basic thoughts including the image of the ideal human being are propounded. Gandhi's concept of 'basic education' will be explained on the basis of some of his writings in *Harijan*.[6] In order to answer the question of whether Gandhi's ideas on education are still relevant in modern India, I will outline some aspects of current challenges concerning education in modern India and discuss possible aspects of Gandhi's ideas that indicate the relevance. A summary of the findings and ongoing questions closes this chapter.

'My life is my message': Gandhi as historical person[7]

At first sight Mahatma Gandhi[8] appears as a fascinating person. Several quotations express Gandhi's person and his notion of philosophy. Chakrabarty (2006: 119) for example depicts Gandhi 'as a practitioner of what he preached'. Gandhi's 'pastoral style in daily life: travelling in third-class compartments, speaking in simple *Hindustani*, wearing self-spun *khadi*, using the imagery of Tulshidas's *Ramayana*' (ibid.: 177)[9] contributed to the distribution of his social and political thought. The most famous quotation is perhaps the one cited above. In the view of Gunturu (1999: 172) Gandhi's statement 'my life is my message' emphasizes the relationship between Gandhi's life and his philosophy. Gunturu describes Gandhi's life as a laboratory. Gandhi's philosophy was thus built on his experiments in daily life.[10]

Mohandas Karamchand Gandhi (1869–1948) was born in Porbandar[11] in India and married at the age of 14. After finishing school he went abroad to receive an education as a lawyer in London (Lang-Wojtasik 2002). Becke (1999) notes that it was in London where Gandhi came not only in touch with Western culture and thought but realized also his own culture. He read for example for the first time the *Bhagavad Gita* (short: *Gita*),[12] a holy Hindu text. Becke points out that Gandhi was very much interested in the study of religion. Beside the *Gita*, Gandhi read the Bible and was inspired by the New Testament and in particular by the Sermon on the Mount.[13]

As Lang-Wojtasik (2002) states, Gandhi returned to India in 1893 but failed as a lawyer in Bombay.[14] He left for South Africa and lived and worked there for the next 21 years. Having experienced racism, Gandhi engaged himself in the rights for the Indians living in South Africa. Kumar (1999) brings in that Gandhi read sociocritical writings such as Ruskin and Tolstoy as well. He then tried to put their ideas of a better society into practice. According to Lang-Wojtasik (2002), Gandhi made his first experiments with a non-violent conduct of life within his first *ahsrams*,[15] Phoenix Farm in 1904 and Tolstoy Farm in 1910. Moreover, Gandhi developed his conception of *satyagraha* (non-violent resistance).[16]

Coming back to India in 1915, Gandhi continued to establish *ashrams* and started *satyagraha* activities (Lang-Wojtasik 2002).[17] Gandhi was not only a practitioner but also wrote about his ideas. Chakrabarty (2006) distinguishes two writings, *Hind Swaraj* (1909),[18] which presented Gandhi's plan of a new society, and Gandhi's writings in *Harijan*. Publishing in *Harijan* for Gandhi was a chance to discuss political issues with like-minded persons and opponents and at the same time to specify his social, political and educational ideas (Chakrabarty 2006). Gandhi did not only define his ideas on education in *Harijan* more precisely, he also suggested the discussion of his ideas on a conference. This conference took place at Wardha, 22–23 October 1937 (Lang-Wojtasik 2002).

To sum it up one can say that Gandhi developed his educational ideas in the view of his personal experiences and in the critical view of the contemporary society. The following part of the chapter integrates Gandhi's person and position in the contemporary period of British colonial rule.

Colonial influences on the Indian education system and Gandhi's position

According to Malinar (1994) the attitude of the British towards the Indian culture changed over the course of the years of British colonial rule. Where in the beginning there was a fascination for Indian culture, this changed to suppression with the increase of influence. The replacement of the Indian education system with the British education system in 1835 is characteristic of the changing attitude of the British colonial power in India. The suppression of Indian culture and tradition expressed itself, for example, in the decision to promote English instead of Sanskrit and Persian. Cenkner (1976: 11) gives an overview on the consequences of the replacement of the Indian education system by saying that '[by] the turn of the century a million Indians had received a Western education either at home in missionary schools and public institutions which had aped Western forms or had gone abroad for education'.

Having received a British education in India and abroad, Gandhi criticized the British education system as unfitting for the Indian context. To him, there was an ignorance of the Indian 'educational experience, such as children integrated with environment, strong pupil-teacher relationships, identity with a people and an appreciation of Indian culture' (Cenkner 1976: 100). Gandhi's critique of the British education system occurs within his social and political thought. In a next step Gandhi's basic thoughts are explained with the focus on his aims of education.

Gandhi's social and political thought and the meaning of education

Gandhi's social and political thoughts are multilayered in a sense as they were rooted in India's tradition, developed during Gandhi's stay in South Africa and later continued in India (Chakrabarty 2006). Corresponding to the Hindu belief, Gandhi considered the self-transformation of a human being as principle life task. However, he reinterpreted the path to self-realization. Gandhi combined the self-transformation of the individual with the transformation of the society and considered the transformation of both as a simultaneous process. By that he made a strong plea for social engagement in society (Kantowsky 1985). To give an overview on his basic thoughts some principles are named and described below.

Swaraj: self-rule

Chakrabarty (2006: 175) underlines that Gandhi's conception of social transformation had its origin in the transformation of the individuals and therefore took into account their specific sociocultural background. He states that 'Gandhi provided a theory of the autonomy of individuals, designed to empower individuals within their traditions and community.' Gandhi reinterpreted the village life in focusing on handicraft, basic democracy and decentralization. On putting the *charkha* (spinning wheel) as a symbol for his conception, Gandhi tied on a common sign and linked people of different parts of India together. In that way his idea of *swaraj* became a movement with the aim of political independence (Chakrabarty 2006). In view of the vision of a new society and political independence education should function as a means to reach the goal of *swaraj* (self-rule) (Cenkner 1976).

Sarvodaya: the uplift of all

Cenkner (1976: 97) regards *sarvodaya*, 'literally the uplift of all', as the central principle of Gandhi's thought. In the process of a social and spiritual transformation of both the individual and the society *sarvodaya* functions as an objective. The simultaneous uplift of all would thus enable the society to reach betterment. Referring to his educational ideas, Gandhi thought that the schools should be self-sustaining and the teaching of a handicraft could help to reach the goal of *sarvodaya*. In doing so one would succeed in reconstructing the village life.

Satyagraha: truth force

A basic principle of Gandhi's philosophy is *satyagraha*. Cenkner (1976: 212) explains: 'satyāgraha: holding to truth, truth-grasping; a truth-force, a soul force; the path followed and the technique developed by Gandhi for change based on truth [. . .].'

Satyagraha describes the process of striving after truth. It was meant as guide to action in human relationships, but as well as technique 'for acting socially and humanely' (Cenkner 1976: 94). To understand *satyagraha* it is necessary to consider Gandhi's basic values, truth[19] and *ahimsa* (non-violence).[20] Cenkner (ibid.) clarifies:

> Truth and nonviolence are interrelated. For Gandhi truth functions as the end and *ahiṃsā* as the means of human activity. The effect of the term *satyāgraha* was to transform absolute truth to relative truth as an ethical norm capable of being formed and utilized within a social context.

Truth and non-violence are seen as basic values that characterize the good conduct of life. The goal of life is the realization of the self, which means the union with God. For Gandhi, God is linked with truth (Cenkner 1976). The transformation of absolute truth to relative truth within the conception of *satyagraha* provides a work ethic for daily life. Truth and non-violence are considered as 'fundamentally relative norms' (ibid.: 95). Therefore compromise appears as basic principle of *satyagraha*. Truth and non-violence have to be first experienced by the individual and then carried out in human relationships. In that way a new society would emerge. Cenkner (ibid.: 94) values Gandhi's ethic as 'creative and open-minded'.

Gandhi's religion of service and his image of the ideal human being

As stated earlier, Gandhi was very much interested in the study of religion (Becke 1999). Cenkner (1976: 88) notes that Gandhi 'sought a concept of God which would be acceptable to all men, religious and non-religious alike'. Inspired by the teaching of the *Bhagavad Gita*, Gandhi formed a religion of service which 'was based upon a profound commitment to the Indian people' (Cenkner 1976: 86). Gunturu (2000) explains the qualities of an ideal human being demonstrated in the *Gita* by giving a short description: 'An ideal human being does not shrink from duty. She is acting, knowing well that human power is limited to the action, at the same time, she is not interested in its fruits' (Gunturu 2000: 142, transl. T.V.).

According to Fischer (1992), an ideal human being is seen as a *Karma yogi*,[21] a human being that acts in even-mindedness and detachment. The *Gita* gives a description of detachment by listing specific qualities in the following way:

> Freedom from pride and pretentiousness; non-violence, forgiveness, uprightness, service of the Master, purity, steadfastness, self-restraint.
> Aversion from sense-objects, absence of conceit, realization of the painfulness and evil of birth, death, age and disease.
> Absence of attachment [. . .] even-mindedness whether good or evil befall [. . .].
>
> cited in Fischer (1992: 51)

The goal of transformation is, following Fischer (1992), the achievement of the union with God. In the union with God the individual reaches perfection, leaves the circle of rebirth and attains *moksha* (liberation). The virtues cited in the verses above indicate the path to reach this goal. Gunturu (2000) states that a human being can attain God through either insight or action. As it is not easy to follow the path of insight, the *Gita* recommends the path of action and *bhakti* (devotion). The central advice of the *Gita* is that a human being should act in renunciation of the fruits of action and dedicate one's actions to God. In that way the human being liberates herself from the law of *karma*[22] (Gunturu 2000). Gandhi's aspiration was the transformation towards a *Karma yogi* (Fischer 1992). Gandhi defined the qualities of a *Karma yogi* as follows:

> He will have no relish for sensual pleasures and will keep himself occupied with such activity as ennobles the soul. That is the path of action. Karma yoga is the yoga [means] which will deliver the self [soul] from the bondage of the body, and in it there is no room for self-indulgence.
>
> Gandhi as cited in Fischer (1992: 50)

Cenkner (1976: 87) interprets the attitude of selfless action as a 'pure form of altruism consisting in unreciprocated activity'. To achieve the stance of non-attachment, *ahimsa* (non-violence) is seen as a means and a condition.

The goal mentioned in the *Gita* is to become a 'man of steady wisdom (*sthitaprajñā*) and stable spirit (*samādhistha*)' (ibid.), one that orients his conduct of life according to these principles. Gandhi inferred his image of an ideal human being from the teaching of the *Gita*. The main focus of Gandhi's educational ideas is therefore the development of the non-violent personality, as Cenkner puts it, 'the *satyāgrahi*' (ibid.: 101).[23] Education should function as the means to 'develop the highest truth possible in the mind, the spirit and the body' (ibid.: 102). In order to present Gandhi's conception of education, some of his writings in *Harijan*[24] are cited and linked up with interpretations of Lang-Wojtasik (2002), Kumar (1999) and Cenkner (1976).

Gandhi's ideas on education: from education as a means to reconstruct the villages to a basic national education plan

The model of the ideal citizen within small autonomous communities

In his paper 'Education through vocation' Gandhi reveals his approach to education. He articulates the purpose and quality of education in saying: 'If we want to revive it today in all its glory, if we are to revive and reconstruct village life, we must begin the education of children with the *takli*' (*Harijan*, 06/11/38, as reprinted in Gandhi and Kumarappa 1951: 10).

In this quote education is linked with the reconstruction of the villages. Education that starts with the teaching of *takli* (a small spinning wheel) is seen as the basis to empower and develop the village life. Kumar (1999: 3) notes that Gandhi's concept of 'basic education' was built up according to his notion of 'an ideal society as one consisting of small, self-reliant communities'. The reconstruction of villages could be achieved 'by training the children for productive work and by imparting to them attitudes and values conducive to living in a co-operative community'. To Kumar, the basis of Gandhi's educational thoughts was the image of an ideal citizen that was 'an industrious, self-respecting and generous individual living in a small community' (ibid.: 4).[25]

Putting handicraft in the centre of the '"basic education" plan' (ibid.: 1) was revolutionary. In Kumar's view Gandhi's ideas on education 'intended to stand the education system on its head' (ibid.: 2). Gandhi altered the conventional notion of teaching in which handicraft was linked to the lowest groups and literacy to the upper groups of the society.

THERESA VOLLMER

Gandhi's conception of education

In his paper 'Intellectual development or dissipation' Gandhi expresses his conception of education. He begins by analysing the situation of students. Gandhi defines his notion of education: I hold that true education of the intellect can only come through a proper exercise and training of the bodily organs, e.g. hands, feet, eyes, ears, nose, etc. (*Harijan*, 05/08/1937, as reprinted in Gandhi and Kumarappa 1951: 12).

Education is seen as a development of the mind but in combination with the training of the body and the senses. Education appears as a creative process. Cenkner (1976: 102) states that Gandhi's approach is 'encompassing the head, the heart and the hands'. Gandhi focuses on a holistic approach on education by saying:

> But unless the development of the mind and the body goes hand in hand with a corresponding awakening of the soul, the former alone would prove to be a poor lop-sided affair. By spiritual training I mean education of the heart. A proper and all-around development of the mind, therefore, can take place only when it proceeds *pari passu* with the education of the physical and spiritual faculties of the child. They constitute an indivisible whole.
> *Harijan*, 05/08/1937, as reprinted in
> Gandhi and Kumarappa (1951: 12f.)

Gandhi clarifies his notion of spiritual education as an education of the heart. Spiritual education and physical education constitute the development of the mind. If there is a single emphasis on the training of the intellect this would be a 'lop-sided affair' (*Harijan*, ibid.) and would lead to distraction. Cenkner (1976: 102) illustrates Gandhi's notion of education of the heart by saying that 'the cultivation of the heart – emotions and feelings – consists in the refinement of human emotions and impulses; it promotes feelings of love, sympathy and fellowship'. Goal of character education following Cenkner is to learn and practice the values of truth and *ahimsa* (non-violence). Gandhi's accentuation on the training of physical faculties in education has to be considered within the aim of character formation. Cenkner (ibid.: 103) postulates 'mind and heart can only be refined if the hand is brought into activity'.

Following this, Gandhi discusses possible consequences and in contrast to this the positive effect of his notion of education. An education that focuses on the development of the physical, intellectual and spiritual faculties would lead to 'a perfect well-balanced, all-around education in which the intellect, the body and the spirit have all full play and develop together into a natural, harmonious whole' (*Harijan*, ibid.: 14). Gandhi explains: 'Man is neither mere intellect, nor the gross animal body, nor the heart or soul alone. A proper and harmonious combination of all the three is required for the making of the whole man and constitutes the true economics of education' (ibid.).

In saying this, Gandhi reveals his conception of man and his holistic approach to education. According to Cenkner (1976: 103) Gandhi aimed to educate the human being 'materially, morally and spiritually'. There was a social orientation underlying his educational plan. Education in Gandhi's view should 'meet all the needs of the people, social, economic, political and cultural' (ibid.: 104). In the last sentence of this chapter Gandhi emphasizes the goal of his educational concept. Children should be educated through a vocation and they should be 'teach[ed] that they live for the common good of all' (*Harijan*, ibid.: 15). The ideal of *sarvodaya* comes to mind. Education should impart values such as '[living] together as a community on the basis of cooperation, truth and *ahiṃsā*' (Cenkner 1976: 104).

The concept of school

Following Cenkner (1976: 104), Gandhi's notion of school as 'builder of the new non-violent society' was formulated on the basis of his experiences in the *ashrams*. While interacting with other children in the school, community children should experience truth and *ahimsa*. The practice of non-violent values should lead to the development of the non-violent personality, the *satyagrahi*. Gandhi considered character formation as main function of school. Cenkner (1976: 101) brings in that Gandhi 'looked upon the development of personality as far more significant than the accumulation of intellectual tools and academic knowledge'. Besides the teaching of a creative activity, Gandhi's concept of schooling contained 'the mother tongue of the student, mathematics, social studies, natural science, music and drawing, and Hindustani' (ibid.: 110). Religious education and the teaching of English were not part of the curriculum. Gandhi stressed oral teaching rather than book learning. Hence he put a strong emphasis on the role of the teacher.

The image of the ideal teacher

Following his philosophy, Gandhi's image of the ideal teacher was derived from the ideal human being presented in the *Bhagavad Gita*. Cenkner

(1976) points out that Gandhi's notion of the ideal teacher was a teacher who lives according to the principles of truth and *ahimsa* (non-violence). A teacher with a non-violent stance was essential for the imparting of character education. Gandhi considered the work of a teacher as sacred work. The relationship between teacher and student was characterized on the one hand by *guru-bhakti* (devotion to the teacher) and on the other hand by a devotion of the teacher to his 'students, to service and to God' (Cenkner 1976: 112). Kumar (1999: 5) notes that Gandhi's model of a good teacher was religion-based instead of 'purely professional'. In the view of Kumar, Gandhi 'was using a familiar Indian motif, that of a guru living in his *ashram* in the company of his disciples' (ibid.). Kumar describes the relationship between the guru and his disciples in the *ashram* as follows: 'In the ideal *ashram* community, the teacher was expected to set an example of the life worth living, and from this high pedestal of daily existence he was permitted to demand any conceivable form of sacrifice from the students' (ibid.).

As we have seen in the beginning, Gandhi relied on Indian tradition concerning the conception of his social and political thought (Chakrabarty 2006). As Kumar (1999) shows, Gandhi's notion of the teacher was as well rooted within Indian tradition. Kumar argues that using the motif of a guru and his disciples was supportive to the distribution of Gandhi's ideas on education. Gandhi favoured a new national education based on the principles of his philosophy. In the following, Gandhi's *Nai Talim* is explored.

Nai Talim: *a conception of basic national education*

According to Lang-Wojtasik (2002), the conception of *Nai Talim* is part of Gandhi's constructive programme.[26] Gandhi's educational ideas are considered as 'lifelong education in five steps' (Lang-Wojtasik 2002: 192, transl. T.V.).[27] As Gandhi regarded the self-transformation of the individual as well as the transformation of the society as principal goals, each step of education incorporated the objective of transformation. Educational institutions were considered as learning environments where individuals could practice a life based on the principles of *swaraj* (self-rule) and *sarvodaya* (welfare for all) on the basis of self-reflection. Education should take place in small independent communities and should be self-supporting. Thus the teaching of a handicraft was central in Gandhi's concept of 'basic education' (Lang-Wojtasik 2002).

Gandhi's ideas on education were discussed on the Wardha Conference in 1937 and an adoption named 'Wardha Scheme or Basic National Education' (Cenkner 1976: 121) followed. It was characterized by 'free compulsory education, craft as the centre of education, the mother tongue as the medium of instruction, and self-supporting education' (ibid.). Even though the Wardha Scheme was adopted by the Indian National Congress and model schools were started, the implementation of Gandhi's educational plan failed. Cenkner (1976) regards a changing political orientation and problems concerning the realization as possible reasons. Likewise, Lang-Wojtasik (2002) outlines among others a lack of rooms, materials and qualified teachers as possible reasons.

The relevance of Gandhi's ideas on education in modern India

In present times, Jha criticizes Gandhi's ideas on education as 'contemporary not modern [and] ideal not practical' (Jha 2007: 129). Conversely and from a European perspective, Lang-Wojtasik (2002) argues that it is meaningful to reflect about Gandhi's concept of education. In the view of current and future educational challenges it offers possible aspects of relevance. In recent times, Kumar evaluates Gandhi's *Nai Talim* under the focus of quality of education (Das 2009). Following this, the question whether Gandhi's ideas on education are relevant in modern India is taken up. Hence, some recent progress and future challenges in modern India are outlined. Afterwards Gandhi's ideas on education are reviewed with the intention to figure out possible aspects of relevance.

Progress and challenges in elementary education in modern India

In 1999 the Public Report of Basic Education in India (PROBE) claimed for universalization of elementary education to achieve a betterment of the situation of individuals and of society (Mander 1999). Universal elementary education was understood as a holistic approach, combining the teaching of career-related knowledge and general education. Among other issues, PROBE revealed bad working conditions for teachers. The work of teachers was influenced by a lack of infrastructure, poor training and guidance and a high pupil–teacher ratio of 1:68. PROBE suggested that public and private engagement in education should bring a change in the notion of education (Mander 1999).

A decade later, several educational programmes were realized, such as Sarva Shiksha Abhiyan (SSA) in 2002[28] and the Right to Education Act (RTE) in 2009[29] to fulfill the demand of universalization of elementary education. Das (2009) summarizes recent progress and challenges in the educational system in India discussed in the book *Concerns, Conflicts, and Cohesions: Universalization of Elementary Education in India*. According to Das the number of school-going children raised in 2004–05 to 93.5 of the GER.[30] This can be seen as progress in enrolment of children. However, there was no change in the rate of dropouts from elementary schools (50.84 per cent). Das considers access to public primary schools as 'highly limited' (Das 2009: 29). The pupil–teacher ratio in primary schools appears on average to be 1:46, but differs between states. Disparities occur within districts and states for example in regard of the quality of education. The expenditure on education remains on a low level of 3.7 per cent of GNP.[31] Das exposes the situation of the dropout children as the current challenge. With regard to the Census of 2001, 34 per cent of India's children, aged 5–14 years, are not going to school. In numbers this would be over 87 million children. Concerning the education of working children there was an improvement in the enrolment ratio.

As we have seen, there is a serious situation among teachers. PROBE stated that there was a lack of infrastructure and guidance and a high pupil–teacher ratio of 1:68 (Mander 1999). Taking the information of Das (2009) into account, this ratio improved to an average of 1:46 between 1999 and 2009. However, Das considers the circumstances of teaching as primary to the betterment of schooling. In the view of the implementation of the RTE, Sarangapani (2011) propounds the importance of quality in teacher training. As long as there are not enough qualified teachers the RTE will not be successful. To promote education to every child in India it would be necessary to understand 'the diversity and complexity of the situations of the children' (Sarangapani 2011: 13). Sarangapani sees the problem in a teacher training that is too narrowly considered. At the present time teacher education provides insufficient knowledge on educational theory and school sociology. There is the need to define the qualities of a teacher and to ameliorate teacher training. Sarangapani states that the conception of the teacher changes in the view of current challenges in modern India. Though the model of a guru[32] 'as an autonomous and thinking practitioner' (ibid.) remains an example, a teacher is not teaching chosen disciples, but rather a person that ensures education of every child in India. Teacher training should provide 'thinking, reflecting and highly motivated teachers who are willing and able to work even in government schools and with very underprivileged children' and likewise enable professionals to become 'agents of change' (ibid.).

Jha (2007) criticizes the present education system as promoting negative qualities rather than encouraging an atmosphere where children are learning together. In the view of current and future changes within the work world and the society Jha claims for a change in the notion of schooling. He suggests reformulating the three Cs of industrial-age schooling, 'compulsion, comparison and competition' into three Cs 'relevant for twenty-first century schooling: choice, consideration and collaboration' (Jha 2007: 135). The main task of the twenty-first century in the view of Jha is the creation of 'a common school system that provides quality education for children of all citizens' (ibid.).

Possible relevant aspects of Gandhi's ideas on education in modern India

Elementary education was of high significance to Gandhi. It was meant to provide abilities related to life and should be imparted through the mother tongue of the child. Gandhi considered learning as a holistic process integrated in the socioeconomic village life. He aimed at the development of the whole personality. By emphasizing the teaching of a craft, character formation and spiritual education, Gandhi differentiated his approach from the conception underlying the current British educational system. Instead of book learning he favoured creative and situational learning. The school as a community was considered as a learning environment where a non-violent behaviour in human relationships could be practiced. Moreover, Gandhi made a strong emphasis on the role of the teacher. Gandhi's conception of education through creative activity favoured children of the lowest groups of the Indian society.

In our days, Gandhi's ideas seem to be relevant not only for children of the weaker groups of the society but for all of the children in India. Children from different sociocultural backgrounds might learn together and learn from each other. As Gandhi considered education a lifelong process, the teaching of a handicraft might offer opportunities to an autonomous life for adults who were deprived from education. Lang-Wojtasik (2002) summarizes four possible aspects. These are the awareness of the meaning of education in society as a whole, the balance between theory and practice, the focus on decentralization and participation and last, the orientation of the educational concept on the needs and the living conditions of the learners. Gandhi's approach opens an alternative in present day teaching in a way that learners and teachers are considered to create a new learning community and participate in the process of education. Nonetheless, Gandhi's model of an ideal teacher is to be seen critically. Teachers in Gandhi's view were living examples of *satyagrahis* (non-violent personalities). They provided education as sacred work, in 'devotion to students, to service and to God' (Cenkner 1976: 112). To Kumar (1999: 4) this appears an 'extraordinary demand'. In the view of the working conditions of teachers in modern India, Gandhi's demand of teachers as living examples of truth and *ahimsa* seems to be unrealistic. Following Sarangapani (2011), the model of the guru as an ideal teacher remains an example but has to be made generally accessible to all children in India. To achieve this, a better teacher education is essential. The ideal teacher in modern India should be a professional aware of his or her responsibility for the future of his students. He should be engaged in his work and consider himself as 'agent of change' (ibid.: 15).

As Gandhi's philosophy of *satyagraha* was based on the demand of compromise, a possible aspect of relevance lays to my mind in enabling individuals to develop a collaborative stance. Thus Gandhi's holistic approach to education might be relevant not only for the development of a personality but also for moral education. Becke (1999) examines as to what extent Gandhi's ethic is suitable to the twenty-first century. He takes Kohlberg's stages of moral development into account.[33] In this concept of six stages, Gandhi is adduced as an instance to illustrate the last stage. Becke values Gandhi's approach as being based on the principle of moral sense. One not only has to conduct one's life according to moral rules but rather has to act based on ethical aspects. This appears to Becke as an invitation to follow Gandhi as an example.

Conclusion and outlook: education for a better world?

Reflecting on education within a global perspective, the question of how education should take place comes to mind. In the European context challenges of globalization brought fields of interests such as peace education, environmental education, intercultural education and the importance of global learning into the centre of the educational discussion (Wulf 2002). How will challenges concerning education be discussed in India? In the horizon of globalization, is it meaningful to continue on Gandhi's ideas on education and how could one provide education according to Gandhi's principles? Is the image of the ideal human being according to Gandhi still relevant?

Gandhi focused aspects of education that motivate us to think of certain aspects of education in the twenty-first century in a critical way. In the beginning of this chapter, a convocation address of N. R. Narayana Murthy was cited. In this speech, Murthy referred to Gandhi's vision of a more socially just society. Murthy proposed the picture of an Indian professional of the twenty-first century following Gandhi's example. Students should become 'useful citizens' (Murthy 2010: 16) and should take responsibility for their society. Education for democracy and citizenship is the goal of the educational programme of Vidya Bhawan Society as well (Dr H. K. Dewan, personal communication, 18 June 2011). This is similar to Gandhi's understanding of education as a holistic approach that focuses not only on the imparting of knowledge but also on the development of personality and a community spirit. Children should be proud of the things they made, and should develop respect for the things made by others. Education should be 'related to the life and the community of the child' and should promote opportunities 'to make them experience an ability to live in the world' (Dr H. K. Dewan, personal communication, 18 June 2011).

Although Gandhi was not an educationist by profession, he developed educational ideas within his *ashrams* in South Africa and wrote about them in *Hind Swaraj* and *Harijan*. Thus Gandhi's ideas on education were based on the reading of religious textbooks and sociocritical writings, educational practices and personal experiences. Gandhi criticized the situation in India and created a vision for a better society. For Gandhi, education had different dimensions, a social and political orientation concerning the betterment of the society and a philosophical orientation concerning the self-transformation of the individual. The conception of man underlying Gandhi's educational ideas was derived from the teaching of the ideal human being in the *Bhagavad Gita*. The goal of education of the individual was to become a non-violent personality, a *saytagrahi*, that lives upon the principles of truth and *ahimsa* (non-violence). Educational institutions were considered as learning environments where individuals could interact with others and practice non-violent values. The teacher in Gandhi's view should incorporate the image of the ideal human being. The teaching of a handicraft should render the educational institution self-supporting. *Swaraj* (self-rule) and *sarvodaya* (welfare for all) are two principles that describe the aim and means of a socioeconomic life in small villages. The relationship between the individual and the society could be practiced by the child within its community. According to Lang-Wojtasik (2002), aspects of Gandhi's ideas on education are similar to the principles of progressive education. The reading and combining of interpretations of two of Gandhi's papers on education in the journal *Harijan* within this chapter exposes the high significance of holistic education that includes the development of head, heart and hands and the emphasis on community learning and creative activity as two main findings. These aspects may remind on educational conceptions of progressive educators such as Pestalozzi, Dewey and Montessori.

Gandhi's ethic of non-violence seems to be relevant not only for India but also for the entire world. Many people are following Gandhi's example. Concerning Gandhi's social and political thought and in particular his views on education, one becomes aware of his unique approach to philosophy. Gandhi oriented his life according to two basic values, truth and *ahimsa* (non-violence). They functioned as guiding principles but as well as goals of life. As truth and *ahimsa* (non-violence) were not considered as universal and had to be experienced by the individuals in interactions, the notion of compromise was basic to Gandhi's concept of *satyagraha* (non-violent resistance). In the view of plurality and complexity there is even today the need of compromise and the development of a collaborative stance. Gandhi's ethic of non-violence provides points of contact to a conduct of life that is autonomous and based on ethical principles. In my assessment, Gandhi's intention of the development of a non-violent personality, a *satyagrahi*, might motivate people to become aware of their identity and personality.

The aim of this article was to give an overview on Gandhi's ideas on education and to answer the question as to what extent they are relevant in modern India. Therefore, Gandhi's person and philosophy as well as current challenges concerning education in India were presented. Although the question of relevance could only be touched upon, this chapter argues that there are aspects that indicate the relevance in present and future times. Some possible aspects as, for example, Gandhi's emphasis on the development of a non-violent personality, were offered. As Gandhi spoke for basic education for all children in India and understood education as lifelong process integrated in the living environment of the individuals, his ideas on education are inspiring in the view of current educational challenges such as the achievement of universalization of elementary education. In my opinion, Gandhi's ideas on education and their relevance in modern India remain a captivating topic worthwhile to continue in an ongoing paper in greater depth.

Notes

1 For a differentiation between formal, informal and non-formal education, see the item on http://www.infed.org/biblio/b-nonfor.htm (30 July 2012).
2 'Philosophy of Education' is a basic course of the dual mode M.A. Education (Elementary) programme. This programme is addressed to professionals in teaching, social work and planning institutions. The M.A. Education (Elementary) programme is realized through cooperation with several educational organizations and research institutions (TISS Information Brochure; see also the M.A.

Elementary (Education) Profile on the website of TISS, retrieved from: http://www.tiss.edu/TopMenuBar/admissions/masters-programmes/m.a.-in-education-elementary?searchterm=elementary (30 July 2012).
3 Following Lang-Wojtasik (2002) *Nai Talim* is a Hindustani term and literally means new education. Kumar formulates Gandhi's educational ideas as 'Gandhi's "basic education" plan' (Kumar 1999: 1) or ' "basic education" proposal' (ibid.: 2). Cenkner (1976: 121) uses the terms of 'Wardha Scheme [and] Basic National Education'. In this article I refer to the terms synonymously.
4 As I stayed at TISS I came in touch with the students attending the course 'Philosophy of Education'. The introduction to the Vidya Bhawan Society was arranged by one of the students. Vidya Bhawan Society is one of the collaboration partners of the M.A. Education (Elementary) programme at TISS, Mumbai (see TISS Information Brochure: 1).
5 Udaipur is a city in Rajasthan, a state in northwest India.
6 *Harijan* was a weekly journal, founded in 1933, that dealt with the current situation and the betterment of future times. It was particularly concerned with the situation of the lowest groups of the society (Chakrabarty 2006).
7 Gandhi (1945), as cited in Gunturu (1999: 172), translation T.V.
8 Mahatma is the honorific title of Gandhi. According to Sharpe *Mahatma* means 'literally "great soul": person of outstanding spiritual attainment' (Sharpe 1985: 177).
9 *Hindustani*: an expression that sums up different Indic dialects, for example the Hindi–Urdu combination, retrieved from: www.thefreedictionary.com/Hindustani on 1 August 2012. *Khadi* means a 'hand-spun cloth' (Chakrabarty 2006: 178) and *Ramayana* is 'one of the two great religious epics of Hinduism (1st cent. B.C.E)' (Cenkner 1976: 211).
10 See also Gandhi (1927).
11 Porbandar is a city in the state Gujarat in northwest India.
12 Cenkner (1976: 209) explains: 'Bhagavad Gītā: The Song of the Lord; a Hindu poem forming part of the epical *Mahābhārata* which teaches liberation by love and divine grace.'
13 Following Lang-Wojtasik (2002), Gandhi read the Qur'an as well, during his stay in South Africa.
14 The official name of Bombay changed to Mumbai in 1996.
15 '*āśram*: a place for spiritual discipline and development within a communal setting' (Cenkner 1976: 209). Whenever possible I indicate the etymological meaning but refer to the English spelling of the Indian words.
16 Gandhi's notion of *satyagraha* will be exposed thoroughly later in this paper.
17 For example the famous salt march conducted in 1930 (Lang-Wojtasik 2002).
18 Gandhi and Parel (1997).
19 Cenkner (1976: 89) explains: '[Gandhi's] concept of truth is not static but a dynamic reality which affects the total lifestyle of man. It is a norm applied to thought, word and deed.'
20 '*ahiṃsā*: non-injury; non-violence; reconceptualized by Gandhi to include a quality of love and redemptive suffering' (Cenkner 1976: 209). There are different forms of writing 'ahimsa'; I refer to the version *ahimsa* used by Gandhi (1984: 9–14).

21 'karma-yoga: the path of activity; a karma-yogin is one who follows the path of activity as his primary spiritual discipline' (Cenkner 1976: 211).
22 'karma: the law according to which every deed has its inevitable consequence, a good deed has a good consequence, and an evil deed an evil consequence; also work, activity' (Cenkner 1976: 210).
23 Cenkner defines a satyagrahi as 'a member of Gandhi's non-violent campaign' (Cenkner 1976: 212).
24 Gandhi's writings are cited according to an edition of his 'Basic Education' that was published by Kumarappa in 1951. In this edition Gandhi's writings were arranged according to subjects (see Gandhi and Kumarappa 1951).
25 This may remind of Dewey's notion of community and learning. See Kumar (1999) for a comparison between Gandhi's and Dewey's approaches to education.
26 The constructive programme developed by Gandhi tries to provide orientation to transfer his social and philosophical ideas into practice. It covers various aspects of the daily life of human beings, but offers preferable changes in the society as well (for an overview see Lang-Wojtasik 2002).
27 These steps are: 'Social Education (Adult Education); Pre-Basic Education (age 3–5); Basic Education (age 6–14); Post-Basic Education (age 15–18); Rural University' (Lang-Wojtasik 2002: 192).
28 Sarva Shiksha Abhiyan (SSA) is a programme initiated in 2002 to ensure universalization of elementary education. It consists of building up new schools, providing additional teachers, teacher training and guidance. (Website Sarva Shiksha Abhiyan; Ministry of Human Resource Development, retrieved from: www.ssa.nic.in on 7 August 2012).
29 The Right to Education (RTE) is a law that was adopted in 2010. It ensures education to every child aged 6–14. (The Right of Children to Free and Compulsory Education Act 2009, pdf.doc, retrieved from: http://it.scribd.com/doc/33735102/Right-to-Education-or-RTE-2009-India-The-Right-of-Children-to-Free-and-Compulsory-Education-Act-2009-India on 9 August 2012).
30 GER = gross enrolment ratio.
31 GNP = gross national product.
32 Besides the guru, Sarangapani mentions Socrates as a model teacher.
33 Kohlberg differentiates three levels of moral development, pre-conventional, conventional and post-conventional. Each level is divided into two stages (Becke 1999: 147).

References

Becke, A. (1999): Gandhi zur Einführung. Hamburg: Junius Verlag.

Cenkner, W. (1976): The Hindu Personality in Education. Tagore, Gandhi, Aurobindo. New Delhi: Manohar Publishers, 73–125.

Chakrabarty, B. (2006): Social and Political Thought of Mahatma Gandhi. New York: Routledge.

Das, A. (2009): Challenges in Ensuring Elementary Education for All [Review of the book: Concerns, Conflicts, and Cohesions: Universalization of Elementary

Education in India, ed. by P. Rustagi]. *Economic & Political weekly*, vol. XLIV, no. 39, retrieved from: www.epw.in/authors/amarendra-das (08 August 2012).

Fischer, L. (1992): The Life of Mahatma Gandhi. New Delhi: Indus.

Gandhi, M.K. (1927): An Autobiography or The Story of my Experiments with Truth. Ahmedabad 1990: Navajivan Publishing House.

Gandhi, M.K. (1984): The Bhagvadgita. Delhi: Orient Paperbacks.

Gandhi, M.K., and Kumarappa, B. (1951): Basic Education. Ahmedabad: Navajivan Press.

Gandhi, M.K., and Parel, A.J. (eds) (1997): Hind Swaraj and Other Writings. Cambridge: University Press.

Gardner, H. (1997): Extraordinary Minds. Portraits of Exceptional Individuals and an Examination of Our Extraordinariness. New York: Basic Books.

Gunturu, V. (1999): Mahatma Gandhi. Leben und Werk. München: Eugen Diederichs Verlag.

Gunturu, V. (2000): Hinduismus. Die große Religion Indiens. Kreuzlingen, München: Hugendubel.

Jha, M.M. (2007): The right to education. Developing the common school system in India. In: Verma, G.K., Bagley, C.R., and Jha, M.M. (eds): International Perspectives on Educational Diversity and Inclusion: Studies from America, Europe and India. Oxon, New York: Routledge, 125–137.

Kantowsky, D. (1985): Gandhi und Indiens Entwicklung heute. In: Kantowsky, D. (ed.): Von Südasien lernen. Erfahrungen in Indien und Sri Lanka. Frankfurt, M., New York: Campus, 31–54.

Kumar, K., UNESCO: International Bureau of Education (1999): Mohandas Karamchand Gandhi (1869–1948), originally published in: PROSPECTS: the quarterly review of education (Paris, UNESCO: International Bureau of Education), vol. 23, no. 3/4, 1993: 507–517, retrieved from: http://www.ibe.unesco.org/fileadmin/user_upload/archive/publications/ThinkersPdf/gandhie.PDF (30 July 2012).

Lang-Wojtasik, G. (2002): Gandhis Nai Talim im Kontext von Education for all. In: Datta, A., and Lang-Wojtasik, G. (eds): Bildung zur Eigenständigkeit. Vergessene reformpädagogische Ansätze aus vier Kontinenten. Frankfurt, M., London: IKO-Verlag für Interkulturelle Kommunikation, 185–200.

Malinar, A. (1994): M.K. Gāndhī und die Frage nach dem Hinduismus. In: Religionsunterricht an höheren Schulen 5: Sonderband: Gandhi, Gütersloh, 268–280, retrieved from: http://www.indologie.uzh.ch/environment/malinar/DocumentsAM/Malinar_Gandhi.pdf (30 July 2012).

Mander, H. (1999): [Review of the book: Public Report on Basic Education in India, by The Probe Team]. *Manushi: A Journal About Woman and Society*, issue 111: 42–43.

Murthy, N.R.N. (2010): The Indian of the Twenty-first Century. In: Murthy, N.R.N. (ed.): A Better India. A Better World? New Delhi: Penguin Group, 9–17.

Sarangapani, P. (2011): Teachers first. The state is not serious about the need for a robust programme of elementary teacher education to realise the right to education. *Frontline*, vol. 28, no. 14: 13–15.

Sharpe, E.J. (1985): The Universal Gītā. Western Images of the Bhagavadgītā. A Bicentenary Survey. London: Duckworth.
TISS (Tata Institute of Social Sciences): Information Brochure: M.A. in Education (Elementary).
Wulf, C. (2002): Kulturelle Vielfalt. Der Andere und die Notwendigkeit anthropologischer Reflexion. In: Wulf, C., and Merkel, C. (eds): Globalisierung als Herausforderung der Erziehung. Theorien, Grundlagen, Fallstudien. Münster, New York, München, Berlin: Waxmann, 75–100.

5

ASCETICISM IN ANCIENT AND MODERN INDIA

Franziska Roggenbuck

> Joining the brotherhood of Sadhus is like going back in time, being reborn in a semi-nomadic 'tribe' of pre-agrarian age. It reflects a nostalgia for humanity's roots, for the simple, harmonious existence.
>
> Hartsuiker (1993: 62)

According to the latest available data, the census of 1931 in British India, only 0.7 per cent of the population of that time, ca. 350 billion people, described themselves as ascetics and only 10–15 per cent of them were female, called *sadhvis*[1] (Gross 2001: 121). A glance into statistics (ibid.) as well as a look into Hindu scriptures offer many terms for Indians living an ascetic lifestyle. They are called *yogis, seers, saints, rishis, mystics* or *tapasvis* (see Bhagat 1976: 4,10f.). Bhagat claims that 'samnyasin [meaning] the one who renounces' (ibid.) is the most common term for a renouncer, despite the fact that different kinds of ascetic lifestyle have mixed throughout time (Michaels 2004: 135). Meanwhile in modern India most sects allow everybody, no matter which age or caste, to become an ascetic, if he or she has found a guru who introduces him/her. The term *sadhu*, Sanskrit for 'good man' or 'holy man', seems to be convenient for a general description of Indian ascetics. Many scholars emphasize the attribution 'holy' when writing about ascetics (e.g. Bedi 1992; Hartsuiker 1993; Linrothe 2006). As *sadhus* are searching for the path of enlightenment, the feeling when *atman* (the self) becomes one with *brahman* (the soul of the world), for many Indians and foreigners they seem to be 'representatives of God [or even] professional mystics' (Hartsuiker 1993: 7f.), who try to gain *siddhis*, magical powers. Michaels (2001) picks up this latter ascription by asking the provocative question whether *sadhus* today are either holy men or freaks. Although he thinks that *sadhus* need to be eccentric in order to 'show their opposition against mainstream society' (Michaels 2004: 8f.), he asserts that nowadays the Western view on Indian ascetics is distorted by contextless photographs, which document an 'Exotismus des Schauderns' (exotism of shudder) (Michaels 2001: 1). In former times, above all during the European Romantic age, imaginations of the spiritual Indian ascetic, remote from the glamour of the world, released dreams of writers, poets and scientists.[2] Nowadays, however, as Michaels (2004) states, tourists' pictures of long-haired, Ghanja smoking, 'naked philosophers' (Hartsuiker 1993: 7) whose bodies show signs of mortification and whose lifestyle is seemingly dominated by contemplation, communicate a counter-picture to the Western ideal of businessman, and thus, rather make Western people scared. Indeed, *Sadhus* offer various associations and a remarkable old-fashioned lifestyle, which could be scary but at the same time makes people curious. Who are these men and women? Which rules do they follow in their daily lives? What are the roots of their belief system? Where does their ascetic lifestyle historically derive from?

In the following article, these questions should become more traceable. The first part of the article will have a closer look on general, cross-cultural definitions of asceticism, followed by the presentation of an ancient[3] Indian concept of asceticism – with a focus on the concept of *yoga*. The third part, which is the main part of the article, will discuss the origins of Indian asceticism by presenting conflicting scientific views. The last part of the article will draw attention to asceticism in modern India, embodied by *sadhus*.

Cross-cultural definitions of asceticism

Etymologically, the word 'asceticism' derives from the Greek word *askesis*, which meant exercise and training for the purpose of strength, skill and mastery in the athletic games (Bhagat 1976: 9).[4] Referring to this definition, Foucault stressed the psycho-emotional aspect of the training. For him asceticism is lifelong exercise on the *self* (Foucault, Technologien des Selbst, cit. in Brenner and Zirfas 1999: 259f.). Brenner and Zirfas rather consider the societal aspect of asceticism by asking the question how ascetic life needs to look like if it wants to be moral. They ask for the ethical dimension of asceticism and finally draw the conclusion that asceticism is an important medium, explained in the expression 'wechselseitige Enthaltsamkeit' (reciprocal austereness) (ibid.: 262) needed in order to practice a new way of morality of reciprocal attention and understanding between people. Already in ancient Greek society, Plato pointed out the ethical aspect of asceticism. He described asceticism as 'in Übung der Gerechtigkeit und jeder anderen Tugend leben und sterben' (living and dying by exercising fairness and all of the other virtues).[5] Michaels orientates his studies on asceticism on Friedrich Nietzsche's basic three point-programme of an ascetic ideal of 'Armut, Demut, Keuschheit' (poverty, humility, chastity) (Michaels 2004: 7f.). He further states that ascetic life, because of its demands of observances like fasting, special diets, times of prayer, lavations and difficult techniques of self-discipline, generally is not easy and even could be called 'art (technique) of simple life' (ibid.: 7). Besides, it always contents a provocative critique of normal lifestyle. Today, he states, asceticism is connoted negatively, because it is linked with self-referring contemplation which does not represent the Western ideal of an active lifestyle (ibid.). However, by highlighting the aspect of simplicity, slowness and resistance, Michaels summarizes aspects of trends which gain more and more influence in postmodern societies, like, for example, the lifestyle of spiritual ecology,[6] which is described by Schumacher-Chilla. However, this modern lifestyle lacks the aspect of resistance.[7]

Referring to Indian asceticism, the Dutch indologist Bronkhorst combines the physical and mental aspects in his definition wherein asceticism 'covers the whole range of physical and mental exercises from extreme mortification to certain forms of "gentle" meditation [. . .] ' (Bronkhorst 1993: 1). In the following, the definition and historical roots of the four main aspects of an *ancient* Indian concept of asceticism will be explained. This concept contends orientations and beliefs, which modern *sadhus* still refer to in daily living style.

The concept of ancient Indian Hindu asceticism

In the first part of his book, Bhagat (1976) gives a detailed, chronological analysis[8] of the origin and evolution of each of the four Sanskrit terms, *tapas*, *vairagya*, *samnyasa* and *yoga*, the four most important dimensions of a concept of ancient Indian asceticism.

The first dimension of his concept is *Tapas* (see Bhagat 1976: 13–28). '*Tapas* is used to comprehend all forms of the pursuit of self-control' (ibid.: 13). Etymologically, *tapas* stems from the Sanskrit root 'tap [which means] to be hot or heated' (ibid.). Thus, *tapas* is something which generates heat. How could this happen practically? The author mentions internal and external practices. Externally *tapas* can be created by sitting near a fire or in the sun or by consuming drugs like Ganja. Internally heat is created by fasting or holding the breath. Resuming the meaning of *tapas* the author asserts that there was a '[historical] evolution of meaning of tapas [. . .] from its mere physical plane, thus it came to be understood as a mental discipline and a moral factor until it was assimilated by the Yoga-system' (ibid.: 27). Furthermore, it can be summarized that *tapas* had two aspects, negatively as self-torture and positively as self-training. He finally states that holy persons like (Gautama) Buddha and holy Hindu scriptures like the Gita (Bhagavad-Gita) and the Yogasutras (from *Patanjali*) favoured the latter point of view. Dolf Hartsuiker also dedicates one chapter of his book about the 'holy men of India' (1993: 109–117) to the topic of *tapas*. He describes *tapas* as the concept underlying austerities and mortifications. It is the 'inner fire' (ibid.: 112) which is opposed to the outer, the sacrificial fire. *Kama* 'the sexual energy, [. . .], the fire of passion, is the main potential source of *tapas* – and at the same time it is its opposite' (ibid.). In order to sublimate and control this 'fire of passion [or this] heat of digestion' (ibid.: 13), the ascetic needs to restrain himself physically. This could be done through special diets, wearing chastity belts, non-speaking or severe mortifications like keeping an arm up or standing on one foot for many years.

The second dimension of Bhagat's concept of ancient Indian asceticism is described by the term *vairaga*, which means 'indifference, non-attachment, detachment, dispassion, desirelessness, passionlessness, freedom from absence of desire and renunciation' (Bhagat 1976: 28). Compared to the body-focused *tapas*, *vairaga* means the 'mental withdrawal from the worldly life' (ibid.). The idea of *vairaga* finds its full development in the *Bhagavad-Gita* and the *Vedanta*.[9] It deals with the question 'How can the mind, which wanders at will, become stable and obedient?' (ibid.: 39). Bhagat underlines that *vairaga* is the precedent of *samnyasa*, which means to finally resign from the world. Gross (2001: 216) supports this connection, by writing that 'the relationship between renunciation (*tyaga; samnyasa*) and non-attachment/dispassion (*vairaga*) permeates the structure of the ascetic belief system.' The concept of *vairaga* recalls the concept of the ancient Greek *Stoa*, a philosophy teaching the aim of liberty from affects, fear and pain through control of affects and passions (see Brenner and Zirfas 1999: 231f.), which contemporarily finds its successor in modern psychological methods like self-managed or guided emotional control. In present scientific literature, there are no further descriptions of how to reach *vairaga* practically. However, as a result of his field research on *sadhus*, which contained many religious talks with them, Gross describes *vairaga* as 'complete dispassion' (Gross 2001: 231), which consists of four degrees. Following Gross, only two of them are important. The first is *samnyasa-vairaga* 'dispassion followed by complete abandonment of all worldly attachments and involvements [. . .], [the second *bhakti-vairaga*] a state of dispassion in which the only attachment left is the desire for realization of God' (ibid.).

The third dimension of Bhagat's concept of asceticism is called *samnyasa*. It generally means 'to resign the world' (Olivelle 1992: 52). It is the Sanskrit word for renunciation as well as the name of one of the stages of the *asrama-system*.[10] The aim of the idea of *samnyasa*, as Bhagat (1976: 60) concludes, is the 'final quest for *atman* (the individual self or soul)'.

Yoga

The last dimension of Bhagat's conception of ancient Indian asceticism is *yoga*. Gross underlines the idea of a connection between *yoga* and asceticism, however, he does not integrate *yoga* as an aspect of asceticism like Bhagat, but puts it on one level with asceticism, which he defines primarily as *vairaga* by saying that 'Yogic and ascetic ideals and beliefs are practically synonymous' (Gross 2001: 234). Thereby he stresses the relevance of *yoga* for the understanding of Hindu asceticism.

Yoga originally means 'union' or 'joining' with the Absolute (ibid.: 232). Bhagat dates back the recognition of the importance of *yoga* for spiritual enlightenment to the times of the *Upanishads*, when there was an 'increasing emphasis [. . .] on the attainment of Supreme wisdom (*jnana*) for liberation' (Bhagat 1976: 55). Besides, he makes clear that the idea of *yoga*, as the practice of meditation, had its origin already in the Indus Valley Culture (2500 BCE) and was an evolution out of the idea of *tapas* (ibid.: 48). Zimmer (1992: 255) points out that there was an interdependency of the earlier *samkhya-philosophy* (written by *Kapila*) and the later *yogasutras* (written by *Patanjali*). For him, they were 'zwei Aspekte einer einzigen Disziplin' (two aspects of only one discipline). Both philosophical systems point out the duality of the world in spirit resp. soul and materiality resp. nature, contrasting the *vedanta-philosophy* which knows *Brahman* as the absolute, non-dualistic world-soul (ibid.: 277). *Patanjali*, who lived approximately in the second century CE, was not the founder of *yoga* but the first who systematized the knowledge about it and wrote it down as the *yogasutras*. The exact date of this collection of prose is controversial, but the three books of the basic paper are dated back to the second century BCE. The fourth book was written in the fifth century CE (Zimmer 1992: 257). Later, *yoga* became an own philosophical system. Today, there are more than two dozen methods or types of *yoga* (Gross 2001: 234). '[Since] Swami Vivekananda and others in the Ramakrishna Mission' (ibid.), *yoga* was organized in four categories: *Karma-Yoga*, *Jnana-Yoga*, *Bhakti-Yoga* and *Raja Yoga*. Patanjali's *Yogasutras* belong to the last one.

What exactly does *yoga* mean? In the explanation of Zimmer, *yoga* deals with the process of detachment and provides practical techniques to reach *moksa* (liberation) or *kaivalya* (simply being) by concentration exercises which are directed inwards (Zimmer 1992: 255). Thus, *yoga* is the 'modus operandi' (Gross 2001: 232), the know-how of ascetic life. In order to understand for which aim this technique is needed, the dualistic world-view of *yoga* needs to be explained first. Zimmer (see 1992: 255–266) describes it as follows. In the understanding of *yoga* and *samkhya* as philosophical systems, the world is a double-system which is irreversible. This bisection consists of *purusha* (life monad) and *prakriti* (inanimate materiality). The *prakriti* becomes manifest in three *gunas*, which could be imagined as three ropes of a hawser. These *gunas*, or qualities of human nature, are *sattva* (the perfect condition), *rajas* (passion) and *tamas* (inactivity).[11] They 'separate the individual soul from God' (Gross 2001: 221). By contrast, the *purusha*[12] is a shining light which lightens the processes of all materiality. It is without form or content. It has no qualities, because this would be part of materiality (Zimmer 1992: 259). Following Zimmer, the *Yoga* philosophy says that each life-monad which connects with the materiality becomes a slave of *samsara* (the cycle of the wandering soul), which is following *karma* (the law of cause and effect). *Yoga* needs to be practiced in order to free the *purusha* from the *prakriti*. This means the inner light or the simple being should be freed from the human nature, which consists of manifold desires.

How to free the simple being from the human nature? *Prakriti*, the human nature, consists of 'ignorance (*avidya*)' (Gross 2001: 221) and aims to reach '*artha*' (wealth), '*karma*' (lust), '*dharma*' (order) and '*moksa*' (liberation) (Bhagat 1976: 45). In order to free the *purusha* from the *prakriti*, every human being first needs to realize these desires. They consist of the 'five spontaneous actions of the soul' (Zimmer 1992: 261–263) and the five *kleshas* (obstacles) (Zimmer 1992: 266–276; Gross 2001: 218). The *five spontaneous actions of the soul* are right imaginations, wrong imaginations, fantasy, sleep and remembrance.[13] The five *kleshas* are ignorance (*avydia*), the imagination that I am me (*asmita*), adherence or sympathy (*raja*), hate (*dvesha*) and to cleave to the will of life (*abhinivesha*).[14] How to overcome them practically? *Yoga* mainly describes techniques and could be understood as a briefing of how to reach enlightenment. Patanjali's *Yoga*-systems is an example for that. It consists of eight limbs (*angas*) including ethical preparation and body exercises like breath control (*pranayma*), positions (*asanas*) and meditation (*dhyana*).[15] His core teaching says, *yoga*'s aim is 'the cessation [suppression] of the modifications [waves] of the mind [by] the going beyond body-consciousness' (Gross 2001: 236). As we could see in the examples of Patanjali's eight limbs, *yoga* primarily deals with the body. The transient body is seen as the 'gateway to hell [and at the same time as] instrument of the spirit' (Gross 2001: 237), which is a paradox of ascetic lifestyle. The body is the vessel, the 'temple of the soul and the soul lying within is the temple of God' (ibid.), and at the same time it should be overcome. However, the *yoga*-philosophy tries to make a compromise by telling that *yoga* 'provides the discipline and direction of the body's function as a doorway (to the absolute)' (ibid.).

But what is the absolute aim of *yoga*? How could this state of enlightenment and liberation be imagined? Following Zimmer, this is described in the last *Sutra* of the third book, where it is said that where the purity of the contemplation (*sattva*) is the same as the purity of the life-monad (*purusha*), there is '[das] für sich sein' (to be for yourself, *kaivalya*) (Zimmer 1992: 266). For a better understanding, Zimmer adds that *yoga* calms down the mind and as soon as this pacification is perfected, the inner human being, the life-monad (*purusha*), will be observable 'gleich einem Juwel auf dem Grunde eines stillen Teichs' (like a diamond at the bottom of a silent lake) (Zimmer 1992: 259). The *yogi* needs to realize that he is not really part of this world of change and hardship, and that he is free and independent from it, though his *gunas* (the three qualities of human nature) are sometimes ensnared. Yoga thinks that all creatures in their substance are 'heiter, erhaben, allwissend und allein' (sanguinely, superior, omniscient and alone) (ibid.: 278) and this is where it is needed to go back to. Generally, Michaels points out the manifestation of individuality in this belief-system (2001: 16). He says that for many Hindu ascetics the 'certitudo salutis' (certainty of salvation) (ibid.) is private. That means the certainty of salvation is evidenced by the self and not, like e.g. in Catholicism, given by God and affirmed by the religious community. The ideal of individual withdrawal is valued higher than in Christianity (see ibid.).

Origins of Indian asceticism

The concept of asceticism describes features of a belief system which is common for all Indian ascetics. After having given an insight of the main philosophical ideas connected to the phenomena of asceticism, its scriptural sources and historical development will be explained.

Samnyasa Upanishads: embedment in Hindu tradition

Indologists and scientists who deal with the roots of ancient Indian asceticism (e.g. Bhagat 1976; Olivelle 1992; Bronkhorst 1993; Freiberger 2009) agree that the so-called *Samnyasa Upanishads* are the '[literary] basis in Vedic revelation for the institution of renunciation (samnyasa) and for the rules and practices associated with that state. They play a central role in the theological reflections and disputes concerning that key institution of Brahmanical religion' (Olivelle 1992: 5). For this reason, the first step of this paragraph is to explain what the *Samnyasa Upanishads* are, how they came into existence and in which historical context they were written.

As mentioned before, *samnyasa* is the Hindu word for renunciation, which is one aspect of the concept of asceticism. The *Upanishads* form 'the concluding section of several Vedic collections' (Olivelle 1992: 3). A synonym term for *Upanishads* is *Vedanta*, which means 'the end of the Veda' (ibid.). The *Veda* itself is a collection of different scriptures, beginning with the *Rgveda* (about 1,200 BCE). The earliest *Upanishads* are dated back to 800 BCE, the latest are dated back to medieval India around 200 CE. The *Vedas* are divided into two sections, the section of rites (*karmakananda*) and the section of knowledge (*jnanakananda*). The *Upanishads* belong to the section of knowledge. No author is known but 'they constitute the temporal manifestations of eternal and transcendent knowledge' (Olivelle 1992: 3). Following Olivelle (1992: 4f.), modern scholarship makes a distinction between the major (classical) *Upanishads* and the minor (later) *Upanishads*. The *Samnyasa Upanishads* belong to the latter category. All in all, the *Samnyasa Upanishads* cover 20 Sanskrit texts, which were written over a time span of 1,500 years. Freiberger (2009: 39–44) explains that Deussen (1897)[16] was the first who translated more than 60 *Upanishads* from Sanskrit to German and formed a category out of seven of them, which he called *Samnyasa Upanishads*. Some years later, Schrader (1912)[17] wrote a critical edition about Deussen's work and finally put 13 more into Deussen's category. Some of them were translated into German and became part of the religious studies of Sprockhoff (1976).[18] Both Sprockhoff and Schrader finally put them into a chronological order. In 1992, Olivelle translated them into English language. The *Samnyasa Upanishads* are 'composite texts' (Olivelle 1992: 8), which means that they contain parts from *older Upanishads* and other texts like the *Puranas*[19] or the *Epics*,[20] too (ibid.). Olivelle alludes to the fact that the *Samnyasa Upanishads* did not 'arise in a vacuum; [but] were part of a broader literary tradition concerning renunciation and related topics in Brahmanical mainstream and in non-Brahmanical traditions like Buddhism and Jainism' (ibid.: 11). He provides a general, historical conspectus of the context in which the *Samnyasa Upanishads* were composed (Olivelle 1992: 11–19). The first organized, non-Brahmin ascetic institution in northern India already existed in the fifth and sixth century BCE and produced literary work which was transmitted orally. Its main content were 'codes of ascetic conduct' (ibid.: 12), like for example, initiation rites.[21] Regrettably, Olivelle does not mention an example or name of this early independent, non-Brahmin ascetic institution. At the same time, within Brahmanism, religious literature was produced in order to explain and assure 'proper performance of the Vedic or domestic rituals [in the *Srauta Sutras* and the *Grhya-Sutras*] [and in order to] inculcate proper personal and social behaviour [in the *Dharma-Sutras*]' (ibid.). Because of the hegemony of Brahmanism, the only way for the ascetic ideas of independent, non-Vedic institutions 'to acquire scriptural authority within Brahmanism was by being incorporated' (ibid.: 15). The reason for the failure of the institution of asceticism to establish an own scriptural tradition was rooted in the hegemony of the Vedic scriptures, which were justified by Brahman theologians. Primarily in the medieval period,[22] after the organization of Brahmanical monastic orders, independent ascetic texts were produced. These scriptures were kind of 'handbooks' (*paddhati*) (ibid.) for monks, dealing mainly with topics concerning rituals. Olivelle clarifies that these handbooks were not part of the *Veda* or the *Smrti* literature.[23] Within the Brahmanical mainstream, the *Samnyasa Upanishads* were the earliest independent works on renunciation. They were written in prose and 'exhibit the pithy style of the Sutra-genre' (ibid.: 17) but later were classified as *Upanishads*.

The content of the Samnyasa Upanishads

The *Samnyasa Upanishads* contain the development of basic conceptions of main terms of today's Hinduism like the *karma*-theory and the idea of *moksa* (liberation), which partly have already been described in the section about *Yoga* above. Despite the fact that the textual originals of the *Samnyasa Upanishads* are churlish and clumsy (see Sprockhoff in Freiberger 2009: 44), without an author, contain largely unmarked citations, and are presented as meta-historical revelation-scriptures (see Freiberger 2009: 39–47), they contain interesting information about rites of renunciation as well as behaviour and customs of renouncers. Besides, they are an abundant source for research on 'inner conflicts of tradition' (Olivelle 1992: 19–58) which becomes clearer in the following presentation of the scholars' discussion, first, if there is any proof of a pre- or non-Arian existence of asceticism, and second, if asceticism developed from a counter-movement against Brahmanism and their *Veda*.

Are the roots of asceticism Aryan or non-Aryan?

Within the scientific community there is a dispute about the influence of the non-Aryan settlers on asceticism. The question, mainly discussed from an archaeological viewpoint, is if either the roots of asceticism could be traced back to the non-Aryan, indigenous, Dravidian peoples of the Indus Valley, who were surprised by the invading 'Aryans' in the second millennium BCE[24] (see, e.g. Bhagat 1976; Gross 2001), or if these settlers did not have any influence on the establishment of the idea of asceticism in ancient India (see Gross 2001).

In a chapter of his book called 'ethno-historical considerations', Gross (2001: 7–47) presents a detailed review of several opinions concerning this discourse. Amongst other things, he draws attention to the widely spread archaeological assumption that the roots of asceticism can be traced back to a Proto-*Shiva*[25] statue[26] 'depicted on three of the several thousand seals uncovered at the Mohenjo-Daro and Harappa' (Gross 2001: 9), which were mentioned in literature for the first time in 1931. This Proto-*Shiva* shows a human figure with horns. It is pictured in a classical meditation-posture that ascetics usually practice. However, there is a lot of scientific resistance to this Proto-*Shiva*-thesis (see Gross 2001: 11). Apart from this assumed archeological evidence of a pre-Aryan existence of asceticism, there exist other ideas which support the opinion of an essential influence of non-Aryans on the development of asceticism. Gross (2001) puts himself on the side of those scholars who conjecture that cultural contact between non-Aryans and Aryans took place. He thinks that asceticism was a resistance movement of the non-Aryans towards the invading Aryans and their developing Brahman belief system.

> Between Aryan and non Aryan populations from the beginning of the Aryan intercursion into the subcontinent [cultural contact has been taken place,] and that it was the colonization subsequent displacement of the autochthonous population, and resulting cultural conflict that contributed to the ascetic and renunciant orientation in the indigenous religion.
>
> Gross (2001: 16f.)

Bhagat (1976: 66–72) points out another clue. He ascribes the concept of *tapas* to the practice of the medicine man called *shaman*, who had an outstanding position in the Indus Valley Culture-society. At the same time, he describes the religious practice of the early *Vedics* (e.g. described in the *rgveda*) as 'pure magic ritualism' (ibid.: 70). He concludes that the Rgvedic *muni's* (seer's) experience is 'comparable to the shamanic ecstasy' (ibid.: 72). By choosing this comparison, Bhagat shows that he is convinced of the pre-Aryan existence of asceticism.

ASCETICISM IN ANCIENT AND MODERN INDIA

Ascetic reformism (fifth/sixth century BCE*)*

Apart from the question if asceticism existed before the Aryans invaded during the second millennium BCE, there is another epoch of Indian history which deals with asceticism: the so-called epoch of 'ascetic reformism' (Michaels 1998: 347f.) from 500 to 200 BCE. In this context, Bronkhorst does not speak about an alleged counter-movement of the non-*Vedic* people against the *Vedic* ones as a reason for the establishment of asceticism. But he talks about the simultaneous emergence of a *Vedic* and a *non-Vedic* asceticism. He explains his view by the example of the development of the *asrama-system*.[27] In his study, he demonstrates 'that the different forms of asceticism that can be distinguished in India belong to (at least) two different currents' (Bronkhorst 1993: 19), the *Vedic* and the *non-Vedic*. They refer to two different textual sources. The *Apastamba Dharmasutras*[28] describe the *non-Vedic* kinds of ascetics, the *parivrajas* and the *vanaprasthas (version I)*. The later *Samnyasa Upanishads* and *Srauta Sutras* describe the second kind of ascetics, the *vanaprastha* (Version II[29]) and the *samnyasa*, which are *Vedic*. Later, the *samnyasa* was included into the *asrama-system* and the four stages of life were put into a strict order, in which the *samnyasa* described the last stage which was reserved for old people who had already gone through the other three stages (ibid.: 29).[30]

Olivelle prefers a view which maintains the duration of cultural developments and the inner dynamics of a culture because of socioeconomic changes. 'World-denying ideals [were not] self-originated [but arose at a particular time] against the background of momentous socioeconomic changes along the Ganges valley' (around fifth/sixth century BCE; Olivelle 1992: 19). He gives an overview of possible socioeconomic reasons which had psychological effects that caused ascetic thinking in the era of the so-called ascetic reformism. There was a food surplus, the population increased, a stable infrastructure of trade existed, and monarchical states and cities were established. For his explanation of the origins of asceticism the last three aspects are the most important ones. They altogether depended on the agricultural bounty of the rich soil of the Ganges Valleys during the *Vedic period*;[31] kingdoms were consolidated along the Ganges Valley (*middle country*). Later, the first states were founded. They contributed to the extension of administrative structures and transport facilities. However, the urban life, in contrast to the former, predominantly village life 'entailed the breakdown of family and kinship networks' and at the same time provided more freedom for individual initiatives' (ibid.: 32). Olivelle further explains that the religious movements which arose in that time, like Buddhism and Jainism, had urban roots. They were the result of the individual taking initiative, which had its model in the individualism lived by the king (as supreme individual in that time) and the merchants, whose enterprises were based on individual initiative and supported by the structures of urban life. 'The individualistic spirit permitted the creation of the first voluntary religious organizations in India' (ibid.: 33). The negative aspect of emerging urban centres was a growing pessimism which resulted in religious movements that based their doctrines on the thinking that human life is suffering (see Piano 2004: 44f.).

How could the rise of pessimism, embodied through religious movements like Buddhism, Jainism and the Hindu ascetics, be explained? In order to answer this question, Olivelle (1992: 33f.), alongside with others, brings up the thesis of Gosh,[32] who states that the move away from a closed community (village) to a more open society (city) increased the need to choose. Hence, 'doubt arises about choosing rightly' (ibid.: 33) which goes alongside with a state of suffering. Bhagat (1976: 83f.) ascribes the rise of the pessimistic worldview to the discontent and unrest of the intelligentsia with the Brahman cult in that time. Divine knowledge (*jnana*) became more important than the performance of rites and ceremonies 'which came to be known as *jnana-marga*' (ibid.). Olivelle consistently points out that this discontent, wherever it comes from, did not come from outside of *Brahman* society but from 'people who chose to remain within that tradition' (1992: 35). Thus, the challenge for old *Vedic* views consisted of a new theology, written down in the *early Upanishads* like the *Brhadaranyaka-* and the *Mundaka Upanishad*. The new set of ideas contained the *karma-theory* as well as the idea of *samsara* and *moksa*. The *Upanishads* therefore developed the thought of the three conditions of consciousness (see Piano 2004: 45–49). The first is being awake, the second is the condition of dreaming and the third is being deeply asleep. Finally, they add as a fourth one the experience of the *self* (*atman*). This doctrine of a possible conscious condition of human beings which will always exist, independent of the physical body, was the base of the invention of a set of new ideas. Moksa, as the final aim, means liberation from the eternal going on of death and new birth (*samsara*). However, the quality of your new life could be influenced by your *karma*, the law of action. In the new worldview, the major activity of the *Veda*, sacrifice, 'came to be considered as obstacle[.] to achieving liberation [which was the] ultimate religious goal of the new world' (Olivelle 1992: 40) and a new equivalent for immortality. Olivelle indicates that this new set of ideas formed an individual-theology (ibid.). Though the new ideas did not fit into the old patterns, the defence of the *Brahman* theology, as for example found in the invention of the theology of debts (see ibid.: 47f.), was not successful. Therefore, a process of assimilation and compromise was successful.

> The most significant structural innovation that facilitated the incorporation of renunciatory ideals and way of life into the Brahmanical world was the change of the mode of the *asrama* system [into an *obligatory* system with the samnyasin as the fourth and last stage of life-order].
>
> Olivelle (1992: 52)

Since the eighth century CE until today, asceticism has undergone many reforms (see Michaels 2004: 131–138). The Guru became spiritual master, and *Bhakti* was invented, as a special kind of devoutness and worship of Gods. In this time, asceticism became monasticism, which had to be administrated. However, *samnyasa*-ascetics as well as Buddhist monks persisted on the idea of the possibility of self-salvation, which can be observed in many variations and differentiations in contemporary India.

The *sadhus'* lives today

As we have seen in the former paragraphs, Indian history provides varying concepts of asceticism throughout the centuries and there are many sources for ascetic thought, above all collected in the *Samnyasa Upanishads*. Nowadays, because of a lack of contemporary field research on Indian asceticism, the study of the ascetics' lives is predominantly theoretical. However, at least two recent field studies offer insight into Indian *sadhus'* contemporary beliefs, knowledge orientations and practices from an in-field-view. Sandra Hausner was wandering with *sadhus* and presents experienced and theoretical knowledge, especially of the *sadhus'* relationship to their bodies in terms of aesthetics and eroticism (see Hausner 2006). Gross (2001), who spent time with *sadhus*, too, edited an ethnographical study about contemporary asceticism in northern India. Gross states that it is difficult to win an overview of today's sects and spiritual orientations, because 'variations in ascetic lifestyle reflect differences in personal approaches to salvation, in the form of sadhana [spiritual praxis], and in religious orientation' (ibid.: 115). Other distinctions are based on varieties of wealth, status and literacy (ibid.).

Nevertheless, Michaels (2004: 162–165), Olivelle (1992: 98–101) and Gross (2001: 112f.) offer overviews of current ascetic sects. According to the scholars, all these sects could be summarized into two currents: those who worship *Shiva* (Saivists) and those who worship *Vishnu* (Vaisnavism) (see Gross 2001: 208; Michaels 2004: 136f.). Those who worship *Vishnu* are called *Ramanandis*. They believe that God, as the highest being, has a personal nature, a form which complies with *Vishnu*. Besides, *atman* (the self) has no identity and a relation with God is only possible through becoming his servant. They believe in the existence of a kind of 'heaven', the only place where salvation is possible. For them, salvation during lifetime is not possible. By contrast, for the *Samkaracharyas* (Gross 2001: 209) the world is non-dualistic. In this, they follow the *Advaita-Vedanta*-doctrine of *Shankara* (eighth century CE). Their religious system is a monistic system. Everything in the world and the world itself are ascribed to one principle, the *brahman* (world soul), which is in unity with *atman* (self). Moreover, they believe that the world is an illusion (*Maya*), thus, every appearance is unreal. Gross (2001: 209) describes this view as follows: 'In your wakening state, you experience the world, but that experience arises from your ignorance. It is a prolonged dream, and therefore unreal.' Salvation could be reached by following the path of knowledge (*jnana*). That means realizing that the eternal *brahman* and the *atman*, the individual self or soul, is one. The *Samkaracharyas* believe that salvation on earth is possible. Michaels (2004: 136f.) points out that they are orthodox monks who defend their *asrama*-system, the prohibition to butcher cows, and the caste-system. Their leaders (gurus) search for closeness to rightwing Hindus. Those two main sect-currents can be distinguished by the signs on their foreheads (*tilaks*). Usually, the *Shivaists* draw their sign horizontal on the forehead (*tripundra*), by contrast the *Vishnuists* draw it upright (*urdhvapundra*) (ibid.).

Although every sect has its own accentuation of philosophy, they share common features, above all rituals. The four most important ones have already been explained in the concept of asceticism, but there are more. Every ascetic follows a *guru* (spiritual leader) who advises his devotee on the convenient kind of *yoga*. Besides, 'Most sadhus undergo *diksa* a formal ritual initiation into renunciant status' (ibid.: 117).[33] Actually, every *sadhu* has to do his daily ritual and spiritual praxis (*sadhana*), which includes *yoga*-exercises, devotional worship and the performance of ritual austerities and *tapases*. Most of the *sadhus* use intoxications like Ganja or Charas (Hashish) and share an itinerant life style. However, at higher age or in monsoon season they usually stay in *asramas* (meditation-monasteries) or remote places like caves. Gross (2001: 417) stresses that only very few go back to their lives as householders, because the majority of *sadhus* 'appear to have become ascetics after a protracted period of acute personal stress or dissatisfaction with worldly life' (ibid.).

Conclusion and outlook

This article is a scientific introduction into the topic of asceticism in ancient and contemporary India. By explaining the cognitive and religious orientations of ascetics, the paradox of the 'immortality of mortality' (Michaels 2001: 15), which forms the *sadhus'* lives becomes clearer. *Sadhus* live in their 'own cultural system [which is a] unified symbolic system' (Gross 2001: 203). For approaching the world view of Indian ascetics, their distinction of profane (social) life (*apavittra*) and their own world which is sacred (*pavitra*) is important (ibid.). In this article, beliefs which constitute this sacred world were described in their historical context of socioeconomic developments. However, many topics of ascetic life and thought could not be discussed in this article, neither the daily rituals and practices of *sadhus* as possible interest of symbolic anthropology (see Gross 2001: 462),[34] nor the more sociological topic of symbolic and economic interaction between *sadhus* and the 'normal' householder-society.[35] The latter topic leads to the more general question of the social function of Hindu ascetics in contemporary Indian society. Does the community of ascetics form a social collecting pond for young men or women who get no work or prefer an adventurous life or search for answers to spiritual questions? Do they conserve traditional values of religious life and thus keep *Brahmanism* alive? There are many questions for further studies. Will asceticism survive in a postmodern, globalized, democratic, capitalist society? Gross, referring to the contribution of asceticism to Indian society, offers an outlook by pointing out that

> asceticism continues to exist as an attractive alternate lifestyle and strategy for personal survival and psycho-social adaptation for many in the subcontinent who are either incapable of dealing with life in any other way or who do not wish to live within the narrow confines of the domestic setting of family, kin, caste, and village.
>
> Gross (2001: 418)

He predicts that *sadhus*, as an anti-structural element of Indian society, will exist as long as the caste-system exists (Gross 2001: 417, 462).

Notes

1 For a closer view on female ascetics, see Khandelwal (2004).
2 Following Michaels (2001: 8–10), during the Romantic age (around the beginning of the nineteenth century) writers, poets, and thinkers like F. Schlegel,

J. Paul, L. Tieck, Novalis, or Hölderlin assembled in Jena (in the middle of Germany, Thüringen) and poetically glorified India.
3 For Bhagat, the adjective 'ancient' covers the time span from the Indus Valley Culture in 2,500 (BCE) to the advent of the Christian era (1976: 8).
4 Bhagat refers to James Hastings (ed.): Encyclopedia of Religion and Ethics II. Edinburgh: 63.
5 Platon, Gorgias 527e, cit. in Brenner and Zirfas (1999: 236).
6 See Schumacher-Chilla (1999: 125f.). The author describes spiritual ecology as a lifestyle which is characterized by distance to daily life of the middle class, accented body styling and eastern religion.
7 For the idea of a lack of the resistance aspect in nowadays ascetic lifestyles see Schumacher-Chilla (1999: 126). Following her analysis, the ideal of proper political action (like it took place, e.g. around 1968) has been substituted by the permanent production of a state which is characterized by the *sensible* individual being and marks a change of culture.
8 The author describes the evolution of each term from the *Rgveda* to the *Yoga-sutras*. For a good overview of the dates of appearance of main Hindu scriptures (in comparison to main European scriptures) see Zimmer (1992: 546–549).
9 Vedanta means 'the end of the Veda' (Olivelle 1992: 3).
10 The technical term for a Hindu's 'order of life' (Olivelle 1992: 52).
11 The *three qualities* of the *guna* are described in more detail in Zimmer (1992: 268).
12 The word stems from the Sanskrit root 'pums' which means 'human being', it also means *atman* (self) (Zimmer 1992: 259).
13 For a detailed description of the Hindu/Sanskrit terms see Zimmer (1992: 261).
14 For further meanings of the Hindu/Sanskrit terms see Zimmer (1992: 266).
15 For a detailed description of the *eight limbs* see Gross (2001: 232–256).
16 Deussen, P. (1897): Sechzig Upanishad's des Veda, aus dem Sanskrit übersetzt und mit Einleitungen und Anmerkungen versehen. Leipzig: Brockhaus, 678–715.
17 Schrader, F.O. (ed.): The Minor Upanisads. Vol. I: Samnyasa Upanisads. Madras 1912.
18 Sprockhoff, J.F. 1989: Versuch einer deutschen Übersetzung der Kathasruti und der Katharudra-Upanisad. Asiatische Studien 43, 137–163.
19 The *Puranas* (Sanskr. for 'old stories') are an important part of written Hinduism. There are more than 400,000 verses and they were written after the *Veda*, but refer to older stories.
20 Like the *Mahabharata* and the *Ramayana*.
21 For a closer look on the initiation rites for ascetics see Freiberger (2009: 47–76).
22 According to Olivelle this is around 600 CE.
23 The *Smrti* 'included many categories of texts without boundaries' (see Olivelle 1992: 15), e.g. ritual texts (some sutras), epics, puranas. 'They were viewed as representing the Vedic tradition'. Central Smrti texts were the *Dharma-Sutras* and their later counterparts, the *Dharma-Sastras* (ibid.).
24 Date of invasion refers to Zimmer's historical overview (1973: 546f.).
25 In Indian mythology Shiva is one of the three main gods, apart from Brahma and Vishnu.
26 Equivalent labelling of this statue is 'horned god' or 'Indus Valley deity' (see Gross 2001: 9).

27 For a close look on the development of the *asrama*-system see also Olivelle (1992: 52–58) and Freiberger (2009: 49–51) as well as footnote 14.
28 The first law codes which were written between 500 BCE and 500 CE.
29 *Version I* means a renouncer, who only needs the ether to live. *Version II* reminds of a householder.
30 The contemporary four stages are *brahmacarin* (student), *grhastha* (householder), *vanaprastha* (forest-dweller) and *samnyasin* (renouncer).
31 See Michaels 1998: 48, the Vedic Period: 1,750–500 BCE.
32 He refers to Ghosh, A. 1973: The City in Early Historical India. Simla.
33 For more information about the initiation rite see Hartsuiker (1993: 4f.) and Freiberger (2009: 47–76).
34 For more information about aspects of daily life of *sadhus* see Bedi 1992: 23–27; Olivelle 1992: 58–107; Gross 2001: 203–295; Freiberger 2009: 76–125 with photography.
35 Gross offers a chapter about this 'nexus', this interaction: 'Religion, Economics, and Reciprocity: The Sadhu-Householder Nexus' (2001: 160–202).

References

Bedi, R. (1992): Sadhus: The Holy Men of India. New Delhi.
Bhagat, M.G. (1976): Ancient Indian Asceticism. New Delhi.
Brenner, A., and Zirfas, J. (1999): Versagende Askese. Zu einer Neuformulierung der Ethik. In: Ch. Wulf (ed.): Paragrana: Internationale Zeitschrift für historische Anthropologie 8 (1): *Askese*. Berlin, 231–268.
Bronkhorst, J. (1993): The Two Sources of Indian Asceticism. Bern.
Deussen, P. (1897): Sechzig Upanishad's des Veda, aus dem Sanskrit übersetzt und mit Einleitungen und Anmerkungen versehen. Leipzig, 678–715.
Freiberger, O. (2009): Der Askesediskurs in der Religionsgeschichte. Eine vergleichende Untersuchung brahmanischer und frühchristlicher Texte. Wiesbaden.
Gross, R.-L. (2001): The Sadhus of India. A Study of Hindu Asceticism. New Delhi.
Hartsuiker, D. (1993): Sadhus: Holy Men of India. London.
Hausner, S. (2006): The Erotic Aesthetics of Ecstatic Ascetics. In: R. Linrothe (ed.): Holy Madness: Portraits of Tantric Siddhas. Chicago: Rubin Museum of Art, 165–173.
Khandelwal, M. (2004): Women in Orche Robes: Gendering Hindu Renunciation. Diss., Albany State University.
Linrothe, R. (ed.) (2006): Holy Madness: Portraits of Tantric Siddhas. Chicago.
Michaels, A. (1998): Der Hinduismus. Geschichte und Gegenwart. München.
Michaels, A. (2001): Heilige oder Freaks? Vom Exotismus in der Wahrnehmung indischer Asketen. In: K. Gernig (ed.): Fremde Körper. Zur Konstruktion des Anderen in europäischen Diskursen. Berlin, 316–355.
Michaels, A. (2004): Die Kunst des einfachen Lebens: Eine Kulturgeschichte der Askese. München.
Olivelle, P. (1992): Samnyasa Upanishads – Hindu Scriptures on Asceticism and Renunciation. New York.

Piano, S. (2004): Religion und Kultur Indiens. Wien.
Schrader, F.O. (ed.) (1912): The Minor Upanisads. Vol. I: Samnyasa Upanisads. Madras.
Schumacher-Chilla, D. (1999): Das Interesse am Selbst. Zwischen Hedonismus und Askese. In: Ch. Wulf (ed.): Paragrana: Internationale Zeitschrift für historische Anthropologie 8 (1): *Askese*. Berlin, 122–137.
Sprockhoff, J.F. (1989): Versuch einer deutschen Übersetzung der Kathasruti und der Katharudra-Upanisad. Asiatische Studien 43, 137–163.
Zimmer, H. (1992): Philosophie und Religion Indiens. Frankfurt, M.

6

CULTIVATING SIMPLICITY AS A WAY OF LIFE

Insights from a study about everyday lives of Tibetan-Buddhist child monks in Ladakh

Tanu Biswas

This article is a brief presentation of some insights which emerged during a research process as part of the MPhil Childhood Studies course with the Norwegian Centre for Child Research. The field of research was a Tibetan-Buddhist monastic community on the Indo-Tibetan border in Ladakh. My exploratory project was to find what it was like to live the everyday life of a child monk through qualitative methodological perspectives and tools.

In the following text, there are underlying assumptions that I wish to make transparent at the very outset. Modern consumerist societies and values are psychologically unhygienic for the individual and the community. Lifestyles based on these values are a deterrent in spiritual pursuits such as developing values of compassion and generosity through voluntary simplicity. By spiritual pursuits I do not mean material religious practice.[1]

The point of departure for this chapter is a brief presentation of Richard Gregg's conviction that simplicity is a factor in creating healthy societies and an advance in civilisation. I proceed by explaining that cultivating simplicity requires social structures and an ambience which nurtures and makes this practice possible for individuals because mundane acts of simplicity[2] do not happen in isolation. The subsequent section presents a clarification of what I mean by 'individuals' which includes children, who according to my research also have preferences for certain lifestyles and may choose a way of life if they receive knowledge of alternatives. This requires social structures which make it possible to provide children with alternatives in terms of the kind of life they want to lead. Within standardised modern societies, children go to school in order to learn to be part of their society and are qualified to choose a way of life only once they graduate or turn 18. Thereafter, I discuss the case of Ladakh as an example of a society with mechanisms, whereby children have the possibility to pursue simplicity as a way of life. In doing this, I endeavour to give the reader an insight into the relational context within which this mechanism functions in the field of study. The last section presents some challenges in sustaining this system, as Ladakh responds to the pressing need of globalising and adapting to modernity and consumerism as a way of life.

My argument is that every culture is based upon metaphysical presuppositions which determine inter-personal relationships including relationships with children and childhood, and with nature. Consequently, I view cultures as an ecosystem which implies that restructuring and inserting new elements (such as modern schooling), which are founded upon different metaphysical presuppositions, cause strain on the roots of the ecosystem.

Simplicity is a necessity for a healthy society

Social philosopher Richard Gregg began discussing the value of voluntary simplicity in the 1930s (1936). He argued that simplicity is a factor in advance in civilisation; along with simplicity, changes in the mode of production and decentralisation of production were essential to secure a permanent advance in culture. He propounded simplicity as essential for non-violence and as aiding the expression of love which is a sentiment accompanied by the realisation of human unity. Although the heart of simplicity is spiritual and found in inner detachment, this inner state must be expressed through outer acts in order to have sincerity, prevent self-deception, strengthen inner attitude and gain further insights for the next step (whatever that may be). In terms of what he calls 'psychological hygiene' simplicity appears to need to be acknowledged as a necessary practice for a healthy society. He justifies his contention that choices need to be narrow based on physiologist Pavlov's experiments on conditioned reflexes with dogs. Pavlov put one of his subjects in a position wherein he had to make several choices with fine discriminations, and this resulted in the dog having a nervous breakdown. The dog had to be sent away to rest for six months in order to be normal again.

Social mechanisms to nurture simplicity

What seems to emerge as the bedrock of simplicity attained through developing inner detachment is the practice of expressing this state through outer acts. These outer acts, no matter how mundane they may be (e.g. drinking a glass of water to quench thirst instead of soda), are not practised in isolation. These acts happen within the context of social structures or a network of inter-related references within which, we as community forming individuals exist. For instance my choice of drinking a soda to quench my thirst is not ahistorical: I have learned through my experiences since childhood to make this choice as I saw the adults around me doing it; it has been done in several social situations and I receive repeated messages through various media in so far as this outer act appears to be the obvious choice I should make when I am thirsty. Apart from a personal history which leads to this habitual outer act, there is a present network of references which supports, facilitates and catalyses such a choice. The can of soda signifies several macro-social interests which are fulfilled when I drink it. To consider just a few—industries such as aluminium, sugar, water, artificial flavouring, advertising, metal recycling, import–export, and so on. Every time an instance arises which calls for me to drink, simply in terms of availability, convenience and norm, the can of soda may appear to be much more accessible to me than a simple sip of fresh water.

This example can be applied to every mundane act that an individual performs. Simplicity in this context becomes a strenuous effort or a matter of privilege. My intention in discussing this aspect of modern existence is to communicate to the reader that simplicity as a lifestyle choice requires social structures and mechanisms which support and catalyse it.

Gregg's contention that simplicity is a necessary practice for a healthy society implies the presence of social structures which ensure that this choice is possible for individuals. By individuals I do not only mean human beings above the age of 18 who legally qualify as adults according to the standardised demarcations[3] of adulthood and childhood.

Individuals as processionary becomings

During my research process with child monks in Ladakh, a key insight which emerged was that, applying a standard paradigm of what childhood or the course of life itself means would prohibit me from accessing world-views essential for my study. Questions such as what is a child and what is childhood are essentially questions about causality. Birth is a precondition for life, which in turn is a precondition for death. This journey is conventionally divided into periods such as childhood, adulthood and old age. The recognition of futurity is based on the recognition of a child's potential to be something predictably different in the future. Thus, we are essentially looking into the realm of causal understanding.

Many conventional adult attitudes towards children are a result of the notion that children are becoming rather than being (Jenks 1996). Thus futurity becomes the defining conceptual, social space of childhood. Children represent the survival of the human species as well as the present generation's investment in the collective future. Childhood as the early stage in the course of human life is understood in reference to future adulthood. Though dependency and futurity are traditional markers of the idea of childhood where adulthood is the final arrival point, in the modern world adulthood cannot be seen as a complete, stable state (Lee 2001). The contemporary era is full of uncertainty about the nature of adulthood and thus childhood cannot be characterised as an incomplete state of dependency making it more complex and ambiguous (ibid.). I mark at this point the causal linearity which metaphysically underpins the dominant, conventional, minority world[4] attitude, i.e. birth leads to growing and ageing which ends in death. Not all philosophical, social and scientific thinking, however, is based on this assumption.

The Buddhist theory of interdependent arising[5] elaborates the process of the cycle of birth. This theory has been given a lot of importance in the Buddhist teachings; the experiential realisation or understanding of this wisdom is equivalent to understanding *dhamma*[6] (Chatterjee and Datta 1968). This implies that there exist a perspective and lived experiences,[7] whereby every individual is a becoming regardless of chronological age.

The hypothesis of rebirth is not the subject of discussion here, nor is its falsification or acceptance indispensable at this stage of enquiry. Essential, however, is an openness to reconsider the paradigm of understanding childhood and what it means to be human in general. I thereby propose a conceptual framework of processionary becomings to understand all beings, including children. The term processionary indicates moving in a procession and in my view lights up an ontological aspect of human existence which has not received any attention in debates within social sciences. It may be compared to the arising and passing away of a flame, which gives us the illusion of one constant flame, but is in fact a rapid processionary succession of moments of causally connected states of flames. It is possible to conceive of our life-course and ourselves as processionary becomings even without the idea of rebirth in so far as we recognise that we are all constantly developing and learning regardless of age. It cannot, however, co-exist with the idea that children are born as a *tabula rasa*. Were one to uphold that the mind of a newborn is an empty slate, it would be logically inconsistent to view all human beings, regardless of chronological age, as ontologically equal in terms of being processionary becomings. This framework further requires that one conceives of the term 'being' itself as a verb and not a noun (Heidegger 1996).

While the above section runs the risk of being read as a derailment, the clarifications presented in it are essential for two reasons. First, to acknowledge how deep rooted the presumption of causal linearity is insofar as it underpins the dominant, conventional, minority world attitude, i.e. birth leads to growing and ageing which ends in death. This logic runs through the veins of modern models of production, relationships and education among other social structures and processes which shape our mundane lives. Second, it is essential to tune our understanding of children because they are no longer to be seen as passive subjects of social structures and processes (James and Prout 1997). The constraints they face are mainly those of members of the socially constructed institution of childhood within a society. In spite of the limitations imposed by adults, children have certain capacities and they may be seen as reflexive social actors or actors within networks of interdependencies (Lee 2001). Another further refined approach is to see them as agents rather than as actors since their actions influence relationships, decisions and social reproduction (Mayall 2002).

Therefore, the choice of simplicity as a way of life does not necessarily need to be a choice made once one becomes a member of the adulthood club. As processionary becomings, it is possible for children to have preferences for certain kinds of lifestyles and choose a way of life if they receive knowledge of alternatives. This presupposes social structures which not only make it possible to provide children with an alternative in terms of the kind of life they want to lead, but also provide support to pursue those choices. Within standardised modern societies, children go to school in order to learn to be part of their society and are qualified to choose a way of life only when they graduate.[8] By the time they graduate of course, the complex can of soda has become a habitual solution to instances that call for a simple drink.

Ladakh: letting children choose voluntary simplicity as a way of life

In my study, I have explored a form of childhood in a society where one may claim to observe two distinct kinds of childhoods, i.e. lay childhood and monk childhood. Contrary to the popular belief that 'children are forced to be monks at a young age and must live terrible lives of austerity', my research in Ladakh revealed that several children voluntarily chose monkhood (the youngest case I discovered was an adult monk who expressed that he began urging his parents since the age of six because he was very attracted to the life and he pretended to be a monk till his parents granted him permission at the age of eight). In a globalising age, as standardised, modern education becomes an important issue for the Ladakhi society, free education and boarding facilities given by monastery schools are also considerations when making the choice. Furthermore, among other reasons there are cases of rebirth, advice from oracles and high monks in the 'best interest' of the child and respecting the wishes of parents why children join the monastery. Some of the children I interviewed told me that they had the desire to help others and therefore became monks; others simply liked the lifestyle or being with other child monks.[9]

Monasteries are indispensable for the culture of Ladakh. At one level they protect and reproduce material aspects of religious expression (texts, rituals, religious objects and so on). However, my engagement reveals to me other possible layers of understanding the function of such an institution within a society. Apart from a narrow identity as religious institutions, I propose viewing them as institutions which give individuals[10] the possibility to express outer acts of simplicity and spiritual pursuit.

I began recognising the monastic institution with its symbiotic relation to the lay society as a strategy or mechanism to foster, practise, and sustain the spiritual qualities of compassion and generosity. Spiritual life in this world-view is a practice committed to meritorious actions which nurture the qualities of the eight-fold path.[11] The bases of meritorious acts – generosity (*dana*), ethical conduct (*sila*) and meditation (*bhavana*) – bind monastic community (*sangha*) and the laity (Spiro 1982). In a broad sense, generosity means embracing actions performed with a generous or giving spirit, but in a specific sense it means giving material support to the monastic community. As the recipients of this support, monks have the responsibility of being a 'field of merit' for the laity. This is achieved by following the eight-fold path of spiritual practice sincerely. In living the life of a monk by practising and teaching *dhamma*, one gives a gift to society and thus reciprocates generosity. Gethin (1998) describes this as a kind of social contract of generosity between society and the monastic community.

While I was in Ladakh, I observed village folk practising generosity by giving time and effort in building the monastery. The Dalai Lama and his delegation were scheduled to visit the village and teach that summer. Therefore, the monastery needed better infrastructure to welcome their principal teacher and all the villages in the block took turns to help achieve this goal. At least one member of the family from each house went to the monastery and did whatever their capacity permitted. During festivals I observed support such as cooking and serving food, tea and refreshments and helping in practical organisation. Folk also distributed money to adult as well as child monks to express their gratitude and generosity. University students discussed Buddhist values and published or helped to publish texts about such discussions. Some of them also studied Buddhism or other aspects of Ladakhi culture so that they could contribute to their society at large. The very act of giving trains the mind to turn away from selfish concerns and loosens attachment (Gethin 1998: 108) or a strong sense of 'mine'. Seen within this light, allowing one's own child to be a monk or 'giving a child' to the monastery may also be an act of generosity towards society.

It would be unreasonable to expect this to be a flawless and effortless process because this is not a congregation of saints. Rather, it is a society of people who value spiritual qualities[12] and aspire to cultivate such qualities through certain traditional mechanisms. There are instances of power struggle, inter-personal conflicts, corruption, and breaches of moral rules, but I found that the overall ambience constructed via their traditional mechanisms is highly conducive to cultivating simplicity as a way of life for all members including children. The participation of adults ensures (among other things) space for children to choose a life of simplicity, on the other hand the participation of children ensures that this process continues.

Ontological challenges of accommodating modernity and becoming global

We have now in front of us a society which has spiritual growth as one of its general purposes. Spiritual growth (at the heart of which is simplicity) within this world-view is perceived as practising morality geared towards being a good human being by developing the attributes of compassion and generosity as taught by the Buddha. To ensure a group of people dedicated to this practice in order to inspire, help and guide others, society has structurally included an institution into its daily functioning. This institution is the monastic community and it has as its members, people who voluntarily choose a lifestyle of simplicity, minimum possession and compassion. However, changes leading to modern life and globalisation[13] observed in Ladakh render monkhood as a lifestyle and simplicity difficult to follow.

> Yes, yes, obviously too much difficult. Now this time many technology, many facilities, many comfortable life . . . everyone wants that. But monk's life, you know, . . . not too much – but use it properly. But 'not too much', this is very difficult. Same question in the future, what will happen we don't know (adult monk, teacher).

The monastic community is actively adapting to accommodate and metamorphose itself to meet the globalising world. One of the ways this is being done is by investing in standardised modern education for its children. At the same time child monks also have increasing access to media and the consumer market. Table 6.1 presents their daily routine, and the pie diagram in Figure 6.1 represents the average amount of time spent on certain categories of activities.

Schooling occupies approximately more than twice the amount of time spent on religious activities. In terms of the children's daily life this is one of the core media of transition; what we see here is the transformation of this unique childhood into a global childhood[14] on a daily basis. Their daily schedule includes television time whereby they are exposed mainly to Indian mass media such as Bollywood films. Little shops around the monastery sell imported[15] consumer products which the children are very attracted to and buy from the money they receive as gratitude for their service to the community. Since the biggest chunk of their day is devoted to modern schooling, most children are bound to move either to the capital city or to other cities outside the region for further schooling.

The challenge for these children as I see it is to find ways to remain a monk and yet to be a modern, global child at the same time. These are very contradictory roles to perform. Modern schooling, commercial films and consumer products are not simply new introductions into their lives. Each of these elements belongs to a network within a very different

Table 6.1 Daily routine of child monks

5:00–5:15	Wake Up	10:30–15:50	School with Lunch Break (12:30–14:30)
5:15–5:30	Morning Exercises	15:50–16:20	Sweet Tea Break
5:30–5:45	Sweet Tea	16:20–17:30	Handwriting and Painting
5:45–6:30	Washing Face and Hands	17:30–18:00	Prayer Reading
6:30–7:30	Learning Prayers	18:00–19:00	Evening Prayers
7:30–8:00	Breakfast	19:00–19:30	Dinner
8:00–8:40	Cleaning One's Room	19:30–20:20	Watch News on Television
8:40–9:40	Morning Prayers	20:20–21:30	Study/Homework
9:40–10:00	Getting Ready for School	21:30–22:30	Watch Television
10:00–10:30	Morning Assembly	22:30	Bedtime

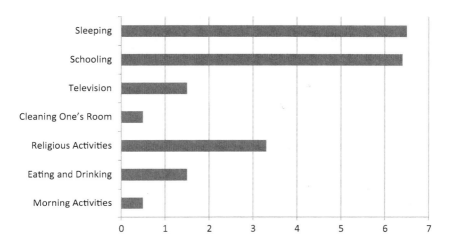

Figure 6.1 Distribution of daily activities

ecosystem with its own underlying metaphysical presuppositions. It is an ecosystem where calculable modern technological and economic growth is the criterion for development and nature is perceived as a storehouse of reserves.

Everything that one needs can be stored in a way so that it induces a view of reserved resources being permanently available on demand (Heidegger 1977). In other words, one begins to experience things as resources which can be stored available on demand whenever the need arises. Consequently, it looks as though it is not we who have to adapt our needs to the process of nature, but it is nature that has to comply with us. Heidegger held that this ordering human attitude has its roots in the rise of modern physics – which is an 'exact science' (ibid.: 303). Consequently, the mainstream modern world-view which I contend is the foundation for globalisation today relates to nature as a calculable force which can be captured, stored and made available to meet our demands. It is based on an understanding of linear causality which is a number-centric or calculable model, whereby only things which can be measured exist or come into being. Obsessive measuring and measurability is a modern scientific practice (ibid.). The paradigm which forms the foundation of a Buddhist world-view is not based on such a quantitative, linear understanding of causality.

Integrating into the modern world therefore, is not a matter of practical structural changes but of the alteration of the ontological relationship one has with his environment as a whole. It implies a shift in the world-view, whereby one is able to see existence itself in numbers, as storable, and understand causality as a linear phenomenon. Non-measurable currencies such as merit-making face a strong challenge in so far as they must succumb to measurable currencies of money-making.

Adapting to modern globalisation is a big hurdle in the monastic pursuit of the eight-fold path. Monks seem concerned about the diminishing population of the *sangha*, because many who find it difficult to remain on the path leave. It becomes increasingly demanding, but at the same time they acknowledge the importance of keeping up with the modern world.

> Dalai Lama said actually we monks are 21st century monks. Ancient monks only study Buddhist philosophy. Nowadays we must learn both Buddhist philosophy and modern education. A monk's life is a precious life, he said. So I got a chance to learn Buddhist philosophy, but I didn't learn modern education . . . no time. Now I try modern education. I haven't finished my Buddhist philosophy. I try to . . . if I get time I will learn some modern education. I think if we don't have modern education, so many people say that monks have no knowledge, that I think is not good (adult monk).

On a daily average, child monks devote more time to learning modernity than to religious and traditional training. One of the principle changes in terms of making the shift to modernity in my observation is that modern monks have to be much more preoccupied with material concerns. As their social ecosystem changes, laity is under pressure to fend for itself and cannot offer generosity as it did before. Getting a job or earning a livelihood on the economic market which in principle is not part of monastic life is making its way into the monastic thoughtscape. Given that right livelihood is one of the directives of the eight-fold path, monks have limited professions they can take up.[16]

> Yes, my situation is different. They [lay youth] have other degrees. I have Buddhist qualifications, if I want a government job they won't recognise my education. So I don't have the same chance. I can work for *gonpas* [monasteries] or get like a *khampo* [monastic degree) position (adult monk, student).

On the other hand, I also found a general optimism among the monks with respect to this demanding transition.

> [. . .] science and Buddhism are alike. Dalai Lama said, Buddhist education and science are like same [. . .] scientists observe all phenomena and Buddhist philosophers are also observers [. . .] Of course there is also a difference, a lot maybe. Buddhist philosophy goes towards peace, modern education goes towards competition. But we are modern human beings, we must know about it (adult monk, student).

Another young monk (student) who appeared to be very committed to his path commented on the challenges of modernity:

> In terms of development, Dalai Lama distinguishes between two kinds, material and spiritual. The 21st century is no doubt materially developed and unbelievable development. I think at the same time such a situation is born, like at one moment everything is ruined – the atom bomb. Material development is good but also very harmful, along with material development if we all can study our faiths and practise it in our daily lives, then this destructive situation of the material development . . . this problem can be resolved.

The twenty-first century *sangha* finds the macro-social structures which sustained it slipping away with modernity. The social ecosystem is altering and this brings new questions about the meaning and role of being a monk. Furthermore, this puts several strategies of pre-serving and practising Buddha's teachings into profound doubt. While the community is concerned and aware of the heavy demands the globalising era has put on them, some remain optimistic about finding new emerging roles in the process.

Conclusion

Be it a can of soda which provides additional alternatives to thirst or the introduction of standardised modern education – these are elements which belong to a social ecosystem, the metaphysical roots of which presume linear causality. Within this paradigm, life begins with birth, ends with death and nature is a storehouse of reserves always available on demand to be consumed. It is through devoting a considerable amount of time to teaching modernity that an ambience can be created wherein a can of soda will appear much more accessible than a simple sip of fresh water.

Converting to modernity does not only imply changing what one does and how, rather it involves changes in one's relationship with existence as a whole. Every culture is founded upon metaphysical presuppositions which determine the way its people relate to each other, including children and childhood, and the environment that they are part of. Consequently, I view cultures as an ecosystem. Restructuring and inserting new elements (modern schooling, consumer economy and so on) which are founded upon different metaphysical presuppositions cause a considerable strain on the roots of the ecosystem.

Simplicity as a lifestyle choice requires social structures and mechanisms which support and catalyse it. If we are to accept Gregg's contention that simplicity is a necessary practice for a healthy society, then this implies the presence of social structures and mechanisms which ensure that this choice is possible for individuals. By individuals I mean all human beings (including children) whom I propose to view as processionary becomings; in other words in a constant process of development throughout the course of life. Through this paradigm it becomes possible to conceive of children as capable of choosing or having preferences for certain kinds of lifestyles.

In the Ladakhi society, children have the choice of a simple life presented to them and supported by their traditional social structures. In modern, industrialised societies such as ours, children do not have this possibility, nor do they receive knowledge of alternatives. The general pattern is that children go to school and qualify to choose a way of life once they become official members of adulthood. The absence of the possibility to choose simplicity in childhood in modernised communities might be one of the areas to look at to find solutions for creating healthier societies. The overall ambience constructed via the traditional mechanisms and structures in Ladakh appears highly conducive to cultivating simplicity as a way of life for the community. The participation of adults ensures space for children to choose a life of simplicity, and on the other hand the participation of children ensures that this process is sustainable.

However, as of today, the process of converting to modernity has begun in Ladakh. To find ways to remain a monk and yet to be a global child at the same time is the biggest challenge for these children as I see it, because these appear to be very contradictory roles. Modern schooling, commercial films and consumer products are not simply new introductions into their lives. Each of these elements belongs to networks within a very different ecosystem with its own underlying metaphysical presuppositions, i.e. an ecosystem where calculable modern technological and economic growth is the criterion for development and nature is perceived as a storehouse of reserves.

For Ladakh and its monastic culture with spiritual ideals the dilemma is to reinvent the practice of simplicity faced with complex choices such as varieties of cans of soda versus a sip of fresh water. For us in the global, modernised world a new dilemma lurks waiting for attention: if our children wanted to walk the path of voluntary simplicity,[17] which social institution would we turn to for support?

Notes

1 Although such practices may benefit individual and social spiritual pursuits.
2 Fundamental in cultivating the quality of simplicity.
3 Confer United Nations Convention on the Rights of the Child.
4 By minority world, I refer to what is commonly called the West, the global north, the developed world or the First World, because geographically and in terms of population it represents a minority.
5 Ignorance is the cause for mental formations to arise. Mental formations give rise to consciousness which is the condition for mind and matter. Mind and matter give rise to sense doors which are a condition for contact. Feelings arise as a consequence of contact. Feelings give rise to craving or aversion due to which clinging arises. Clinging gives rise to becoming which gives rise to birth. Birth is the condition for ageing and dying. If ignorance is not eliminated at an experiential level, the cycle keeps on repeating itself (Chatterjee and Datta 1968; Sharma 1960).
6 The metaphysical principle of nature which is deeply interwoven with ethical conduct. In theory, Buddhism has no God, but the principle of *dhamma*.
7 In societies such as Ladakh which are founded upon such metaphysical grounds.
8 Or reach a legal age in so far as they qualify to be a member of adulthood.
9 Each individual may leave the monastery if he decides to do so.
10 This of course includes children.
11 The noble eight-fold path consists of cultivating and maintaining the right view, right intention, right speech, right action, right livelihood, right effort, right mindfulness and right concentration (Sharma 1960; Chatterjee and Datta 1968).
12 For example, compassion, generosity, non-attachment, non-violence and so on.
13 Term used as defined by the *Oxford English Dictionary*, i.e. the process by which businesses or other organisations develop international influence or start operating on an international scale.
14 Adhering to a standardised idea of a universal childhood. This concept can be expanded to accommodate several characteristics, however, some characteristics are considered indispensable for this identity: first and foremost, the child is defined by chronological age, i.e. he/she is below 18 years. Second, he/she goes through the process of systematic schooling and is not encouraged to work. Third, the global child is a consumer of at least one multinational product. And last, the child learns English.
15 From other Indian states. Products are usually owned by non-Indian companies or multinational corporations.
16 Politics and business, e.g., are not advised.
17 Not necessarily as a religious practice.

References

Chatterjee, Satischandra, and Datta, Dhirendramohan (1968): *An Introduction to Indian Philosophy*. Calcutta: Calcutta University Press.

Gethin, Rupert (1998): *The Foundations of Buddhism*. Oxford: Oxford University Press.

Gregg, Richard B. (1936): *The Value of Voluntary Simplicity*. Wallingford, PA: Pendle Hill Publications.

Heidegger, Martin (1977): *Basic Writings* (David Farrell, ed.). New York: Harper & Row.

Heidegger, Martin (1996): *Being and Time* (trans. Joan Stambaugh). Albany: State University of New York Press.

James, Allison, and Prout, Alan (1997): *Constructing and Reconstructing Childhood: Contemporary Issues in the Sociological Study of Childhood*. London: Falmer Press.

Jenks, Chris (1996): The Postmodern Child. In: J. Brannen, and M. O'Brien (eds): *Children in Families*. London: Falmer, 13–25.

Lee, Nick (2001): *Childhood and Society: Growing Up in an Age of Uncertainty*. Buckingham: Open University Press.

Mayall, Berry (2002): *Towards a Sociology of Childhood: Thinking from Children's Lives*. Buckingham: Open University Press.

Sharma, Chandradhar (1960): *A Critical Survey of Indian Philosophy*. London: Rider & Company.

Spiro, Melford E. (1982): *Buddhism and Society: A Great Tradition and Its Burmese Vicissitudes*. Berkeley: University of California Press.

7

THE LEGENDS OF ST. THOMAS AND THE EXTENSIONS OF THE MAGIC/MIRACLE DICHOTOMY IN THE STORIES ABOUT KADAMATTATH KATTANAR[1]

Susan Visvanathan

This chapter is concerned with the aspects of magic in Syrian Christian Society as a narrative around the everyday pursuits of the recognition of the unfamiliar. I use data from various sources to understand why the theme of magic appears in the life of the St. Thomas Christians of Kerala. They are divided into many segments but their customs are often marked by the dramatic. The stories around Kadamattath Kattanar are well known to all and often reproduced in film, play, graphic novels, newspapers, cartoons and TV serial shows. The paper was begun as a prefatory paper for field work in 1980 and has been expanded for various reasons. I preface the paper with a letter from the eminent historian and linguist, Prof. Istvan Perczel, written to me in the course of our correspondence on the story of Kadamattath Kattanar, a legend I had first encountered as a child visiting relatives in Kerala, and later as part of my field work.

Istvan Perczel, Professor of History and Ancient Languages at Budapest, wrote to me on 17 July 2008:

> Dear Susan,
> Thank you for this! Here is the translation of the Syriac text:
> 'The holy bones of Priest Manisha (?) of Kadamattam, which were found here on the first of the month Adar (March), in the year 1990 of Our Lord, were placed here.'
> Do I understand the Malayalam correctly when I read something like this?

'In 1990, on the 1st of the month of March, there were found the holy remnants of a Father'?

Now I have several questions:

Do I misunderstand the Malayalam, when I read kandedukkappetta as 'were found'? Then, the name would be missing from the Malayalam, simply speaking about 'a Father'.

In the Syriac I read the name of the buried person as Priest Manisha of Kadamattam, but the Kadamatthath Kattanar's name was Paulos.

Do I understand well that in 1990 people found the bones of an unidentified person at the location where this commemorative inscription is placed and that now they think these are the remnants of the Kadamatthath Kattanar?

Now the question is where these bones were found. Was it in the southern wall of the church? Because if it is so, then, we may safely identify the bones with those of Mar Denkha, which, according to the Malayalam Church history, the Kadamatthath Kattanar placed in the southern wall. Mar Aprem would be very happy to learn about this, because the burial places of the Nestorian bishops are usually unidentified (Mar Gabriel, who died in 1732, if I am not wrong, is buried in the Cheriyappally in Kottayam, but – as the church belongs to the Orthodox – he is not commemorated at all).

This is really exciting! I am awaiting your answers.[2]

One of the significant aspects of the changes sought by the synod of Diamper was the repudiation of the belief in astral signs and witch craft. However in the 1980s, when my data was collected for the purposes of writing my doctoral thesis, the Christians believed in the stories told to them about one Kadamattath Kattanar. His exploits were still recounted in the form of stories, cartoon scripts, plays, and then, in the twenty-first century, as a TV-film.

We must remember that Thomas the Apostle himself was associated with rites which veered between magic and miracle. It is said that the first disciple of Thomas the Apostle in Kerala was a young Brahmin boy from the village of Niranam. He was returning home in the early morning having worshipped at the temple, when he met the Apostle Thomas who asked him if the gods ever heard his prayers. The boy replied that they were carved from stone but he worshipped them because his father did so, and his grandfather before him. 'It is the custom of the country. And if I did not go every morning my mother would give me no food.'

Thomas instructed him in the ways of the Christian faith and the boy returned to him often. When he was baptised by Thomas, his father drove him out of his house. The boy was ordained as priest and named Thomas after the Apostle.

According to legend, the majority of the conversions made by the Apostle were of Brahmins. Were there Brahmins in Kerala during the first century AD? K. P. Padmanabha Menon says that this is a disputed question, but he is inclined to believe that Brahmin colonization took place very early, perhaps earlier than the first century (Menon 1924: 24). The Raja of Kodungaloor gave Thomas permission to preach the gospel and gave him gifts of money. The Apostle is said to have built seven churches – at Kodungaloor, Quilon, Chayal, Niranam, Kokamanglam, Parur and Palayur. The Raja also became a Christian. The legends say that the Brahmins were infuriated at seeing their Raja becoming a Christian. But Thomas performed many miracles and the conversions continued. Here is a version of a legend recorded by Zaleski. This version is still a very popular narrative in terms of its form, since an MPhil student, Ashok Kumar, produced a verbatim account in a classroom discussion in my course on Historical Method in Sociology in JNU in 2006, saying that his grandmother had told him this story (in Malayalam of course, when he was a young boy). Zaleski writes:

> Then in July, on the day of the full moon, he went to the Brahmin quarter. He was passing by a pond which was sacred and many Brahmins were bathing. They took water in their hands and threw it into the air. Thomas asked them why they did so and the Brahmin replied 'We are offering it to the Gods.'
>
> Thomas said 'Do not the Gods reject your offering? See the waters fall back into the pond?'
>
> The Brahmins said 'Such is the nature of the water, it was made so, that it falls always down.'
>
> The Apostle then took some water into his hand, and threw it into the air. And the drops remained suspended shining like so many gems, then fell at Thomas' feet in a shower of beautiful flowers whose fragrance filled the whole place. Many of the Brahmins then followed the Apostle who instructed and baptised them.
>
> Zaleski (1912: 132)

This happened according to tradition at Palayur. Those Brahmins who remained attached to their traditional faith left the place, cursing it and swearing that they would never return or eat or drink from that place – it was cursed. Fr. Hambye S.J. writes that a Brahmin family called Kalathu Mana keeps a document, Nagargarandhavaryola, where it is written, in

'Kali Year 3153 (52 CE) the foreigner Thomas Sanyasi came to our village (*gramam*) and preached there, causing pollution. We therefore came away from that village' (Perumalil and Hambye 1972: 370f.).

Another legend describes a procession in Parur – a multitude following an elephant with an idol carried ceremoniously on its back, and accompanied by drummers and musicians. Several in the procession recognized Thomas as 'the magician who corrupted the people of Palayur' and they crowded around him threateningly. But then the sky darkened, according to the legends, thunder came from the clouds and the people were frightened.

When the time came for St. Thomas to leave for Mylapore, where the legends say he died, the people went and could not reconcile themselves to the fact that their Muttapen (old father) was leaving them. His departure is described by these legends in very ceremonial terms. The people followed him as he rode in a cart driven by two white bullocks. They were disconsolate because the Apostle had foretold his martyrdom and they knew he would never return to them again (Zaleski 1912: 139f.). He would 'return', however, in memory and ritual, in the miracle healings and the liturgies, and sometimes people would even 'see' him (see Visvanathan 1993: 72).

One of the central problems the story of Thomas raises is that of the stranger. Nowhere does Thomas the renouncer really stay, nowhere does he belong. The commands he obeys are never temporal, but always purely of the Spirit – 'and he who does not take his cross and follow me is not worthy of me' (Matthew 10:38). The Gospel of Luke records 'And he said to them, Take nothing for your journey, no staff, nor bag, nor bread, nor money and do not have two tunics. And whatever house you enter, stay there and from there depart' (Luke 9:3).

The stranger, as Simmel argued, is the potential wanderer who is tied down for a time with a particular group in a specifically bounded space. The stranger – and the *sanyasi* is precisely that – is essentially quasi-social for he can never overcome the demand to move on, he will never be settling. This threshold identity gives him a certain freedom of action, speech and thought. It is his difference from the group that makes him powerful, that creates tension, which allows him to leave for his wandering.

Some of the legends express the ambiguity of Thomas's identity. Hostility, curiosity, respect, awe and love are some of the emotions recorded in the legends. Perhaps these can be understood in terms of the relationship and the distinction between magic and religion, sorcerer and priest.

The appellation 'sorcerer' sounds hostile when looked at from the perspective of a stable association of believers centring around a transcendent God. Was Thomas seen as a magician?

The legends emphasize the use made of discourse and instruction, of teaching the ethic of peace, gentleness and humility, which embodied the Christ's life. Thomas was directly in the tradition of the Christ, and as with Jesus, miracles were part of the spiritual mission rather than proof of it. According to the legends, the people loved Thomas, they crowded to hear him and followed him wherever he went, for he worked great miracles (Zaleski 1912: 130).

But the legends of Malabar also describe certain acts of Thomas which do not seem merciful or beneficent or expressive of Christian humility.

When a Brahmin gave him a cruel blow, St. Thomas predicted 'Thou will soon lose the hand that has struck me.' A few days later a mad dog (in some versions a tiger) bit off the hand of the Brahmin. When the latter repented the hand healed, showing not even a scar. Not surprisingly, in A.J. Klijn's edition of the legends, the Raja of Mylapore locks up his wife in order to keep her safe from the magical rituals of St. Thomas, who bewitches with oil, wine and water (Klijn 1962: 146).

The legends represent the fact that Thomas's acts are considered by some to be the authentic works of the God of Thomas. Therefore the multitudes who follow him believe in his teachings and treat him as a priest. To describe him as magician or priest thus seems to be offered in the legends as value judgements.

Furthermore, Thomas as the renouncer threatens the conceptual order of Hinduism, and it is not surprising that the legends continually emphasize the roles of Kings and Brahmins. Both J.P.S. Uberoi and Veena Das (1977) have shown this to be central to the issue of Hinduism in its relationship to the formation of sects. Susan Bayly in her classic work attempts to understand the relationship between Hindu Kings and Christian subjects (Bayly 1989).

Even if we accept the oral traditions and the legends of Thomas's visit to Kerala as a curiosity, there is evidence of Christian presence here as early as 345 CE. This refers to the coming of immigrant Christians of Middle Eastern origins. According to the tradition, they were led by one Thomas of Cana who brought with him 70 families from Jerusalem, Baghdad and Nineveh. These immigrant Syrians according to the Kerala legends did not inter-marry with the indigenous St. Thomas Christians, but merely supported them in their religious life. The King gave, it is said, to Thomas of Cana an area of jungle land and built there for him church and houses; also 'seven kinds of musical instruments and all the honours, and to travel in a palanquin and that at weddings the women should whistle with the finger in the mouth as do the women of kings, and he conferred the privilege of spreading carpets on the ground and to use sandals and to erect a pandal and to ride on elephants' (Brown 1982: 74). Many of these were seen to be high-caste privileges. This link with the immigrant Christians was reinforced by the arrival of Syrian prelates through the centuries and had a variety of ecclesiastical consequences. The Indian Church of St. Thomas was drawn by this association into a number of controversies not of its own making which were to affect its existence and identity. Every schism affecting the Persian Church was to have its effect upon the Syrian Christian Church in Kerala. As the Church of Persia also claimed to have been founded by Thomas the Apostle, this led to an allegiance between the Indian and Persian churches. By the ninth century, India was under the control of the See of Seleucia Ctesiphon, and the most important prelates who visited Kerala (Quilon) were Mar Sapor and Mar Prodh. Tradition states that the Christians of Kerala were reinforced once again by immigrants from Persia at this time (Podipara 1970). Copper plates record the privileges given by the King (Ayyan of Venat) to the Christians (Brown 1982: 74).

There were other travellers too who came to Kerala in search of ancient Christians and spices. Marco Polo, who came probably in 1293 to Quilon, was one of them, and he found both Christians and Jews. John of Monte Corvino had been another such traveller. Then there was Jordanus, who in 1328 was consecrated by the Pope as Bishop of Quilon and sent to the Nascarene. (The St. Thomas Christians were called Nazranis, followers of Jesus of Nazareth.) In 1328, Odoric of Undine came to Quilon and Mylapore. John de Marignolli came in 1348. Leslie Brown cites him:

> On Palm Sunday 1348 we arrived at a very noble city of India called Quilon where the whole world's pepper is produced. Now this pepper is grown on a kind of vines which are planted just as in our vineyards [. . .] nor does it grow in forests but in regular gardens, nor are the Saracens the proprietors but the St. Thomas Christians. And these latter are the masters of the public weighing office [. . .].
>
> Brown (1982: 83)

Kathleen Morrison, in her paper 'Environmental History, the Spice Trade, and the State in South India', published in *Ecological Nationalisms*, suggests that prior to the cultivation of pepper in gardens it has been wild pepper that was collected by foresters and brought to the sea side towns for purchase and trade (Morrison 2005: 46–48).

The 'discovery' of a sea route to India with the coming of Vasco da Gama (cp. Subrahmanyam 1997) to Kerala marks the beginning of the Portuguese period in Syrian Christian history (Panikkar 1959: 30; Visvanathan

1993: 14). From this moment on, the identity of the St. Thomas Christians would undergo a change. In the meeting of Orthodox Christianity with imperialism, commerce and the Latin rites of Portuguese Christianity, its autonomy would be continually threatened (Menachery 1973). There would be allegations of heresy against it, attempts to ritual unification, then bifurcation and schism. It would encounter the Protestant interpretations of Christianity through the British colonists, and more splits would occur. One of the greatest ironies would be the questioning of the authenticity of the legend of St. Thomas in Kerala (Visvanathan 1993).

As long as the Christians in Kerala remained in their local enclaves, participating in a plural culture, which was both ranked and separate, visited by peripatetic Middle Eastern bishops, they remained autonomous. Certainly they were part of the fabulous imagery of what it was to be Oriental. They were sought out because they were 'Other'. This notion of 'otherness' allowed them their unique ceremonies, liturgical language and cultural self-definition. It was an autonomy that came from maintaining separation, difference, reciprocity and dialogue. But when they as Orthodox Christians were assimilated into the ritual colonization of both Catholicism and Protestantism, they began to lose confidence. The last 400 years have been a period of staying alive as a unique cultural expression of India's idea of pluralism and difference. We must not lose it to the new metaphors of homogeneity *or* alienation.

Legends tell us to listen. In the listening we discover voices, words, tones, nuances, cadences, timers, patterns and reasons. When we listen to the 'Other' in the dialogical sense that Martin Buber offered we hear stories that are strange, but not alien. Because every listener is capable of both empathy and diagnosis, is both subjective and distanced. Every legend thus calls out. This is why Roland Barthes says that hearing is physiological, but listening is psychological – and of course social, because it involves the deciphering of signs and symbols (Barthes 1985: 245). Interestingly, Barthes says that 'listening is intimacy, the heart's secret. Sin.' This curious linkage is made by his intuitive understanding of the religious attitude. He argues, 'A history and a phenomenology of interiority (which we perhaps lack) should here form a history and a phenomenology of listening for at the very heart of a civilisation of sin interiority has developed steadily' (Barthes 1985: 250).

Can we really understand what Barthes calls transgression as engendered by God's gaze? A sociology of religion must attempt both of these: understanding the voice of the 'other' *and* diagnosing the sources of religious anger. This means looking at the fusion of language, space and time in a new way. The work of Istvan Perczel has been extremely important to the writing of history in Kerala, since Perczel, out of love for the subject, set about digitalizing the archives of the St. Thomas Christians on the hunch that not all the records of the Christians might have been burnt by the Portuguese, who had accused the St. Thomas Christians of being heretics. Perczel communicated this intuition to the monasteries by offering to help them in archiving their ancient documents, and he was allowed access to even those materials which had been hidden away for 400 years.

Independently of this project, one of the most interesting documents that have appeared in print are the notes of one traveller, Dutch in origin, who kept a chronicle of the early 1600s while travelling in Malabar and Ceylon. His work is published as *Description of the Great and Most Famous Isle of Ceylon* (Baldaeus 1996). The work that I quote here at length is extremely interesting with regard to the question of the interpolation of narratives and the manner of dissemination of sacred histories, whether canonical or legendary. Baldaeus writes:

> The Malabars write upon the leaves of the wild palm trees with iron pencils; their letters are very ancient, and distinguished into short or running letters long ones, vowels, consonants, diphthongs, letters used only in the beginning of a work, such as are used only in the middles, and such as are used only in the end, as will more clearly appear out of the annexed cuts. And feeling that the Malabar letters have hither to not appeared in public print, wither in Holland or Germany, it will not be amiss to allege the reasons thereof, and to show that this language is no less worth our care nowadays than the Hebrews, Chaldean, Arabian, Persian, Samaritan and other languages.

The main reason why the Malabar language has remained so long unknown to us, is because that country was not conquered by the Dutch country till in the years 1661, 1662, 1663, from the Portuguese; and it is not their custom to send any ministers into those places, where they are not sovereign masters (Baldaeus 1996: 663).

Baldaeus (ibid.) then writes that he got a good interpreter who was skilled in both Malabar and Portuguese languages, and served him well for eight years. The reason for Baldaeus's interest in learning Malayalam was for purposes of establishing commercial interests through religious intervention.

He not only found the Malabar language difficult to learn because of the vast number of letters, but the language expressed that 'the Indians are not so unpolished as some Europeans represent them, and that they treat one another (especially persons of quality) with singular civility and respect' (ibid.: 665).

Baldaeus describes the ability of the Portuguese to contribute to language shifts and debates in mission history.

> Thus 1622, a Syriac Dictionary was published at Rome, by John Baptist Ferarius, a Native of Siena; and the Syriac grammar of Georgius Ameira, a famous divine and philosopher of the college of the Maronites, born near the Mount Labanus. And 1628, Abrahamus Ecchelensis obliged the World with his Introduction to the Fundamentals to the Christian Faith, in the same Language. Whence it is evident that the Roman clergy exceed ours, in their zeal of propagating the Roman Religion; though on the other hand it must be allowed that their Plenty furnishes them with sufficient opportunities of performing those things which the Reformed ministers for want of means are forced to let alone. I have seen diverse Books printed with the Portuguese characters, in the Malabar language, for the instruction of the Paruas, one whereof I keep by me to this day; though at the same time I must confess that in case we should follow the same method, in printing with our characters, though in their Language, it would not have the same effect, they being much more bigoted both to the Roman Clergy and the Portuguese Language, for that I have met with some of the Paruas who spoke as good Portuguese as they do at Lisbon. For the rest, the Products of Cranganor are the same as in the other parts of Malabar, except that now and then they meet with some Gold Dust, but in no great quantity. (ibid.: 631)

The Synod of Udeyemperoor or Diamper took place in 1599 and is popularly associated with the destruction of the Nestorian heresies and archives of the Christians by the Portuguese. But just as Istvan Perczel wishes to argue, the records of the pre-Diamper obliterations did exist, for Baldaeus had seen them.

> The Christians of St. Thomas teach their children in their very infancy these following heads concerning St. Thomas. St. Thomas was the Man who first abolished idolatry; it was he that baptiz'd them, and taught them the true Faith, and to profess God the Father, the Son and Holy Ghost. They also tell you, that he converted the three kings of the East (one of whom, call'd Perumal,

they say was King of Ceylon) and that St. Thomas' body was transferred from Maliapour to Edessa in Mesopotamia. (ibid.: 638)

Baldaeus also writes:

> But setting aside all these uncertain relations, the most secure way (founded upon no small probabilities) is that St. Thomas was actually in these parts and converted a great number of people to the Christian faith which contradicts that bold assertion of the Roman Catholicks, that all nations have received the Christian Faith from Rome it being beyond all question, that at the time of the arrival of the Portuguese in those parts under de Gama, the Inhabitants declar'd themselves to be Christians from most ancient times, desiring the Protection of the King of Portugal against the Pagans, and in token of their Obedience presented him with a Silver Scepter gilt. Nay, the Church of Rome can't boast of that Honour, even of all parts of Europe itself, since the Kings of England and Scotland, Lucius and Donaldus embraced the Christian Faith 124 years after our Saviour's Nativity, without having the least communication with the church of Rome. [. . .]
>
> The Christians of St. Thomas remained many years in the Primitive Purity of the Christian Religion, till in time, for want of good Pastors, they began to be infected with some Pagan Superstitions, and were in most imminent danger of losing the Remnants of the Truths of the Gospel, had not Martome a native of Syria, taken care of the decayed fate of Christianity in these parts, and being seconded in his endeavours by diverse other Teachers out of Syria, Babylonia, Chaldaea and Egypt, the Syriac Language was introduced, and the former purity of religion restored among them, till in time the Nestorian heresy got footing in Syria, and was from thence transplanted hither, as is sufficiently evident from the Records of the Malabars. (ibid.)
>
> This Martome (signifying in their Language as much as Lord Thomas) being respected by the Kings of Cranganor (Kodungaloor) and Coulang (Kollam) and by the Christians of St. Thomas in general, was declared by them their Head: and the bishops of Cochin, Coulang and Cranganor, being afterwards sent for out of Syria, there introduced the Syriac language, and acknowledged the Patriarch of Alexandria or Babylon for their Metropolitan, till at last they submitted to the Pope of Rome. For the Supreme Ecclesiastical Head of the Indians (at the persuasion of the Portuguese)

did in 1562 acknowledge the Supremacy of the Pope of Rome, provided they might continue in the former free exercise of their religion, which was confirmed in the Synod of Goa, where they would not content to the least alteration of any of their Church Ceremonies. But after the Decease of this Bishop, his successor 1599, embraced with the rest of his clergy in another synod the Roman Faith. (ibid.)

Baldaeus was writing in 1622, published in Dutch in 1672 and in English in 1703. His work is available in reproduction of antique book form in a 1996 Indian edition.

The refusal of the Christians of Kerala to lose all their customs to Rome is the obvious reason for the Koonen Kurisu episode of 1653, and the shifting away from the pomp and ceremony of Rome. As social anthropologists and historians know, there is also much which is not talked about. Traces, as Marc Bloch (1954) would write, is all we have to follow the clues of the past and of tradition. The following lines are from my field work log, penned in August 1982.

12.8.1982

Although most families when asked of their heritage will hark back to 52 A.D., to Thomas the Apostle, and to the Brahmins, evidently assimilation across caste lines did occur, and there are instances when lower castes were absorbed within the higher status Christians. But in such cases, their past was remembered, and alliances with better placed families were not possible, unless they suddenly came into a lot of wealth or when one of them acquired education of a very superior kind.

One of the most eligible of families known for their unusual prosperity were some generations ago extremely poor. In fact, one of the residents of the Angadi while speaking of their own difficult times said that some generations ago, they would give what excess vegetables they had to this particular family, who would give in return a coconut or some other item from their own yard. Their wealth today is attributed to the marriage of one of their people with a family that was blessed by Parimalla Tirumeni. As the Tirumeni was travelling one night by boat, he asked the boatmen to row the boat to shore as he wished to visit the family that lived there. It was mid-night and the boatman said hesitantly, 'Tirumeni, let us return in the morning, they must be sleeping now.' But Parimalla Tirumeni was insistent and when they went to the house and waited outside they heard the family at prayer – at the *padrathri namaskaram*. The Tirumeni blessed the startled family and said that they would be prosperous in the coming generations. A daughter of this family was married into the Puthengadi family, because the man she was married to had a B.A. degree – a rare achievement in those times. Since her marriage into the Angadi family they shot from obscurity to positions of great economic power.

The mysticism of Parimalla Tirumeni and the Shakti that even now is associated with his personality is attributed to the love God had for him and for the fasting and abstinence that characterized the Tirumeni's life. He sacrificed all pleasures of the flesh, and indeed was given to creating periods of Lent of his own, which he followed assiduously living on pepper water for long periods at a time. The miracles attributed to him are many, and easily and often remembered. He is a living saint, and every house carries a framed picture of the ascetic gentle face, with its long beard and the Semitic nose, and in his hand the Tirumeni carries a hand-cross and in the other a shepherd's crook.

Kadamattath Kattanar on the other hand is a much more ambiguous figure, when compared to St. Thomas the Apostle, or Parimalla Tirumeni. He is believed to have lived in the fifteenth century, when Malabar was still visited by itinerant bishops from the Middle East. Hidden manuscripts are the subtext of survival of customs thought to be unacceptable to those in power, and in the following materials we will find this appearing.

Kadamattath Kattanar is remembered by old women who tell small children about him, rather as entertainment stories. He is the trickster figure, one who actually fooled the devil, and the stories about him are amusing, a little foolish, but often remembered. He fooled Kayamkollam Kochoonoony for instance, one of the most famous robbers of his time, a type of Robin Hood figure. As he was sailing on the river one day, he saw a boat approaching, and made for it intending to rob its passengers. In that boat sat Kadamattath Kattanar. His boatman, seeing Kayamkollam Kochoonoony approaching, told the Kattanar that he recognized the thief, and they should try to get away. But the priest insisted that they do not change course, and instead went forward to meet the robber. As their boats came close to each other, Kadamattath Kattanar hypnotized Kayamkollam Kochoonoony and said, 'I have no clothes, no money, no food!' and before the robber knew what was happening he found that instead of robbing the passenger of the other boat he had willingly given to him everything that he had in his possession, that he had been swept clean of all that was in his boat except the clothes he stood in.

Another story tells how the Kattanar while on his travels met a Namboothiri who had heard of his magic powers. So he tied up the boat in which the priest was to travel in the higher branches of a tree, and when the priest requested that he bring it down, the Namboothiri refused saying that he wished the priest to exhibit his prowess. After some gentle persuasion, the priest discovered that the Namboothiri had no intention of listening, so when next the Brahmin looked toward the tree, he found that the Brahmin ladies of his house had come out of seclusion and were climbing up the tree. He was utterly ashamed and begged that the Kattanar should not cause him and his family this loss of face and dignity, and that the ladies should be sent back to the privacy of their house. The Kattanar did so, and the boat was restored to him, and the ladies returned to the inner rooms of their house.

A third incident describes how a Tirumeni visited the Kattanar in the wilds of the North of Malabar far away from the comforts of urban civilization and suddenly said, 'How nice it would be if we could get some grapes.' At this, the Kadamattath Kattanar produced a bunch of grapes, most perfect and luscious from nowhere at all. The Tirumeni asked for an explanation, and then said 'These things are not for us, for we are Christians, and you must never play with these forces again. What you have learnt from the devil you must eschew.' He desired that Kadamattath Kattanar should bring to him all the books that he had got of black magic and that these should be brought before him and burnt. The Kattanar bought all to be burnt, except two which he hid in the shoes that he was wearing. When the Tirumeni asked whether he had brought all before him, the Kattanar said 'All of them are in front of the Tirumeni,' which was a true statement concealing however the fact that two of the manuscripts were concealed in his shoes.

It is extremely interesting that witchcraft is seen to be a view of the world acceptable to Izhavas or Tiyyas. Gilles Tarabout's path-breaking essay looks at the way in which witchcraft is part of modern traditions among alcohol merchants, where seva or service to kutti chatthan (little demons) is not at all derogatory. Tarabout is very clear that what is devil to some is god to another, and in fact like Veena Das (1977) is critical of the Durkheimian preoccupation with the hierarchy of the sacred and profane, the good sacred and the malevolent. In the case of Kadamattath Kattanar, the story goes, he served the devil in order to trick him, in order to learn the craft, so that he could utilize it for his own purposes, which were not malefic. In the analyses of the blurring of terms, Gilles Tarabout writes,

> Let us consider the example of Cattan, a god already mentioned and called often also Kutticattan ('small baby' Cattan). He may be worshipped either as a lone figure, or as a pair or yet as hordes of Kutticattans (10, 12, 336, 390, 400, or more still), in which case he is the leader of the horde and represents simultaneously its totality. This child of Siva, brought up by a Parayan woman (or according to some claims, a tribal woman in the mountains), has a dubious reputation throughout Kerala. He may routinely display his power by polluting food with hairs or bits of finger nails, by transforming water into urine, by polluting statues of gods, by provoking spontaneous combustions of clothes or hay-stacks, and by various other mischievous acts in bad taste.
>
> Tarabout in Vidal et al. (2003: 229)

Tarabout further provides 11 reasons why the occult may be a part of everyday events, requiring consultation with specialists. These are wrath of the gods, wrath of family deity, wrath of serpents, wrath of one's forbears or ancestors, wrath of one's master, wrath of Brahmins, influence of planets in a malevolent fashion, wrath of unsatisfied deads, preta or ghosts, evil eye, poisons administered through mantras and the act of an enemy through a sorcerer (ibid.: 226). Do Christians continue to share the customs and beliefs of their neighbours? The data from Kadamattam seems to suggest they do. In *Christians of Kerala: History Belief and Ritual among the Yakoba*, I discuss how Ezhavas or toddy tappers, working as household servants, use witchcraft as a means for controlling the excesses of the Syrian Christian landlords who often ill-treated them. Satan is unleashed, for the chathan appears in a very fearsome form, the Ezhavas are paid to 'tie up the devil' through possession and ritual actions. An Ezhava woman recounted the story to me in 1981:

> At night, my father's father and his brothers all gathered in Chakko's house to perform the magic. The pounding of the herbs and the preparation of the medicines began. They saw there was just one villaku (lamp) and the men started singing and beating

the drum. Just then there were loud shouts at the gate. Chakko Saar had returned without warning. His wife started shivering and trembling; after all, she had wanted this done behind his back. She had wanted Satan to be tied up before her husband returned. Chakko Saar came in with his big stick and said 'Eddo aa ra?' (Hey, who is that?), and began to swing the stick around. Everyone left in a hurry except my grandfather's brother who was beginning to leap, having become possessed by the devil; as Chakko Saar descended on him with the stick, my relative said, 'Have you recognised me?' in a very menacing tone. For the first time Chakko Saar felt fear, for the question kept being repeated. 'Have you understood me, do you know who I am?' He said, 'I will give whatever you ask: but go away.' So the devil said, 'Ask my pardon.' Chakko Saar did so, and after that the curse was removed, and life returned to normal. Since it had been my grandfather's brother who had been responsible for tying up the devil, we were given a privilege for two generations – our family's needs for rice were met by them.

Visvanathan (1993: 89)

In the following section, I will show how the presence of witchcraft is recorded in the Mannanam document (provided by Istvan Perczel and written after 1816 and before 1830), where it is written.

With the order of Mar Hirihānátthios (Ignatius) in Antioch, a man called Thomas, a merchant from abroad, came here and brought here bishops, priests, men, women and children and, with all of them, he came to Kodungalloor and met the mahāraja Cheruman Perumal and bought, by agreement, land for churches and for a city. The foreigners and the local people together built there a church and the city named Mahódévarupattanam (the City of the Great God). While they were residing there, the foreign bishops gave the ranks of bishops (vispumar) and priests (pathiri) to many persons in Malankara. After that, they also established churches at other places. In these times, when Christianity (the religion of baptism) was flourishing, in the year 825 of Jesus, a merchant called Ióh (that is, Job) brought, from a foreign country, two bishops whose names were Mar . . . (here a place is left blank, apparently the scribe or author did not know the name of the bishop and wanted to supply it later – one would expect here the name Sapor or Shahpur) and Mar Aprót (Aphraat). They ruled over the Christians (mámódisákarar or those baptised) for some time.

A few years later, two or four persons, who studied at depth the books of the devils, came from abroad to Malankara. Their names were known as Mārābhanmár [Mar Abba's]. One of these, who were called, Mar Dehaná (that is, Mar Denhā), a sorcerer (kšudraka<ra>n), taught sorcery to a priest from the Pozhiyedutthu family (tharavad) in Kadamattam (here: Kat,amuṟṟam). The two of them, by the help of the devils, wrought many miracles. At that time the sorcerer called Mar Dehaná died. His disciple, the Kadamattam priest (Kat,amaṟṟatthukaran pathiri) took the bones of the sorcerer whose name was Mar Dehaná and placed them in the southern wall of the Kadamattam church. He made him a god (deyvamákivaccha), offered him burnt offerings (homam), [Hindu-type] worship (pújá) festive food-offerings (ulla útthu,t,ghošamáyit) and he showed many wonders and miracles. By sorcery he caught the devils and conquered them. On those who stood against them [apparently against the group of the Kadamattam priest] befell many sorts of calamities and dangers.

So while he was doing these great things, this sorcerer taught another priest who was his nephew, to worship this sort of devils and to perform the burnt offerings and the worship (the pújas). Then, from the time of the death of the senior priest until today there is the tradition that there always must be a priest to worship the name of Mar Dehaná, the sorcerer, and to maintain the aforementioned (customs). While this tradition was in force, it happened that there were no male children in that family. Then, members of the family (tharavad) of the Mar Thoma Metropolitans (metran) were adopted in the Kadamattam Pozhiyedutthu family. So until today the present Mar Thoma Metropolitan[3] is the one who has to venerate the devils of Mar Dehaná. Also, this man has somehow made others believe many falsehoods and he is a man who, having subdued the devils by sorcery, has wrought many miracles. Since he is such a man, many people, being afraid of opposing him, would keep silence. Those people who are in the Kadamattam family, are the worshippers of the devils and they are keeping a house as the seat for the devils.[4] This fact is known to all the Syrians in Malayálam and also to those who obey the Puttenchira and the Varapuzha Metropolitans (metran) and to the Nairs who are living near Kadamattam.

Until now nobody from this Kadamattam family (tharavad) has become a bishop. The present Mar Thoma Metropolitan was not given episcopal ordination by other bishops and, therefore, to obey this man is very sorrowful. The bishop who, at present, is residing in the North, in the Chavakkad District (Chavakkatthu shímayil) (shíma means a foreign country outside the Cochin Kingdom), is a very poor and humble man; still, there is the completeness of episcopal ordination in him. So I request the merciful Queen Sáyú[5] to save us by issuing an order to obey that man. I think that, if we have to obey the present Mar Thoma Metropolitan, it would be better for us to live on begging.

This document is extremely interesting because it shows the venom between parties who sought to separate from one another. For the time period that it represents, feuding was at its most violent.

Clearly, the document shows that church politics pervades the sense of ethics and values invested in marking difference in belief. My visit to Kadamattath was on the assumption that interviews would help me to better understand the narrative materials I had, which are offered here as a description. Together, they corroborate the evidence that magic and sorcery have practical value for those who believe in them. They also suggest that faith is the catalyst when it comes to the Church's interpretation, regarding the transformation to miracle through the gentle mediation of Mary. The parish priest, as we shall see, believes that apocrypha is neither endorsed nor legitimated by the Church, but nor is it denied.

Kadamattath village lies 30 km from Ernakulam town. The white church is extremely beautiful. It is ancient; the inhabitants of the village say it dates from the sixth century. Of course there have been modifications, but it certainly stems from the pre-Portuguese period. It is dedicated to Mary, who according to legend rescued the Kattanar or priest from the devil. The story goes, retold to me by villagers in 2009, that while he was grazing his cows the devil took him and they went down the well and entered padallam or purgatory. But then, having learnt the arts of magic, he escaped and with the devil and his allies chasing him, he reached the Church of Mary, and managed to gasp 'ammae' (Mother) at which a rooster flew out of his mouth. This rooster is a predominant symbol, even today in this church, both as a creature to be slaughtered in sacrifice as well as in art work present on the church walls. It is clearly a phallic symbol of sorts, representing ego, sexuality, basic desires, the omen of crowing at the time of Peter's denial of Christ and so on. Even in the creaking of doors I hear in the Kadamattath Palli the hollow sound of cock's crowing. The Church of Mary is crowded with miracle seekers. When I visit it (14.3.09), it is Lent, and only Hindu devotees who do not know that it is Noimbu or Lent have come to the Church hoping to sacrifice or slaughter the cock.

When 'sacrifice of the cock is acceptable', people bring the cock, which has its head chopped off, to that ancient well, and the rest is offered to the Kattanar. It is then cooked and presented along with five kinds of savoury foods (fried lentils) and with an offering of Madhyam (alcohol) to Kadamattath Kattanar and then eaten by the sacrifiers. This is the Jacobite Syrian/Orthodox assimilation of the 'chattan sewa'. The dominant culture of Hinduism is integrated into the larger tradition of Orthodox Christianity (Mundakuzy 1982) where, in this church, Mary is venerated. The Hindu aspect of the temple is the most interesting thing about it, since it has the iconic aspects of the fifth century traditions where the symbols of the lamps, walls, tiled roofs seek to integrate it into the dominant culture of the region. For instance, 'Like domestic architecture, church architecture also borrows from the Hindu perception of the natural world. But unlike domestic architecture, it simultaneously draws from the Jewish tradition. The Christian church resembles in its internal structure the Jewish synagogue. However, the construction of the church takes place in the manner prescribed by the Thaccu Shastra (a book of rules in verse on building practice), and the rules followed are those adapted from the building principles for the temples. In the façade of the church, the cultural elements of Hinduism, Christianity, and the Syrian tradition are clearly in juxtaposition' (Visvanathan 1993: 9).

I ask the priest (Kattanar Joseph of the Syrian Jacobite denomination) about the distinction between magic and miracle. For him, the encounter between the devil and Kadamattath Kattanar and the consequent saving of his soul by his plea to Mary is a miracle, 'albhoodam'. To this priest, the Kadamattath Kattanar is saved from the devil because of his plea to Mary. However, he is very clear that the Church does not accept Kadamattath Kattanar's story as part of its orthodox canon. He is definitely seen by the Church to be outside of it. However, the young priest who is a parish priest, as well as a well-trained theologian, says that the Church understands the transmission of local histories from 'mouth to mouth' and it respects tradition. The phrase he uses, 'mouth to mouth', certainly communicates intimacy and familiarity as folk stories do. Legends, myths, the oral histories and records of communities are passed down very carefully, often suggesting by-heart renderings which begin to have corresponding structures in narratives, whether written, printed, or remembered. What then is faith? Can one evaluate or measure or weigh experience? The priest asks me this, when I interrogate him in friendly conversation. People have miracles happen to them, which change their lives. He takes out a notebook from which he reads out several stories. Like many St. Mary Orthodox and Syrian Christian Churches, peasantry is mainly concerned with problems of fertility, bearing of children and their safe passage into the world. The people who come to him for advice are from distant places in Kerala as well as those who have jobs in America or the Gulf countries. 'It's not magic, certainly not,' he says. These are stories of faith, and of prayers answered. He asks me to stay in the village for a few days, and he will introduce me to the daily petitioners. Kadamattath Palli (Church) according to him is the Church of Mary, and Kadamattath Kattanar a beneficiary of her great love.

There has been a tendency to schism in the Orthodox and Syrian Jacobite churches, taken together referred to as 'Yakoba' (see Visvanathan 1993). Here, too, that schism is historically more than apparent. The two 'Parties' (or *Katshis*, to be translated as segments) after eight years of a lock-out and quarrels and a court directive, now co-exist. They have a parish of 2,500 families, not counting the visitors. The priest take turns to use the church, since a court order enjoined them.

Several steps below is the church which is built where Kadamattath Kattanar's home once stood. Next to it is an old well where the slaughter of roosters takes place. This ancient custom, which enjoins men and women to 'party' with Kadamattath Kattanar, is actually a vestige of social custom for North Kerala, where women also may drink occasionally. The assumption is that it is a cultural practice, not leading to drunkenness or debt. It is part of the unrecorded survival of customs and histories of the Malayalies. The ritual cook who accompanies me to the well says that 'whisky and brandy are consumed' when I ask him what he means by Madhya. When I say, 'Women, too?' he says, just a drop, a licked finger, that is all, communicating that anything more would seem scandalous to me. Quite often, anthropologists have reported that respondents tell them what they wish to hear. I instinctively laugh about Kadamattath Kattanar escaping from the devil; I can imagine him scurrying up the old well which we are looking into. The ritual cook says, 'It's true, not a laughing matter.' There is anxiety in his eyes, and that too is part of the tradition which suggests that when saints are insulted there is a backlash of bad luck. He continues, 'anyone who feels they are bewitched can call on the Kadamattath Kattanar, and he will help them. Just say "Kadamattath" and he will help.' The priest I interviewed says that people of all religions come here, and they hope to find relief from agonies. He does not turn anybody away. The priest as counsellor is how I see him. Father Joseph listens to them and gives them advice. He makes me wait while he finishes speaking to two women who have approached him for a private audience. They have come from Verapoly and are Catholics, and yet, they speak with the parish priest of the Patriarch's Party of the Syrian Jacobites. He speaks with hundreds of such people, all of whom are either looking for miracles or have experienced them.

Because of the Church quarrels there are four churches in the same vicinity: (1) St. Mary's Church, (2) The Kadamattath's House (now a Church), (3) Patriarch's Party Chapel and (4) Orthodox Party Chapel. The last two were built when the first two were closed. Once opened, by legal decree, each party used churches 1 and 2 alternatively every Sunday, since these formerly were the sacred and contested sites. Now the chapels are used by those who meditate, the Orthodox chapel having pictures of Parimalla Tirumeni who is one of their most valued contemporary saints. Kadamattath Kattanar's skeleton was supposed to be found under the boards when St. Mary's Church was being renovated, but the nineteenth-century church tracts digitalized for the monasteries by Istvan Perczel in the 1990s and the translation of the casket engravings (provided in the letter to me cited on the first page of this essay) suggest that it is the skeleton of a powerful sorcerer bishop from the Middle East that is interred. This iron casket (skeleton intact according to the priest) is decorated and lit up like a Christmas tree. It is located on the left-hand side of the altar in St. Mary's Church, and to this casket, or to St. Mary's tranquil presence encapsulated in the myth of patronage and protection, the people pray.

Also consider an essay published by William Dalrymple in an anthology edited by Shinie Antony (2009) called *Kerala Kerala*. It is on the syncretistic nature of belief in the Orthodox and Jacobite Syrian Churches in Kerala and refers very specifically to Mannarkad Palli which had been the focus of my attention in *Christians of Kerala* in Chapter 8, where I contrast canonical rituals with those relating to St. Mary, who appears as giver of favours to Hindus and Christians alike. Dalrymple (wishing to follow up that work which was written in 1983 by me as data collected from Kottayam) in his inimitable style discusses the syncretistic aspect of Hindu Christian rituals.

> Bhagavati, they explained, was the pre-eminent Goddess in Kerala, the most powerful and beloved deity in the region. In some incarnations, it was true, she could be ferocious. But in other moods, Bhagavati could be supremely benign and generous to her devotees, the caring, loving, fecund mother; and this was how her followers usually liked to think of her. [. . .] In this form, Bhagavati is regarded as a chaste virgin and a caring mother, qualities she shares with her sister, whose enclosure lies a short distance down the road:
>
> 'Yes, yes, the Virgin Mary is Bhagavati's younger sister,' explained Vasudeva, the head priest, matter-of-factly, as if stating the obvious.
>
> 'But for sisters don't they look rather different from each other?' I asked. A calendar image of the Goddess was pinned up behind

Vasudeva showing Bhagvati as a wizened hag wreathed in skulls and crowned with an umbrella of cobra hoods. In her hand she wielded a giant sickle.

'Sisters are often a little different from each other,' he replied. 'Mary is another form of the Devi. They have equal power.'

He paused: 'At our annual festival the priests take the Goddess around the village on top of an elephant to receive sacrifices from all the different people. The Goddess visits all the places, and one stop is the church. There she sees her sister.'

'Mary gets on an elephant too?'

'No,' he replied. 'But when the Goddesses visit each other, the sacrifice in the church is just like the one we have here: we light lamps and make an offering of neelam at a particular place in the compound. The priests stay in their church, but the trustees and congregation of the church receive us, and make a donation to the temple. Each year they give some money, and a tin of oil for our lamps.'

'So relations are good?'

'The people here always cooperate,' he said. 'Our Hindus go to the church and the Christians come here and ask the Goddess for what they want. Almost all days they are coming, for everyone believes the two are sisters.'

This was something I had seen for myself ever since I had arrived in Mannarkad, a small village 80 km to the south of the Keralan capital, Cochin. In the large courtyard of the church – newly rebuilt and enlarged around a mediaeval core – many of the worshippers had turned out to be Hindu rather than Christian.

Dalrymple (2009: 17–19)

This syncretism has been the virtue of religious faith. While ideologies and isms constrain and bind in enclosures, faith and belief are more open, more osmotic, more tender in their mutual concern. Faith is personal; while it draws from collectivities and tradition, the real question of their viability depends on the larger structures which serve them, either in protecting or in constraining or in letting them be.

Notes

1 My thanks to Prof. Istvan Perczel of Central European University, Budapest, and Prof. Pius Maleykandathil of CHS, JNU. Veena Das, George Gispert Sauch, Gilles Tarabout, Geeti Sen and Jaya Bhattacharji Rose have read the draft

version in its incipient stages across a time span of 1980 to the present. Segments of this paper have been published in IIC Quarterly (1997) and Museindia.com (2013). In its final version, Christoph Wulf and Michael Sonntag have been a great help in making it available to a new audience, and I am immensely grateful for their interest in this work.
2 Cp. *www.hindu.com/mag/2008/09/14/stories/2008091450170500.htm* website link for an interview with Istvan Perczel (accessed on 21 October 2013).
3 Mar Thoma VIII (1809–16).
4 Obviously, the author is speaking about the house where Paulos Pathiri of the Pozhiyedutthu family, the famous Kadamattam Priest, was born. People venerated the place until recently, when the house was demolished, and in its place, a chapel was built. The inhabitants of Kadamattam keep bringing offerings to this chapel, to earn the favours of the Kadamattam Kattanar (information received from Rev. Dr. George Kurukkoor).
5 An honorary title of the Queen of Kochi.

References

Baldaeus, Philip (1996): *Description of the Great and Most Famous Isle of Ceylon*. Delhi: Reprint Asian Educational Services.

Barthes, Roland (1985): *The Responsibility of Forms: Critical Essays on Music, Art, and Representation*. New York: Hill and Wang.

Bayly, Susan (1989): *Saints, Goddesses, and Kings*. Cambridge: Cambridge University Press.

Bloch, Marc (1954): *The Historian's Craft*. Manchester: Manchester University Press.

Brown, Leslie W. (1982): *The Indian Christians of St. Thomas*. Cambridge: Cambridge University Press.

Dalrymple, William (2009): *The Strange Sisters of Mannarkad*. In: Antony, Shinie (ed.): *Kerala Kerala: Quite Contrary*. Delhi: Rupa & Co., 17–30.

Das, Veena (1977): *Structure and Cognition*. Delhi: Oxford University Press.

Klijn, Albert F. J. (ed.) (1962): *Acts of St. Thomas*. Leiden: Brill.

Menachery, George (ed.) (1973): *The Thomas Christian Encyclopedia*. Madras 1998: BNK Press.

Menon, Padmanabha K. P. (1924): *History of Kerala*. Vol. 1. Ernakulam: Cochin Government Press.

Morrison, Kathleen (2005): *Environmental History, the Spice Trade, and the State in South India*. In: Cederlof, Gunnel, and Sivarmakrishnan, K. (eds): *Ecological Nationalisms: Nature Livelihoods and Identities in South Asia*. Ranikhet, Delhi: Permanent Black, 43–64.

Mundakuzhy, Rev. Thomas P. (1982): *Our Church, Malankara St. Thomas Oriental Orthodox Church of India*. Mavellikara: St. Paul's Mission Press.

Panikkar, Kavalam M. (1959): *Asia and Western Dominance*. Bombay: Asia Publishing House.

Perumalil, Hormice C., and Hambye, Edward R. (eds) (1972): *Christianity in India*. Alleppey: Prakasam Publications.

Podipara, Placid J. (1970): *The St. Thomas Christians*. Bombay: Darton, Longman and Todd.

Subrahmanyam, Sanjay (1997): *The Career and Legend of Vasco da Gama*. Delhi: Cambridge University Press.

Vidal, Denis, Tarabout, Gilles, and Meyer, Eric (2003): *Violence, Non-Violence: Some Hindu Perspectives*. Delhi: Manohar.

Visvanathan, Susan (1993): *Christians of Kerala*. Madras: OUP.

Zaleski, Ladislas (1912): *The Apostle St. Thomas in India*. Mangalore: Codiarbel Press.

8

IN-BETWEEN PLACES: THE NATURAL ZOO AS A CULTURAL PLACE

Meera Baindur

My research is in the broad area of Environmental Humanities and the interface between the concepts of nature and culture. A large part of my activity during the 'Passage to India' exchange programme was exploring places and blogging about them. In some ways I was 'displaced' from my home country and was occupying an in-between place. Berlin was my home, yet not my home. This essay includes 'in-betweenness' in its structure, as the actual paper is written in between my journal entries (in italics) on the visit to the Berlin Zoo. Zoological gardens are places where boundaries between nature and culture are fuzzy and one cannot apply distinct binaries to evaluate or judge them as one or the other. The zoological garden is ontologically a cultural place but its components or constituents are natural elements such as trees, animals and plants. This chapter traces the in-betweenness of zoos through the story of Knut, the polar bear in the Berlin Zoo and the history of zoos in general.[1]

On the history of zoos: collections of animals

The tickets to the Berlin Zoo were printed with pictures of birds and animals and it looked like a colourful souvenir I could put away in my scrapbook. As I followed my friends through the large gates, past the ticket-checking personnel, I was one of a few hundred people entering the Berlin Zoo that day. This was my first 'sight-seeing trip' inside the city of Berlin.

Vernon N. Kisling Jr. (2001), in his book on the history of zoos, informs us that human beings attempted to keep wild animals as early as 10,000

BCE, along with the first attempts at domestication of animals. This just might have been a process where some animals were selected to live with human beings and some were found unsuitable for domestication. The collecting of different types of animals began later. Kisling (ibid.: 7) adds that, 'however, "collections" of wild animals were not assembled until the earliest urbanised civilisations began about 3000 BC.'

Many animal collections also formed parts of gifts and tributes to the conquerors of other kingdoms and the value of the tribute being greater in case the animal was perceived as exotic. In a descriptive passage from the *Mahabharata*, one of the ancient epics of India, we find a list of animals, gifts to the emperor Yudhistira from his vassals including wild animals, camel herds and many other animals (cp. Sabha Parva Book 2: Mahabharata). The earliest zoo (Kisling 2001: 7) recorded in history was the collection of African animals by Queen Hatshepsut of Egypt (ca. 1479–58 BCE) brought from the punt region (now a part of Ethiopia). We know from the temple paintings of this period that it may have been the first collection that was open for public viewing. We do know that private royal animal collections did exist before, such as those of Shulgi, the ruler of Urs (now south-eastern Iraq), but they were for the pleasures of the royal court only. There were also collections of sacred animals that belonged to the temples (cp. Turner 2005: 13f.). All of these places that animals were displayed in were called by different names over time but fundamentally, they always were concerned with having animals on display. Kisling (2001: 7) points out:

> Animal collections evolved into menageries during and after the European Renaissance period (1456–1828), and then into zoological gardens beginning in the nineteenth century (1828 to present). In hindsight, however, earlier collections may also be considered menageries or zoos. Modern usage of these words applies to any collection of wild animals, including those collections existing in the past.

From 'mere display' to the 'scientific study' of animals in a garden

The Berlin Zoo is spread over a large area with wide open spaces, pathways and display boards showing maps and information (in both German and English) about the enclosures and the animals on display. As we walked past the large herbivores (Elephants, Camels and Giraffes), my colleague, who studies animal behaviour and social interactions in monkeys, kept up a running commentary on the different animals, their geographical distribution and strange facts about them a philosophy student like me may have not known.

The study of animals and their classification became central to Natural history in the early half of the eighteenth century. Carolus Linnaeus (1707–78) is credited with the establishment of the modern scientific method of classification and naming of plants, animals, minerals and diseases. With increase in trade and explorations to other continents, more and more varieties of plants and animals were discovered, prompting natural historians like Linnaeus to send trained pupils as observers to record and describe in detail as well as to bring back samples of the plants and animals of the different explored countries (cp. Ben-Menahem 2009 (1): 1330). The private animal collections were replaced by institutionally managed collections during this period. The move was both political and social, and reflected the changing ideas about 'science' during the eighteenth and nineteenth centuries.

Characteristic of this period is the transformation of Curiosity which was a part of the flaws of character, along with Hubris, into a noble virtue. Sarukkai (2009: 762) writes:

> From the seventeenth century positive values get attached to curiosity. [. . .] Hobbes also used curiosity to distinguish humans from animals and thus puts curiosity in a constellation of ideas such as rationality which served to make this distinction in Aristotle. For Hobbes and Descartes, curiosity was the origin of the search for knowledge.

This development of 'science' as a discipline encouraging curiosity about the world in general did initiate the scientific study of animals (zoology) during that period. We find that one of the official documents, a Zoological Society of London prospectus dated 1 March 1825 stated:

> It has long been a matter of deep regret to the cultivators of Natural History, that we possess no great scientific establishment either for teaching or elucidating Zoology; and no public menageries or collections of living animals where their nature, properties and habits may be studied. In almost every other part of Europe, except in the metropolis of the British Empire, something of this kind exists.
>
> cited in Kisling (2001: 61)

Kisling draws from this document to show how the idea of a zoological garden promoted the scientific study of animals. He writes:

> This prospectus also asserted that the society would 'offer a collection of living animals, such as never yet existed in ancient or modern times' and that it would benefit Britain to offer 'a very

different series of exhibitions to the population of her metropolis', one that could be used for the 'objects of scientific research, not of vulgar admiration'.

ibid.: 62

The motivation of scientific curiosity which legitimised the act of watching exotic animals earlier was now considered a vulgar spectacle. By contrast, the scientific method of observation in the form of animal studies in zoos was construed as legitimate pursuit of the rational human being. The setting up of the zoological gardens thus seems to have been influenced by the re-cast idea of curiosity that supported proper methods of science.

Sarukkai (2009: 7) writes of this development of 'methodical curiosity' in the sciences:

> For Descartes, the problem was in unmethodological curiosity and so he constructs methods which will control 'blind curiosity'. Over the course of the seventeenth century, curiosity gets established as something natural, something innate which characterizes human thought and action. It is not an accident that this period also saw the invocation of duty towards attaining knowledge.

Turner (2005: 18) explains that in eighteenth-century England the study of wild nature otherwise called 'first nature' was given renewed significance by the philosophical school known as empiricism. He writes: 'There was a steady swing from Cartesian rationalism to the empiricism of Bacon, Hobbes, Locke and Hume. In the nineteenth century, this led to a botanical appreciation of plants. Gardens became an example in the discussion of man's relationship to nature.'

The word 'zoo' is an abbreviation of the term zoological garden. Like a botanical garden that houses plants and trees from all over the world, a zoological garden (or zoo) houses animals of different kinds. In German, another word for zoo is 'Tiergarten', which literally means 'animal-garden' and actually is the name of the district where the Berlin Zoological Garden is located. The word 'garden' in the phrase 'zoological garden' warrants a closer look.

The place between nature and culture

As we sauntered along, a board with an arrow announced, 'Arctic foxes and polar bears'. Polar bears . . . My heart must have skipped a beat. To actually see a live polar bear in Berlin was a welcome opportunity. Instead of trudging miles in the freezing arctic cold or alternatively watching a moving picture on a flat screen in the comfort of my city home, I comfortably get see a live polar bear in Berlin Zoo! From my own interest in environmental issues, I already knew that the polar bear was a mascot for the cause of mitigating global warming. The ecologists are concerned that melting polar ice caps would maroon these large carnivorous bears on islands of ice, threatening their very existence. As I neared the large rocky enclosure, I was more than satisfied. Polar bears, their fur white as snow were taking a bath in the warm sunlight, ambling along the rocks, or just resting, watching us watch them. The arctic foxes were in another enclosure with the brown bears. As I look at the brown shaggy animal, the brown bear chose to suddenly stand up on its hind feet and tower over the watching humans. All of a sudden I smelt raw meat. I turned back to see a wheel barrow behind me. It was filled with the bear's lunch – dead rabbits and birds. The title of an environmental-philosophy essay of James Hatley's came to my mind – 'The Uncanny Goodness of Being Edible to Bears'. I had a phenomenological moment of being bear's food (meat) for a few seconds then the irrational fear filled moment passed and the human rationale took over. I began to click pictures with my mobile phone camera.

Gardens are places that are between nature and polis, our built settlements. Rolston (2005: 62) claims (as does Aristotle earlier) that human beings are naturally political and build themselves a *polis* in which they can socialise. According to him, the architectures of nature and culture are different, and culture will always seek to improve nature, this management intent spoils the wilderness. Cultural processes by their very 'nature' interrupt evolution, he claims. Yet one cannot deny that human beings have dimensions within themselves which relate to the wild or the rural. The parks and the gardens seem to create a 'wild' or natural area for the urban dweller to fulfil this need. One may speculate that this need is perhaps what draws the visitors to the zoos. These gardens and green areas within an urban area are much visited as they bring the natural landscape to that halfway point between human-made and entirely natural. The normal reaction of urban dwellers to the wild is one of threat and fear and there are communities that would be happier with plastic plants and trees. Yet these halfway wildernesses, places that are hybrid between nature and culture are set against the background view that tamed nature is more worthy than either the pure wild or the totally built environment.

Yi-Fu Tuan (1975: 156) also points out that for the people of the city, the public places of a city are less meaningful than the countryside and wildernesses. He writes:

The assertion is obvious and yet may sound surprising, for many well-educated and vocal people of urban background have come to believe that meaning in a place gains almost in proportion to its lack of people. In this view, sparsely settled farmlands are somehow more meaningful than cities, and wilderness areas more meaningful than farmlands.

Explaining this urban preference for wilderness, he (ibid.) further adds:

To people of urban background, farms and wildernesses are aesthetic and religious objects. A special verbal and pictorial syntax, the creation of many talented artists, exists to articulate rural and wilderness experiences from the visitor's viewpoint.

Though Tuan is talking specifically about the paintings and colour slides as visual syntax, a zoo is also such a carefully designed or staged representation of wilderness within a city, nature in an urban area. Are such gardens natural or cultural? The landscaped gardens are an urban phenomenon certainly and zoos are a special type of such garden places with animals. In his history of gardens, Turner mentions that early collections of animals were maintained in gardens. 'People have always sought to understand the natural world and enclosures have assisted the quest by containing collections of plants and animals. The earliest spaces of this type were known as *pairidaeza* (literally "around-wall")' (Turner 2005: 11).

It is interesting to examine here how the idea of the 'wild' is constructed in urban areas through the construction of parks, particularly zoological gardens. The idea of 'wild animals' brings to the layman the imagination of the forest and wilderness more easily than neat rows of tulips in a garden bed. The nature that zoos represent is – created nature – a restored or maintained natural surrounding which the philosopher Elliot refers to as 'faked nature'. He argues that any humanly designed entities are at best feeble attempts to copy nature (Elliot 1997: 105).

Without giving in to this extreme dichotomy between nature and culture, we could also look at the idea of cultural as being related to human purposes. Within the life-world of human beings, zoological gardens do not exist for or by themselves. The zoo is designed to fulfil a human purpose, that of looking at the animals placed in enclosures (for education or aesthetic or scientific study), which makes the place cultural for us. The term cultural is appropriate here because it includes the aesthetic appeal of nature and not merely its utilitarian values.

A zoo is an example of a new kind of *hybrid place* where the porous boundaries between nature and culture seem to fulfil a cultural purpose.

The zoo is a place where nature (as represented in particular by the wild animals and their 'natural enclosures') is present. But the zoo itself is a museum, a cultural exhibit that is totally created for human purposes, be it for education, conservation of a gene pool or the study of animal behaviour. Though zoological gardens are meant to house and study animals in general, we find that a majority of the zoos prefer to house exotic species. For the lay person, the idea of exotic means alien, uncommon, strange or rare; for the zoo expert, the term is to be understood in a more technical sense. Exotic for the expert refers to the geographical origins of the animals, to the fact that their natural range is found in parts of the world other than where the zoo and its exhibits are. However, it must be emphasised that the zoo is not like a scientific *laboratory* of a zoologist or ethologist. One of the main functions of a zoo is to display these exotic animals for the general public. A zoo that does not open its gate for public viewing is rare.

I walked away towards the souvenir stall that seemed to be a polar bear special shop, hoping to pick up a message T-shirt or something small for my friends back in India. I saw a picture postcard of a cuddly white bear cub reclining on a green blanket. 'KNUT' said the caption in block letters. 'Knut? Who's Knut?' I was puzzled that one animal had so much popularity in the zoo and he was famous enough to have a souvenir stall all for himself. When I asked the store-keeper about it in broken German, she replied in perfect English, 'Knut was born in this zoo, so he is a special bear.' Was Knut a Berlin bear, or a polar bear, or a polar bear born in Berlin? Later, browsing through the internet from many articles and news stories, I found out about Knut. Born in captivity in the Berlin zoo, on December sixth, 2006, this polar bear cub called Knut has been the centre of many controversies surrounding the ideas of 'natural' 'wild' and ethics of human-animal interaction.

A polar bear is exotic because it does not naturally occur in the regions around Germany. In other words it is alien to the local geographical region. This idea of exotic comes from a particular understanding of the concept 'ecological species'. This is a concept of species in which a species is a set of organisms adapted to a particular set of resources, called a niche, in the environment. According to this concept as defined by Ridley (2004: 353), 'populations form the discrete phenetic clusters that we recognise as species because the ecological and evolutionary processes controlling how resources are divided up tend to produce those clusters.' So when an animal is displaced from its natural niche it is 'alien' to the place. In a zoo, most animals are exotic and 'displaced' from their natural habitat. Despite the best attempts of zoo managers to recreate their natural surroundings it is evident that this is not the natural habitat of the animal in nature. Even if zoos manage to recreate ice and snow within a large arctic glass dome, they cannot avoid the miniaturisation effect. The best zoo enclosure is another artificial niche, created by humans and maintained by sustained effort of cost and energy.

Lee (2005: 22) suggests that according to a particular view in environmental philosophy known as holism or ecocentrism, 'ecology in general, and habitats and ecosystems in particular, play a vital part both in the emergence and the maintenance of a species.' The polar bear in Berlin is a representative of the species *Ursus maritimus*. But this polar bear, devoid of the Arctic landscape and seascape is actually a 'non-polar' bear. Even without invoking ideas of wild and non-wild, the zoo animals may be natural kinds, but they are culturally different from the bears foraging for fish in the Arctic regions. They are human artefacts, placed on display. Like reconstructed Greek pillars in the museum, they are show pieces for study, education and entertainment. The difference between the pillars and the bears is that these animals are alive.

Arguing for an environmental ethic that addresses the value of nature from a non-anthropocentric perspective, Elliot (1997: 97) posits that original nature cannot be replaced by these restored artefacts. These increasing trends to bring nature into the city represent an aspect of the human–nature relationship which portrays nature as an artefact, adding to the glory of human technology that recreates the pristine beauty of the wild for us in our urban backyard.

The human destruction of the environment resulting from depletion of resources prompted George Marsh to write *Man and Nature: Or, Physical Geography as Modified by Human Action*, one of the first modern books (published in 1864) concerned with the need for environmental conservation (Kisling 2001: 18). The changing interest towards the study of ecology and conservation led to zoological gardens redefining themselves as being centres of ecological education and conservation awareness. Kisling (2001: 40) writes that the trend towards conservation parks is a reflection of related social, environmental and technological changes. Captive breeding has created the idea of zoos being a sort of a modern Noah's ark where animals can be preserved and bred within zoos in controlled environments, perhaps to repopulate the depleting wild populations. Most zoos justify their programmes around creating awareness about conservation and environmental issues. It comes from the idea of preservation of type. Elliot (1997: 107) writes:

> [. . .] we might distinguish between type-preservation and token-preservation. In the case of preservation, type-preservation will always involve token-preservation. The point of the distinction is merely to signal that there is a particular reason for

some token-preservations, namely that they are, in addition, type-preservations. So, one token-preservation may be compellingly justified to carry out more than another. This may be because some type of ecosystem is threatened and would be made safer through that particular act of token-preservation. Token-restoration of various kinds is one way in which the type-preservationist goal might be secured.

So a token 'wild animal' will help preserve the type polar bears in the arctic region being threatened by melting polar ice caps. Given this argument, it becomes easier to see why rarer animals are important for the zoo. On the other hand, zoos that are actually engaged in captive breeding or wild life rescue to replace wild populations are very careful to maintain the animals in very non-human surroundings. The exposure of such animals to human beings is minimised to a great extent to allow the animal to adapt to the forest or other habitats easily. The animals on display however are used to human presence.

As I bought the cute card and a cute keychain, I found Knut items were marked with a copyright. It was estimated that in 2007 from the sale of tickets and Knut-branded merchandise, Knut generated more than 5m (£4.4m; $7m) euros in extra income for Berlin zoo. Reports also estimate that the stocks of Berlin zoo went up after the cub Knut was registered as a trademark of Berlin zoo. Is Knut a form of urban capital, a brand?

Latour (1993) detects two contradictory processes at work in modern societies – the increasing proliferation of hybrids mixing nature (physical objective world) and culture (the human subjective world). On one hand there is an attempt to keep these two terms pure and pitted against each other, yet there continuously occurs an intertwining between them. 'Here lies the entire modern paradox. If we consider hybrids, we are dealing only with mixtures of nature and culture; if we consider the work of purification, we confront a total separation between nature and culture'. Latour (1993: 30)

This attempt to mix and yet keep apart is continuously present in a zoo. The animals in captivity are portrayed as tokens of their species that live in the wild. Are they actually wild animals? People may argue that animals in a zoo are natural and that they are just in a different habitat. Others may raise the issue that like exhibits in a city museum, they are no longer wild. That was the issue with Knut. As any wild cub in the polar region rejected by its mother may simply die, so also the cub Knut in the zoo must have been allowed to die. Would the cub have been rejected at all in the wild? Knut's upbringing raises so many ethical questions regarding the close interaction between human beings and their wild wards. What is the status of these halfway wild animals in the human world and in human conceptualisation? To understand this we must turn to the philosophical stream called ontology. Ontology indicates the kinds of things there are in the world, how to distinguish them and their role in framing our conceptual schemes.

We are clear that animals and other organisms are not like tables and cars. They are natural kinds. Lee (2005: 19) defines natural kinds and processes thus: 'Naturally occurring entities and processes are precisely those which have come into existence, continue to exist, and go out of existence, entirely autonomously, and therefore independently of human intentionality and agency (and of supernatural agency for that matter).' An animal or a plant, though not exactly like a lake, a rock or a mountain are still instances of natural kinds. Living organisms are those natural kinds that not only exist *by themselves*, but also exist *for themselves*; fulfilling a life trajectory. They grow, mature, reproduce and actively nourish and protect themselves from destruction. They are said to be autopoietic.

I was standing inside a dome in the zoo with glass walls and the other side was filled to half with water. A Hippo baby slowly swam across the pool and sank down underwater, its feet striking the floor of the tank and raising the mud. I had never seen a Hippo underwater. I watched the animal gracefully treading through water and watched it swim across the large tank across my glass screen view. I had an 'underwater Hippo baby' photograph to show off to my friends.

Arguing that the term 'wild animals in captivity' is a misconstruction from an ontological viewpoint, Lee (2005: 81–88) posits that once the animals are placed in a zoo, their ontological status changes, they are no longer independent of human intentionality. He insists that the animal caught from the wild first becomes decontextualised and then recontextualised according to human design and intention. He suggests that they are biotic artefacts. Where in the wild can one see arctic foxes at such close proximity to brown bears? A large part of the decontextualisation is the displacement of the animal from its natural geographical habitat. The recontexualisation of the animal occurs within the structures of the zoo. As I noticed during my visits there, the design of the enclosures (with glass domes or walls that have replaced the older kinds of iron bars in most zoos), the space that is provided for activities, partial concealment areas, feeding and watering spots, ponds, rocks, shrubbery – everything is arranged as a part of the display background. The cage is now a showcase, as in most parts of the Berlin Zoo; these are larger in size and suited for a living display. The zoo enclosures are designed in such a way as to enable zoo visitors to look at the animals. Elements of the design also ensure that the animals are content and happy in these enclosures with enough distractions for play or movement. Some zoos feed the animals in public view, some make sure that at least for a part of the day the animals are available to the viewing public. The public is not concerned with the ontological status of the wild animal. For the lay person, as long as the tiger looks like a tiger in the forest, it is a wild animal. For purposes of conservation and education, a token 'living model' of a wild tiger is placed in a glass enclosure. Lee suggests that the zoo keepers are careful to maintain the outward appearances of the wild animals. He writes:

> Zoo theorists and zoo keepers, therefore, deliberately intend and ensure that their exhibits retain the morphological characteristics which their wild counterparts possess in order, first, to sustain the claim that they are 'wild' but happen to be exhibited to the public in zoos, second, to uphold their central justifications of zoos in terms of ex situ conservation and education-for-conservation.
>
> Lee (2005: 76)

Knut represents not himself, but the wild polar bears in the Arctic region who are threatened by melting polar icecaps. The fact that Knut himself was born in the zoo and may have never been to the polar region is not of importance for the awareness-education about polar bears as a threatened species. On the other hand, the politics of Knut's ownership and the profits from his popularity are all firmly based on the fact that he was *born* in captivity. Knut is wild as a representation, a mascot for his species. But he is not wild; he is owned, brought up and cared for by human beings. His fate is intertwined with the politics of the Berlin Zoo.

Of politics and polar bears

Knut was feeding on some fishes in the enclosure but there were so many people surrounding him, many more than those around the other polar bears or the brown bears, which seemed equally interesting to my eyes. I caught just a glimpse of Knut in between many heads of people in front of me and after one or two more unsuccessful attempts to see him for longer, I unconcernedly walked away and enjoyed the rest of animal watching day. Watching some of the animals watch me, I wondered if they 'knew' they were displaced. I for one was an Indian, who had voluntarily displaced herself to Europe, always aware my 'home' was far away. Like the animals' enclosures, my room in Berlin was miniaturised too. From a large six room territory called my home, now I was residing in a small hostel room a few squares in size. I had the same view of the adjoining building from my one window to the world every day. But as a human being I was of course free to go out, have adventures and explore the city or the country. The animals would remain in the zoo. Knut will stay in Berlin. Or will he not?

Knut was born at the Berlin Zoo to 20-year-old Tosca, a former circus performer from East Germany who was born in Canada, and her 13-year-old mate Lars, who was originally from the Tierpark Hellabrunn in Munich. His birth and the surrounding ethical debates gave rise to an endless stream of nature journalism – a steady stream of photographs, essays, pictures and articles on Knut followed in what was dubbed as 'Knutmania'. It is no wonder than that Knut brought both cultural and economic values to the Berlin Zoo. It is no surprise that in July 2008, it was announced that the Neumünster zoo in northern Germany, which owns Knut's father, was suing the Berlin Zoo for the profits from Knut's success. Neumünster had previously tried to negotiate with Berlin Zoo, but was now seeking a court ruling in their favour. Zoos are much more than just cultural, they have become political. The political implications of a city owning an exotic zoo animal is equally relevant today as it was in medieval periods to own and care for these exotic animals.

On one hand it seems that the media representation of such issues feeds into the way the zoo as a place is constructed culturally. On the other hand, it also seems possible that what is written in such newspaper articles are mere representations of what is already present in people's minds. Trying to find out if the cultural construction came first or the representation in people's minds is a question that is unanswerable.

The dichotomy between nature and culture is not a clear one. It is a continuum that ranges from the human-free autopoietic being such as a tree to the completely human-dependent sign board. The animals in a zoo are not artificial, their context, the place is. The place called the zoological garden or conservation-education park, or by any other name is an in-between nature-culture place. We as human beings will interact with animals in the zoo at various levels. We, human beings give them our meanings, make them appealing for us to look at and in return we become their caretakers. They continue to follow their life trajectory. We culturally relate to them as wild pets, endangered species or as objects of study. It is for us that these animals in a zoo are cultural. They are the hybrid wild.

I walk past the other enclosures of tigers, lions, jungle cats, snakes, amphibians and fire ants. As I walk away from the zoo, a broken monument, destroyed during the World War stands outside the aquarium. The displaced stones and broken order stand in stark contrast to the neat structures of the building behind it. *All the animals are busy at fulfilling their existences. The difference is that they now are sharing a place that I belong to, being seen by me and my fellow beings, fulfilling our needs. There is a saying in Hindi which comes to my mind that I translate here: 'The Peacock danced in the jungle, but nobody saw it.' The animals in zoo are seen admired and appreciated. They are paid for, cared for and perhaps loved too.*

Epilogue

As I reedit this paper for publication, I am back in India doing research and teaching – well placed as one could say – and a great many things have happened at the Berlin Zoo. On 19th March, 2011 Knut the polar bear died. An infection in the brain caused him to drown in the pool. I saw the news on television and was reminded of my visit and this essay that I wrote in Berlin. In fact, Knut's current status as an artefact has come full circle. Arguments against the idea of stuffing Knut were raised; the museum instead mounted the real fur on a statue for display. They also have a bronze statue in his honor. The Website of the Natural History Museum has photographs of the mounting process and states that after the free public display for a few days, 'Knut will be added to the scientific research collections of the Museum and be displayed in another exhibition not before 2014 (cp. BBC report 2011). The exhibition entitled "The Value of Nature" will include Knut under the aspects of his extraordinary popularity and his role as ambassador for an endangered species.'

Perhaps the most important idea of the natural is the idea of life ending, of death. Knut has overcome this not once but twice. The first time, the zoo came to his rescue saving him from a biological death. The second time, after the biological demise he has been conserved immortalised in bronze and also in fur. Knut the polar-Berlin bear is no more but Knut the brand and his artefact value survives.

Note

1 I am grateful for DAAD scholarship that allowed me to be a part of the student exchange programme with Free University, Berlin, from October to December, 2009. I would like to acknowledge Prof. Sundar Sarukkai for his encouragement and guidance during this research. I would also like to thank Prof. Christoph Wulf and my friends at FU Berlin.

References

BBC report. (2011): *Star German Polar Bear Knut Dies*. 19 March. Retrieved 22 March 2013. http://www.bbc.co.uk/news/world-europe-12796359.

Ben-Menahem, A. (2009): *Historical Encyclopedia of Natural and Mathematical Sciences*. 6 vols. Berlin: Springer.

Elliot, R. (1997): *Faking Nature: The Ethics of Environmental Restoration*. London: Taylor & Francis Routledge.

Kisling Jr., V. N. (2001): Ancient Collections and Menageries. In: V. N. Kisling, Jr. (ed.): *Zoo and Aquarium History: Ancient Animal Collections to Zoological Gardens*, 1–48. Boca Raton: CRC Press.

Latour, B. (1993): *We Have Never Been Modern* (trans. by C. Porter). Cambridge, MA: Harvard University Press.

Lee, K. (2005): *Zoos: A Philosophical Tour*. Hampshire: Palgrave Macmillan.

Ridley, M. (2004): *Evolution*. 3rd ed. Malden: Blackwell Science Ltd.

Rolston H., III. (2005): Environmental Virtue Ethics: Half the Truth but Dangerous as a Whole. In: P. Cafaro, and R. Sandler (eds): *Environmental Virtue Ethics*, 61–78. Lanham, MD: Rowman & Little Field.

Sabha Parva, Book 2 (1933–66): *The Mahābhārata, for the First Time Critically Edited*. In: V. S. Suktankar, S. K. Belvalkar, and P. L. Vaidya (eds): Poona: Bhandarkar Oriental Research Institute.

Sarukkai, S. (2009): Science and the Ethics of Curiosity. *Current Science* 97 (6): 756–767.

Tuan, Yi-Fu (1975): Place: An Experiential Perspective. *Geographical Review* 65 (2): 151–165.

Turner, T. (2005): *Garden History: Philosophy and Design, 2000 BC-2000 AD*. London: Taylor & Francis Routledge.

Part II

DANCE, THEATRE AND MEDIA

9

CUTTING INTO HISTORY: THE 'HINDU DANCER' NYOTA INYOKA'S PHOTOMONTAGES

Tessa Jahn

This essay springs from my interest in a phenomenon that may be understood as a passage from Europe to India and back again: the wandering of images and imaginations about Indian culture into early European Modern Dance.

In the so-called West the turn of the nineteenth to the twentieth century came with a huge market for exotica and a flood of photographs depicting 'remote and exotic' countries, India being only one amongst many. The well-established technique of photography was used as major means – easily reproducible and transportable – for creating, gaining and trading knowledge about foreign cultures.[1] Photography became a major source for information in the academia and the public, and as I am going to point out, subject to intense involvement for Modern Dance artists, who used it as material for their creations, for the publication and contextualization of their work.

The 'avant-garde' of European dance in the beginning of the twentieth century – namely Isadora Duncan, Loïe Fuller, Ruth St. Denis – the 'prime movers' as Joseph H. Mazo[2] puts it, all had their 'original narration' of how they found the source of their movement. Most strikingly, the one diving into exotic fantasy worlds of literature as well as into anthropological research, the North American dancer Ruth St. Denis, sets her 'original myth' in an encounter with an exotic picture: the cigarette commercial poster 'Egyptian deities' in 1904.[3] According to her autobiography *An Unfinished Life* it inspired her to create *Radha*, her first own piece of dance and one of the first modern adaptations of Indian mythological narration and cultural framing in the 'West'.

In this context, the poster anecdote functions as a manifesto, which underlines the importance of pictures for the dancer's process of creation. Additionally, photography played a vital part in shaping and promoting St. Denis's dances, and as her husband Ted Shawn points out in the 1920 book *Ruth St. Denis: Pioneer and Prophet*,[4] had been her first step towards the new creation. Soon in 1904, St. Denis had made a photograph in costume. She then accompanied the two-year creation process of *Radha* with several sets of photographs, finally using one of them to present her piece to the theatre owners of New York in order to convince them to book her. *Radha* premiered in 1906 at the New York Theatre, New York.[5]

The following years and the success of *Radha* made her create several more pieces set within Indian culture. Her choice of costumes and poses bears a remarkable resemblance to Byam Shaw's illustrations for the exotic poem compilation *India's Love Lyrics* by Laurence Hope (Adela Florence Cory).[6] Besides these illustrations quoted as one of her inspirations,[7] St. Denis also mentions the *National Geographic* Magazine as one of her sources containing 'hundreds of pictures in color of all the Oriental peoples – authentic, beautiful, a mine of information'.[8]

This involvement with photographic images as sources of authentic information but also authenticating means in the promotion of dance creations can also be found in the work of the French dancers Jeanne Ronsay and Nyota Inyoka. The latter is the example I want to focus on the following pages.

Today rather unknown, the 'danseuse hindou' Nyota Inyoka worked in Paris between 1917 and 1955. Born 1896 in Pondicherry (India) to a French mother and an Indian father, Nyota Inyoka grew up in France.[9] She stepped onstage in her self-taught dance style in 1917 at the Folies Bergères for the first time and continued performing all over Paris, soon touring Europe and the USA. Although until now her oeuvre has not been reviewed by historical dance research, in her days she was a well-known dance artist and a much in demand expert in what was conceived of as 'Hindu dance'.[10]

Indian by birth but European by education, Inyoka claimed and was acknowledged to have the ability to translate between both cultures, French and Indian. Known as an expert in Indian dancing in her later years, she actively shaped the image of 'the' Orient in Europe, while explicitly relying on European research accessible in the libraries and museums of Paris. In this constellation her imagination of India and Indian dance emerged, whose status as ancient culture and assumingly unbroken tradition seems to have provided a suitable frame for her project to 'revive' the dance:

les danses de nyota.inyoka:

- d'origine indienne, nyota.inyoka s'inspire de la mythologie épique et religieuse de l'Inde; elle ajute à ses recherches l'étude

de l'iconographie et de la sculpture antique de l'égypte, de l'assyrie, de toutes les grandes civilisations d'orient [. . .]
- par son art elle nous apporte l'ambiance qui émane des légendes du passé; elle en traduit à nos yeux les gestes millénaires et nous les offre renouvelés, vivants, accessibles.
- sa conception de la danse reposant sur un idéal élevé, *nyota. inyoka* 'danse l'orient, mais un orient pur'.[11]

This statement taken from one of her programmes marks the originality of her dance creations, but also places them in a context of history and tradition. This tradition is put forward as being contained in her body (being Indian by birth) as well as in her expertise in the study of Indian culture. Both capacities seemed to enable her to understand the essence of 'the' Orient and make it understandable for the European audiences through her work. Most interestingly, this setting can also be found in the context of a number of photomontaged images combining dance photographs with archaeological and architecture photos from India as well as with Rajput paintings,[12] which function, I argue, as visual manifestations of the 'original myth' of her dance.

In this context the dance can be conceived of as part of what is known as 'visual culture',[13] especially as decades later it becomes visible to us in preserved and collected photographic montages and collages. So another aspect to be made explicit is my own activity re-viewing those images.

As dance history research itself relies on photographic documentation of its subject – the dance, which is necessarily transitory and fugitive – basic methodological questions arise, which I want to sketch only very briefly in this essay: how can the photographic image become a source for research in dance history? What kind of information does the photograph provide us? And how can the interaction of bodies and pictorial records be described?

Approaching photographic records from a dance historian's view

Dance research has not yet offered a consensual way of dealing with pictorial documents of its subject. Other than the general disregard of or mistrust towards photographic records in historical dance research,[14] I understand photos of dance with Claudia Jeschke as 'Material in der Auseinandersetzung mit Tanz',[15] in which dance is reconstructed within the other medium, its conditions, modes and techniques. Going further, I suggest that dance photography aims at making the dance movement's characteristics visible through diverse pictorial strategies and contextualizes it in the picture itself as well as in its presentation, thus accumulating meaning(s).

Following this understanding, a photograph is to be seen as a pile of layered facts and meanings, which are to be taken into account. In order to uncover those layers configuring the interaction of the moving body and the image in photography, its mediality and material characteristics, its modes of representing movement, and its interpretative contexts need to be considered. I focus these three aspects in three descriptions: first, the photograph's content as well as its pictorial aspects such as motif, lines, colour and textures are examined. Shifting the perspective to a movement-orientated approach towards photographic records of dance, I use a combination of the system of movement analysis called *Inventarisierung von Bewegung* (IvB)[16] with a description of the onlooker's perception guided and dynamized by the photographic composition. The position of bodies and limbs, their range of movement and muscular activity depicted within the image's composition mark out body configurations and their visual dynamics. As final step the sediments of the photograph's history and context(s) will be discussed examining photos as means for creation and visual uttering of knowledge.

Similar but different: bodies in movement in Nyota Inyoka's photomontage

Montaging pictures

In the photograph we see the French dancer Nyota Inyoka set against the backdrop of a time-worn, partly damaged South Indian stone relief 'Women adoring the Buddha Suggested by Throne and Feet'.[17] It shows a group of five women arranged in two side groups of two each with one woman in their middle. All depicted figures kneel with bending torso in gradual variation of bow, bodily orientation and line of sight.

The women's crouching position and their compact body posture conjoin them. Their arms stay in a normal scope of movement, creating compact body postures with equally distributed muscular strength. The depicted bodies correspond to each other through similarities in size, proportion, and dress, sameness in colour (all in black and white) and repetition of movement-lines. At first glance, the picture evokes the impression of a frieze in its rhythmic alignment and the manifold views on bodies. Looking closer, however, Nyota Inyoka's outline marks a literal cut in the materiality of bodies and their image, contrasting sharply to the relief's stone-carved bodies and their strong black and white contrasts by the diffused light on the dancer's soft body. Through the techniques of photography and montage independent pictures of bodies are not only combined, but their contents, composition, and (photographic) surfaces are blended into one another, yet exhibiting the act of their combination.

Montaging movement

Although Nyota Inyoka seems to blend into the picture very well, still her body and movement range is marked as different. The centre of the photograph is taken by her kneeling figure, bending her torso to the left side,[18] arms extended in middle distance from her body. She wears a metallic gleaming bustier, loincloth with drapery and ornaments around neck, head, wrist and upper arm. Her hair is tied back, her head tilt to the upper right, her glance directed at the distance passes by the viewer. The light focuses her torso, left arm extended across her body to the lower right and left leg turned towards the left side lead the viewer's glance in opposite directions. Right arm and leg, slightly shadowed, form a rounded line running from her knee on the floor via the bent side of her torso through her arm towards the upper left. Although her limbs are not extended fully, the placement of knees, hands and head depicts a wide range of movement and combines lines projected in diverse directions, accentuating the middle axis of her body. The viewer's glance is directed from the centre, thus accentuated and put into 'limelight' additionally, to all sides of the photo.

In the relief, the figures' legs and knees support the body in its kneeling position. Their bow is oriented downwards and towards the centre only, palms held together in a prayer-gesture, their arms tend symmetrically towards either up *or* down in one body. In contrast, those of Nyota Inyoka oppose each other in asymmetrical extension. Her posture is supported mainly by right leg and knee, while only the left toes touch the floor, a position that implies great mobility. Inyoka's bent torso continues with her raised right arm, her left arm extended downwards together with the tilted head form counter lines, which indicate a twisting tension in her body and multidirectional movement. While the carved female bodies curve in well-ordered sequence from the outside towards the centre, depicting a tightening contraction, the dancer in the middle takes up their movement, centres it, and re-projects it to several directions at the same time.

The depiction of movement in the relief can be read as sequential stages of bowing to the floor in a representation of worship. The onlooker's glance is led towards the middle, where it comes to a rest at the quiet point of the movement: the actual touching of the floor in the deepest bend of the torso, above which one sees the decorated feet and a throne symbolizing

Buddha. The religious symbolization is accentuated visually: it forms the static central viewpoint, and manifests the ritual context of the movement displayed.

In her photomontage, Inyoka covers the lowest position and the endpoint of the relief's visual lines. The position of the most intense moment in adoration is modified into a centripetal-centrifugal spiral without an end. Inyoka perpetuates the bending movement, shifts its direction and creates a different representation of the movement's temporality.

Most strikingly, besides the clearly chosen imitation of dress, is the represented movement into which Nyota Inyoka inserts her body. This movement gets montaged through imitation of the basic body posture and its variation, which includes her and sets her apart at the same time. The uniformity and sequence of bows in the relief's figures are cut against counter tensions and movability in Inyoka's body shown in a multidirectional spiral.

Montaging contexts

The fragment Nyota Inyoka combines with her own image stems from a photograph of an ancient relief found at the Buddhist Stupa of Amaravathi, South India, situated in what was called 'Madras Presidency' during the British rule. Although it remains unclear where she actually took it from, the plain frontal setup in front of a monochrome black backdrop hints at the standard catalogue setting of archaeological photographs around 1900. The stone fragment was recorded in 1882 by James Burgess (1832–1916, sometimes also spelled 'Jas' or 'Jass') on his mission to survey and preserve the archaeological sites of the colony of India and got soon included in the collection of the Madras Government Museum, India.

It is quite probable that Nyota Inyoka came about drawings of this stone in James Burgess's publications (1882 and 1887)[19] during her studies at the library of Musée Guimet. Although we find a number of photographs using a black backdrop similar to Inyoka's montage in 1887's issue, unfortunately, there is no photo of the 'Women adoring the Buddha Suggested by Throne and Feet'. But we may be quite sure she was well acquainted with archaeological books and the conventional setup of scientific photography of that time. Till now I have been unsuccessful in finding the exact photograph Nyota Inyoka could have chosen, but the Catalogue of Madras Government Museum[20] issued in 1942 includes a photographic reproduction of the stone fragment in question, however, without the black backdrop.

Considering these facts, it might be even inferred that Inyoka chose the arrangement in front of a black background for her photomontage. As a further modification of the 'original' picture, the lower half of the fragment is cut off as it displays only bare stone. It seems to have been of less importance to her to display the unaffected artefact in a surveying view than to focus on the scene depicted in it. Still the scientific context remains present through visual conventions as a meaningful framework chosen for her dance in the photomontage.

This framework is provided by two layers present in the 'original': first, an archaeological photograph of a fragment documented within the colonial project of an Archaeological Survey of India, which led James Burgess to travel through the country, engaged in excavation and documentation of his findings. The second layer is the representation of the ritual practice of women worshipping Buddha on an ancient relief.

Additionally, we find two layers of time inscribed in the photograph conjoined with the dancer's body – for us from the past, for Inyoka and her audience contemporaneous – and the fragmentary relief bearing obvious marks of age. This co-existence of different bodies from different times plays with the indexicality of a photograph and uses what Elizabeth Edwards calls 'virtual witnessing'. Edwards coins the term for the particular constellation of the image, its origin and its use: 'Photographs are exactly replicable statements on immutable mobiles, in that they transport a mechanically inscribed indexical trace, replicating information uncorrupted over space and time'. It creates a form of virtual witnessing 'you see what I saw.'[21] This 'virtual witnessing' becomes 'I move how they moved and show it to you now' in Inyoka's photomontage.

Although the ritual context stays present in her photomontage, Inyoka shifts the attention to the practice of dancing. The clearly artificial co-existence of the dancer's body and the historic relief in one photographic representation puts both forward as relics or artefacts and links them with cultural history. The dancer and her cultural action – dancing – get visually historicized by a photograph taken from an archaeological context. The construction of knowledge about Indian movement styles and body configurations as a practice of a long cultural history becomes strikingly visible and is connected as well as contrasted with Inyoka's dance.

For this transfer of her body into an archaeological photo, she chooses a photograph that is part of the construction of the view on India, its inhabitants, their history, religion and physicality within the visual discourse of colonialism.[22] Inyoka projects an ancient body on herself, takes up its image of movement, and varies it by inscribing a modern body by means of montage.

Conclusion

Inserting herself into what is marked as Indian history, Nyota Inyoka creates a vision of dance rooted in ritual practice and being subject to scientific discovery. She stages her 'rediscovery' of a sacred ancient body alluding to archaeology's unearthing of historic artefacts. In a highly modern pictorial strategy, such as photomontage, Inyoka visualizes an *archaeology of movement* framing her work as choreographer and dancer. Directed at the viewer and his/her acquiring of knowledge through photographs she interacts materially with photographic records and envisions a self-perception of her dance through photomontage. The artist literally 'steps into' the discourse of images on India with her very own particular means: her body in movement, which is confronted with the photos' meaning as she imitates and varies it. Nyota Inyoka puts the photograph's content and context in relation to her actual dance practice, which is then transferred back into photography by cutting into the photo itself in a montage of images, of movements and of histories.

Notes

1 See Pinney (2008); Edwards (2007); Banta and Hissley (1986).
2 Mazo (2000).
3 St. Denis (1939: 51ff.).
4 Shawn (1920).
5 Shelton (1981).
6 Hope 2001.
7 Shawn (1920: 64).
8 St. Denis (n.d.: 10).
9 Décoret-Ahiha (2004: 239).
10 During the first decades of the twentieth century a growing number of Euro-American dancers appeared onstage forming what can be labelled the exotic genre of early Modern Dance. Within this development the subgenre of 'numéro hindou' (see Décoret-Ahiha 2004: 131) evolved, bearing on what was called 'Indian culture', which comprised a territory from West-Pakistan to Indonesia with its manifold variations of religion, mythical narrations and arts.
11 See Fonds Nyota Inyoka at the Département des arts du spectacle, Bibliothèque nationale de France, Paris.
12 See Fonds Nyota Inyoka at the Département des arts du spectacle, Bibliothèque nationale de France, Paris; Box 1; without date and photographer's mark.
13 I rely on Nic Leonhardt's work (2007), which explores late-nineteenth-century theatre as a reception and production site for images within the theoretical framework of visual culture.
14 See Adshead-Landsale and Layson (1983).
15 Jeschke (2002: 9).
16 Jeschke (1999).
17 Shivaramurti (1942, Plate XXXVI No.2).

18 All descriptions take the dancer's body as spatial frame of reference, not that of the viewer's perspective on the photo!
19 Burgess (1882, Plate 11; 1887, Plate XLIX No. 3).
20 Shivaramurti (1942).
21 Edwards (2007: 49).
22 For detailed studies of visual discourses on India see Pinney (2008); Karlekar (2005); for the use of photography in archaeology see Banta and Hissley (1986: 72–99).

References

Adshead-Landsale, Janet, and Layson, June (eds) (1983): *Dance History. An Introduction*. London.

Banta, Melissa, and Hissley, Curtis M. (1986): *From Site to Sight. Anthropology, Photography, and the Power of Imagery; A Photographic Exhibition from the Collections of the Peabody Museum of Archaeology and Ethnology and the Department of Anthropology*. Harvard University, Cambridge.

Burgess, Jas (James) (1882): *Notes on the Amaravati Stupa*. Archaeological Survey of South India No. 3. Madras (Reprint by Prithivi Prakashan, Varanasi 1972).

Burgess, James (1887): *The Buddhist Stupas of Amaravati and Jaggayyapeta in the Krishna District, Madras Presidency surveyed in 1882*. Archaeological Survey of South India No. 6. London.

Carter, Alexandra (2004): *Rethinking Dance History. A Reader*. London.

Décoret-Ahiha, Anne (2004): *Les danses exotiques en France, 1880–1940*. Pantin.

Edwards, Elizabeth (2007): Shifting Representation. The Making of the Ethnographic in Nineteenth Century Photography. In: Bayerdörfer, H. P., Dietz, B., Heidemann, F., and Hempel, P. (eds): *Bilder des Fremden. Mediale Inszenierungen von Alterität im 19. Jahrhundert*. Berlin, 41–62.

Hope, Laurence (2001): *India's Love Lyrics. Including the Garden of Kama*. Reprint from the 1906 edition. Amsterdam.

Jeschke, Claudia (1999): *Tanz als Bewegungstext. Analysen zum Verhältnis von Tanztheater und Gesellschaftstanz (1910–1965)*. Theatron No. 28. Tübingen.

Jeschke, Claudia (2002): Tanzforschung: Geschichte – Methoden. Tanzforschung zwischen Aktion, Dokumentation und Institution. In: Gesellschafts- und Volkstanz in Österreich (Hg.): *Musicologica Austriaca. 21. Jahresschrift der Österreichischen Gesellschaft für Musikwissenschaft*. Wien, 9–36.

Karlekar, Malavika (2005): *Re-Visioning the Past. Early Photography in Bengal 1875–1915*. Delhi.

Leonhardt, Nic (2007): *Piktoral-Dramaturgie: Visuelle Kultur und Theater im 19. Jahrhundert (1869–1899)*. Bielefeld.

Mazo, Joseph H. (2000): *Prime Movers: The Makers of Modern Dance in America*. Princeton.

Pinney, Christopher (2007): The Phenomenology of Colonial Photography. In: Bayerdörfer, H. P., Dietz, B., Heidemann, F., and Hempel, P. (eds): *Bilder des Fremden. Mediale Inszenierungen von Alterität im 19. Jahrhundert*. Berlin, 19–39.

Pinney, Christopher (2008): *The Coming of Photography in India*. New Delhi.
Shawn, Ted (1920): *Ruth St. Denis – Pioneer and Prophet. Being a History of Her Cycle of Oriental Dances*. San Francisco.
Shelton, Suzanne (1981): *Ruth St. Denis. A Biography of the Divine Dancer*. Austin.
Shivaramurti, C. (1942, repr. 1956, 1977): Bulletin of the Madras Government Museum – Amaravati Sculptures in the Madras Government Museum. Vol. IV. Madras.
St. Denis, Ruth (1939): *An Unfinished Life. An Autobiography*. London, Bombay, Sidney.
St. Denis, Ruth (n.d.): *Oriental Dances and Technique*. Unpublished manuscript, Jerome Robbins Dance Division of the New York Public Library.

Archives

Bibliothèque nationale de France, Département des arts du spectacle, Paris.
Centre national de la danse, Paris.
Jerome Robbins Dance Division of the New York Public Library, New York.

10

THE COMMUNE-IST AIR: LIVING THE EVERYDAY IN TIMES OF STRUGGLE

The case of the Indian People's Theatre Association's Central Squad

Sharmistha Saha

This chapter is concerned with the Commune-ist. Its phonetical affinity to the word 'communist' is obvious and one might even wonder if that is the path this chapter aims to traverse. However, I would like to clarify from the beginning that I aim at specifically studying the Commune in the light of the Indian People's Theatre Association's Central Squad (IPTA CS) which was located at Andheri in Mumbai and functioned between 1943 and 1947.[1] It is in the context of how a certain lifestyle of living in a commune becomes a belief system that the suffix '-ist' has been added to the word commune. Here it could be highlighted that the suffix '-ist' is often used to signify a certain adherent of a belief system, practice, ideology etc. Before moving to a study of the Central Squad, I would like to lay down a theoretical framework such that our later study is facilitated and as the meaning of the term commune-ist unfolds, it stands distinctively against the word communist.

The word 'commune' immediately emits several connotations. It suggests a community, the common or even communism. Its historical significance lies in the way the idea of the commune has been implemented with political intent. The commune has been seen as that which dissolves the nation-state but at the same time as lacking 'statist capacities'. Functionally, its ability to overturn that which is normative makes the idea of the commune appealing. However, this revolutionary character of the commune is only relevant in conjuncture, for example in case of the Paris Commune. So then, what exactly is a Commune? Is it when a group of people consciously live together?

Karl Marx explains otherwise. In *Grundrisse: Foundations of the Critique of Political Economy* he asserts that forms of social life that may appear quintessentially irreparably divided and individuated are actually communal.[2] Hence for him the process of a commune might not involve an *act* insofar as an *act* could be understood as an action consciously taken forward by an agent but rather he identifies the 'original' commune in the Asiatic, ancient, Germanic and Slavonic forms as pre-capitalist mode of living. He discusses it in terms of social relations of kinship/clan where it comes to exist as a result of 'the communality of blood, language and customs'. The commune comes to represent itself, subjectively, as a unity in which propriety rights residue.[3] In this form of commune, according to him, surplus labour performed, predominantly on communal land, is appropriated by the entire clan. This sort of a commune and related forms of subsistence have often been called 'primitive communism'. On the other hand, talking about the Paris Commune, Marx talks about 'self-government'. 'It is the people acting for itself by itself' he says.[4] The Paris Commune that came into existence on 28 May 1871, following the defeat of France in the Franco-Prussian War is seen in his words as 'the reabsorption of the state power by society as its own living forces instead of as forces controlling and subduing it, by the popular masses themselves, forming their own force instead of the organized force of their suppression – the political form of their social emancipation [. . .] This form was simple like all great things.'[5]

Although essentially the two forms of communes discussed here highlight 'communality', that is they share-in-common something, for example land, space etc. at the same time *being*-in-common is emphasized, a 'substance-less substance'.[6] This 'substance-less substance' has been the 'thing' of curiosity also for anti-colonial movements, when *being*-in-common required to be emphasized, as against difference or even beyond the common something.[7] Mahatma Gandhi in the context of the Indian anti-colonial struggle clarifies his position in this regard in the *Hind Swaraj*, which he himself translated into English as Indian Home-Rule, a small booklet written in 1909 in the form of a dialogue between two characters, The Reader and The Editor. When asked by The Reader what he has to say to the nation, Gandhi asks, 'Who is the Nation?' and subsequently answers, 'it is only those Indians who are imbued with real love who will be able to speak to the English [. . .] without being frightened, and only those can be said to be so imbued who conscientiously believe that Indian civilization is the best and that the European is a nine days' wonder.'[8] However, his nationalistic commentary on the Indian civilization is not limited to the idea of 'real love' for it alone, rather it is impregnated with the idea of *swaraj* or self-rule. *Swaraj* is not only political *swaraj* or self-government but also individual *swaraj* or self-mastery. Regarding the idea of village *swaraj* he writes: 'My idea of village swaraj is that it is a complete republic, independent of its neighbours for its own vital wants, and yet interdependent for many others in which dependence is a necessity,'[9] an idea similar to what Marx calls the 'original' commune. But associated to this idea explicitly in the case of Gandhi is the idea of self-governance. To experiment with his method, Gandhi started seven *ashrams*, two in South Africa and five in India, in the beginning of the twentieth century, which were spaces of self-governance for him. They were spaces of social emancipation as Marx claimed in case of the Paris Commune. 'With members drawn from many castes, classes, religions, occupations, regions, and languages, *ashrams* provided retreats to those who wished to join a community dedicated to a new form of life, a life of simple living, service, and political activism.'[10] He called such mode of life *Satyagraha* or holding firmly to truth, where *satya* means truth and *agraha* means insistence or holding firmly. The followers of this path were called the *Satyagrahis*. During the independence movement of India these *ashrams* played an instrumental role in creating public opinion especially amongst masses. A Satyagrahi was in that sense a commune-ist as it were.

Coming back to the context of the commune in the light of IPTA CS, we need to highlight that this space of the commune that functioned for a very short period of 4–5 years, was an act of performing out a space where social relations were reinvigorated within the historical conjuncture of an anti-colonial movement. On the one hand, it was proclaimed as the 'Gandhian Ashram with pluses'[11] by the General Secretary of the Communist Party of India (CPI) Puran Chandra Joshi (PC Joshi) while on the other, it was criticized as the model of 'primitive communism' by Rajani Palme Dutt of the Communist Party of Great Britain.[12] This chapter highlights how the space of the Central Squad commune not only aimed at a 'communality' that was based on borrowed principles from the CPI but also constantly responded to anti-colonial upsurge within the surroundings of which it functioned in creating and performing the '*being-in-common*'-ness.

On 1 June 1943, the formation of the Indian People's Theatre Association or IPTA was declared at the first national conference of the CPI. But the Central Squad of the IPTA came into existence a little later when a group of performers of the IPTA Bengal Squad had come to perform at Bombay to collect money for the Bengal famine in mid-1944. It was rather on the request of some of the members of the CPI and some performers from the Indian ballet dancer Uday Shankar's troupe, that the Central Squad was founded. According to PC Joshi, it was to achieve more 'professional expertise' in the cultural work for 'freedom' not only from the British but also from various societal norms within the wider panorama of world politics that the Central Squad was started. The men and women in the squad were mostly from students' political movements. Some members lived in the commune with their families. One such member was Ravi Shankar who had joined the squad in August 1945.[13]

At the commune, life was disciplined and focused mainly at the work of the troupe. Gul Bardhan (1995), one of the female members, writes in a memoir about her days in the IPTA:

> Our first class would begin at 7 o'clock in the morning. We would exercise till 9 o'clock and then break for one hour for breakfast and cleaning the house. From 10 to 1 we would again practice till lunch break. In the afternoon from 4 o'clock, after tea, we learnt new movements and practiced compositions. We would break for tea again at 6 for half an hour and then continue till 9 or 10 at night. In a sense our routine was fixed by the kitchen bell.

Preeti Banerjee, another member, notes that the ones who were in the music group would get up a little earlier for regular riyaz (rehearsal). 'The moonlight would still be there when I would wake up [. . .] Reddy [. . .] Ravishankar [. . .] his wife (Annapurna) [. . .] Sushil would sit on the swing and do the riyaz of his flute.'

The members would often sit back after the rehearsals were over at night, to help making the costumes and other accessories necessary for the performances. Pictures of their activities in the commune such as costume making etc. were published in the magazine called *People's Age* which was the mouthpiece of the CPI. It became necessary to render the private public in order to establish its significance as work for the nation. In one such newspaper report published in the *People's Age* on 13 January 1946, Balraj Sahni, a member of the IPTA, wrote:

> Typical of the spirit of bold experiment which characterizes the IPTA are the costumes. As the curtain went up on the dress rehearsal I was struck by their glamour. The patterns are entirely new and the colours extraordinarily pleasing. It took Chittoprasad (the artist whom all readers of People's Age know quite well already) two months to design them. Incredible as it may sound these costumes are mostly made of gunny cloth [. . .] The IPTA has neither the means nor the desire to go to the black market for silks.

However, according to Preeti Banerjee, a performer of the Central Squad, not only gunny cloth but other materials were also used.[14] After lunch during the break period women would help in kitchen work. Holidays were very rare during their stay at the commune and especially during the period when a 'show' was to be held soon, the performers would hardly get time to breathe. However, Gul Bardhan writes,

> [. . .] once in a while we would get a holiday and I would run to Bombay to see three films one after another in the four-anna section. And at twelve o'clock at night I would stealthily climb a tree and enter the bungalow. Abani-da[15] used to visit us around ten o'clock to see whether the whole group was in bed or not. So I used to arrange the bed beforehand in such a way that it looked as if someone was sleeping in it. [. . .] Other members would go and spend their five rupees (the monthly allowance was 40 rupees according to most of the members of which one had to pay for food separately) on a good meal.[16]

The rituals of everyday were carefully choreographed, in order to not only meet the needs of the performances but also create national subjects. The entire process was voluntary. The banalities of life gained significance in order to not only establish the significance of what was being done as having importance in national life but also purge theatre and dance of the prejudices that were attached to it mainly in the middle class urban population. The details of everyday were linked to ethical issues of social significance. The public discussion of such details aimed at bridging the gap between the performer/activist/revolutionary and the masses. It was in the manner of the Gandhian ashram that life was being performed in order to create democratized spheres of public interaction especially against Colonial government.[17]

Within the limited scope of this chapter, it would not be possible to discuss the several processes of the Central Squad which re-contextualized the everyday life of the Central Squad performers from mundane inconsequential activities to work that was worthwhile. However, to highlight the transformation that was happening I would like to quote from an interview of Preeti Banerjee. In an interview with Dhruv Gupta she notes: 'Before this we had done different kind of work outside – we were not used to staying inside the house and practicing for hours. Joshi (the general secretary of the CPI) had told us then – now your true work is to play the *tanpura* (stringed musical instrument) and devote your time to *riyaz* and rehearsing your steps.'[18]

The *riyaz* or rehearsal not only was for a good 'show' but, as PC Joshi said, for them was also 'true work' – a work that would eventually lead them somewhere – they were not sure exactly where – but a place and time which would become as true as their work in their present. And this nostalgia for the truth – a future of their own gave them the impetus to deal with their difficult lifestyle 'inside', an 'inner domain' – dislodged or rather subsumed any form of closure and opened up the space for a metamorphosis, transformation, innovation, reorganization, restructuring or revolution. However, it should not be assumed that this is what exactly happened. On reading the IPTA Central Squad performances and the narratives of the Central Squad, one finds how the re-contextualization transformed into textualization of those very narratives and performance modes that once held potential of revolution. Let us look at the performances of the IPTA Central Squad.

The Bengal Squad that came to perform in Bombay in mid-1944 had the sole purpose of sociopolitical good in mind. As has been already mentioned, it had come to collect funds for the Bengal famine that had affected a huge population in the area of the then Bengal Presidency. PC Joshi mentions in a memoir of Balraj Sahni that, although these performances had vigour and had opened up new horizons, what they inevitably suffered from was 'amateurishness'. He writes about the IPTA that was formed in 1943 and had already started functioning, often as small groups, even before it was formally declared to have been founded, under the patronage of the CPI:

> What made the IPTA really well-known then and famous later was their choir of patriotic songs from all the languages of India together with folk songs with a social content and moving tunes [. . .] We had deliberately adopted the policy of young Left intellectuals with cultural talent, to learn, perform and popularize the folk heritage of the various parts of our vast and ancient land [. . .][19]

However, as PC Joshi notes, it was to achieve 'professional expertise' in the 'work of the nation' that the Central Squad was founded. Hence the aim of the Central Squad, as was chalked down by the general secretary PC Joshi, was to etch the formal aspects of the performances. The congregation that created the IPTA Central Squad hence comprised many experts in dance, music, etc. who did not necessarily agree with the ideological inclinations of the Communist Party but agreed to join the Central Squad on the grounds that the group had already acquired some name in its work for the nation and also substantially contributed to the anti-colonial movement. Shanti Bardhan, the choreographer of the Central Squad, who was already a trainer at the Uday Shankar India Cultural Centre, Abani Dasgupta, a musician again from the Uday Shankar India Culture Centre, who joined as the music director of the Central Squad and who was later joined by the ace *Sitarist* Ravi Shankar, therefore, became names associated to the IPTA Central Squad in order to give it the professional expertise it required. Here it needs to be mentioned that 'Uday Shankar India Culture Centre' at Almora was opened by Uday Shankar, a ballet dancer himself, with an aim of creating a modern school for dance and music training. He had been immensely inspired by the idea of giving a national form to the performing arts of India. With the financial support of some friends, independent sponsors[20] and the money he collected from his performances he founded the 'Uday Shankar India Culture Centre' at Almora, which started working on 3 March 1940, modelled on the Dartington Hall in England. Uday Shankar appointed stalwarts of dance forms like Kathakali, Bharata Natyam, Manipuri and also of music in his centre. Rabindranath Tagore was striving to do the same in Shantiniketan and Rukmini Devi Arundale was reviving Bharata Natyam at Kalakshetra that she founded in 1936. According to Sudhi Pradhan, Uday Shankar's work was also informed in the 1940s by the 'floating news' of 'his Bengal's dying people'.[21] He collected money for the Bengal famine through his performances at Delhi. Influenced by the socialist maxim that had given rise to socialist realism in Russia, Brechtian alienation techniques and other modernist cultural movements in Europe like German Expressionism (the influence of which becomes apparent in Shankar's film *Kalpana*), whose experiences he had gathered during the extensive tours in Europe, he had earlier created the ballet Labour and machinery. In Delhi in one of his performances through a symbolic use of the sickle he tried to portray that the socioeconomic problem in India was essentially linked to the peasant and farmers. *Janajuddho*, the mouthpiece of the CPI, reports on 23 November 1943:

> [. . .] the world famous dancer Uday Shankar is going to Bombay along with his troupe. His manager has informed the leadership of Bombay IPTA that he is going to present his dance in front of the working class with nominal charges of tickets. Most of the money collected from the ticket sale will be given to the IPTA – the IPTA will spend this money on the victims of the Bengal famine [. . .] We hope that the efforts of a world class artist like Uday Shankar would inspire other artists.

Such presentations also brought him criticisms such as Uday Shankar has left the 'throne of the pure golden art' and has become a sociopolitical 'propagandist'.[22] However, when due to lack of funds the Almora centre had to be shut down, Shanti Bardhan, Abani Dasgupta and many others joined the IPTA Central Squad and it could also be argued that they brought along the aesthetics of the ballet form that Uday Shankar had by now mastered.

IPTA's rationale could be identified by its most invigorating slogan 'People's theatre stars the People.' This slogan in its humanistic passion creates the new social icon of the national 'people'. Typical to any performative ritual, the first performance of the first season of the IPTA CS started with the 'Call of the Drum'. The souvenir for this performance claims it to be 'Dance of Invocation for the Youth of India, rousing them to patriotism.' This was followed by the song composed by Ravi Shankar 'sare jahan se achha' – a 'people' better than any other 'people' as it were; 'hum bulbulein hain us ki, woh gulsitah humara' or we are its nightingales and it is our garden abode. The claim to difference lay in the very beginning of proclaiming the *being*-in-common within the abode or home. The difference was claimed by not only declaring it, but also establishing it. 'She died of hunger' – a solo dance in classical style portraying the sorrow of a peasant of Bengal who arrives home to find that his wife and companion has died of hunger acts as a newspaper report of the events that were taking place in Bengal.

The Bengal famine of the early 1940s was known to be a man-made famine whereby more than 60 million people died only in Bengal. The exploitation of the people by the British was one of the key elements to affirm difference and declare the British Rule as illegitimate. *Being*-in-common was performed in tabloid form depicting the various forms of cultural life of the different folks of India. According to Sunil Munshi who was among the audience at some of the performances of the IPTA Central Squad, the performances were a collection of items one after the other, not necessarily interlinked by any logic of narration.[23] The aesthetic of these tabloids was borrowed from the picture tabloids which were published in the magazine of the CPI regularly. These picture tabloids highlighted the lives of 'working class', 'peasants' and 'real people' of India. Thus, 'Lambardi Dance' – 'A simple folk dance of the Lambardis, a gypsy tribe living in Hyderabad State', 'Dhobi Dance' – 'A folk dance commonly seen among the Dhobis of Andhra', 'Collective Farmers' Harvest Dance' – 'This incorporates folk dances and music of more than one province of the Punjab, of Bengal, of Andhra and of the U.P.', 'Ramleela' – 'The troupe present a scene from the story of Ramchandra in a folk form very commonly seen in the UP villages', of the first season and 'Sentry Dance' – 'The guards in the Frontier

Provinces as they dance together at night in peace time', 'Gajan' – folk dance of Bengal in which 'Shiva and Parvati, with their followers compete in dancing', 'Khadaun' – 'A classical form of dancing with intricate foot-work, with wooden sandals' and 'Chaturanga' of the Northeast and Bengal, 'Holi' – 'A glimpse of the colour festival in UP [. . .]' of the second season, were incorporated as ethnographic tabloids. The aim was to create a singular narrative interweaving 'communities of location' or networks of relationship formed by face-to-face interaction within a geographically bounded area to 'communities of interest' or networks of association that are predominantly characterized by their commitment to a common interest – in this case an interest of identifying a nation in the *communality* or sharing-in-common of diversity that in turn created that 'substanceless substance' of *being*-in-common.

From 1945 onwards IPTA CS came to be known as the Central Cultural Troupe. Now a Squad can be understood as a crew, squadron or cadre (a term made famous by communist use) that performs a function and brings a certain action to its completion, whereas a troupe is one that is a band, an ensemble that performs, but that performance is not guided by any function that it consciously carries forward. By the beginning of the second season of the CS performances, the activist fervor had been eclipsed by a need '(to give) philip to creative activity',[24] although it continued to maintain its *historical* tour of the new 'people' even in its second season. Both the ballets *Spirit of India* which the souvenir writes 'is a ballet based on the story of India since the advent of the British' of the first season and *India Immortal* – 'gives a picture of India from the earliest times to the present days touching momentous events that form the landmarks in the cultural history of India' (Pradhan 1979: 379, 386) – were demonstrations of a journey towards a 'people' *to be*, from a 'people' *that has been*. IPTA CS performances exemplified a federation of *people(s)* whose icon or 'star' is the 'people' itself, meaning that the supreme power of representing lies in the hands of this 'people' that it stars. But compared to the first season of its performances, in the second season this 'people' does not remain a common 'man' anymore but becomes the 'artist' who invokes not 'man' but a higher power in order to craft the 'people' using his artistry through 'intricate' work. But in both cases, the objective is naturalized by a historical logic of a 'spirit' of India and then a more self-determined 'immortal' India that imbibed its determination from a 'glorious' historical past.

> *Aj shonabo ki kahini srihina bharatbhumir*
> *Sampode shourjey chhilo jar sreshtho ashon dhoronir*
> *Shatto nyayer deep jalilo buddho namey raj tonoy*

Kabir hetha hindu muslim Milan-bani bilay
Raja Ashok badshah Akbarer raj ki hoe smaran
Shanti shukh o nyay dharmey sharthak proja palon. (Spirit of India)[25]
(What story would I tell you about the once beautiful land of Bharat/ Wealth and valor had made it the best in the world/ Buddha lit the candle of truth and justice/ Kabir spread the word of hindu–muslim unity/ Does one remember the rule of Raja Ashoka and Badshah Akbar/ The rule of the subject was based on peace, happiness and the *dharma* of justice.)

This tendency of giving form to the 'substance-less substance' in the name of a spirit or an inner being of a certain locatable people on the basis not only of 'real love' as Gandhi would have it but also of creation of difference, a dual creative process of not any dialectical movement but rather an obsession with an almost photographic tabloid-like form, shifted the concerns of the IPTA CS commune. Many members not only of the CS but also of the CPI went through a phase of doubt about the role of such a commune. This phase of doubt could be somewhat identified from the ballets of the two seasons. The narrative of *The Spirit of India* of the first season was borrowed from the earlier famine plays like 'Nabanna' (New Harvest) and 'Antim Abhilasha/Jaban Bandi' (Last Wish). In that sense it was more of a narrative that was still under the effect of a historical reflex that motivates the other famine narratives. But at the same time, this performance of the CS was one of the first few performances that hints towards a glorious 'past' of a united India, but even then that 'past' remains limited to 'tales of heroism' alone, rather than the representation of any pre-existent cultural monumentality. The narrative ends leaving the possibility of an act to change the existent modalities of 'being'. Apart from the famine narrative that the IPTA had been using successfully in mobilizing relief funds as well as anti-colonial sentiments, the performances in this season included *They Must Meet Again*, whose theme was directly taken from the CPI's agenda of 'sovereign national constituencies' elected by universal suffrage on the basis of linguistic regions (modelled on the Russian Leninist model of mini-nationalities) and electing in their turn an all-India Constituent Assembly, with each region or 'nationality' retaining a right to secession.[26] The narrative of a singular history in *The Spirit of India* at the wake of a demand of 'sovereign national constituencies' hence becomes a representation of the agenda of CPI, as it was at this point that CPI also demanded for such 'constituencies', which in turn would elect 'an all-India Constituent Assembly'. With these performances the IPTA CS had gained much popularity, and Ravi Shankar and many others of Uday Shankar's Almora Troupe joined the group. During this phase the second season ballet of the CS was produced which was called *Immortal India*. It 'gives a picture of India from the earliest times to the present days touching momentous events that form landmarks in the cultural history of India. It starts from early worship of the Himalayas and passes through past impacts of culture to modern times.' The obsession with a national culture increases in the performances of the second season of the CS giving it a monumentality that it did not have earlier. Both Ravi Shankar, the director of music in this season, and Shanti Bardhan, the director of dance in the season, mention 'our rich cultural heritage, handed down from generation to generation' (Pradhan 1979: 383) in the notes written for the brochure by them. In this ballet, a worker dreams of 'puja' and 'invocation dance' in the Himalayas, rivers-land-harvest, Buddhists-Muslims-Chaitanyas – 'all our people flourish together'. A magician charms this *people* with his magic flute. 'Traitor plans against the Nawab with the Magician – Nawab is overthrown and crown given to traitor – traitor and magician together rob the people . . . Individual revolts of the people against this oppression are suppressed by the magician – the people rise once again in an attempt to revive their own culture.' The ballet ends with the black marketeers and hoarders 'devour(ing) the food and cloth themselves and dance(ing) in frenzy – the dream (of the worker) is shattered – one women with a child in her arms rises alone questioning whether life will always be dark [. . .] but the answer is heard that the people unite, will rise and will fight to be free' (ibid.: 388). Thus, a singular narrative driven by the existence of a 'national culture' and shared experience of exploitation by the foreign 'magician' runs along the linear thread of fictional/real accounts.

At this point it is necessary to note that the CPI between 1942 and 1945 had received serious setback as a popular political movement as a result of the continuous tension that it faced due to the contradictions of Nationalism's localized logic and Communism's universal dialectic. While British policies during this period of war remained extremely repressive and reactionary, Britain also happened to be an ally of the socialist state Soviet Russia, when Hitler invaded Russia. After a lot of hesitation, in January 1942 the CPI lined up with the international communist movement calling for support to the anti-fascist 'people's war' even while reiterating the standard Congress demands for independence and immediate national government. But such a dual position of both support of war, whose effects were directly making an impression in India in terms of socioeconomic consequences, and also, antagonism towards the colonial rule of the same British government, although that no more remained a precondition for support to the national movement, on the one hand helped lift the ban on the party, making it easy for the party to work, and on the other hand, made the party extremely unpopular. The performances of the IPTA CS and the call for 'unity' in order to form a national community on the grounds of the existence of a singular linear past in the post-war situation was a strategy also to win back the people it had lost during the war years. Preeti Banerjee remembers: 'In 1942 the party made a huge mistake – during the movement (Quit India), our cultural movement could break that isolation [. . .] the isolation due to the position on "people's war" could be overcome because of our cultural effort.'[27]

Thus through a coalition of histories the CS created a performance of paradox whereby, on the one hand, it upheld the liberal democratic rhetoric of nationalism through the use of linear narratives and on the other hand highlighted issues that were thought to be in alignment with the Marxist universal logic of a classless society. The huge success of the IPTA CS performances of the first two seasons was not merely due to its complete potential to represent a national culture that the national bourgeoisie aimed for, or due to the sincere socioeconomic issues that these performances often talked about in concurrence with the CPI's often chaotic agendas, but more fundamentally it was a result of a *communitas* that it created for itself. By *communitas* is meant 'a direct, immediate and total confrontation of human identities'[28] whereby it (the *communitas*) allows performance to 'play' with the audience's fundamental beliefs, without producing immediate rejection. For it is 'the ludic nature of the audience's role that allows it to engage with ideological difference, that allows rules to be broken (via authenticating conventions) while rules are kept (via rhetorical conventions). This paradox links theatrical performance to carnival and other forms of public celebration' (Kersaw 1992: 28). The IPTA CS performances thus became unique in their successful juggling with different 'identities' and 'ideologies'. PC Joshi writes:

> The Central Troupe of the IPTA was just coming into its own not only politically, professionally and organizationally, but also earning a reputation for attempting something unique and distinctive in our cultural life. It is then, during the end of 1947, that a sectarian offensive inspired by the incorrigibly Left comrade Ranadive was put into operation through the good-hearted but narrow minded treasurer, Ghate. As the treasurer, he complained that too much of the central funds were being wasted in cultural work by subsidizing the IPTA troupe while its earnings were nominal.[29]

Gul Bardhan remembers this period:

> In 1946 we did an all-India tour and went to Lahore with *India Immortal* [. . .] The left in the party felt that the Central Squad was a white elephant. 'So much money is spent and they won't even work for Party propaganda' (apparently they were asked to do a performance on the two nation theory, which was not even the CPI's agenda, but what is possible is that they were asked to do a performance on 'sovereign constituent nationalities' as against a federal system that the Congress had proposed) [. . .] So, after a very successful all-India tour with *India Immortal* the Party disbanded the Central Squad. During our tour we received a lot of appreciation everywhere we went and because of our work a large number of intellectuals and artists came closer to the Party and many became Party supporters. But the Party did not realize that. When we returned to Bombay we were told that it had been decided to disband the Central Squad. Naturally the sword first fell on Shanti Bardhan and four others who were not party members. They had to leave. There was no debate or discussion. So Shanti-da, Ravi Shankar, Abani-da, Sachin and Narendra Sharma left together. All the members of the Central Squad felt very sad and sorry about the whole thing. We felt that this was absolutely wrong but we were too young to speak against the leadership.
>
> Bardhan (1995: 42)

One of the reasons for the party's high-handedness regarding this issue was its newly found self-confidence. After the war years, especially after the victory of Soviet Russia over the fascist powers, CPI could move on from its 'people's war' line to more populist regional agendas in order to recover from the damage that their party line had caused them in terms of popularity during the war years. They pioneered the Kisan Sabha[30] movement, trade union activities, in providing leadership to the Telangana[31] movement in Hyderabad, Tebhaga[32] Movement in Bengal, movements in Kerala etc. which ultimately resulted in their emerging as 'the principle contenders of the Congress in several provinces' in the election of 1946.[33] But at the same time continuous attack on the communists with regard to their earlier anti-Quit India Movement and 'people's war' positions, bitterness resulting from the trials of the Indian National Army (INA) war prisoners (who under the leadership of Subhas Chandra Bose asked for the help of Japan, an ally of Germany in liberating India), and condemnation of their violent actions against the government by the Congress and mainly by Gandhi, often created isolations (in spite of their position of a Congress, Muslim League and Communist united leadership against the Imperial forces) which resulted in a ghetto-like mentality amongst many of the CPI members, and this also created the need to shield itself more sternly even in their involvement with the CS as they dictated the terms with frequent 'do this, edit that'[34] vigilance.

After the IPTA CS was disbanded Shanti Bardhan, Ravi Shankar, Sachin Shankar and Narendra Sharma joined the 'Indian National Theatre' of the Congress where they produced *Discovery of India* conceptualized by Jawaharlal Nehru. The rest of the troupe continued with their work at Andheri and produced a third season of performances in 1946–47. Preeti Banerjee recalls:

> I have forgotten the names of the items, actually these are memories of long ago, although I remember the names of the ones that we performed earlier – those of 45–46 [. . .] the songs would be composed by Benoy-da [Benoy Roy], others would add folk tunes of different regions – Dashrathlal would add folk tunes of Bihar, Prem [Dhawan those of Punjab]. Benoy-da would write the songs and the Hindi ones would be written by Prem [. . .] These were not performed for many days though.[35]

The third season of the performances were more propagandist in nature. The two main ballets of this season, *Naval Mutiny* and *Kashmir*, were directly conceptualized from the party's position on the Royal Indian Navy (RIN) mutiny in Bombay on 18–23 February 1946, and its agenda of forming 'sovereign constituent assemblies'. In an interview with Dhruvo Gupta taken in 1988 she remembers:

> [. . .] we had prepared a ballet on the RIN mutiny in Bombay. We would begin with the song 'jana gana mana' [this became the national anthem of India after Independence]. The British government had banned all the items of this season including 'jana gana mana'. The song 'vande mataram' would be allowed. We would secretly perform the ballets by changing their names. Nobody would rent us auditoriums [. . .] we made our own stage within the compounds of the house at Andheri, where we would perform the ballets. We would invite the navy personnel.

Reba Roychoudhury mentions some other items they had performed in this season like 'Gandhi-Jinnah phir miley' on the talks between Gandhi and

THE COMMUNE-IST AIR

the Muslim League leader Jinnah on the issue of separate nation-state formations, and 'New Village', where a village woman kills an exploitative feudal lord etc.[36] The use of communist propaganda became apparent not only in the contents used during this period but also in the apparent use of communist symbols. For example, in the ballet called 'New Village', one of the songs explicitly refers to the red symbol.

> . . . *hindu muslim bhed mitaiboi shob mil korboi kamo Beet gayi hai sab durdinwa Ek shonge jiiboi ek shonge morboii Chahe jae poranwa Kisan Sabha ke baat manbei kor bai shob kahanwa*
> *Hum uraibei lal nishanwa.*[37]
> (. . . we shall destroy the clash between the Hindu Muslims, together we shall diminish it/ The bad days are gone/ We shall live and die together/ Let our lives leave us/ We shall listen to Kisan sabha and do as has been said/ We will flow the *Red symbol*.)

Although for some time the CPI financially supported their work but within a year of disbanding the CS, the remaining members were asked to go back to their own regions and 'use whatever you have learnt' (Reba Roychoudhury talking about what PC Joshi had told them) in their work at the regional IPTAs.

IPTA CS had lost its earlier vigor in its third season of performances as the day of liberation of India from the rule of the British government approached nearer. When Dhruvo Gupta asked Preeti Banerjee for the reason behind this she replied, 'I think it was not the failure of the IPTA alone – rather our failure in everything – the private ego had become more important than the collective, the fall within the group, one should see it adding to all of these.'

According to Shanta Gandhi,

> the entire IPTA period movement was basically based on humanism, a humanism of a very left orientation. Marxism had played a very leading role. People connected with the communist party that had been the driving force in this and it was through these people that the movement was linked up with the people's movement like Kisan movement, Trade Union movement, student's movement, women's movement [. . .] there was no difference of goal in getting the British out [. . .] This was not possible after Independence [. . .].[38]

IPTA CS had set out to form a *national community* through the use of the narratives of real/fictional, linear/tabloid-esque paradoxical understandings of history. The efficacious objective of the CS in the multiplicity of contextualities and ideologies driven both by nationalism and universalism at the same time did succeed in creating a huge support base among the people, which I have called *communitas*, borrowing from Victor Turner. But in itself the troupe of the CS could not remain a 'community' as a result of the very clashes that created a *communitas* for them. The commune-ists who once believed in the possibilities of such a space slowly started getting disillusioned as a more concrete image of the nation appeared. This new image was not that of an alternative space, but rather a space free of any elements of difference to the British – the *raison d'être* of their coming together. The proposal in post-independent India was to disassociate theatre from any specific political programme and to rethink it comprehensively in relation to the remote and proximate past. In the 1956 Drama Seminar organized by the Sangeet Natak Akademi, a government institution for the promotion of performing arts, it was felt by erstwhile members of the IPTA like Balraj Sahni that colonial and late colonial theatre institutions were no longer usable and it was necessary to anticipate a future theatre radically unrelated to its colonial past.[39] Hence the commune-ist air in colonial India that once held possibilities of questioning power, in the form of performing banalities and *living* or rather *acting* everyday out while performance for an audience was rehearsed, was ultimately abandoned. In a new-India, the commune was replaced by the nation itself that had already discovered itself as it were.

Notes

1 The Commune was started in 1942 by the Communist Party of India for its members.
2 Amariglio (2010: 330).
3 'Marx does not privilege the idea that the direct producer of surplus is an individuated, labouring subjective entity over a subjectivity in which, or through which, the commune/clan is the unity to which the term direct producer can be applied. The notion of a direct producer, or worker, is seen as a historical product' (Amariglio 2010: 333).
4 Marx (1980: 130).
5 Ibid.: 153.
6 Curcio and Özselçuk (2010: 308).
7 For Maurice Blanchot (1988), this could be the simple absence of conditions which he calls the negative community. Agamben (2009) sees the possibility of politics in this absence, something that rejects all identity and every condition of belonging.
8 Indian Opinion (Gujarat Columns), 11–12–1909, 18–12–1909: 66.
9 Harijan, 26–7–1942, 76: 308–309.
10 Hoeber Rudolph and Rudolph (1967: 152).
11 Joshi (1974: 59).

12 Ram Rehman quotes the incident from Sunil Janah's unpublished autobiography in the 14th PC Joshi Memorial Lecture delivered by him on 'Sunil Janah, Photographer and PC Joshi: the Making of a Progressive Culture' in 2010.
13 According to the Second Souvenir, the pamphlet of the IPTA Central Squad (cp. Pradhan 1979). According to a report by Balraj Sahni in *People's Age* published on 13 January 1946, it was 1946.
14 In an interview with me on 4 May 2010 at Kolkata.
15 Abani Dasgupta was a musician of the Central Squad. *Da* is a way of addressing the older men (often in the sense of brother, but not necessarily).
16 Bardhan (1995: 40).
17 However, it would be too far-fetched to argue that all social normatives were questioned in the context of the commune. Heteronormative binaries were often not only not addressed but rather reinforced in the daily banality of activities. I have in mind the accusation of Reba Roychoudhury, a performer of the Central Squad, in her autobiography *Jibaner Tane Shilper Tane*. She wrote about an occasion where she felt discriminated by the general secretary PC Joshi for not looking good enough (not being of 'fair' skin like Preeti Banerjee).
18 Gupta (1988: 5) (translation from Bengali mine).
19 Joshi (1974: 63–65).
20 Including Alice Boner, Michael Chekhov, Mr. and Mrs. Leonard Elmhirst, John Martin, Jawaharlal Nehru, Sir Ferozkhan Noon, Sir Chinubhai Madhavlal Ranchhodlal, Romain Rolland, Sir William Rothenstein, Leopold Stokowski, Mr. Whitney and Lady Daphne Straight and Rabindranath Tagore.
21 Uday Shankar was Bengali.
22 Pradhan (1977).
23 Sunil Munshi interviewed by me at Kolkata on 14 August 2009.
24 Ravi Shankar in the Second Souvenir of IPTA CS, cp. Pradhan (1979: 383).
25 Roychoudhury (1990: 37).
26 The CPI had made its positions clear earlier in 1942 in an article 'National Unity Now' published in *People's Age* on 8 August by asserting that the Muslim League leadership was 'playing an oppositional role vis-à-vis imperialism in a way somewhat analogous to the leadership of Indian National Congress itself . . .'
27 In an interview with me taken in 2010.
28 Turner (1982: 47).
29 Joshi (1974: 69).
30 Name of the peasant's front founded in 1936 at the Lucknow session of the Indian National Congress. It demanded the abolition of the existent feudal system and other oppressive taxes on the peasants. Although founded by the initiative of the left inclined individuals of the Congress, it came fully under the control of CPI in 1942 around the time CPI was fully legalized.
31 The Nizam of Hyderabad wanted an independent status as was enjoyed by the princely states during the independence of India. A movement was created called 'Join India' in order to include Hyderabad within the Indian nation against the Nizam's wish. Peasants joined the movement under the leadership of CPI which came to be known as the Telangana rebellion. The peasants wanted the abolition of the feudal system. In 1948, the Government of India with the help of the Indian Army assimilated Hyderabad into the nation in an operation called 'Operation Polo'.

32 The Tebhaga Movement was initiated by the Kisan Sabha in order to increase the share of crops of the peasants from the landowners. Tebhaga which literally means one-third share was their demand that they would give to the landowners against the half of the crop share that they gave.
33 Sarkar (2006: 426).
34 Shankar (2006: 127).
35 In an interview with me on 4 May 2010 at Kolkata.
36 In an interview with Khaled Choudhury (from the collection of *Natyashodh Sansthan*, Kolkata; date unavailable).
37 Roychoudhury (1990: 45).
38 In an interview with Pratibha Agarwal on 28 August 1984 (from the collection of *Natyashodh Sansthan*, Kolkata).
39 Dharwadker (2005: 38).

References

Agamben, Giorgio (2009): The Coming Community. Trans. Michael Hardt. In: Theory out of Bounds. Vol. I. Minneapolis: University of Minnesota Press.

Amariglio, Jack: Subjectivity, Class, and Marx's 'Forms of the Commune'. In: Joseph Childers et al. (eds): Rethinking Marxism: Special Issue on the Common and the Forms of the Commune, Volume 22, No. 3, July 2010: 329–344. Routledge Taylor and Francis Group.

Bardhan, Gul: What a Tremendous Movement It Was... In: Seagull Theatre Quarterly, Issue 7, October 1995.

Blanchot, Maurice (1988): The Unavowable Community: Trans. Pierre Joris. New York: Station Hill Press.

Curcio, Anna, and Özselçuk, Ceren: Introduction: The Common and the Forms of the Commune. In: Joseph Childers et al. (eds): Rethinking Marxism: Special Issue on the Common and the Forms of the Commune, Vol. 22, No. 3, July 2010: 304–311. Routledge Taylor and Francis Group.

Dharwadker, Aparna Bhargava (2005): Theatres of Independence: Drama, Theory, and Urban Performance in India since 1947. Iowa City: University of Iowa Press.

Gupta, Dhruv: Charer doshok: uttal shomoy. Acharya, Anil (ed.): Vol. 4, 1988. Anushtup: Kolkata.

Hoeber Rudolph, Susanne, and Rudolph, Lloyd I. (1967): The Coffee House and the Ashram Revisited: How Gandhi Democratized Habermas' Public Sphere. In: Rudolph, Lloyd I., and Hoeber Rudolph, Susanne (eds): Postmodern Gandhi and other essays: Gandhi in the World and at Home. Chicago, London: University of Chicago Press, 140–174.

Joshi, Puran Chandra (ed.) (1974): A Dedicated and Creative Life. New Delhi: Vikas Publishing House.

Kersaw, Baz (1992): The Politics of Performance: Radical Theatre as Cultural Intervention: London, New York: Routledge.

Marx, Karl (1980): On the Paris Commune. Moscow: Progress Publishers.

Pradhan, Sudhi (1977, October): Gananatya Sangho o Uday Shankar. Kolkata: Gananatya.
Pradhan, Sudhi (ed.) 1979: Marxist Cultural Movement in India: Chronicles and Documents (1936–1947): New Delhi: National Book Agency.
Roychoudhury, Sajal (1990): Gananatya Katha. Kolkata: Mitra and Ghosh Publishers.
Sarkar, Sumit (2006): Modern India 1885–1947. New Delhi: Macmillan.
Shankar, Ravi (2006, December): *Raag Anuraag*. Kolkata: Ananda.
Turner, Victor (1982): From Ritual to Theatre. New York: Performing Arts Journal Pub.

11
FINDING A PATH
Notes on political forms between locality and globality in India's contemporary 'art world'

Sarah Ralfs

I spent three months in India as an exchange PhD student at the Tata Institute of Social Science in Mumbai, one month of which I travelled through the south of India.

My research topic while in Mumbai, and later in various other areas in India, was the question of political art forms in local contemporary artistic practices. I was interested in the ways such practices deal with the social structures, problems, paradoxes and complexities of India's diverse and heterogeneous society; how they refer to relations between the local, the nation state and the global; and how they balance traditional and contemporary artistic forms arising from new technological media.

In the following, I would like to introduce and discuss three different examples of contemporary cultural and artistic productions, each of which deals in different ways with questions, problems and potentials of the plurality of cultural and social tradition, of tradition and change, of the local and the global and of the political potentials of artistic practice in terms of an adequate critical addressing of the problems, conflicts and issues in India's complex and versatile contemporary society, embedded and interwoven in global structures, patterns and conflicts. All three case studies present different artistic practices, media and forms and come from various places in India.[1]

Pad.ma[2]

The discovery of my first example, the Internet database Pad.ma, offered me the opportunity of navigating and mapping, of finding a path within India's advanced critical contemporary art practices and alternative cultural productions.

Pad.ma is the acronym and URL for Public Access Digital Media Archive. It is run by the Mumbai-based film collectives and artist groups Majlis, Point of View and Camp as well as the Alternative Law Forum in Bangalore. The Berlin-based collective 0×2620 has installed the page with specific software for digital archives, which they developed by themselves.

The archive consists of various documentary films and videos portraying people, spaces, social environments and conflicts in India and its neighbouring regions and countries while choosing different focuses and lenses. From religion to art, culture, war, poverty, social infrastructure, work and everyday life you find a variety of topics and issues. The material is generated and produced by the film collectives and various other filmmakers not only from India. You also find historical films in the database as, for example, the collection of Afghani films from the Afghan Film Archive in Kabul, exhibited through the Pad.ma-interface in dOCUMENTA 13.

The documentary footage is uploaded as unedited raw material. Following the idea of direct cinema, the films and videos are shot by small teams of one to three people, while the terms of production are made transparent through dense annotation. All dialogue from the variety of Indian languages (e.g. Hindi, Marathi and Gujarati) is transcribed into English. The technical operations of direction and framing are described with these explanations and appear in a side frame, along with the translations of the spoken text, while you are watching. These attempts to elucidate the work stem from a general concern to avoid audio-visual exploitation, obfuscation or (false) representation. There is no interpretation, added narration or affection by voice over. Nor are there any other devices used to influence the viewer.

This way the filmmakers try to achieve a new kind of visibility and to conserve their voices and positions within a global cosmos and its orders and patterns of representation. On the one front, they decline to format their work for entertainment or commercial purposes. On the other, they resist the reproduction of global power structures and asymmetries transported by those conventional patterns and structures of representation and narration.[3] These joint ethical-aesthetic principles are combined with and embedded in questions of artistic and cultural production like authorship, copyright, collectivity, distribution and accessibility, exploring them in alternative, innovative and advanced ways.

The Pad.ma material, available to anyone with access to the Internet, is allowed to be reproduced and used as artistic or scientific material. It can be re-edited, re-arranged and re-contextualized with other materials and can further be uploaded and published in the archive if minimally annotated and transcribed.

The idea of common production is bound to the premise that the material itself implies more than a single producer. All users can expand and extend the material by commenting, re-editing and re-contextualizing the audio-visual narrations (of an alternative and under-represented worldview). As Maximilian Linz notes in his Pad.ma profile, this 'could at least theoretically be continued infinitely, because on the basis of the present material in the archive the thread could be taken up over and over again, while differently every time'.[4] The aim of the archive is not to achieve an end or to produce closure, but to generate openness and enable connections. Again quoting Linz: 'Pad.ma keeps the past present in order to remind that the history of the real is not a finished narration, but an open process for which nobody could claim authorship nor copy right.'[5]

Ninasam

My second example differs from the first in various ways, but I 'discovered' it through the digital archive Pad.ma, so I assumed that they must share some general ideas and principles of cultural and artistic production and decided to visit the theatre institution Ninasam in the hinterland of the South Indian state Karnataka in December 2012 as part of my journey to encounter innovative, politically conscious and emancipatory theatre, performance groups and practices.

Ninasam was founded in 1949 and started as a cultural exchange and amateur theatre amongst a group of inhabitants of the village Heggodu and its surrounding under the name Nilakanteshwara Natyaseva Samgha, the name of a local goddess. The theatre group has remained at the heart of the institution. Under the acronym Ninasam the institution has become gradually more professional and more public as it has extended its field of activities to include an annual cultural symposium with established intellectuals, inclusive of workshops, film screenings and publications[6] within the following decades. The Ninasam Theatre Institute was founded in 1980 as a training place for young theatre scholars. Its alumni work as a touring company named Tirugata, travelling to local villages and in tribal regions every year from October to March. After the death of founder K.V. Subbana, who is vividly remembered and whose ideas still have a strong impact on the current work at Ninasam, his son Akshara V.K. is leading the institution.

Ninasam has three stages, two of which are smaller and located on a campus comprising a meadow. From outside, the campus buildings – stages, library and student hostels – could easily be mistaken for beautiful stables. The third, huge stage is built outside of the fenced-in area and opens onto the village's main street forming a semicircle together with an administration building, canteen, guest hostel and a small publishing house. All of the buildings have been made in the local style. They ideally correspond to the climate conditions and perfectly fit into their environment with bricks fabricated from Karnataka's red soil.

The foundation of Ninasam is tightly bound to the independence movement of India. In his essays on the work and ideas of Ninasam, its founder K. V. Subbana describes the ideas of Gandhi as the conceptual source from which Ninasam came into being: 'It was a vision at once microcosmic and macrocosmic, envisaging peace and development for the villages and thereby assuring the entire world of the same. It was an extraordinary and yet utterly practicable utopia where decentralisation, non-violence, freedom and democracy embraced every single human being as well as the whole of mankind in one sweep.'[7]

Ninasam is an outstanding cultural institution especially with regard to its position: settled in Karnataka's hinterland, it is founded, guided, run and conducted by the local population, and is embedded in their life, routines and ideas. It is unique in its balance between self-government, self-determination and openness towards a broader intellectual culture, influences of which enter but ideas and concepts tend soon to be adapted by and interwoven with local practices, problems and questions. It seems to be, then, a serious attempt to avoid the lower end of the hierarchical city-countryside divide, and so to be of global significance. In this aim of balancing local concerns and larger patterns, the work at Ninasam re-maps the division of Indian theatre culture and provokes the hegemony of the metropolis. Ninasam noticeably influences the atmosphere and culture of its environment and vice versa as it gives space for people living in the countryside to develop and preserve their traditional and contemporary cultural practices, and to shape and re-shape their forms of self-representation, examination and administration.

During my stay at Ninasam I had the opportunity to witness a theatre performance of Maxim Gorki's *The Lower Depths* by current students of the theatre institute, forming only one part of Ninasam. Although not representative of the larger institution's work, the performance offered a first impression of the institute's style of artistic education and their ideas of theatre today.

The institute offers 10 to 15 young students aged 15 to 30 scholarships for one year, during which they are trained as actors and theatre practitioners. It always has been an explicit aim of the institute that these students then could return to their home villages to run their own theatres there. Most of the students come from the villages of Karnataka,[8] and teaching is held in the local language Kannada. All students live on campus during their studies.

The performance of *The Lower Depths* I visited was the outcome of an acting class. The play had been translated by the teacher into Kannada.[9] The setting had been shifted to an imago of a local Indian family. The stage showed the interior of the family's kitchen, which also functioned as living room and bedroom. One of the highlights of the show was the opening scene when the stage lights slowly began to glow to signify the rising sunlight in the early morning and one actor after the other was slowly moving in every corner of the stage, where you had not expected and seen anyone before. This appeared as an apt image for the density of people sharing public and private spaces in India.

For the rest of the staging, the acting style appeared to be a bit old fashioned and conservative. Old fashion here does not mean a strong bound to local traditional theatre forms but the opposite: in spite of all endeavours for and accentuations of the local specifics the orders and hierarchies of a globally powerful theatrical dispositive seem to have even stronger effects on the aesthetic of the performance and its normative implications. In other words, the aspects of the performance of the play, which appeared to be problematic to me, are neither singular nor specific for the work at Ninasam and its theatre institute, but due to a specific concept, idea and practice of theatre, which (still) seems to have strong effects on various places of theatre practices all over the world.

The students seem to be trained in the style of the Konstantin Stanislavski school, a so-called psychological realistic mode of acting, according to which the students try to approach their characters by imagining and imitating their state of mind, their psychological dispositions and conditions and then try to feel their (imagined) feelings. Seemingly a strong accompaniment to this theatre concept everywhere in the world, the actors smoked and pretended to be drunk, which neither the actors nor the audience, predominantly coming from the village, seemed to practice normally, and here one could ask how much this play, even in its adapted version, has to do with people's local life and experiences and what would be the use, the tension or enrichment of a local adaption restricted to translation, stage design and some site-specific anecdotes.

In their style of acting, the actors did not appear to be encouraged to behave self-consciously or to determine for themselves a critical or distanced position within their play and actions.[10] They appeared driven to please the teacher and to fulfil his instructions, who by himself seemed to follow a European nineteenth-century theatre concept, where interpretation and representation of the drama determine a hierarchical order of the performance elements. The authority of the text is not necessarily questioned by a site-specific or contemporary shift and adaption and does not guarantee artistic contemporaneity nor advantage, which was obvious here as well as in the majority of German and European theatre practice today. In this theatrical dispositive, the director comes into being as someone who stages his theatrical interpretation of the drama. Author and director (as well as conventions and traditions) serve as authorities, as the central instances of logos. The students/actors become subordinate agents. The work of the avant-garde movements and more specifically of the so-called 'post-dramatic theatre'[11] has been turning against these orders and divisions. They question hierarchical functions and call for the equality of elements and a critical, self-aware and emancipatory practice of all the participants involved in the artistic event. It would be useful to integrate these ideas into the education of acting students in India, in Europe and elsewhere in the world so as to enable and encourage people to take responsibility for their artistic actions and practices. A pure artistic training in virtuosity, agility, conformity and obedience does not seem to be a proper standard for (artistic) education. Instead, imparting of knowledge, encouragement of critical thinking to obtain independence are at least equally important skills to be taught and supported.[12] This not only because technological possibilities might replace certain artistic traditions and enable new forms of expression and connection to the world, but also because they enable artistic practice to differentiate, to change and to revise relations of power, domination and violence as well as the hegemonies of mainstream culture and its monopolies.[13]

Kochi-Muziris-Biennale

Finally, I'd like to sketch some impressions from the Kochi-Muziris Biennale,[14] India's first art biennial that took place from 12 December to 13 March 2012/2013 in and around the harbour cities Kochi and Muziri in the South Indian state of Kerala. The biennial exhibited a wide variety of contemporary visual art from all over the world as well as by numerous native and local artists in order to 'pay homage to India's traditions and heritage by embracing its history of poetry and performance, whilst inviting audiences to experience new cultural and artistic expressions'.[15] The various shows took place in galleries, public spaces and site-specific installations, while the main quarters were located in the disused and partly decayed harbour storage and warehouses at Fort Kochi. A programme of discussion panels and talks accompanied the exhibitions. Generally, the biennial continued and varied different curatorial approaches familiar from other biennials such as Manifesta or the Berlin Biennale and at the same time successfully sets its own locally specific parameters in terms of concepts, practices and focuses. The biennial was co-funded by private and public sponsors as well as by the Government of Kerala. At least in the first weeks it did not charge any entrance fee. Already after the second weekend the organizers could announce having hosted 50,000 visitors, the majority being local residents. According to the spokesman of the biennial, and corresponding with my own observations and conversations with other visitors at the biennial, many were experiencing an exhibition of contemporary art for the first time. In confronting the often abstract ways of aesthetic communication of contemporary art, they also could have found themselves encountering novel forms and alternative modes of conceptualization, focus and perception in regard to the social environment and the specific concerns and patterns of local daily life.

The displayed work of Amar Kanwar, *Sovereign Forest*,[16] e.g. deals with guerrilla fighting in Orissa by the tribal population of the area against the Indian Government. The clashes were triggered by the destruction of habitat and forests, as well as the disruption of local ecology, by large industrial companies for the purpose of bauxite mining. In response to the fighting, Kanwar installed a variety of audio-visual media and materials. In a long, dark room a film was projected on one end portraying the area and its people in a sequence of quite slow, beautiful pictures. Pictures of the demonstrations and confrontations were projected as slides onto huge books on sidewalls. Kanwar lends a strong expression to the plurality of growth and life when he installs 266 varieties of indigenous seeds on the walls, which function as a sort of biological archive and as a memorial for the prevention of land speculation. In his installation the relation of form and theme is precisely balanced and one can sense a concentration on the reflection and usage of the media specifics, like indexicality, conservation and time transformation, enabling the evocation of a specific relationship to the past, certain modes of remembrance and melancholia as well as political agitation, with both enfolding aesthetic entanglement. The elements themselves expose simultaneously a world and its conflict, and their own materiality, forms and aesthetic operations. The work inscribes itself at the same time in political and aesthetic debates and thereby exemplifies their constitutive interaction, exposing the aesthetic dimension of politics as well as the political force of aesthetic questions. In doing so, the work lends the conflict, but more so the landscape and people for whom it demonstrates solidarity, specific aesthetic modes of perception, sensibility and visibility.

The work of Amar Kanwar described here is exemplary for a whole series of works shown in the exhibition and of the biennale's attempt to develop and present ways and forms of aesthetic expression and communication, which generate multidimensional entanglements of art, aesthetics and politics, provoking and changing the possibilities, modes, forms and patterns of representing and perceiving the world, via questioning, criticism and displacement of traditional hegemonies.

Destuffing Matrix, a 12-channel video presented by Camp,[17] the collective that co-founded Pad.ma, is presented on four flat screens vertically installed and depicting the packing and loading of import and export goods in the industrial harbour of Kochi. The clip runs on an eight-minute loop. It begins with one split screen at the top left showing the unloading of steel scrap as it is noisily hurled towards the spectator. One channel after the other subsequently illuminates different procedures of loading and unloading carried out by the shipping agency workers. Further information, such as, what kind of goods are loaded, their weight and value, the destination and whether it's an import or export become temporarily projected in white block letters across the images. The main business is the export of coconuts and raw materials, while the import goods are predominantly – as outrageously it is still common for so-called developing countries in the actual division of power structures in the world – steel scrap of the holders of economic power and industrialized countries.

Slowly one screen after the other turns black until a single screen in the middle shows one carrier waiting for a door to finally close on the completely loaded container. He seems to be on his own. It is already dark outside and he is illuminated by electric light.

Destuffing Matrix offers insight into the normally opaque procedures and practices of the significant harbour business of the firms of carriers as a scene of global trade market as well as the under-represented, exhausting and undermining labour of the carrier workers via a tense aesthetic form and its own political implications. The technical virtuosity of the installation transforms the depicted scenes into a self-confident statement and stages form as medium of an emancipatory artistic practice, while subverting the hegemonic order of the current mapping of the world.

Finally

All examples given have in common that each in its own way displays the complexities of cultural production communicated in a globalized yet nationalized world order, which in its functioning heavily relies on controlled borders. Each case challenges the concepts of nation state, of foreign-domestic dichotomies and of fixed identities. Uploading footage in Pad.ma, people might beforehand be as unfamiliar with their subject and the localities of filming as any visiting scholar. But their concern is another: their work shifts the attention to the circumstances producing divisions within society that only later come into being as naturalized cultural, ethnic or religious difference. The work of Ninasam highlights the manner in which a site remote from all major cities can become a centre of art production, interweaving the local with the global in unforeseen ways. Finally, the work of Amar Kanwar demonstrates how the indigenous people of Orissa and the landscapes they inhabit are gradually being extinguished via expropriation of their land by the Indian government and by multinational corporations, themselves claiming to represent the 'original' interest of the Indian people in economic growth and wealth.

Notes

1 Of course this is just a tiny and non-representative selection of a completely diverse, heterogeneous and complex cosmos of India's multiple and impossible for me to overview artistic productions which would fit into this issue too.
2 http://pad.ma/
3 See the overall informative and revealing comparative study by Maximilian Linz with whom I researched together in India and who in his study is comparing the orders of representation of the Dharavi-slum in Mumbai in Pad.ma and in German television (Linz 2012).
4 Ibid. All translations of this text by myself.
5 Ibid.
6 The publication sector is called Ninasam Matukate. Most of their publications are in the state language Kannada and include many translations of theatre texts, too.
7 Subbanna (2009: 29).
8 As the current director of Ninasam, Akshara V. K. explains in a documentation shown to us during our stay, many of the students did not speak English fluently so that they could not achieve higher education access, but by the diploma of the institute they continue their qualification.
9 Consequently my observations refer to the style of acting, the body language, the volume and intensities of voices, the stage design and what can be understood of the plot by these non-linguistic aspects. Without understanding the language one could still grasp quite a lot because of various cultural connections and interrelations beyond national languages.
10 The students' class lasts from early morning to late evening and even during their performing period they were rehearsing every day all day long before the show started. Some appeared to be very exhausted, but they did not seem to formulate their states of being nor their ideas.
11 For post-dramatic theatre, see Lehmann (2006); see also Fischer-Lichte (2008).
12 For education of actors in Germany today, see Weiler and Roselt (2011) as well as Roselt (2013), 'Nachahmung im Theater ist kein Frevel'.
13 I would like to remark that I visited this single production only. The institute's work in the context of other traditional theatre forms like the local Kannadian

Yakshagana might be completely different and my arguments might not be accurate here. But the specialist for Yakshagana at Ninasam is the same teacher who directed this production of *The Lower Depths*. And second: a critical attitude towards every form of tradition could be a useful basis for new forms of emancipatory and self-determined cultural and artistic practice.

14 http://kochimuzirisbiennale.org/
15 Quoted from the programme.
16 The work has been shown at the DOKUMENTA 13 in Kassel in 2012 too, but in its locally specific display in Kochi is gaining new site specific connotations, contexts, perspectives and ways of perception.
17 http://kochimuzirisbiennale.org/camp/

References

Fischer-Lichte, Erika (2008): *The Transformative Power of Performance. A New Aesthetics*. London, New York: Routledge.

Lehmann, Hans-Thies (2006): *Postdramatic Theatre*. London, New York: Routledge.

Linz, Maximilian (2012): 'Was wir von der Welt wissen wollen'. In: *Fabrikzeitung*, November 2012, Nr. 286.

Roselt, Jens: 'Nachahmung im Theater ist kein Frevel'. In: *Hildesheimer Thesen III, Was die unfreiwillige Gemeinsamkeit zwischen Stadttheater und Freier Szene bringen kann*, http://www.nachtkritik.de/index.php?option=com_content&view=article&id=7426:hildesheimer-thesen-iii-&catid=101:debatte&Itemid=84 (accessed 25 August 2013).

Subbanna, K. V. (2009): 'Ninasam: The Springs of Inspiration'. In: N. Manu Chakravarthy (ed.): *Theater and Community*. Heggodu: Akshara Prakashana.

Weiler, Christel, and Roselt, Jens (eds) (2011): *Schauspielen heute. Die Bildung des Menschen in den performativen Künsten*. Bielefeld: Transcript.

12

THE MESSAGE OF THEIR PICTURES

An essay on photographs taken by Indian auto-rickshaw drivers

Julia Thibaut

> It is always the image that someone chose; to photograph is to frame, and to frame is to exclude.
>
> Susan Sontag[1]

This essay is an attempt to analyse the message of a photograph that was considered to be good or liked by the photographer. In order to do this, a collection of photographs, all taken by auto-rickshaw drivers in Indian cities, was analysed by studying the photograph's composition. The photographs were taken during an exchange programme between students from Germany (Berlin) and India (Bangalore).[2] The project was realized thanks to the support of students from Bangalore and Mumbai.

During the study, the drivers were asked to go to a location in their city where they would like to take the pictures. This was done in order to give the drivers control over the subjects of the photos, instead of having them simply photograph what happened to be in front of their lens. The drivers were accompanied by the author of this article and an interpreter (a student from Bangalore or Mumbai). The interpreter also explained to the drivers how to operate the digital camera. The drivers were asked to choose from the pictures they had taken those ones they considered to be good or which they liked. The composition of these photographs was compared with the composition of the photographs the drivers did not prefer, to distinguish the drivers' favoured visual expressions from visual expressions they did not like.[3] Finally, recognizable characteristics of these preferred visual expressions were analysed in relation to the driver's social background or status, i.e. the social status of auto-rickshaw drivers in large Indian cities. This was done in order to find out if the drivers' background indicates a meaning or message of their preferred visual expression.

The participants of the project

The photos were taken by 11 auto-rickshaw drivers in four cities of India: three drivers each in Bangalore, Mumbai and Delhi, and two drivers in Ahmedabad. To be able to communicate with the drivers a local interpreter was used, even though most of the drivers spoke some English. The drivers were asked randomly at public places[4] to participate in the project. Initially, almost all of the drivers were surprised at being asked; about one-third of them refused to participate.

The participants were aged between 26 and 47 and all male (there were no women seen driving auto-rickshaws). All of the participants were married and had to support a family of three to five people. Most of the participants worked 7 days a week, 8–14 hours a day and took only a day or two days off a month. All participants started working between the ages of 15 and 16; therefore half of them moved from the village where they grew up to the city. One of the participants owned his vehicle, two used vehicles owned by their relatives and the others had rented a vehicle from a commercial car hire. As none of the drivers had his own camera, a digital camera was lent to them for the purpose of this project. In order to ensure the drivers would not lose income by partaking in the project they were compensated for their expenditure of time at their normal rates.

The locations depicted for the photographs

The vast majority of places the drivers chose for their photographs were parks or park like areas and gardens: the well-known 'Botanical Gardens – Lal Bagh' (also known as the 'Red Gardens') in Bangalore,[5] the 'Jayaprakash Narayan Park' at Mathikere in Bangalore,[6] the 'Hanging Gardens' in Mumbai,[7] and a smaller garden attached to a neighbourhood in Malabar Hill, Mumbai,[8] and the 'Science City' in Ahmedabad/Gujarat, including its surrounding park.[9] Other than that a few temples were photographed: the Bir Hindu Temple in New Delhi,[10] the Akshardham Temple in Delhi[11] and the Vaishno Devi Temple in Ahmedabad.[12] Due to rules prohibiting photography inside the temples all of these photographs depict the temples' exteriors. Therefore there are far more pictures of parks and gardens, also because it was possible to stroll through the parks while taking photographs. Finally, there are a few pictures of the ocean and beach in Mumbai,[13] there is one picture of a participants' car in Mumbai,[14] one picture of a traffic island in Ahmedabad,[15] one picture of the Red Fort in New Delhi,[16] and one picture of a space shuttle in the 'Science City' in Ahmedabad/Gujarat.[17]

There could have been photographs of shopping malls, as there was a young rickshaw driver (about the age of 18) who said that he wished to photograph a mall, but after being asked to actually take the photos he declined, saying it wasn't allowed. Another driver declined, saying that he didn't know a nice place in the city of Mumbai, even though he's been working there for almost 30 years.

In explaining their choice of locations, most of the auto-rickshaw drivers mentioned their personal background; as opposed to talking about the city's appearance or the cultural heritage of the location, for instance. They spoke of visiting parks with their family, of playing in gardens with their children during their off-days, or of meeting friends when they were younger, before they had started a family. While strolling through the parks some drivers pointed out several details like stone figures, which looked like animals, children or a family (cf. Figures 12.1, 12.18, 12.19 and 12.26), dustbins having the shape of a penguin, or flowerbeds of various types (cf. Figures 12.23 and 12.24) etc.

Figure 12.1 Family made of stone, Jayaprakash Narayan Park, Bangalore, Mathikere

Figure 12.2 Man with newspaper and radio, Hanging Gardens, Mumbai

The act of taking a picture was sometimes combined with a pointing expression and a grin at the thing or area that was about to be captured. One driver laughed at a man sitting on a bench in a park, listening to music from a radio and reading the newspaper, he took his picture (cf. Figure 12.2); another driver saw a women meditating on a bench under a canopy, he pointed at her and took a picture of her. Many pictures are of lawns, hedges, flower arrangements, stone figures, trees, and walkways. There are some people captured in several pictures, walking through the park or in front of a temple as visitors, but they are rarely in focus.

The drivers' preferred perspective

Each driver took about 10–40 pictures, as there was no upper limit on the number of pictures they were allowed to take. After the drivers were done with taking pictures they were asked to review them (using the screen of the digital camera) and to point out the ones they preferred. In doing so, each driver selected less than four pictures as 'good' or 'liked' by him, again, there was no upper limit on the number of selected pictures.

Reviewing the preferred photographs it became obvious that they were distinct from the others not only in their subject, but also in their composition. While each driver may have taken many photographs of similar lawns, hedges and flowerbeds, for instance, one of these photos was then preferred. That means, the selection made it apparent that *how* a thing or place was displayed was just as important as *what* thing or place was displayed.

One of the drivers, choosing the 'Botanical Gardens – Lal Bagh' in Bangalore as the place for his photographs, took pictures of hedges trimmed in the shape of different animals. He pointed out the different hedges, explaining which animal each hedge represented, while explaining that he had liked them ever since he himself had been a child. Some of the hedges were shaped like a bear, some like a swan, some like birds, giraffes, elephants etc.[18] The driver explained that his son would like to play with him in the garden, and that he would like to spend some of his weekends with his family around here.

The driver captured the hedges two times (cf. Figures 12.3 and 12.4). One of the two pictures was then his favourite photograph. Besides the hedge animals, he took photos of flower arrangements, walkways and a huge glass house. But unlike the hedge animals, none of these were tied to a personal history.

Figure 12.3 Hedge animals, Botanical Gardens Lal Bagh, Bangalore (preferred version)

Figure 12.4 Hedge animals, Botanical Gardens Lal Bagh, Bangalore (not preferred version)

The two photographs depict the hedges from two different points: Figure 12.3 is taken from a footpath next to the hedges' lawn and with three different hedges in the picture; Figure 12.4 is taken from a second footpath, slightly farther away, with the lawn and a single hedge directly in front. The first picture is the driver's favourite photograph. But what distinguishes it from the other photograph?

The background of Figure 12.4 is divided into a left and a right group of trees, in between these two groups there is a bright spot of the sky. This spot is the brightest part of the photograph. In contrast, the background of Figure 12.3 shows a dense layer of trees, blocking the sky. Even though there are gaps in this layer (and a few dots of sunlight shine through) the brightest part of Figure 12.3 is a bright-green section of the lawn, in front of the hedge in the centre of the picture. A second bright spot is in between the central hedge and the hedge on the right, and a third one (though less brighter than the other two) above and to the left of the central hedge. These three spots in Figure 12.3, as well as the hedges, almost form the corners of a triangle (cf. Figure 12.5). Additionally, the triangular forms are circumscribed by smaller plants and edges of the footpath at the bottom left and right corner of the photograph (cf. the black marks in Figure 12.5).

JULIA THIBAUT

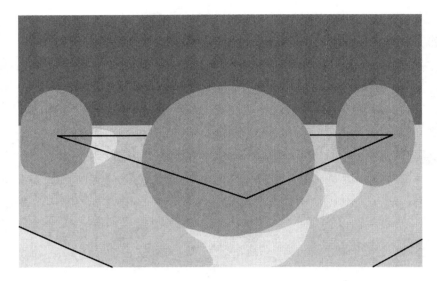

Figure 12.5 Approximate composition of Figure 12.3

Due to this structure, the main difference between Figures 12.3 and 12.4 is the presence (respectively absence) of the bright spot in the background of Figure 12.4. The brightness of the spot makes the whole photograph comparatively darker; leaving room only for the (bright green) lawn, upon which the hedge is growing and a small section of the boundary of the footpath (cf. Figure 12.6). Even though the hedge-animal is in the centre of the picture, it is as if the view does not rest on it; as if the eyes don't know where to stop. The view moves up and down from the bright spot to the lawn to the boundary of the footpath and back again, searching for something to focus on; which makes for an unsteady expression of the photograph.

The triangular structure of Figure 12.3 binds the composition together, giving the photograph a steady and clear look. The eyes tend to focus on the hedge in the centre, while the hedges on the left and right side frame it or almost point towards it. It looks as if the viewer knows where to focus on. This means, the preferred photograph shows something in particular, it points out the hedge in the centre, using the triangular structure of the composition to frame it. Whereas the not preferred photograph shows no particular thing and leaves the viewer uncertain about what to look at.

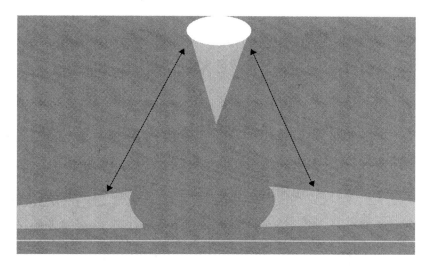

Figure 12.6 Approximate composition of Figure 12.4

The tendency towards a clear expression

Similar to the previous driver an auto-rickshaw driver from Ahmedabad chose, of two photographs, showing the Vaishno Devi Temple in Ahmedabad, the photo that gives an unambiguous look at the temple. Both photographs show the same section of the temple's external walls and the entrance area, they differ only in their perspective (cf. Figures 12.7 and 12.8).

The preferred photograph (Figure 12.7) can be divided, almost like a pie, into three parts: the lower two-thirds of the photograph showing the temple's walls and entrance area; the upper third of the photograph showing a massive white cloud; and, also in the upper third of the photograph, wedged between these two parts a section of clear blue sky (cf. Figure 12.9). The intersection of these three parts is located at the top of the temple, left above the centre of the photograph; it is decorated with a red flag. Beyond the pie-like structure the photograph shows more details: a fence at the feet of the temple, two little white domes at the photo's left- and right-hand side, four other red flags spread around the temple, and a dark green canopy at the upper left-hand side. Notwithstanding these elements, the pie-like structure of the photograph leads the viewer to look at the top of the temple. It is as if the three parts point towards the centre, highlighting the temple's massive stone walls.

Figure 12.7 Vaishno Devi Temple, Ahmedabad (preferred version)

Figure 12.8 Vaishno Devi Temple, Ahmedabad (not preferred version)

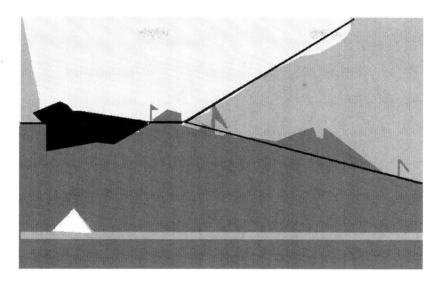

Figure 12.9 Approximate composition of Figure 12.7

This is in contrast to the picture that the driver did not prefer (cf. Figure 12.8). About two-thirds of the photograph show the blue sky and the white/gray clouds, while only the lower right corner of the photograph shows the temple. There is no structure, figure or shape that leads the viewer's look to the temple. The photograph points out more or less each of its details. The eyes move from the sky and the clouds at the upper half side to the temple walls and the dark green canopy at the lower right to the tops of the trees at the lower left side and back again. There is no thing or object to rest upon; the view tends to circle unsteadily around the centre of the photograph (cf. Figure 12.10). All in all, the driver preferred (like the previous one) a photograph that shows the chosen place clearly and obviously, instead of having it being a part among others.

This case is again similar to the one of a driver from Mumbai, who took almost 25 pictures of a smaller garden attached to a neighbourhood in southern Mumbai. Of these 25 photographs the driver indicated three as his favourite ones. Whereas two of the three photographs were of things the driver captured only once (a playground for children and a small bridge, cf. Figures 12.20 and 12.21), there is one photograph of a place the driver captured many times, but from different perspectives. He indicated only one of these as good or liked by him.

Figure 12.10 Approximate composition of Figure 12.8

The preferred photograph shows a dark green archway (made of a hedge) in a section of the lawn, from a central perspective (cf. Figure 12.11). Compositionally, the picture can be divided into three roughly triangular parts (cf. Figure 12.12): a stone footpath, occupying the lower right corner of the picture; a green garden arrangement from the lower left corner to the central right part of the picture (including different sections of lawns, a tree, hedges and archways); and a light grey sky from the upper right corner to the upper left corner of the picture. The dark green archway in the centre of the picture is particularly well defined. The bright green lawn behind the archway shapes its interior, the bright white sky frames the archway from above and the stone footpath frames it from below. These elements combine to draw the viewer's gaze to the centre of the picture.

In contrast, one of the photographs the driver did not prefer shows a wide, central section of hedges, plants and trees (two archways are only visible sideways) (Figure 12.14). The picture can be divided, like the preferred one, into three parts: a gray stone footpath at the bottom of the picture; various trees, plants and hedges, occupying the entire central section of the picture; and a light grey sky at the top of the picture. The large central band of hedges, plants and trees is framed above and below by the sky and the footpath. This frame draws the viewer's gaze to the central area

Figure 12.11 Garden, Malabar Hill, Mumbai (preferred version)

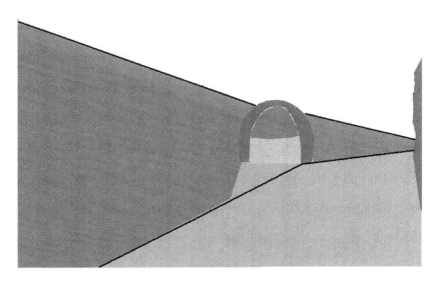

Figure 12.12 Approximate composition of Figure 12.11

Figure 12.13 Garden, Malabar Hill, Mumbai (not preferred version)

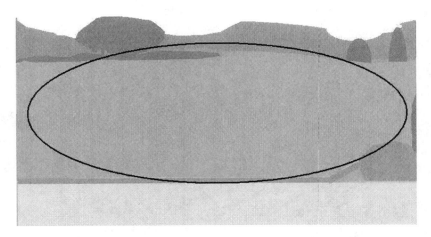

Figure 12.14 Approximate composition of Figure 12.13

of the photograph. But unlike the preferred photograph (within this section), there is no specific focus point where the eyes can rest. The picture captures the chosen place widely and leaves the viewer ambiguous about what to look at.

Showing one particular thing

With the pictures analysed so far it is apparent that the drivers favoured photographs with a clear, unambiguous expression; pictures which point out one thing or place precisely, instead of showing an area vague or unclear. This pattern was seen in the other photographs taken during the course of the project as well. Whenever the drivers had multiple photos of the same thing or place, and could choose between a clear and steady expression and an ambiguous, unsteady expression, they chose the clear one. However, in those cases where the drivers had only one photograph of a certain thing or place they liked, they chose that photo, whether its composition was unambiguous or not. This means that the drivers implicitly expressed a priority of subject over composition. Whereas their preferred way to (visually) express a thing or place they liked was a clear and steady one.

Places oppositional to the drivers' working conditions

Against the backdrop of this result the question arises *why* the drivers preferred photographs which show a thing unambiguous and clear. Why did they generally prefer pictures which point out one particular thing over others which show the place they chose for their photos widely and within that place nothing in particular? In other words: what makes the drivers want to show (clearly, steadily) one particular thing?

The parks and park-like places, the beach in Mumbai and the temples the drivers chose for their photographs are places that are calm and quiet, compared to the traffic situation on the streets in cities like Bangalore, Mumbai, Ahmedabad and Delhi. The drivers took photographs of places that are almost opposite to their daily work environment. The streets in large Indian cities are usually jammed, loud and polluted. The parks and temples are segregated from the streets and therefore comparatively quiet, neat and less crowded. Additionally, the auto-rickshaws are three-wheeled scooters that aren't protected from traffic voice and pollution. This means, the drivers are usually much more exposed to the traffic situation than occupants of enclosed cars.[19]

Due to the fact that the drivers work 8–14 hours a day, almost 7 days a week, travelling on loud and jammed streets, their choice for quiet and neat places looks as if counterbalancing their daily life environment. None of the drivers chose a place for their photographs right next to a street, even though some had to travel half an hour from where they were asked to participate in the project to reach their chosen places.[20]

Furthermore, a survey of Dinesh Mohan and Dunu Roy, analysing the labour conditions of auto-rickshaw drivers in Delhi in 2003, rates the drivers' current situation as difficult: 'Over the past year TSR [three-wheeled scooter rickshaw, J.T.] drivers have been complaining about their working conditions (especially lack of availability of CNG) [compressed natural gas, J.T.], about rise in costs of operating their vehicles and have been demanding an increase in fares.'[21] Mohan and Roy explain that the drivers 'have even gone on strike to make these demands but the problem persists'.[22] This situation makes the drivers feel not being recognized by society adequately: 'A paucity of facilities and the inadequacy of the fares forces TRS drivers to struggle for their survival and this has given them the public image of being dishonest and rude. Many TSR drivers resent this image deeply and feel that their struggle to support families as decent human beings is not being recognized by society.'[23] Mohan and Roy add, that this is 'reflected in the fact that 61 per cent of them have to support a family of 5–8 persons'.[24]

An indication of the photographs' message

During the time the participants of the project went to the places they had chosen for their photographs most of them talked about their working conditions, their situation at home or their families. They said, for instance, they had only a few days off in a month to spend with their wife and children, or that they usually did not go on vacation. Even if none of the drivers complained about his working conditions (on the contrary, most of them were happy to have a job at all), some of them indicated they could not afford the park entrance for their families and therefore went in the morning, when admission is free, or that they wished to find a better job and to be able to support their families properly. One of the drivers even said he would leave the country to find a better job. Almost all of the participants pointed out they had to leave school when they were 15 or 16 in order to work and to support their families.

According to these working conditions, the drivers' preference for a clear and steady visual expression can possibly be seen as a hint at their social unsteadiness. The remarks of the drivers participating in the photo-project indicate that their present social situation is similar to the one described by Mohan and Roy. The drivers wish for a better job and their lifestyle avoiding park admissions and spending only a few days off in a month (for instance) appears deprived and precarious. The fact that the drivers' strikes to demand an increase in fares, as Mohan and Roy say, have not been effective so far, is also confirmed by G.R. Medan, who analyses the recent status of cooperatives organized for Indian auto-rickshaw drivers. Medan rates the cooperatives' effect for rickshaw drivers as of no avail: 'However, due to illiteracy of the members and lack of support by voluntary workers they did not make any satisfactory progress.'[25]

Against the backdrop of this social status, the drivers' photographs are possibly a visual expression of what the drivers miss in their daily life. The clear and steady compositions of their preferred pictures seem to be opposed to their unsteady, precarious working conditions (concerning the rise in costs, the inadequacy of their fares, their image of being dishonest or not to be recognized by society appropriately). In this sense, the photographs point out what the drivers miss in their daily life: steadiness, stability and maybe calmness. The straight and clear expressions of their preferred photographs, unambiguous about what to look at, could be seen as a demand for a less ambiguous, less precarious or for a steadier life.

Appendix

Collection of the drivers' preferred photographs (not mapped above):

Figure 12.15 Botanical Gardens Lal Bagh, Bangalore

Figure 12.16 Glass-house, Botanical Gardens Lal Bagh, Bangalore

Figure 12.17 Lake, Botanical Gardens Lal Bagh, Bangalore

Figure 12.18 Cows made of stone, Jayaprakash Narayan Park, Bangalore, Mathikere

Figure 12.19 Children made of stone, Jayaprakash Narayan Park, Bangalore, Mathikere

Figure 12.20 Children's playground, Garden, Malabar Hill, Mumbai

Figure 12.21 Garden, Malabar Hill, Mumbai

Figure 12.22 Beach, Mumbai

Figure 12.23 Hanging Gardens, Mumbai

Figure 12.24 Hanging Gardens, Mumbai

Figure 12.25 The car of a participant, street in front of the beach, Mumbai

Figure 12.26 Dinosaur made of stone, Science City, Ahmedabad, Gujarat

Figure 12.27 Space Shuttle, Science City, Ahmedabad, Gujarat

Figure 12.28 Traffic island on the way to Vaishno Devi Temple, Ahmedabad

Figure 12.29 Bir Hindu Temple, Delhi

Figure 12.30 Red Fort, New Delhi

Figure 12.31 Akshardham Temple, Delhi

Notes

1. Susan Sontag: Regarding the pain of the others. New York 2003: 37.
2. The exchange programme was between students of the Free University of Berlin and the National Institute of Advanced Studies in Bangalore. It was funded by the German Academic Exchange Service and took place between June and December 2009.
3. Ralf Bohnsack describes that the detailed composition of a photograph, here referred to as 'visual expression', indicates the photographer's habit, if the photographer likes the photo or considers it to be good. A comparative analysis with pictures the photographer does not like clarifies what the preferred photography is about. For the reason that no other group, apart from the auto-rickshaw drivers, was asked to take part in the study, the preferred photographs of the drivers are compared with their own, not preferred photographs. Cf.: Ralf Bohnsack: Qualitative Bild- und Videointerpretation. Opladen, Farmington Hills 2009.
4. Auto-rickshaw drivers usually are parking their vehicles at public places, waiting for passengers.
5. Cf. Figures 12.3, 12.4, 12.9–12.11; see also Appendix.
6. Cf. Figures 12.1, 12.12 and 12.13; see also Appendix.
7. Cf. Figures 12.2 and 12.17; see also Appendix.
8. Cf. Figures 12.11, 12.13, 12.20 and 12.21.
9. Cf. Figure 12.26.
10. Cf. Figure 12.30.
11. Cf. Figure 12.31.
12. Cf. Figures 12.7 and 12.8.
13. Cf. Figure 12.22.
14. Cf. Figure 12.25.
15. Cf. Figure 12.28.
16. Cf. Figure 12.29.
17. Cf. Figure 12.27.
18. Most of the hedges were poorly trimmed and hard to recognize for someone who didn't already know what they were supposed to be.
19. Except for the drivers from Mumbai all participants of the project were drivers of these three-wheeled scooters. Due to a restriction that doesn't allow the scooter-rickshaws in southern Mumbai all drivers from Mumbai used four wheeled vehicles (cf. the car of a participant from Mumbai in Figure 12.25).
20. Other than that, the drivers are used to passengers travelling to places like parks and temples as they are common tourist attractions; thus, they might have chosen these places by force of habit. In this context, the drivers were asked to participate in the project by a student from India and a student from Germany; the latter might have appeared like a tourist.
21. Dinesh Mohan, Dunu Roy: Operating on Three Wheels. Auto-Rickshaw Drivers of Delhi. In: Economic and Political Weekly, Vol. 38. No. 3, 18–24, January 2003, pp. 177–180, URL: http://www.jstor.org/stable/4413089.
22. Ibid.
23. Ibid.: 179.
24. Ibid.: 177.
25. G.R. Medan: Co-operative Movement in India. Daryaganj, New Delhi, second, revised edition 2007: 397.

13

TRANSMITTING CULTURE WITHIN LINGUISTIC ALTERITY

Nika Daryan

The following considerations attempt to visually pinpoint the logic of contingent alterity as one structuring operative principle of India's social space. The structural-analytical separation of this anthropological phenomenon can only be done theoretically and analytically, because it is not possible to distinguish the human practice from everyday life.

Theory, as 'an instrument of experience' and as a monitoring tool, is the key word of this paper. The structural image shown here tries to apply theoretical knowledge to personal and body-based experience. After years of using and living these experiences they are, if we follow Bourdieu, part of the habitual dispositions of a social actor. The following presentation of some significant aspects of Indian society is the result of experience-based knowledge acquired in some of India's different social fields (academic field, cultural field and public space) during a period of six months. Besides, this paper aims to discuss some concepts of my PhD project. This doctoral thesis deals with the role of media in mimetic processes as a foundation, as an actual and prospective paradigm of the theories of education in German *Bildungstheorie*, theory of education. As a theoretical work, it aims to describe and to localize different dimensions of present educational structures, which have to be seen as missing links in educational concepts especially when we look at processes such as informal learning and the growing significance of learning processes in non-school culture.

This educational importance of media includes the basic problem of using the term – no matter if as a scientific and epistemological term or as part of common sense; so far neither the cultural studies nor the social sciences have a basic conceptual formulation of 'media'. In recent years, a branch of science has developed which allows working with an open concept of media to understand the various forms and dimensions of a medium. The new approach of the French mediology, particularly the work of Régis Debray, is this new methodological and theoretical basis for a transcultural and interdisciplinary discourse on media and their role in society, particularly in educational processes. A medium is a particular vector of a process of transmission. Therefore the study of cultural transmission of meanings, religions, political and socio-economic ideas in society and across societies over a period that is usually measured in months, decades or millennia is indispensable. This approach allows bringing to light the function of a medium in all its forms. According to *mediological* understanding, not only the new media (television, Internet, newspapers etc.), but every cultural object may be a medium for making sense (cp. Debray 2000). 'Transmitting Culture' is the object of study, similar to the language, the religious tradition and the particular social order of a society.

The meaning of the Other

The experience of the Other is a significant part of human life. Moving in different social spaces is becoming constitutive for the habitual development of social actors. But if the new social space is entered once, it turns out that to stay is a difficult task. The vast amount of unknown sensory stimuli makes it hard to enter this new world. Perception is flooded by strangeness. Once you start asking what exactly is 'strange', the depiction of this otherness opens up the complexity of the experience. The easiest answer would be the environment; the climate is different and the people look different as well – actually you are different, you look different! Once you enter a strange environment, it is no longer the new environment which is strange, but it is you who is representing the otherness of this space.

The Other may appear as a friend or foe, as an enrichment or as something abnormal. This perception is always the result of the knowledge or ignorance about the Other. This knowledge is highly dependent on the historical experiential context of a culture with strangers and strange phenomena. Anyway, the self and the Other presuppose each other. To ignore this genuine human phenomenon would result in severe social problems (Wulf 2001: 153).

The egalitarianism of Western civilization strengthened by the technical-industrial progress and dominance of scientific ideas led to the claim of the assimilation of the Other. The otherness of foreign cultures was not accepted (ibid.). The relationship to the Other is characterized, first, by value judgements, which may have individual as well as collective dimensions; second, by the respective way of alignment with the Other, which is strongly embedded in the overall cultural context of a society. These two points make up knowledge of the Other. Especially if the other is not directly tangible due to spatial distance so that direct contact is not feasible,

TRANSMITTING CULTURE WITHIN LINGUISTIC ALTERITY

usually only the indirect consequences of interaction with others are experienced (Wulf 2001: 155).

Some mediological reflections on the phenomenon of diversity in the social space of India

In India, social space is structured by cultural alterity and diversity. On the surface you already see a religious and linguistic diversification. Nearly everywhere in India the structuring power of the different religious belongings (Hinduism, Islam, Jainism, Buddhism, Sikhism etc.) and the diversity of languages is to be found. In contrast to our social space, religion in India's public space is transmitted through many channels. Religion has always been an important part of India's everyday life and has a massive structuring impact on the habitus of social actors. Physically, religion is present in everyday life in transportation, building entrances, on the streets and at offices. Figure 13.1 gives an example, showing the different combinations of writing systems with language and to which social field they belong.

Figure 13.1 Advertising on the occasion of the Hindu deity Krishna's birthday – Varanasi, August 2010

The presentation of the event of Krishna's birthday is communicated through a Sanskrit-based writing system in Hindi language, but the hymn is in Sanskrit using the Latin writing system. The sponsor 'Bank of Baroda' uses the English as well as the Hindi medium. Obviously, Hindi with the Sanskrit-based writing system is the dominant language of the religious field of Hinduism. With regard to Hinduism, the most widespread religion in India, you can see an interesting relationship between language and religion. In addition to Hindi and English, Sanskrit is of fundamental significance for Indian society. This Indo-Aryan language does not only form the basis of Hindi, regarding its writing system and etymology, but also form the basis for many other languages spoken in India. The corpus of Sanskrit literature encompasses a rich tradition of poetry as well as scientific, philosophical and Hindu religious texts, which still represents a knowledge-base for most of the Indian population. Sanskrit continues to be widely used as a ceremonial language in Hindu religious rituals in the forms of hymns and mantras. Many words and concepts of this language can be traced far back and allow some traditional cultural categories to stay alive without significant transformation. In fact, people who grow up with Hindi or any other Indian language use conceptual categories, identities, and quantities which do not have a 'real' equivalent in their daily life. They are part of a habitual disposition, even if the social fields have changed, particularly in relation to the pervasiveness of the English language with its own composition of cultural categories, which is increasingly dominating the economic and academic fields.

The existence of a linguistic plurality is specific to India. This fact opens the possibility to get a different understanding of the structural role of languages (as a medium) as a main institution of a society and has far-reaching implications for the most diverse fields.

In the Western world the building of modern nations coincided with the dominance of one established language and the displacement of other spoken languages (dialects) on the national territory (cp. Castoriadis 1987). The establishment of only one language by, e.g. the public school system leads to the implementation of this language as a specific institution with its own composition of cultural categories. In contrast, the linguistic plurality in India is part of a social actor's daily life; the social space in India has a multilingual nature. For example, in the intellectual field, several languages are in use, but the major scientific writings are in English. During pre-school time an educational subject gets in contact with at least three different languages (Hindi, English and the regional languages of the respective State, like Urdu or Panjabi). It is possible to visit a Hindi medium school and to study at an English University or vice versa. New Media

TRANSMITTING CULTURE WITHIN LINGUISTIC ALTERITY

in India, especially electronics, advertising and telecommunication technologies are distributed in social space. Both English and Hindi are used as language of mass media. They co-exist and they dominate the different social fields. The left part of Figure 13.2 shows canvassing in Hindi language with a Sanskrit-based writing system. The right part shows a movie advertisement in Hindi language but with the Latin writing system.

The fifth summer school at the Institute of Philosophy and Humanities of the Manipal University under the topic of 'the Idea of Justice'[1] is another example for the Indian phenomenon of linguistic alterity. Here, the observer was able to see what kind of linguistic and thereby cultural troubles the actual academic and intellectual field is confronted with. Reading the Western thinkers showed the difficulty of a match between the English terms, including their associated cultural meanings, and Hindi language with its own cultural categories. Speakers from different scientific backgrounds tried to sensitize the participants for the fact that if we do not have a word or term for something, this cultural object or thing, regardless of whether the object is materialized or not, is not 'visible' for us. A number of participants were familiar with Western philosophical concepts of the human and social sciences (especially European philosophers like Kant,

Figure 13.2 Canvassing and movie advertisement – Mumbai, November 2010

Heidegger and Benjamin), but they were not aware of the fundamental otherness between epistemological and anthropological concepts in different cultures. It became clear that Western concepts based on categories that do not have equivalents in India. To find etymological correspondences between terms in different languages turned out to be nearly impossible. The intellectual epistemological tradition of India is different from the Western dualism with its highlighting of the Cartesian tradition and its confrontation of body and mind, of reason and experience or the dualism of theory and empiricism (cp. Sarukkai 2005). Step by step, this Western–Indian difference was shown in various presentations, highlighting the culturalism of languages and especially of meanings as well as of theoretical concepts in the perspective of different social sciences.

The foundations of Western philosophy and especially its formal logic were the starting point of this critical view. In the following, the results and major concepts are presented in brief. Following Sundar Sarrukai, we may say that logic is an analysis of arguments and the connection of sentences (cp. Sarukkai 2002). Logic addresses the formal structure or the relation between signs and is not necessarily referring to the meaning of cultural categories. What if English terms in analytic philosophy do not match with cultural signs or categories in India? To read something is to understand its meaning, and the limits of language are the limits of reality. What cannot be verbalized is not part of one's own world. Wittgenstein said: depending on how you use words, you give them different meanings. As the participants were asked which Hindi word is used synonymous with the English term of justice, something significant came up. Nyáya is a word used in everyday's language meaning 'justice', whereas etymologically it means 'logic'. While the word did not change, its meaning did. Also, a relationship between justice and logic emerges differing drastically from its counterpart in the English idiom.

Habitus and the role of mimetic learning

If we now try to understand these observations within Bourdieu's concept of habitus, it will lead us to a more sociological and thus to a more practical view. The habitus of a social actor is the basic structure of his perception, his actions, his taste and his language. The habitus combines structured and structuring structures (Bourdieu 1996: 126). The habitus of a social actor is structured by the different forms of capital which he owns and has incorporated. It is the main part of the world making and refers to the limits of his reality, to what is possible or impossible. Language or language skills are also part of the cultural capital. More specifically, it is the linguistic capital (Bourdieu 1991: 50). In this concept, language has a strategic function. The more cultural capital a social actor has incorporated, the better his language abilities and his position in social space (Bourdieu 1983).

Cultural capital is incorporated in large part through mimetic processes, because mimetic learning is a basic form of cultural learning (cp. Gebauer and Wulf 1955). Mimetic ways of world making (cp. Goodman 1978) play an essential role as part of the educational structure of a social actor. In educational processes, there is an overlap of this way of world making with other ways like the poietic and the performative. Regarding the fundamental difference between Indian and Western societies in terms of the structural feature of alterity in India in contrast to the homogenization processes of Western nations and the resulting problems in the transport of cultural concepts from one culture to another through language, a practical example may be used as an interface of Western educational theories and their practical implementation in the social space of India.

The 'Shiksha Samarthan Project' in Phagi[2] is an initiative by Digantar[3] to improve the quality of education in (rural) government schools. Until now, the history of educational achievements of India in general, in particular in Rajasthan, is one of mixed success. This project has made encouraging progress in raising schooling participation in rural areas. The reason is to be found in its strategy and may be described as a practical application of mimetic theory. To quote from the current brochure: 'Our earlier interventions and experience of working with government schools has indicated that change in government schools is possible if we collaborate with teachers and demonstrate to them alternative classroom practices.'

The main objective is to improve quality of education in government schools and to create viable academic support structures. By working directly in schools with children and teachers they demonstrate alternative classroom practices in primary schools.

To achieve a pedagogical school environment, the 'Samarthaks'[4] continuously engage in dialogue with the school participants, and beyond that, they try to involve the community in this process. The Samarthaks accompany the teachers and students through the school and suggest alternative practices in the traditional structure of school days. They directly participate in the activities, and therefore, act as role models. By their physical presence, they serve as a source of mimetic processes. The cultural capital, which they have acquired through training in Digantar programmes, is now part of their habitual structure. By the presence of their habitus and its structuring power they structure the social field of school. It is important that these pedagogical assistants are from the same region as the school's participants. They have the same habitual structures, but a different

Figure 13.3 Children and the Samarthak in the schoolyard of the primary public school in Phagi

cultural capital. So they can act as mimetic reference points. Figure 13.3 shows a typical situation in the school break. Educational fundamentals such as justice and equality can be transmitted through group games. In a society with traditional social disparity, such simple educational concepts may exert a tremendous influence on children.

It is through the human body, that educational concepts materialize themselves. This is a body-based manifestation of culture. The habitus of the pedagogical assistant is an interface between Western and Indian structures, it represents a hybrid form, which the children can use as a reference point. Language as a medium of transmission needs the human body, because there is an insurmountable relationship between body, language and culture. The capacity for mimesis enables social actors to learn culture without being aware of these different dimensions. Most social spaces show a strong trend to homogeneity, so that this relationship may not be visible. In contrast, alterity is a structural paradigm of India's social space and a state sui generis, which allows observing anthropological phenomena no longer visible in most of the Western societies.

Notes

1 This paper arose from my participation in the summer school.
2 Phagi is a village about 60 km from Jaipur, the capital of Rajasthan.
3 Digantar is a voluntary non-profit organization engaged in education, guided by the principles of justice and equality. The term Digantar in Sanskrit implies 'beyond the horizon' or a change in direction. They are searching for alternatives in education and are one of the partners in the MA (education) program of Tata Institute for Social Science.
4 Samarthaks are pedagogical assistants.

References

Bourdieu, P. (1983): Ökonomisches Kapital, kulturelles Kapital, soziales Kapital. In: Soziale Ungleichheiten (*Soziale Welt* Vol. 2), 183–198. Göttingen.

Bourdieu, P. (1991): Language and Symbolic Power. Cambridge, MA.

Bourdieu, P. (1996): Reflexive Anthropologie. Frankfurt, M.

Castoriadis, C. (1987): The Imaginary Institution of Society. Cambridge, MA.

Debray, R. (2000): Transmitting Culture. New York.

Gebauer, G., and Wulf, C. (1955): Mimesis. Art -Culture - Society. Berkeley et al.: California University Press.

Goodman, N. (1978): Ways of Worldmaking. Hassocks.

Grosjean, F. (1984): Life with Two Languages: An Introduction to Bilingualism. Cambridge, MA.

Sarukkai, S. (2002): Translating the World: Science and Language. Delhi.

Sarukkai, S. (2005): Indian Philosophy and Philosophy of Science. Delhi.

Wulf, C. (2001): Einführung in die Anthropologie der Erziehung. Weinheim, Basel.

Part III

EDUCATION, SELF-EDUCATION AND HUMAN DEVELOPMENT

14

IN LINE

A photo essay on entering a school in Bangalore[1]

Christos Varvantakis

This chapter is concerned with the processes of applying discipline to pupils who enter the school. In its form, it is a visual study of this process. It is concerned with the mechanisms that are set in motion in order to apply an order to the pupils at the process of entering a school, lining up for the morning prayers and finally entering the classroom.

The concept of lining up students, either as an embodied practice or as a practice imposed by school authority, seems to be of primary importance for the learning of discipline in general. In following Tim Ingold's problematization of the line, we assume that: 'In modern societies, it seems, straightness has come to epitomize not only rational thought and disputation but also the values of civility and moral rectitude' (2007: 2). Straightness represents development. If bodies can be put in order, thoughts can be put in order and eventually a whole society can.

This particular case of line making seems to be of a quite difficult kind. The 'dots' needed to be lined here are pupils, in ages ranging from five to sixteen. Figure 14.1, below, where pupils are photographed from above (the photographic lens assuming the view of one of many CCTV cameras which are installed in the school) during the break, is not really confined to the borders of the picture frame; the image spreads and it expands; just like its subject, pupils that play during break, is impossible to stay inside a fixed frame. This is what I mean by saying that those are difficult dots to line up.

This is primarily a visual study of the subject, and as such it is bound to be confined by the photographer's gaze and his aesthetics. It intends not to interpret but to communicate knowledge which may be better communicated through images and has by no means moral evaluative intentions. MacDougall, in his extensive work in a boarding school in India, has also been concerned with what he conceived as social aesthetics. In his visual study

Figure 14.1 Pupils play during break

he encounters frequently motives of homogeneity and similarity; instead of turning a blind eye to those reoccurring themes in fear of creating stylized stereotypes, he instead, attempts to visually study their importance. There is something at stake here of course, best expressed perhaps in the words of Susan Sontag: 'Even when photographers are most concerned with mirroring reality, they are still haunted by tacit imperatives of taste and conscience' (2002: 6). MacDougall takes defiance into the act of looking, advocating the importance of observation. 'As a filmmaker I cannot separate my aesthetic sensibilities from how I see people, and indeed I think it is our duty as filmmakers to be as honest as possible in how we see. This is very difficult – to put aside all the ways that other people, and documentary conventions, and the established academic disciplines would like us to see. To look, and to look carefully, is a way of knowing that is different from thinking' (2002: 100).

There has been a fair amount of skepticism on the role of photography in science, most of which is centred around the supposed photography's distorting filtering of the so-called real life. 'Life is not about significant details, illuminated a flash, fixed forever. Photographs are' (Sontag 2002: 81). In particular in anthropology, despite the overwhelming initial adaptation of the medium (consider for instance its extended use in the Torres-Straits expedition), photography never played a satisfactory role in anthropological enquiry during the twentieth century. With some notable exceptions, most of which derive from the last decades, photography was used as illustration or decoration for the ethnographic texts. This uneasy relation is largely due to the stigmatization of photography as an instrument used extensively by evolutionary anthropologists – from whom anthropologists of the second part of the twentieth century were seeking to disassociate themselves (Ingold 1994; Morphy 1994; Morphy and Banks 1999). It has been noted rather early, however, by anthropologists such as Mead and Bateson, for example, that there are aspects of culture that cannot be conveyed with words alone (Bateson and Mead 1942; Mead 2003). This agenda has been brought forward passionately during the last decades, notably by David MacDougall (1988, 2003, 2006) and Elizabeth Edwards (1999); yet, as these scholars point out, if anthropologists want to address visual aspects of culture, they'll need to address the image in its own terms as well. In short, to look, as well as to see.

* * *

It seems that a desired guideline as well as outcome of education in India is discipline (Pathak 2002). For me, this journey started with a discussion with a group of students (*leaders*; see Figures 14.5 and 14.6) during fieldwork. One day, just after the morning prayers were over, I was approached by two of them; they knew who I was, they knew I was coming from Germany, and they wanted to know what I was thinking about India.

Pupil A:	What do you think of India, what's different from Germany?
Ethnographer:	I think there's a lot of discipline.
P A:	(*Looking at the other pupil*) Discipline?
E:	Ehm, yes.
P A:	Here in India?

They smiled at each other, estranged, conspicuously; perhaps I was calling disciplined something that they considered self-evidently undisciplined. They never bother talk to me again, thinking perhaps I was stupid.

When, later on, I was putting together the pictures for the present chapter – a paper supposed to be a study of the morning rituals in a private school in Bangalore – I found myself terribly troubled with sequencing the pictures. Words like 'order', 'sequence', 'narration', were dominating my notes for this chapter; gradually, I realized that it were the very images which impose this need for order on my thinking. What I had made photos of was a process of lining, of putting things in order. The very ritual of morning prayers is a performance of unity, which is expected to be expressed through discipline and synchronization. Bittner writes: 'The school starts with a ritual, where all pupils are coming together to welcome their teachers, congratulate their schoolmates, sing the state and school hymn. These morning-prayers show in intensification the governing practices of a school. The morning-prayers represent the meaning of schooling, as it is a collective process, where everyone has his or her position and has to behave in a synchronized way within the norms, e.g. in a respectful manner.' The mechanisms which are set in motion, from the time of entering the school up to leaving the schoolyard for the classroom, in order to produce or encourage this synchronization, are the focus of this chapter.

In discussions after fieldwork, Martin Bittner was concerned about how much of what we saw was set up due to our presence there. However, and since this is a visual study of discipline, if all was a show it was a very disciplined one; if the authorities of the school or indeed the pupils themselves chose to appear in their good clothes, well, this is then how their good clothes look like – or how I saw them.

Around 7:30 a.m., the pupils arrive at school. They first have to wait on the street outside of the school, in order to enter the school in order. Entering the school seems to be important for the lining of the morning prayers. The children would arrive either with their parent's vehicles or with hired rickshaws – only a few of them by foot. Parents sometimes stay to overview

Figure 14.2 Arriving at school[2]

A PHOTO ESSAY ON ENTERING A SCHOOL IN BANGALORE

the process of entering the school, some of them staying until their children are well within the school – adding up to pupils and school staff as the audience of the performance of entering the school. Pupils of the kindergarten are directly admitted to the school and do not have to wait in line.

Figures 14.3 Entering the school in a line

Figures 14.4 Entering the school in a line

Mostly the security men (rather than the teachers or the students themselves) are directing the operation of keeping the students in line as they enter the school. A significant aspect of the discipline is connected to waiting. It is a very difficult task to maintain a line of young pupils in relative order. The youngsters inventively or by rights of age frequently attempt (and sometimes succeed) to skip the queue.

The *leaders*[3] are in charge of guarding the inner gate of the school after the morning prayers has begun – again, pupils of the kindergarten are excluded, as they are not expected to have incorporated discipline sufficiently. Pupils who arrive late are made to wait outside the gates and will afterwards somehow be punished by the leaders for having arrived late. Additionally, there is a sign at the gate, asking the students to turn off their mobile phones. Although one cannot expect such a request to be taken very seriously by Bangalore kids from middle-class families, it seems to correspond to the closing of the gate; aiming at a control of the flow as well. Closing the door and switching off the phones mark time as well as territory.

Figure 14.5 Latecomers at the inner gate of the schoolyard

A PHOTO ESSAY ON ENTERING A SCHOOL IN BANGALORE

Figure 14.6 A pair of leaders writing down the (noteworthy) news of the day

The distillation, selection and presentation of the news is a process of lining up as well. The rules are simple: the leaders[4] should not write about crime – although they will certainly come upon it while reading the chapter, as they will come upon politics etc. They are expected to possess the wisdom which will allow them to separate useful news from uninteresting or harmful ones. Like the control of entering the schoolyard in a specific flow appears to be important for the shaping of lines, just the same seems to be the case with the flow of information.

His gaze is directed towards the schoolyard; outside the ever-growing city of Bangalore. He sits just on the borderline, on this minimal sitting place that a border affords. A border which separates inside from outside. His gaze at the school, his mind presumably not quite there yet; a schoolyard is a strange place I think when I look at this image. It is an outside in relation to the classroom and yet an inside in relation to the world outside of the school walls. A space that's changing functions, an inter-space in one sense and a non-place in another. A place eventually suitable for lining and the learning of lining to take place.

When I mention these thoughts to my colleague Martin Bittner, he agrees; 'Yes, of course,' he says, 'architecture is education.'

Figure 14.7 Pupil waiting for the morning prayers to begin

Interlude: architecture is education

Figure 14.8 Details of the school building

Figure 14.9 Details of the school building

Figure 14.10 Details of the school building

Figure 14.11 Details of the school building

> Visible, wild nature is a jumble of random curves; it contains no straight lines and few regular geometrical shapes of any kind. But the tamed, manmade world of Culture is full of straight lines, rectangles, triangles, circles and so on (Leach 1976: 51).

* * *

> The man of reason walks in a straight line because he has a goal and knows where he is going; he has made up his mind to reach some particular place and goes straight to it (Le Corbusier 1924: 274).

The lining of the pupils does not end with the end of the morning rituals: they also have to walk into the classroom in an order. As with Figure 14.14, there's someone who overviews this process. In this case, the overviewer's height, in line with the power of his position, allows him to overview the symmetry of the image he has in front of his eyes. Accordingly, the photographer, a bit more elevated, sees another symmetry, where the overviewer balances the line of students. One persistent question however is: who's mimicking whom when they hold their hands behind their backs?

Figure 14.12 Morning prayers

Figure 14.13 Morning prayers

Figure 14.14 Morning prayers

Figure 14.15 Morning prayers

A PHOTO ESSAY ON ENTERING A SCHOOL IN BANGALORE

Figure 14.16 Leaving the schoolyard for the classroom

Notes

1 The material for this article has been gathered through a research in Bangalore, India, in the summer of 2009, funded by DAAD and supervised by Prof. Christoph Wulf, to whom I'm grateful for offering me this position. This text, however, wouldn't have been published without the invaluable assistance of my co-researcher Martin Bittner who shared his thoughts, his comments and his notes with me throughout the writing of this chapter.
2 The name of the institution has been erased at the request of my research colleagues.
3 A note on the leaders. The school is divided into four houses. Each house has its team of leaders. Students with not only good grades but overall good behaviour and leadership skills as well are chosen and asked by their teachers to become leaders, a suggestion which is usually accepted, for, as some leaders mentioned, it is a source of pride.
4 A note on the leaders – continued: the leaders are wearing buttons depicting their function (leaders or assistants) and the colours of the house they represent. They were assigned several duties concerning peripheral aspects of school life and they are expected to maintain an overview of their fellow pupils' activities (see Figures 14.5 and 14.6). Because of their duties, they are excused from participating in the morning prayers, or of coming late in the class. Yet, a leader who will arrive late at school one day will not do his duties on that day, for others not to follow his example.

References

Bateson, G., and Mead, M. (1942): *Balinese Character: A Photographic Analysis*. New York: New York Academy of Sciences.

Edwards, E. (1999): Beyond the Boundary: A Consideration of the Expressive in Photography and Anthropology. In: Morphy, H., and Banks, M. (eds): *Rethinking Visual Anthropology*, 53–80. Wiltshire: Yale University Press.

Ingold, T. (1994): Introduction to Culture. In: Ingold, T. (ed.): *Companion Encyclopedia of Social Anthropology: Humanity, Culture and Social Life*, 329–349. New York: Routledge.

Ingold, T. (2007): *Lines: A Brief History*. New York: Routledge.

Leach, E. (1976): *Culture and Communication: The Logic by Which Symbols Are Connected*. Cambridge: Cambridge University Press.

Le Corbusier (1924): *Urbanism*. Paris: Edition Cres.

MacDougall, D. (1988): *Transcultural Cinema*. Princeton: Princeton University Press.

MacDougall, D. (2002): Comments on the Email Exchange between David MacDougall and Anna Grimshaw regarding the review of With Morning Hearts. In: *Visual Anthropology Review* 18: 1–2.

MacDougall, D. (2003): Beyond Observational Film. In: Hockings, P. (ed.): *Principles of Visual Anthropology*, 115–132. New York: Mouton de Gruyter.

MacDougall, D. (2006): *The Corporeal Image: Film, Ethnography and the Senses*. Princeton: Princeton University Press.

Mead, M. (2003): Visual Anthropology in a Discipline of Words. In: Hockings, P. (ed.): *Principles of Visual Anthropology*, 3–10. New York: Mouton de Gruyter.

Morphy, H. (1994): The Anthropology of Art. In: Ingold, T. (ed.): *Companion Encyclopedia of Social Anthropology: Humanity, Culture and Social Life*, 648–685. New York: Routledge.

Morphy, H., and Banks, M. (1999): Introduction: Rethinking Visual Anthropology. In: Morphy, H., and Banks, M. (eds): *Rethinking Visual Anthropology*, 1–35. Wiltshire: Yale University Press.

Pathak, A. (2002): *Social Implications of Schooling. Knowledge, Pedagogy and Consciousness*. New Delhi: Rainbow Publishers.

Sontag, S. (2002): *On Photography*. New York: Penguin Books.

15

GOING TO SCHOOL IN INDIA

An ethnographical research at two schools in Bangalore

Urs Kübler

The Indian school system consists of a wide ranging variety of schools. They are known under designations like governmental village school, public school, private schooling, alternative school and a lot more. The charging of school fee, the use of special languages, the quality of educational transaction or the social intercourse are only some of the items in which they differ from each other.

This article is a comparison between an alternative[1] and a mainstream school in Bangalore, India. The topic of the study is the school culture,[2] as it appears in the social intercourse, the daily run and the lessons. Additionally, a view on the school building, the classrooms and the surrounding of the school, as it contributes to these conditions. My purpose was to get an inside view of the Indian school system, with its pedagogical ideas, hierarchical structures, social interactions and material conditions. It is a spotlight in a more ambitious part of the school system, as both schools, alternative and mainstream, are private, charge school fee, have a middle class clientage and use English as language. This might not be very representative, as perhaps a great amount of village government schools[3] use regional languages for the teaching and are not well resourced with materials and teaching staff, but these distinctions might not hinder the search for some lively existing ideas and practices of teaching and education in India. Perhaps it might even be helpful to study more advanced approaches of learning and education to figure out concepts and valued ideas of education.

The main object of the ethnographic research was the mainstream school, which is a Composite College that includes a class range from lower Primary over Higher Primary to High School, as well as a nursery with an extra Montessori section. So children could stay for 13 years in this institution. Our research group mostly went to the school on Monday, to accompany the morning assembly, and then attended one of the fifth classes through their school day, which normally ended near to three o'clock in the afternoon. Furthermore we visited school celebrations like the founders day or stayed for a day in another class for comparison. Our main method was shared observation added by two video cameras. Additionally, we made interviews with pupils, teachers, the principal (director), and a group discussion with some teachers of our mainly investigated class.

In between, I visited for some days also an alternative school, a little bit outside Bangalore. Here I was not allowed to use a (video) camera, as long as the pupils stayed there. I took down my notes only by writing and memory protocols. This very familiar school had open classrooms, mixed classes and also a nursery. Next to the visit of the lessons, I accompanied project groups by preparing their contributions for the 'independent day' in the free spaces around the school, had an interview with the principal, who is also working as teacher, and some in-between talks with teachers or administration staff. At this school, I was much more integrated in the events, when, for example, I was asked about German history at the end of a social science lesson or the pupils wanted me to comment on their projects. Last but not least, I participated at some ball plays, because I got invited as soon as the lesson ended.

The article starts with a narrative description[4] and reflection of the mainstream school and its daily run, followed by a description and reflection of a typical lesson of this school. Afterwards I do the same with the alternative school, which then leads to a discussion in the way of a comparative analysis of both, the mainstream and the alternative school's reflections. In the final conclusion I try to describe the relationship of both schools and to outline their typical elements.

The reader should be aware that the descriptions and reflections are filtered through my eyes and my mind. As I was in India for the first time, I didn't know much about the meanings of common habits or customs, and I was not free from subjective prejudice or bias. But nevertheless, to be a stranger was also an advantage for an ethnographic study. Seeing them for the first time, I was very attentive concerning situations and their meanings. Getting used to the circumstances often leads to habituation and things begin to appear ordinary, naturally or self-evident (Hirschauer and Amman 1997).

The mainstream school inside Bangalore

The building, the school day

The mainstream school in Bangalore is located in a well of living quarter in the belt around the inner city of Bangalore, on a street away from the main roads. The pupils come by walk, were brought by auto rickshaws, which sometimes pull six to eight and more of them at a time,[5] or by bus or motorcycles. Before the school opens the gates at twenty past eight, they have to build a queue before the gate, for entering in a line. The construction of this line is controlled by a member of the administration staff, who sometimes touches or beats the pupils with a wooden stick to get them in the right formation. By the opening of the gate, the pupils pass the school building on their left side and go to the inner schoolyard. Doing this, they have to pass some of their schoolmates, which are called 'leaders' and take care that everybody conforms to the rules. This may refer to the tidiness of the school uniform or the shoes, but also whether they walk on the right or left side of the way according to age and sex.[6] On the right side of this way there is a small stretch of land with some green plants, a playground for the nursery and some free resting places, where pupils have to wait when they arrive after the beginning of the morning assembly.

On the left side of the way there is first a private house also covered by green plants, then the administration building, the nursery rooms, the big and convoluted primary building and at last, after an inner schoolyard, which includes a roofed and an open part, there is the high-school building. The houses look very dry and functional. They consist of washed concrete, have up to two floors, small stairs and a small hallway before the classrooms. There is no further hall or space, and everything seems very tight and narrow, an impression enhanced by the large number of pupils who share the rooms and buildings. In most of the rooms there is a picture of the school's founder, his child which is strongly connected to the historical foundation of the school, and a famous guru. Furthermore there is a calendar, which often has overhanging edges due to the ventilators situated on the ceiling of the rooms. Next to the entering way and before the administration office there are two blackboards, on which some students write the thought of the day, a quiz[7] and some news about current events. Posted on a billboard next to these there are some copies of newspaper articles. The classroom furniture consists of small tables and benches, which can't be moved, a teacher's table next to the billboard, a cupboard for learning stuff and a shelf for the food packages that the pupils are carrying from home. Otherwise, there is not much shaping of the rooms and spaces of the building.

After entering the inner courtyard, the pupils ran around playing and talking for some minutes, until two teachers begin to order them in lines, using their arms and whistles like traffic policemen. Slowly the classes begin to stand in lines, always oriented to a big stage which is part of the roofed courtyard. This process takes more than 10 minutes until the whole school stands well arranged. While the male teachers take care for the lining up of the whole school, the female teachers take care for the classes they belong to. Finally one of the teachers takes the microphone on the stage and the assembly can begin.

First the teacher gives some commands through the microphone, telling the pupils to change their stand between a straight and a relaxed way.[8] Then one of the pupils who stays on the stage to lead the assembly declares the thought of the day, which is repeated by all pupils. Afterwards another pupil reads a quiz, which somebody has to find out and answer through the microphone. This is followed by some national and religious chanting and a silent prayer. Coming to the end, all of the birthday children introduce themselves to the assembly, which subsequently repeats by singing a birthday song for them. Finally, the birthday children shake the hand of the principal and get a candy from the stage-teacher. The assembly is finished by a collective greeting of all the teachers by the pupils. Line by line the pupils leave to their classrooms.

Now the pupils have to face the progression of seven subjects which always last about 45 minutes for each subject, and in between they have one break of 30 minutes. Change of lesson is sometimes fluent, when teachers shake hands at the entrance. Sometimes the class has to wait alone. Then some leaders, who are ordered for this duty, observe their classmates and draw up check lists of their misbehaving fellows on the board. They always find a lot who seem to be too loud or loose, and these pupils are expected to get some punishment from the next teacher.[9] Another way to pass the break between two subjects is to sing together. This is guided by some pupils in the front.

The main break for half an hour is at 12 o'clock, after the first four lessons. During this time, many pupils go to the toilet first and wash their hands before eating their meals, which they carry in their food boxes from home. They have to take it from the shelf in the back of the classroom where it is stored in the morning. Because of the tight and narrow space of the classrooms and the whole school building, the break starts with busy crowding until everybody is able to sit at his place for eating. Sometimes the teacher stays in the classroom, sharing the meal. The pupils can talk and behave in a less observed way, and when the meal is finished, they have nearly 10 minutes for free, during which the class can relax. Some talk to each other, ask the teacher for leaving the room, perhaps get a visit or run around. The teacher, who mostly is still present and works at his table, doesn't care too much during this period.[10] Only at the end of the break, he leads the pupils to a further silent period, where everybody lays down his head and upper part of the body on the table to have a rest.[11] The teacher probably leaves the room now, leaving back some pupils responsible to surveil this procedure again by writing down the names and making check lists of rule breakers.

The class schedule[12] on Monday is English, Kannada, Math, Moral Science, Social Science, Physical Education and General Science. The lessons are mostly structured by an intensive communication between the teacher and the class. A lot of times, the teacher asks and the pupils to answer together. If they answer individually, they normally have to stand up. Most of the teachers use schoolbooks, which all of the pupils own, but despite this they recite the book's exercises and texts, so that the pupils can memorize or write down the exercises by listening to the voice of the teacher. Some still take the book or look at the neighbour's notebook. Interestingly, the teacher often after a question also recites the correct answer. Mostly the lessons are divided into a more communicative part, during which the teacher recites and explains in an interactive manner and by integrating the pupils through comprehension questions or memorizing tasks, and a following part characterized by individual work, during which exercises are written down. Still, here, it seems pupils are allowed to copy from the classmate.

Despite these typical teaching methods in this class, or at this school,[13] there are a lot of differences between the individual teachers in the way of creating their subjects, for example, the use of a beginning and a closing ritual of the lessons. Some celebrate it very strictly, some just don't use it. This holds more or less for the use of praise or punishment, too. It seems to be very common to touch or hit the pupils' body for getting them to comply with an order, or to punish them for rule breaking, disturbing or inattentive behaviour. Still some don't do it. The other way round, some teachers put a strong emphasis on praising the pupils for correct answers or well-done performances. Sometimes they demand the classmates to applaud. Another difference is to be found in the handling of loudness during class, depending on the use of punishment or the call for discipline at the time of presentation of the subject.

Apart from their classes, the pupils belong to one of three school groups, the so-called houses. Every house has its own name, colour and dress, which the pupils wear on a special day of the week instead of their common school uniforms. Just like the classes, the houses are organized by leaders who are appointed by the teachers and take care for the adequate behaviour of their house-mates. Being a leader is a chance to become a responsible member of society, as the principal and some teachers explain. The houses compete against each other in sportive activities, and there are also competitions with other schools.

The school celebrates some cultural events, like founder's day or Independence Day. There are a lot of group performances in dancing, singing and other stage programmes. The pupils prepare these presentations on the school ground, mostly after the classes, but sometimes they get free time in between the lessons. Founder's day, for example, is a whole day-long celebration which is strongly focused on the presentations of these different acting groups, who show very elaborate performances which always are applauded enthusiastically.

Reflection

The school has a high degree of mass organization, which is established by guidelines for correct behaviour. The official social converse is ruled by discipline and punishment. The items of correct behaviour are advised by principles which convey the right manners for all pupils. How to dress, how to walk, on which place to be, which body posture to have, and how to behave are prescribed for a lot of situations. To be a good pupil means to behave in a predefined way, and the one who is successfully doing this has a chance to become a leader. This means to supervise the schoolmates in the compliance of correct behaviour. In the official school discourse a leader has the ability to guide other pupils, and the appointment of a pupil to a leader position is an educational method which should support him to become a responsible member of society. Next to being a good role model, he has to monitor his fellows and report their misdoings to the teachers who probably will speak out some punishments.

The underlying concept of such an educational system, which leads to the idea of an ideal-typical behaviour, has a hierarchical impact, as the one who is more successfully doing this is the better one and furthermore has the chance to reach a superior position.

Next to this principal guided and hierarchically organized items of social life, the use of rituals and ritual elements[14] is another topic of the school's culture. Standing or walking in line, performing the morning assembly, the handling of welcome and leave-taking in the lessons, the collective singing in the break or the celebration of school events like founder's day are examples for the embedding of ritual elements in everyday school life. These common rituals amalgamate the many individual pupils to a unique or uniform figure. This opens, next to further functions of rituals like the establishing of hierarchical levels or steady habits, the possibility to merge in a bigger group of fellows. This effect of synchronization may impact the feelings for each other in the way of losing a bit of the individual boundaries between the participants or releasing from the act of defining oneself in distinction to the others. A partly loss of the self and a feeling in the way of a flow[15] may be possible. Reaching this kind of consciousness can lead to a transforming process, which affects the individuality of the pupils and is related to the educational targets incorporated in the school culture.

How pupils deal with these circumstances of being ruled by principals, getting pressed into hierarchical structures and taking part in ritualized activities is a question which leads to the explication of a further culture inside the school, the pupils culture. Do they grow into this school culture to a high extent or do they just use it to figure out their own performing and communication practices, and how do teachers react? The high level of discipline by the pupils, which is connected to the system of leaders and the threat and execution of punishment, is subverted by a lot of minimal interaction activities, performed in between or during the official elements of school structure. Reading under the table, hassling while standing in the line, ignoring the teachers' announcements and talking to classmates is frequently found and represents an experience in and of the school differing from official purposes and official school culture. Individual development takes place in the dispute and handling of the given circumstances. This might lead to the result of disciplined pupils, but not necessarily. The pupils show a lot of enthusiasm and excitement if they are allowed and enabled to by the teachers.

General science as first lesson of the day, starting with a yoga exercise

The pupils, coming from the morning assembly, enter their classroom, sit down or drink some water out of their bottles. The girls sit on the left side of the middle gang, the boys on the right one. With the teacher approaching her table, all pupils rise. She stays some seconds in front of the class just looking, while the room is getting silent, then she calls out 'Good morning'. The pupils chorally recall 'Good morning!', and after one more short break she calls 'Sit!', which is followed by the pupils. Some moments later, they are storing their luggage under the tables, the teacher again calls in a sharply manner: 'Ok, sit straight, close your eyes!' As the children do so, she walks the middle floor between the tables and pushes some of the pupils for correcting their posture.[16] Then, with an in between break of about 10 seconds, she gives the alternating commands: 'Breathe in!' and 'Breathe out!' The pupils are following and while breathing out exclaim a long-lasting 'Ohm'. Apart from that, the class is silent and one can hear the loud voicing of the neighbouring class[17] and some more sharp commands of the teacher, who takes care for correct posture, closed eyes and absolute silence. Sometimes she abruptly strikes a loosely sitting child again to bring it back in right position. After about eight times of breathing in and out, the pupils change the exercise by putting their fingers on their eyes and their thumbs into the ears. Some more breathing rhythms later, the pupils rub their hands to get them warm and hold them on their necks and faces. The teacher stops the yoga exercise with a short 'Relax'.

After the yoga exercise, the teacher checks the attendance of the pupils. In alphabetical order, each of the nearly 50 pupils stands up shortly and calls out his or her name. While the teacher now has to drop something from the cupboard, the pupils talk silently for one or two minutes. Then a birthday child wearing ordinary clothes stands up with a plastic box full of sweets and moves to the front. He gives a sweet to the teacher and the class starts to sing 'Happy Birthday' for him. Afterwards they clap and count the number of years of his age. Then he goes around, distributing his goodies. Some of the pupils shake his hand or talk a bit to him.

Now the science lesson starts. The teacher demonstrates the meaning of 'force' by pushing a chair back and forth on the floor. She asks the pupils about this, who mostly answer chorally by repeating her explanations. Then she pushes the chair again, but now a pupil has to push it back to her. She writes the different kinds of push and pull forces down on the table:

Any push and pull-force

1 Moves any object
2 Moving objects can be stopped
3 Change of speed
4 Change of direction

Additionally, she gives some examples like the rickshaw drivers, who drive slowly when they drive up the hills of Bangalore. As a next step she describes and writes down different kinds of force:

Types of force

1 Muscular force
2 Magnetic force
3 Electro static force

The pupils repeat by reading or answering the written text chorally. Then the teacher gives the advice they should be able to answer questions concerning this at all times, before she wipes it off. In the following, she asks for an example of muscular force. The pupils answer individually while briefly standing up. She asks about magnetic force, and a lot of pupils call out answers. 'Ah, good, how very well!', she praises.

The next step is an experiment. Some pupils have to rub a ruler on their hand, while their classmates are very engaged in commenting this.

They stand up, spread out their body over the desk and cry out answers concerning the experiment. It seems they like to be involved. The teacher now gives examples to the whole class, and the pupils identify the kind of force chorally. 'Forces that open a door?' – 'Muscular force!' the pupils answer. The teacher starts sentences and the pupils finish them in common. Sometimes, when the class gets too restless, because of talking or playing under the desk, the teacher gets a loud and definite voice, but quickly returns to her usual intonation.

In the last part of the lesson, the teacher writes down some questions to be answered, with the advice to copy them correctly. The pupils ask for also getting the correct answers, but the teacher refuses.[18] She walks from desk to desk, controlling the exercise books and sometimes marking them inside. After the ringing of the bell, a pupil reads his answers loudly, and the teacher gives advice for the next lesson. Then she takes her stuff and cleans the blackboard before leaving the room. The pupils stand up and chorally exclaim: 'Good day, Miss.'

Reflection

After coming from the morning assembly, the class performs another ritual setting, the yoga or meditation exercise. It is a body-focused, rhythmical exercise synchronizing the classmates who stay in close contact with their body. The different phases focus breathing, maintaining of concentration and body posture. As everybody does the same during this exercise, the individual activities are at a low level, and the classmates come or flow together in a shared activity. But this is limited, as the teacher goes around, poking some of the pupils. They still have to be aware of their body posture. The poking also shows that the individual pupil is not the sovereign of his or her body, as the teacher can touch him without forewarning. By her touching and prescribing the postures and sounds of the pupils, the body appears as a medium of education and agitation for the teacher and the school culture she represents.

Before starting the actual science lecture, there are two more ritual procedures: the roll call and the birthday celebration. Both constitute class community and social intercourse. The supervision of attendance performed by the roll call is a very purposive procedure. As everybody has to function in a straight and formal way, the act of surveillance seems to be more important than the appreciation of the individual pupils. The gesture of controlling creates an atmosphere of compulsion. The activity of the pupils is a strict result of the given presetting. The birthday celebration, now for the second time after the morning assembly within the frame of the class, is also formalized, but provides a lot more free space to chat, move loosely and behave spontaneously. The pupil is in a central position.

Giving the science lecture, the teacher uses a chair to demonstrate the meaning of force. After this, she refers to instances like the rickshaw driver to establish a connection to the everyday experience of the pupils. Physical experiment and reference to everyday life are measures to maintain the pupils' grasping of the phenomena. But the lesson is predetermined, and by exactly repeating the explanations, the pupils have to reproduce the prescribed conceptions. The experiments are done only by the teacher or some of the pupils. Rote learning and reiteration constitute the main didactical basic with the purpose of an exact repetition of the given input.[19] As the pupils repeatedly beg for predetermined answers to write them down in their exercise books, it seems that they like[20] this kind of rote learning and getting predetermined answers. Exact repetition and doing exactly the same seems to be a structural element in the school culture.

The pupils have exactly defined codes of conduct concerning their activities, their body posture and the way they take part in the lesson. Observation and controlling by the teacher are changing from very strict to more lavish. The pupils use this to slip out of their predetermined rolls and pursue some parallel activities or modify the respective kind of interaction in their preferred sense. Then they just cry out answers or follow some other activities under the desk.

The alternative school near to Bangalore

Introduction

For three days, I visited an alternative school out of Bangalore. Here I only made memos by writing them down, as they didn't want me to use video cameras or recorders. During these three days I received a welcome speech, guidance through the building, had some talks with teachers in between and an interview with the principal. Furthermore, I had talks and plays with some of the pupils in the breaks. During my stay, there have been lots of group projects in order to prepare for Independence Day. This caused an extraordinary timetable at these days. I also visited two or three classes, due to the fact that there was no easy comparison with the fifth class of the mainstream school, as here there were classes of mixed age.

The building/the school day

The alternative school is situated about half an hour outside of Bangalore, by car. Most of the children get carried by special school buses, which pick them up directly at their residences around the city. This will take more than one hour until the bus has picked up everybody. There are less than 50 pupils and nearly as many children in the nursery, which is situated in the rooms downstairs. Before the start of the school day at 8.30 a.m., the children run around, mostly in the schoolyard on the right side, the size of which is bigger than that of the building and on which a very stable looking basketball hoop is affixed. Besides, the schoolyard consists only of flat soil and is framed by trees and a hedgerow, a fence and the sidewall of the school building.

The school building is made of red mud bricks and natural stone. The rooms lie around an inner courtyard, which is half roofed and open to the surrounding on two sides. Different sorts of green plants are cultivated in the roof-free part, next to a mosaicked floor, which has several levels. The roofed part offers some seating accommodation and is used for different purposes, like eating in the break, school projects or just standing around. The building rests on pillars connected by arches replacing conventional walls. Instead of a door, the rooms have an arch to enter through,[21] which connects to the inner courtyard by crossing an arcade. Whereas the walls between the nursery rooms are opened by arches, the ones between the classrooms are closed. Downstairs on the left side are the nursery rooms, a kitchen and a bathroom, on the right side the teacher's and administration rooms, upstairs are the classrooms and a library. In the classrooms there are corkboards on the walls, next to pupils' paintings, and on the blackboard still is yesterday's written text. Surrounding the school, there are lots of free spaces; at a distance, there are some agriculture fields and another school. As this place is somewhat out-of-town, the access road is not tarred.

For the morning assembly, the teacher and the pupils come together on the first floor. Everybody sits, stands or leans on a wall in the space between library and staircase, and after an informal greeting, the principal tells about the affairs of the day or the week. The pupils sometimes interrupt her by making a plea, and their involvement is requested, as the principal finally asks them to commend her statements. The exchange can also be used to address personal affairs, if somebody wants to, and this can open up a common discussion or sharing of experiences and knowledge about a topic.[22] Until the end of the assembly, I couldn't notice any formal ritual elements.

At nine o'clock the lessons begin. Here, too, everything proceeds more informal, as I couldn't observe any ritual performances at the beginning or the end of a lesson. There is neither a bell nor any choral activities or speaking. By visiting some lessons, I got the impression that the pupils more or less can do what they want. If they follow the teacher's impartation or do something else, like throwing balls of paper, sleeping on the desk or just leaving the room for some time, teachers do not intervene in these kinds of activity. Some of the teachers just leave them, some try to involve them by continuously raising up questions about the topic, directed to one pupil after another. Doing this, they try to promote the progress of the lesson and involve the pupils in discussions.

The timetable includes conventional courses like science, chemistry, math, social science, English, Hindi, Kannada, etc. In between, after 45 minutes, there is a short break, which some of the pupils use for a ball game at the schoolyard. Lunch break lasts about an hour, and on some days parents involved in the school's happenings cook some warm meal which is eaten together in the inner schoolyard. Pupils, teachers and the nursery staff are sitting or standing around in mixed groups, as there is no formal eating furniture. As usual, pupils address the teachers by their forename.

When preparing a celebration like Independence Day, as during my attendance, for one and a half hour in the morning, the whole school is practicing all around on the school ground. There is dancing, singing, writing of banners or acting. The projects are across classes, and the pupils appear very active, while the teachers tend to adopt the role of mediators. They concede the pupils a lot of free time. But there is not only harmony, as for instance one of the older girls, who guides a drama group, is very desperate when one of her actors refuses to play his role any longer. Or a group of older boys reject to take part in Independence Day, as they think it is boring.[23] They have to confront much discussion over some days, with the principal and some teachers, about their kind of participation or attendance at Independence Day, but for the whole time they didn't take part in any of the projects. Just to do something, they decided to make paper folding during the practice time. Another confusing event was contributed by a very dedicated mother, who brought a whistle to practice the marching.[24] Hearing the sound of the whistle, some of the older pupils groaned loudly, as they couldn't believe to hear such a sound at this place. Afterwards they sit down, refusing the order to establish a row formation. Completely different from this are the younger children, mostly from the nursery, who enthusiastically practise the marching, which later on brought up the idea of a steady marching group for regularly practicing. These divergent attitudes often lead to breaks and produce a mood of desperation, as the processes got stuck. Then time goes on without working on the subject.

To finish the school day, the classes come together for a further short-term assembly at the same place as in the morning. There is a short exchange about the actual state of affairs, before saying good bye and leaving for the two or three buses waiting before the building to take the pupils, but also some teachers and parents back to their homes in and around Bangalore. By trudging through the suburbs, the pupils have to stand the noise and smell of the Bangalore traffic, which can last up to one and a half hour. Inside the small buses there is a familiar atmosphere, as teachers, parents, pupils and the bus driver make a lot of cross communication. There is talking, singing, laughing and sometimes silence next to the sound and vibration of the engine. From time to time some of the pupils leave the bus.

Reflection

Arriving at the alternative school, after crossing some of Bangalore's highways, is like coming to a small and beautiful island. The wide spaces around, the natural environment, the silence and the building itself with it natural stones, the brick arches and the open spaces compose a nice atmosphere. The building and the rooms appear tidy and harmonically arranged. The whole atmosphere seems very familiar, as everybody knows each other and the pupils play in groups. They wear individual clothes, address the teachers by their forename and add to the discussion about daily affairs. All these are indicators for a low-level hierarchical system. Discussion is the way to solve problems, and the pupils don't have to face punishment or to comply with the power of disciplinary action. They are involved in many decisions and are required to choose own solutions.

This may bring forth very active pupils who create own ideas and advocate their rights by taking part in the daily policy. This educational concept of adopting responsibilities in the lives of the pupils also leads to a lot of idleness, as the pupils don't follow the lesson or disturb teaching by doing something else. Perhaps the big amount of time used for discussion and being unaware of the lesson's subject is necessary to create this alternative model, which is hardly delegated top down. In this way, the school is an open experiment because it can't predict what will come out by including the pupils in many responsibilities.

The school doesn't practice much ritual elements in a traditional way. The morning assembly has the mood of an informal meeting or work coordination. There is no synchronized activity, but it opens a space to share common experiences between the teachers and the pupils. Bringing together different kinds of views about a topic, and in a sense about the world, is perhaps next to classroom work and project practicing another model of learning, which needs this special kind of open space. In this way the morning assembly is low level, but still specifically ritualized and opens a space for a learning style characterized by a less functional way of carrying together experiences and knowledge of the attendants.

On the whole, the school has a democratic culture by including the pupils in decision making and by strengthening them to stand for their personal rights without avoiding problematical situations. This is probably possible by the assurance not to be punished or disadvantaged when doing this. And it coincides with the handling of personal contact respecting the individuality of the particular pupil and his learning speed, which is quite possible considering the low amount of pupils. All in all, this shapes the culture of the school, everybody seems to be privileged.

First lesson, starting after the morning assembly

The first lesson after the morning assembly in a class with younger pupils (aged about eight to ten years) is science. The teacher leaves the classroom again soon after arriving. The pupils are sitting at their places, talking or doing something. Nobody looks after anybody else. When the teacher comes back, she carries a pocketknife and starts to cut through a plastic bottle. The boys first have to wash their own bottle before they follow this lead and also cut the upper part of them. After this, they put the cut part crosswise inside the basic part of the bottle.

Then the class leaves downstairs, where they stand around in the inner courtyard and a little bit outside the building, boys and girls separated, while the teacher again leaves. The boys start to show their body power by imitating a smash-through of the bottles by hand (the bottles are already cut) or kick them around. The girls sit or stay together and talk. One time they give me a sign to come to them. As the teacher comes back, the whole class enters the faculty and administration rooms. On a comfortable seating accommodation the pupils sink down, while the teacher takes cellotape from the secretariat to fix name tags on the bottles. As they sit very relaxed on the black leather sofas, it seems that this is neither new nor special for them. After putting the name tags on the bottles, we leave for the schoolyard where the teacher instructs the pupils to search small stones, which should be put inside the bottle. Meanwhile, the boys have started to play a bit of football. Kanu,[25] a member of the administration who just came to hand out some tea for the associate staff, indignantly interrupts them by ordering to stop the game. The boys follow and start to search for stones.

After some further explanations and the filling of the bottle with some stones and a bit of water, the children have created a water-level gauge, which now has to be fixed in a solid way on the ground. Thus, the class leaves the school ground through a hedgerow onto a big field which seems to be unused. Here the bottles are put on the ground by consolidating them with stones from the field. A girl who found a big roof tile tries to smash it by dropping it on the ground. She is not successful and some of the girls come together and try to help her. Several attempts and a discussion later, they figure out to break the tile by crushing it with some other stones. The tile now splits into pieces and the girls place them around the bottom of the water-level gauges. While this happens, one of the boys marches around carrying a big bamboo cane on his shoulder. 'Who needs help? I'm a soldier', he calls out over and over. As he meets the girls group they deny his offer. After leaving the field back to school, another boy, left behind, begins to ask the teacher about his construction by shouting after her, but she doesn't react any more.

Reflection

The classroom offers much space and there seems to be no fixed configuration of the two-person tables. Some children sit alone, and I can't discover any male–female assignment. After the teacher leaves, there is no great change of behaviour, but as some of the pupils rest with their head on their hand and elbow, writing, reading or doing nothing, it seems that they just follow their own purpose, more or less aware of the teachers temporary absence. Being back, the teacher cuts the plastic bottle, in a mode of just doing it for herself, without any demonstrative gesture. She cuts the bottles for some of the pupils who want her to do it. These pupils stand around the teacher-table, observing her handling knife and bottle, others remain at their own table, not showing much attention for the teacher's practice.

Interestingly, this teacher doesn't spend much activity in keeping the pupils in line or taking care if they focused on the subject submitted in the lesson. She does not only leave the class at several times but is mainly involved in her own attachment to the lesson's item. However, it doesn't appear as not taking care of the pupils or not being really interested in them, but rather as being highly aware of this situation. It seems that she practices a teaching style which is based on mimetic learning, being involved in the lesson's subject and not laying much stress on observing and disciplining the pupils.[26] She is mainly trying to get them focused by doing the 'act of focusing on the practice' on her own. Not all of the pupils are involved in the teaching, and most notably the boys drop out, especially in situations outside the classroom.

Spontaneously, another member of the administration staff interrupts the boys' football match while the teacher is present. This might be no familiar help or anything similar to that but rather seems to be the result of a lack of clarity in the sphere of competence and the educational concept. This is underlined by my talk with a teacher and the interview with the principal. While the principal emphasized there are different concepts of teaching, especially when comparing the newcomers who more or less still carry the concepts of their former schools and the older teaching staff. In contrast to the older teaching staff, the new teachers say that the pupils should at least 'stay by the subject', which should not be subverted.

Kanu's intervening in the football match refers to this 'staying by the subject', as his interruption brings the boys back to 'the subject' of the lesson, the filling of the bottle with small stones. The football match may be seen as a loss of the lesson's subject and thus seems to legitimize his right to penetrate into the science teacher's sphere of responsibility.

The handling of the 'stay by or loss of the subject' seems to be a focal point in the teaching concept of this school. For a part of the administration staff or some teachers the 'loss of subject' seems to be the starting point for the application of measures which apart from this should also regulate the self-responsibility of the pupils. Another part of the teaching staff still prefers not to regulate this behaviour. The football match intervention is an example for the handling of this contradiction between two of the schools' educational topics, the self-responsibility of the pupils and the 'stay by the subject'. While this contradiction seems to be aware in the school's discourse, as two members of the teaching staff tell me about it, there seems to be no concerted action in the handling of this phenomenon.

The short stay in the administration rooms does not show much distinction between pupils, administration and teaching staff. The class behaves very homelike and casual entering the administration sphere and there seem to be no formalized rules of conduct. When the pupils loosely sink down on the sofas, they behave very relaxed and eased, which may be seen as an indicator of an anxiety- and tension-free relation between the groups. At least, this shows that their relationship is not ruled by formalized body postures. The administration and teacher rooms are not a restricted area, as I experience a further time during the interview in the principal's room. A group of pupils knock and enter the room to state a complaint about a recent school day's extraordinary duration and successfully negotiate a school-free Saturday, meanwhile my interview is interrupted.[27]

Last, but not least, this lesson is an example of a more practical and haptic learning style, which is not enhanced by extraordinary facilities but by the fantasy and improvisation of the teacher and the helpful manifoldness of the school's surrounding. All pupils build their own water-level gauge, which they can observe the following days. They have to solve problems like the fixing of the bottle on the ground or the smashing of the roof tile, which brings some of the girls together in a common activity. There seems to be an emphasis on social and practical skills and learning by own experiences with the lesson's topic.

Discussion/comparative analysis

It seems to be a big difference to visit the mainstream or the alternative school, both located in Bangalore. The difference starts on the way to school with the experience of the school building and its surrounding. Each school is a small cosmos in itself, with its own different ways of functioning and involvement of the pupils in the social context. Going to the mainstream school, pupils are confronted with many codes of conduct, with simultaneous group activities like standing, walking, praying or singing, with moral slogans, with teachers and some classmates in charge of them, and disciplinary sanctions if they fail to comply with the rules. The school has more than 1,000 pupils, and since space is narrow, there is not much place for the single pupil. The degree of adaptation to norms and rules of conduct is very high.

In contrast, the alternative school has a lot of room and a very familiar atmosphere. As there are only about 50 pupils, everybody knows each other, the pupils call the teachers by their forenames and in the break they sit and eat together in the inner schoolyard. The pupils wear personal clothes and they have no rituals with synchronized performances. They are encouraged to take over responsibility for themselves as for their school affairs, and discussion is the way to solve problems or conflicts. The school offers conditions for a personal contact between teachers and pupils which influences educational and learning processes and probably helps to reduce the quantity of rules of behaviour.

The mainstream school is hierarchically structured, the teachers have absolute authority over the pupils, and among these there are also different levels, as the leaders have to take care of or control their schoolmates. This comes along with the idea of an ideal behaviour or an exemplary kind of development worthwhile for everybody.[28] As there is a defined way of behaving, there is also a defined way of what to learn. The pupil should be able to learn and reproduce the predetermined contents taken from the schoolbooks. Rote learning is the main activity of the pupils, and the educational idea seems to be the development of knowledge in the sense of factual knowledge. By using experiments or examples of the life of the pupils the teacher tries to enhance the understanding of the phenomena, but still she delivers given facts. There is hardly any reflection or discussion about the subject matter, just repetition. Good pupils are pupils who know much and behave correctly. They confirm with the official school culture and try to support it. Doing this, they are told to become successful members of society. In this way, this school is an institution that supports and maintains given ideas of knowledge, education and behaviour. The individuality of the respective pupil is not important, but the maintaining and preservation of special ideas and ideals. This is the best for everybody, and to realize it a hierarchical system is needed.

At the alternative school, the school culture is less hierarchical. The pupils are challenged to find their own ways of participation, as the teacher is not regulating their habits, behaviours or body postures. Discussion is the way to solve conflicts and to find common solutions, and the pupils have to learn to find their own perspectives and to confront each other. As the teachers are not so much interested in the repetition of given facts, they ask the pupils more about their own opinions and statements. This is a challenge to rethink and reflect about the particular items. Furthermore, they have some practical experiences, as they make experiments on their own or in groups. This dealing and coping of exercises in small groups involves the pupils in social intercourses and leads to social and practical skills. These skills are also supported by some more items of the school's culture, like the calling by forename among all school members, the common meal and the open rooms and spaces. Less hierarchical structures, active participation and social involvement should lead to the development of responsibility for themselves as for school affairs, which is one of the main items of this school culture.[29] All in all, the school is not so much interested in conveying established ideas as in developing the individuality of the pupils.

Another great difference between the two schools is the handling of ritual elements. Each day in the mainstream school is filled with rituals or ritualistic elements. They are structured in a more conventional way, which means they consist of shared common activities that are practiced in synchronized formations. The synchronization may involve the voice and speech, the body posture and the movement of the body. It can be an interplay like the teacher–pupil interaction or a total synchronization like the singing or the silent prayer in the morning assembly. The rituals are helpful to establish an arrangement and a structure for the crowds of pupils and their activities, and they constitute the school culture in the body of the pupils.

The alternative school has no rituals of this conventional synchronized form implemented in daily routine. But this doesn't mean they have no rituals at all, as their social intercourse contains ritualized elements, too. For example, the morning assembly can be seen as a ritual to enable a free conversation between the pupils and the teachers. Its open and loose form supports a kind of debate, discussion or compilation of facts which is dedicated to the school's idea of an open and low hierarchical way of learning and communicating. The ritual arrangement of this morning assembly allows space for the participants to bring in their individual perspectives in a forum which partially regulates the school affairs and enables new kinds of learning, like the common collecting and sharing of knowledge and experiences, in which the teacher and pupils are more or less equal.

Both schools use ritual elements which are structured due to their ideas of learning. While the 'everybody does the same' rituals of the mainstream school support a learning style, which tries to convey a perfect form applying for everybody, the rituals of the alternative school allow space to facilitate individual development. As rituals are not functional elements of the syllabus, they represent the respective school culture, and, furthermore, implant it in the life of the pupils. The obvious high amount of rituals or ritual elements in the mainstream school can perhaps be explained by its philosophy of giving or 'implanting' an ideal kind of knowledge and behaviour. But since a ritual is not a functional instrument, it is not easy to determine the influence of rituals or ritual elements on the participants. The partly loss of individual boundaries and the flow effect of the synchronized rituals practiced by the mainstream school may also have a strong impact on the development of the individual pupil. Then again, not to grab or represent the own perspective in a ritual offering some space for this may detain individual development. Thus, the rituals and ritual elements have a more holistic character which can't be subsumed under the 'official' ideas or ideals of the schools.

Part of the school's culture is the pupils' culture, i.e. the handling of given circumstances by the pupils. Whereas the pupils of the mainstream school create a subculture, which perhaps helps them not to become a 'designed' pupil shaped by the rules of behaviour, the alternative school does not seem to have such an elaborate pupils' subculture. As the pupils here don't have to hide their habits, interests and communicative practices, they are not compelled to create their own delimited culture. Their loosely, unwilling or disturbing behaviour is for the larger part not sanctioned by the teachers. An exception is the 'stay by the subject' which is handled in different ways by the teachers. But there seems to be an element of subculture in the teachers community, since they don't have a common concept of handling this topic[30] and the pupils don't hide their 'absence from the subject' from them.

As well as the rituals or ritual elements, the existence of a pupils' subculture might possibly lead to a strengthening of the pupils' individual development, which in this case would subvert the school culture in both cases, as the alternative school, to enforce the individual development of their pupils, does not have an outlined pupils' subculture, and the mainstream school, interested in creating an ideal form of development, just creates a strong pupils' subculture. Both schools might also create educational topics not corresponding to the school's purposes.

Conclusion

Whereas the mainstream school represents the educational system of the society with its social, political and economical impacts, the alternative school is an attempt to find solutions for some of these educational standards they consider to be worth to be improved. In this way, the mainstream school is the starting point of the alternative school to find far-reaching solutions and reasonable adjustments according to its educational ideas or ideals. Maybe in one or two decades some of these ideas will find their way into the mainstream schools, just like today's methods of the mainstream school may be evaluated more progressive than those of some decades ago.[31]

From this perspective, the comparison of both schools puts a spotlight on the current conditions of school culture in India, where it comes from and where it probably tends to go. For sure, the school culture of the alternative school is only one of a lot more indicators for a possible development of the school system, but it is a space where new kinds of school community and teaching methods are figured out in a practical way and can be validated. To improve the school system, in 1989 the Indian government founded the National Institute of Open Schooling (NIOS) which tries to implement basic alternative learning approaches in mainstream schools (Raghavan 2007: 46).

If we proceed from these parameters, we may assume that the Indian school system contemporarily has a high degree of hierarchical systems, works with threat and punishment, is very much based on rote learning and tries to push the pupils in predefined kinds of behaviour. But in the long run it tends to change to lower hierarchical structures, tries to give the pupils more responsibilities and participation, enhances social and practical experiences and has a stronger focus on the individual development of each pupil. Whether these developments will enter the mainstream school system depends on a lot more factors, but the outcome of the competition of old and new methods surely is one of them.

Another item of this survey was the insight that a school culture is no formation to be functionally modelled. It has holistic elements, like ritual settings or subcultural elements, which have unpredictable effects and resist functional usurpation. Purposes, intentions and the corresponding methods for achieving educational targets do not totally coincide with the expected outcome, the modelling and shaping of the pupils' personality. The pupils do not totally adopt the system they are confronted with. They find ways to subvert or underrun the instances and circumstances of their schooling environment everywhere, and in this way, they create their own small rooms and terms of activeness.

Notes

1 The term 'alternative' is used in the sense of progressive teaching methods (Ullrich 2008: 77).
2 The term 'culture' in relationship with school refers to a complex interaction of norms, values and premises on the one side, and their arrangement and precipitations on the different levels of the school's organization on the other side (cf. Esslinger-Hinz 2010: 13).
3 On the state of schooling in government village schools, see Sarangapani (2003: 11).
4 I reproduce the field data as a narrative description to create a lively picture of the school life (Geertz 1987; Girtler 2001: 19).
5 Normally they are built to transport two or three people.
6 One of the reasons for the different paths may be the protection of the small children who visit the nursery.
7 A thought was, for example: 'A guilty conscience needs no accuser, a quiet conscience makes one severe.' The quiz at this day was: 'Which is the first newspaper published in India? Ans: Bengali Gazette.'
8 The commands were 'Attention please!' and 'Stay at ease!', and in my view they had a military character.
9 Not every teacher is doing this, some just want the names to get wiped off, some have them to write exercises or they have to stay during the next lesson. By the interview with the pupils we got told or rather showed further and harder punishments.
10 Nevertheless, the class is not so agitated when the teacher is present.
11 This was not a common habit at the school.
12 Of a fifth standard class.
13 I also found similar didactics in another fifth and a seventh class.
14 In rituals, as I use this concept, practical and physical knowledge is required through mimetic processes. The sustainability of their educational impact is due to their repetitive, symbolic and performative character (Wulf et al. 2004: 9).
15 For the flow effect, see Csikszentmihalyi (2007).

16 Because of their closed eyes, the pupils can't anticipate this.
17 The decision for practising a yoga exercise depends on the respective teacher.
18 As the pupils ask several times, it seems that they are used to get an answer.
19 For the concept of rote learning, see Sarangapani (2003: 164).
20 They do not only like it, they are also used to it.
21 The laboratory, library, kitchen, office and therapy room are the only rooms that have doors.
22 At one morning assembly, a pupil pointed out that a classmate had seen sea turtles and asked if this person will share her experiences. This led to an extensive exchange of knowledge and experiences regarding sea turtles.
23 Taking this statement as a starting point, I asked them what they find interesting, and they told me that they like Ninjas.
24 Marching is commonly a basic event at Independence Day in Indian schools.
25 The name is changed.
26 For the concept of mimetic learning, see also Gebauer and Wulf (2003).
27 By the way, this was a demonstration of the school's discussion culture, which according to the principal is a basic communication style and an important skill to learn for the pupils at this school.
28 Pupils who successfully comply with these standards can become leaders. For the school's administration, this means that they are able to take responsibility for their classmates, and by learning this, they will become worthy and successful members of the society. What the leaders in fact do is to control if their mates conform to the rules, and, furthermore, to deliver them up to restriction and punishment.
29 For responsibility as a key skill related to social life and as a grounding for democratic society, see also Bräu (2008: 179).
30 This pedagogical dispute casts a light on the difficulties and challenges the administration- and teaching staff have to cover when practicing a low-level hierarchy in their collegial work.
31 For the changeability of school culture, see also Esslinger-Hinz (2010: 26).

References

Bräu, Karin (2008): Die Betreuung selbstständigen Lernens. Vom Umgang mit Antinomien und Dilemmata. In: Breidenstein, Georg, and Schütze, Fritz (eds): *Paradoxien in der Reform der Schule. Ergebnisse qualitativer Sozialforschung*. Wiesbaden: VS-Verlag, 179-199.

Breidenstein, Georg, and Schütze, Fritz (eds) (2008): *Paradoxien in der Reform der Schule. Ergebnisse qualitativer Sozialforschung*. Wiesbaden: VS-Verlag.

Csikszentmihalyi, Mihaly (2007): *Flow. Das Geheimnis des Glücks*. Stuttgart: Klett-Cotta.

Esslinger-Hinz, Ilona (2010): *Schlüsselkonzepte von Schulen. Eine triangulierte Untersuchung zur Bedeutung der Schulkultur an Grundschulen*. Bad Heilbrunn: Klinkhardt.

Gebauer, Gunter, and Wulf, Christoph (2003): *Mimetische Weltzugänge. Soziales Handeln – Rituale und Spiele – ästhetische Produktionen*. Stuttgart: Kohlhammer.

Geertz, Clifford (1987): *Dichte Beschreibung. Beiträge zum Verstehen kultureller Systeme*. Frankfurt, M.: Suhrkamp.

Girtler, Roland (2001): *Methoden der Feldforschung*. Wien: Böhlau.

Hirschauer, Stefan, and Amman, Klaus (eds) (1997): *Die Befremdung der eigenen Kultur*. Frankfurt, M.: Suhrkamp.

Raghavan, Neeraja (2007): Ripples That Spread: Can Innovations of Alternative Schools Spread to Mainstream Education? In: Sarojini, Vittachi, and Raghavan, Neeraja (eds): *Alternative Schooling in India*. New Delhi: Sage, 45–52.

Sarangapani, Padma M. (2003): *Constructing School Knowledge. An Ethnography of Learning in an Indian Village*. New Delhi: Sage.

Sarojini, Vittachi, and Raghavan, Neeraja (eds) (2007): *Alternative Schooling in India*. New Delhi: Sage.

Ullrich, Heiner (2008): Zur Aktualität der klassischen Reformpädagogik. In: Breidenstein, Georg, and Schütze, Fritz (eds): *Paradoxien in der Reform der Schule. Ergebnisse qualitativer Sozialforschung*. Wiesbaden: VS-Verlag, 73–94.

Wulf, Christoph et al. (2004): *Bildung im Ritual. Schule, Familie, Jugend, Medien*. Wiesbaden: VS Verlag.

16

'THE TREASURE OF LIFE LIES IN HARD WORK'[1]

Insights into the discursive practices of becoming educated and developed in schools in South India

Martin Bittner

Prologue

In 1492, Columbus was sent out from Europe by ship to discover a passage to spice-producing India, and by mistake he found a sea route to America. In 1498, Da Gama preceded the task, explored the Indian Ocean and laid the foundation for the colonization and politicization of the Indian Ocean. Thus, the basis for the intercommunion between Europe and India was created in pre-modernity.

Forster's (1924) *A Passage to India* was the literary effort to understand India on its own terms and signified the European (and mainly British) influence in India. His work can be read as a criticism of politicized ideas, as he depicted ruling and economy as modern illusions.

The student-exchange programme *A New Passage to India* (2009–13) refers to the political knowledge and the (early) interrelations between India and Europe, too. The programme (implicitly) aims to impart their historically based and to reconsider their political relations. The relations between India and particularly Germany will prosper from the communication, translation and interpretation of thoughts, ideas, discourses and knowledge. The experience of contradiction and contrariety (among other experiences) is not to be faced with a superiority of technology (pre-modernity) or with the entitlement of power (modernity) but with the observation of the self and the other in its otherness and the outline that knowledge has to be seen in its historical and constructed relations (post-modernity).

Introduction

The transnational organization UNESCO defines a general target for the United Nations, which is: *becoming educated and developed*. It is a slogan and an important idea, with relevance to the Indian Nation. In India the slogan became a paradigm for many actors participating in governmental and non-governmental institutions. Becoming educated and developed then is a combination of the transnational idea and the distinct knowledge of the Indian society. As this perception of reality differs concerning social status, age, religion, caste, political convenience, gender, living place, time etc. of the perceiving person, there seems to be an interrelation between education and development bringing up different practices. These practices are following an implicit but also discursive knowledge of how to gain the aim of societal development. If we are considering to observe the practices of schooling and contemplate history by means of the archaeology of knowledge (Foucault 1969), we have to take into account that the aim of becoming educated and developed can only be realized through a plurality of discourses and practices.

Up until colonialism the access to education and knowledge was restricted. Only Brahmans, the highest caste were supposed to produce and deal with a greater knowledge. Then between 1867 and 1941 the colonial rulers influenced and shaped the educational system to advance their mostly economic aims. Since the Independence of India (1947), education is known and claimed to be the important and essential task in the development of national unity. This is why education became part of the national constitution.[2] By this the educational system frames the social formation of society (Beteille 2007). These are only elementary references in a wider history of the state to indicate the diverse discourses about education and its practices. The practices, ideas, beliefs and the (scientific) knowledge of the past are interwoven with educational practices in India nowadays. 'Here is a society with its political agenda: the agenda of a modern nation striving for equality and democracy' (Pathak 2002: 51ff.). As Indian society acknowledges that it wants to develop its country, it has to answer the question of how to educate the future generation. The answer is given in its social practices and effects the implementation of education and teaching of a predominant knowledge. This chapter focuses on the practices of schooling by describing different educational institutions, looking for an answer to the question of the exchange programme, 'What is India?' Two different school cultures and their practices will be described to exemplify the discourse of becoming educated and developed.

Reflecting on school, Pathak (2002: 15f.) gives two ambiguous dimensions of the practices of schooling. The first dimension contradicts the agenda of equality, but follows a capitalist discourse. 'They make one believe in competition, social divisions, and in one's success at the cost of someone else's failure.' The second dimension considers the potentiality of the learner, without placing a precise cultural demand on the individual. Educators support individuals in their self-development and let them create the future according to their own perspectives. This dimension follows a discourse of modernity, as it highlights a democratic, open and less predetermined perspective on schooling. 'It is believed that the school is an agent of social change; it leads to modernity. Moreover it makes social mobility possible' (Pathak 2002: 15).

Educational practices represent specific discourses in different times and places. The fulfilment of a practice can only succeed if the practice is related to the orders of discourse (Foucault 1969). While practices form the discourses, the discourse vice versa determines the teaching practices. The subjection of the individual, the arrangement of a pedagogic space and the construction of knowledge result from a practice framed and guided by discourses (Arvind 2008). This is why educational practices will be described as discursive practices. Practices not only have to follow discourses but may also have a performative character. Educational practices follow a (discursive) structure and stage the teleological and educational aim on an implicit and explicit level. Practices by their performativity extend into the future. Through observation, description and reconstruction of practices I will show how practices facilitate *Bildung* (Wulf and Zirfas 2007). I will argue that discursive practices cause the positioning, shaping and performing of the individual. Under conditions of power, this process has to be described as subjection (cf. Butler 1997).

The different discourses on schooling and education cover a conflictive problem within the Indian education system. When Sainath (1996: 47) was reporting from the poorest districts of India, there were 'schools without teachers. Or schools without teaching. Or schools with no students. Or, simply, [they were] no schools at all'. Contradicting this description, the Eleventh Five Year Plan for Education Sector reports a positive development on schooling.

> The number of primary schools (PS) in the country increased from 6.6.4 lakh in 2001–02 to 7.68 lakh in 2004–5. In the same period the number of UPS [upper primary schools; M.B.] increased at a faster rate from 2.20 lakh to 2.75 lakh. The sanction of 2.23 lakh new PS/UPS, 1.88 lakh new school buildings, and 6.70 lakh

additional classrooms has made a big dent in reducing the school infrastructure gap.

Eleventh Five Year Plan 2007

Besides this positive development the report still shows the deficiencies of schooling in India, even though Sainath (1996) warned the society with his reports 10 years earlier that the aim of getting educated and developed is not at all an easy task to succeed. Quantitative evaluations and journalistic investigations like these show that the number of primary schools is not adequately covering the spreading of society and thus indicate a general practice of unequal requirements.[3] The implementation of the programme 'Education for All' was to decrease these differences and their effects, but from different studies we know that government syllabus, evaluations and degrees only reproduce inequality. 'This seemingly highly localized conflict is of significance because it points to the ways in which participants in development held "education" accountable to the multiple subject positions they occupied, and to the material politics of their lives' (Klenk 2003: 109). This article will not carry on the extensive discussion about education and the education system in general, but will describe and analyse the practices of becoming educated and developed in specific contexts.

Doing ethnography in Indian schools

The following study of two different types of schools does not by any means represent the variety of schooling in India.[4] Taking into account the orders of discourse and the construction of knowledge (Foucault 1969), this study focuses on practices that are embedded in the school and represent a discursive knowledge. Discursive practices follow specific mechanisms and regularities. They are powerful, meaningful and action-guiding as they effect and produce subjectivity in social situations. My analysis refers to the general subject of the social meaning of schooling in social and educational sciences. The chapter will not give a macro-analytic answer, but adapt the question to another understanding of social situations by focusing on a theory of practice (Reckwitz 2002). The survey will focus on the impact of schooling for the child and on the connected practices of teaching. Within an ethnographic approach, the interest in the discursive practices will be clarified.

The ethnographic fieldwork was done by a white-western researcher easily to be identified as someone with a foreign cognitive and experiential background. An alienation of the researcher is inevitable at this stage (Amann and Hirschauer 1997). The visible and addressed foreignness has an impact on the understanding and construction of the social situation of research. A researcher is thus disturbing the field, but by putting across a special interest in the *Other* in doing research the field is forced to reproduce the valid and intelligible practices of its own (Reuter 2002). In the field, a performance and construction of the social order can be understood as a representation of the attributed best practices that are following a discursive knowledge. The representation of the practices and the performance of the social order of the field highlight some requirements which have to be covered in terms of methodological approach and the method of analysis. Self-reflection and reflections on the role of the researcher are essential to understand the practices and mechanisms in the field (Agar 2008). Reflection as a method of analysis means to translate the observed practices into a different system of enunciation. The description of the practical knowledge in the field, the transcript of a recorded voice has to be seen connected to the circumstances of translation. It is through these processes of translation that a cross-cultural investigation and a reconstruction of practices and discourses are permitted (Wulf 2006). Field-notes, audio-recordings, interviews, video-recordings and focus groups are the methods and sources of data gathering to answer questions concerning the practices of education for all in an ethnographic study. These multidimensional methods of field interaction and data gathering and the reflexive analyses of these ethnographic data can be seen as an answer to the crisis of representation and act to transform ethnography within the theories of performativity into post-modern reflexive ethnography (see Ogbu 1981; Rabinow 1993; Krüger 2000; Wulf et al. 2010). Ethnographic work contains different stages of compressed time fieldwork (Jeffrey and Troman 2006). While my first example is concerning interview data, thoughts will be presented based on the interview, field-notes, participant observation and an analysis of by-the-field-produced-documents. The second example of the practices of becoming educated and developed in India is based on a nine-week ethnographic study. During this stay, the communication practices, interactions, actions and occurrences in a classroom had been video-taped. In addition, interviews and focus groups had been audio-recorded as well as field-notes had been collected from participant observations. I will start with the first example.

Development through multilingual education and self-education

The Sri Aurobindo Society (SAS) with its chief administrative offices in Puducherry,[5] capital of the Indian Union Territory of the same name, is very much engaged to mediate to the world the philosophy and ideas of *Sri*

Aurobindo and his spiritual collaborator *The Mother*.[6] Following their integral philosophy and their educational concepts, SAS takes care of them by supervising a centre for children from early childhood to adolescence. During a two and a half hour interview with a member of Sri Aurobindo Society we[7] got to know about the practices of education and development. Our introduction to the member of SAS was arranged by a colleague[8] from the National Institute of Advanced Studies (NIAS), an institution where collaborative work within the different fields of sciences and humanities is encouraged, following the idea of bringing governmental and academic knowledge closer together, to face complex issues of Indian and global society. Although the SAS is not a government institution, it engages with global and local issues of India.

The interview at SAS for the main part was a description by the executive member of the arguments concerning education. There were only few and very short narrations. Only when it came to the question of bureaucratic acceptance of the school-concept, the interviewee gave a narration of how the final certification of the school called 'completed knowledge' was acknowledged as a degree by the government to enter the Indian Institutes of Technology (the prestigious academic institutions in India). The composition of the interview[9] enables a reflection on the main arguments and descriptions, while through narrations we could analyse the action guiding orientations. Based on this interview, I will elaborate on the practices and discourses on education that govern the SAS.

Language plays an important role in their concept of education, since the interview was about the ideas and concepts of the Sri Aurobindo *international* centre of education. Already in its early years the child is taught its first foreign language. In kindergarten the children are taught French from the age of three onwards. They will continue with different languages by their own choice in the following years of school education. French is one of the most important languages since in any level of schooling all natural sciences will be taught in French only. In higher school levels children are taught English, because it is the medium to teach further subjects like literature. The pupils in school will be taught Tamil, as it is the local language of the district where the school is situated. They will also learn the ancient language Sanskrit to read the Indian epics and learn about philosophy. They are invited to choose a fifth or even sixth language, as their parents may speak a language which has not been part of the curriculum, or simply out of interest. The different languages which are taught give a pedagogical answer to the sociohistorical order children are growing up in. By teaching more than one language and by not starting with the individual mother tongue of the learner, the Sri Aurobindo international school responds to the specific social significance of language. It is self-evident and expected that every Indian citizen is able to speak more than one language. Insofar the choice of languages is at the centre of education, it is linked to a specific discursive knowledge, which will be explicated in the following lines.

The teaching of French represents and refers to a historical knowledge. Puducherry was a French colony from 1673 to 1954 and even nowadays this is still a factor in this region of India. The architecture, the cuisine or the way of living have a French tinge; forty percent of the population in Puducherry still have a French citizenship. To teach French means to acknowledge the historical and cultural process of colonialism and its impact on the practices and the self-conception of people in this region of India. What was said about French could be said about English, too. Considering the history of India and the British colonization, English became a language representing a specific relationship to a world where global principles of economy are ruling. Teaching English in India is thus not so much related to a mere historical knowledge, but 'is implicated in relations of power and dominance' (Peirce 1989: 406). English promotes the integration of the pupil into a predominant *social class*, as it is compulsory for the growing middle class to speak this language (Das 2007).[10]

We may now understand the teaching of Tamil not only as a local requirement, but in its further function to integrate the subject into a social class. Knowing Tamil, French and English enables individuals to connect to those who do not speak all the three of them. This means that the knowledge of languages and the aquestion of teaching a language instead of another one not only is question of grammar, pronunciation and literacy, but gives insights into sociocultural history and shows the greater meaning of the subject in its cultural-historical development. The different languages have an effect on how someone thinks and argues as well as on the self-conception of persons. Language puts the subject into discursive power relations. Sanskrit as the fourth compulsory language is not only a literary language but a spoken language in SAS. Sanskrit linguistically provides the basis for a *pure* Hindi instead of Urdu or Hindustani. Knowing Sanskrit enables the subject to perceive the Indian society within the conflicting unity.

Teaching languages is a discursive practice, it teaches the subject which language to use to elaborate a specific theme. As using a language restricts the information within the barriers of that language, the discursive mechanisms of boundary and regulation operates within the language. Multilingualism thus, not only enlarges the possibilities of communication but also organizes and structures knowledge.

In the interview, our informant not only described the educational practices of language teaching and the rest of the curriculum, but was very much engaged to discuss the role of technology for Indian society and its impact on the practices of schooling. For him, the developmental status of technology displays that the Indian society is highly developed. He not only was elaborating on this but raised antithetic questions: 'How far can we develop?' He did not answer the question directly but aimed to make us think about it in the future. In the conclusion he linked it with the anthropological question of 'How to find a greater meaning in life?' and by this referred to the discourse of getting educated and developed in a non-hegemonic context. To teach in a non-hierarchical way would thus mean to help the pupil to encourage self-learning processes, not to follow a given syllabus, not to impose education skills, but to let pupils choose the subjects of interest and by this help them to develop their inherent qualities. Thus the manifestation of the self is the central target of this educational practice. However, the self is not an individual but part of the unity of the universe, as the interviewee here referred to Buddha. This holistic perspective is represented in the aim of developing an 'entire body' – physical, emotional, intellectual and spiritual parts combined. The answer to the social question of how to become developed and of how far can we go has to be seen as a distinguished differentiation of a self-concept as a main aim of schooling. Educational practices of teaching languages and highlighting the role of the corporal self encourage the recollection of the Indian past by incorporating historical knowledge. Through practices of teaching the representatives of SAS ask their pupils to change consciousness to develop the future corresponding to the history of Indian knowledge. We have seen the practices of language-teaching and the discussion about development as the pronunciation of a self-concept of education. Foucault (1988) had depicted these technologies of the self as a praxis of early Christianity and the Old World. The practices of schooling of SAS can be seen as intercommunion in the progression of the passages to Europe and the passages to India.

Education through discipline and social pride

In the second example, I will depict another understanding of becoming educated and developed. It takes place in a private school in a metropolitan city. The contact for this ethnographic study was again given by an administration employee of NIAS. This school was chosen because in private schools the majority of the subjects are taught in English, which enables the researcher to listen to and talk to the actors in the field. Again language plays a role in the field, not only for the researcher but also for the field itself. The teachers are arguing that English is not only compulsory but sufficient for the pupils. From higher primary onwards (means fifth Standard) they force the pupils to learn and speak English. Their aim is to prepare them well for high school. The school has described their clients as 'children from all backgrounds'. According to how they explained and practised language teaching, it acquires the function of opening a space of possibility for the pupils. English imparts a selected knowledge about the self, its origin or social background; it even gives the (erroneous) impression of social affiliation. Teaching English equalizes the chances of getting developed and educated for the pupils, thus a democratic discourse is represented in the practice of teaching English.

Besides the idea of negating the social background and affiliation the school has a history that still has an impact on the pupils and not only represents but reproduces their social affiliation, too. This history is remembered in every classroom, where a picture of the school founder's short-lived daughter is placed above the blackboard. She was expected to become a great thinker and a genius. As her parents were surrounded by educationalists and men of letters, they had an optimistic philosophical blend of mind and were encouraged to start one of the first educational institutions in this area after their daughter's death. As schools represent the educational answers for the social questions of society, this school brings up its own answer within the framework of their discursive knowledge. It is given in the everyday teaching practices, the architecture, material objects and booklets. The daughter's memory picture in every classroom is to remind the pupils that they could become geniuses, too. During the 1940s, founding a school was of some importance for an upcoming academic, intellectual middle class in India that settled down in a tranquil area of the city and wanted to raise their children in a protected environment to become *the best citizens*.[11] Development was promoted by the idea of education, as we have seen earlier. But this school also represents the influence of the British rule, i.e. educating a specific social class and imposing English language to govern Indian society as well as its (economic) policy. Nonetheless, this school also shows the dedication of people whose idea of education for an independent, democratic Indian nation was on the rise. This contradiction between a rising self-awareness of the Indian nation and the admired British influence is still to be seen in the following depiction of the practices of teachers and pupils in the present-day school.

In addition to the field-notes, which were the main sources for the case study in the last section, video-taping and audio-recording will be the basis of the presentation of this field. Videography as a tool in ethnographic fieldwork is predetermined if we take into account the simultaneity and sequentiality of social actions (see Wagner-Willi 2004). Videography cannot be chosen in every setting of research and it takes more time to prepare the participants in the field. But it helps to enable a more detailed reconstruction of practices. To get to know the perspectives and orientations of pupils and teachers in addition to the video data, focus groups were initiated, one group discussion with six teachers and five group interviews with two pupils each.

In a performative understanding of the social order, the discursive knowledge of schooling is represented in practices and assertions. Schooling has always to be redefined, remembered, quoted and enacted by the individuals engaging in it. Thus, every morning school starts with morning prayers (Figure 16.1), where all pupils come together at the school yard to welcome their teachers, congratulate schoolmates having birthday on the day and sing the state and school hymn. These morning prayers show the governing practices of a school in a compact form. They represent the meaning of schooling as a collective process, where everyone has their position and has to behave in a synchronized way within the norms, e.g. in a respectful manner. 'This disciplining of bodies, both at the time of the morning liturgy and later on in the classroom, is regulated by the concept of *śista*. Commonly translated as "discipline"' (Benei 2008: 77f.).

This knowledge is also represented in the focus group with teachers. The following transcript shows the shared understanding about schooling and the significance of teaching pupils in the age of fifth Standard.

Teacher 4 (T4)[12] describes herself as an experienced teacher, as she has worked for six years in this school. T6 had working experiences as a post-graduate assistant before she came to this school 11 years ago. T3 has working experiences in two different schools and has worked in this school for the past 18 years. All of the teachers mentioned that they got married, left their jobs and stayed at home to care for children for a duration of two to ten years before entering this school. T6 is teaching Science and English and is the class teacher of the fifth Standard we did research in. T4 is teaching Social Science in this class and is the class teacher of the ninth Standard. T3 is teaching Hindi language in this class. All teachers have experience in primary and high school teaching but feel very happy to be in this age group of 9–13-year-olds.

T4: I have been working earlier as a lecturer, also as a high school teacher in various schools. Here also I worked for one year as a high school teacher. And here with this age group students, I really feel, lead them in the right path in the sense this

Figure 16.1 Morning prayers at the schoolyard

> is the age when they do both bad and good things . . . the manners what we talk about . . . the value process . . . the phenomena, the concepts we teach them they should understand properly the phenomena, whether it is maths, science, socials . . . So you tell them exactly what it is . . .
>
> *T3 and T6:* Not only the subjects, . . . even the manners, the way they move, talk to you, how they get along with others, how they behave . . . Suppose you are a guest and you enter the class, they should know what to do when a guest comes, how to act, how to react . . .

The conversation in this sequence was very intensive, charged and affective. The teachers do not represent their individual attitudes but the shared collective knowledge. That is why we can read this discussion as a discourse of one voice. On the one hand, schooling is about teaching the subjects which are pre-assigned by the state or governmental syllabus, following an agenda which focuses on the individual learner, and on the other hand, schooling can be seen as the defined place and time where pupils develop manners, interests, emotions and habits, that produce an adequate member of society.

By giving the example of 'a guest comes' they also indicate that the situation of a researcher in the class is of importance for the children and teacher, as in their practices they have to give evidence of the history and discourses of the school. In their description it becomes clear that discipline is the main discursive practice to follow.

> T6: At this age you are the godfather. So they will follow you. They try to choose the right path . . . in an orderly way. They will be watching you. One day, two days, three days, fourth day they will think we also should do things in an orderly way . . . Slowly, all these things they observe and learn more, rather than oral. Whatever we teach, more than that they observe and learn. This is the age when you are soft they will also be soft. When you are [*not clear*] When you are disciplined they will also be disciplined. Like that.
>
> T3: That's what we say. Discipline comes first.
>
> IM: Discipline comes first?
>
> T3: That's what we say. More than studies, discipline is first.

As T3 formulates the conclusion of this theme, discipline is one of the main aims in the school practices. That means, the strength of teaching the different subjects is to confront them with exactitude and also strengthen their manners and behaviours. The reason of behaving exactly lies in the perception from outside and shows the belief that only by exactitude appreciation is given. As teachers point out, pupils should present themselves in a well mannered way, as they represent not only themselves but also the teachers and the teachers' qualities, as well as the institution. To be responsible for oneself and the other is demanding. Teachers' good qualities were represented through respectful behaviour of pupils, who give the right answers and understand what the teacher is explaining. Thus repeating chorally what the teacher had said or to give an answer in the affirmation of the teacher's knowledge is a discursive practice that forces the pupil to subjectify him or herself within the discourse of discipline. The necessity for discipline is represented and understood not only by the teachers but also by the pupils; it is an incorporated knowledge. In an informal talk with a female pupil from ninth Standard, who has a leading position in the school, it was explained as follows.

G9: But generally foreign countries are known for their (cultural and) civilized way of living compared from that to India. Like how India is known for its culture and tradition and foreign countries are full of discipline and the way of living culture and civilized, dignified. Of course Indians are . . . but it is comparatively less than other countries. [abridged] India is second on world's top population and all that, so gradually inherent our economic progress and all that, apart from that India is mainly known for its culture and religion. Comparing to other countries it's a developing country.

Exactitude paired with discipline and a cultured civilized way is seen as the key concept for the acknowledgement as a developed country. By developing one's self (in the frames of exactitude), one believes to transform the perception from developing to developed country. This is why the practices of education are focused on discipline and the cultural knowledge of India.

In addition, the discourse about India is not only explicitly known by the representatives of the school but is also present in the Social Science textbooks.[13] Even though the teaching practices are following the educational aim of changing habits, schooling in this school compiles with the predominant modern discourse. In the Social Science textbook the following themes (implicitly) play a central role: equality (including but not respecting diversity), discipline (not always as self-discipline but as a hierarchy of a limited number of persons governing the others) and knowledge (where it is most important to make pupils understand a certain perspective, to generate knowledge is not done by discussing but by copying and following the teacher).

'THE TREASURE OF LIFE LIES IN HARD WORK'

The pupils listened to the teacher and discussed the Vedic system, they copied part of their textbooks into their workbooks and answered the questions: 'Why did the parents of the later Vedic Age prefer a male child than (!) a female child?', 'What are the qualities of a "good citizen"?' By completing such activities pupils are supposed to learn that they have to follow the rules to change for the better and thus to bring development to themselves, their family and their country. Since it is necessary to think about the civic life and to learn that one thing depends on the other, the Social Science teacher (ST) introduces the subject to the pupils (ep). Doing this, the framework of what to think and what to feel is modelled by the teaching.

ST: So social science teaches us how man develops and fifth to sixth to seventh you will learn how India grew (as it is), did you understand? Our concern is talking about the . . . progress of the Indian (present). ((*not clear*)) You have to attend – you have to know your India first. Okay . . . So that's why you have to attend compulsory social science . . . because you must, you all should know your India first . . . how great it is . . . and how we must be proud to be born in this land called?

ep: India
[abridged]

ST: The system we have should ever be the best ((*not clear*)) make you a good citizen.
[abridged]

ST: You can spoil us if you become a terrorist, you can spoil us if you become a (*not clear*) . . . ; if you become a very good scientist . . . you are making India more proud. If you are becoming a very good teacher, lecturer (*not clear*). If you can make it good and better, yes, work for that but don't make it . . . worse. Did you understand. So every person should understand so every country has its own count, ah: history. That's why in India we have so much of historical stories to tell you; to make you understand that India was so prosperous, that India was so well, that India was having everything.

As there is a need for further thinking about civic life and regulation, the teacher asks the pupils to realize that change is slow but constantly ongoing. In the perception of ST any change is supporting development. With her introduction the teacher not only communicates the importance of development, but also presents the educational relevance as this knowledge has to be passed down the generations. However, the discourse of possibilities of development is restricted by the disciplinary practices and the discourse of acknowledgement.

Conclusion

The difficulty of writing about India is due to the fact that the debate on Indian schooling is not only located in India, but is related to Western debates, as it was explicitly articulated in the informal talk with the female student. If we take into account the explicit knowledge and the perception of India as 'a modern nation striving for equality and democracy' (Pathak 2002: 51), teaching practices are orientated towards this discourse. But the discursive practices are taking into account implicit dimensions of development also, e.g. that the school has to 'decolonise the mind and retain the cultural spirit of India' (Pathak 2002: vii). By analysing the aspects of the governmentality of development and the disciplining practices of getting educated, this chapter showed conflicting views and practices in Indian schooling. This represents the difficult task of preserving knowledge beyond generations and a process of transformation, e.g. from a developing country to a developed country.

The purpose of this chapter is to describe a specific perspective on India by reflecting about schooling in India. If we ask the question of who is the author and who has the right to speak (Butler and Spivak 2007), the practice of translation (not only language but thoughts, understandings) becomes constitutive to generate a *new passage to India*. The focusing of discursive practices provides a researcher-dominated perspective and concentrates on the practices related to the knowledge of the field and the subjection of the actors in the field. By doing so, the description of India as a post-modern society (Sarrukai 2001; Viswanathan) arises from the very experiences India itself presents (Varshney 1997).

Notes

1 Moral saying that was written on the blackboard in the front of a classroom in an Indian primary school and shadowed the pupils during the whole school day. Such moral issues were explicitly presented not only by these interior decorations but also by teaching Moral Science (MSc). Normative and moral issues were implicitly presented in all teaching practices, most interestingly while teaching Social Science (SSc).
2 http://www.education.nic.in/constitutional.asp#Fundament.
3 See, e.g. the report of Azim Premji Foundation (2004): The Social Context of Elementary Education in Rural India (http://www.azimpremjifoundation.org).
4 Vasavi (2009) classifies 11 types of schools.
5 Known as Pondicherry until September 2006.
6 'The Mother' was born as Mirra Alfassa in Paris, France. After a first period of education and transformation she met Sri Aurobindo in 1914 and recognized him as a spiritual leader. In 1926, Sri Aurobindo called her to guide, lead and develop the Sri Aurobindo Ashram, which is a strong and very widely engaged spiritual community.

7 This work has been done together with my colleague Urs Kübler.
8 As we stayed at NIAS, we came in touch with the people working there and they became colleagues to us.
9 The method of qualitative interviews and the differentiation of text given by Schütze 1983.
10 Susan Visvanathan explains that English stands for freedom, because it belongs to nobody.
11 Benei 2008 also elaborates the concept of the good citizen by analysing the impact of language, bodies and emotions.
12 Teachers will be presented either with numbers or with the subject they teach to allow anonymity.
13 See Wong (2002) for the role of school textbooks and cultural authority.

References

Agar, Michael H. (2008): The Professional Stranger: An Informal Introduction to Ethnography. 2nd ed. Bingley: Emerald Group Publishing.

Amann, Klaus, and Stefan Hirschauer (1997): Die Befremdung der eigenen Kultur. Ein Programm. In: Hirschauer, S., and Amann, K. (eds): Die Befremdung der eigenen Kultur. Zur ethnographischen Herausforderung soziologischer Empirie. Frankfurt, M.: Suhrkamp, 7–52.

Arvind, Gaysu R. (2008): Institutional Context, Classroom Discourse and Children's Thinking: Pedagogy Re-examined. Psicologia & Sociedade 20 (3): 378–390.

Benei, Véronique (2008): Schooling Passions. Nation, History, and Language in Contemporary Western India. Stanford: Stanford University Press.

Beteille, Andre (2007): Classes and Communities. Economic and Political Weekly, March 17, 945–952.

Butler, Judith (1997): The Psychic Life of Power. Theories in Subjection. Stanford: Stanford University Press.

Butler, Judith, and Spivak, Gayatri C. (2007): Who Sings the Nation-State? Language, Politics, Belongings. London: Seagull Books.

Das, Gucharan (2007): Aufbruch ins 21. Jahrhundert. In: Riemenschneider, D. (ed.): Reise nach Indien. Kulturkompass fürs Handgepäck. Zürich: Unionsverlag, 120–136.

Forster, Edward M. (1924): A Passage to India. Cambridge: Penguin Books.

Foucault, Michel (1969): The Archaeology of Knowledge. London, New York 2002: Routledge.

Foucault, Michel (1988): Technologies of the Self. In: Martin, L.H., Gutman, H., and Hutton, P.H. (eds): Technologies of the Self: A Seminar with Michel Foucault. Amherst: University of Massachusetts Press, 16–49.

Jeffrey, Bob, and Troman, Geoff (2006): Time for Ethnography. In: Troman, G., Jeffrey, B., and Beach, D. (eds): Researching Education Policy: Ethnographic Experiences. London: The Tufnell Press, 22–36.

Klenk, Rebecca (2003): 'Difficult Work': Becoming Developed. In: Sivaramakrishnan, K., and Agrawal, A. (eds): Regional Modernities. The Cultural Politics of Development in India. Oxford, New York: Oxford University Press, 99–121.

Krüger, Heinz-Hermann (2000): Stichwort: Qualitative Forschung in der Erziehungswissenschaft. Zeitschrift für Erziehungswissenschaft 3: 323–342.

Ogbu, John U. (1981): School Ethnography: A Multilevel Approach. Anthropology & Education Quarterly 12 (1), Issues in School Ethnography: 3–29.

Pathak, Avijit (2002): Social Implications of Schooling. Knowledge, Pedagogy and Consciousness. Delhi: Rainbow Publishers.

Peirce, Bronwyn N. (1989): Toward a Pedagogy of Possibility in the Teaching of English Internationally: People's English in South Africa. TESOL Quarterly 23 (3): 401–420.

Rabinow, Paul (1993): Repräsentationen sind soziale Tatsachen. Moderne und Postmoderne in der Anthropologie. In: Berg, E., and Fuchs, M. (eds): Kultur, soziale Praxis, Text. Die Krise der ethnographischen Repräsentation. Frankfurt, M.: Suhrkamp, 158–199.

Reckwitz, Andreas (2002): Towards a Theory of Social Practices. A Development in Culturalist Theorizing. European Journal of Social Theory 5: 243–263.

Reuter, Julia (2002): Ordnungen des Anderen. Zum Problem des Eigenen in der Soziologie des Fremden. Bielefeld: Transcript.

Sainath, P. (1996): Everybody Loves a Good Drought. Stories from India's Poorest Districts. New Delhi: Penguin Books.

Sarrukai, Sundar (2001): Mathematics, Language and Translation. Meta XLVI (4): 664–674.

Schütze, Fritz (1983): Biographieforschung und narratives Interview. Neue Praxis 13 (3): 283–293.

Varshney, Ashutosh (1997): Postmodernism, Civic Engagement, and Ethnic Conflict: A Passage to India. Comparative Politics 30 (1): 1–20.

Vasavi, Anita R. (2009): New Imperatives in Elementary Education. Journal of Human Development 3 (1): 133–142.

Wagner-Willi, Monika (2004): Videointerpretation als mehrdimensionale Mikroanalyse am Beispiel schulischer Alltagsszenen. ZBBS 5: 49–66.

Wong, Sandra L. (2002): School Textbooks and Cultural Authority. In: Levinson, D. L., Cookson Jr., P. W., and Sadovnik, A. R. (eds): Education and Sociology. An Encyclopedia. New York: RoutledgeFalmer, 533–537.

Wulf, Christoph (2006): Anthropologie kultureller Vielfalt. Interkulturelle Bildung in Zeiten der Globalisierung. Bielefeld: Transcript.

Wulf, Christoph, and Zirfas, Jörg (2007): Performative Pädagogik und performative Bildungstheorien. Ein neuer Fokus erziehungswissenschaftlicher Forschung. Weinheim, Basel: Beltz, 7–40.

Wulf, Christoph et al. (2010): Ritual and Identity. The staging and performing of rituals in the lives of young people. London: The Tufnell Press.

17
THE IMPACT OF SCHOOL ENVIRONMENT ON FUTURE ASPIRATIONS OF HIGH SCHOOL STUDENTS IN INDIA

Beatrice Lange

In a country like India, where 'diversity gives rise to people with very different kind of family backgrounds and demographic characteristics' (Singh 2010: 230), it has been observed over the last few decades that children do not receive equal educational opportunities and prospects (cp. ibid.; Lakshmi 1989: 21f.). In the Constitution of India is written that education is a fundamental right and that equality of educational opportunities should be provided for all individuals living in a democratic social system (as per note of the *Directive Principles of State Policy*; cp. ibid.: 19ff.).[1] The Annual Status of Education Report (ASER 2011) recently disputed various conditions in schools and challenged the issue of a single 'Indian education system' and how education for all could be provided (cp. ibid.: 4, 18).

Research in India has shown that success in school plays a very important role in defining a child's future and unequal educational opportunities lead to unequal future related prospects among the scholars (cp. Varma 1998; Verma et al. 2002: 501). According to a quantitative study conducted by Verma, Sharma and Larson, young students face a 'highly competitive examination system' (ibid.: 500) which implies that they suffer from higher degrees of anxiety (cp. ibid.: 501; Raina 1983). In the context of this study questions have been raised regarding 'the effects of the school system on the total wellbeing of young people' (Verma et al. 2002: 501). Considering the duration of a child attending school,[2] one can presume that the school environment involves a high degree of influence, positive and/or negative, on the emotional state and experiences of an adolescent in his or her daily life (cp. ibid.).

Certainly, young people differ on various levels regarding their 'experiences, their perspectives and their hopes for the future' (Bansal 2013a: 10). For instance, scholars in their early twenties, in a phase between school and after-school, change educational statuses and personal relationships diversely and frequently (cp. ibid.; Rindfuss 1991).

Especially before leaving school, young people have many questions regarding personal and worthwhile goals in life (cp. Bansal 2013a: 15). Studies on personal future orientations have indicated that higher SES[3] high school students reflect on a definite orientation to making long-term plans and prepare proactively for the future. Lower SES groups, conversely, tend to maintain less reflective systematic long-term planning (cp. Misra and Jain 1988; Chandra 1997; Arulmani et al. 2003: 196f.). Given the importance of schools and the main factor considered in this chapter, it should, however, also be important to review other aspects of socialization such as the socioeconomic status in the Indian context, the role of family backgrounds, and the community (cp. ibid.: 195).

This chapter is an extract of a reconstructive study conducted in India (2012) that examines the impact of school environments, particularly boarding schools[4] in the secondary education level, on future aspirations of young students in India. It attempts to answer the question: *How does different schooling affect children's aspirations?* The presented results indicate that certain future related responses are consistent: achievement orientations and the pressure of decision-making concerning after-school future orientation.

Child development: factors of socialization

Child development is seen as an ongoing process of interactions concerning different influences. The General Systems Theory states that human beings correlate with the environment and surrounding world in the course of their developmental years (cp. Ramey et al. 1982; Bronfenbrenner and Morris 1998). Thus, if positive changes have been made in the early childhood, then positive long-term aspects can be achieved (cp. Clarke and Campbell 1998: 319).

The Social Cognitive Career Theory (SCCT)[5] deals with the 'manner in which beliefs about personal efficacy operate within a system of sociocultural and socioeconomic influences to affect career decision-making behaviour'. Structuring a personal career is a process by different social cognitive mechanisms. These mechanisms[6] are reciprocal, interact with each other and tend to be influenced by 'environmental forces such as differential socialization and by the internalization of these forces' (Lent et al.

1994; Arulmani et al. 2003: 195f.). It is important to consider the diversity of influences in the process of socialization. Therefore, the Social Learning Theory of Career Decision-Making (Mitchell et al. 1979) examines the impact of *factors like environmental conditions and learning experiences* on career-related decision-making. It says that the development of cognitions and beliefs influences the professional development (cp. Krumboltz 1979, 1994; Arulmani et al. 2003: 196).

It has been demonstrated in various studies that *schools* play an important role when it comes to socializing young students during their educational processes (cp. Wiater 2007; Köller 2007). Hence, schools need to ensure fostering the students' expertise such as social skills during their educational processes (cp. Wiater 2007). Lakshmi (1989: 11) points to the essentials of secondary education, when it comes to train young people in being effective members of society. In this regard, capabilities of scholars, including abilities, aptitudes, attitudes, interests and characters, must be developed during this stage of their schooling. After leaving the level of secondary education, a young person enters 'life knowledgeably and mentally alert' (ibid.).

High school education needs to provide possibilities of a preparation for the future. High school level learners should in the least be given the capability of vocation and be educated for business and life orientation (cp. ibid.: 13). This is associated with the fact that students attending the same school have commonalities in their history of socialization (cp. Bohnsack 2010; Nohl 2012). Schools have an influence on 'customs, beliefs, rituals, conventions, expectations and demands, combined with instruction and the setting of examples' for their scholars (Barrow and Milburn 1986: 205) and they become one main influencing factor in evolving children's capabilities, and therefore, education should be based on children's needs and interests (cp. ibid.: 38). On the other hand, *teachers* are central figures in the educational processes in schools and particularly responsible for the success of an educational system (ibid.; Rao 1989: 1). They interact daily with the students and it is expected that they provide sufficient time and support for them. They should approach students' individual needs and problems which they are facing during the course of their school career (cp. Verma et al. 2002: 507).

As youth studies have shown, *peer groups* also play an important role regarding similar biographic commonalities. In boarding schools (which were investigated in my 2012 study), parental authority is replaced by peers, who interact privately on school premises, by living up desires and fantasies (cp. Bansal 2013b: 260). This socializing collective interaction is determined by the setting of the school (e.g. classrooms, bedders) and not by choice as in other instances when the membership in a group is chosen by the child (e.g. a friendship network) (cp. Hartup 1992: 272).

According to Mitchell et al. (1979), a *community*[7] is a further influencing element regarding future and career planning. Communities persuade a 'social process of learning' when transmitting career belief patterns to the youth (cp. Arulmani et al. 2003: 201). Aspirations are formed by social and cultural patterns of a society and social change (cp. Bansal 2013b: 251f.). Within a community, it is primarily the *home environment* which contributes to the development of a child. Children from affluent homes with better facilities face fewer difficulties in learning processes than those in poorer conditions (cp. Lakshmi 1989: 22). Therefore future related beliefs involving life choices 'are affected by the attitudes of the young person's family and community to further education, job acquisition, and to the future as a whole' (Arulmani et al. 2003: 202). Bansal (2013b) points to *families* who extend influence and authority to the 'self-definitional attempts' of a child, trying to outline a place and position in society. A family encourages the right for young people to define own lifestyles, ideas, plans, actions etc. on their own interests, needs and motives. Conventionally, an Indian family has been a provider of economic and emotional support as well as an indicator for social positions of its members. In India, the institution of the family has been, and will continue to be, socially and psychologically one of the most significant influencing elements throughout a child's development (cp. Bansal 2013b: 251f.).

All that raises several questions regarding strategies and choices and how they are influenced by the above mentioned factors, like families, social networks and communities, as well as personal identities and interests of a young person, all of them within socioeconomic contexts, which are constantly changing (cp. Ball 2003; Nambissan 2010: 286). Nambissan (2010: 288) notes that aspirations concerning education and schooling always interact with 'mobility strategies in the changing context of globalization and the role that they [families] see education (of specific kinds/qualities) playing in this process'.

Considering the above mentioned socializing factors, the reconstructive study, using the qualitative method of group discussions, explored the following questions: what do children from specific schools think about (their) future? Can their thoughts be associated with the environmental conditions and learning experiences?[8]

Methodology

While observing educational challenges in India during the research stay in 2012, I developed an individual interest in future aspirations and perspectives of young Indian students. To find out more about the processes that underlie implicit orientations of young students and also to reconstruct collective orientations in a particular 'conjunctive experiential space' (cp. Bohnsack 2010: 105) group discussions were conducted in May 2012 in international boarding schools in the urban area of Delhi.[9] The focus groups[10] were approached by addressing this topic and consisted of young students in the eleventh to twelfth grade (aged 16–18). It was an opportunity for the children to reconsider their individual situations and perspectives towards their future and to reflect, discuss and share thoughts and fears among each other in their familiar school environment. For initiating the discussions in the beginning and approaching the insights and understanding about this theme, the first question was designed to engage them into the process (cp. Anderson 1990: 245ff.).

The discussions have been analysed by using the Documentary Method (Bohnsack), including the Formulating and Reflecting Interpretations. The Formulating Interpretation deals with decoding and formulating the topical structure of the transcript, whereas the Reflecting Interpretation means the reconstruction of the framework of orientation within the groups' habitus (cp. Bohnsack 2010: 110f.). By implementing these interpretation procedures, the 'structure or patterns of orientations underlying the practical action' can be identified (Bohnsack 2010: 106).

High school students expressing future aspirations

Boarding school (1) 'the world is not very easy to handle'; four participants[11]

Cf: Hmm (.) school life is (.) is always like eh very good like a part memory I mean like if kind where eh like we can have fun we can enjoy (.) but after school life we have to take things *seriously* very more seriously and that's () get over () what we have to and what () I feel (3)

I: C-ould you ehm explain more what you mean with th-ings that you have to take seriously what kind of things you mean

Cf: Hmm we have to focus (.) More on like e-h our career like where we have to go where we have to leave take a next step and that step will have to be eh like if we go or *now* (.) we have to decide and we have to make up our mind (.) to know like because eh (.) right now in school everything is easy but when we go outside in the world things will not be so easy (.) I mean the world is not eh (.) very easy to handle is what it feel (.) soo like it will *do* have hard time also (.) so (.)

Df: In school so many tutors are there to guide us but once we leave the school once we go out of the school then we have to like take care o-f ourselves in every aspect (.) we have to take our own decision everything so (.) it becomes that I- we have to be serious (.) and there is always this fear that we might take a wrong step so (.)

During the phase of topical structuring, certain topics have been mentioned and repeated by the participants such as the importance of making a decision about what will happen after school. Referring to the study on orientations to the future (Arulmani et al. 2003), the SES school students of this group also tend to make a long-term plan, or rather find a decision which helps them to define their life span proactively. There is a clear contrast between school life and life after school, which the students of this particular focus group associate with strong seriousness. The main association that has been ascertained by the students is achievement orientation. They seem to expect strict requirements and challenges they would have to fulfil after leaving school:

Am: In *school* (.) we have learn- we have learned some *scares* so when we pass out school we have to (.) *prove* ourselves because eh *college* (.) to get admission a good college we- should prove ourself that's what we *are* (.) because *college* is the only thing which eh gonna (.) put us *somewhere* and land us *somewhere* at some point where we can start our *life* (.) because at the age of twentysecond twenty third (.) twentytwo twentythree (.) I think most of them (2) have only decided what they wanna do what they wanna *be* (.) but at *this* stage it's like (2) *really* important time (.) time span where we you take important decisions of your life

I: ⌊mmh (.)

Am: If you go wrong at this point eh the future will not be easy (.) That's what I think because getting good eh getting admission is in a good college is *not* easy

I: ( ) you explain th:e process

Am: Actually I se::e for *me* it's a bit easier because I come in obc other backward classes so for *me* it's a bit easier but people are in general caste [class?] It's a bit difficult because our cut off is a bit less but for science people it's *difficult* because eh we have colleges like IIT ( ) institute of technology they won't take people who are not that capable of (.) forming that good (.) So it's *not* e:asy to get admission at good college mmh to get a good *job* to get a good *placement* what matters I think is college [. . .]

Am: It wouldn't be *easy* to:o (.) eh come on that place we are planning to be but (.) to be on that place *hard* work is very important I think eh after *ten* years getting a job will not be easy because () government is planning to give hundred percent () to all the companies all the multinational companies so if there are gonna rule after ten years the market they will control us to get jobs (4) is all the small industries () closed down (4) to:o get a job after *ten* years will not be easy (.) you'll w-ork *really* hard

These schools, where they share similar experiences, seem to influence their beliefs and patterns towards the life after school, their personal futures. The school environment seems to give the students a reference in terms of tutorials, good care and safety, almost as being cut off from the outside world of the school.

According to Bansal (2013a: 11) a 'graduation farewell' is no longer a guarantee for a sizeable section of young students to change from the world of 'explorative learning to the world of committed work'. Hence, working experiences of many young people are interrupted by phases of 'returning to school' or 'taking time off' combined with periods of paid work. In regard to this discussion, the students fear a competitive world which requires hard work and will not be as safe as going to (this) school. The students debate about the dependence on institutions such as colleges and also the existing castes in the societies that are able to decide about their personal careers.

Boarding school (2) 'plan for our future'; six participants

Dm: We should plan for our future we should know that ((moaning/interruptions)) (.) ehm (8) eh ((@Bm@)) (.) passing school we have to go where and then (.)
Af: ˪ Firstly we should have a (.) *goal*
Dm: ˪ and after that what we have to do (.) we should *have* some idea that w:what we are going to do
Af: ˪ We should have enough *knowledge* for that goal
Bm: Ya (.) because (.) we have to study long () ((moaning))
Em: We should have (.) possible goals ()
Af: We need to study (1) *hard* for it
I: ˪ What do you mean with possible goals
Em: That (1)
Af: @What do you mean by that@ (2)

Concerning the second discussion, an orientation with high external expectations towards 'doing something' was examined. Some topics that structured the interpretation were relevant to the students if they were frequently mentioned. Students of their age should have a plan containing specific future goals, which is rather a theoretical explanation and does not explain their everyday practice. At this point, a collective orientation was implemented regarding future related orientations (cp. Bohnsack 2010: 105).[12] The students seem to agree on what is attributable to their specific common environment. The aspect of finding a decision before leaving school is coherent with findings in the first discussion. First of all, there should be a (long-term) goal, which requires hard work in order to be reached. The pressure of decision-making for young students is always embedded in 'a competitive world, the self-worth of an individual is dependent on how well he or she compares with others which keeps bringing forth self-conscious doubt about "how good one is" and a sense of shame over one's inadequacies and failures' (Bansal 2013b: 265). Furthermore, anxiety towards exams increases and forces them to 'live in fear that one poor exam performance will permanently harm their future success in life' (Verma et al. 2002: 507).

Bm: Ehmm (2) we can (.) like (.) we can do *now* you are asking what we can do *now* (.) we can:n have place to (2)
Af: ˪ we *need* to have the
Bm: Make the people aware about global warming ozone or something else ((moaning)) (3) so that () especially (.) especially the Samosa and ehm (.)
Af: ˪ shout up (2) shout up (5)
Bm: ˪ ((speaking Hindi)) (2)
Dm: Start
Af: ˪ First we need to have that (.) enough knowledge for it (.) then we can:
Cm: ˪ enough money (?)
Dm: And we have to apply that in our live also ((speaking Hindi)) that (.) we plan () not going to do that in three days
Bm: ˪ Mmhh
Dm: ˪ apply that in our lives we are not able to achieve our goals (2) we will ((moaning)) between this goal and (.) like eh:h

Another analysed and commonly known fact is that, one needs to study hard in order to reach possible goals in one's life span. This seems to be another school-related pattern, which implies a chronology of actions: acquirement of knowledge, imagination of a goal and as a result the implementation of that goal. At this point, the discussion is highly interactive, and therefore implies an inclusive modus within the group, a so-called 'interactive density' (*organization of discourse*; Bohnsack 2010: 105, 111).[13] Concerning the acquired knowledge, the students theorize to a high degree. Their arguments seem to be a theoretical point of view and do not provide an indication of their everyday practice. If transferal of knowledge into life has not yet taken place, goals could not be reached (according to the students). The aspect of knowledge that is needed to achieve goals is, at this point, stagnant and demonstrates two aspects that have been used as a contrast.[14] As mentioned in the previous section, the easy school life constitutes a positive frame, whereas the serious life after school is a negative frame. Tutors who individually mentor the students in this school seem to be very important for the students.[15] They assume that such guiding tutors would no longer be available after leaving school and this evokes fear and strengthens the impression of seriousness concerning their future. In addition to that, the students seem to be under a severe pressure in making decisions about their futures and being responsible for themselves. They say that in schools they have developed scare concerning future related decision-making.

It has been shown in the Reflecting Interpretation that the students collectively focus (or imagine) on similar issues especially regarding their early twenties, such as finding a decision of what should and what has to be achieved in future. This time frame seems to play a very important role for them when it comes to thinking about future-related decisions. At this stage, the interpretation allows a perception which demonstrates a biographic commonality among this focus group. A comparison between at least two group discussions needed to be done for the purpose of finding similar observations and to validate these findings (cp. Nohl 2012: 6):

- Aspects of seriousness (in making a decision)
- Achievement orientations
- Pressure to come to a decision before leaving school which involves high expectations
- The importance of hard work in order to reach goals set during the early twenties
- Proceeding according to a plan and using knowledge learnt at school.

Conclusions and contribution to the field

The youths of the focus group belong to (private) boarding schools with high fees in the urban area of New Delhi, and the pressure of 'finding the right decision' and empirical findings such as high achievement orientation can be connected to former findings which say that 'higher family income students wish to get higher education [and] similar occupational or professional skills as their parents have' (Veena 1988: 42).

The analysed findings of the qualitative study presented in the section above reveal an interrelation of causes and effects among different socializing factors, but primarily the impact of the school environment on future decision-making. This shows again that 'school has a major impact in shaping the daily lives of middle-class urban Indian adolescents' (Verma et al. 2002: 506).

School is an important socializing factor, nevertheless variances in individual achievements may be ascribed to 'differences in factors beyond the individual's responsibility (inequalities due to individual circumstances also referred as inequality of opportunity)' (Singh 2010: 231).

India has a rapidly growing economy, facing a globally interdependent system of high technology, confronting the population with First World labour demands. Therefore parents and their children find themselves in processes underlying this fast changing contemporary world and its newly developed orientations which are different from those of the past years in India (cp. Bansal 2013b: 257). Schools in India have to deal with complex and diverse conglomerates of students, facilities and opportunities. 'In India, it is not the rupture but the stretching of traditional values that becomes a means for the young person to realize his dreams for life' (Kakar and Kakar 2007: 15).

The results of this study are of relevance for educationalists and people who are interested in developing a deeper understanding of how school environments as educational institutions play an important role as main influencing factors regarding children's future in India.

Notes

1 For further aspects to the caste and social inequalities see Jodhka 2010.
2 '[. . .] it is found that at least 10 per cent of the children do not enter the schools at all' (Mali 1989: 11).
3 Socioeconomic status.
4 'Any school providing accommodation and meals for the majority of its pupils' (IED: 22).
5 Based on Albert Bandura's (1986) Social Cognitive Theory.
6 'selfefficacy, outcome expectations and goal setting behavior' (Arulmani et al. 2003: 196f.).
7 'Community' here means 'particular area or place considered together with its inhabitants [. . .] a rural community and/or local communities [. . .] the people of a district or country considered collectively, especially in the context of social values and responsibilities' (OD 2013).

8 Perceptions and incorporative knowledge of that kind can only be addressed through qualitative empirical analysis in group discussions. For Documentary Method and Group Discussions, see Bohnsack (2010). For other qualitative methods, e.g. Narrative Interview and Documentary Interpretation, see Nohl (2010). An exemplary extract of a documentary analysis will be presented in the following pages.
9 'These private un-aided schools are mostly located in urban areas, and charge much higher fees than the government or local body schools. Since these private schools mainly cater to the richer sections of the population, their rapid growth is indicative of increasing education inequality in India' (Pal and Ghosh 2007: 16).
10 'A focus group is a group comprised of individuals with certain characteristics who focus discussions on a given issue or topic' (Anderson 1990: 241).
11 For further details on the transcript conventions used in this paper, see Bohnsack et al. (2010: 365).
12 For further details about collective orientations and the 'conjunctive experiental space', see Bohnsack (2010: 105).
13 At this point, a strong intervention on the part of the interviewer needs to be mentioned, who influenced the discussion by asking prepared questions from the questionnaire.
14 Empirical comparison horizons (*negative und/oder positive Vergleichshorizonte*; for more, see Bohnsack 2010: 242).
15 The impact of tutorial activity in schools of different types may have contrary results (cp. ASER 2011: 5).

References

Anderson, G. (1990): Fundamentals of Educational Research. London: Falmer.

Arulmani, G., van Laar, D., and Easton, S. (2003): The Influence of Career Beliefs and Socio-Economic Status on the Career Decision-Making of High School Students in India. International Journal for Educational and Vocational Guidance 3 (3): 193–204.

ASER (2011): Annual Status of Education Report (Rural). Provisional 16 January 2012. Facilitated by Pratham. Online in: URL: http://www.asercentre.org/.

Ball, S.J. (2003): Class Strategies and the Education Market. The Middle Classes and Social Advantage. London, New York: RoutledgeFalmer.

Bandura, A. (1986): Social Foundations of Thought and Action: A Social Cognitive Theory. New Jersey: Englewood Cliffs.

Bansal, P. (2013a): Identity in Youth: Conceptual and Methodological Underpinnings. Youth in Contemporary India 2013, Springer India, 9–38.

Bansal, P. (2013b): Youth in India: Identity and Social Change. In: Youth in Contemporary India 2013, Springer India, 235–269.

Barrow, R., and Milburn, G. (1986): A Critical Dictionary of Educational Concepts. An Appraisal of Selected Ideas and Issues in Educational Theory and Practice. New York: St. Martin.

Bohnsack, R. (2010): Documentary Method and Group Discussions. In: Bohnsack, R., Pfaff, N., and Weller, W. (eds): Qualitative Analysis and Documentary Method in International Educational Research. Opladen, Farmington Hills: Barbara Budrich, 99–124.

Bohnsack, R., Pfaff, N., and Weller, W. (eds) (2010): Qualitative Analysis and Documentary Method in International Educational Research. Opladen, Farmington Hills: Barbara Budrich.

Bronfenbrenner, U., and Morris, P. A. (1998): The Ecology of Developmental Processes. In: W. Damon (series ed.), and R. M. Lerner (vol. ed.): Handbook of Child Psychology: Vol. 1. Theoretical Models of Human Development (5th ed.). New York: Wiley, 993–1028.

Chandra, S. (1997): Problems and Issues of Child Labour in India. Social Change 27: 3–4.

Clarke, S. H., and Campbell, F. A. (1998): Can Intervention Early Prevent Crime Later? The Abecedarian Project Compared with Other Programs. Early Childhood Research Quarterly 13: 319–343.

Hartup, W. W. (1992): Peer Relations in Early and Middle Childhood. In: Van Hasselt, V. B., and Hersen, M. (eds): Handbook of Social Development: a Lifespan Perspective (Perspectives in Developmental Psychology). New York: Plenum Press, 257–281.

India Education Diary (IED): Eden of Education. http://indiaeducationdiary.in/Boarding-Schools-in-India/index.asp.

Jodhka, S. S. (2010): Engaging with Caste: Academic Discourses, Identity Politics and State Policy. Indian Institute of Dalit Studies and UNICEF (New Delhi, India).

Kakar, S., and Kakar, K. (2007): The Indians: Portrait of a People. New Delhi: Penguin Books India.

Köller, O. (2007): Die deutsche Schule im Lichte internationaler Schulleistungsuntersuchungen (TIMSS, PISA, IGLU, DESI). In: Apel, H. J., and Sacher, W. (eds): Studienbuch Schulpädagogik. 3., überarb. u. erw. Fassung. Bad Heilbrunn: Julius Klinkhardt, 138–154.

Krumboltz, J. D. (1979): A Social Learning Theory of Career Decision Making. In: Mitchell, A. M., Jones, G. B., and Krumboltz, J. D. (eds): Social Learning and Career Decision Making. Cranston, RI: Carroll Press, 19–49.

Krumboltz, J. D. (1994): Improving Career Development Theory from a Social Learning Theory Perspective. In: Savikas, M. L., and Lent, R. W. (eds): Convergence in Career Development Theories: Implications for Science and Practice. Palo Alto: CPP Books, 9–31.

Lakshmi, S. (1989): Challenges in Indian Education. New Delhi: Sterling Publishers Private Ltd.

Lent, R. W., Brown, S. D., and Hackett, G. (1994): Toward a Unifying Social Cognitive Theory of Career and Academic Interest, Choices, and Performance. Journal of Vocational Behaviour 45: 79–122.

Mali, M. G. (1989): Education of Masses in India. Delhi: Mittal Publications.

Misra, G., and Jain, U. (1988). Achievement Cognitions in Deprived Groups: An Attributional Analysis. Indian Journal of Current Psychological Research 3 (1): 45–54.

Mitchell, A. M., Jones, G. B., and Krumboltz, J. D. (eds) (1979): Social Learning and Career Decision Making. Cranston, RI: Carroll Press.

Nambissan, G. (2010): The Indian Middle Classes and Educational Advantage: Family Strategies and Practices. In: Apple, M. W., Ball, S. J., and Gandin, L. A. (eds): The Routledge International Handbook of the Sociology of Education. London: Routledge & Francis Group, 285–299.

Nohl, A.-M (2010): Narrative Interview and Documentary Interpretation. In: Bohnsack, R., Pfaff, N., and Weller, W. (eds): Qualitative Analysis and Documentary Method in International Educational Research. Opladen, Farmington Hills: Barbara Budrich, 195–217.

Nohl, A.-M. (2012): Interview und dokumentarische Methode: Anleitungen für die Forschungspraxis. Qualitative Sozialforschung. 4., überarbeitete Auflage. Wiesbaden: Springer VS Verlag.

Oxford Dictionaries (OD) (2013): http://oxforddictionaries.com/definition/english/community.

Pal, P., and Ghosh, J. (2007): Inequality in India: A Survey of Recent Trends. Economic & Social Affairs. DESA Working Paper No. 45. ST/ESA/2007/DWP/45.

Raina, M. K. (1983): Biochemical Consequences of Examination Stress. Indian Educational Review 18 (2): 17–39.

Ramey, C. T., MacPhee, D., and Yeates, K. O. (1982): Preventing Developmental Retardation: A General Systems Model. In: L. A. Bond, and J. M. Joffe (eds): Facilitating Infant and Early Childhood Development. Hanover, NH: University Press of New England, 343–401.

Rao, R. B. (1989): Educational Environment in India (A Multidimensional Study). Allahabad (India): Chug Publications.

Rindfuss, R. R. (1991): The Young Adult Years: Diversity, Structural Change, and Fertility. Demography 28 (4): 493–512. Published by: Springer. Article Stable URL: http://www.jstor.org/stable/2061419.

Singh, A. (2010): The Effect of Family Background on Individual Wages and an Examination of Inequality of Opportunity in India. Journal of Labor Research 31 (3): 230–246. Published online: 4. June 2010. Springer Science + Business Media, LLC 2010.

Varma, P. K. (1998): The Great Indian Middle Class. New Delhi: Penguin.

Veena, D. R. (1988): Education Systems: Problems and Prospects. New Delhi: Ashish Publishing House.

Verma, S., Sharma, D., and Larson, R. W. (2002): School Stress in India: Effects on Time and Daily Emotions. International Journal of Behavioural Development 26: 500–508. DOI: 10.1080/01650250143000454 (22 March 2013).

Wiater, W. (2007): Theorie der Schule. In: Apel, H. J., and Sacher, W. (eds): Studienbuch Schulpädagogik. 3., überarb. u. erw. Fassung. Bad Heilbrunn: Julius Klinkhardt, 29–52.

18
SUGARCANE MIGRATION AND THE IMPACT ON EDUCATION

A perspective on seasonal migration in Maharashtra and the linkage to children's education

Sandy Hallmann

Mobility in general and migration in particular is a worldwide phenomenon often discussed as inevitable part of life in the history of mankind (see, e.g., Chattopadhyaya 1987; Mathew et al. 2005; Deshingkar and Farrington 2009). Whether looking at moving tendencies of early nomadic people searching for nutrition and residence (Piper 2010), nearly 60 million people who left Europe for America in the twentieth century in forecast of a new life (Hoerder et al. 2008) or thousands of inhabitants leaving their hometown because of nature catastrophes or political persecution, migration in general reflects human endeavour to survive in the most challenging conditions, either natural or man-made. But while most academic literature refers to international migrants only (including refugees, asylum-seekers, emigrants and immigrants), data is rare for internal migration facts (see, e.g., Chattopadhyaya 1987; Deshingkar 2009; HDR 2009). However, the predominant part of migrants does not go abroad at all but moves within the own country (see, e.g., HDR 2009: 1). This is true not only for worldwide movements but reflects Indian reality as well (Deshingkar 2009). Therefore, this report argues the important impact on internal migration influencing both social and economic development of the country and the people.

Against the background of the capability approach presented by Sen and Nussbaum and with special reference to the sugarcane workers in Maharashtra, the chapter describes positive as well as negative effects on the phenomenon of internal migration. Moreover, the attention is drawn to a very special migration group often neglected in the past: the migrating children (see Smita 2011: 316). Thus there are many cases of voluntary migration in search for better economical conditions and self-determined life in adulthood (HDR 2009). Most of the migrating children are forced to follow their parents, while leaving their educational status behind. These children are not represented in official data (see, e.g. Census of India 2001). For this reason, the article does not only present migration facets in general, but try to answer the question as to how seasonal migration in particular affects the education of Indian children and how policy reflects this issue in recent strategies.

So the chapter starts with the presentation of key features emphasizing past ideas and recent trends of theoretical migration framework in part 1. Part 2 argues differences as well as similarities in migration definitions and concepts first, before presenting the definition of seasonal migration as understood in this context. The available macro data largely shaped by National Census and National Sample Survey are shown and discussed in part 3. In part 4, the focus lies on seasonal migration facts with special reference to sugarcane harvesting in Maharashtra. Part 5 considers the difficult aspects on education of migrant children against the background of the Right to Education Act (2009). Last but not least, the article turns to the term of special school (Sakhar Shalas) offered by non-governmental organization Janarth (NGO Janarth) and the discussion of future possibilities dealing with the education of migrant children on a policy level.

A theoretical framework of migration

Before dwelling on educational aspects of seasonal migrating children it seems necessary to reflect the complex phenomenon of migration itself. Therefore, previous theories are presented in a brief overview before dealing with recent developments. Until now, there exists a large number of theories and models which proposed to describe human migration in general. In the twentieth century the beginning was made by Ernst Georg Ravenstein who was convinced of an inner migration (in Britain) depending on 'laws' (Ravenstein 1885). In fact, his work was not only the first mentioned study on human migration itself but the birth of a long era finding an adequate migration theory while putting down different reasons and consequences of human moving decisions. Nevertheless, almost one century had passed before in 1966 the often quoted 'push and pull' model entered the stage. But although Everett S. Lee's paradigm was (and still is) mentioned to be adequate for analysing facts pushing migrants away from their home residences and pulling them to new destination resorts (Lee 1966), the 'push and pull' model can hardly be seen as a theory on its own (Kröhnert 2007: 1).

Actually, there is the risk of over-simplifying the process of migration which does not include external and impersonal forces only but is caused by objective, normative and psycho-social factors as well. Meanwhile, a lot of macro-theoretical affine experts tried to create even special formulas (see, e.g. Lowry 1966) for describing and calculating migration in order to make the phenomenon calculable.

Nowadays, more and more micro-theoretical models displace those early efforts. In fact, a conglomerate of multidisciplinary researchers including experts from demography, geography, sociology, anthropology, ethnography and others try to understand the impact of sociological tendencies (see Giddens 1984), political issues (see Fine 2001) and – referring to India – the role of caste, class, gender and power relations shaping migration processes (see Mathew et al. 2005). Some of the scientists also try to analyse 'how migration shapes society' (Deshingkar and Farrington 2009: 5). According to that, Sonja Haug emphasizes the importance of new migration theories including individual and social network aspects as well as the reasonable combination of micro- and macro-theoretical studies (Haug 2000: 30). This shift seems to break a new ground concerning the link of human development and migration, leaving behind the dominant bad press on negative effects only and concentrating on the migrating individual instead.

Against this background, the Human Development Report (HDR) is not meant to be a further step in migration theory but one of the first documents combining migration processes with the capability approach (see HDR 2009). Once introduced by the Indian economist and Nobel laureate Amartya Sen as a theory of justice and further developed by US philosopher Martha Craven Nussbaum, the capability approach constitutes a broad normative framework for both: the evaluation of individual well-being and social arrangements.[1] Thus, the approach does not only design policies and proposals about social change in society but often go together with empowerment strategies as well (see, e.g., Alkire 2002: 131).[2] So, referring to migration, people do not only have the capability to decide where to live and when to move but the act of movement itself needs a large amount of capable strategies. In fact, the ability for changing the place of residence is a fundamental component of human freedom in India as well as in most countries of the world (see Deshingkar 2009; HDR 2009). Therefore human mobility is understood 'as a positive and not only a negative freedom' (HDR 2009: 16). Nevertheless, the topic of migration remains complex at any time, needing more concretion in this chapter.

The terms of internal and seasonal migration

Due to the complexity and with the absence of a universal theory, definitions of migration remain vague, sometimes even controversial and contradictory. Just to give an example, most terminologies differ enormously in the variable of space. Whereas the United Nations Economic Commission for Europe defines migration as a move from one area to another usually crossing administrative borders (UN/ECE 1993); other authors outline the change of residence within the national border (e.g. Chattopadhyaya 1987). On this account, scientists as well as politicians have to clarify in advance whether dealing with international or internal migration. As mentioned above, the attention in this chapter is turned to the latter.

As a matter of fact, migration processes do not differ in space only but in time as well. In fact, there is a large amount of migrants making their change of residence not a permanent one. Instead an increasing number of people leave their home just for a few months (or years) looking for sufficient employment, manageable weather condition, better education, religious freedom or health-care opportunities before returning to their native places (see Deshingkar and Farrington 2009). In order to categorize this diversity, Zachariah once distinguished not only between short-term and long-term movement but between permanent, semi-permanent, periodic, temporary and casual migration (Zachariah 1964: 250).

Thus, while migration in general is not easy to define, the problem is even worse concerning this chapter's purpose. In fact, there are only very few people dealing with the subject of seasonal migration in India. Haraprasad Chattopadhyaya, for example excluded it completely from his case study of Internal Migration in India because in his point of view such temporary movements 'do not involve either a change of birth-place or a change of residence' (Chattopadhyaya 1987: 4). Meanwhile, the Dutch sociologist Jan Breman (1990) inspired a whole generation of scientists dealing with the topic of short-term migration. Following his footprints, the neo-classical economist Michael Lipton (1980) searched for the impacts and drives of migration arguing that migration from rural to urban regions does not necessarily go hand in hand with an increase in income, while Shekhar Mukherjee (2001) from the Institute of Population Sciences in Mumbai gives some recommendation on how India may deal with seasonal migrants in future. The most recent and exhaustive publication however was published by Priya Deshingkar and John Farrington (2009). In their work, the two authors finally concentrate on the basic question of how 'circular migration' (including seasonal migration) can reduce poverty in overwhelmingly poor rural areas of India.

According to their term of circular migration and in absence of an appropriate definition, seasonal migration in this article is meant to be 'a temporary move from, followed by return to, the normal place of residence, for purposes of employment' (Deshingkar and Farrington 2009: 1), dependent on the growing seasons.[3] Actually, this implies a very narrow migration concept referring to economy-affected seasonal migration from one village to another in Maharashtra only.[4]

The data-basis – national census and national sample survey

Although migration flow in India is nothing new (Deshingkar 2009: 1), studies have been very few in the past. In fact, the migration rate was not considered to be an important demographic issue compared with the increase of the country's total population (Bose 1983: 137). Nevertheless, the information on international and internal migration has been collected with the first National Census (NC) in 1871 (see Chattopadhyaya 1987).[5] Due to little interest, in the beginning it was confined only to people enumerated not in their place of birth (POB). So it took another 100 years before the Census introduced an additional question. Since 1971 the NC provides migration data based on place of birth (POB) *and* place of last residence (POLR). Consequently, a person is defined as migrant if his/her place of birth or of last residence is different from the place of enumeration.[6] The following data just gives an overview of the migration in India in general.

Referring to the last published data in 2001, Census counted the total number of 314,5 million internal and international migrants by last residence (Census of India 2001). This is nearly one-third of India's population (1,028 billion in 2001) and indicates an increase of 37 per cent in comparison to 1991.[7] In Maharashtra meanwhile the total number includes 42 million migrants; more than two-thirds of them (34 million) moving intra-state. But although in all censuses the internal migration in general and rural to rural migration streams in particular are the most important ones, short-term migration remains undetected in the data. Including migrant numbers with a duration of more than one year only, the provided data for total India is 8.8 million; for Maharashtra 429,574 persons. While 193,880 of them moved because of economic reasons, another 144,173 moved with the household (Census of India 2011).[8]

Because of the lack of short-term migration data, the National Sample Survey (NSS) creates the second main source of primary migration data in India. In fact, the 55th round of NSS in 1999–2000 is meant to be the first chapter defining temporary migrants including 'persons staying away from usual place of residence for 60 days or more for employment or better employment or in search of employment' (NSSO 2001). So, while short-term migrating people stay invisible in National Census, the NSSO estimates at least 10 million temporarily Indian migrants. Deshingkar and Farrington however point out a number of 100 million circular migrants by adding up the rates of major sectors including textile and garment industry, employment workers, mine workers, brick-kiln workers and agricultural staff (Deshingkar 2009: 28; Deshingkar and Farrington 2009: 16). Nevertheless, there seems to be a large estimated number of unreported cases, while the rate of migrant children is not counted anyway – neither in NC nor in NSS.

Hence, most of the description in secondary migration literature is based on these two documents only. According to Deshingkar and Farrington (2009: 2ff.), this lack of data prevents experts from attaining diversified conclusions in their research. Therefore, this chapter does not only refer to the last two decades of National Census of 1991 and 2001 and the available NSS data, but to some additional data from Janarth as well, a non-governmental organization mainly focusing on short-term migration in rural areas of Maharashtra with emphasis on children's migration.[9]

The case of Maharashtrian sugarcane cutters

An overview of sugarcane industry in western Maharashtra

Representative of dozens of states and districts in India, Maharashtra has been chosen for this chapter.[10] As the most developed state in India it was a hub of migration at any time. Now and then it provides a dynamic environment for both migration streams, inter-state as well as intra-state, no matter whether from rural or urban areas. But while inter-district and inter-state migration to urban centres – for example to Mumbai (former Bombay) – have always remained a matter of serious concern for researchers, planners and policymakers, the total number of intra-district rural-rural migration is hardly known. Nevertheless, there is a widespread number of circular migrants especially from the Marathawada region as well as Ahmednagar, Nashik and Jalgaon (see Wadiker and Das 2004).

Besides that, Maharashtra holds the largest amount of sugar industry producing 40 per cent of India's sugar output (Deshingkar 2009: 21). Following official statistics from the Maharashtra State Sugar Cooperative Federation, there are at least '1.6 million sugarcane farmers growing the crop on 0.7 million hectares of land, producing 60 million tonnes of sugar' every year (ibid.). Often the 172 sugar factories are managed by cooperative farmer societies providing employment directly or indirectly to 15 million people (migrants and non-migrants). While Deshingkar (2009: 21) estimates an amount of 1 million migrating cane-cutters, Smita (2011: 327) offers a number of 650,000 people including 200,000 children. Most likely the exact data lies somewhere in between.

Who moves for sugarcane cutting?

Whereas traditional circular migration metiers like stone quarries, salt pans, brick kilns or rice mills mostly attracted (or 'pulled') male family members to new receiving villages for paid work, in recent decades more and more families were forced to leave their rural homes. Especially in Marathawada regions, today's families threatened by economical indebtedness and food insecurity are leaving their native residence for the 'sugar belt', namely the surrounding area of Nasik, Ahmadnagar, Pune, Satara, Sangli, Kolhapur and Scholapur (Smita 2011).

In fact, women and children constitute a high proportion of migrant population in sugarcane sector. While searching for the reasons, Wadiker and Das suppose a simple causation chain including more people meaning more employment and more income (Wadiker and Das 2004: 2). Only persons of juvenile and senile age groups are less mobile and stay at home basements whereas children of nearly all ages accompany their parents. Although they are not officially paid for work (which is officially prohibited and regulated since the Child Labour Act in 1986), employers as well as contractors benefit from the 'family labour' (Smita 2011). Therefore the percentage of boys and girls migrating with their parents is balanced till the age of 10. Up to this age however, more girls than boys are found in sugarcane sites because parents do not want to leave the girls alone without male protection (see Desai 2005). Sometimes girls even migrate only for the purpose of cooking, washing and taking care of younger siblings while all the other family members are working on the field (Wadiker and Das 2004: 4).

Referring to the definition above, the most important reason for seasonal migration is financial difficulty. In fact, examining the socioeconomic background in general, the profile of people migrating for agricultural labour includes the most marginalized and impoverished sections of society. In India this refers to Scheduled Castes (SC), Scheduled Tribes (ST) and Other Backward Castes (OBC) owning little or no land.[11] Whether these groups can actually benefit from migration mainly depends on 'the mode of recruitment, skill and wage levels and the ability to access remunerative work' (Deshingkar 2009: 47). Due to the classification, sugarcane families generally belong to coping migrants often not only being poor but uneducated and unskilled and therefore hardly improve their living conditions (Deshingkar and Farrington 2009: 20ff.).[12]

The migration scenario and the migration site

Looking at the starting point of migration, sugarcane cutting families usually are recruited by a contractor. Against an advance payment of 10,000 to 20,000 Rupees (145 to 290 Euro) offered in the post-monsoon period when the need for money is the greatest (Deshingkar 2009: 43), the family often takes the money and leaves the village for the duration of six months. But while earnings from such work are meant to be 'good' in comparison to other migration sectors, the living conditions on the work site are extremely poor. Citing a famous statement of Jan Breman, 'even dogs are better off' than sugarcane cutters measured against the harsh living conditions (Breman 1990).

After arriving at the migration site, the family usually stays 'in a small conical hut or *kopi* made of a bamboo mat and poles' (Smita 2011: 332). Meanwhile 50 to 500 *kopis* form an *adda*, the living site of migrant workers situated near the sugarcane field. During the *koyatas* (work units) the workers cut the cane (from 4 a.m. till noon) while children up to five years 'put the cane into a pile, and collect and bundle the sugarcane tops' (ibid.). While some of the bundles are sold on the market as fodder for animals, most of them are carried by men or women for transport to further processing. According to Smita, at least 15–20 adults as well as 12–15 children of all ages create such a *koyata* (ibid.).

So while migrant workers in general exert cheap labour for very little payment, sugarcane workers provide the ultimate flexible workforce to employers who can hire and fire them whenever wanted (see Deshingkar 2009: 29). In fact, '[b]eing away from their homes and villages and leading uprooted lives, the first thing that migrants lose is their identity as citizens' (Smita 2011: 335). Actually, they do not only leave their traditional environment but their right for participation in *panchayats* (important village councils), in free service of public health as well as the entry to Public Distribution System (PDS) or Below Poverty Line (BPL) grains offering food ration cards for the poorest (ibid.). A recent research study done by Prashant Bansode from Gokhale Institute of Politics and Economics (GIPE) even points out that migrant sugarcane cutters are better off staying at their native villages than at places where they migrate in search of employment. The associate professor mentions that their quality of life deteriorates sharply with their basic human rights at destination work sites compared to the normal quality of life at their source villages (Bansode 2011). With regard to the capability approach and human development however, one of the most serious costs is related to migrating children missing the second semester of school overlapped by the migration cycle from November till April/May (Smita 2011: 318).

Seasonal migration and its impact on education

The interaction of seasonal migration and the right to education act

As mentioned above, the decrease of rural livelihood in many parts of India, including Maharashtra, forces hundreds of thousands families to leave their homes and villages in search for work. Because of little support in the village or the urgent need for money, many adults take their children along with them, usually making them drop out of school and therefore closing the only opportunity for an alternative future besides the sugarcane factory. Following a study accomplished in six districts and 6,406 households from 25 sugar factories by the Centre for Development Research and Documentation, at least 200,000 migrated children have been identified – half of them in the age group of six till fourteen (see Deshingkar 2009: 22).

This exactly covers the age addressed in the Right to Education (RTE) Act of 2010 (passed in September 2009). Beginning with 1 April 2010, the State of India provides eight years of free and compulsory education to each child from six to fourteen years in a school of the child's neighbourhood. Since then, financial cost that prevents children from accessing school have to be borne by the state. So the Maharashtrian state as well as every other state has the duty of enrolling the child as well as ensuring attendance and completion of schooling (Government of India 2009). Meanwhile the RTE Act goes together with one of the Millennium Development Goals (MDG) as well as the signature on the Convention on Rights of the Child including the achievement of universal primary education by 2015 (1989) (see Govinda and Bandyopadhyay 2011). But despite these political 'statements', Indian policy draws little attention to migrant labour children so far.

Asking primary teachers in a small village next to Tuljapur about this issue, they often approve the lack of policy action. Just for evidence, a teacher has shown the enrollments of her class. While 46 children have been registered, only 20 were sitting in class. 'Some work on the field, others left with the family. Although we have to register the children since 2010 we only list them in the first weeks of semester. So there are no remarks of absent children' the teacher Ashwita Borajanti explained.[13] Of course this case is not adequate for generalization, but it conforms with studies of Janarth. Unfortunately the state governments do not collect own official data of seasonal migrating children, so the basic source concerning migrant children remains the village, town or school register. But although there are student numbers as seen in the example, the children on the move are not counted, neither in sending nor in receiving villages (Wadiker and Das 2004: 6).

Meanwhile inadequate numbers and therefore less attention are not the only problem migrated children and their families are faced with. Referring to Smita, sending schools as shown in the example neither enroll migrated children on exam records nor provide extra afford by offering special learning material. So, while arriving at school with the end of sugar-harvesting season homecoming children usually are not encouraged to continue their studies but seem to be gradually dissociated from the education process (Smita 2011: 338). In fact, it is even worse within the work site (or receiving) schools because often there are no schools at all, especially near the *kopis*. And even if there exist some institutions where students could continue their semester, usually the local authorities do not take care of the special needs of migrant children.

To sum up, migrant children are external to both school systems because 'neither the home nor the work district takes responsibility for their education' (ibid.). Therefore most migrating children do not take part in the difficult reality of sugarcane work only but continue the vicious circle of seasonal migration because of short-handed abilities and substandard education.

Educational interventions in Maharashtra

Making child migration visible not only in society but in future policy seems to be one of the main goals referring to Deshingkar and Smita (Deshingkar 2009: 48; Smita 2011: 342). A first step in this direction was made by the Sarva Shiksha Abhiyan (SSA) which in 2001 recognized seasonal migration children as a category of out-of-school children living under the most difficult circumstances (see Wadiker and Das 2004: 9). This classification was needed to include short-term migrating children to the Education Guarantee Scheme (EGS) and Alternative and Innovative Education (AIE). Both programmes offer a number of facilities to make education accessible in difficult living conditions including challenged children, those from minority communities or religions *and* migrant children. With the help of AIE and EGS, for example mobile schools, examinations on demand, bridge courses as well as residential camps are offered. Taken altogether, those activities can facilitate education in future times (Deshingkar 2009: 48). While there are different organizations responsible for the implementation of SSA all over India, in Maharashtra the Mahatma Phule Sikshan Hami Yojna (MPSHY) was made mandatory in 2002 for the issue of sugar mills and the education of children working in the sugarcane fields. But due to Wadiker and Das (2004), at the moment the MPSHY programme does not cover even 10 per cent of the migrant children.

The case of the Right to Education Act as well as the MPSHY programme show, however, that passing a law or governmental order alone is not enough to ensure the education of migrant children. Though the responsibility of providing education is well recognized in principle, the governmental practice lags far behind achieving the goals of a universal education for children up to 14 years. Meanwhile, following the different proposals for the enlargement of child migrant education provided by Smita, there is a need for an adjustment in the learning environment at schools as well as for an improved collaboration of civil society and local government. Otherwise the development of seasonal hostels in villages, schools at work sites as well as summer bridge courses and the strengthening of local government schools are not realizable (see Smita 2011). Because there are not many examples of NGO's dealing with seasonal migration and education in particular, the last section presents the education model of Janarth.

Sakhar shala – a model of migrant education by Janarth

In 2001, the NGO Janarth – situated in Aurangabad – initiated a pilot project opening 10 schools next to sugar factories in Ahmednagar district. Because sugar factory owners as well as contractors and local government did not take responsibility of migrant children, they started the initiative in two cooperative sugar factories with the perspective to retain at least some children 'in the quality education process and decrease the dropout rates caused by migration' (Wadiker and Das 2004: 11). From November 2001 till April 2002 the total amount of 882 children in school-going age were educated in 10 *Sakhar Shalas*, also known as second semester schools (ibid.: 12). Only two years later (2003–04) the organization covered 73 schools in 20 sugar factories and 4,256 students already (ibid.) whereas Deshingkar (2009: 49) indicates a number of 126 *Sakhar Shalas* and 15,000 children.[14] Getting children from all over Maharashtra, these schools do not experiment with the courses but follow the curriculum adopted by governmental schools.

But although the number of schools on the work sites increases steadily, the progress is slow in comparison to growing rates of seasonal migrating families. Janarth itself gives different reasons for this phenomenon. Due to a Strength Weakness Opportunity Threat (SWOT) analysis in 2004, the Sakhar Shala model is highly accepted in migration population and even supported by some sugar factories.[15] Nevertheless, it remains difficult to get the total amount of children working in *koyatas* or staying in the *kopi*. As a result not all children are recognized by Janarth teachers. Moreover, not the same but different groups of children enter the work site every year (due to the recruitment of the contractor). So the teachers have to deal with different cohorts coming from different village schools every year. This makes schooling difficult and the monitoring of school careers in the native villages impossible (see Deshingkar 2009: 50ff.).[16] Besides the difficulty of variable student numbers however, the finances provided by MPSHY are another threat concerning the project because at the moment resources are insufficient for both: teachers as well as school infrastructure.

Despite all these difficulties however, the Sakhar Shala model seems to be an adequate alternative to migrant children continuing their education during the migrating season and therefore providing a further step to the fundamental Right to Education for every child. Meanwhile Janarth takes part in the Child Right's committee, which can be used for representation purpose as well as acquiring other NGO's pursuing the aim of the univerzalization of elementary education not only in Maharashtra but all over India.

Discussion

In the end, the complex effects associated with human movement in general and seasonal migration in particular make it difficult to summarize the presented phenomenon in just one sentence. But referring to the question how seasonal migration affects children's education and how policy reflects this in Indian context, there exist at least two different ways of giving an answer.

Summarizing the chapter from a macro-theoretical point of view, it is not questionable that migrant labour in general and seasonal migration in particular make an enormous contribution to Indian economy. In fact, there is an increasing number of families going for sugarcane cutting which seems to be a regular and reliable option for better living conditions. So, many families even think of it as their main occupation. But although the phenomenon of seasonal migration is slowly recognized as an important factor influencing social and economic development, migrants themselves remain on the periphery of society. Searching for adequate literature and available studies, the dimension on missing data becomes quite visible. This is true for official papers as well as (inter-) national research programmes and field works. In fact, most of the studies referring to Indian migration are merely descriptive, not analytic, neither theoretical nor integrative. So the gap in data seems to be at least one argument for the lack of policy awareness concerning the effects on internal migration in general and the problem of the education of migrant children in particular.

Looking at the micro level instead, the preceding sections have shown migration processes which are not negative per se. In a positive sense, seasonal sugarcane harvesting for example brings a minimum of economical security for many families and therefore often prevents malnourishment and further indebtedness in their native villages. Despite those positive impacts, most of seasonal migrants work and remain in extremely difficult conditions while school-aged children are threatened disproportionately high by child labour and school drop-outs. But as proved by Janarth, seasonal migration does not have to be a limiting factor for the fundamental Right to Education. In fact, schools like the presented Sakhar Shalas as well as bridging courses, examinations on demand and a growing responsibility from governmental schools give a first idea of future development to the special treatment of migrant children.

Finally, education processes in India as well as in any other country of the world go hand in hand with both: individual as well as social development. Therefore, it seems to be a special need to revive the rural economy and society through local resource mobilization including migration in the purpose of better livelihood and self-help strategies. Due to the capability approach it has to be the highest aim to prevent children falling irreversibly into the annual cycle of migration because of inherited poverty and non-education but to empower them to go their own way into a self-determined life.

Notes

1 Some aspects of the capability approach can even be traced back to concepts of Aristotle, Adam Smith, John Stuart Mill and Karl Marx (see Sen 1985; Nussbaum 2003). Nevertheless, the approach in its present form has been pioneered by Amartya Sen and more recently by Martha Nussbaum.
2 Empowerment in the context of education includes the increase of people's ability to bring about change. Moreover, it contains the ability of individuals as well as social groups to engage with, shape and benefit from political as well as other processes (see Cheater 1999: 1ff.).
3 Besides seasonal sugarcane harvesting a lot of migrants are needed in other seasonal industries like salt production, cotton ginning and fruit processing. The

seasonal nature of production depends on a large variety of factors including non-conducive climatic conditions and cropping patterns.
4 Meanwhile, there exist dozens of other categories to classify migration processes including, for example, labour migration, refugee migration, and migration because of globalization as well as individual, group or family migration (see HDR 2009: 25) and different incentives encouraging migrants to leave their native place.
5 The Census of India is meant to be not only a census in classical meaning but a mirror on social, cultural and economical aspects of this multiethnic, multilingual and multicultural country. Therefore it 'gives a snapshot of not only the demographic but also the economic, social and cultural profile of the country at a particular point of time' (Census of India 2011: 2).
6 The National Census only provides migrant numbers but no flows which actually would be more important not only for this article but for Indian policy as well.
7 Although the recent Indian population is 1.2 billion people (2011), this paper refers to the 2001 data. The data on migration from Census 2011 were not published with the editorial deadline of this paper.
8 In Census 2001 as well as in 1991 the migration reasons have been classified into seven main groups: (1) work and employment, (2) business, (3) education, (4) marriage, (5) moved at birth, (6) moved with family or household, and (7) others. Usually marriage among females and employment among males can be identified as main migration reasons followed by accompanying parents or any other family members.
9 Janarth literally means 'for the people'. It is a non-governmental organization (NGO) active in Gangapur and Aurangabad district (Maharashtra) since 1988. The major focus lies on education especially for migrating children (Wadiker and Das 2004).
10 The author stayed some weeks at Tata Institute of Social Sciences in Mumbai and Tuljapur including field-trips in the rural area next to Scholapur and Aurangabad in May and June 2011. Therefore the interest was drawn to Maharashtra. Meanwhile, some interviews have been taken with teachers and mayors in schools and villages in the context of rural-rural migration and the impact on children.
11 People from Scheduled Castes and Tribes belong to the poorest stratum of Indian society not only according to economic benefits but social acceptance as well. Although this article mainly refers to economic reasons forcing people into migration activity, obviously there are many other circumstances resulting in internal or seasonal migration. In a study of untouchability in rural India, for example, Shah et al. point out that 'wherever possible, Dalits [also: Untouchables] have individually and also collectively migrated from their ancestral villages in order to escape continued humiliation and oppression' (Shah et al. 2006: 145).
12 According to Deshingkar and Farrington there are two different kinds of migration. The first one is named *coping* migration including uneducated or less educated men and women migrating mainly for survival reasons. Their movement sometimes helps them to manage extremely risks but seldom leads to better living standards. In India people from Scheduled Castes (SC), Scheduled Tribes (ST) and Other Backward Castes (OBC) are disproportionately high represented in this migration type (Deshingkar 2009: 18). Besides that *accumulative*

migration mostly of educated people often allows some accumulation of assets, savings and investment and therefore improves the living conditions (see Deshingkar and Farrington 2009: 19).
13 The interview was done in a small school in a village next to Tuljapur. Thanks to Tata Institute of Social Sciences in Tuljapur for the provided translator.
14 While the institution of Sakhar Shalas is an arrangement only suitable for school-aged children, Janarth at the same time offers some childcare services as well, known as *balwadi* in the Indian context (Wadiker and Das 2004: 12).
15 Developed by Albert Humphrey in 1960s, the SWOT analysis is a strategic planning method used to evaluate strengths, weaknesses (or limitations), opportunities as well as threats involved in a business venture or – in case of Janarth – in a project. It is quite important to specify the 'objectiveness' of a business venture and identify the internal and external factors that are favourable and unfavourable to achieve the aims (see Paul and Wollny 2011: 81ff.).
16 In awareness of the difficult integration of migrant children in their home schools, Janarth additionally has built seasonal hostels in nine high-migration villages. Started in 2005, this is just another attempt preventing the migration of children and making school attendance possible (Wadiker and Das 2004).

References

Alkire, S. (2002): Valuing Freedoms: Sen's Capability Approach and Poverty Reduction. New York.

Bansode, P. (2011): Seasonal Rural Migration: Quality of Life at Destination and Source. Pune.

Bose, A. (1983): Migration in India: Trends and Policies. In: A. S. Oberai (ed.): State Policies and Internal Migration: Studies in Market and Planned Economies. London.

Breman, J. (1990): Even Dogs Are Better Off: The Ongoing Battle Between Capital and Labour in the Cane-Fields of Gujarat. Journal of Peasant Studies 17: 546–608.

Census of India (2001): India D-series, Migration Tables, Registrar General and Census Commissioner, India, New Delhi. Available: http://censusindia.gov.in/Tables_Published/D-Series/Tables_on_Migration_Census_of_India_2001.aspx/. Accessed May 9, 2012.

Census of India (2011): Migration Tables. Available: http://censusindia.gov.in/. Accessed May 12, 2012.

Chattopadhyaya, H. (1987): Internal Migration. A Case Study of Bengal. Calcutta.

Cheater, A. P. (1999): The Anthropology of Power: Empowerment and Disempowerment in Changing Structures. London.

Desai, M. (2005): Janarth Sakharshala – The Sending Village Report. Working Paper No. 23. Pune.

Deshingkar, P. (2009): Human Development Research Paper 2009/13: Migration and Human Development in India. London.

Deshingkar, P., and Farrington, J. (2009): Circular Migration and Multilocational Livelihood Strategies in Rural India. Oxford.

Fine, B. (2001): Social Capital versus Social Theory: Political Economy and Social Science at the Turn of the Millennium. London.

Giddens, A. (1984): The Constitution of Society: Outline of the Theory of Structuration. Berkeley.

Government of India (2009): Right to Education Act. New Delhi.

Govinda, R., and Bandyopadhyay, M. (2011): Access to Elementary Education in India: Analytical Overview. In: R. Govinda (ed.): Who Goes to School? Exploring Exclusion in Indian Education. New Delhi, 1–86.

Haug, S. (2000): Klassische und neuere Theorien der Migration. Arbeitspapiere Mannheimer Zentrum für Europäische Sozialforschung, Nr. 30. Mannheim.

Human Development Report (HDR) (2009): Overcoming Barriers: Human Mobility and Development. New York.

Hoerder, D., Lucassen, J., and Lucassen, L. (2008): Terminologien und Konzepte in der Migrationsforschung. In: K. J. Bade, P. C. Emmer, L. Lucassen, and Oltmer, J. (eds): Enzyklopädie Migration in Europa. Vom 17. Jahrhundert bis zur Gegenwart. München, 28–53.

Kröhnert, S. (2007): Migrationstheorien. Berlin. Available: http://www.berlininstitut.org/ fileadmin/user_upload/handbuch_texte/pdf_Kroehnert_Migrationstheorien.pdf. Accessed May 8, 2012.

Lee, E. S. (1966): A Theory of Migration. Demography 3(1): 47–57.

Lipton, M. (1980): Migration from Rural Areas of Poor Countries: The Impact on Rural Productivity and Income Distribution. World Development 8 (227): 1–24.

Lowry, I. S. (1966): Migration and Metropolitan Growth: Two Analytical Models. San Francisco.

Mathew, K. S., Singh, S., and Varkey, J. (2005): Migration in South India. Kolkata.

Mukherjee, S. (2001): Low Quality Migration in India: The Phenomenon of Distress Migration and Acute Urban Decay. Paper presented at the 24th IUSSP Conference, August 2001, Brazil. Available: http://iussp.org/Brazil2001/s80/S80_04_Mukherji.pdf. Accessed May 15, 2012.

National Sample Survey Organisation (NSSO) (2001): Migration in India. Report No. 470 (55/10/8), 1999–2000, National Sample Survey Organisation, New Delhi, Ministry of Statistics and Programme Implementation Government of India. Available: http://www.mospi.gov.in/mospi_ nsso_rept_pubn.htm. Accessed April 27, 2012.

Nussbaum, M. (2003): Capabilities as Fundamental Entitlements: Sen and Social Justice. Feminist Economics 9 (2/3): 33–59.

Paul, H., and Wollny, V. (2011): Instrumente des strategischen Managements: Grundlagen und Anwendung. München.

Piper, E. (2010): Mobilität. In: Ch. Wulf (ed.): Der Mensch und seine Kultur. Hundert Beiträge zur Geschichte, Gegenwart und Zukunft des menschlichen Lebens. Köln, 198–202.

Ravenstein, E. (1885): The Laws of Migration. Journal of the Statistical Society 48: 167–235.

Sen, A. (1985). Commodities and Capabilities. Amsterdam, New York.

Shah, G., Mander, H., Thorat, S., Deshpande, S., and Baviskar, A. (2006): Untouchability in Rural India. New Delhi.

Smita (2011): Distress Seasonal Migration and Its Impact on Children's Education. In: R. Govinda (ed.): Who Goes to School? Exploring Exclusion in Indian Education. New Delhi, 315–360.

United Nations Economic Commission for Europe (UN/ECE) (1993): International Migration. No. 3. Genève.

Wadiker, J., and Das, M. (2004): A Report on Sakhar Shala – An Education Program for Children of Migrant Laborers in Sugar Factories. Model Developed by Janarth. Mumbai.

Zachariah, K.C. (1964): A Historical Study of Internal Migration in Indian Sub-Continent, 1901–1931. Bombay.

19
EDUCATIONAL EXPERIENCES OF STUDENTS WITH DISABILITIES IN HIGHER EDUCATION
A case study of a German university[1]

Nageswara Rao Ambati

Background of the study

The idea that the state should be generally responsible for the welfare of its citizens with disabilities is comparatively new. Traditionally, the German welfare model is based on the medical model, which focuses on individualized cures, rehabilitation and treatment (Heyer 2002). Later on, the civil rights model evolved as a critique of the social welfare model. Disability policy, under a rights model, focuses on ways to make social environments accessible and reform the existing social institutions to include people with disabilities (Heyer 2002). The basic assumption is that once contact with the persons with disabilities increases through neighbourhoods, workplace, integrated schools etc. discriminatory attitudes and the necessity for legal intervention would decrease. In policy terms, the rights model replaces parallel track with equal opportunity and anti-discrimination, and segregation with integration. The primary enforcement tool is the law. Accordingly, people with disabilities are transformed from passive patients and welfare recipients to people with civil rights that are enforceable by law (Silvers et al. 1998).

The much discussed paradigm shift in German transition from medical solutions to social change, from pity to power, and from charity to rights has now been acknowledged and the German government adopted the US disability rights model. The enactment of Social Code Book IX (Rehabilitation and Participation of Disabled Persons) in 2001 was a significant step, and marked a change of paradigm in German disability law. The act aims 'to promote the autonomy of the disabled and ensure their equal participation in society, and to avoid or counteract disadvantages'. This new orientation was the result of the 1994 amendment of the German constitution's Article 3, which included the prohibition of discrimination on grounds of disability. Now we will see how the paradigm shift in disability policy affected the provision of support services for students with disabilities in German higher education institutions and its impact on their educational experiences.

The Federal Republic of Germany is made up of 16 federal states 'Länder', as a result of German unification through a treaty between the Federal Republic of Germany and the German Democratic Republic on 3 October 1990. Each federal state or 'Land' has its own constitution and government. Educational legislation and administration of the educational system are primarily in the responsibility of the federal states. After the constitutional reform in 2006, the German state has only minimal influence on educational policies in Germany (KMK 1982).

According to the recommendation of the Standing Conference of the Ministries of Education and Cultural Affairs of the *Länder* all educational institutions follow a code of practice which aims at improving the educational conditions of students with disabilities (KMK 1982). These recommendations primarily seek to bring about the integration of students with disabilities in the existing structures of higher education institutions, rather than suggesting segregate solutions such as 'universities for students with disabilities' or courses of study designed especially and exclusively for students with disabilities (KMK 1982).

According to the official statistics, approximately 292,000 German students and foreign students with a German education were enrolled in their first semester in the year 2005. Similarly the national Association for student's affairs (Deutsches Studentenwerk, DSW) periodically conducts a survey on the social situation of students, including those with disabilities in higher education institutions in Germany. These samples are regarded as being representative, and data are based on anonymized information of the surveys about students. The latest survey was conducted in the summer semester 2000 (DSW/HIS 2001). According to this survey, 2 per cent of all students consider themselves as having disabilities, and 13 per cent have chronic disease. Of the students with chronic disease, 8 per cent have chronic psychological disease, 17 per cent disease of the muscular-skeletal system and supporting tissues, and 52 per cent suffer from allergies and diseases of the respiratory tract. The data given can only be taken as a basis for legitimizing or improving further support services for students with disabilities in higher education institutions (DSW/HIS 2001).

Review of literature

Students with disabilities (SWDs) represent an emerging population in higher education institutions, whose perceptions and experiences in higher education are ultimately shaped by their sociocultural experiences, the existing environment and the availability of specific facilities required by them for pursuing their higher studies. The literature included in this study is based on the e-resources available in the library of the Free University Berlin (FUB). A great deal of research in the West has been conducted on diverse issues of students with disabilities in higher education institutions. This review is focused on the factors affecting positive and negative educational experiences of such students with disabilities in higher education institutions. But unfortunately it was found that there is a dearth of research studies in the German context. This section first examines the policies and support services provided by the higher education institutions for students with disabilities. The second part deals with their educational experiences in higher education institutions.

Studies by Hall and Tinklin (1998) and UNESCO (1999) indicate that most of the higher educational institutions now have institutional policies for students with disabilities. But the ways in which policy implementation is monitored vary greatly among institutions. Various forms of advice, guidance and support are now available to students with disabilities, but more could be done to increase public awareness on this issue. Weiss and Repetto (1997) indicate that post-secondary institutions are continuing to move towards providing necessary individualized support services to students with disabilities. After such students learn to take full advantage of these support services, they will improve their chances of receiving the training and education needed to be competitive in the job market.

Hall and Tinklin (1998) have found that the main challenge to higher educational institutions is to combine recognition of the individuality of students and their needs with policies and actions which are more than piecemeal attempts to resolve difficulties. A similar study conducted by Riddell et al. (2005) has identified four issues for higher education institutions to address: (a) pre-orientation support, (b) staff's commitment to facilitating a barrier-free curriculum, (c) consultation with and empowerment of students with disabilities and (d) a commitment on the part of higher education institutions to develop support services for students and planning for their personal development. A UNESCO (1999) study also found that there was no uniformity in universities in terms of the financial and human resources to respond to this challenge. The researcher suggests that the first step towards providing equal access for all students is the will to address the diversity of needs of students and to create a supportive environment accordingly. A similar study by Vickerman and Blundell (2010) found that students' learning and teaching assessment was restrictive and this appeared to be due to the inappropriate learning resources, lack of modification of teaching by teachers, lack of discussion with students with disabilities regarding their problems and needs related to learning and assessment strategies that significantly place them in a disadvantaged position in higher education. Bierwert (2002) opines that requesting for an accessible classroom was often stressful to the students with disabilities. In a similar study, West et al. (1993) found that the majority of students indicated that they had encountered barriers to their education, including lack of understanding and cooperation from administrators, faculty, staff and other students, adaptive aids and other accommodations, as well as inaccessibility of buildings and grounds.

Overall, the review of studies shows that there are several factors or barriers which affect the social and educational experience of students with disabilities in higher education institutions. Despite the significant progress in legislations and policies for the students with disabilities in higher education institutions, many of them are still faced with various challenges in completing their studies successfully.

Research design and methodology

The present qualitative study is exploratory in nature. It was conducted with students with disabilities at FUB. Qualitative research allows for a naturalistic approach to this study. Qualitative forms of investigation tend to be based on recognition of the importance of the subjective, experiential 'life world' of human beings, describing the experiences of people in-depth (Burns 2000). This study attempted to discover the higher educational opportunities available to students with disabilities including support services, legislations, rights, funding support from different organizations and the resulting impact on their educational experiences.

Objectives of the study

1 To understand the disability from the students' perspective based on their experiences.
2 To identify the enabling and hindering factors affecting the educational experiences of such students in higher education institutions.

Research setting and population

The researcher selected FUB to conduct this study. His opportunity to visit the University was provided by the 'Passage to India' programme run by the DAAD (German Academic Exchange Service) from October 2010 to January 2011. Subjects of the study were students with disabilities who enrolled in the academic year 2010–11 at FUB.

Data sources and methods

This study is based on both primary and secondary data. Due to the lack of research on students with disabilities in the German context as well as the lack of corresponding literature in the English language, the researcher could not find much secondary data or adequate literature on the subject. The secondary data include papers from the OECD (Organisation for Economic Cooperation and Development) Conference on Higher Education and Disability held in Grenoble in 1999, educational reports of the German government, which were found online, and reports and official websites of Studentenwerk. The information in the published conference proceedings and reports was, therefore, encoded, entered and processed. For this study, primary data were collected from five students with disabilities at FUB.

Sampling method

The study used the snowball sampling technique to collect data. Snowball sampling – also known as chain referral sampling – is considered a type of purposive sampling. It was very difficult to get details about students with disabilities from the disability office due to issues related to confidentiality. That's why the researcher used snowball sampling. In this method, students with disabilities with whom contact has already been made use their social networks to refer the researcher to other students who could potentially participate in or contribute to the study. Due to the short time available, the researcher could collect data from only five students with disabilities.

Data collection and analysis

The researcher used semi-structured interviews to collect the data from the students. An interview guide was developed, based on the research questions of this study. The interview questions focused mainly on funding opportunities, provision of support services to students with disabilities, and the factors affecting the educational experiences of these students. Almost all of the discussions were open-ended to explore issues which respondents of the study considered to be important. The discussions and interviews were audio-taped and video-recorded. The researcher compared the information for analysis and interpretation (Charmaz 1994) and transcribed, coded and analysed the data through thematic analyses and according to how the common themes seemed to be emerging. Participation in this study was voluntary. The researcher explained to the participants at different stages the aims and objectives of the study and at each stage special care was taken to explain the nature of informed consent and their right to withdraw from the study.

Limitations of the study

- A major limitation is the lack of availability of relevant literature in the German context, as well as in English language, since very few empirical studies have been undertaken in Germany.
- Due to the time limit of the study as well as its objectives the researcher focused mainly on factors which have an impact on educational experiences at institutions of higher education.
- In addition, the sample of student participants may not fully represent the diverse types of disabilities in this university. Thus the results may vary across students with different disabilities.

Findings of the study

From the data gathered, three main categories of findings emerged. These include: (1) understanding of the disabilities from the student's perspective, (2) institutional commitment to support students with disabilities and (3) student's positive and challenging educational experiences. These are discussed below.

Understanding and defining disability from the students' perspective

In this section, the researcher has attempted to provide an understanding of the concept of disability from the students' perspective, based on their experiences or their own understanding. Understanding their disability, needs and problems appears to be essential for the empowerment of such students. Respondents of the study believed that it is better to inform the disability coordinator and their teachers about their impairments and specific needs at the beginning of their studies. They also believe that their impairments impact not only their educational experiences, but also their social relations and personal experiences. However, the degree of self-understanding their disability varied among the respondents. Some of them described their disability based on terms of impairment, whereas a few of them described that the nature of their disability depends on the availability of support services by the university, which affect their day-to-day educational experiences. The following are the responses:

> I am a totally blind person. I cannot see anything or read by myself, and I always need my friends or personal assistants for help or some assistive devices for my academic activities. I could not do all the activities which are considered as normal for others. (Bent, totally visual impaired)
>
> My visual impairment is making me to lag behind my friends as far as studies are concerned. But in order to succeed in my studies, I need good support and have to face so many problems like spending much time for scanning, editing or asking friends for collecting material and also for recording it on the tape-recorder. All these problems are just because of my disability. (Ivos, partially sighted)
>
> The major challenge for me is to make the necessary adjustments in order to survive in this critical environment which is created for individuals without disabilities. Regarding my disability it depends on the role of the university management system in providing support services and adjustments as per my needs which would enable me to access all educational facilities. (Urs, mobility impairment)
>
> Initially, when my sight was reducing I felt my life won't go smoothly anymore. But the availability of support services at school as well as in this university makes me feel that still I am independent. I am now no longer anxious about my eye sight and studies. (Nika, partially sighted)
>
> Even though people treat me as disabled, I do most of my things without depending on others, except a few things due to some limitations of the body. I do believe that everyone is having some limitations or the other. So I don't like to be considered myself as disabled. (John, mobility impairment)

Overall, the understanding of the term disability varied among the students. For some respondents disability was based on their impairment which affects their educational experiences. For some respondents it was understood within the context of norms of mainstreaming society or the environment with which he or she lives. But all respondents highlighted that their supporting system in Berlin and within the university management has played a major role in shaping their educational experiences.

Factors affecting the educational experiences of students with disabilities in higher education

Educational experiences and success of the students with disabilities depend not only on the availability as well as accessibility of facilities and support services, but also on challenging situations at higher education institutions. This section is focused on each of these factors, in order to demonstrate how they impact the higher education of these students.

Support services for students with disabilities

Support services for students with disabilities is multifaceted, involving issues of availability of resources and their accessibility, training of academic tutors and staff, awareness about diversity and areas of special needs, effective referral services, as well as emotional and pastoral support for students with disabilities to disclose disability to and minimize the sense of stigma (Tinkling and Hall 1999). There were several support services for these students at FUB. The university prescribed a set of procedures, in order to integrate these students and to improve their educational experiences. According to the disability coordinator:

> Once students with disabilities have been selected for a particular programme at the university, they are required to submit medical proof document, which states that person has disability as per social code IX. These students can also discuss their needs and problems at the disability office, in order to get services.

From the data it was found that the key areas of concern for the participants included: counselling, academic, personal and financial services.

Counselling Services: Some of the respondents reported that counselling services is important for them to access all kinds of support services from the beginning to end of the course. Robert had this to say:

> I had problems when I joined here to find out where I will get support. I obtained so many applications to get help but it is very

difficult to meet so many people and tell everything from the beginning to each and every person. I don't know whom to contact, how to contact and where to contact. Since the campus is very big and there are so many departments, it was very difficult for me to find out. Finally, I met the coordinator of disability affairs, who assessed my needs and informed me about the various kinds of support services that could meet my special needs and requirements.

Similarly, another student, Urs, stated that the disability coordinator played an important role in solving his problems. He said:

In my case, I can't meet the disability officer every time. But I consult him through email and phone. When I joined here and discussed my problems, he sent me a list of places, including class rooms, academic places which are accessible to me in the entire campus. He also suggested to me how to access academic buildings and informed me about the location of stair cases, ramps, and lifts and toilet facilities in the campus.

It was also found that students discuss their needs and problems including: (1) effective use of support services available at the campus, (2) teaching and learning resources including technical, personal assistance and (3) available financial resources.

Personal assistants: It was found that provision of personal assistants was considered as most important service. For four students (out of five interviewees), this support was significant. All respondents in this study reported that they are getting the services of personal assistants for their studies. These personal assistants were arranged by the disability coordinator and financed by the Studentenwerk. As the Disability Coordinator put it:

Law says that all students with disabilities will get personal assistants as per their special needs. In most of the cases we arrange students/personal assistants from their class with the intention that only classmates know better about their needs and render more help to these students along with their work.

All the respondents believe that these personal assistants were greatly impacting their educational experiences. Nika said:

I am getting a personal assistant from the university. She is my friend and classmate and is helping me in my studies by scanning and collecting material from the library, writing notes for me. She reads and writes for me and also helps me if I need something related to my studies. Since I am getting support from the university, I can follow lectures much better. It makes it easy to study well. Otherwise, I would have to spend a lot of time for collecting and scanning material.

According to Urs:

I am getting 10 hours personal assistance for my studies at the campus. He helps me to carry my books, writing notes and collecting material from the library and opening the building doors.

From an analysis of the students' narrative it was also understood that these personal assistants help them in pushing wheelchairs and moving up and down the ramps on the campus. Since not all buildings do have adopted automatic doors, it is very difficult for many students to get in and out of the classrooms and other places. Interestingly, these findings show even though most of the buildings and classrooms are accessible to these students, they could not complete their studies successfully without their personal assistants. This support made their life at the campus easier. They also felt comfortable knowing that there is always a person who can assist them in their studies and in accessing academic buildings, cafeteria, leisure centres etc.

Alternative Testing and Testing Place: All students with visual impairment responded that taking an alternative test or modifications in testing and an alternative quiet room where an assistant was writing their exams was a very crucial support for them. They were also allowed extra time during the examination. These students inform the disability officer prior to their exams. Then, the disability officer talks to the concerned teacher and makes all preparation for students to write exams as per their special needs. Denims, a respondent, had this to say:

Last time, my professor allowed me write exams in a word document file as I requested at the disability office. I am very comfortable with writing exams with technical assistance. Speech software helps me to write exams. It worked well. I didn't ask for anyone's help to write my exams and I even finished my exam without asking for extra time. Therefore, I believe that this kind of support makes me feel that I am independent.

Bent, another respondent, said:

> Getting extra time during the exams is very helpful to me. Sometimes the students who are assisting me to write exams are not good at speed writing. For me, too, it is very difficult to explain and tell fast. Most often, I take extra time not only during exams but also for assignment submissions. Taking extra time makes me feel better and do well in my studies.

All students felt the availability of this kind of academic support is a very important factor which positively impacts their educational experiences. During the course of their academic life, they had positive experience with the staff in the library. A common experience shared by many students was that librarians were very helpful. Bent's comments are representative of the group's experiences. He noted: 'Whenever I go to the library, the staff helps me in searching, issuing and returning books, and making photocopies. They also help me in accessing assistive devices within the library, and guiding me around the site.'

At the same time, students with visual impairment also mentioned that they had positive experience with the teaching faculty. They also reported that teachers give useful material in advance; they put material in black board (a website which contains details of the course, material, lecturers and presentations) in advance. The following statement by Robert represents this experience.

> In the beginning of the course, I went to my teacher after the class with the letter given by the disability officer, which mentions the special needs and requirements in the class and facilities I was supposed to get. That day onwards, he/she is aware of my needs and allows me to take extra time, arranges alternative places for exams and allows me to write exam in computer with speech software.

Assistive Technology: Assistive technology is one of the ways to help students with disabilities compensate for their difficulties and support them in a number of academic areas. The provision of assistive technology changes the educational experiences of these students in higher education (Goldberg and O'Neil 2000; Burgstahler 2002). Assistive technology helps students in reading, writing, note-taking, assignments, or writing tests, scanning and saving material. In fact, it has increasingly become apparent that the advantages of the use of the new information technology and assistive devices improve the physical and learning capabilities of these students more than those of students without disabilities. Bent noted:

> Before coming to this campus, I used the Braille machine and normal paper for my studies. But due to the amount of text and things you have to write with this machine, this is not very easy and helpful. You would have to use a lot of paper. I would say you would have a whole room full of papers but you do not know the location of the particular text or material. You need to check each and every paper. I think computer technology makes it very easy to write, scan and organise material.

Financial Support: Students whose parents do not have enough financial strength get financial assistance in all German Universities for their studies. Nearly 20–25 per cent of the students get this fellowship. Students with disabilities get it for a longer period of time. In case they could not finish their course due to their disability, their fellowship will be extended. Students with disabilities need more financial support for their studies in order to get support like scribes, writers and personal assistants. According to the disability officer at German University:

> As per the law and University guidelines students with disabilities are often eligible to apply for financial assistance or disabled students allowance (DSA). This assistance depends on the type of disability and its needs. It helps them to procure their assistive devices or equipments or to employ readers or scribes and personal assistants. This assistance is funded by the Studentenwerk as per their contract with the university management and the government.

Respondents in this study stated that the disability coordinator helped them in getting information about the financial resources and application procedures. The application process involves the assessment of the needs of students and its approval by the disability coordinator. Those who received financial aid through recommendation of the disability coordinator purchased assistive devices including scanner, computers and speech software. This support reduced the amount of work they have to put for Braille writing. Now they do not need to depend on others for recording material and it also helped them to save time and become independent at least concerning their studies.

Accessibility and Transport: The issues of accessibility and physical barriers continue to exist in higher education institutions for students with disabilities. This includes lack of access to buildings, classrooms and other places on the campus. A study by Shevlin et al. (2004) reported that students with disabilities experience variable access within higher education institutions and physical access remains a serious obstacle to full participation. Paul's (1998) study indicates that students who use wheelchairs struggle with inaccessible classrooms and restrooms. A study by West et al. (1993) also shows that barriers identified by students with disabilities were inaccessible buildings and classrooms, and lack of other accommodations.

In the current study, findings show that access for these students, particularly for mobility impaired wheel chair users, improved at FUB, since in 1992 the Senate (city government) passed guidelines for a more disabled-friendly city. The goal of the guidelines was to foster and encourage the equal participation of all disabled and non-disabled residents and visitors in the city's diverse social, economic and cultural life. As a result most of the buildings including public and private offices, educational institutions, railway stations, and other transport facilities have been made user-friendly and accessible to all.

Here, the coordinator of disability affairs plays an important role in suggesting the university management and planning section to provide a friendly environment for students with disabilities. The disability officer noted one of his experiences:

> Few years ago, we had discussions about wheelchair users in the chemistry department. Because it was a question of accessibility how a student with wheelchair can work in the laboratory in the chemistry department. Then we had some discussions with the concerned student, his teachers, university management, our law department and the university security department. We worked together to find a solution. Finally, we found the solution in the law saying that we have to support each student with disability. The law department also said that it is not a question if the student can study but how he can study and it is not a question of support, but how we support him. Finally, we made some accessible environment and some equipment like modifications in the laboratory, which would make the wheelchair user do his work himself while sitting in the wheelchair, and we allowed him to continue his study. He does not compulsorily have to work alone. He will get some assistance from his fellow students and his personal assistant. Finally, we succeeded in this case. We became the first laboratory where wheelchair students also can study this kind of courses. Two years ago, I think, he completed his course and

right now one more new student with wheelchair has enrolled in the same department. Now it is much easier for him and also for us because in the first case we have done and provided all facilities and accessibility to the laboratory.

The study by Brown (1992) also suggests that for a student with disability to have a successful and positive educational experience in higher education two issues need to be addressed: availability of specialized services to 'maximise the students' ability to participate fully in the chosen course of studies' and 'the campus must be physically accessible'.

In the current study, students with mobility impairment may rely on wheel chairs, or electrical motor cars for transport to go to their universities. Urs uses an electrical motor car to move around at the university. If his classes are in different places in the academic building (a huge building at the selected University), he drives from one place to another including classrooms, computer centres, restaurants and libraries. He can access the buildings with his motor car, because they have ramps and lift facility along with staircases. Urs noted:

> Most of the places in my academic building are accessible to me. I even got special parking facilities for my motor car in all the places I visit. However, once I visit my academic buildings entirely, there are so many doors to get through. Unfortunately not all doors are automatic or electronic doors. Since I have problems with legs and hands, I do face some problems. I cannot open any door in order to get my motor car through. So, at the beginning of my course, the disability coordinator arranged one student from my class as my personal assistant. Since our both classes and time tables are the same, he knows when and where I need his help to get inside or help in pushing in difficult places. Other than this, I am getting transport service, which is founded by the government social aided fund. I get this service to reach my campus. This bus service has been especially arranged for persons with disabilities in Berlin. All these facilities make it much easier for me to get around and outside the campus.

Challenges faced by students with disabilities at FUB

Despite so much progress and provision of support services students with disabilities are still facing many barriers which affect their educational experiences in higher education. Most of the challenges they discussed in detail in this section include: (1) not having dormitory or hostel facilities within the campus, (2) physical environment and accessibility, (3) lacking financial opportunities and (4) attitudes of teachers and peer group.

Physical Environment and Accessibility: Many students with disabilities feel that the university is a challenging environment. FUB extended effort to integrate students with disabilities by enabling them to participate in educational activities with different support services. Today, most of the buildings are accessible and are equipped with ramps, lift facilities etc. But still there are some buildings and departments that remain inaccessible, because there is no way to adapt them, or these adaptations require more funds. Urs opined that most of the buildings are accessible, having special parking facilities in most of the places.

Some participants with visual impairment reported that it is very difficult to move in the university. Since it is very huge campus, non-availability of hostel facilities within or near the campus makes it difficult for them to attend classes, going to the library or to restaurants in the campus. Bent noted:

> Even though I took mobility training before coming here and having a personal assistant, my initial days in the course were very horrible to me. We cannot expect the personal assistants to be with us for most of the time. Sometimes in some places in the campus, till I reach the destination I don't know whether I have reached the right place or not. But somehow, I am managing everything and have the belief that I will complete my studies successfully.

All the respondents in the study are staying neither inside the campus nor in their homes. Since the selected university is not providing dormitory or hostel facilities within the campus, students with disabilities often have a difficult time to reach the campus. Even though they have special transport services, it is very difficult for them to come to the campus every day. The worst thing was that the special bus for them is running according to the university time schedule. But in case they wish to spend more time in the library or within the campus, this won't be possible. Thus, it also hinders maintaining friendships and social relations within the campus.

Paucity of Financial Resources: Financial resources are an important factor to integrate students with disabilities in any educational institution with all support services. The more an institution spends money for a friendly environment, including adaptations, ramps, lifts and assistive devices and technical and personal assistance, the less negative experiences students will have. The disability officer reported that there were some financial problems in supporting and fulfilling the special needs of all types of students with disabilities:

> We are having much problems with sign language interpreters. We are getting financial resources from Berlin government, some part comes from the university management, and another part comes from the Studentenwerk. In order to solve this problem, we had some discussions with sign language interpreters, university management and the Studentenwerk. As a result of the discussion, we are planning to renew the contract with the Studentenwerk in the coming year in order to meet the expenses for sign interpreters.

Attitudes of Teachers and Peer Group: Attitudes play an important role in the success or failure of students with disabilities in higher education institutions. Attitudes of teachers, peer groups, non-teaching staff and the administration, as well as student services coordinator, can all have a profound effect on the social and educational experiences of students with disabilities in higher education institutions (Nathanson 1979), since general educator's willingness to include these students in regular education classes is critical to the success of inclusion. A number of studies have stressed the importance of understanding teachers' attitudes, their awareness about the needs and problems of students with disabilities in higher education (Cook and Semmel 1999; Wilson and Lewiecki-Wilson 2001).

In the current study, no respondent did report any negative experience with teachers. But the experience of the disability coordinator was contrary to that. Many times he found it difficult to work together with university teachers (more than 500). He noted:

> If a student comes here and gives me some document regarding disability and tells me about his/her problems or needs, I will explain in my letter to the particular teacher the situation of the students and their needs and availability of some provision to them. Ninety per cent of teachers agree and they provide all kind of support including extra time, alternative place.
>
> The rest of the teachers won't agree with me and says that is not fair to grant extra facilities to some people and not for all. This is due to their lack of understanding about the disabilities and their special needs. We also failed in some cases like invisible disabilities of students with some psychological problems who need some

support like extra time or extensions but teachers didn't agree in a few cases. Since some disabilities are not visible, it is very difficult to convince teachers to support students. Teachers say that these students do not have any problems and if they want a disability certificate they get it easily. So they didn't believe some students with invisible disabilities.

In a similar way, these students encountered some negative attitudes from their peer group. Nika noted: 'Sometimes I had to come across misunderstandings among a few of my friends who said that I am using all disability benefits without having any disability.'

Copeland et al. (2004) reported that peer support programmes helped them to understand more about students with disabilities and improved their attitudes towards them. Overall, the findings of the study indicate that peer support programmes helped the respondents of the study to effectively address the challenges related to the inclusion of students with disabilities and promoted their access to general education.

Discussion and conclusion

This section presents a discussion about the facilitating and hindering factors influencing the educational experiences of students with disabilities in higher education. The findings of the study show that the understanding of the term disability varied among the students in this study. For some participants, disability was based on their impairment which affects their educational experiences. This finding is supported by the work of Olney and Brockelman (2003) in many ways. They suggest that one is disabled according to the situation, not as a constant state of being. This is supported by respondents of the current study; many of them reported that they felt disabled within the context of norms of the mainstream society or the environment in which he or she lives. Some of them describe themselves disabled where they don't have teaching and learning support services. Second, it was found that the positive educational experiences of participants depend on the efficiency and functioning of the disability coordinator. Overall, we understood from their educational experiences that they were integrated into higher education and the support services needed to facilitate their academic performance. This finding is supported by the study of Tinto (1975), which suggests that the greater the degree of student integration into the academic system of the university, the more likely the students with disabilities will persist to complete their studies successfully. Other research studies, like Weiss and

Repetto (1997) and Hall and Tinklin (1998) arrive at a similar conclusion. In this study, the following support services or factors facilitated the positive educational experiences for students with disabilities at the university: (1) services of the disability officer, (2) availability of support services, (3) university coordination with other agencies like the Studentenwerk and (4) attitudes of faculty and peers towards the students with disabilities.

Another key conclusion is, while all the participants had positive educational experiences, they also had to face a number of challenging situations at the university. This is evident from the experiences shared by students with disabilities, and the disability coordinator at FUB. Findings from this study and studies conducted by Marder and D'Amico (1992), Wagner (1993) and McBroom (1997) clearly show that the significant increase in the number of students with disabilities in higher education institutions over the past two decades is accompanied by an equal concern for the academic failure of a number of these students. These researchers contend that many factors could possibly contribute challenging situations for students with disabilities at higher education. It is important for policymakers to understand those challenging situations that affect the educational experiences of students with disabilities.

Implications for policy

This study has sought to provide policymakers an insight into the factors affecting the educational experiences of students with disabilities in higher education and the need to respond in several ways to enhance the conditions of these students. One major area of policy is focused upon management issues important to address the challenges faced by students with disabilities. First of all, the university management should review the current policy and make changes in the existing system. Support for students with disabilities should be decentralized in the entire campus. Instead of having a single support cell in one place, there should be more advocacy and support centres or networks which could help students with disabilities. The second important point for policymakers is that the persons who are employed as disability officers or coordinators should be full-time employees. In order to properly understand the problems of students with disabilities and improve their educational experience it is better if they are employed on the basis of certain qualifications like knowledge, awareness and work and educational background related to disability issues. Another implication is that policy should provide additional funding resources in order to meet requirements of all types of special needs like sign language interpreters, to buy new assistive devices or equipments, to create adaptations or friendly environments in laboratories and install automatic doors in all places. One final implication for policymakers is that there should be additional funding for training of persons to help students technically and provide in-service training to create awareness among the teachers about the needs and problems of students with disabilities.

Future researchers can draw from this study to examine how the experiences of these five students relate to those of the larger population, and also how these experiences can lead to better social interaction and academic success. There is a significant need for further research on the academic success of students with disabilities in higher education institutions.

Note

1 The author would like to thank the respondents of the study for giving their time and sharing educational experiences with him. He is grateful to the DAAD (German Academic Exchange Service) programme and its coordinators Prof. Padma Sarangapani, TISS, Mumbai and Prof. Christoph Wulf, FU, Berlin, for giving him an opportunity to study in Berlin. He also wishes to thank his supervisor for her thoughtful and insightful comments. He is also indebted to his family members and friends who helped him during his stay in Berlin. An expanded version of this article was recently published as 'Paradigm shift in German disability and its impact on educational experiences of students with disabilities in higher education' in *Asian Journal of Research in Social Sciences and Humanities*.

References

Bierwert, C. (2002): Making accommodations for students with disabilities: a guide for faculty and graduate student instructors. *Center for Research on Learning and Teaching*, University of Michigan, No.17, 2002.

Brown, J. T. (1992): *Access to equity: the next step for women students with disabilities on the college campus*. Unpublished doctoral dissertation, Teachers College, Columbia University.

Burgstahler, S. (2002): *The role of technology in preparing youth with disabilities for postsecondary education and employment*. Unpublished manuscript.

Burns, R. B. (2000): *Introduction to research methods* (4th ed.). Sydney: Longman.

Charmaz, K. (1994): *The grounded theory method: an explication and interpretation*. In B. G. Glaser (ed.), *More grounded theory methodology: a reader*. Mill Valley, CA: Sociology Press.

Cook, B., and Semmel, M. (1999): Peer acceptance of included students with disabilities as a function of severity of disability and classroom composition. *The Journal of Special Education* 33 (1): 50–61.

Copeland, S., Hughes, C., Carter, E., Guth, C., Presley, J., Williams, C., and Fowler, S. (2004): Increasing access to general education: perspectives of participants in a high school peer support program. *Remedial and Special Education* 25: 342–352.

DSW/HIS (2001): Sozialerhebung. Available at www.studentenwerke.de (accessed November 2010).

Goldberg, L., and O'Neil, L. M. (2000): Computer technology can empower students with learning disabilities. *Exceptional Parent* 30 (7): 72–74.

Heyer, K. (2002): The ADA on the road: disability rights in Germany, Law & Social Inquiry. *Journal of American Bar Foundation* 27 (4): 723–762.

Hall, J., and Tinklin, T. (1998): Disabled Students in Higher Education, *Scottish Council for Research in Education*, 61, Dublin Street, Edinburgh. http://www.scre.ac.uk.

KMK (1982): Empfehlungen zur Verbesserung der Ausbildung für behinderte Hochbegabte. Neckar-Verlag, Villingen-Schwenningen. In: OECD (2003): *Disability in higher education*. Paris: Organization for Economic Cooperation and Development, 109–148.

Marder, C., and D'Amico, R. (1992): *How well are youth with disabilities really doing? A comparison of youth with disabilities and youth in general*. Menlo Park, CA: SRI International.

McBroom, L. W. (1997): Making the grade: college students with visual impairments. *Journal of Visual Impairment and Blindness* 91 (3): 261–271.

Nathanson, R. (1979): Campus interactions, attitudes and behaviors. *Personal and Guidance Journal*, December, 57/58: 39–62.

Olney, M., and Brockelman, K. (2003): Out of the disability closet: strategic use of perception management by select university students with disabilities. *Disability and Society* 18 (1): 35–50.

Paul, S. (1998): Identifying the career development needs of college students with disabilities. *Journal of College Student Development* 39 (1): 23–32.

Riddell, S., Tinklin, T., and Wilson, A. (2005): New labour, social justice and disabled students in higher education. *British Educational Research Journal* 31 (5): 623–643.

Shevlin, M., Kenny, M., and Mcneela, E. (2004): Participation in higher education for students with disabilities: an Irish perspective. *Disability & Society* 19 (1): 15–30.

Silvers, A., Wasserman, D., and Mahowald, M. B. (eds) 1998: *Disability, difference, discrimination: perspectives on justice in bioethics and public policy*. Lanham, MD: Rowman and Littlefield.

Social Code (SGB) Book 9 (IX) (2001): Rehabilitation and participation of disabled persons. *In International Disability Rights Monitor: Europe 2007 Report Card*, International Disability Network, Chicago.

Tinkling, T., and Hall, J. (1999): Getting round obstacles: disabled students experiences in higher education in Scotland. *Studies in Higher Education* 24: 183–194.

Tinto, V. (1975): Dropout from higher education: a theoretical synthesis of recent research. *Review of Educational Research* 45 (1): 89–125.

UNESCO (1999): *Provision for students with disabilities in higher education: a survey*. Paris: UNESCO.

Vickerman, P., and Blundell, M. (2010): Hearing the voices of disabled students in higher education. *Disability & Society* 21 (1): 21–32.

Wagner, M. (1993): *Trends in postsecondary outcomes of youth with disabilities*. Menlo Park, CA: SRI International.

Weiss, K.E., and Repetto, J.B. (1997): Support services for students with disabilities. *Community College Journal of Research and Practice* 21 (9): 709–720.

West, M., Kregel, J.E.E., Zhu, M., Ipsen, S.M., and Martin, E.D. (1993): Beyond Section 504: satisfaction and empowerment of students with disabilities in higher education. *Exceptional Children* 59: 456–467.

Wilson, J.C., and Lewiecki-Wilson, C. (2001): *Embodied rhetorics: disability in language and culture*. Carbondale, IL: Southern Illinois University Press.

20
A FRESH PERSPECTIVE ON INDIGENOUS TOOLS FOR INCLUSIVE EDUCATION

Mallika Swaminathan

The history of inclusive education has often been the site of many paradigms. The three more dominant of these have been the psycho-medical, sociopolitical and organizational paradigms. Educational programmes across many countries of the world have a mix of paradigms; however, it is the sociopolitical paradigm which seems to be the one which is more preponderant. A shift in the design of educational programmes towards the social context rather than the individual's differences, with a focus on a unitary education system dedicated to providing quality education for all is gaining prominence.

Over the years, the concept of inclusive education has been broadened to encompass more than just children with disabilities, and this particularly so, by researchers like Skrtic et al. (1996) who argued that inclusive education goes far beyond physical placement of students with disabilities in general classrooms. The confusion that exists within the field internationally arises, in part at least, from the fact that the idea of inclusive education can be defined in a variety of ways (Ainscow et al. 2000). It is not surprising therefore that progress remains disappointing in many countries. For example, in her analysis of national education plans from the Asia region, Ahuja (2005) notes that the idea of inclusive education was not even mentioned.

Discussion and debate on the topic of inclusive education often seems to direct towards the view point that this issue is not an unproblematic one, both conceptually and practically (Hegarty 2001). It is also important to note that, even in the developed world, not all educationalists have embraced the inclusive philosophy and some are resistant to the idea (Fuchs and Fuchs 1994; Brantlinger 1997; Freire and César 2003). However, the pursuit and the process towards achieving it are gradually building the consensual notion that the characterization, purpose and form of inclusive education reflects the relationships among the social, political, economic, cultural and historical contexts that are relevant to any particular country. Ongoing initiatives of the UNESCO aimed at enhancing the quality of learning and promoting inclusive education involve inclusion of indigenous groups and their ways. This includes a strategy for the elaboration of high quality, culturally relevant textbooks and learning materials in the languages of the learning community, and recommendations for influencing educational policies and practices worldwide. The UN Permanent Forum on Indigenous Issues is an advisory body to the Economic and Social Council, with a mandate to discuss indigenous issues related to economic and social development, culture, the environment, education, health and human rights and its focus on culturally and traditionally relevant elements is unmistakable (United Nations Permanent Forum on Indigenous Issues, UNPFII). In resonance with this trend, research along these lines and its focus on the ethos, attitude and culture of the educators and the school community is well documented (Carrington 1999; Phiri 2004; Subban and Sharma 2005). However, in comparison with the above mentioned study, the culture, ethos and attitude of the society as a whole towards this subject have not received adequate attention.

In the review *Education That Fits* (Mitchell 2010), there are many propositions of which two are of particular relevance to this chapter. One of them is that inclusive education exists in historical contexts in which vestiges of older beliefs co-exist with newer beliefs and also that it is embedded in a series of contexts, extending from the broad society, through the community and family. It is in this context that I present this chapter about indigenous tools in the process towards inclusive education.

Education for all is a fundamental requirement in any democracy. This is particularly important when considering that the community of differently abled people is constantly increasing in number and in diversity. Though internationally the concept and practice of inclusive education have gained importance in recent years and are increasingly understood more broadly, the gap between theory and practice seems to be getting harder to bridge. Special education pundits around the world are battling with the sociopolitical and financial limitations of the field.

Exclusion may start very early in life. However, a holistic vision of education could help to keep this at bay. Research shows that early intervention is imperative. Comprehensive care and support programmes improve children's well-being, prepare them for primary school and give them a better chance of succeeding once they are in school.

In their *International Study of Inclusion in Education*, Booth and Ainscow (1998) define inclusive education as 'a process of people enquiring into their own context to see how it can be developed and it is a process of growth. It is a social process that engages people in trying to make sense of their experience and helping one another to question their experience and their context to see how things can be moved forward.' A corollary to this could be the added need for socially responsible critical thinkers who are willing to challenge the conventional ways to look at incorporating a system with new and more holistic methods. Such a system would perhaps be one that will not remain confined to the narrow definitions and interpretation of inclusive education, especially in view of the world's present economic and financial conditions.

'Inclusive Education: The Way of the Future', a 'holistic' approach of UNESCO, was advocated to improve educational opportunities for children who are excluded. This holistic approach implies the reinterpretation of core educational concepts through a highly complex and delicate social and political process. In particular, it challenges governments to review the content and scope of concepts that have strongly permeated the educational agenda in the last 20 years. The outcomes of the 48th International Conference on Education (ICE) also underscored the need for a holistic approach to the design, implementation, monitoring and assessment of educational policies.

India, the most populous democracy in the world, has committed itself to many of the programmes of UNICEF. It is a signatory and participant in the United Nations Rights of the Child (UNESCO 1989), the Jomtien Declaration on Education for All (UNESCO 1990), United Nations Standard Rules on the Equalisation of Opportunities (UNESCO 1993), the Salamanca Statement and Framework for Action (UNESCO 1994), the Dakar Framework for Action (UNESCO 2000) and the Kochi Declaration (UNESCO 2007). In spite of its participation and commitments at international forums on inclusion and its own national policies and legislations (Right to Education Act, August 2009), inclusive education in India is still a distant dream to be achieved.

For a long time now, inclusive education has been seen purely from a pedagogical and/or medical perspective. There is an obvious need to disengage from this and balance it with other sociocultural parameters and to move the concept of inclusive education forward. It could not be more appropriate in time than now, when social models are slowly taking precedence over the medical model in this field. A move towards a holistic paradigm instead of a reductionist one might bring a greater understanding of the multidimensional ways in which the requirements of inclusive education could be addressed.

In this chapter, I put forth a fresh and more 'holistic' approach and perspective towards the issue of inclusive education in India. I examine the traditional prenatal practices of India and bring under focus certain aspects of these practices that are hugely relevant to education and learning.

Recognition of pregnancy as a life-cycle stage that requires special attention is common to all human societies. What constitutes appropriate management of pregnancy varies cross-culturally, from numerous mandates for behavioural change and a long list of taboos to minor modifications of pregnant women's diet or activity patterns. Elaboration of the cultural logic of proscriptions and prescriptions for pregnancy was once a popular research topic for anthropologists interested in either diet or reproduction, but this interest has waned since the mid-1980s.

In his book of 1960, *The Rites of Passage*, Arnold van Gennep examines the role of rituals in demarcating transitional phases in life like birth, puberty, marriage etc. Using this concept as a starting point, I examine the role of prenatal practices that are a part of the sociocultural rituals of India. These rituals are called Samskaaraas in the Sanskrit language.

The Vedas belong to the earliest documents of the human mind and form the bedrock of the way of life for most Hindus in India. The Samskaaraas are a part of the Dharma Shastras[1] which are an important component of ancient Indian literature. These were composed by the very early seers to help guide the common man through his life. Sixteen practices were prescribed covering the span of a human's life. There are many such Samskaaraas prescribed for the cycle of life and three of them are prenatal Samskaaraas. They are called (1) Pumsavanam, (2) Valai kaappu and (3) Seemantonnayana. These are primarily to celebrate conception, motherhood and pregnancy. Some of the main features of these celebrations include a stress-free ambience for the mother-to-be, good nutrition, music and pointers for a healthy and happy time of gestation.

No Indian ritual is quite complete without food. It can be seen in the photo above that there is a hearty and healthy meal for all at the end of the prenatal celebration. Food and nutrition as an integral part of it show that the focus on health and nutrition was an important aspect of these Samskaaraas. Though of very ancient origin, they have features that are not alien to our modern times.

Not strangely though, these seem to include some of the salient features of modern-day research and science as the important aspects that contribute positively towards fetal health. It is this set of three prenatal Samskaaraas that I want to consider. Inclusion in education is concerned with an individual's effective participation in society and reaching his or her full potential, and inclusion often requires a shift in people's attitudes and values. This perspective is the most important in this chapter. It is indeed interesting to see that attitudes and values have been highlighted

Figure 20.1 Children present at Seemantonnayana are helping to pound the herbs for the health of the pregnant lady

Figure 20.2 Various members of the society participating in celebrating motherhood, of which adorning the mother-to-be with glass bangles is one

A FRESH PERSPECTIVE ON INDIGENOUS TOOLS

Figure 20.3 Meal at the end of the prenatal celebration

when the issue of reaching one's full potential is discussed. This is carried through even further when it comes to identifying barriers in the process of education. In this process towards education, the need and relevance of exploring the indigenous strengths of the peoples of the world and their traditions seems imperative (Booth and Ainscow 1998).

The discussion on the prenatal Samskaaraas and the need for a holistic and culturally sensitive approach towards inclusive education lead me towards the two main issues of this chapter. The first one is that certain important practicing aspects of the prenatal Samskaaraas like maternal health and nutrition and an anxiety free period of gestation are vital to fetal development and hence to learning itself; the second one is that inclusion is the instructional design of the Samskaaraas, hence its practice could impact inclusive education in a relevant manner.

In the context of this chapter, I use the phrase 'instructional design' to denote that branch of knowledge concerned with research and theory about instructional strategies and the process for developing and implementing those strategies. In simpler terms they stand for not only sharing the body of knowledge as to 'what' to do to lead a meaningful life but also 'how' to do it for all.

This chapter looks at the elements of the prenatal Samskaaraas that have direct relevance for learning and education. It also lays a special focus on the instructional design of the Samskaaraas and examines how it supports inclusion as an integral part of its lifelong educational process.

In tracing the evolution of special education in India, one has to start with the system of general education and also of what today we loosely understand by the terms 'education' and 'learning' and how they were understood and practiced in ancient India.

In the Vedic system of education which is probably one of the oldest in the world, the student was required to live with his teacher until his education was over. The education of the girl child and that of the disabled, figure prominently in this ancient system. The epics of India are famous for their reference to in-utero learning and inclusion of the disabled. Ancient Indian universities like Takshshila were sensitive to the needs of the socially and physically disadvantaged. Modern day India was the birth place of the popular method called the 'Madras System', which later became famous in England and was conceived for the socially disadvantaged.

'Learning is a process that lasts a lifetime, both in its duration and its diversity', the Faure Report claims in 1972. 'While lifelong education is considered to be the cornerstone of educational policies, the learning society is seen as a strategy aimed at committing society as a whole to education.' *Learning: The Treasure Within* (1996), or the Report of the Delors commission on Education, proposed a holistic and integrated vision of education based on the paradigms of lifelong learning and the four pillars of learning: to be, to know, to do and to live together (UNESCO.org, The four pillars of learning).

If all the above would be gathered together and given a name, then the Sanskrit word Samskaaras would be most befitting. The word Samskaaraas can be understood as the rites of passage prescribed in the Vedic context. Though many in number, 16 of these Samskaaraas are well known and practiced even today. These are prescribed to mark and facilitate the passage from and into certain important stages of development in life. Even though their precise origin is lost in antiquity, it is certain that they originated in social needs and only much later did they acquire their religious garb. We see how, in the education of man through the lifelong learning process of leading a meaningful life, the Samskaaraas do not isolate the individual but integrate him or her into society, and hence give the opportunity to grow even when he or she is a functional part of it. The 16 Samskaaraas that spanned the entire life period are divided into five groups: the Prenatal, Childhood, Educational, Marriage and Funeral Samskaaraas. The spectrum of rites and rituals relate directly to the formation of personality.

It is indeed interesting to see that there are three prenatal Samskaaraas, giving that stage in life significant importance. Even though the Sanskrit names for these are Garbhadana, Pumsavana, and Seemantonnayana, they are called differently all across the Indian sub-continent. The fetal environment and its eventual importance in the future development of a child have been given great priority in the Vedic line of thought. Learning in the womb is not an alien concept here. The main aim of the Samskaaraas was to create conditions for the development of an integrated personality which could adjust to the surrounding world and lead a life worth living.

I have looked at the two aspects of maternal health and nutrition along with a stress-free gestation period, which are two salient aspects of the practice of the prenatal Samskaaraas. This chapter will focus on all those small yet relevant practices and beliefs that make up the prenatal Samskaaraas and the essence ensconced in them.

The Samskaaraas originated primarily because of a sociocultural need for a healthy society where there was respect for all. Traditional prenatal practices are not exclusive to India. Prenatal practices of cultures throughout the world are varied and colourful. India has its share of myths and traditional beliefs about learning in-utero. Research in the field on cognition and prenatal environment has made huge strides in the last three decades. It has now been known for long that prenatal stress can result in cognitive deficits like autism but also hinder fetal brain development (Kinney et al. 2008). It has also been well established that prenatal malnutrition can adversely affect the development of the brain. Ayurveda, the ancient Indian medical science, describes 'safe motherhood': 'Motherhood is the basis of family life which, in turn, is the backbone of all the orders of society. Hence, family life remains protected if the woman is safe and protected' (Charaka Samhita).[2] Particularly concerning the importance of maternal care, it adds, if a pregnant woman is taken care of as advised, she will give birth to a child which does not have any diseases – a healthy, physically strong, radiant, and well-nourished baby. In the modern world, the same is expressed in the words that there is considerable evidence that malnutrition in early life can have an adverse effect on the developing brain (Morgane et al. 1993). During various critical periods in the development of the central nervous system, malnutrition has been shown to affect the morphology, physiology and neurochemistry of the brain and this may have important implications for future health and cognitive function (Winick et al. 1972).

Despite all this knowledge along with the policies and legislation over the years, the scene of inclusive education in India is dismal. This, however, does not in any way mean that primary education for all has not been on the Indian agenda. Many governmental and nongovernmental schemes have been launched over the years but have achieved marginal amounts of success. Especially in the past few decades, schools have mushroomed all across India. It is doubtful, however, if mere quantitative expansion of educational facilities implies that this target will be achieved. With over 194 million children in some 1.2 million habitations (http://www.worldbank.org/en/country/india) to be brought into the fold of education, it is a challenging task by any standards. To be added to this is the fact that disability is a complex subject in India and it is very difficult to find reliable data about the prevalence of disability. Its conceptual understanding and management are both socially and culturally defined. Policies and pledges are easy to make but implementation may be difficult and goals hard to achieve, especially in a vast and populous country such as India.

To explore what the understanding of inclusive education was, to see up to what extent schools had been able to make successful progress along the process of inclusion, and to know what in their opinion were the obstacles or barriers in this pursuit were the reasons for my school visits. The schools that I had chosen were from a wide spectrum and the aim was to collect data as authentic as possible from the concerned school community. The spectrum was determined by starting at the level of public schools totally funded by the government through to private schools that were largely autonomous but had in some way to maintain and show that they were following the national policy and directives on inclusion. In the middle of the spectrum were partly funded schools for children with challenges. The data gathered from these sources were used to find out (1) what was it that people really valued in terms of what they could get from a school and (2) what did they think was the biggest obstacle in their path towards achieving it. The need to visit schools and to be able to understand their thinking with regard to this topic was what, in my opinion, anchored the relevance and importance of a study such as this one.

The feedback from all the group discussions, interviews and discourses points towards some significant directions. One major point is that exploring indigenous ways of interventions is quite accepted in India. Though some expression of doubts regarding its relevance were present there were many who thought that exploring indigenous ways for their possible potential was nothing to feel apologetic about. Moreover, there was the opinion that something old did not always have to be redundant in today's modern times, hence further research along these lines could result in new perspectives. Government policies should take the path of exploring indigenous options and potentials. There are many old cultures in this world full of traditions and rituals that may have the potential to teach us to live, grow and learn together. The need to understand and know more about the indigenous systems and their possible benefits seems to be strong. This came across in a clear fashion. To explore the potential of the prenatal Samskaaraas seemed to be a good subject to pursue. It may be important to start asking if inclusive education could be seen as located within the ambit of social inclusion in India and its traditional practices. We have been looking at inclusive education as fundamental to the growth of social inclusion. It might perhaps be interesting to now look at it from the reverse perspective of the social inclusive thought processes and practices as a tool in the process of implementing inclusive education in India.

I would like to conclude this chapter with the thought that indigenous ways of intervention to facilitate the process of inclusive education, particularly in India, might be a perspective that could have a lot of potential. This paradigm of learning to understand and live a life of inclusion could be a very effective springboard, particularly for societies that have such inherent indigenous strengths, in the process of pursuing inclusive education.

Notes

1 The Dharmashastras are the ancient law books of Hindus which formed the basis for the social and religious code of conduct in the past.
2 Charaka Samhita is an early text on Ayurveda (Indian traditional medicine).

References

Ahuja, A. (2005): EFA National Action Plans Review Study: Key Findings. Bangkok: UNESCO.

Ainscow, M., Farrell, P., and Tweddle, D. (2000): Developing policies for inclusive education: a study of the role of local education authorities. International Journal of Inclusive Education 4 (3): 211–229.

Booth, T., and Ainscow, M. (1998): From Them to Us. An International Study of Inclusion in Education. London, New York.

Brantlinger, E. (1997): Using ideology: cases of non-recognition of the politics of research and practice in special education. Review of Educational Research 67 (4): 425–459.

Carrington, S. (1999): Inclusion needs a different school culture. International Journal of Inclusive Education 3 (3): 257–268.

Freire, S., and César, M. (2003): Inclusive ideals/inclusive practices: how far is dream from reality? Five comparative case studies. European Journal of Special Needs Education 18 (3): 341–354.

Fuchs, D., and Fuchs, L.S. (1994): Inclusive schools movement and the radicalization of special education reform. Exceptional Children 60 (4): http://www.questia.com/library/journal/1G1-14858478/inclusive-schools-movement-and-the-radicalization.

Gennep, A. van (1960): The Rites of Passage. London: Routledge & Paul.
Hegarty, S. (2001): Inclusive education: a case to answer. Journal of Moral Education 30 (3): 243–249.
Kinney, D. K., Munir, K. M., Crowley, D. J., and Miller, A. M. (2008): Prenatal stress and risk for autism. Neuroscience & Biobehavioral Reviews 32 (8): 1519–1532: http://www.ncbi.nlm.nih.gov/pubmed?term=Crowley%20DJ%5BAuthor%5D&cauthor=true&cauthor_uid=18598714.
Mitchell, D. (2010): Education that fits: review of international trends in the education of students with special educational needs. http://www.educationcounts.govt.nz/publications/special_education/education-that-fits/executive-summary.
Morgane, P. J., Austin-LaFrance, R., Bronzino, J., Tonkiss, J., Diaz-Cintra, S., and Cintra, L. (1993): Prenatal malnutrition and development of the brain. http://www.ncbi.nlm.nih.gov/pubmed/8455820.
Phiri, M. P. (2004): An Investigation into the Attitudes of Head Teachers and Teachers towards the Inclusion of Children with Special Educational Needs in the Mainstream School in Four Education Regions of Zimbabwe. University of Hull, UK.
Skrtic, T. M., Sailor, W., and Gee, K. (1996): Voice, collaboration, and inclusion: democratic themes in educational and social reform initiatives. Remedial and Special Education 17 (3): 142–157.
Subban, P., and Sharma, U. (2005): Understanding educator attitudes toward the implementation of inclusive education. Disability Studies Quarterly 25 (2): http://dsq-sds.org/article/view/545/722.
Winick, M., Rosso, P., and Brasel, J. A. (1972): Maternal nutrition and prenatal growth. Experimental studies of effects of maternal undernutrition on fetal and placental growth. Archives of Disease in Childhood 47 (254): 479–485: http://www.ncbi.nlm.nih.gov/pmc/articles/PMC1648258/.

21
PERCEPTION AND INFERENCE

Friederike Schmidt

Perception: a fundamental issue of pedagogical practice

One central topic of the pedagogical process is the support of people in their development. In the various educational contexts, this main pedagogical theme is connoted quite differently, for instance school education compared with social work. In the context of school, this basic topic is particularly related to so-called formal knowledge, whereas it is also linked to personal development, life perspectives or social interactions. Social work on the other hand does not primarily refer to formal knowledge, even if this may be part of the social work practice, e.g. homework support. Rather, the practice is concentrated on the social development of the clientele, which may mean help concerning skills like dental or personal hygiene, housework, child care, drug abuse and so on. But despite these differences, one can generalize the pedagogical task and function as a support of personal development and growth.

This major issue of pedagogy assumes that pedagogues have to be aware of not only the possibilities and resources of the clientele, but also their problems and difficulties. Thus, the perception of the pedagogues gets an important role in the pedagogical practice, or to be precise, is the fundamental basis along which the pedagogical process is unfolded. Against the background of their view, pedagogues formulate educational objectives, develop offers of support, modify and dismiss these. They see the clientele's development and by the same token call it into question and generate prognoses. This is not only a requirement raised in specific situations, for instance when pedagogical aims are generated, or as in the context of social work, help is applied at the social welfare office. In fact, it is an essential element of daily pedagogical practice. Permanently, pedagogues have to observe their clientele, have to understand them, have to recognize and interpret them. On the ground of their view they handle them, help, encourage and admonish them. Therefore, when reflecting on this field of action, perception is a theme of enormous importance.

The fundamental role of perception for the pedagogical process claims an encompassing debate about it and cannot be reduced to a discussion about methods as in the debate about diagnostics one can find in the German context of social work.[1] For, a debate of methods signifies a specific perspective, i.e. points out only a specific aspect of perception and is not able to catch the immanent logics of this action. Rather, the enormous importance of perception in the pedagogical context claims fundamental theoretical researches as well as empirical studies.

It is conspicuous that the German analysis is concentrated on Western theoretical positions, whereas other theoretical discourses are only rarely noticed. Needless to say that perception is not only a topic of Western theories, but also theme of debates in other contexts – sometimes in a similar way, sometimes along different aspects and with a different impetus. Fundamental theoretical perspectives on perception are thus found in Indian philosophy, in which perception plays an important role, e.g. in the Nyâya school of philosophy,[2] which raises important questions: on which basis do we perceive the other? What is the initial point of our view? Do we actually see what we are aware of?

Perception and inference: an insoluble relation?

Perception is about sense, cognition, understanding, recognition and as such cannot be explained only with our concrete sensory cognitions, i.e. our seeing, hearing, smelling etc. If it were so, it would be inexplicable why two persons perceive different things while looking at the same object, or why a person perceives a specific item, e.g. a house, although he/she actually sees only a part of it, e.g. the front side. Perception is more than what we actually hear, see and so on, even though it is essentially dependent on these sensory experiences. In fact, perception is insolubly bound to actual sensual cognitions and inferences.[3]

This relation between concrete perception and inference plays an important role in Indian philosophy, e.g. in the Nyâya system or in Buddhism.[4] Thus, and referring to the philosophical discourse of the Nyâya, fundamental questions may be raised: what do we recognize while perceiving? According to which information is our view enfolded? Is perception possible without inference? These are significant questions concerning the visual senses, whereas they can be discussed in the following only partly. Basis of this analysis is an example Matilal elaborates in his research about perception in Indian philosophical discourse[5]: the legend of the Vatsa King

Udayana, whose senses were deceived by his opponent, the King Pradyota of Avanti.[6]

King Udayana goes out on an elephant hunt with his army. Along the way he recognizes an elephant, and since he is an expert in taming elephants by playing his lute, he orders his army to stay back while he himself, playing his lute, is moving towards the elephant. While getting nearer, Udayana realizes the mistake he made when interpreting the object as an elephant. For it is not an elephant that stands in front of King Udayana, but a counterfeit, a wooden replica of the forequarter of this animal, behind which a group of armed soldiers of the enemy king is hiding. Due to his misperception, or to be precise, to his mis-inference, King Udayana gets captured by the enemy king, King Pradyota.[7]

Even though this saga may be variously interpreted, concerning our interest in perception, two aspects demonstrated by this example have to be recognized: first, there is a gap between what we recognize and what we claim to perceive, or like Matilal points out, there is a '"gap" between what we see [. . .] and what we in fact infer from a piece of some sensory datum or evidence' (Matilal 1986: 256). Second, due to what we recognize our perception may be wrong, i.e. does not match with what we are looking at.

Concerning the first aspect, it can be verified that the gap between our seeing and inferring is not specific for extraordinary situations as in the case of King Udayana, but is a general characteristic of perception. When recognizing something, e.g. a house, our perception goes far beyond our sensual cognitions, i.e. what we see. Looking at a house, we do not see the whole house but a part of it, maybe the front or the back side. Thus, there is a difference in what we actually recognize and what we believe or assert to perceive. But instead of being precise in what we see or instead of relating to what we in fact view, or finally, instead of collecting more parts of the situation, we affirm that this part we are aware of is significant enough to give us information on what lies in front of us. This can be seen as a form of generalization of the part. The specific component we cognize is universalized to an aspect with significance.

As part of our perception, it seems that this gap between what we actually see and what we infer, and linked to this the generalization of the part, is not only located on a reflective level of perception, but rather, it is founded in the tacit knowledge which structures perception.[8] It is nothing that we develop with a specific will or intention, although this might of course happen, but is perception itself and therefore is mainly not discussed, at least not in our interactions in daily life. In fact, most of the times we are not even aware of this gap. Matilal indicates this when he notices, 'if I have to assert that I see not the moon but only the front side of the moon, then there seems to be some oddity creeping into our understanding or our use of the term "see".[9]

Besides, the example of King Udayana shows that in reference to our concrete awareness our perception may be false. Even if Udayana is a victim of an intended illusion, i.e. his misperception was provoked by the enemy king, which may limit the significance of the example, his case of mis-inference shows a specific problem of perception: due to our cognition a false inference may be generated and lead to a mistaken perception. It has to be noticed that in most cases misperception is unproblematic. Mostly, it is not even recognized or can be solved without greater effort. However, as the example with King Udayana illustrates, this inference-based perception or this generalization of a perceived extract may also lead to serious difficulties and therefore has to be discussed.

In addition, this characteristic of perception has a specific significance in the pedagogical context. As shown, Udayana misinterpreted the situation, which has fatal consequences for him, because his mis-inference presumably means success for his opponent, King Pradyota, and eventually has consequences for Udayana's kingdom. But in a sense, Udayana, as the main actor of this story, is a victim of his own mis-inference and has to accept responsibility for that. In pedagogical contexts, this inference-based perception has a different meaning than in the case of Udayana. Even if the clientele gets the ability to elaborate how they feel, think, experience and interpret their lives, it is the pedagogical view according to which pedagogues act and deal with the clientele, support them, and not seldom initiate relevant, existential steps for the clientele, e.g. when pedagogical support is applied on the basis of the pedagogical view.

Therefore, the example of Udayana shows some relevant issues concerning perception that have to be recognized in the pedagogical context. Pedagogues have to be aware that their perception is based only on an extract and that their view necessarily resembles an inference that may be false. They have to recognize that they cannot see everything but only a part of it, and from this inevitably have to infer. Thus, they have to reflect on their perspectives and to analyse based on which their view is generated. Relevant questions then are: how can we avoid being a victim of our actual cognition? How can we avoid misinterpreting what we see or what we thought to see? What does one actually recognize and how can one perceive things 'correctly'? Furthermore, what does 'correctly' mean in general and in this particular case? Correctly, i.e. for the clientele, is according to a pedagogical perspective or for the society? Finally, can we universalize our perception of a part at all? Why does one see a specific problem? Which is the basis of that perspective?

According to my own research on the pedagogical view, these questions can be related to an implicit logic of perception, along which one enfolds one's view. My empirical study shows that we do not perceive things or other persons randomly and our view cannot be reduced to an individual intention or will. In fact, our perspective has a collective implicit logic, along which we enfold it. For a better understanding of this argument, a reference to my research is made.

Tacit logics of the view: a reconstruction of the perception of pedagogues

My main interest is how pedagogues perceive their clientele. This 'how' is meant literally, as I am not interested in the methods the pedagogues have learned in their education and how they transfer them into practice. Rather, my study reconstructs the tacit logics of perception and is thereby interested in the collective implicit orientations of the pedagogical view.[10]

The study is based on an empirical research set out in the framework of the Documentary Method – a method of empirical research, along which the implicit level of acting is analysed.[11] The central question of the study is: how do social workers perceive their clientele?[12] Thus, the perspectives of the pedagogues towards young adults (aged 18–27) as a specific pedagogical target group were of particular interest. The research is located in the context of the social work, viz. social welfare support for homeless adults. Basis of the study are nine group discussions with pedagogical teams of this social welfare programme.[13]

Although the focus of research was first related to the group-specific implicit perceptional orientations, the data show that the pedagogues' view is structured by an implicit logic one can find in all discussions. This logic is structured by three elements, according to which the other, the clientele, is seen: (professional) self-image (a), knowledge (b) and focus (c).

(Professional) self-image

The group discussions show that the perspective of the pedagogues is implicitly structured by the *(professional) self-image*. This element of their implicit 'logic of perception' cannot be reduced to an intended and staged self-presentation as the self-image is commonly understood. Besides the more reflective dimension of the self-image, this element of perceptional logic is expressed in our acting itself, i.e. in the way the other and self present themselves. Thus, the self-image 'decides' about our perception as it implicitly structures the view. This self-image is thereby never simply bound to the individual person. It is enfolded and generated through interaction, and thus, is collective. According to the data, one can differentiate between two types of professional self-images: on the one hand a self-image of the expert, and at the same time recognizing the clientele as deviant resp. abnormal. The own perspective represents the only one (self-image-Type I); on the other hand a self-image also of an expert, but one who accepts the clientele, tries to understand them and at times tries to declare normal what they do or think (self-image-Type II).

Knowledge

The perspectives of the pedagogues are based on a complex *knowledge*-foundation, to which they as a group refer and elaborate on. According to this knowledge, they view the clientele and interpret them. The comparative analysis[14] of the group discussions consequently shows that the groups refer to similar knowledge, even though they elaborate this differently. There are six knowledge groups to differentiate: background milieu (Knowledge-Type I), development (Knowledge-Type II), health (Knowledge-Type III), education (Knowledge-Type IV), gender (Knowledge-Type V) and discrimination (Knowledge-Type VI). Against the backdrop of these topics the clientele is viewed and interpreted in multiple perspectives.

Focus

The third layer implicitly structuring perspectives is a collective *focus*. While presenting their experiences with the clientele, the different pedagogues refer to this focus. They concentrate on specific themes and aspects, which they discuss again and again. Thus, the actors generate a specific focus, along which they perceive the other, i.e. the clientele. The results of the empirical study show a main focus of all groups articulation: the scope of action of the clientele. The group perspectives are differentiated into two types of focus: focus on the attitude of the clientele (Focus-Type I) and focus on the capability of acting (Focus-Type II).

Even though the specific content of the reconstructed logic has to be related to the actual context, the central result of the research may be generalized: there is a collective implicit logic of perception, and its basic structure contains three elements: self-image, knowledge and focus.[15] According to these results, some more questions have to be raised concerning the discussed insoluble relationship between actual cognition and inference: is inference necessarily rational? Is inference to be reduced to an analytic or reflective judgement? Or do inferences follow a specific implicit logic as this study assumes? And, referring to the study, is inference a product of an individual person or does it have a collective dimension? How is it possible to understand and comprehend what the other (presumably) infers?

Conclusion

Aim of the following is to raise issues concerning perception that are mostly neglected in German educational science: what are we aware of when perceiving the world, e.g. objects or other persons? Do we actually see what we are aware of? Following the approaches of Indian philosophy, one has to relate these questions to a relationship between perception and inference. Even though this chapter could only refer to some aspects of this debate, it may be emphasized that our perception goes beyond what we actually see. We see a part, but are aware of the whole and normally we do not recognize this gap. In fact, it is an aspect of our perception in daily life, along which we unfold our view, making interaction possible. Referring to my own research, I link this aspect with an implicit logic, along which actors unfold their perspectives. On this basis, inference-based perception is developed along an implicit logic. Thus, the reflection of our cognition, i.e. what we see and what we perceive, has to involve an analysis of our implicit logic of perception.

Furthermore, Indian philosophy formulates several aspects concerning this relationship between actual perception and inference that could not be discussed, e.g. the debate between Nyâya and Buddhist, which is noted in the Nyâya-Sûtra[16] 2.1.30–35. Main topic of this passage of the Sûtra is, 'whether or not our sensory perceptual awareness involves an inference' (Matilal 1986: 257f.). According to this dispute, further questions concerning the relation between perception and inference have to be raised: what do we perceive and what do we infer? Can we perceive things without inferring, as the Nyâya assumes, or does our perception involve an inference, as the Buddhist assumes? Does seeing then mean inferring, or in Matilal's words (1986: 256), 'Is every case of seeing a case of inference?' And, is the whole inherent in the parts, as the Nyâya supposes, so that we perceive the whole, e.g. a tree, although we actually just see the part, e.g. a branch? In view of limitations of space, these questions have to remain unanswered here, but they show that Indian philosophy offers an enormous amount of issues considering perception that, in the context of German educational science, point out new perspectives on this essential element of pedagogical practice.

Notes

1. Cf. Urban (2004); Ader (2006).
2. Nyâya is a school of logic and debate, whereas it is also the name of a method of arguing which was established in this philosophical school and which is comparable to the Aristotelian syllogism. The Nyâya-School is characterized by two main periods, viz. Pracina-Nyâya and Nyâva-Nyâya. Pracina-Nyâya was founded by Gautama around the second century AD, whereas the period of Nyâva-Nyâya was established by Gangesa Upadhyaya in the thirteenth century. The second phase lasts till now, although, as Bhattacharyy points out, major developments of the Nyâva-Nyâya were already completed by the eighteenth century with the commentaries of Gadadhara Bhattacharyy (cf. Bhattacharyya 1974: 329).
3. Cf. Matilal (1986: 255).
4. Cf. ibid.: 257–275.
5. Cf. ibid.
6. The story of King Udayana's tricked perception is adapted from the Sanskrit play *Swapnavasavadatta*, generally attributed to the Sanskrit playwright Bhasa. There are different presentations of this story, e.g. the description of Varadpande (cf. 2005: 60). The one I refer to is noted by Matilal (cf. Matilal 1986: 256).
7. Obviously, this legend reminds us of the saga of the Trojan Horse (cf. Varadpande 2005: 60).
8. Cf. Bohnsack (2010: 100).
9. Matilal (1986: 257).
10. Within the framework of Praxeological Theories acting is not just a question of rational reflective will or intention, rather, it is organized and structured by a tacit knowledge that the actor mainly does not recognize or reflect but is expressed in the way one acts (cf. Bourdieu 2001; Gebauer and Wulf 2003; Hörning 2004). Thus, acting has its own implicit logic, which organizes and structures the actor's view of the other, and is therefore, an important issue for pedagogues and educational science. This tacit logic of practice is never just the logic of a single person but collective and funded in the contexts actors are included in (cf. Bohnsack 2008: 108).
11. The Documentary Method is a method for qualitative field research developed by Ralf Bohnsack in reference to Karl Mannheim's Sociology of Knowledge as well as to Garfinkel's Ethnomethodology (cf. Bohnsack 2008). Its topic is to analyse implicit knowledge expression in the way one acts. So, for the Documentary Method it is not only interesting what one says or does, but how. Group discussions are a good device to get an access to implicit collective orientations structuring acting (cf. Przyborski and Wohlrab-Sahr 2008: 101–115).
12. In fact, this was not the question posed to the pedagogues as it relates to a reflective layer of experiences. Concerning the research interest in the implicit layer, the central question of the study had to be asked differently, i.e. indirectly. The social workers were asked to tell about their experiences with the clientele. However, in the run-up they were informed about the research interest in perception.
13. Group discussions allow a reference to the collective dimension of acting. Relating to the Documentary Method, the group discussions in the study were based on the concept of self-regulation in the sense that not the researcher but the group members decided how to discuss the principle topic of the study. They

gave their own priorities and did this by mimetic acting. In the way the members did this and dealt with the study's issue, implicit collective orientations, implicit collective logics of perception were expressed (cf. Bohnsack 2008: 208).
14 The comparative analysis is the main instrument of interpretation of the Documentary Method to reconstruct the implicit orientations of actors (cf. Bohnsack 2008: 188).
15 According to the central topic of this article, the fundamental theoretical embedding of the empirical study is left out. But briefly it may be noticed that in a fundamental theoretical perspective these elements characterize the implicit logic of perception by various dimensions: it has to be seen as a mimetic, discursive and habitual logic, or better as an interplay of these three dimensions. The self-concept has to be seen as an expression of the mimetic logic-layer, the knowledge as an expression of the discursive logic-layer and the focus as an expression of the habitual logic-layer. This differentiation of the logic-layers has to be seen as an analytic distinction, for in the practice of perception these elements correlate with each other. They cause and determine each other.
16 The Nyâya-Sûtra is the doctrine of Nyâya. It is a book of logic, in which short formulated aphorisms (Sûtra) are phrased. The Nyâya-Sûtra is mainly attributed to Gautama, the founder of Nyâya, whose book provides a basis for all later interpretations of this philosophical school. It is characteristic for orthodox Indian philosophy that the Sûtras, the interpretations of the Vedic rules and doctrines, are commentated and sub-commentated. These commentaries work out subtleties and classifications, but do not fundamentally modify the Sûtras. Important commentators and sub-commentators of the first Nyâya period are Pakshilasvamin, also called Vatsyayana, and his debate with the Buddhist Didnâga Nyâyabhâsya, Uddyotakara and his interpretation *Nyayavarttika* (cf. Geldsetzer 2010: § 15), Vâcaspati Mishra and his work *Nyayavarttikatatparyatika*, a commentary on Uddyotakaras *Nyayavarttika* (cf. Todeschini 2010: 50) and Jayanta Bhatta and his interpretation *Nyayamanjari* (cf. Geldsetzer 2010: § 15). The most relevant commentators of the Nyâva-Nyâya are Gangesha Upadhyaya, the founder of this new direction of the Nyâya, with his work *Tattvacintamani*, Vasudeva Sarvabhauma, Raghunatha with the interpretation *Didhiti* (cf. Geldsetzer 2010: § 15) and Gadadhara.

References

Ader, S. (2006): Was leitet den Blick? Wahrnehmung, Deutung und Intervention in der Jugendhilfe. Weinheim, Munich: Juventa.

Bhattacharyya, S. (1974): Some Features of Navya-Nyáya Logic. In: Philosophy East and West 24 (3): 329–342.

Bohnsack, R. (2008): Rekonstruktive Sozialforschung. Einführung in qualitative Methoden. Opladen. Farmington Hills: Barbara Budrich.

Bohnsack, R. (2010): Documentary Method and Group Discussions. In: Bohnsack, R., Pfaff, N., and Weller, W. (eds): Qualitative Analysis and Documentary Method, 99–124. Farmington Hills: Barbara Budrich.

Bourdieu, P. (2001): Meditationen. Zur Kritik der scholastischen Vernunft. Frankfurt, M.: Suhrkamp.

Gebauer, G., and Wulf, C. (2003): Mimetische Weltzugänge. Stuttgart: Kohlhammer.

Geldsetzer, L. (2010): Die klassische indische Philosophie. Vorlesungen an der HHU Düsseldorf. SS 1982, WS 1993/94, WS 1998/99. Online document available at: http://www.phil-fak.uni-duesseldorf.de/philo/geldsetzer/indotit.htm (18 December 2010).

Hörning, K. H. (2004): Soziale Praxis zwischen Beharrung und Neuschöpfung. Ein Erkenntnis- und Theorieproblem. In: Hörning, K. H., and Reuter, J. (eds): Doing Culture. Neue Positionen zum Verhältnis von Kultur und sozialer Praxis, 19–40. Bielefeld: transcript.

Matilal, B. K. (1986): Perception. An Essay on Classical Indian Theories of Knowledge. Oxford: Clarendon Press.

Przyborski, A., and Wohlrab-Sahr, M. (2008): Qualitative Sozialforschung. Ein Arbeitsbuch. Munich: Oldenbourg.

Todeschini, A. (2010): Twenty-Two Ways to Lose a Debate: A Grecian Look at the Nyâyasûtra's Points of Defeat. In: Journal of Indian Philoscphy 38: 49–74. New Haven: Springer.

Urban, U. (2004): Professionelles Handeln zwischen Hilfe und Kontrolle. Sozialpädagogische Entscheidungsfindung in der Hilfeplanung. Weinheim, Munich: Juventa.

Varadpande, M. L. (2005): History of Indian Theatre. New Delhi: Abhinav Publications.

22

WHEN THE SOLUTION BECOMES PART OF THE PROBLEM: THE ROLE OF EDUCATION IN SOCIAL CONFLICTS

Observations in the Indian context

Iris Clemens

In March 2007 two men, most probably at least one of them was a school teacher, were holding a school bus with around 30 pupils in the capital of the Philippines, Manila.[1] Their request was rather unusual for kidnappers: the state should guarantee proper education for some 145 students from a school in a poor and disadvantaged district of Manila. The kidnappers wanted to attract attention for the urgent problem of the malfunctioning educational system for the underprivileged.

In fact the inertia of the government towards education for the underprivileged is a common phenomenon in many countries. In consequence since the awareness for education has increased, education itself has become a battlefield in many parts of the world, especially where education has the reputation of being the way out of poverty, oppression and marginalisation and towards modernisation, welfare and wealth. This is particularly true for countries in transition and once so-called developing countries, where the social gap between the winner of the globalisation and the loser is extremely big (Subrahmanian 2005). Supported by large campaigns of global players like the World Bank or OECD, education has become a symbol for future expectations and hopes (Resnik 2006). However, taking into consideration that the increasing number of degree holders has sharpened competition on the job market and developments like liberalisation has led to a decrease of white-collar governmental jobs in countries like India, an educational career often cannot fulfil the expectations of social and economical mobility

(Jeffrey et al. 2004). Nevertheless, in the rising states like China and India the symbolic power of education is enormous (for India Béteille 2002). As a result of the disparity between the high reputation of education on the one hand and the restricted access to it on the other, education holds a lot of potential for conflicts within these societies. Therefore, the aim of this article is to point out some aspects of the role of education in social conflicts in countries in transition. As a concrete example the context of India is chosen.

The Indian context

Education in India

India is a striking example for the analysis of social tensions resulting out of inequality in the access to and success in education. The illiteracy rate is 34 per cent in a country where the effort to develop nuclear weapons has long heavily influenced the research agenda and the scientific system (Raina and Habib 2004). Whereas the excellent IITs – Indian Institutes of Technology – are best known in the whole world and Indian researchers are ahead in the area of biotechnology, for example, more than 353 million are illiterates and 32 million children are out of school (Mehrotra et al. 2005). The comparison with China demonstrates the problem of the lopsided development in India: both countries had similar problems in the late 1940s like mass illiteracy and endemic poverty. However, today India is far behind China with respect to elementary education: compared to 34 per cent of illiterates in India, China today has only 5 per cent (PROBE: 12). On the other side, India sends about six times more students to the universities and other higher educational establishments than its neighbour China (Varma 1999: 55). 'In fact', the Indian author Pavank Varma states, 'there is little doubt that the lopsided development of education in India is directly linked to the structure of Indian society, and that the inequalities in education are [...] a reflection of inequalities of economic and social powers of different groups in India' (ibid.). In India, the term of 'Whither Education' has been created to describe this undesirable trend.[2]

But even for those kids going to school, the situation is often quite far away from being desirable as the dropout rate is high and the quality of education especially in public schools is often poor. Although the school enrolment for the first class is more or less 100 per cent today, already in the third class approximately 30 per cent have left school and in class seven not even half of all kids left over. Important to see is the big difference between urban and rural areas: while 83 per cent of kids from an urban background complete elementary school after the fifth class, only 57 per cent from the rural areas do (Seventh All India School Education Survey 2007).

Apathy of the parents towards education is one widespread explanation for the problem. But in a big survey in 1996 (PROBE Report), the huge majority of parents from a backward rural area agreed that education is important for their children. The survey was undertaken in five northern Indian states (Himachal Pradesh, Uttar Pradesh, Rajasthan, Bihar and Madhya Pradesh) and four of these states are the worst-performing in terms of elementary education (only Himachal Pradesh is performing better). More than half of all out-of school children in India live in these states (PROBE). In fact, the conditions for these parents who are willing to send their children to school are certainly not supporting their intentions. To single out only one aspect of the difficulties these parents are facing with regard to the education of their children, the 'myth' that elementary education is free of cost has to be destroyed: North Indian parents spend about Rs 318 per year on average to send one child to a government primary school: on fees, books, slates, clothes etc. at which the fees are indeed only a negligible part. Having in mind that most of the poor families in India have more than one child, an agricultural labourer in Bihar with three children in school age would have to work round about 40 days per year just to send them to primary school (PROBE: 16), and the average real expenditure for education is even said to be much higher, say the authors of the PROBE Report. Other difficulties (in details Srivastava 2007) are long ways to schools, absence of the teachers, very bad infrastructure (no equipment like blackboard, toilets, chairs etc. sometimes not even a building, see Verghese 1995), high teacher–student ratios, discrimination of lower castes and Muslims in the classroom (Holzwarth et al. 2006) and so on.

Taking this into account, adding that the offered quality of primary education is very often awful if teaching activities are taking place at all (Gupta 2002), it would be understandable if even more parents would refuse to send their children to school. It is not unusual that after five years of school attendance in a single teacher village school with the teacher more or less absent a student is not even able to read or write (PROBE; Aikara 1998). So, even the smallest hopes of the parents, for example that their son could manage the finances of the family are not fulfilled. On the other side his working power was missed, he didn't learn a handicraft in the meanwhile and the money spent for his education might have been used for medicine or other required investments.

Education as a valuable good

Nevertheless, education has an extremely high reputation in India and it is a hard-fought good. Due to historical reasons education has a special position in the Indian society. With the most probably unique phenomenon of the Brahmins as the intellectual elite heading the caste system, education was connected to hierarchy since ages (e.g. Weber 1988; Oldenberg n.d.a, n.d.b; Kaviraj 1992). Education was even prohibited in pre-colonial times for the low castes and the casteless (Nancharaiah 2002). The colonisation has further consolidated the situation, as the occupying force included only some Brahmins into their educational system on behalf of the demand for administrative staff and excluded the rest of the people from the educational institutions they established (Bhattacharya 2002). It was only in the course of the occupation and mainly due to missionary interests that the British Empire got involved in general education to some extend in India, but the half-hearted attempts have not been very successful. After independence in 1947, the new government wanted to overcome the old discrimination, especially of the untouchables and the tribal people. Education was one major point on the agenda, and a reservation system with positive discrimination for the so-called backward communities was implemented. Seats in higher education institutions and jobs in government positions were reserved for these groups (Rolly 2002). However, 60 years later, the situation has not changed fundamentally. Caste discrimination is still very striking especially in rural areas, and educational institutions are heavily affected (Kulke and Rothermund 1998). The situation shows 'the apathy of the Indian elite towards education for the common people', as Acharya (1998: 230) states.

The fight for education is in full swing, too. In 1990, the protests from higher-caste members against a recommendation of a commission to further increase the reservation quota for the backward communities led to the resignation of the Prime Minister Vishwanath Pratap Singh in the end (Srivastava 2007). And regularly the struggle for education culminates in self-immolations of students from higher castes, accepting such a horrifying death to protest against the educational policy and their reduced chances to get a seat in an institution of higher education. Hunger strike is another common tool to fight against the reservation system. Other alarming signs are the regular suicides committed by students failing to get a university seat[3] or in case of exam failure,[4] and the recent approach to include also the IITs in the reservation system has led to an outcry and is seen by parts of the society as an attack on the developmental chances of the whole country (Radhakrishnan 2007).

Resignation of a prime minister, hunger strikes, self-immolations of students, these examples show the dramatic relevance education has in the Indian society and the enormous emotional intensity of this fight for education. The importance of education in the Indian context can also be shown on the individual level when for example within only one generation education becomes the most important criterion for the highly structured process of arranged marriage (Karve 1993). Education has replaced caste or even religion as the former most powerful criterion for a suitable match (Dube 1997; Merz 1999; Clemens 2004). The 'Cultural Production of the Educated Person' (see Levinson and Holland 1996) in the case of India is characterised by extremely positive connotations. In consequence my presumption is that besides of course powerful economical considerations, the enormous influence of education on the construction of the self and the social identity in this context is at least partly responsible for the intensity of the described conflict, too. This will be discussed in the next section on the basis of an empirical study which focuses on the urban Indian context.

Empirical study of the laymen's understanding of education and an educated person

Theoretical conception

In 2003, I did a field study on laymen's understanding of education and its influence on individual and social constructions in Hyderabad, capital of Andhra Pradesh in the South of India. The study consists of 26 open, problem-orientated interviews with a sample of well-educated (degree holder) urban, Indian middle-class people: employee, unemployed and housewives. The meaning construction of education and an educated person, the attributions, associations, biographical hopes and ideas or even 'fantasims' (Boesch 1991) related to education have been analysed (in detail Clemens 2007). The understanding of 'meaning' is orientated on the sociology of knowledge (Schütz 1974) and accordingly conceptualised as a basic category for any human action and society. The concept of 'semantics' by Niklas Luhmann (1998) as a kind of *generalised meaning at a higher level* or a *store of possible themes of communication* available to a given social system adds a cultural perspective to the production of meaning. The semantics is always structurally coupled with the society in which it has occurred, and accordingly the evolution of ideas is interrelated to the social evolution. Therefore, evolutions of idea are not accidental, but if they are 'stored' in the semantics at least for some time for further communication, part of the culture itself. In consequence it can be assumed that the meaning of ideas like education will vary between different societies and that it is coupled to the specific social structures (Clemens 2007a).

Additionally one can assume that the attributions to education in a certain context will deeply influence the educational aspirations of the people.

There is a great difference, if educational success of a child is affecting the honour of the whole family like in parts of Asia for example (Kim 2004), or if failing in school is taken as a rather normal incident what can be assumed for parts of the German society, marginalised groups which are more or less excluded from society and the regular job market in the second or even third generation. The construction of education and an educated person shall influence social observations and individual behaviour in many aspects in consequence.

Findings

I will focus only on selected parts of the findings here. With regard to the figure of *Sanskritisation* (Srinivas 1989) in the Indian literature, I called the emerging pattern of argumentation in the interviews *Educationalisation* (Clemens 2007). The argumentation follows the logic of perfectibility (Luhmann and Schorr 1979) through education. The interviews show that this includes the beliefs that only education can ensure: (a) intellectual development, (b) moral development, (c) development of an intact, decent and individualised personality and (d) development of competencies like social behaviour and communication competencies, as well as being helpful to other people. Conversely, an uneducated person is seen as a kind of unfinished, not fully developed human being, and the arguments found in the study suggest that he or she is at a level somewhere between a human being and an animal. 'He will be a total parasite', as an employed male, stated in the study. This also implies to some extent that an educated person is a better person from a moral point of view, not just with respect to the pure competencies. In consequence, a satisfying conception of identity needs to refer to a successful educational carrier nowadays in this context. Education as reference for identity construction is also vital for the identity construction of the disadvantaged – the uneducated persons who have feelings of inferiority and see themselves as excluded from the process of civilisation.

To see the brisance of these findings one has to reflect not only the low literacy rate but also the judgement that the interviewed persons only describe someone as 'educated person' if he or she is at least a 'degree holder' (bachelor or diploma). There are no valid statistics, but only 5–6 per cent of recent generations are involved in higher education (Pinto 2002: 182), and so, may be 1–5 per cent of the population are degree holders in India. The rest is excluded from the category of 'educated person' in the perspective pointed out by the study, and therefore from being a fully developed human being. An analogy can be drawn between the dichotomy of educated–uneducated and an older one, specific to the Indian context: the dichotomy clean–unclean (Dumont 1976), underlying the caste system. The three main characteristics of the dichotomy clean–unclean: hierarchy, social separation and division of labour are now more and more established and supported through education. In consequence, there are hints for the hypothesis that education is replacing caste in social structuring and as leading social identification. This change of the leading observation pattern regarding social recognition and self-construction I want to call *Educationalisation*. The findings of Jeffrey et al. (2004) in their ethnographic field research, comparing educated Muslims and Dalits, tend to a quite similar interpretation when they state: '*Education is a particularly attractive development idea because it offers marginalised groups a model of achieved status distinct from ascribed definitions of respect*' (p. 975; for a detailed differentiation of the historical shift from ascribed definitions of respect to achieved ones in Europe see especially Bourdieu.1987).

The reference to the concept of perfectibility through education and the differentiation between human beings and animals, between 'valuable beings' and 'parasites' clearly uses older meaning patterns and ways of thinking rooted in the caste ideology. At the same time new meaning forms are established, based on an older duality but better adapted to the demands of a modern society with functional differentiation instead of a stratified organisation (Luhmann 1987), where respect and recognition is granted now because of the own achievement instead of a bequeathed status. The semantics implies connectivity to more democratic and modern argumentations, as it empowers the individual as creator of its own destiny. The status as educated person and accordingly as 'fully developed human being' is the merit of one's own efforts and has therefore an egalitarian legitimation. In reverse, this semantics may also suggest some responsibility of the individual in the case of failures in the educational carrier.

The semantics of perfectibility through education is also used by the unemployed interviewees. Their argumentation is that, although education has not helped them to settle down in life and for economical success, they have improved their personality and only due to their education they have become decent, valuable individuals. The conflicts related to education get another connotation through observations like this. Being excluded from education, or having reduced chances for a seat in university due to the reservation system, is an elementary danger not only regarding economical facts, but also for the social recognition and identity and therefore for being accepted in society. This makes it understandable why the struggle for education and equality in the access to it is hard-fought even to death in India: it is not only an economical question – white-collar salaried employment is even reduced due to the economical liberalisation in India – but also a question of being accepted and valued as a full human being.

An additional perspective: the role of privatisation

Privatisation is one more aspect of the hard-fought field of education in India which may intensify the conflicts. Because of the malfunctioning of governmental schooling, privatisation is on the run, and this is true not only for the cities, but also in the poor rural districts. Two main reasons are given by the PROBE Report: breakdown of government schools and parental ability to pay. But this is true only partly. For example, in Himachal Pradesh, were parents could afford private education but governmental schools functioning well, only a few private schools are established. In reverse, in central Bihar poverty is endemic, yet private schools are widespread, because the parents are disillusioned with government schools according to the report. In this vicious circle the expansion of the private sector further undermines the government school system, as fewer and fewer students, only the poorest and most probably less supported ones, will join them. This leads to the situation that children of the Untouchables and other underprivileged groups (like also Muslims) go to the government schools (Tooley and Dixon 2003) while higher caste children go to private ones, a two-track schooling system, like Shiva Kumar (2003) describes it. And the differences in quality of education and educational opportunities for privileged children and for those with an underprivileged background are further increasing very fast (Nambissan 1996; Vaid 2004). Regarding privatisation, Lukose (2000) describes a struggle for education as a public good or a private commodity and asserts that the argumentation for education as private commodity wanted to obscure the political dimension of the problem. This argument seems to fit quite well to the earlier mentioned shift from ascribed definitions of respect to achieved ones. If education is a private affair, the individual is responsible for herself and her educational carrier.

Although the government tries to regulate the participation of the underprivileged in private education by the reservation system (Rolly 2007), the ongoing privatisation of the educational sector must be intensively observed. Where the government school system is insufficient and undermined by privatisation, other educational providers can extend (for Bangladesh Kusakabe 2007). Especially in rural areas where the problem is most striking, a spreading of religious motivated schools can be observed. Like a study in Uttar Pradesh shows, especially Muslims tend to choose a religious school – the so-called Madrasas – for their children to protect them against discrimination in public schools, or because these schools are cheaper and they trust that these schools will teach their children the right ethics and norms beside the religious instructions. Going to a Madrasa, the young men tend to wear the traditional clothes and they have chances to be placed in a job through connections related to the community. In reverse, while showing their religious affiliation openly they often face encroachment from police and discrimination on the official job market (Jeffrey et al. 2004). This might lead to an ongoing separation and implies another potential for social conflicts in the future, as it can challenge national integrity.

Especially with regard to the earlier described observation of the connection between education and a positive social identification, social recognition and the impact of education for the construction of identity in India, the withdrawal of government from the educational sector and the filling of the gap for example by religious institutions must be observed very critically.

Notes

1 http://www.spiegel.de/panorama/justiz/0,1518,474304,00.html. (all websites accessed on December 2014).
2 http//www.indowindow.com/sad/article.php?child=29&article=29.
3 http://cities.expressindia.com/fullstory.php?newsid=89330.
4 http://www.hindustantimes.com/news/5922_954254,0015002200000001.htm.

References

Acharya, P. (1998): Law and Politics of Primary Education in Bengal. In: Bhattacharya, S. (ed.): The Contested Terrain. Perspectives on Education in India. Hyderabad: Orient Longmann.

Aikara, J.A. (1998): National survey of achievement at the end of primary stage. Bombay: Tata Institute of Social Sciences (mimeographed).

Béteille, A. (2002): Hierarchical and Competitive Inequality. *Sociological Bulletin* 51 (1): 3–27.

Bhattacharya, S. (2002): Introduction: An Approach to Education and Inequality. In: Bhattacharya, S. (ed.): Education and the Disprivileged. Hyderabad: Orient Longman.

Boesch, E.E. (1991): Symbolic Action Theory and Cultural Psychology. Berlin: Springer.

Bourdieu, P. (1987): Die feinen Unterschiede. Kritik der gesellschaftlichen Urteilskraft. Frankfurt, M.: Suhrkamp.

Clemens, I. (2004): Education and Women: About Castes, Marriage Markets and the Illusion of Deconstruction. *Man in India* 84 (3–4): 247–255.

Clemens, I. (2007): Bildung – Semantik – Kultur. Zum Wandel der Bedeutung von Bildung und Erziehung in Indien. *Frankfurter Beiträge zur Erziehungswissenschaft*, Monographien 7.

Clemens, I. (2007a): Globalisation and the Need for Cultural Perspectives in Educational Sciences. In: Philosophy of Education: Research Areas, Paradigms, Methods. Special Issue of the *Critique & Humanism Journal*, Vol. 26 (special issue): 171–186.

Dube, L. (1997): Women and Kinship: Comparative Perspectives on Gender in South & South-East Asia. New Delhi: Vistaar.

Dumont, L. M. (1976): Gesellschaft in Indien. Die Soziologie des Kastenwesens. Wien: Europaverlag.

Gupta, N. K. (2002): Need to Boost Primary Pupil Achievement: A Strategy of Education for All. *Indian Educational Review* 38: 115–138.

Holzwarth, S., Kanthy, S., and Tucci, R. (2006): Untouchable in School. Experiences of Dalit Children in Education, Youth Speak: Knowledge Community on Children in India, draft version.

Jeffrey, C., Jeffery, P., and Jeffery, R. (2004): 'A Useless Thing!' or 'Nectar of the Gods?' The Cultural Production of Education and Young Men's Struggles for Respect in Liberalizing North India. *Annals of the Association of American Geographers* 94 (4): 961–981.

Karve, I. (1993): The Kinship Map of India. In Uberoi, P. (ed.): Family, Kinship and Marriage in India. New Delhi: Oxford University Press, 50–73.

Kaviraj, S. (1992): Kolonialismus, Moderne und politische Kultur: die Krise Indiens. In: Matthes, J. (ed.): Zwischen den Kulturen? Die Sozialwissenschaften vor dem Problem des Kulturvergleichs. *Soziale Welt*, Sonderband 8, Göttingen: Schwartz, 219–238.

Kim, U. (2004): Factors contributing to academic achievement in Korea: psychological, relational, social and cultural perspectives. Lecture at the German Institute for International Educational Research, Frankfurt, 29 May 2004.

Kulke, H., and Rothermund, D. (1998): Geschichte Indiens. Von der Induskultur bis heute. München: Beck.

Kusakabe, T. (2007): Madrasa Education in Bangladesh – Competition Against the Primary Schools. Paper presented at the 13. World Congress of the Comparative Education Societies, Sarajevo, 3 July 2007.

Levinson, B. A., and Holland, D. (1996): The Cultural Production of the Educated Person: An Introduction. In: Levinson, B. A., Foley, D. E., and Holland, D. C. (eds): The Cultural Production of the Educated Person. New York: University Press, 1–25.

Luhmann, N. (1987): Soziale Systeme. Grundriß einer allgemeinen Theorie. Frankfurt, M.: Suhrkamp.

Luhmann, N. (1998): Gesellschaftsstruktur und Semantik. Studien zur Wissenssoziologie der modernen Gesellschaft, Bd. 3. Frankfurt, M.: Suhrkamp.

Luhmann, N., and Schorr, K.-H. (1979): Reflexionsprobleme im Erziehungssystem. Stuttgart: Klett-Cotta.
Lukose, R. (2000): Private-Public Divides. Seminar, October 2000. http://india-seminar.com/ 2000/494/494%20ritty%20lukose.htm.
Mehrotra, S., Panchamukhi, P., and Srivastava, R. (2005): Universalising Elementary Education in India: Uncaging the 'Tiger' Economy. New Delhi, Oxford University Press.
Merz, R. (1999): 'What's Love Got to Do with It?' – Social Networking through Marriage in Andhra Pradesh, India. *Internationales Asienforum* 30 (3–4): 335–357.
Nambissan, G. B. (1996): Equity in education? Schooling of Dalit children in India. *Economic and Political Weekly*: 1011–1022.
Nancharaiah, G. (2002): Dalit Education and Economic Inequality. In: Bhattacharya, S. (ed.): Education and the disprivileged. Hyderabad: Orient Longman.
NCERT: 7th All India School Education Survey 2007. New Delhi: NCERT.
Oldenberg, H. (n.d. a): Die Literatur des alten Indien. Stuttgart: Magnus Verlag.
Oldenberg, H. (n.d. b): Religionen des Veda. Stuttgart: Magnus Verlag.
Pinto, A. (2002): Culture, Values and Dalits in Higher Education. In: Bhattacharya, S. (ed.): Education and the disprivileged. Hyderabad, Orient Longman.
PROBE: Public Report on Basic Education in India. Oxford: Oxford University Press.
Radhakrishnan, S. (2007): Rethinking knowledge for development: Transnational knowledge professionals and the 'new' India. *Theory and Society* 36: 141–159.
Raina, D., and Habib, S. I. (2004): Big Science and the University in India. In: Raina, D., and Habib, S. I. (eds): Domesticating Modern Science. A Social History of Science and Culture in Colonial India. New Delhi, Tulika, 199–225.
Resnik, J. (2006): International Organizations, the 'Education–Economic Growth' Black Box, and the Development of World Education Culture. *Comparative Educational Review* 50 (2): 173–195.
Rolly, H. F. (2002): Bildungsrecht und Bildungspraxis religiöser und linguistischer Minderheiten in Indien. Frankfurt, M.: P. Lang.
Rolly, H. F. (2007): Educational Policy for Higher Education of Linguistic and Religious Minorities in India. Paper presented at the 13. World Congress of the Comparative Education Societies, 3.-7.09., Sarajevo.
Schütz, Alfred (1974): Der sinnhafte Aufbau der sozialen Welt. Frankfurt, M.: Suhrkamp.
Shiva Kumar, A. K. (2003): Common school system: End apartheid in education. *The Times of India* (New Delhi), p. 12.
Srinivas, M. N. (1989): The Cohesive Role of Sanskritization and Other Essays. Delhi: Oxford University Press.
Srivastava, A. (2007): Dynamics of Schooling. New Delhi: NCERT.
Subrahmanian, R. (2005): Education Exclusion and the Developmental State. In: Jeffery, P., and Chopra, R. (eds): Educational Regimes in Contemporary India. New Delhi: Sage Publications, 62–82.
Tooley, J., and Dixon, P. (2003): Private Schools for the Poor: A Case Study from India, CfBT (Centre for British Teachers): 1–27.

Vaid, D. (2004): Gendered inequality in educational transitions. *Economic and Political Weekly*: 3927–3938.
Varma, P. K. (1999): The Great Indian Middle Class. New Delhi: Penguin Books.
Verghese, N. V. (1995): School Effects on Achievement: A Study of Government and Private Aided Schools in Kerala. In: Kumar, K. (ed.), School Effectiveness and Learning Achievement at Primary Stage: International Perspective. New Delhi: NCERT, 260–288.
Weber, Max (1988): Gesammelte Aufsätze zur Religionssoziologie II. 7. Aufl. Tübingen: UTB.

Part IV

HOMOGENIZATION VERSUS DIVERSITY

23

SOCIALISATION IN THE CONTEXT OF GLOBALISATION

How adolescents in India deal with global processes

Benjamin Wagener

Over the last two decades, an ever-growing segment of the Indian population has been deeply affected by extensive economic, social and cultural change, that is to say, by globalisation (cf. Das 2002). This term theoretically refers to 'complex and contradictory interactions of global, regional, and local aspects of social life' (Karunakar 2011: 156) caused by worldwide fluxes of goods, people and information. As in other emerging nations, globalisation brought both benefits and drawbacks to the Indian society. It gave birth to a wealthy middle class (cf. Nayar 2007) while conversely caused worries about growing economic and social disparities as well as about the loss of cultural values and traditions (cf. Sahoo 2008; Mohan 2011). The latter concerns are especially related to the youth who is considered as being increasingly interested in the so-called Western lifestyle, i.e. an 'ultra-consumerist orientation [. . .] owing to the deep penetration of satellite television and cable networks in urban as well as rural areas and slums' (Mohan 2011: 219). Advocates of this point of view argue that the socialisation of the youth, in a traditional sense, is threatened by the influence of globalisation as it 'has forced an overhaul of the existing value system in order to link the tastes of the average person, particularly the young and adolescents of the middle classes, with their counterparts in Western Europe and North America' (ibid.).

However, there is an academic disagreement on how globalisation actually affects the socialisation of young people (cf. Hornstein 2001: 527f.). In this debate, socialisation at the stage of adolescence is understood as processes of cultural identity formation as well as social evaluation and localisation (cf. ibid.; Jensen et al. 2011).[1] On the one hand it is argued that globalisation has minimal effects on the socialisation of adolescence since processes of socialisation would primarily take place locally, i.e. at school, with family and among peers (cf. Hornstein 2001: 527f.). On the other hand globalisation is assumed to be a macro-context of socialisation processes as any environmental system crucial to socialisation gets affected by global processes: society (e.g. international political agreements), institutions (e.g. international schools), interactions (e.g. interactions between immigrants and locals) and individuals (e.g. cultural identity formation) (cf. Nestvogel 2000).[2] Nevertheless, the question of how global processes affect socialisation has been discussed almost exclusively in a theoretical manner. Although empirical research on this topic was already claimed 10 years ago (cf. Scheunpflug 2003: 116), the sociocultural research field still lacks data generated by appropriate methods (cf. Fritzsche 2012).

This chapter presents selected findings of an empirical study on the influences of socialisation on adolescents in a globalised context. Based on a qualitative approach, it investigates how young students in India experience processes related to globalisation and how they integrate them into their own world models.

The first part gives an introduction to some current sociological and anthropological perspectives on how globalisation affects the individual. The methodological background of the study is depicted in the second part. The last two sections present the results of the analysis and draw conclusions for further investigation of socialisation in a globalised context.

Globalisation and the change of sociocultural contexts: current sociological and anthropological perspectives

While in the mid-1980s the term *globalisation* was mainly used to describe economic changes (e.g. Levitt 1983), it became more and more relevant to anthropology and other social sciences at the beginning of the 1990s (cf. Eriksen 2003: 1). From a multidisciplinary perspective, globalisation is defined as a multidimensional process which has a massive influence on economic, political, social and cultural factors (cf. Sahoo 2008; Giddens 2001; Gosh 2011). Examining the different Euro-American and Indian sociological and anthropological discourses on the various impacts of global processes on individuals and their sociocultural contexts allows to identify four major theoretical notions.

One of the most discussed observations on globalisation is *the (re) production of social inequality* (e.g. Giddens 2001: 28; Mohan 2007; Beck 2008; Sahoo 2008). Proponents of globalisation argue that it enables the so-called developing and emerging countries to grow economically through an increased participation in the global market; a process eventually leading to a worldwide increase of social equality (cf. Nayar 2007: 133). When examining the rates of violence, crime and labour conflict between 1950 and 2005, Nayar points out, in the case of India, a positive correlation between economic liberalisation, economic growth and the decline of social inequalities. In contrast, Sahoo (2008: 136) argues that the 'relentless march of globalisation, mandating economic deregulation and liberalisation [in India], effected a truncation of the state's role as the regulator of economic activity and provider of social services.' The truth is that throughout the few decades of liberalisation of the Indian market the overall poverty rate dwindled (cf. World Bank 2009) and the economic boom gave birth to an Indian middle class (cf. Ghosh 2011: 155). However, the gap between rich and poor, between urban and rural areas, remains remarkably high (cf. World Bank 2009). As for socialisation, this heterogeneous development leads to unequal chances for adolescents and young adults to participate in the society, e.g. to access education facilities and/or work opportunities[3] (cf. Sahoo 2008) and to build their own social role (cf. Erikson 1968).

Another very much-discussed repercussion of globalisation is *the time-space distanciation* (cf. Giddens 1991: 21). As the use of information and communications technology (ICT) widens, information, images and representations are shared across nations and cultures. It is assumed that one main effect of this process is 'the intersection of presence and absence, the interlacing of social events and social relations "at distance" with local contextualities' (ibid.). As a result of the Indian population's increasing access to mass media, an ever-growing segment of the society is exposed to international information, global news, movies or music (cf. Ghosh 2011: 157ff.). Besides obtaining digital information on international issues, many Indians – especially the middle class in urban and semi-urban areas – experience the consumption of imported goods and services such as Western fashion or fast food (cf. ibid.). Western sociologists and anthropologists assert an increase in complexity concerning the individual's living environment because of simultaneity and fusion of local and global processes (cf. Wulf 2002: 81), which Robertson (1995) called 'glocalisation'. When it comes to the socialisation of adolescents, Hornstein (2001: 527) connects the increase of social complexity with tensions and contradictions that adolescents have to face as they live at the crossroads of their local environments and virtual realities.

The declining significance of the nation state is seen as a further consequence of globalisation (e.g. Giddens 2001: 24; Wulf 2002: 78). It is argued that the single nation-state has lost not only much of its economic and political influence but also its role as a source of cultural identity (cf. Wulf, ibid.). In this regard, Friedman (1994: 86) points out a crisis of cultural identity territorially defined and routed in the nation-state. When talking about India, referring to the 'Indian culture' is inappropriate as the country is a constantly changing blend of many religious beliefs – mainly Hinduism, Islam, Buddhism and Jainism – languages and diverse ethnic representations (cf. Mohan 2011: 215). However, Mohan extracts three essences of 'Indian culture' which he sees as threatened by Western cultural imperialism: *communitarianism*, characterised by 'communitarian relationships such as [. . .] family, kinship, caste, village' (ibid.); *spiritual ethos, worldly concerns and moral values*, marked by an 'emphasis upon the realisation of an ultimate spiritual ideal, i.e. unity with the cosmos without undermining material achievements' (p. 216); and *creativity and the spirit of accommodation*, i.e. creating new and accommodating to 'multiple currents and traditions' (p. 217). Mohan argues that the globally spreading Euro-American value system, its inherent consumerist culture as well as its trend towards individualism attack the communitarian ideal, create a hedonistic and materialistic mentality – which particularly affects the youth – and produce a mass culture in which 'lives become even more boring and unfulfilled' (p. 220).

In contrast to this rather pessimistic notion of cultural change, often described as 'Westernisation' or 'Americanisation', Western as well as non-Western writers assert *the rising significance of locality* for cultural identity formation (e.g. Olwig 2003; Ghosh 2011). It is argued that the decline of the nation-state's significance does not result in the rise of a global culture (cf. Wulf 2002: 79; Gosh 2011: 172) and thus does not lead to the development of a global cultural identity (cf. Friedman 1994: 86). In his comprehensive analysis of cultural development in India, Ghosh (2011) agrees with the assumption of a certain homogenisation of culture in urban and semi-urban areas due to the 'cultural globalisation'. However, he describes this process as having 'helped in accelerating the growth of cultural self-consciousness and cultural identities by exposing us [the Indian society] to a wide variety of sociocultural forms of life' (p. 171) and therefore resulted in 'a renewed "sense of belonging" at the local level' (p. 166). As a consequence, it is argued that the debilitation of former national identities leads to the formation of new identities based on locality and on the experience of cultural plurality (cf. Friedman 1994: 86; Ghosh 2011: 172).

These four summarised notions on the effects of globalisation on the sociocultural contexts of individuals imply a worldwide social reorganisation in the sense of cultural change. According to Giddens (2001: 31), this social change is characterised by instability, risks and paradoxes in which the individual experiences a feeling of continuous uncertainty. Following this point of view, Kirkwood (2001: 10) worries about the conditions as well as the results of socialisation of adolescents in the twenty-first century:

They will experience some of history's most serious health problems, inequities among less-developed and more-developed nations, environmental deterioration, overpopulation, transnational migrations, ethnic nationalism, and the decline of the nation-state. The new age will challenge their emotional, intellectual, and physical well-being.

Referring to this normative and rather pessimistic prospect, the investigation of whether (cf. Hornstein 2001: 527) and how globalisation affects the socialisation of adolescents is highly important.

Methodological background of the study

Globalisation rendered engaging with different cultures and global issues a necessity for sociocultural research in international contexts (cf. Schriewer 2000: 511). Unfortunately, previous studies in this field of research often failed to produce valid results because of inadequate methodologies considering cultural varieties to be distinct differences between homogenous units (cf. Matthes 1992: 7; Schriewer 2000). Due to the increasing cultural mixing process induced by globalisation, appropriate methodologies should be based on a notion of culture that encompasses complex interactions and the overlapping of different cultural elements (cf. Fritzsche 2012: 96). In addition, an inadequate reflection on cultural bias – resulting in the exploration of 'the other' from the observer's subjective point of view (cf. Matthes 1992: 7) – is a further challenge faced by sociocultural studies. In this regard, research should focus on the participants' interpretative acquisition of cultural plurality and be based on a praxeological methodology considering culture as a knowledge-based and socially constructed reality (cf. Reckwitz 2005: 94ff.).

The question of how adolescents in India experience globalisation-related processes and integrate them into their own world models is linked to two kinds of social knowledge. First, it is a matter of theoretical representations of global processes which can be expressed explicitly by the individual (cf. Bohnsack 2010: 100). Second, it is a question of implicit knowledge 'that underlies everyday practice and orientates habitualized actions independently from subjective intentions and motives' (Pfaff 2010: 46). Therefore, the research question uses the *Documentary Method* which aims at reconstructing both kinds of social knowledge: the explicit knowledge also known as common sense knowledge and the implicit knowledge or tacit knowledge (cf. Bohnsack et al. 2010). Moreover, this method meets the requirements of sociocultural research to control the researcher's culturally biased point of view in two aspects. For one thing, it enables the participants to reveal their own points of reference. For another, the continuous use of comparative data analysis – a special feature of the method – aims at restraining ethnocentric interpretations of the 'other culture' (cf. Fritzsche 2012: 106f.; for further details on the methodological aspects, also see Bohnsack et al. 2010).

In order to examine the adolescents' explicit and implicit knowledge, data collection was based on non-directive group discussions, in which the participants mutually expressed their social knowledge on the topic and revealed their 'collective pattern of meaning' by doing so (Bohnsack 2010: 106). Following the praxeological sociology of knowledge, this collective pattern of meaning is 'based on (implicit) shared experience[s] and the weltanschauung of social actors [. . .] underlying and orientating habitualized social action' (Bohnsack et al. 2010: 21; for further details on the method of group discussion in the context of the Documentary Method, see Bohnsack 2010). The exemplary analysis in this chapter only refers to data collected from ninth grade students from English medium schools in India in May and July 2012: one public school in New Delhi and one international school located in a rural area in the state of Rajasthan. Students from the English medium schools were chosen as participants because they are English speakers. Also, recruiting from pre-existing groups such as school classes was easier. The selection of the two school types was based on the observation that global processes particularly affect the social structures in urban areas in India as well as in international institutions, e.g. international schools (cf. Introduction). Each group consisted of five participants of the age of 14–15 – two females and three males in the *urban group* (New Delhi public school) and one female and four males in the *international group* (international school in Rajasthan) – selected by their teachers.

As mentioned above, the data analysis is based on the *Documentary Method* which consists of several working steps. First, creating a thematic overview of the audio-recorded group discussions, selecting and transcribing relevant passages, identifying and summarising topics – the *Formulating Interpretation*. Second, decoding orientation frames – the *Reflecting Interpretation*. Last, highlighting the commonalities and specifics of certain groups – the *Comparative Analysis* (for further details on the working steps, see Bohnsack 2010). The results presented in the following chapters refer to both the students' theoretical knowledge on globalisation and their practical knowledge or orientation frames.

Thinking about globalisation from ethical perspectives

Asked about their thoughts on globalisation, both groups expressed theoretical concepts on the topic. In their discourse, the students of the *urban group* compare globalisation with the use of social networking sites.

Im: e::hm what do you think about globalisation (2) which ideas do you have about this topic?
Bm: It's a great way to communicate (2) like
Af: ⌐Social networking sites
Bf: ⌐Social networking sites[4]

The students appreciate the possibility of interacting with others beyond local and national borders, especially with friends or relatives who live away from them. They draft a positive image of this process by implicitly highlighting the community-building or community-preserving function of social networking sites. The theoretical concept of globalisation developed by the students is strongly linked to their experience realm, their everyday practice, marked by a 'glocal' process (cf. Robertson 1995): using Facebook, an American-based social networking medium.

Compared to the *urban group*, the members of the *international group* depict the following idea of globalisation:

Em: In general would be (.) ehm development of the economy. (.)
I: Aha (.)
Em: Eh eh mainly actually;
I: Ya (.) what do you mean?
Bm: ⌐(Like)
Am: Ya to make (.) economies one;
Em: ⌐Different
Am: To unite them.
I: //mhm//
Am: Trade amongst different countries. (.) if you talk about e- economics it-is sort of like that. but ehm (2) if you talk about it in *general* it's *sharing* of *cultures* (.) ehm from (.) different countries amongst each other. and sharing of values; sharing of ehm (.) products () (sacred) stuff. from different countries to other countries. (.) ya so that's why this () making the world one

The students of the *international group* differentiate between two understandings of globalisation. On the one hand they present a definition focused on economic factors, which they consider to be conventional – and later on even morally questionable. On the other they introduce their own theoretical concept of globalisation including international cultural exchanges and sharing of ideas and goods. Using the conditional ('would be', 'actually') implies that their conventional definition falls too short. By doing so, Am and his schoolmates distance themselves from this economic idea of globalisation. Besides, this indicates that they assume their own notion to be more comprehensive – and later in the discussion process even of higher value. Compared to the *urban group*, their theoretical concept of globalisation adopts a meta-perspective taking global dynamics of different social dimensions into account, i.e. culture, economy and consumption. Nevertheless, both groups theoretically link globalisation to forms of sociocultural communication and, as a consequence, to an international convergence or even cultural unification (*international group*: 'making the world one').

Without being asked, the students in both groups provide evaluative interpretations of the assumed effects of what they define as globalisation. This process can be compared to Erikson's (1968) concept of social evaluation, meaning that adolescents critically assess their social environment on their way to identity. The students of the *urban group* dichotomise globalisation by drafting two opposing images of the effects of globalisation on the individual and (Indian) society. They repeatedly link their notion of globalisation to Facebook, which they consider to be an anonymous medium of communication involving the potential hazard of misuse.

Af: They tortu::re like if (we are chatting with) () and (). (.) they would like torture us and force us to do (.) we- eh what we should not do. (.) and in pressure or something we got dep- we get depressed (.) which (leads) to something (.)
Am: Suicide
Af: Suicide and (.) we (.) do something wrong (.) and then the society like (.) they also torture (.) and then we're in (.) pre- pressure.

The idea of globalisation expressed by the students implicitly reflects an increase in social complexity which is represented, to put it in Giddens's words (2001: 31), by an uncertainty about or a fear of 'the great unknown'. The hypothetical worst-case scenario depicted here appears to be based on a concept of globalisation characterised by a deep distrust of 'the unknown'. In this regard, 'the unknown' represents the danger of violation of the individual. Therefore, the protection of the individual serves as the reference point for the students' assessment of globalisation. This reference point can also be identified in the students' presentation of their positive image of globalisation:

Bm: Today's youth also uses Facebook (.) for like protesting against like molesting sexual harassment nowadays it's very common (.)

When thinking about globalisation, their frame of reference or realm of experience mostly consists of stories about actions related to their peers and relatives as well as occurrences in the Indian society.[5] Although the students introduce Facebook as a 'global' medium they implicitly emphasise the significance of 'local' practices. This pattern can also be found in the students' 'modus operandi' (Bohnsack 2010: 101) discussed in the next chapter.

In contrast to the *urban group*, the students of the *international group* only draft a negative image of the effects of globalisation on the individual. From their point of view, globalisation failed to pursue its original idea aiming at boundless cultural exchanges and the reduction of social inequality. They consider individuals as victims of powerful and corrupt global actors who prize economic goals above the respect for human rights.

Cm: Like the recent news you must have heard (.) recent news; one girl in Australia; (.)
Bm: ⌞Cheating (.) cheating
Cm: she got food poisoning from one KFC meal
Ff: ⌞(Corruptions)
I: //mhm//
Cm: And KFC has to pay her eight million dollars.

Unlike the *urban group*, their perspective on globalisation – from a spatial point of view – seems to be more 'glocal' (cf. Robertson 1995) since they take narratives from India and other countries into account. The *international group* students show a deep distrust of globalisation as a result of a moral evaluation with social equality and reciprocal respect used as criteria.

Adolescents in both groups assess globalisation with a more or less nuanced and critical mindset. The interviews do not indicate any unreflective dealing with global processes, at least not on the common-sense level, as feared by some 'cultural globalisation'-pessimists (e.g. Mohan 2011). However, it is assumed that evaluations occurring at the explicit level as well as self-theories or identities differ from implicit value systems that determine our everyday actions (cf. Bohnsack 2013).

Dealing practically with uncertainty: sticking to one's kind versus saving the world

How do the interviewed adolescents practically deal with their images of globalisation in their everyday life? By investigating the implicit knowledge underlying the habitualised actions of both groups one can identify similarities and differences in the students' orientations. Both groups have in common that their actions are somehow related to their distrust of globalisation. However, the interviewed groups present different orientations towards their reactions on their distrust.

Am: ˩It depends completely on the user how he uses the Facebook
Af: ˩uses yes
Im: Ok
Am: If he uses it ()
Bm: ˩if he has a control on him- himself (.) then it could be an () criteria of like eh (god sent) but (.) if he like eh some people like unknown people
Af: ˩add unknown people and share his thoughts (and posts and views) (.) and it's not (good).
Am: So global (.) globalisation is (a good thing) but if the user uses it (wrong) then (I) see it as a problem.

The students of the *urban group* are oriented towards 'acting on familiar ground'. They draft a negative image of getting into contact with 'the unknown', which they consider as a threat. Therefore, their positive image of 'using' globalisation is linked to familiarity-oriented actions. This implicit orientation can also be identified when the students talk about the benefits of globalisation and give a short description of how they use social networking sites:

Bm: ˩Social networking like it all- it allows an ultimate understanding (when) it always keeps in touch (.) like (.) ah in the society that we're able to take our friends () and relatives live very far from us like some in Dubai or some in there some in there (.) so we can (.) like without (.) spending money () in phones (.)

When briefly outlining some advantages of globalisation, they refer to communicating with peers and relatives on Facebook. In regard to their distrust of globalisation this 'sticking to one's kind'-orientation, to put it in simple terms, might serve as a protection against the assumed 'global threat'.

In contrast, the students of the *international group* describe the exchange of different cultural perspectives and traditions as necessary to accomplish what they consider to be the true purpose of globalisation: living in a world marked by harmony and respect for the 'cultural other'. The following passage on interacting with an international schoolmate illustrates the students' positive orientation towards engaging with otherness:

Cm: ⌊Global values we (.) talk with each others like (.) he is an international student he talk to us he is our friend; (.) we learn his culture his tradition; we learn that; we know some (things) about his country (.) ((some thuds in the background)) (and) he told us.
I: ⌊//mhm//
Am: We learn different different things about different cultu:res (.) e:hm example like how (personal respect) () (out of) a different country: (.) so it helps a lot that way;
Bm: It's not like (.) if he-is (.) from another country (.) if he does not know how to speak the language of our country. It-is not like that we gonna say him (.) stupid things in our language; (.)

The 'international student' implicitly represents the 'cultural other' whose otherness has to be explored and whose theoretical and practical knowledge have to be learnt by interacting with her/him. In contrast, the students' negative image of dealing with globalisation is characterised by a discriminatory and humiliating behaviour towards 'cultural others' as discussed in the previous chapter. Regarding the realisation of their ideal image of globalisation, the students implicitly experience themselves as being capable of proactively changing the negative aspects of globalisation, as depicted in the following extract:

Am: Ehm I just wanted to add like ehm (.) globalisation (.) we talk about it ((bell ringing)) right now it's going to an extent where it's (.) not helping but harming the people.
I: //mhm//
Am: So (.) hm (we've) what we have to look for now is how to stop it

The *international group* example illustrates the meaning of 'global socialisation' from a systemic perspective (cf. Nestvogel 2000). In this example, global processes especially influence the adolescents' micro-system. The interviewed students are part of an international institution. Through contacts with students from other countries and various cultural backgrounds, the interviewees got acquainted with the cultural specifics of their peers. These interactions seemingly have a crucial effect on the formation of their social identity, i.e. shared values and common mindsets, but also on their everyday practices. However, it cannot be ascertained whether the experience of cultural plurality leads to the adoption of other cultural practices and concepts (cf. Friedman 1994: 86) or to 'a renewed "sense of belonging" at the local level' (Gosh 2011: 166).

On the contrary, the adolescents from New Delhi (*urban group*), a city considered as cosmopolitan and multicultural, do not describe such intercultural experiences. Apparently, their common micro-system (particularly interactions in school) includes different experiences leading to different collective identities and day-to-day practices, as described above.

Conclusion

The findings of the exemplary analysis of group discussions with adolescents in India demonstrate that global processes have certain effects on the socialisation of young people. As they describe their realms of experience, the interviewed students refer to the simultaneity of global processes and local living environments, also called 'glocal' experiences (cf. Robertson 1995). This illustrates how meaningful globalisation is for them: it is part of their life and not just an abstract concept. Their critical evaluation of social change resulting in a deep distrust of globalisation contradicts the pessimistic and general assumption that the youth naively deals with globalisation-related processes (cf. Mohan 2011). However, the action-related orientations towards their distrust of globalisation are different in the two studied groups. These differences are probably rooted in the different realms of experience of the students, especially in experiences they share at school. This finding speaks against the idea that schools do not provide socialising environments in a globalised context as they are considered as local systems (cf. Hornstein 2001: 527f.). The comparative analysis of two different school types underlines the influence of interaction processes on social identity formation as well as on action-related orientations taking place in institutions, e.g. schools. The example of the international school students supports such a systemic approach of the impacts of globalisation on socialisation as developed by Nestvogel (2000). From this perspective, interacting with 'cultural others' in an international school apparently affects the students' explicit and implicit knowledge, e.g. values and value-based actions. However, whether or not the experience of cultural plurality leads to the adoption of other cultural practices as well as to the formation of a new cultural identity still remains an open question. Nonetheless, the results indicate that the investigation of socialisation processes in a globalised context is worthwhile, especially when it comes to the normative issue of young people's skills for dealing with the challenges of globalisation (cf. Giddens 2001; Kirkwood 2001: 10). In this regard, doing cross-cultural research using open methods that focus on the participants' interpretative acquisition of cultural plurality is essential in order to overcome an ethnocentric point of view (cf. Fritzsche 2012).

Notes

1 This notion of socialisation is closely tied to Erikson's (1968) concept of the formation of an adolescent's identity. In this regard, 'forming a cultural identity involves adopting the beliefs and practices of one or more cultural communities' (Jensen et al. 2011: 286). At the stage of adolescence the individual is faced with the need to critically evaluate her-/himself and her/his social environment in order to develop a particular social role (cf. Erikson 1968; Jensen et al. 2011: 286).
2 Nestvogel (2000) enhanced dominant theories of socialisation (cf. Bronfenbrenner 1979; Geulen and Hurrelmann 1980), which disregard the influence of globalisation on human development, by a world-systems perspective.
3 In this regard, Nestvogel (2000: 183f.) draws a distinction between the standard of institutional education in industrial countries and ways of informal learning, e.g. in the context of child labour commonly occurring in several parts of the world. From a world-systems perspective overcoming the norm of formal education both kinds of learning might be considered as equivalent socialisation processes. However, the separate consideration of child labour underlines the exploitation of children often even being created by globalisation (cf. ibid.).
4 The speakers are identified by capital initials and a small 'f' or 'm' to indicate gender. For further details on the transcript conventions used in this paper, see Bohnsack et al. 2010: 365.
5 When talking about protesting against sexual harassment, the students refer to the frequent sexual assaults occurring in India.

References

Beck, U. (2008): Risikogesellschaft und die Transnationalisierung sozialer Ungleichheit. In: Berger, P. A., and Weiß, A. (eds): Transnationalisierung sozialer Ungleichheit, 19–40. Wiesbaden.
Bohnsack, R. (2010): Documentary Method and Group Discussions. In: Bohnsack, R., Pfaff, N., and Weller, V. (eds): Qualitative Analysis and Documentary Method in International Education Research, 99–124. Opladen, Farmington Hills.
Bohnsack, R. (2013): Habitus, Norm und Identität. In: Helsper, W., Kramer, R.-T., and Thiersch, S. (eds): Schülerhabitus. Wiesbaden (in press).
Bohnsack, R., Pfaff, N., and Weller, V. (eds) (2010): Qualitative Analysis and Documentary Method in International Education Research. Opladen, Farmington Hills.
Bronfenbrenner, U. (1979): The Ecology of Human Development: Experiments by Nature and Design. Cambridge.
Das, G. (2002). India Unbound: From Independence to the Global Information Age. New Delhi.
Erikson, E. H. (1968): Identity, Youth, and Crisis. New York.

Eriksen, T. H. (2003): Introduction. In: Eriksen, T. H. (ed.): Globalisation. Studies in Anthropology, 1–17. London.

Friedman, J. (1994): Culture Identity and Global Process. London.

Fritzsche, B. (2012): Das Andere aus dem standortgebundenen Bilde heraus verstehen. Potenziale der dokumentarischen Methode in kulturvergleichend angelegten Studien. In: ZQF 13 (1–2): 93–109.

Geulen, D., and Hurrelmann, K. (1980): Zur Programmatik einer umfassenden Sozialisationstheorie. In: Hurrelmann, K., and Ulich, D. (eds): Handbuch der Sozialisationsforschung, 51–68. Weinheim.

Giddens, A. (1991): Modernity and Self-identity. Oxford.

Giddens, A. (2001): Entfesselte Welt. Wie die Globalisierung unser Leben verändert. Frankfurt, M.

Gosh, B. (2011): Cultural Changes and Challenges in the Era of Globalization. The Case of India. In: Journal of Developing Societies 27 (2): 153–175.

Hornstein, W. (2001): Erziehung und Bildung im Zeitalter der Globalisierung. Themen und Fragestellungen erziehungswissenschaftlicher Reflexionen. In: Zeitschrift für Pädagogik 47 (4): 517–537.

Jensen, A. L., Arnett, J. J., and McKenzie, J. (2011): Globalization and Cultural Identity. In: Schwartz, S. J., Luyckx, K., and Vignoles, V. L. (eds): Handbook of Identity Theory and Research. Vol. 1, 285–301. New York.

Karunakar, P. (2011): Threat of Globalization to Indigenous Peoples' Culture and Identities in India. In: Fourth World Journal 10 (2): 153–166.

Kirkwood, T. F. (2001): Our Global Age Requires Global Education: Clarifying Definitional Ambiguities. In: The Social Studies 91 (1): 10–15.

Levitt, T. (1983): Globalization of Markets. In: Harvard Business Review 61 (3): 92–102.

Matthes, J. (1992): 'Zwischen' den Kulturen? In: Matthes, J. (ed.): Zwischen den Kulturen. Die Sozialwissenschaften vor dem Problem des Kulturvergleichs, 3–9. Göttingen.

Mohan, B. (2007): Social Exclusions: Challenges for New Social Development. In: Journal of Comparative Social Welfare 23 (1): 69–79.

Mohan, K. (2011): Cultural Values and Globalization: India's Dilemma. In: Current Sociology 59 (2): 214–228.

Nayar, B. R. (2007): Social Stability in India under Globalization and Liberalization. In: India Review 6 (3): 133–164.

Nestvogel, R. (2000): Sozialisation unter Bedingungen von Globalisierung. In: Scheunpflug, A., and Hirsch, K. (eds): Globalisierung als Herausforderung für die Pädagogik, 169–194. Frankfurt, M.

Olwig, K. F. (2003): Global Places and Place-identities – Lessons from Caribbean Research. In: Eriksen, T. H. (ed.): Globalisation. Studies in Anthropology, 58–77. London.

Pfaff, N. (2010): Gender Segregation in Pre-Adolescent Peer Groups as a Matter of Class: Results from Two German Studies. In: Childhood 17 (1): 43–60.

Reckwitz, A. (2005): Kulturelle Differenzen aus praxeologischer Perspektive. Kulturelle Globalisierung jenseits von Modernisierungstheorie und Kulturessentialismus. In: Srubar, I., Renn, J., and Wenzel, U. (eds): Kulturen vergleichen. Sozial- und kulturwissenschaftliche Grundlagen und Kontroversen, 92–111. Wiesbaden.

Robertson, R. (1995): Glocalization: Time-Space and Homogeneity-Heterogeneity. In: Featherstone, M., Lash, S., and Robertson, R. (eds): Global Modernities, 25–44. London.

Sahoo, S. (2008): Globalization, Social Welfare and Civil Society in India. In: Journal of Comparative Social Welfare 24 (2): 133–141.

Scheunpflug, A. (2003): Stichwort: Globalisierung und Erziehungswissenschaft. In: Zeitschrift für Erziehungswissenschaft 6 (2): 159–172.

Schriewer, J. (2000): Stichwort: Internationaler Vergleich in der Erziehungswissenschaft. In: Zeitschrift für Erziehungswissenschaft 3 (4): 495–515.

World Bank (2009): Has India's Economic Growth Become More Pro-poor in the Wake of Economic Reforms? Policy Research Working Paper 5103. Retrieved from: http://elibrary.worldbank.org/content/workingpaper/10.1596/1813-9450-5103 (4 August 2013).

Wulf, C. (2002): Globalisierung und kulturelle Vielfalt. Der Andere und die Notwendigkeit anthropologischer Reflexion. In: Wulf, C., and Merkel, C. (eds): Globalisierung als Herausforderung der Erziehung. Theorien, Grundlagen, Fallstudien, 75–100. Münster, New York, München, Berlin.

24
POWER TO THE PEOPLE: A LONG ROAD TO CONSCIENTIZATION

Maria Schneider

Rise of empowerment

In 1970, Ester Boserup changed the attempt to help women to gain gender equality through her Book *Women's Role in Economic Development*. She showed that although women make decisive contributions to subsistence economy, they get more and more marginalized in all spheres of life.

The *Humphrey Institute of Public Affairs* observed that 'while women represent 50 per cent of the world population, they perform nearly two-thirds of all working hours, receive one-tenth of the world income and own less than one per cent of the world property (Jitendra N. Bhatt 2006).'

The census of India in the year 1971 showed that women made up 48.2 per cent of the population but only 13 per cent of economic activity. Female workforce in the unorganized sector was about 94 per cent. Mostly they work in agriculture, agro-forestry, fishery, handicrafts and so on (Pattnaik 1996: 42).

After the book was published, the United Nations decided to give mandate to all member countries to help women to gain equality, development and peace. Before Boserup's book, international aid focused on getting women trained in traditional work patterns such as sewing, spinning, agriculture and training in hygiene. In general, women worked in the unorganized sector. Boserup revealed that it is much more helpful to integrate women better into international or national aid projects rather than to make them more productive (United Nations 1998). Reflecting the situation back in the 1970s, the UN decided to change their approach more towards development rather than rise of productivity or welfare. Initially, the approach accepted existing social structures and emphasized how to better integrate women into existing development initiatives.

In 1980, the United Nations Development Programme (UNDP) set up a special women division, *International Development Strategy for the Third United Nations Development Decade*. Here again a change of the approach took place. The chapter emphasized a more active role for women not only seeing them at the end of the aid chain. Women should be integrated in all aspects of economy and at all levels in the programme enrolled by the UNDP. Some of the aspects included industrialization, food and agriculture, science and technology and social development; all of them should involve women (Joekes 1990: 147ff.).

Since 1990, the *UNDP Human Development Report Office* publishes an annual *Human Development Report* (HDR) to measure and analyse developmental progress. The *Human Resource Development* (HRD) philosophy supports investment in women to increase their efficiency and productivity, in order to increase their economic and social status.

Another approach is the *Human Development Concept* (HDC); it emphasizes the quality of life or well-being as an aspect of investment in women. This approach especially emphasizes education, health, nutrition and better quality of life (Patel n.d.).

In 1985, the perspective on women widened to gain more equality, development and peace. The *OECD* (Organization for Economic Co-operation and Development) development Centre was concerned that the perspective was still more focused on welfare. More attention should be paid to the 'home economics approach and focus on income-generating activities which are relevant and useful to the women participating'. Also, it quoted a lack of information about the roles and activities women play in their families or communities. Research information should be used to develop further projects (Weekes-Vagliani 1985: 52ff.).

One of the research frameworks was the *Harvard Analytical Framework*, which came up with the so-called 'efficiency approach'. Men as well as women should benefit from development aid. This should help to make development aid much more efficient.

Criticism on the Women in Development (WID) approach is large and wide. One of the most frequently raised objections is that WID does not sufficiently emphasize the larger social context affecting women's lives and their roles as mothers as well as participants of the community. In contrast to the Harvard Framework Approach, the WID supports only the female population. The approach does not go far enough and does not touch the roots of gender inequalities.

To tackle that problem, in 1980, a gender analysis helped to bring the *Gender and Development* (GAD) approach on its way (UN 1998). The GAD helped to develop a broader view on relationships rather than focusing straight on women's issues (Campillo 1993: 34).

Another milestone in the history of women's empowerment was the *United Nations Decade for Women* 1976–1985 (UN, Beijing). In that time, the *Convention on the Elimination of All Forms of Discrimination against Women* (CEDAW) was written. Three big conferences were held during the Decade for Women. The last one in Nairobi (1985) caused a series of member states to schedule a removal of gender discrimination in national laws by the year 2000. Not only the convention was written in that decade, also as a result of the international focus on women in 1975 a number of institutions were established:

- *The International Research and Training Institute for the Advancement of Women* (INSTRAW)
- *United Nations Development Fund for Women* (UNIFEM)
- *Women's Studies Resource Centre*, South Australia

In 1995, the fourth women's conference was held in Beijing (UN, Beijing 2). Since then, a five-, ten- and fifteen-year Review and Appraisal were published. Main topics were *National level review of implementation*, *Regional 15-year review processes*, *Global 15-year review process in the 54th session of the Commission on the Status of Women* and *Related intergovernmental processes*. In the Review and Appraisal the *United Nations Entity for Gender Equality and the Empowerment of Women* investigates how and if the 38-point *Beijing Declaration* is implemented (UN, Beijing 3).

In 2010, the *United Nations Entity for Gender Equality and the Empowerment of Women* was established (UN Women). 'In doing so, UN Member States took an historic step in accelerating the Organization's goals on gender equality and the empowerment of women. The creation of UN Women came about as part of the UN reform agenda, bringing together resources and mandates for greater impact. It will merge and build on the important work of four previously distinct parts of the UN system which focus exclusively on gender equality and women's empowerment' (UN Women).

Putting all this together in the *Millennium Development Goals* (MDGs), the United Nations and 23 international organizations showed a strong will to achieve and promote gender equality and empowering women.

Not only since the last 50 or 100 years, people and especially women have fought for their freedom, for justice and especially for equality with men. The UN defined Gender Equality as follows: 'equality is the cornerstone of every democratic society that aspires to social justice and human rights' (CEDAW). This emphasizes the importance of equality between genders and shows how important the topic is to the highest and powerful League of Nations.

In 1995, the *UN HDR* looked at gender equality in terms of capabilities like education, health and nutrition. Besides such capabilities, facilities offered in the economic sphere and in decision-making processes should lead to equality.

In 2012, the *World Bank* concludes that equality consists of equality of opportunities and equality of outcomes (World Bank 2012: 4). This includes equality in wages for work and access to human capital and other productive resources. One very important aspect of equality that was mentioned neither by the UN nor by the UN HDR is the equality of voice that means the ability to influence and contribute to the developing process.

To sum up the facts one can outline three domains that are important for gender equality. These are capabilities, access to resources and opportunities, agency or the ability to influence and contribute to outcomes. These three capabilities are interrelated, if one gains access to resources they will try to gain influence on the use of the newly gained resources.

A feminist critical remark on the WID, WAD and GAD models

From the feminist perspective the WID, WAD and GAD models show very clearly the paradigm shift completed by the UN and other NGOs. Vibhuti Patel, an Indian scholar at the University Department of Economics of SNDT Women's University, Mumbai, depicts this paradigm shift. In the WID model, women were often treated as mere beneficiaries of the spent money. In WID, women play a minor part in the wide range margin of economy. Women were treated as auxiliary labour force, allowed to help overcome a period of crisis and then were expected to step back and let men take over again. The WID is more about economic growth than enabling women to gain equality.

Woman and Development (WAD) model shows a shift in perspective. Women are not just beneficiaries, but should play a more active role in the developmental work they are doing for themselves and in general. It is not enough to get women into the role of labour force. State and a proactive approach by the civil society through NGOs should empower women against the forces of patriarchal class society. This approach became very powerful during the 1990s.

The GAD model emphasizes gender relations and tries to empower not the women in general but the weak ones. On the one side, gender is socially constructed, on the other side gender relations are power relations. Power can be seen as a very important analytic category. Gender inequality can be measured by the current sex-ratio, literacy rates, health and nutrition indicators, wage differentials and ownership of land and property. 'The implicit relations are those embedded in relations of power and in hierarchies and are more difficult to measure. Located in the household, in custom, religion, and culture, these intra-household inequalities result in unequal distribution of power, control over resources and decision-making, dependence rather than self-reliance and unfair, unequal distribution of work, drudgery and even food' (Kapur-Mehta 1996: WS80).

Molyneux in her remarkable work *Mobilization without Emancipation* (1985), describes the transformation from development towards empowerment. One of her main points is the distinction between women's 'practical needs' and 'strategic interests'. She combines 'practical needs' with conditions of living, their workloads, roles and responsibilities. Her concept also relates to women's biological make-up. If provision of maternity protection and childcare centres, nearby water supply, stoves for efficient cooking and training in sewing and weaving are available to women, they can take care of their 'strategic interests'. Very often 'strategic interests' arise from the mechanisms of women's subordination to men. Hence it is important to understand the current power structure in order to search for strategies to dismantle them. Not surprisingly, socialist feminists' criticism was that the development approach prefers to support 'practical needs' and neglects 'strategic interests'. Another critical point is that the development perspective primarily remained in areas of economic concern neglecting the power dimensions of gender relations. Only to adjust the economic situation of women to get them into employment is not likely to bring them on par with men. Apart from bringing women in an equal position with men, the economic status of women does not say much about their happiness and the impact on their role and status. Therefore one important impact is her say in the decision-making processes, her participation in the domestic as well as communities' power structures. To get women a word in decision-making processes could lead to the rise of women's empowerment perspective (Sharma 2000: 21f.).

Inspired by Molyneux's work, Longwe (1995) designed an analytical framework of 'gender awareness' which paved the way for a stricter empowerment perspective. This framework is depicted in Figure 24.1.

It takes account of the social, economic, psychological and political dimensions altogether. Another important point is that this framework can be read as gender-neutral. For male as well as female persons seeking empowerment the dimensions of welfare, access, conscientization, participation and control are important. One can read the framework from top to bottom, as an example how it could be to be an empowered person. One is in control of one's life and levels of power. Next is participation in the progress of

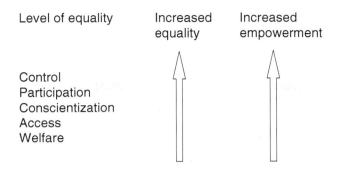

Figure 24.1 Longwe based on Sharma (2000: 22)

decision-making about different aspects of life, for instance choice of residence or profession and so on. The third point is about conscientization and is the most important one because it holds the key for empowerment. It is about the knowledge and critical awareness of the structures of discrimination, exploitation and oppression in which one is placed.

Conscientization has three aspects. The first one involves 'generating awareness' among women about inequalities between men and women regarding material welfare like nutrition, mortality rate and gender ratio access to resources, education, property and labour; participation in decision-making processes within the family and community and the most important, control about someone's own life, choices, labour and decisions. Second, it is the perception that 'gender gaps' are neither given by God nor natural and thus are modifiable. The last aspect of conscientization is about mobilizing and organizing women to bring empowerment on its way. 'Access' is about finding a way to access resources and benefits. At the bottom line stands material welfare. In this framework, conscientization holds the key for real empowerment among humankind. It is just not enough to be free from hunger, diseases, unemployment and homelessness.

Obviously, Longwe's framework neglects the idea of seeing women as mere beneficiaries, thus depicting the process of empowering as a more complex one. Similarly, Kabeer interprets the process as a power relation that needs transformation towards women having more power over their own lives rather than men having less power over women (Kabeer 1990: 8). According to Beteille, 'the main point behind empowerment is that it seeks to change society through a rearrangement of power' (Beteille 1999: 591).

Empowerment: the best possible

The empowerment approach holds a much greater promise than welfare or development approaches. First, the multidimensional construct of development suits the challenges in life well. Empowerment is not just about gaining power but includes several other dimensions like economic, social, political and – very important and often forgotten – psychological dimensions. Social empowerment emphasizes strengthening health, education, freedom and the possibility to realize one's potential.

Economic empowerment connotes productive resources and benefits, property, employment and income regardless of gender differences. Political empowerment is about establishing equality in decision-making processes at all levels and structures of power, from the local to a global level. Psychological empowerment is to reinforce the ability to overcome feelings of helplessness, to gain self-esteem and to get a sense of efficacy.

Friedmann (1992) makes a similar distinction when it comes to the term of power. Social, political and psychological are the dimensions Friedmann shows. Similar to the empowerment approach, the three dimensions are interlinked.

Bystydzienski (1992) has a different point of view concerning empowerment. He emphasizes more the process taking place when people are trying to improve their position. Empowerment helps oppressed persons to gain more control over their own living in regard to taking part in the development of activities.

Indian context

The first part of this chapter was very much about classifying the term of empowerment. It showed that the progress of empowerment underwent different stages among the United Nations, significant NGOs and Governments. As mentioned earlier, the point of view of women who are seeking empowerment has changed. Earlier in the process, the goal has been to improve women's economic situation. It was assumed that a proper financial situation would help to encourage women. Unfortunately, this was a mistake. So the campaign moved forward to a more holistic approach. Now, not a special gender was the starting point for help but the view widened to a gender-neutral support. Still, more women are recipients of state or international aid than men. More important, it became clear that without changing social, economic, psychological and political dimensions, empowerment remained just a nice and notable idea. Especially for the Indian context, the religious dimension plays a big role if empowerment programmes should be successful.

In the Sixth Five-Year Plan (1980–1985), for the first time an entire chapter was dedicated to 'Women and Development'. Previously, the supported strategy has been 'Women and Welfare'. For the first time, the Indian Governance promoted the shift from a welfare to a development approach. The next Five-Year Plan (1985–1900) marks a second shift in the approach favoured by the Indian State, by pronouncing the 'Socio-Economic Programmes for Women" The third and most significant landmark came with The *National Perspective Plan for Women 1988–2000* which sought to integrate and co-ordinate the diverse schemes of women's development into a holistic perspective. Like the UN programmes, the Indian State tried to build a framework that includes social, economic, psychological and political dimensions. On the political level, the Indian government installed a quota, saying that one-third of the seats in locally elected bodies are reserved for women. Unfortunately, the *Bill of Reservation of Women in the Indian Parliament and State Assemblies* on a nationwide quota did not pass when it was submitted in 1996 and in 1998. One day after International Women's day 2010, Women's Reservation Bill passed, ensuring 33 per cent reservation to women in Parliament and state legislative bodies (The Hindu 2010).

The Constitution of India has made many contributions to women's equality:

- Article 14: Guarantee of all Indian women equality.
- Article 15(1): No discrimination by the State.
- Article 16 and 39(d): Equality of opportunity.
- Article 39 (d): Equal pay for equal work for both men and women.
- Article 51 (A) (e): The state renounces practices derogatory to the dignity of women (Kalyani Menon-Sen 2001).

The women's movement started in the 1970s. Twenty years later, with the help of grants from foreign aid agencies, *Self Employed Women's Association* (SEWA) has played a major role in women's rights movement in India. In 2001, *Swashakti* meaning Year of Women's Empowerment was launched by the Government of India.

The situation of women and girls in the last 10 years has improved beyond doubt. Still there is a lot more to improve. A closer look at education shows that the female literacy rate is rising but still far lower than its male counterpart (Singh 2007: 3). One reason could be that far fewer girls are enrolled in schools than boys and even if they are going to school many of them drop out before finishing the tenth grade (Kalyani Menon-Sen 2001). A similar picture may be drawn for labour conditions. In 2007, 32 per cent of the female labour force[1] were employed, compared to more than 84 per cent of the male counterpart (Bhalla and Kaur: 7). A different question is equal payment, assured by the Indian government in Article 39 (d). Men are still far more than women when it comes to paid labour. In the software industry, more than 30 per cent of the labour force may be female (Singh and Hoge 2010: 200ff.). They are even in terms of wages or position at the work place. The situation in rural parts of India looks different. Most women work at the biggest industrial branch, agriculture and allied industrial sectors. There, nearly 90 per cent of the total labour is done by women (Sustainable Development Dimension). In agriculture, it is estimated that more than 50 per cent of the total labour is done by women. According to a World Bank report from 1991, women have an employment level of more than 90 per cent in dairy production. In forest-based small-scale enterprises, a little bit more than half of the work is done by women (ibid.).

When it comes to discrimination against women and girls, the biggest topic is probably dowry. Dowry is paid by the bride's family. Mostly it is money; items of daily use, mostly kitchen and cooking equipment or realties. In case of realties, the husband or the husband's family is the new owner. In 1961, payment of dowry was prohibited under Indian civil law. Fifty years later, the payment of dowry is still an often practiced ancient custom causing lots of problems. At least a dozen wives die each day in 'kitchen fires' (Iqbal 2007). Dowry puts a lot of financial pressure on the bride's family. It is one of the reasons for families to favour sons over daughters.

This preference of sons is another issue getting much international attention. Sex-selective abortion is the practice of terminating a pregnancy based upon the predicted (in this case, female) sex of the baby. In India, this is not allowed by law but reality shows that this does not help to prevent parents from getting rid of their unborn or born daughters (Ridge 2010). According to the decennial Indian census, the sex ratio in the 0–6 age group in India went from 104.0 males per 100 females in 1981 to 105.8 in 1991, 107.8 in 2001 and 109.4 in 2011. The 2011 census showed that the ratio of girls to boys under the age of six years old has dropped from 927 girls for every 1,000 boys in 2001 (Census 2001) to 918 girls for every 1,000 boys in 2011 (Census 2011).

Not surprisingly, India ranked 134 out of 187 in 2011 at the Human Development Index (HDI) enrolled from the UNDP.

The first parts of this chapter dealt with the concept of empowerment and possible impacts for women. Also it gave an overview over the current situation women face in India. The following part is about the implementation of the empowerment approach in India. Without doubt, the situation of women needs improvement. The Government of India, the United Nations and several NGOs are working for the goal to improve the situation of women. The following lines are about one of those many associations fighting for improvement.

Stree Mukti Sanghatana

During a university exchange I came to meet and see the work of the *Parisar Vikas Project* at the *Tata Institute of Social Science* in Mumbai. *Stree Mukti Sanghatana* (SMS) initiated the *Parisar Vikas* programme. The NGO is located in Chembur, Mumbai. Chembur is a suburban neighbourhood located in eastern Mumbai, 22 kms from downtown Mumbai. Retail outlets and other industries are located in Chembur. The Chembur market is very close to Chembur railway station. Both offer a large scale of goods and services on street sales. Apart from the many street salesmen Chembur has a shopping mall, multi product stores, several retail and factory outlets. Chembur has to fight large pollution problems. In an Indian ranking of the most polluted industrial areas it ranked 46th (Varma 2008). The ground water is polluted, too. The nearby Deonor dumping ground is causing health problems for the residents due to fires and smoke (The Indian Express 2008).

SMS was established in 1975 and is a women's liberation organization. It has directed its efforts towards improving conditions for women primarily by creating awareness in the society about women's issues. Since its inception, SMS has made significant contributions to the women's movement in Maharashtra (state of India) through various activities (SP Working Paper 2005: 29). SMS applies a three-folded approach concerning financial, environmental and social issues.

The women run through an environmental entrepreneurship programme which helps them to gain skills in organic manure making, gardening, leadership development and formation of cooperatives etc. As said earlier, Parisar Vikas's aim is to make underprivileged women aware of their rights. In 2000, an important dialogue with rag pickers was initiated. Rag pickers are mostly female. Their situation is one of the worst in India. Rag picking women in Mumbai are isolated, often in poor health and lack important life skills. Mostly they never attended a school and their social status is low. They aren't integrated into the social structure and often just leave home for working. Usually, children of rag pickers do not go to school, like their mothers didn't. These families lack knowledge about health care and hygiene, both for themselves and for their children. Ideas about saving money are rare. Many families depend on loan sharks when it comes to unforeseen incidences like illness. Society is looking down at them due to their social status and caste.

In SMS terms rag pickers are called Parisar Bhaginis which means neighbourhood sisters. The Parisar Bhaginis and their children get the chance to improve their education or health condition through literacy classes, health and social awareness campaigns.

Once a month, groups of women meet for social gatherings, where the women get the chance to talk about their hopes and dreams; about questions they can't ask elsewhere; about parenting or simply about work. Every month, the women save some money, which was nearly impossible before. Without an identity card one does not get a bank account and therefore the only way of saving money is to keep it at home. Another concern SMS deals with is about insurances and access to government schemes for poor urban people.

Another big concern of Parisar Vikas is to educate children of rag pickers. With help from *Pratham* (NGO), pre-primary education has been made available by establishing a kindergarten. Furthermore, six crèches were opened, one of them near Deonar dumping ground. Children get training in reading, writing, maths, etc. They also get study support like scholarships so that they can continue to go to school. Libraries were also set up. Six centres for adolescent sensitization programmes were established. In these centres role-plays take place about subjects relevant to the teenagers. Topics could be stress management, family life education, bad habits and addiction and early marriage. There are also vocational trainings for health workers and sewers.

So far, eight family counselling centres could be opened. There, families get information about family planning issues, health and educational matters or they get help in improving their personal or family situation.

SMS cooperates with other like-minded organizations for inputs especially in health and educational activities. SMS gives its attention mainly to:

- organization and training of the female rag pickers,
- improving the standard of living of female rag pickers by recognizing their problems,
- developing new techniques for treatment of waste,
- creating zero waste situation in cities by appropriate waste recycling techniques.

The first step was to give every woman who wanted to participate in the programme an identity card and to provide them with special training in waste handling, collection, transportation of waste to pits and pit management. They also got training in alternative skills, like composting and gardening etc. The women learn about their role when it comes to the waste management system. The training elucidates women's rights, rights for education and, especially in the Indian Context, knowledge about caste issues. The work of SMS includes a regular health check-up for the whole family. SMS also encourages women to devise an economic plan. The training includes education about responsible parenting. This point is especially important since very often it seems that social status does not change over the generations.

The training took place every Wednesday and Saturday and lasted for 16 days. During that period the women also got medical treatment at municipal hospitals, if necessary. When the training is finished, the Parisar Bhaginis know the difference between wet and dry waste. The former is going to be converted into compost and could be sold at local markets. The latter is going to be recycled. Women collect the waste at special garbage bins set up in Mumbai. Compost will be used for gardens and to maintain plant nurseries. They sell the garbage directly to customers, without interim dealers, so that the women's income is higher. Another important point is that the women are in control about all aspects so that they do not feel dependent.

The project was funded by the UK-based NGO War on Want. They contributed Rs 20 Lacs[2] for a period of four years.

SMS established a useful garbage dividing system. Furthermore, 13 garbage wards are spread over the city for establishing a zero garbage status. Additionally, Parisar Vikas managed to construct and maintain biogas plants (Nisargruna).[3] One of them is running at the *Tata Institute for Social Science*. Normal biogas plants can just transform human waste and cow dung. The Nisargruna is able to process all biodegradable waste. Wet waste from the Tata Institute is used at the canteen as fuel for heating and generating electricity.

Project at Tata Institute for Social Science

Some of the rag pickers work at the canteen, called SMS canteen, at the *Tata Institute for Social Science*. At the university, there are two such SMS canteens. Students and staff can buy snacks, meals, chocolate and drinks. The meals are prepared by Parisar Bhaginis. Meals served are typical Indian and Marathi food like dal, samosa, Indian bread, potatoes, egg, rice with curry or gravy. All is freshly cooked and served. During lunch one has to hurry to get a meal. Lunch meals are quickly sold out. Parisar Bhaginis women are dealing with cooking and buying ingredients, serving and cleaning. The atmosphere in the canteen is warm and welcoming. Non

Maharati[4] speakers sometimes struggle to understand the menu card, but the Parisar Bhaginis women are always as courteous as possible. At the canteen there is a woman as cashier. This woman never cooked or cleaned or served. The other way round, the women who cooked, served or cleaned never worked as a cashier.

When it was clear to me that I would write an article about empowerment in India and about the SMS project, I tried to get in contact with somebody in charge. Fortunately, I could meet a student from the Tata Institute. Yanath helped to build two more Nisargruna. We had a good talk about the Nisargruna and the SMS canteens. Furthermore, he gave me some information about *Parisar Vikas* and *Stree Mukti Sanghatana* and the impact these projects have on the women involved. He also helped me to arrange an interview with three women from the SMS Canteen. I wanted to hear and see by myself how the project changed the life of the former rag pickers and if it is possible to detect some ideas from the empowerment approach. Laxmi, a student from Tata Institute, helped me to translate from Marathi into English and vice versa.

One of my interview partners was Leela.[5] She has worked for four years at the SMS canteen and was not sure about her age. I estimated her age between 40 and 45 years. Purnima was 29 and likewise has worked for four years in the canteen. Before that, she had stayed at home. Through her sister-in-law she came to know the project and organization. She was looking for a job and found one that suits her. Leela used to sell garlic before she joined the project. Laxmi, Rafina, Purnima, Leela and Sita, a former rag picker now also working at the canteen, were sitting with me in front of the canteen. When I asked the second question, Sita started answering for Leela and Purnima. Throughout the whole interview these two were looking at Sita before they told me anything. The question asked was if there is any improvement in their lives since they work at SMS. They answered that they felt more independent and had the feeling that they do not depend on somebody else. Their self-esteem changed and the process of changing felt very good. Very interestingly, Sita at first did not tell her name nor told anything about her time at SMS. From time to time she emphasized very clearly and loudly that the women's life had improved a lot since they joined the project. When I asked for any training or education, Leela and Purnima denied. Rafina attended an education programme since some months. There still is a split between the group of women at SMS. Women who went to school or have some knowledge of writing and math are given the job as cashier. The others do all kinds of work, cleaning, serving and cooking. So far, the SMS programme does not intend to enable women without any education to improve in basic arithmetic or in writing.

Discussion

Empowerment is a complex topic containing economical, social, political and psychological ideas and notions. The term empowerment has been established over the last decades. Especially in Longwe's framework it is obvious that conscientization is the key for empowerment. The most important detail in the process of empowerment is whether one has power over one's own action, to have self-confidence and to believe in oneself. The project presented shows very clearly how important it is to teach women a sense of conscientization and self-confidence. Of course one cannot forget the social constraints. Especially at this point, further projects need adjustment. The concept of empowerment is based on the idea of creating capabilities for the ones having none or few. If that happens, the process of empowerment will be successful. As the Italian pedagogue Maria Montessori put it, 'Help me to do it by myself!'

Notes

1 'Labour force refers to the 15–59 age group that reports that they are working, or looking for work, according to the "weekly status" definition of employment' (Bhalla and Kaur: 7).
2 1 Lac = Rs 100,000; Rs 20 Lacs are about €.28.860
3 The following link shows an example of a Nisargruna: http://www.thehindu.com/sci-tech/science/efficient-way-to-turn-waste-into-resource/article4006137.ece.
4 Maharati is the local language. Every state in India has its own language with different grammar and vocabulary. In north and central India, the spoken language is mostly Hindi. English is common throughout India.
5 Names in this chapter are changed.

References

Arnold, F., Kishor, S., and Roy, T.K. (2002): Sex-Selective Abortions in India. Population and Development Review 28 (4): 759–785.

Beteille, A. (1999): Empowerment. Economic & Political Weekly 34: 589–597.

Boserup, E. (1970): Woman's Role in Economic Development. London: Allen & Unwin.

Bystydzienski, J. (1992): Women Transforming Politics Worldwide Strategies for Empowerment. Blooming Transforming Politics Worldwide Strategies for Empowerment. Bloomington, Indianapolis: Indiana University Press, 24–40.

Campillo, F. (1993): Gender, Women and Development. A Framework for IICA's Action in Latin America and the Caribbean. Instituto Interamericano de Cooperación para la Agricultura.

Friedmann, J. (1992): Empowerment. The Politics of an Alternative Development. Oxford: Basil Blackwell.

Joekes, S. P. (1990): Excerpts on Women in Development: International Development Strategy for the Third United Nations Development Decade. INSTRAW study. New York: Oxford University Press.

Kabeer, N. (1990): Gender, Development and Training: Raising Awareness in Development Planning. GAADU Newspack 14.

Kalyani Menon-Sen, A., and Shiva Kumar, K. (2001): Women in India: How Free? How Equal? United Nations. Report commissioned by the Office of the Resident Coordinator in India.

Kapur Mehta, A. (1996): Recasting Indices for Developing Countries: A Gender Empowerment Measure. Economic and Political Weekly 31 (43): WS80–WS86.

Longwe, S. (1995): Gender Awareness: The Missing Element in the Third World Development Program. In: C. March, and T. Wallace (eds): Changing Perception: New Writings on Gender and Development. Oxford: Oxfam, 149–157.

Molyneux, M. (1985): Mobilization without Emancipation? Women's Interests, the State, and Revolution in Nicaragua. In: Feminist Studies 11 (2): 227–254.

Patel, V. (n.d.): Human Development and Gender. Mumbai: Women's University.

Pattnaik, A. K. P. (1996): Women in Development. In: Tripathy, S. N. (ed.): Unorganised Women Labour in India, 42–52. New Delhi: Discovery Publishing House.

Sharma, S. L. (2000): Empowerment without Antagonism: A Case for Reformulation of Women's Empowerment Approach. Sociological Bulletin 49 (1): 19–39.

Singh, S. (2007): Schooling Girls and the Gender and Development Paradigm: Quest for an Appropriate Framework for Women Education. Journal of Interdisciplinary Social Sciences 2 (3): 1–12.

Singh, S., and Hoge, G. (2010): Debating Outcomes for Working Women. Illustration from India. The Journal of Poverty 14 (2): 197–215.

The Hindu (2010): Rajya Sabha passes Women's Reservation Bill. Chennai, India.

Weekes-Vagliani, W. (1985): The Integration of Women in Development Projects. Paris: OECD Publishing.

World Wide Web References

Bhalla, Surjit S., and Kaur, R.: http://www.lse.ac.uk/asiaResearchCentre/_files/ARCWP40-BhallaKaur.pdf. (June 20, 2013).

Bhatt, J. N. (2006): Gender Justice: Human rights perspective triumph or turmoil; victory or vanquished: http://www.ebcindia.com/practicallawyer/index2.phpoption=com_content&itemid=1&do_pdf=1&id=938.

CEDAW: http://www.pdhre.org/conventionsum/cedaw.html (May 29, 2012).

Census (2001): http://web.archive.org/web/2004060621364C/http://www.censusindia.net/results/provindia2.html (May 29, 2012).

Census (2011): http://southasia.oneworld.net/news/india-census-data-reveals-lowest-child-sex-ratio-in-64-years#.Ui2iEcbIbDw (May 29, 2012).

The Indian Express (2008): Residents protest fire at Deonar dumping ground. (March 25, 2008).

Iqbal, A. (2007): Bride Burning – in the name of dowry: http://aishaiqbal.blogspot.de/2007/02/bride-burning.html (May 29, 2012).

Ridge, M. (2010): http://www.csmonitor.com/World/Asia-South-Central/2010/0308/Gender-selection-In-India-abortion-of-girls-on-the-rise (May 30, 2012).

Sustainable Development Dimension: Asia's women in agriculture, environment and rural production: http://www.fao.org/sd/WPdirect/WPre0108.htmhttp://www.fao.org/sd/WPdirect/WPre0108.htm (May 30, 2012).

SP Working Paper (2005): http://www.scribd.com/kshitij_raj/d/50850429/11-Parisar-Vikas-Programme P.29 (May 29, 2012).

United Nations (1998): Shifting views of women and development. Africa Recovery: http://www.un.org/en/africarenewal/bpaper/boxseng.htm (May 29, 2012).

United Nations, Beijing 1: http://www.un.org/womenwatch/daw/beijing/ (May 29, 2012).

United Nations, Beijing 2: http://www.un.org/womenwatch/daw/beijing/fwcwn.html (May 29, 2012).

United Nations, Beijing 3: http://www.un.org/womenwatch/daw/beijing/beijingdeclaration.html (May 29, 2012).

UN Women: http://www.un.org/womenwatch/daw/daw/index.html (May 29, 2012).

Varma, G. (2008): 43 Industrial Clusters imperiled in India. Daily News and Analysis. http://www.dnaindia.com/india/report-43-industrial-clusters-imperiled-in-india-1327305 (May 29, 2012).

World Bank (2012): https://siteresources.worldbank.org/INTWDR2012/Resources/7778105-1299699968583/7786210-1315936222006/Complete-Report.pdf (June 19, 2013).

25
THE NEW AND YOUNG INDIAN MIDDLECLASS
Life between traditions and Western values

Christiane Müller

Trying to get access to and understanding about Indian culture, society, history and reality while being in Mumbai, I soon was confronted with the subject: young Indians, being the first generation living their life out of traditional patterns. At first sight, similarities to this young urban Indian generation seemed to exist more to my parents-generation than to my own: breaking narrow rules and traditions, searching for new ways of living and fighting for more personal freedom reminds of the agenda of the movement of 1968. But at the same time technology has extremely changed – the 1960s with Internet and mobile phone would have been completely different for sure – and the objectives of the new search are very different in the end.

I got interested in the biographies of those young Indian people. How do they cope with the gap between tradition on the one hand and self-development and individual life conception on the other? Or is this *gap* just interpretation out of my Western socialization point of view? And if there is a gap, would that fact automatically mean a conflict for them? Or is it just another one of the country's inherent contradictions, which they can easily overcome in their life?

This chapter mainly has two concerns: first, the methodological ideas and access I used. The important point hereby is not the content of the interviews, but the conclusions about doing qualitative social research in a different cultural setting. Second, the Indian middle class itself. I will give a historical overview of its development and roots, and finally an orientation concerning the present day and some peculiarities of this class relevant to Indian society.

Methodological confusions and tricky access

Together with Ronja Wäsch, we did seven narrative interviews[1] with young Indian men of the new middleclass, aged between the mid-twenties and the mid-thirties. While having the idea of doing biographical-narrative interviews in the way I knew, we immediately got confronted with some differences and seemingly cultural peculiarities. It made me think that – generally speaking – we cannot transfer methodological concepts one-to-one to another cultural setting. There were two main points of 'disturbance' for doing the interviews: the first concerns the female–male constellation, and the second, the conception of self-reflection.

First, there happened to be only male interview-partners. The public in India is very male dominated even in Mumbai. And as life there differs very much depending on your being a man or a woman, we decided to focus on the male perspective, not least because our access to men was much easier than finding enough women for a similar request.

Bourdieu says, if one tries to understand what one is doing when entering an interview-relation, in the first instance this will be the attempt to recognize the effects one is provoking automatically through this *invading and intervening* which always is somewhat arbitrary and constitutes the starting point of any exchange (especially by the way to present oneself and the interview, by giving or refusing encouragement etc.) (Bourdieu 1997: 781).[2]

To me, these effects seem to be even stronger in our case: being women (and more than that, white-skinned, evoking a lot of additional unwanted attention in India) in a country where there are cultural and moral codes in a girl–boy situation; where eye-contact easily gets misunderstood as flirting instead of being a simple sign for paying full attention and listening. Where you unknowingly might ask about a very sensitive topic and still get an answer, because your interview-partner just is very polite. How do these facts influence the interview?

Second, the fact that probably had the main impact on the results of the interviews is that in India there is no concept of individuality comparable to the one we are used to in a Western context.[3] We basically grow up with self-reflection, self-development – a life-long way to self-perfection.

Being aware now that traditionally there is a completely different notion of individuality in the Asian area, it becomes obvious that a biographical-narrative interview, with only one opening question at best case scenario, is very likely to be unsuccessful. So we decided for a methodological compromise: a mixture between a narrative and a guideline-based interview. After the entrance-question with the request to tell his life, we improvised questions according to what the interviewee said. According to our topic, 'a life between tradition and Western values', we focused on questions about what sorts of Western/modern influences are appreciated and which traditions are considered to be important on a personal level. Are there any conflicts between tradition and modern lifestyle? And if so, when and where do they become visible? And last about the role of the family in one's life, relationship and friendship.

Having made these experiences, I may say that there cannot be something like a universal method which can be used in every cultural setting for doing qualitative social research. Cultural and social differences in society-structures must be kept in mind for finding an understanding approach and a different focus on Asia. Realizing this is a precondition for doing research.

The following lines may be seen as an extract of the studies I did to understand this country that is so difficult to understand. I am aware of the fact that it is just one perspective, but it shall give a brief introduction into the phenomena of the Indian middleclass and some cultural backgrounds.

Short middleclass history

India is a country full of contrasts. This is straightaway obvious, among other things, in the contrast between the rich and the poor and in conflicting ways of life according to either ancient traditions or notions of Western-world progress in the big cities. While in rural areas life is structured by religious values and, despite official repeal, by the old caste-system, people in urban areas get more and more chances for multiple ways of living and alignment to Western-capitalistic lifestyles.

The people of this new way of living are mainly members of the so-called 'new middleclass' (Varma 1998; Kreuser 2002). In the beginning of the twenty-first century, this new class emerged under the influence of some economic liberalizations and also due to the access to the new Western[4] media and the Internet.

However, the Indian middleclass is not a new phenomenon. It dates back to the times of British colonialism. From 1835 onwards the English started to create a native elite. Its members were supposed to be mediators between the colony rulers and the Indian population and should help to control the masses.

> It is impossible for us, with our limited means, to attempt to educate the body of the people. We must at present do our best to form a class who may be interpreters between us and the millions we govern; a class of persons, Indian in blood and colour, but English in taste, in opinions, in morals, and in intellect.
>
> Macaulay (1835)

This English-created Indian middleclass did not only learn the language of the occupants. It started to copy the lifestyle of the Englishmen, who were convinced of their own superiority, in the hope to find admittance to the selected circle of society-members.

> They sought access to the employment opportunities it provided; they were appreciative of the civilizational values it stood for and envious of its material achievements; they hankered for social acceptance within the paternalistic framework it promised and were unashamedly emulative of the lifestyle of those sent to govern them.
>
> Varma (1998: 5)

Thus being guided by the life of the English, already in the nineteenth century a cultural conflict emerged for these members of the Indian middleclass: turning away from their traditional origins and their solidarity with their country and its people, they were not respected by the invaders as equivalent (cf. ibid.: 6f.).

Consuming for boom: the new middleclass

Since 1991, the Indian middleclass took on greater significance through some economic reforms heading for more integration of Indian economy into the world economy and an opening towards the Western world (cf. Varma 1998: 171ff.). Their propensity to consume was discovered and became a main condition for an economical boom. In the beginning of the twenty-first century, the proportion of the Indian middleclass amounted to about 10 per cent of the country's entire population.[5] These figures might seem sort of small, but it is the class with the biggest economic and political influence (cf. Tieber 2007: 213).

Rachel Dywer, professor for Indian Culture and Film, subdivides the Indian middleclass into three categories. In the context of this chapter, only the first two of them – the old and the new middleclass – are of some importance.

According to Dywer, the old middleclass nowadays would work mainly in bureaucracy, medicine and journalism, be secular, have cultural capital,[6] a civil mentality and a democratic political attitude. They would control the cultural values of India, since they worked in the administration, educational system and cultural institutions (cf. Tieber 2007: 123ff.).

In contrast to the old, the new middleclass (Dywer also calls them 'Bombay's Rich') would work mainly in the media sector. Different from the old middleclass, they would have economical, but hardly any cultural capital. Nevertheless, it would be the new middleclass that sets the new standards in India's public culture. They define what is culturally recognized and by that challenge the values of the old middleclass. This cultural conflict is to be seen in the refusal of the 'new' culture by the old middleclass (ibid.: 123ff.).

Since the membership to this new middleclass in a wider sense is defined through consumerism,[7] economical capital seems to be the most important thing to achieve (cf. Varma 1998: 170f.). As a consequence, the boarders of the caste-system gradually got (and still get) looser, especially through the increasing importance of the IT-sector.

A problematic side of this materialistic development is shown by the Indian author and ambassador Pavan K. Varma in his book about the Indian middleclass: the lifestyle of the elites[8] is becoming a role model for the Indian middleclass, for which the Gandhi-era with its maxim of simple life is over. 'Now it was state policy to "open" the economy to the objects of desire. Consumerism was sanctified because the middle class' ability to consume was an index to progress. Material wants were suddenly severed from any notion of guilt' (Varma 1998: 175).

Varma poses the question, why hunger, diseases and poverty of millions of people do not make a lasting impression on the privileged classes. While they are living their hedonism, the poor get poorer and the rich richer (ibid.: 196ff.). So there is a tension between increasing materialism and wealth for some and the social and environmental disasters for the others.

But tension does not only emerge on the publically visible political-social side, it also emerges in the interior of this class. This comes into view when a whole generation of young Indians is moving between the temptation of material possessions with all their comfort on the one side, and traditional values on the other. According to Kreuser, the new middleclass – different from the old – is not secular adjusted and combines consumerism with religious traditions. The worlds of 'sari and short skirt' seem to be compatible for the young generation. They would easily combine *American Style* with *Indian Taste*, go to the ceremonies in the temple and next watch MTV at home (cf. Kreuser 2002: 74).[9]

Despite all these new freedoms, especially those of the personal way to live apart of the narrow traditional system and to be oriented towards the Western lifestyle in the metropolis, the manners between man and woman still seem to follow a strict moralistic, religious and conservative behaviour code. Representations of love and sexuality are still a taboo and are expressed in the classical Bollywood movie only encoded in the obligatory song and dance sequences (cf. Borsos 2010).

Even though there is a lot of change in India, there also is a 3,000 years old mythological-religious tradition still present, conveying the idea of values and structures to the everyday life of a Hindu (cf. Gudermuth 2003: 10).

All in all, one may say that on the one hand, new biographical concepts seem to become more and more conceivable, as well as they are realized – so there is more freedom to create your life according to your imaginations. On the other hand, there are but few role models for this kind of individuality in Indian society, and a lot of predetermined expectations by the family and assigned responsibilities to deal with at the same time.

So, for example, an arranged marriage still is appreciated by many young people of the new middleclass and does not necessarily seem to bring them into conflict with a Western orientated lifestyle. That might be rooted in the fact that in South Asia a person traditionally is not seen as an individual, but as a part of a whole. So love relations are not seen as the exclusive relationship between two individuals, but refer to all family members (cf. Gudermuth 2003: 123).

Ultimately, the concept of individuality is a Western model that gets increasingly adapted, lived and by that newly designed by the Indian middleclass. But in the end this difference in the notion of individuality might be the biggest difference between *the West* and *the East* and needs to become a strong point of awareness when trying to understand a different cultural setting.

Notes

1 Narrative interviews were first developed by Fritz Schütze and got popular especially through the Sociology department of the Chicago School. For detailed further information see Bohnsack (2008: 91ff.).
2 My translation, since there is no English translation of this text. German orig.: 'Wenn man versucht zu verstehen, was man tut, wenn man eine Interviewbeziehung eingeht, bedeutet dies zunächst einmal den Versuch, die Effekte zu erkennen, die man unwillkürlich durch dieses *Eindringen und Sicheinmischen* ausübt, welches immer ein wenig beliebig ist und den Ausgangspunkt jeden Austausches bildet (besonders durch die Art und Weise, sich und die Umfrage zu präsentieren, durch zugestandene oder verweigerte Ermutigungen usw.).'
3 I will get back to the concept of individuality in the passage about the new Indian middleclass.
4 The term 'western' refers here and in the following to the whole Western world, including Europe and USA, with its attached values like freedom, individualism, democracy, capitalism and free enterprise economy.
5 Figures concerning this class differ very much. According to Müller, the number most frequently quoted in India is 300 million. So nearly one-third of the population would be neither poor nor really rich in relation to average Indian incomes. If you compare this to Western incomes, the middleclass still would amount to 60 million people – more than the French population (cf. Müller 2006: 24f.).

6 The author refers to Bourdieu's categories of capital (economical, social, cultural and symbolic capital).
7 According to Müller, it still needs some time till India overcomes the caste-system completely. But especially young Indians would substitute caste-thinking step-by-step by individualism and materialism (cf. Müller 2006: 21).
8 These trends are set not only by the rich in politics and free economy, but also by the stars of Bollywood.
9 In that respect, following the Indian news, I would think that the 'easy combination' of modern and traditional lifestyle described above is possible for the lucky privileged urban few and thus is rather an exception than a general rule.

References

Bohnsack, Ralf (2008): Rekonstruktive Sozialforschung. Opladen, Farmington Hills: Barbara Budrich.
Borsos, Stefan (2010): Geraubte Küsse. Notizen zum Filmkuss im Bollywoodfilm. http://www.schnitt.de/211,0060,02 (January 23, 2011).
Bourdieu, Pierre (1997): Verstehen. In: Das Elend der Welt (ed.). Zeugnisse und Diagnosen alltäglichen Leidens an der Gesellschaft. Konstanz: UVK, 779–822.
Gudermuth, Kerstin (2003): Kultur der Liebe in Indien. Leidenschaft und Hingabe in Hindu-Mythologie und Gegenwart. Münster: LIT.
Kreuser, Gabriele (2002): Der Schlüssel zum indischen Markt. Mentalität und Kultur verstehen, erfolgreich verhandeln. Wiesbaden: Gabler.
Macaulay, Thomas B. (1835): Minute on Indian Education. http://www.columbia.edu/itc/mealac/pritchett/00generallinks/macaulay/txt_minute_education_1835.html (February 10, 2011).
Müller, Oliver (2006): Wirtschaftsmacht Indien: Chance und Herausforderung für uns. München: Hanser.
Tieber, Claus (2007): Passages to Bollywood. Einführung in den Hindi-Film. Berlin: LIT.
Varma, Pavan K. (1998): The Great Indian Middleclass. New Delhi/New York: Viking.

26
RISK-TAKING AND ENTREPRENEURSHIP IN INDIA
Implications of social and cultural norms for poverty alleviation policies

Alexander J. Wulf[1]

The aim of this study is to contribute towards developing an in-depth theory of the social and cultural norms that govern risk-taking and innovative behaviour in India, a field in which there has been little research to date. Qualitative data on this aspect of Indian entrepreneurial culture were collected in the Bangalore, Chennai, Delhi and Mumbai industrial regions. The study is mainly based on qualitative expert interviews and participant observation of entrepreneurs. The chapter introduces the whole study and presents first findings from an in-depth analysis of the risk-taking behaviour of two Indian managers. The chapter is part of a larger comparative study whose aim is to compare the social norms that govern risk-taking behaviour in India, Japan and Germany.

Introduction

Risk and risk management are often regarded as technical issues. To date they are primarily discussed from a legal and economic perspective (Bernstein 1996; Steele 2004). The failure of many sophisticated theoretical approaches to risk management was characteristic for the recent financial crisis. Institutionalized risk management systems could not prevent major economic losses and the ensuing threats to the global financial system (Taleb 2007). One of the main reasons for the failure of these systems was their lack of response to cultural issues and social norms. Even though both matters are important determinants of excessive risk-taking behaviour they are neither well understood nor taken into account by common risk prevention approaches (Fraedrich and Ferrell

1992; Rao 2006). An understanding of different risk mentalities may therefore help to prevent excessive risk-taking and subsequent crises in the future. However, if on the contrary the social norms and the cultural values that govern risk-taking behaviour are too strict, this also adversely affects society. It may not allow businessmen to engage in innovative behaviour (Memili et al. 2010), which to a certain extent involves risk-taking and the transition of existing social norms (Dess and Lumpkin 2005). Hence, innovators and employees of innovative businesses are constantly subject to the tension between the need to adhere to social norms and cultural values and the necessity of taking risks in order to innovate. An understanding of this principle problem may contribute towards creating a socioeconomic environment that encourages appropriate risk-taking and stimulates innovation. In the long term this leads to economic growth and the welfare of society (Schumpeter 1949, 1975).

To establish a risk management practice that embraces cultural considerations, we have to understand how managers from different cultural backgrounds think and feel about risk. We may learn about principal differences in attitudes towards risk across countries by observing the approaches that managers take in their struggle to cope with risk and the uncertainty they face. These observations will not only teach us about differing risk cultures, but also help us to identify and characterize those cultural traditions and social norms that form an individual's risk mentality (Hofstede et al. 2010). This knowledge will guide us through the variety of global risk mentalities and may serve as a starting point for adapting risk management practices to the cultural challenges that globalization brings about.

India, the world largest democracy, is a country with a long history and rich culture. Even though the country shares many political and economic problems with other developing countries it has an astonishingly unique character. India's religious beliefs, rituals, traditional social structures and cultures are incredibly complex (Gupta1994: xi). A small-scale, qualitative study like the one presented in this chapter faces the problem that it is extremely difficult to pay respect to this complexity, while still making generalizations about Indian business culture. I therefore classify my empirical results as exploratory. Exploratory empirical research is an approach to the analysis of empirical data that aims to develop theories rather than to test them. It is motivated by a desire to search for clues and evidence about the phenomena at stake, thereby maintaining the greatest possible flexibility throughout the analysis in order to obtain new insights. Exploratory empirical research is necessary because it identifies relevant issues for future research (Flick 2006: 11–12). Nevertheless, Indian businessmen generally do share a common body of beliefs, attitudes and expectations that is essentially cohesive and uniquely Indian. Even though over the past decades Indian managers more and more adopted Western style approaches to management, there is and probably always will be an intrinsically Indian way to management. For example, in contrast to the Western tradition, the Indian approach does not only appraise the rational but also embrace the spiritual. Indian businessmen are also exceptional in bringing together self-interest and social affection in a way that is alien to other, for example, Western approaches to management (Gupta 1994: 23, 48).

In the following sections I will first discuss my methodology and research design and then introduce the two companies and their Chief Executive Officers (CEO), who are the main subjects of this chapter. I will then present the main statements from several in-depth interviews with these CEOs on their risk-taking behaviour and Indian management philosophy in general. I conclude with a summary of my main findings and how these may contribute to our understanding of the Indian risk mentality.

Methodology

This study employs a qualitative, exploratory research design. Its aim is to investigate how the social and cultural norms that govern risk-taking behaviour in India affect innovative behaviour. I selected my interview partners in a way that would allow me to obtain an illustrative picture of Indian risk mentality. Applying the grounded theory approach (Corbin and Strauss 2008), I recruited new interview partners throughout the research. I thereby continuously adapted my selection criteria according to the results of my analysis of the previous interviews. This gave me the flexibility to construct a corpus of interview data that was capable to cover the complexity of Indian risk mentality, despite the difficulty of this task (see also the introduction). Once the topics and patterns that were upcoming during the interviews started to repeat and including additional interviews that would not have led to new insights, I stopped my data collection. My corpus had reached saturation and was sufficiently large to allow an initial analysis of Indian risk mentality (Bauer and Aarts 2000). The first interviews were conducted with interview partners easy to reach. These were managers of small and medium-sized family-owned businesses, who were recommended to me by fellow academics, colleagues and friends. One main source for recruiting the first interviewees was a befriended attorney who recommended the clients of his law firm, where he worked as a managing partner, to me. Once I had gained an initial feeling for Indian risk mentality I tried to get in touch with managers of enterprises that were, for example, larger in size, operating in certain industries or regions, or had other characteristics that were of special interest to my research project. As these interview partners were harder to reach, I had to turn to official contacts to get in touch with them. These were, for example, chambers of commerce, embassies, business directories, and business contacts of other interview participants. In what follows, I present the first, preliminary findings from interviews with two Indian managers.

Risk-taking and poverty: life experiences of an Indian businessman

The following interview is an example of a manager who was forced into business life by material needs. His main motivation in business is to ensure the well-being of his family. The interview illustrates how a lack in formal university and management education is offset by a vision of personal goals and a strong desire to succeed. One key outcome of the interview is that a manager's perception of risk and his personal risk-taking behaviour substantially depend on his personal social and economic background. Connected to this is the insight that a person's economic situation and his personal visions may play an important role in overcoming the fear to take risk.

About the company

Lightning Protection Company was founded in 2004. On its webpage, the company describes itself as a supplier and service provider for lightning and power protection equipment. Its headquarter is located in India's capital, New Delhi. Lightning Protection Company has another branch office in India's technology hub Bangalore and maintains a distribution network across the country, for example, in Chennai, Coimbatore, Hyderabad, Mumbai and Trivandrum. The company's main revenues come from the import and subsequent trading of electric equipment. A smaller part of the revenue comes from consultation and installation service and the manufacturing of a few own products. Lightning Protection Company's main customers are from the defence, power, telecommunication and transportation industry. The company has two co-CEOs, one of them is the company's founder and the other is his partner who joined the company a few years after its foundation. Both share equal responsibility and run the business like a partnership. The company states that it has drastically increased in value over the last years now reaching a total capital of more than INR 35,000,000 (€485.470/$641.320).

About the interviewee and interview setting

My interview partner is the founder and one of the two co-CEOs at Lightning Protection Company. At the time of the interview he was about

35 years old. The interviewee comes from a simple family. His father was the owner of a small store which just made enough money to buy food for the family. Being the oldest son it was the interviewee's responsibility to take care of his three sisters and his much younger brother. At the early stages in his career, his main economic concern was to earn enough money to support the family and to get his three sisters married. Because of this burden he could only attend high school for 10 years. After graduating, he was not able to go to university but nevertheless managed to obtain a diploma in electrical engineering by completing a short-term course. Recently his business has developed well. The interviewee states the main reason for his success was that he had no other chance but to succeed; his whole family was depending on him. Due to the relatively small age difference between me and the interviewee, the interview atmosphere was very relaxed. Throughout the interview, the interviewee was very friendly and answered all questions straight forward in a down-to-earth manner. He explained that he has never participated in an academic study before and showed some pride to be interviewed.

There were several meetings between me and the CEOs of Lightning Protection. Most of the meetings took place in India but we also met twice when he visited Germany for business purposes. However, the main interviews on which the following analysis is based were conducted during two meetings in India. The first one took place after the interviewee had invited me for lunch at a luxury hotel in Bangalore. The second considerably shorter interview took place during a visit to one of the interviewee's business partners in Delhi to whom he had recommended me for a further interview. After we had finished our lunch in the hotel's restaurant, we went to a meeting area located in one corner of the hotel's lobby, a large hall. We were largely undisturbed during the entire interview except for some general noises coming from the hotel's lobby. During the entire meeting, the interview's attorney (who had helped me to arrange the interview) was present. Throughout the interview the attorney remained in the background except for a short comment towards the end of the interview. Some time had passed between both meetings and the interviewee had reflected on my questions. He felt the need to elaborate on some topics that we had talked about during our first meeting.

Results from the interview

The interviewee's self-perception as a businessman is strongly connected to his social background. He emphasizes that for him it was not a voluntary decision to go into business. He had no other option because his entire family was economically dependent on him. The interviewee explains that this may be the very reasons why he became successful in business and at risk-taking. To clarify, he tells me the following parable which expresses a sense of religious belief in fate. A lion and a rabbit live in the jungle. They are good friends and they always spend their time together. One day a flood comes ruining all food supplies. The lion says to the rabbit: 'Listen, you are my friend, but God created me in a way that I have to hunt. I am made like this. So I have to eat you. Do you understand? Didn't God make me like this?' The rabbit responds: 'Yes, God made you like this. But why do you want to eat me? We have been friends for so long.' The lion responds: 'I have no food. I am hungry, I need to eat something. I am made to hunt if I am hungry. That is how God has made me.' The rabbit responds: 'Ok. I understand. God has made you to hunt rabbits when you are hungry. But God also made me to run for my life if I am hunted. Do you agree, this is how God has made me?' The lion responds: 'I agree. So you run and I will hunt you. We will both do what God has made us for.' So the rabbit starts to run, the lion chases it. The rabbit runs very fast and the lion can't catch it. The rabbit then crawls into a hole under a tree, where it is safe from the lion. When the lion arrives at its hideout it says 'Come out'. The rabbit responds: 'No, you will eat me if I come out.' Lion: 'No, you are faster than me, I see I can't catch you, I won't eat you, we can be friends again.' The rabbit comes out and the lions says: 'I don't understand it. I am made to hunt if I am hungry and still I couldn't catch you because you were faster. How can that be?' The rabbit answers: 'Well, the reason is, we were both doing what God has made us for: I was running, you were hunting. But I was running for my life, you simply to feed your hunger.' The interviewee argues that this story is also his own story. He had no other option than to take risks and to succeed in business life simply because his whole family depended on him. These social considerations now also determine his overall attitude towards risk taking. 'In my business life, I always take very calculated risk. Emotionally you are bound to a lot of responsibilities, with your parents, your brothers, sisters, wife, wife's parents and everything. So you have a responsibility on your shoulder at the stage of starting your career. We have to take risk keeping all this into the back of our minds: if I slipped down, whether I would be able to cater the basic needs of my people surrounding me.'

Nevertheless, the interviewee accepts risk taking as a necessity in business life, stating that 'if there is no risk, there is no survival.' Emotionally, risk decisions do not upset him because he believes that occasionally risk decisions may turn out wrong but in the long term taking risks always pays off. On the contrary, when he takes risk he often gets excited because taking risks is for him tantamount to realizing a plan that he had carefully laid out and envisioned. 'When I take this kind of decisions, I feel excited: "Okay, I am investing in my dreams." So, even my wife says "you are a big dreamer." You know Abdul Kalam? He is the father of scientists in India, he is one of the renowned scientists, who said "dream a lot, dream will come into thoughts, thoughts will come into action and ultimately the action will come into result".' The interviewee states that usually he does not explicitly puzzle out the best solution to a situation that involves risk nor does he take preconditions for the case that a risk materializes. For him it is sufficient to envision his overall goal. When doing so, he considers whatever is necessary for the realization of this goal and he accepts the risks that go hand in hand with his plan. For this reason, the interviewee argues that to envision a goal and to dream about its realization in every detail is an essential precondition for successful risk taking. 'Unless and until you don't dream you don't plan. So when we invest, when we take risk, the risk has been already previewed as if you made a film in your mind. And if you are investing in your film it is not an unknown risk, it has already been taken care of in your brain. [. . .] I never mind the result, I never mind whether it's going to cheat me [. . .] That would mean that you will never ever be able to take any decision in your life. So I feel excited when I do it because it's my dream and I am investing in it. Yeah, always I feel excited to do that.'

Risk-taking, the caste system and the North–South Indian divide: thoughts of a social entrepreneur

The following interview describes the interviewee's general observations on the Indian risk-taking mentality. The interviewee is in a good position to comment on how regional and caste difference affect individuals' risk-taking behaviour. In his earlier professional life, he was in charge of screening officer candidates in the Indian armed forces – among others for their risk-taking and decision-making abilities. Also, his present work in the education sector brings him together with a large variety of young trainees from different social backgrounds and from across India. The interviewee's generalizations on Indian risk mentality are based on his own observations. They are introduced to provide the reader with a general orientation on the influence of social and cultural values on risk-taking behaviour in India. Future research has to show whether these generalizations also hold for the entire population of Indian managers.

About the company

Vocational Education Company is a social enterprise established in 2009. It provides education to disadvantaged social groups, especially to high school drop outs and illiterates who cannot otherwise succeed on the job market. Students are recruited from across the country through a far-reaching network that also covers rural areas. Selection criteria are the motivation and the aspiration of students and not their formal qualifications which many of them lack. The company's aim is to teach skills that are required by the market and that will help students to obtain lifelong employability in the formal or informal sector of Indian economy. The company's vocational training focuses on practical skills that are taught in a semi-formal way in cooperation with partners from the business community. It primarily cooperates with eight industrial sectors, among them agriculture, construction, trade, IT and accounting. The company operates more than 65 nationwide centres and has up to now taught over 18,000 students in its training programmes. It is financed by public and private funds.

About the interviewee and the interview setting

My interview partner is the head of operations of one of Vocational Education Company's largest training centres. At his branch, he has responsibility for around 120 employees. Before he took up his position at the company he held several different positions in various industries. He began his career in the Indian army where he was among others involved in screening officer candidates. After leaving the armed forces, he started his own travelling company which offered adventure and extreme sports tours. He then joined a start-up company that sold corporate travel and housing solutions across India. Shortly after the interview, the interviewee left Vocational Education Company and started his own enterprise in the same field. The interview took place in an industrial area of Delhi. The company's branch office is located in a medium-sized business building that is entirely occupied by the company. The building is functional and lacks architectural finesse. Even though the interview took place outside regular business hours many employees were still vigorously pursuing their work. The interviewee is a charismatic leader of about 50 years of age. He wears casual business attire and smiles a lot throughout the interview. The interviewee is very motivated to participate in the interview and he eagerly develops and contributes his own thoughts.

Results from the interview

The interview primarily addresses the social and cultural issues that affect risk-taking in India. The interviewee points out that already when he served in the Indian Armed Forces he noted differences in the risk-taking abilities of officer candidates according to castes and regions. Even though these differences were not clear cut and there were always exemptions, general tendencies could be identified that also held later on in his business life. He argues that, generally speaking, people from North India are risk-loving, whereas people from South India are rather risk-averse. These differences in risk appetites may partly be explained by the historical developments in these regions. In North India there has been more migration and social unrest than in the South. People were forced to migrate and whenever they came to new places they had to build a new life and start businesses to sustain their living. '[T]here have been wars, [. . .] in '71, lots of migrants came into Delhi [. . .] When these guys came in, first thing they started was business, because there were no jobs. And their ability to take [. . .] risks is much higher because they [. . .] invested wherever they could and they kept exploring. So that sense of exploring, I think the risk-taking abilities are inherited from that.' The interviewee explains that in contrast to the North, the South of India was historically less affected by wars and migration. This made people more cautious and also affected how they explore business opportunities. 'In fact, when you go to Bangalore, you will find a lot of North Indians going downwards into the South. But you will find very few South Indians coming up to the North and taking over businesses.' The interviewee points out, however, that the ongoing globalization of the business world influences these regional tendencies. The interaction with Western companies in India and Indian employees who are sent abroad bring new ways of thinking to the traditional Indian business world. To substantiate this thought the interviewee quotes the example of Infosys, a major Indian IT company. He claims the company traditionally, i.e. under the management of its co-founder Narayana Murthy, was rather conservative, but this changed as soon as the company spread its activities around the globe, especially when it reached for the US market.

The interviewee then turns on to talk about how caste membership affects individuals' willingness and ability to deal with risk. It shall be noted that the Indian caste system is a complex social system. The interviewee's descriptions can therefore only serve as a starting point to explain how caste membership affects risk-taking behaviour. For example, especially in South India the caste system may be more complex and it may thus not be possible to describe this system in a comprehensive manner by the introduced four castes categorization scheme. Nevertheless, the interviewee states: 'I would agree that castes play a role [. . .]. Basically there are four castes: Brahmins, who are at the top. Then you have the warriors, [. . .] who have always been fighting for winning battles. Then you have the people who do business. And then you have the lower castes. That is how our society is divided. [. . .] Every strata of the society has different ability to take risk.' The interviewee explains that by tendency individuals from the Brahmin (priest) caste are risk-averse. 'In the history of our culture, they have occupied high positions [. . .] and they were supposed to be preaching to us and they [. . .] were generally comfortable in life. [. . .] They have got whatever they wanted and they probably won't like to lose it. Whatever interaction I've had with them, risk taking abilities have been very, very low. Generally, they would not get into any kind of venture. You find these people working [. . .] in government jobs, you know, these kinds of things where there are no risks.' In contrast, the interviewee explains members from the Vaisya (merchants) caste are good risk takers. 'When you talk of risk taking ability in terms of business then you will find this merchant class that comes in, who have been doing business for a long time. [. . . They] probably go for more calculated risks. They would weigh. Before taking a risk they would think like a hundred, thousand times.' According to the interviewee, individuals from the Kshatriya (warriors) caste are also risk takers, but only in some circumstances. For example, they may take risks when serving in the armed forces, but when it comes to business they are by tendency rather risk-averse. 'These guys have gone through a lot of changes, [. . .] there have been wars where these guys have migrated, they have fought wars. So their ability to take risks is higher. [However, they lack] understanding of business [. . .], chances of failure of risk been taken by these people is much higher than the risk been taken by, say, the merchant class [. . .]. ' According to the interviewee, members of the other lower castes and the untouchables are also less able to take business risk, primarily because they lack any connection to the business world. '[They] have been exploited over a period of so many years, you know. So probably for a very long period of time they didn't even understand, they could never reach that level where they could actually get into this business kind of work. Even today, when you go to rural India, you'll find that these guys are still much below, I would say, poverty line. The opportunities for them are very, very limited.'

Finally, the interviewee attempts to explain how these regional and social differences in people's risk-taking abilities come into existence. He argues that risk-taking ability is predominantly determined by social norms and not by education or other factors. For example, a Brahmin is not directly taught by his parents to avoid engaging in any risky economic activities. Instead, the process that makes him or her risk averse works differently, more subtle. In case of a failed risk-decision, the consequences of social pressure and stigmatization will be much worse for a Brahmin than for a member of the merchant caste. This will thus prevent him or her from engaging in any risky business activity. The same holds true for members of the warrior caste – a loss in business may lead to a loss of social status and is therefore not acceptable. '[F]or the upper castes, culturally their family name is a big thing. In case they fail in anything, let it be education or business or whatever, it's considered very big. So people will look and point fingers that he is the guy who failed. So I see a connect in that, culturally. [. . .] So he is averse to all this. But for the merchant class which is doing business throughout, for them it's a part of life. Everybody in their group knows that his business may come up, may fail. So, it's not that big deal.'

Some conclusions on Indian risk culture and implications for poverty alleviation policies

It has been demonstrated that explaining Indian risk-taking mentality is a difficult endeavour. The two above introduced interviews shed light on the complexity of this task and identified some core themes that are relevant to the risk-taking behaviour of Indian managers, among them are: poverty, religion, caste membership and regional differences. The first interviewee, the CEO of Lightning Protection Company was forced to take risks as part of his struggle to improve the economic situation of his family and of himself. In general, in business life risk-taking may be regarded as an unpleasant activity. Having had no other choice than to work his way out of poverty, the first interviewee overcame any initial resistance he may have had and started his own company. He describes his will power as a matter of religious belief and fate: he had no other choice but to succeed. Over the years of running this enterprise he managed to develop a positive, playful attitude towards risk-taking. This allowed him to feel more comfortable when he had to face economic uncertainty and take critical business decisions. Using this approach he managed to realize his personal goals and build a profitable enterprise. The second interview with a major branch manager from Vocational Education Company portrayed the great complexity of Indian risk mentalities. The interviewee showed an in-depth understanding of the social and cultural factors that affect risk-taking behaviour in India. To describe some general tendencies in the Indian risk mentality, he drew from the experience that he had gained when he was screening applicants and trainees with various social backgrounds and from all Indian regions. The interview clarified that due to the high complexity of this task the presented description of Indian risk mentalities can only be regarded as first, exploratory step. Further research with more interview partners from different castes and regions of India has to be carried out to refine these exploratory findings.

The research results presented above allow me to formulate an advice for poverty alleviation policies. The focused ethnographic study on the CEO of Lightning Protection Company demonstrated how entrepreneurship can serve as an effective remedy for poverty. If the social and economic circumstances permit, individuals with an entrepreneurial spirit can work their way out of poverty and create welfare for themselves, their families and society as a whole. However, there are many prerequisites for starting a business and these may not be easily fulfilled. Especially in a developing country like India a lack of education and capital may prevent new ventures from flourishing. My research results suggest that business unfriendly social and cultural norms may further add up to these hurdles. The interview with the CEO of Vocational Education Company revealed that the norms which prevail in certain castes can sometimes seriously limit an entrepreneur's ability to engage in potentially fruitful economic activities. Taking risks and eventual failure are sometimes condemned and excessively punished even though both necessarily go in hand with doing business. Potential entrepreneurs may therefore hold back because they fear a loss of status and expulsion from the community. Cooter and Schäfer (2012) argue that a prime cause for poverty in developing countries is these countries' inability to bring together capital and ideas. According to them, long-term economic growth can only take place if a country is able to effectively encourage the funding of innovations. Innovators must be able to trust investors with their ideas and investors must be able to trust innovators with their money. Cooter and Schäfer argue that in absence of strong legal institutions both parties are reluctant to contract with each other, because they fear betrayal and a loss of investment. They explain that this is the principal problem that prevents the economies of developing countries from growing (ibid.: 27–28). Building on this thought, we may argue that – if they are too rigid – also the cultural and social norms discussed above may prevent innovators and investors from coming together. In other words, if these norms neither allow innovators nor investors to take appropriate economic risk both groups will be unable to cooperate. In result, innovation will be suppressed and substantial economic growth unnecessarily prevented. Overcoming business unfriendly norms should therefore be a key policy goal for combating poverty in India, no matter whether these are caused by the caste system or the historical developments in certain regions.

Note

1 The author participated in the exchange not with a grant from the DAAD but with the help of a scholarship awarded to him by the Friedrich-Naumann-Foundation. A first version of this article was published in IABE San Francisco Conference Proceedings, 15, 2015 (4), 21–33.

References

Bauer, M., and Aarts, B. (2000): Corpus Construction. A Principle for Qualitative Data Collection. In: Bauer, M., and Gaskell, G. (eds): Qualitative Researching. London: Sage, 19–37.

Bernstein, P. (1996): Against the Gods. The Remarkable Story of Risk. New York: John Wiley and Sons.

Cooter, R. D., and Schäfer, H.-B. (2012): Solomon's Knot. How Law Can End the Poverty of Nations. Princeton: Princeton University Press.

Corbin, J., and Strauss, A. (2008): Basics of Qualitative Research (3rd ed.). London: Sage.

Dess, G., and Lumpkin, G. T. (2005): Entrepreneurial Orientation as a Source of Innovative Strategy. In: Floyd, S., Roos, J., Jacobs, C., and Kellermanns, F. (eds): Innovating Strategy Process. Oxford: Wiley-Blackwell, 3–9.

Flick, U. (2006): An Introduction to Qualitative Research. London: Sage.

Fraedrich, J. P., and Ferrell, O. C. (1992): The Impact of Perceived Risk and Moral Philosophy Type on Ethical Decision Making in Business Organizations. In: *Journal of Business Research* 24 (4): 283–295.

Gupta, A. (1994): Indian Entrepreneurial Culture. Its Many Paradoxes. Pune: Wishwa Prakashan.

Hofstede, G., Hofstede, G. J., and Minkov, M. (2010): Cultures and Organizations. New York: McGraw-Hill (3rd ed.).

Memili, E., Eddleston, K., Kellermanns, F., Zellweger, T., and Barnett, T. (2010): The Critical Path to Family Firm Success Through Entrepreneurial Risk Taking and Image. In: *Journal of Family Business Strategy* 2 (5): 1–37.

Rao, S. (2006): Understanding Risk Culture and Developing a "Soft" Approach to Risk Assessment Methodologies. In: Morel, B., and Linkov, I. (eds): Environmental Security and Environmental Management. The Role of Risk Assessment. New York: Springer, 201–210.

Schumpeter, J. (1949): Theory of Economic Development. Cambridge: Harvard University Press (3rd ed.).

Schumpeter, J. (1975): Capitalism, Socialism and Democracy. New York: Harper Colophon.

Steele, J. (2004): Risk and Legal Theory. Oxford: Hart Publishing.

Taleb, N.N. (2007): The Black Swan: The Impact of the Highly Improbable. London: Penguin.

27
THINKING ABOUT CLIMATE CHANGE
Young people from Ladakh responding to global warming: an explorative study

Sofia Getzin

Preventing dangerous interference with the climate system worldwide, the Copenhagen Accord documents the *2 degrees goal*. The UN agrees that deep cuts in global emissions are required to reduce global emissions so as to hold the increase in global temperature below 2°C, and take action 'to meet this objective consistent with science and on the basis of equity' (UN 2009: 2). India with its 1.2 billion people represents 17.5 per cent of the world's population (Census of India 2011: 38) and thus is an important global player in questions of anthropogenic impact on global climate change. India will continue to be severely impacted by climate change issues precisely at a time when it is confronted with huge development imperatives (cp. Government of India 2009: 2).

According to the 4th and 5th Assessment Report of the Intergovernmental Panel on Climate Change (IPCC), the thinning of the (Himalayan) Glaciers can likely be attributed to global warming due to increase in anthropogenic emission of greenhouse gases since the 1960s (IPCC 2013: SPM-13; Parry et al. 2007: 10.6.2). In the western Himalayas, a decreasing trend of summer monsoon rainfall has been observed in the same period of time (cp. Sontakke et al. 2008: 1057f.). Another observed trend in the glaciers of Indian Himalayas is that during the last three decades of the twentieth century a degeneration of glacier mass has happened (cp. Raina 2009: 6f.).

Ongoing global warming suggests that CO_2 in the atmosphere needs to be reduced from its current 385 ppm to 350 ppm, but likely even less than that (cp. Hansen et al. 2008). In May 2013, the mean concentration of carbon dioxide in the atmosphere surpassed 400 ppm for the first time since measurement began (NOAA 2013). Pushing the global balance to dysfunction by temperature rise above 2°C could change all these climatic phenomena that used to define our lives concerning habitat, vegetation, agriculture and harvest etc. One big part of influence to sustain the future of our climate is up to political and industrial decision-making. The OECD and International Energy Agency (IEA) point out that of all the BRICS countries, in 2010, India has the lowest CO_2 emissions per capita with 1.4 tons (OECD and IEA 2012: 24), but its shares are likely to rise in the coming years (cp. ibid.: 19). Although per capita emissions are very low compared to many OECD-countries, due to the population number, India accounts for more than 5 per cent of global CO_2 emissions and in 2035 will easily account for 10 per cent (cp. ibid.: 23). Another important part of influence is up to the actions of everybody. In a high-population country like India, understanding the young generation's attitudes towards climate change, global warming and environmental protection is crucial to promote sustainable development within the future. Following the Brundtland 1987 definition, the 'classic' term of sustainable development meets the present 'without compromising the ability of future generations to meet their own needs' (cp. WCED 1987: 1). Since the 1992 UN Rio Conference on Environment and Development, it is generally accepted that sustainable development calls for a convergence between the three pillars of the concept: *economic* development, *social* equity and *environmental* protection (cp. UN 2010: 6).

This article introduces sections of an empirical investigation of young people's attitudes towards climate change and global warming. In a qualitative study conducted in Ladakh, Jammu and Kashmir, it has been investigated how young people respond to local climatic changes in their day-to-day life, while living in a highly sensitive ecosystem – the Himalayas. The following questions will be analysed within this article: *Do young people in Ladakh respond to climate change? What attitudes do they have towards climate change and global warming?*

Climate change: India's position and impact

While the Copenhagen Accord points out the need to achieve the two degrees goal, it recognizes that the frame for peaking emissions is longer in the South, bearing in mind that social and economic development and poverty eradication are the first and overriding priorities of the South and that a low-emission development strategy is indispensable to sustainable development (UN 2009: 2). In the 2009 statement about India's position on climate change issues (cp. Government of India 2009: 3), the official position towards greenhouse gas emissions was emphasized: India is the third largest greenhouse gas emitter after the US and China. But the emissions are limited in a way that the per capita emissions will not exceed those of the countries of the North. This restriction 'effectively puts a cap on our emissions', says the statement of the Indian Government, 'which will be lower if our developed country partners choose to be more ambitious in reducing their own emissions' (ibid.: 3). Subsequently India's so-called 'own perspective on climate change issues' and understanding of global equity towards development is given: 'It is India's view that the planetary atmospheric space is a common resource of humanity and each citizen of the globe has an equal entitlement to that space. The principle of equity, therefore, implies that, over a period of time, there should be a convergence in per capita emissions' (ibid.: 6). A recent statement of the BASIC-countries (BASIC Ministerial Meeting 2013) demands strong ambitions to reduce per capita emissions: the ministers expressed that the countries of the North who have taken commitments under the second commitment of the Kyoto Protocol will raise their ambition level in 2014 'in consonance with science and their historical responsibility' (ibid.: 1f.).

In the 2012 Second National Communication of India towards the UNFCC it is summarized that the rapid economic growth, expanding industrialization, increasing incomes, rapidly rising transport and modernizing agriculture are leading to a high growth in energy use in India and meanwhile causing serious environmental concerns and reasons to be concerned about climate change (cp. Government of India 2012: IIIf.). The large population depends upon climate-sensitive sectors (e.g. agriculture). Any adverse impact on water availability due to recession of glaciers, decrease in rainfall and increased flooding in certain areas would cause a range of serious problems (cp. ibid.).

In a note about the impacts of climate change on the Indian economy, the European Parliament identifies water and agriculture as the most vulnerable sectors to climate change, both necessary for improving livelihoods (cp. European Parliament 2008: i.). Rainfall patterns and the melting of the Himalayan glaciers will directly influence the availability of water (cp. ibid.). The following figures are a few projections of core facts towards India's vulnerability to climate change: an increase in surface temperature of 0.4°C has been observed on the national level during the last century (cp. ibid.: 1). The regional patterns of monsoon rainfall have been measured: certain parts with increasing rainfall (e.g. the west coast) oppose parts with decreasing rainfall (e.g. the Northeast). The sea level increases between 0.4–2 mm/year (cp. ibid.). The IPCC indicates that one of the most significant changes occurs in water resources: the glacier-fed river systems of the Ganges, Indus, Brahmaputra and other rivers are highly influenced by the melting of the Himalayan glaciers. The current trend suggests that these rivers could likely become seasonal rivers in the near future as a consequence of climate change and could likely affect the economies in the region (cp. Parry et al. 2007).

Perception of climate change in India

Leiserowitz's[1] UNDP summary analyses what is currently known about perceptions, opinions and behaviours on global climate change (cp. Leiserowitz 2007: 34). India turns out to be a special case: on the one hand, a notable number of people in rural areas of India remain unaware of the issue of climate change, as it is conceptualized by modern science (cp. ibid.). On the other hand, together with the European Union and Brazil, a significantly greater concern about this issue was measured than in comparison to China or the United States. In India, as well as worldwide, the highest concern was about human health, water shortages and extreme weather events (cp. ibid.: 35). Specifying the work on India, Leiserowitz and Thaker (2012) conducted a representative survey amongst 4,031 Indian adults to investigate the state of public 'climate change awareness', beliefs, attitudes, etc. A few central results of the study are that 80 per cent of the respondents said that *the amount of rainfall in their local area had changed*, either increased or decreased. Thirty-eight per cent responded that *the monsoon had become more unpredictable* (ibid.). Concerning global warming awareness and beliefs, Leiserowitz and Thaker summarize that the majority of the respondents (61 per cent) are *very* or *somewhat worried* about global warming (ibid.: 23). The difficulty to measure climate risk perception by percentage is expressed in various findings from different surveys. The most recent data from the World Values Survey indicates that around 80 per cent of the Indians perceive global warming to be *somewhat* or *very serious* (Running 2012: 10) while living in a high climate risk country (Harmeling and Eckstein 2012: 20). Coming back to Leiserowitz and Thaker's findings, 56 per cent said that *global warming is caused by human activities*, while 31 per cent said it is *caused by natural changes in the environment*. Remarkably large majorities (around 60 per cent) said that *global warming and its effects would harm future generations, plant and animal life and people in their surroundings* (Leiserowitz and Thaker 2012: 1f.). A noteworthy result is that the respondents were evenly divided between those that emphasized either *individuals can make their own destiny* or *everything in life is the result of fate* (ibid.: 2).

The results indicate that worry and concern towards climate change is strongly connected to the educational level. The group of *very worried* respondents has a constant size amongst all educational levels. The group of *somewhat worried* respondents decreases from the level graduates to non-literates, while the group of *don't know, not at all worried* and *not very worried* respondents increases from graduates to non-literates (ibid.: 23).

Particularly, research on local knowledge in the western Himalayas of India by Vedwan and Rhoades (2001) shows that perception of climatic change is shaped by the dynamic nature of human–environment relationship in this area. It is also connected to traditional sources of knowledge like the weather calendar (ibid.: 113). They suggest that in order to understand how humans respond to climate change, essential investigations on people's perception on climate change and environment in general should be conducted. Local knowledge should be incorporated in any strategy to mitigate the impact of climate change (cp. ibid.: 117).

Risk response, emotions and climate change

Kollmuss and Agyeman (2002: 257) developed a model of pro-environmental behaviour and highlighted the important role of emotional involvement: internal factors that influence a pro-environmental behaviour are not only knowledge but at the same time *feelings, fear, emotional involvement* as well as values and attitudes. Research on environmental values describes a trichotomy of environmental concern: egoistic, altruistic and biospheric. Egoistic concern is focused on the individual while altruistic concern focuses on people beyond oneself. Biospheric concern focuses on all living things including the biosphere (cp. Schultz 2002: 7).

Simultaneously with external factors such as political, social and cultural factors, these internal factors lead to pro-environmental behaviour (cp. Kollmuss and Agyeman 2002: 257).

Leiserowitz explains why climate change, feelings, fear and emotional involvement alone do not activate immediate response: 'If you're walking through the woods and you hear the crack of a stick behind you, your body immediately goes into fear response, a fight or flight response. Climate change isn't that kind of a problem. It's not an immediate, visceral threat. [. . .] We can look out the window and there's CO_2 [. . .] pouring out of tailpipes, pouring out of buildings, pouring out of smokestacks. And yet we can't see it, it's invisible' (Leiserowitz and Moyers 2013: 2). Thus, the nature of the perception of climate change problems is not a visceral respond. This indicates that the reaction of many people is not a fear response as provoked by the crack of a stick in the woods even though it is a highly threatening issue.

Findings from the 2005–2008 World Values Survey indicate that personal exposure to climate risk neither changes the individual concern for global warming (cp. ibid.: 17), nor is it necessarily connected to the readiness to act pro-environmentally (cp. Running 2012: 4). Results from the field of research on behavioural and environmental decisions suggest a connection between the perception of risks and the decisions to take actions that reduce or manage perceived risks: Weber[2] (2006) provides evidence for the claim of causal importance of visceral reactions towards risks. Referring to the work of Peters and Slovic (2000) on the affective and analytical information processing in choice of gains and losses (ibid.: 1472f.), she points out that effect and especially negative effect are 'the wellspring of action' for environmental decisions (Weber 2006: 104). She describes that emotions like worry or fear motivate us to remove ourselves from the particular dangerous situation. The two existent processing systems in *homo sapiens* have a different speed and effectiveness in dangerous situations: as mentioned above, the intuitive, automatic and fast *associative system* that responds to 'the crack' integrates uncertain aspects of the environment into affective response (e.g. fear, dread, anxiety) and thus represents risk as a feeling (cp. ibid.: 105). The second system, the *analytical processing system*, is slower and requires conscious awareness and control (cp. ibid.). Its use for a given situation is not triggered automatically. According to the importance of emotions for the way we think and for rational decision-making, Damasio's work *Descartes' Error* illustrates that the two processing systems work parallel and interactive. Analytical reasoning can only be effective when guided and assisted by emotion and effect (cp. Damasio 2006: 227ff.; Weber 2006: 105). The case of global warming is an example where the lack of integration of the outputs of these two systems may result in less concern than advisable since the analytic system identifies global warming as a serious concern, but the affective system fails to send early warning signals (Weber 2006: 105). For an appropriate risk assessment there are two pathways: the first pathway is personal experience and the second is statistical description. On the one hand, many people base their visceral reaction to the risk of global warming on personal experience, so the perception of the risk will be low because they are not alarmed by the risk of global warming (ibid.: 108). Climate scientists, on the other hand, are aware of the details of global climatic changes by statistical descriptions and thus will consider global warming as a high risk (ibid.). Bringing together findings from Leiserowitz and Weber, possibly only the potentially catastrophic nature of climate change has the potential to activate a visceral reaction to the risk (cp. ibid.: 113f.).

Methodology: group discussions and the documentary method

In May and June 2012, climate change perceptions of young people have been investigated in the Himalayan region Ladakh. Sections of two group discussions among secondary school students of public schools in the Himalayan region Ladakh are exemplarily analysed and attitudes towards climate change identified. Group discussions have been implemented with students, aged 15–18, five participants each.

In the group discussions, the object of examination is how the statements differentiate within processes of negotiation with others. By clarifying one's own point of view, the *implicit* attitudes ('orientations') are strengthened and come to the surface (Bohnsack 2000: 370). For understanding these attitudes, the researcher initialized the group discussion by asking the participants about their experiences with environment and climate change. According to Mannheim's sociology of knowledge, groups revert to common biographical experiences that are based on the so-called 'conjunctive space of experience' (cp. ibid.). The more the students share a similar set of knowledge, e.g. one culture, similar social, environmental and economical background, the more likely they develop and articulate common definitions about these contingencies and a resembling strategy of how to handle them. This common frame of reference appears in the 'conjunctive space of experience' (Bohnsack 2010: 105). Although the group is not the place of the genesis of collective opinions, the discussion is a place of representation and articulation of these opinions (Bohnsack 2000: 373).

The technique of documentary interpretation has been developed by Bohnsack and defines the relation 'reflexivity', where every expression has a character of a representing index or a document for an underlying pattern of meaning. It refers to a change from asking 'what' to asking 'how' (cp. Bohnsack 2010: 102). Changing the approach leads to a transit between observations of first ('observation') and second order ('observation of observation'). Thus documentary interpretation defines two different types of knowledge: the knowledge that can be explained by the participants and the knowledge that is 'taken for granted', the *knowledge of experience* (ibid.: 102f.). This second kind of knowledge often cannot be expressed directly, but the participants understand each other 'without any need to explicate it to each other' (ibid.: 103).

In order to reconstruct attitudes towards climate change and global warming, understanding the earlier mentioned 'conjunctive spaces of experience' is crucial. The documentary method contains the following analytic steps (cp. Bohnsack 2007: 325ff.): (1) *Formulating Interpreta-*

tion (a. *Topical Structuring* – identification of 'focusing metaphors': sections of low/high interaction and b. *Detailed Formulating Interpretation* – identification of focusing metaphors/reformulation of the imminent, the communicative-generalized sense of the discussion). (2) *Reflecting Interpretation* – comprehends the documentary, not articulated 'deeper sense' of the statements and interactions/reconstructs the 'how' of the conversation and the *framework of orientation*. (3) *Comparative Analysis* – recognizing the same pattern in homologue semantic structures.

In the following sections the empirical research of young people's attitudes towards climate change and global warming in the Himalaya region in India will be introduced.

Personal idols and climate perception (Group 1)

Bm: and he also loves nature and he tells me er- th- you know the ways how to plant trees how to preserve them how to er- take care of them and just because of him I have learned a lot how to plant trees and today I am doing my bit o save the nature (.) because I am deeply concerned about the global warming
I: //mmh//
Bm: and everyone is scared that 2012 will be the end of the world
Am/Cf: ˪@(3)@
Bm: as it is told as it was predicted prophesized by Nostradamus
I: //mmh//
Bm: I think it's true (.) because this year it is you know many people are afraid even in x, Ladakh most of the people are afraid
Am: ˪because of the (   ) cloud burst of x
I: //mmh//
Bm: ˪ ()
Am: normally it th- there would be a cloud burst as you know there are cloud burst one in humid temperature warm temperature and humid conditions so you can see it's a very not unknown thing unknown climate- then we can say that er- because of the er- global warming and er- global warming has such a big impact that more than at the cold places cold er- polar regions than on the equatorial regions which are warm.

The anecdote of *Bm*'s own engagement in planting trees is strongly connected to the idol-function of his grandfather and his knowledge, both mentioned earlier in the discussion.

The second reason to get involved in environmental activities seems to be the fear of global warming. Emphasizing this with the term 'deeply concerned' is central for the ability and motivation to behave action oriented. Expressing concern is the most common reaction to climate change rather than a visceral fear response as provoked by 'the crack of a stick in the woods' (cp. Leiserowitz and Moyers 2013).

In the explication, the group connects the need to face global warming as a real problem with the fear of natural disasters. They mention that the prophecy of the end of the world 2012 could be true because of the still very present memory of the devastating cloudburst and its impact. Findings from Weber (2006: 105) from the field of risk perception show us that especially negative risks are the 'wellspring of action'. Opposing this, fear and belief in the prophecy of the end of the world result for 'most of the people'. The laughter of some of the participants shows agreement with *Bm*'s explication but could also emphasize subtle irony to the explication with the prophecy. If they took this seriously they would probably not laugh. They show solidarity with the memories of most of the people from Ladakh. As Vedwan and Rhoades (2001) point out, the perception of the environment is coined by the dynamics of human–environment relationship. In this area, this thesis can be confirmed by the findings. Personal and people's destiny is strongly connected to the environmental future and possible disasters, because livelihood depends on the environment.

Explaining the impact of global warming on cold regions as the climatic sensitive Himalaya region of Ladakh, the group points out that global warming is generally perceived as an important problem. These findings accord with the finding that the local population identifies a change in rainfall patterns – cloudburst is perceived as a terrifying as well as an unusual phenomenon (cp. European Parliament 2008; Leiserowitz and Thaker 2012; Sontakke et al. 2008).

The negative experience of the cloudburst leads to environmental commitment amongst the self-proclaimed 'educated students' within *Group 2* as in the second example:

Perception of knowledge about climate change (Group 2)

Am: er- we can do many things er- to //no// sav- er- conserve the environment to some extend //no// and many peoples are illiterate you know the people doing ( ) //no// they are not aware of what is wrong and what is right and er- being a student er- I personally can go to the village an- and I can come with my message to the village; people of

	the village //no// what is the wrong and what is the right I think this is where we can- er- spread the awareness er-
Ef:	└ya
Am:	to the people (6)
I:	have you experiences with that?
Df:	ya
Am:	ya of course I ha- once I you know I get down all the people of village an- er- and I told them that er- not to use er- you know that fossil fuel very much and er- it's effect our environments you know it's leads to the greenhouse effect which er-
I:	└//mmh//
Am:	certainly you know er- it's er- increase the temperature of all and will lead to global warming (.) ya an- and I //no// I many times we went to others village ya I sort ( )
I:	└//mmh// (3)
Df:	we also used to participate in rallies to conserve from schools

Both of the sections have a high metaphoric density and are so-called 'focus metaphors' with a high level of interaction and dramatization (cp. Bohnsack and Przyborski 2010: 234). The sections of the discussions are both organized univocal – participants talk parallel, intersecting and complementally as well as consensus orientated (cp. ibid.: 239).

In a *comparative analysis*, here exemplarily introduced, both of the groups show common interpretive dimensions:

(1) *Reasons for commitment: 'Having a role model' or 'being role model oneself'* – Both sections show different ways to respond to global warming and climate change. The section of *Group 1* explained the role model as a member of the family. Commitment appears as a result of the personal background. A person that is 'deeply concerned' learns from another very engaged person (the grandfather) who has the knowledge to do 'good things'. Solidarity with the fears of 'everyone' towards natural disasters triggers engagement.

Group 2 shows opposing attributes – commitment appears as an outcome of the perception of one's own obligation due to the privilege of being educated. The group emphasizes the status of 'educated' students with the privilege of education. This privilege imposes the duty to act responsible upon them. 'Of course' *Am* replies when he was asked if he had own experiences. They address global warming by educating other people. This point of view is emphasized as a collective attitude because *Am* includes the participants ('we') in his anecdote. Talking univocal (mutually complemented) and adding the experience in school rallies, they include themselves. Opposing *Group 1*, they understand the privilege of education as a responsibility to behave as a role model and more than this to expect the other people to act appropriately after sharing one's message about not using fossil fuels to protect global warming. A rather elite understanding of privileges and the 'right' attitude triggers taking care of spreading knowledge about climate change.

(2) *Education and knowledge* – In both of the discussions, having the skills and the knowledge to do good seems to be central for the participants. *Group 1* emphasizes skills to act pro-environmentally, e.g. planting trees. They identify the perception of climate change as knowledge-based.

In the conclusion of *Group 2*, they express that pro-environmental behaviour and the 'right' attitude occur according to the educational level of a person. They conclude that people in the villages do not know what is right and wrong due to their illiteracy. They emphasize that consciousness determines action and are even more explicitly focused on knowledge about the topic than *Group 1*. For them, knowledge and education are privileges; they operate for a pro-environmental attitude, and in their explanation illiteracy consequentially brings about 'not knowing what's right or wrong'.

Leiserowitz's 2007 paper points out that many people in India's rural areas remain unaware of the issue of climate change. This finding cannot be confirmed by the results of this study because they are not only aware, but even very concerned with climate change issues. De facto, they mention the interrelation of the level of concern and the educational level. They say the 'people from the village' do not know much about climate change. This goes along with Leiserowitz's 2007 representative findings (cp. ibid.: 34). According to Leiserowitz and Thaker's 2012 work on India and climate change, the participants of this empirical investigation probably are part of the 7 per cent of the population that describe themselves as knowing 'a lot' of the issue (ibid.: 20). The division as mentioned in their 2012 work between those who said 'individuals can make their own destiny' as opposed to 'everything in life is a result of fate' is identified within the two sections of the discussions: on the one hand the participants clearly describe themselves as having the ability to act and to respond to climate change. On the other hand, *Group 1* identified 'most people' as believing in a prophecy and fate.

(3) *Emotional response and climate change* – The emotional dimension in both of the discussions underlies the other interpretive dimensions and is rarely directly explained by the participants.

In the section of *Group 1*, the participants talk about the cloudburst and the fear of another natural disaster. Losing beloved family members, friends and houses just a few years ago is still a very present memory. Due to their knowledge, they know about the scientific causes of climate change and cloudbursts that makes them act responsibly. This contradicts the almost religious belief in the prophecy of the end of the world of 'most of the people'.

Group 2 shows primarily pride as an emotional reaction to responsibilities following the privilege of knowledge. They can spread and share the message with the 'people of the village'. Acting pro-environmentally within Group 1 compensates one's own worries towards the consequences of global warming and within Group 2 shows a strong sense of duty.

Conclusions

The exemplarily analysed sections of the discussions taken from the Himalayan region sample show the response of the young participants towards climate change in their day-to-day life. The three identified interpretive dimensions illustrate how the participants discuss reasons for commitment, their viewpoint on role models and the importance of knowledge and education. The emotional dimension is probably the most difficult to identify. The data clarifies that even their emotional stance is connected to their knowledge about climate change, e.g. having role models/trying to be role models themselves and actual commitment to the issue. These findings go along with other findings, especially of Leiserowitz (2007) and Weber (2006). The groups show a reaction to perceived climate risks in their environment and find different ways to respond to the perceived risks. While Group 1 has an experience-based emotional connection to environmental topics, Group 2 responds in responsibilities following their perceived privilege of education.

Notes

1 Anthony Leiserowitz is one of the most popular researchers on Climate Change Perceptions from the Yale Project on Climate Change Communication.
2 Elke U. Weber, working for Research on Environmental Decisions at Columbia University is an expert in behavioural models of decision-making under risk and uncertainty in environmental decisions.

References

BASIC Ministerial Meeting (2013): Joint Statement issued at the Conclusion of the 14th BASIC Ministerial Meeting on Climate Change. http://envfor.nic.in/assets/XIV_BASIC_Joint__Statement_FINAL.pdf.

Bohnsack, R. (2000): Gruppendiskussion. In: Flick, U., von Kardorff, E., and Steinke, I. (eds): Qualitative Forschung, 369–384. Reinbek.

Bohnsack, R. (2007): Dokumentarische Methode. In: Buber. R., and Holzmüller, H. H. (eds): Qualitative Marktforschung. Konzepte – Methoden – Analysen, 231–330. Wiesbaden.

Bohnsack, R. (2010): Documentary Method and Group Discussions. In: Bohnsack, R., Pfaff, N., and Weller, V. (eds): Qualitative Analysis and Documentary Method in International Educational Research, 99–124. Opladen, Farmington Hills.

Bohnsack, R., and Przyborski, A. (2010): Diskursorganisation, Gesprächsanalyse und die Methode der Gruppendiskussion. In: Bohnsack, R., Przyborski, A., and Schäffer, B. (eds): Das Gruppendiskussionsverfahren in der Forschungspraxis, 233–248. Opladen, Farmington Hills.

Census of India (2011): Provisional Population Totals. India, Paper 1 of 2011. New Delhi.

Damasio, A. R. (2006): Descartes' Irrtum. 4th ed. Berlin.

European Parliament (ed.) (2008): Climate Change and India: Impacts, Policy Responses and a Framework for EU-India Cooperation. Brussels.

Government of India (2009): The Road to Copenhagen. India's Position on Climate Change Issues. Retrieved from: http://pmindia.nic.in/Climate%20Change_16.03.09.pdf.

Government of India, Ministry of Environment & Forests (ed.) (2012): India. Second National Communication to the United Nations Framework Convention on Climate Change. New Delhi.

Hansen, J., Sato, M., Kharecha, P., Beerling, D., Berner, R., Masson-Delmotte, V., Pagani, M., Raymo, M., Royer, D. L., and Zachos, J. C. (2008): Target Atmospheric CO_2: Where Should Humanity Aim? In: Open Atmospheric Science Journal 2: 217–231.

Harmeling, S., and Eckstein, D. (2012): Global Climate Risk Index 2013. Who Suffers Most from Extreme Weather Events? Weather-Related Loss Events in 2011 and 1992 to 2011. Bonn.

IPCC (eds) (2013) Working Group 1 Contribution to the IPCC Fifth Assessment Report. Climate Change 2013. The Physical Science Basis. Summary for Policymakers. http://www.climatechange2013.org/images/uploads/WGIAR5-SPM_Approved27Sep2013.pdf.

Kollmuss, A., and Agyeman, J. (2002): Mind the Gap: Why Do People Act Environmentally and What Are the Barriers to Pro-Environmental Behavior? In: Environmental Education Research 8 (3): 239–260.

Leiserowitz, A. (2007): International Public Opinion, Perception and Understanding of Global Climate Change. In: UNDP (ed.): Human Development Report 2007/2008, Occasional Paper. Yale University.

Leiserowitz, A., and Moyers, B. (2013): Transcript of: January 4, 2013. Anthony Leiserowitz on Making People Care About Climate Change. http://billmoyers.com/segment/anthony-leiserowitz-on-making-people-care-about-climate-change/.

Leiserowitz, A., and Thaker, J. (2012): Climate Change in the Indian Mind. Yale University/George Mason University.

NOAA (eds) (2013) 'Carbon Dioxide at NOAA's Mauna Loa Observatory Reaches New Milestone: Tops 400 ppm'. http://www.esrl.noaa.gov/news/2013/CO2400.html.

OECD/IEA (eds) (2012): CO_2 Emissions from Fuel Combustion. Highlights. 2012 ed. Paris.

Parry, M. L., Canziani, O. F. J, Palutikof, J. P., van der Linden, P. J., and Hanson, C. E. (eds) (2007): IPCC Fourth Assessment Report: Climate Change 2007. Impacts, Adaption and Vulnerability. http://www.ipcc.ch/publications_and_data/ar4/wg2/en/contents.html.

Peters, E., and Slovic, P. (2000): The Springs of Action: Affective and Analytical Information Processing in Choice. In: Personality and Social Psychology Bulletin 26: 1465–1475.

Raina, V. K. (2009): Himalayan Glaciers. A State-of-Art Review of Glacial Studies, Glacial Retreat and Climate Change. New Delhi.

Running, K. (2012): Examining Environmental Concern in Developed, Transitioning and Developing Countries. World Values Research 5 (1): 1–25.

Schäffer, B. (2011): Gruppendiskussionen. In: Bohnsack, R., Marotzki, W., and Meuser, M. (eds) Hauptbegriffe Qualitativer Sozialforschung. 3rd ed. Opladen, Farmington Hills, 75–80.

Schultz, W. P. (2002): Environmental Attitudes and Behaviors Across Cultures. In: Online Readings in Psychology and Culture 8 (1): 1–12. http://scholarworks.gvsu.edu/cgi/viewcontent.cgi?article=1070&context=orpc.

Sontakke, N. A., Singh, N., and Singh, H. N. (2008): Instrumental Period Rainfall Series of the Indian Region (AD 1813–2005): Revised Reconstruction, Update and Analysis. The Holocene 18 (7): 1055–1066.

UN (2009): Copenhagen Accord. Copenhagen.

UN (2010): Sustainable Development: From Brundtland to Rio 2012. Background Paper. New York. http://www.un.org/wcm/webdav/site/climatechange/shared/gsp/docs/GSP1-6_Background%20on%20Sustainable%20Devt.pdf.

Vedwan, N., and Rhoades, R. E. (2001): Climate Change in the Western Himalayas of India: A Study of Local Perception and Response. In: Climate Research 19: 109–117.

WCED (1987): Our Common Future. Oxford.

Weber, E. U. (2006): Experience-Based and Description-Based Perception of Long-Term Risk Why Global Warming Does Not Scare Us (Yet). In: Climate Change 77: 103–120.

28
HEALTH PROMOTION AND DIVERSITY
Theoretical reflections and personal experiences in everyday India[1]

Markus Wiencke

My stay at the Tata Institute of Social Sciences in Mumbai and my participation in a two-week summer school on social justice at the Manipal University took place towards the end of my PhD work in clinical cultural psychology at the Free University of Berlin (Wiencke 2011). In this chapter, I will discuss how this three-month stay in India helped to provide new perspectives on the topic of my dissertation: health promotion. I will first sketch out the central aspects of my dissertation and then describe their relevance concerning my experiences in India.

Social dimensions of mental health

The chronically mentally ill have to deal with significant disruptions in their biographies (cf. Estroff 2004). While many indications exist that a 'positive' practice of making sense influences the process of recovery significantly (cf. Davidson et al. 2005; Amering and Schmolke 2007), many studies also point out the context dependency of the construct of schizophrenia (cf. Zaumseil 2006).

I thus set myself the goal to examine in my dissertation to what degree there are phenomena that can be attributed to the construct of schizophrenia tied to a specific context. I will pursue the question of how it may be possible to deal with the diagnosis of schizophrenia as a person and under what conditions a 'positive' significance may be derived. To investigate this question empirically, I have chosen three specific settings by means of which to examine the more general concept of context. I understand 'setting' as the interaction between material conditions, discourses and the emotional-physical participation of an individual in social events. The studies took place using participant observation (Spradley 1980) and 72 problem-centred interviews (Witzel 1989) on the ground, in August and September 2004 in a Candomblé and Umbanda temple in Brazil (Wiencke 2009), and for two months each in the two socioculturally very different settings of a German psychosomatic clinic, where a discourse on spirituality was included in the treatment (2006), and in a Mapuche community psychiatry in Chile (2007). Working with a grounded theory research strategy – and much indebted to Strauss's (1998) approach – I have developed a heuristic model that describes the necessary conditions in the three settings, under which schizophrenia cases may develop a 'positive' practice of making sense. Cultural factors and cultural differences were taken into account as possible influences not only on the empirical level but also on the level of theory building.

The three settings have three relevant features in common: (1) they demonstrate phenomena that can be assigned to the construct of schizophrenia; (2) the social community plays a central role; and (3) in the therapeutic treatment, spiritual dimensions are relevant. At the same time they are embedded in very different local value systems.

In the collected data, specific patterns emerged between the meaningful practices in the settings and the changes in the convictions of the participants. These patterns were similar to concepts of health promotion such as self-efficacy (Bandura 1997), dispositional optimism (Scheier and Carver 1992) or sense of coherence (Antonovsky 1979, 1987). But the emphasis in these latter concepts is on the health promotion value of cognitive processes in individuals. By contrast, my data revealed significant evidence that in the studied settings, the health promotion value could be found in processes embedded in social events. To explain these relationships between people and social contexts, I referred to very different theoretical perspectives found in the literature. I developed a theoretical basis in my work with the empirical data and the literature, including Manfred Zaumseil's (2006) concepts for the context dependency of the schizophrenia construct, Bettina Hannover's (2000) context-dependent self, Rudolf Moos's (2003) power and fragility of a setting and the differentiation between sense and meaning as developed by Erich Wulff (1992). In the data, indications could also be found that health promotion processes were tied to a participant's physicalness. Thus, there emerged ties to concepts that are described in the literature on ritual and mimesis (e.g. Csordas 1997; Wulf 2005).

Against this backdrop a concept of health and health promotion thus emerged in my work with the empirical data. Figure 28.1 provides a visual overview.

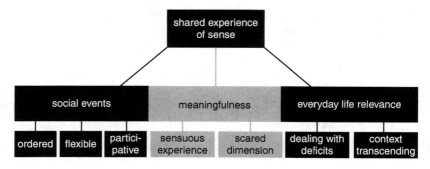

Figure 28.1 Shared experience of sense

My concept of health and health promotion, 'shared experience of sense', has three components: 'social events', 'meaningfulness' and 'everyday life relevance'. The table above shows on three levels the differentiation of the developed concept. The three colors reflect the three levels and not the three settings.

In my work, I see health promotion in the relationship between the individual and social events in the physical environment of the setting and everyday life in which an individual takes part emotionally and physically. I thus speak of a 'shared experience of sense', which is produced in the performative practices of the settings in which an individual physically takes part (the upper level in the table). In the settings an individual participates physically in meaningful practices that may be described as dramatic-physical performances and that differ in the 'how' of their performance. In different manners, with different performance styles, social worlds of meaning are produced in the performances. What makes them special, the core meanings created together in the setting by the persons in the performance, is described in the next level of the table.

An individual experiences self as part of a social event in which a health-specific sense of meaning is constantly restaged in performative practices (this aspect is shown in the table as 'social events'). The data shows numerous statements that refer to three aspects that are generated in the social events and are necessary for an experience of sense.

The first aspect is that social events are 'ordered' in a way specific to the setting. In social practices, the individual experiences a specific order of meanings in which he or she may situate their illness. This can lead to a subjective comprehension of the illness.

The second aspect is the term 'flexible'. In social performance, participants experience in a plastic manner the blurred boundaries between the objects of social meanings of the settings. Social meaning – and thus their illness as well – appears to the participants as a network of relationships that can be dealt with flexibly and can be affected.

The third aspect may be summarized under the term 'participative'. In social practices, an individual experiences that he or she may in a participative manner access resources, such as social support.

When all three aspects concur, an individual may come to the conclusion that he or she is experiencing the same effects that are mediated in the meaning of the social events: namely that it is beneficial to their health to participate in these social practices. Health is thus a social phenomenon.

Many statements in the data suggest that individuals who participate emotionally and physically in the performative practices often have intense sensory experiences. This may result in a social event being experienced as embedded in a spiritual context. These are experiences of embeddedness in shared meaning systems. An individual can thus come to believe that their involvement in this social event of which they feel part of is meaningful (which I understand as 'meaningfulness' in the table).

In this context, the data suggest that in the performative practices of the settings, the deficits in the everyday lives of the participants are dealt with in a manner appropriate to their daily lives. Participants experience social events in the setting very intensively, both emotionally and physically. At the same time, they recognize that these social events are also anchored in the social meanings of their daily lives. Individuals can cope with their illness not only in the setting but also in everyday life – that is, within their family and their usual living conditions (identified as 'everyday life relevance' in the table).

In the following, I would like to illustrate this concept of a 'shared experience of sense' based on material from the Chilean community psychiatry. To this end, I will present a thick description of the work of the community psychiatry, which has been practicing in this form since the beginning of the 1990s. The patients live in their families and are visited there and treated by the psychiatric staff. In addition, in the psychiatric clinic located in a small town, medicines, psychoeducation and to a limited degree psychotherapy are offered. About 700 patients diagnosed based on ICD-10 (WHO 1993) are in treatment. Of the 127 patients who have been diagnosed with 'schizophrenia', 67 are ethnic 'Mapuche'. In the 1992 census, of the 14 million citizens of Chile one million individuals over the age of 14 identified themselves as Mapuche. Their name can be translated as 'people of this land' (Schindler 1998:

71). The Mapuche patients lived in communities of between 30 and 200 households, i.e. with several hundred to several thousand people. Usually, a social worker visited them every two weeks in their houses for between 20 and 30 minutes. If the patients were to be given medication in the course of the visit, the social worker was accompanied by a medical assistant. The driver of a pick-up truck bearing the words 'Salud Mental' completed the medical team. The driver was dressed in a white coat, the two female staff wore everyday clothes. The social worker had a badge hanging around her neck bearing her name, photograph and function in the psychiatric clinic. In the following scene, the medical team is additionally accompanied by me and an intern who translated for me in interviews. Initially, the social worker approached the house alone to ask if the student and I may accompany her, which was always answered in the affirmative. The driver stayed in the truck.

In this specific instance, the farm consisted of two approximately 25m² large wooden houses built at right angles to one another, and another smaller house. Next to the houses, pigs and chickens ran around in a fenced garden. There were also several dogs and cats. When we arrived, the patient remained in one of the wooden houses, where he was repairing a bicycle. We therefore initially only greeted his parents. After a short conversation with the social worker, the father left for the field armed with a hoe. Now the social worker asked the mother about the family situation in general. She added that the young man may remain in the house if he wanted to. Then the woman went in to talk with her son. He came out about five minutes later and greeted us warmly. The strong young man was dressed in a T-shirt, jeans and a baseball cap on his head and appeared a little bit shy. The social worker asked him how he felt, how he had slept and whether he saw images or heard voices. He explained how at night voices spoke to him and that he saw strange things. In answer to the social worker's question, whether the voices were in his head or outside, he answered 'outside'. He only heard and saw the voices and images at night but he had headaches during the day. When asked if he was taking his medication regularly, he answered in the negative. The social worker replied that in principle this was okay; but that it was important, however, that he observed his condition and took the medication as directed, should psychotic symptoms appear. She suggested that we come back in a few days for an interview. The young man said, however, that he must help with the harvest and did not have any time.

In the exchange between the psychiatry staff and the Mapuche patients and their families, situation-specific meanings of schizophrenia emerge that are tied to sensory experienced human interaction. In their contact with the staff, the patient and his family acquire practical knowledge in terms of the medication required to stabilize the structures of meaning in everyday life that may be threatened by his psychosis.

Experiences in India

Against the background of the recovery concept (cf. Amering and Schmolke 2007), I explored under what setting conditions it becomes possible, despite biographical disruptions, to arrive at a 'positive' practice of making sense. The concept of 'shared experience of sense' depicts a practice of making sense that can be promoting health in schizophrenia (and in other severe mental disorders). For a person to achieve this 'positive' practice of making sense is dependent on him or her participating emotionally and physically in social events in certain settings. In this context, I have elucidated the bridges that the therapeutic settings create to everyday life. Based on the supporting structure of the therapeutic setting, an individual is empowered to cope with their illness in everyday life, which, depending on the context, may mean very different things. This is what I understand in my work as 'health promotion'. My methodological approach was indeed based on mental health, but the data pointed repeatedly to the fact that mental and physical health were inseparable. Therefore I propose an extension of my initial thesis with a tie to emotional, physical and social events for a possible understanding of 'health'. The concept of 'shared experience of sense' locates the promotion of health in the physical environment of a setting and at the same time in day-to-day events. In the interaction of objective conditions and subjective participation in shared practices relevant to everyday life, an improvement in health may take place.

My conception is based on therapeutic settings. The treatment practices in the three investigated settings draw on local lifestyles and try to influence these lifestyles in terms of promoting their medical benefit. With my concept, one may accordingly find relationships between changes in contextual conditions – understood as a setting – and changes in lifestyle. At this point the question arises of what form everyday health promotion, in a broader understanding of the context, can take beyond the context of the therapeutic setting. My own sensory experience of the diversity of everyday life in Mumbai made it clear to me that the role of everyday life relevance in my concept of 'shared experience of sense' needs to be differentiated further. An appropriate point of departure may be seen in the tension between public and private spaces and in the question of how diversity is dealt with, as I would like to demonstrate in the following narrative.

In Mumbai, I experienced how boundaries between public and private spaces dissolved in everyday activities. By means of several examples, I will describe three aspects of this experience of dissolution that in my mind will be relevant for further research. The first aspect concerns 'dealing with gender'. On campus, male and female students were housed separately in two parts of a building. A guard ensured that no student crossed to the other side. I was thus breaking an official rule every time I visited the female members of our group in their rooms. This separation also existed in the local trains, in which there were special cars for women. I never saw any Indian couples kissing in public. In many conversations with local students, I was told that their parents would find a marriage partner for them. I was particularly irritated by the view expressed by one student that his parents knew him very well; and because of their greater life experience they thus knew better than he himself which woman would suit him. On the other hand, many young men and women expressed their discontent about these arranged marriages; they wanted to choose their partner by themselves but often feared social exclusion should they speak out too loudly. On campus, many students dealt flexibly with these rules. I was repeatedly told about relationships (in part tolerated by parents) before marriage, about sexual activities among university students and I personally observed students flirting with one another in the fitness room and in the cafeteria. This flexible 'dealing with gender' also included a somewhat irritating experience in the public space of the local train and on the street, namely the appearance of gaudily made up and colourfully dressed transvestites who – clapping their hands in a specific way, brushing their hands through the hair especially of younger men and caressing their faces – asked for money.

The second aspect that I would like to elucidate is addressed here as well, namely what one might call 'public physical contact'. It appeared common practice that the transvestites begged for money in a particularly performative way, in which they touched others in a very intrusive but not arbitrary manner, remaining within the closely defined boundaries concomitant to their social status. For me, travelling in Mumbai was associated with unavoidable physical contact. Even if I was lucky and the train stopped so that the doors opened directly in front of me, I was immediately pushed aside by the disembarking masses. Boarding the train was only possible by means of shoving aside the other bodies pressed on mine. Even on the train, I was usually in direct contact with other bodies, which were constantly in motion, leaving the train, boarding it or simply making room for others. Walking in the night, I often had to dodge people sleeping in the middle of the sidewalk. At night in the train stations as well, I invariably had to skirt the bodies of people sleeping on the floor.

With this latter phenomenon, I would like to introduce the third aspect, for in my mind it were the private lives of poor that mingled most with public spaces. Illegal slums in Mumbai are often located next to the train station and along the tracks, where people live in small makeshift accommodations built of boards, concrete blocks, plastic and corrugated iron. Travelling by train, I probably was irritated most by children playing on large piles of rubbish in front of these hovels or by the chickens pecking for food in the garbage, while rats scurried between the tracks. I saw the residents of these slums relieving themselves in the narrow space between their shelters and the tracks, where they also washed their clothes and prepared food. In an oddly tragic manner, one was able to participate in the lives of these people. Perhaps the best term for this third aspect is 'public home life'.

From these observations one can derive further questions on the differentiation of everyday life: how does therapeutic practice in specific settings, done with the goal of promoting mental health, interact with private and public spaces? Do conflicts between these spaces exist? In addition, my experiences in India have led to questions of how diversity in everyday life can be taken into greater account than it has been to date in my concept of a 'shared experience of sense'. I explored very different parts of Mumbai and met people with very different biographies. I lived on the campus of an elite research institute, visited modern shopping centres with members of the Indian middle class and went to clubs, where people were paid to turn the taps on and off in the washrooms so that guests could wash their hands. I also visited slums and was a guest of poorer students of the Tata Institute in their small houses, visited Hindu temples, took part in Buddhist meditations and ate in tourist restaurants. In the public spaces of the streets there was a great diversity. Five to seven rows of cars, trucks with colourful ornamentation, buses, auto-rickshaws, motorcycles, bicycles and oxcarts filled the four to five lanes wide roads. The traffic was in constant flux, with drivers looking for narrow gaps to pass left or right and turning left recklessly even of a red light across six rows of oncoming traffic. This impressive diversity could be found on many other levels as well. In addition to large shopping centres, there were smaller supermarkets, kiosks, street vendors with carts selling several types of fruit down to dealers who only had boiled eggs to offer to the customer. The streets were filled with a multitude of smells, of plants, fruits, vegetables and spices, sometimes of car exhaust, perfume and incense, and often the slightly putrid smell of monsoon rain. When I went to local markets, I could observe how chickens were slaughtered in front of the customer or I could go a few stalls further and buy a computer and the most modern of software. I was surrounded by a cacophony of voices in English, Hindi, Marati and a dozen more languages, running engines, ringing cell phones, music and car horns. It was a sensory miscellany, arranged in a manner that could barely and only in very fuzzy terms be grasped rationally. My body learned to move in this diversity – to move with the bodies around me. My participation in a two-week summer school on 'social justice' at the Manipal Centre for Philosophy & Humanities, Manipal University allowed for a more rational approach. On the one hand, the summer school allowed me, after three weeks in Mumbai, a necessary physical and sensory retreat from city life to reflect on myself and the place I found myself in. On the other hand, it was an important introduction to key aspects of Indian society. The structuring principle of society that was most present for me and at the same time the most inconsistent in this presence was that of the social hierarchy associated with the caste system (cf. Dumont 1976). The summer school was attended by about 50 undergraduate and graduate students and assistant professors from various parts of India, all of them belonging to different castes and economic classes. Professors from diverse disciplines such as philosophy, medicine, economics, law and management discussed the concept of social justice as it was applied in their discipline. I was fascinated by the personal involvement of the participants in the discussions and the repeated references to the concept of caste and the associated inclusion in and exclusion from private and public spaces that they often experienced firsthand. Some lower caste members of the group described, for example, that they had experienced professional obstacles because of their caste or that in their villages they were forbidden to enter the houses of members of the upper castes.

Perspectives

In my dissertation, I situated health promotion between subjective experience and the objective distribution of power and resources embedded in everyday life, albeit from the perspective of therapeutic settings. The described observations from Mumbai were intended to show that the sphere of everyday life relevance in the concept of 'shared experience of sense' needed to be differentiated further. Above all it is unclear how the described 'dissolution of boundaries between public and private spaces' – with the three aspects of 'dealing with gender', 'public physical contact' and 'public home life' – and the phenomenon of diversity affect 'coping with an illness in everyday life', such as to give access to the necessary resources for this purpose. One suggestion voiced at the summer school was Amartya Sen's (2001) reflections on social justice, summarized in the hypothesis that your freedom depends on those capabilities of functions that you value in your life – and that you have good reason to value. A capability set describes the freedom that individuals have to realize alternative combinations of functions, or in other words, to realize different lifestyles. The functions include simple issues, such as the meeting of basic health needs including clean drinking water and sufficient food. Sen's concept provides a heuristic orientation for developing a connection, by means of values, between access to objective resources in everyday life with my observed tensions between public and private spaces and lived diversity. I perceive these observed phenomena thus as dynamic lifestyles. Values influence the range of possible actions and choices in day-to-day contexts in different ways. For example, the caste system can, depending on the local context, constitute an obstacle for one individual, while providing another individual with the social capital to access resources. In this situation, the concept of 'entrepreneur' as it exists in everyday Indian life occurred to me as instructive. There were magazines with the word in the title and the streets were filled with entrepreneurial activities. At the Tata Institute, students could take courses in 'social entrepreneurship'. Using Sen's terms, I define 'social entrepreneurship' as a capability set used to increase the number of one's own and other's options in everyday life. The selection of relevant capabilities is in turn strongly tied to the values inherent to the local context. In the terminology of my dissertation I see 'social entrepreneurship' as an attempt to achieve a 'positive' practice of making sense, and in this context I am interested in how the acquisition of the relevant skills interacts with private and public spaces and the diversity of everyday life. My two research questions are: to what degree does 'social entrepreneurship' change access to resources and existing power structures in everyday life? How do values affect the range of possible actions and choices available to social entrepreneurs?

I have completed interviews with 18 social entrepreneurs in Mumbai and New Delhi. They were between 19 and 53 years of age, eight of them were female and ten male. The entrepreneurs had very different biographical backgrounds: some came from the slums, others from the upper class with degrees from elite universities. Some wanted to change their immediate environment, while others were interested in more comprehensive changes. They were active in such diverse areas as HIV prevention and intervention, youth work in the slums, recycling of used clothing, improving informal labour conditions or in developing an Internet platform for NGOs. Their projects were at various stages of development, some of them in their very initial phase, while others had already established organizations with more than 100 employees.

The data have yet to be sufficiently analysed. A preliminary focus is on the tension between the hierarchical caste system and conflicting values such as equal rights and self-determination. My second focus is on changes in everyday life concomitant to social entrepreneurship. The lives of some interview partners have become much more public and global. They have been on television; they have been portraited in newspapers and they lecture at conferences in Europe or the United States. The data provide indications on how the possibilities for changing lifestyles – including changes in access to resources – are influenced by social value systems and how these in turn are changed by social entrepreneurship. In this sense, my own experiences in India have made me aware that 'coping with an illness in everyday life' is a dynamic process that interacts in many ways with the private and public spaces of everyday life.

Note

1 My thanks to Charlotte Trenk-Hinterberger for her helpful advice and to Andreas Hemming for his translation.

References

Amering, M., and Schmolke, M. (2007): *Recovery. Das Ende der Unheilbarkeit.* Bonn: Psychiatrie-Verlag.

Antonovsky, A. (1979): *Health, Stress, and Coping: New Perspectives on Mental and Physical Well-Being.* San Francisco: Jossey-Bass Publishers.

Antonovsky, A. (1987): *Unraveling the Mystery of Health – How People Manage Stress and Stay Well.* San Francisco: Jossey-Bass Publishers.

Bandura, A. (1997): *Self-efficacy: The Exercise of Control.* New York: Freeman.

Csordas, T.J. (1997 [1994]): *The Sacred Self: A Cultural Phenomenology of Charismatic Healing.* Berkeley: University of California Press.

Davidson, L., Sells, D., Sangster, S., and O'Connell, M. (2005): Qualitative studies of recovery: what can we learn from the person? In: R.O. Ralph, and P.W. Corrigan (eds), *Recovery in Mental Illness: Broadening Our Understanding of Wellness,* 147–170. Washington, DC: American Psychological Association.

Dumont, L. (1976 [1966]): *Gesellschaft in Indien: Die Soziologie des Kastenwesens.* Wien: Europaverlag.

Estroff, S. (2004): Subject/subjectivities in dispute: the poetics, politics and performance of first-person narratives of people with schizophrenia. In: J.H. Jenkins, and R.J. Barrett (eds), *Schizophrenia, Culture and Subjectivity: The Edge of Experience,* 282–302. Cambridge: Cambridge University Press.

Hannover, B. (2000): Das kontextabhängige Selbst oder warum sich unser Selbst mit dem sozialen Kontext verändert. In: W. Greve (ed.), *Psychologie des Selbst,* 227–238. Weinheim: Beltz.

Moos, R.H. (2003): Social contexts: transcending their power and their fragility. *American Journal of Community Psychology* 31: 1–13.

Scheier, M. F., and Carver, C. S. (1992): Effects of optimism on psychological and physical well-being: theoretical overview and empirical update. *Cognitive Therapy and Research* 16: 201–228.
Schindler, H. (1998): Neuere Fachliteratur über die Mapuche. *Zeitschrift für Ethnologie* 123: 71–90.
Sen, A. (2001 [1999]): *Development as Freedom*. Oxford: Oxford University Press.
Spradley, J. P. (1980): *Participant Observation*. New York: Holt, Rinehart and Winston.
Strauss, A. L. (1998 [1994]): Grundlagen qualitativer Sozialforschung. Datenanalyse und Theoriebildung in der empirischen soziologischen Forschung (2nd ed.). München: Fink.
WHO (1993 [1992]): Internationale Klassifikation psychischer Krankheiten ICD 10. Bern: Huber.
Wiencke, M. (2009 [2006]): *Wahnsinn als Besessenheit. Der Umgang mit psychisch Kranken in spiritistischen Zentren in Brasilien*. Preface by Manfred Zaumseil. Berliner Beiträge zur *Ethnologie, vol. 18*. Berlin: *Weißensee Verlag*.
Wiencke, M. (2011): Kulturen der Gesundheit. Sinnerleben im Umgang mit psychischem Kranksein. Eine Anthropologie der Gesundheitsförderung. Preface by Manfred Zaumseil. Series Kultur und soziale Praxis. Bielefeld: transcript.
Witzel, A. (1989 [1985]): Das problemzentrierte Interview. In G. Jüttemann (ed.), *Qualitative Sozialforschung in der Psychologie*, 227–255 (2nd ed.). Weinheim: Beltz.
Wulf, C. (2005): Zur Genese des Sozialen. Mimesis, Performativität, Ritual. Bielefeld: transcript.
Wulff, E. (1992): Zur Konstitution schizophrener Unverständlichkeit. Beitrag zu einer subjektkonstruktivistischen Theorie des 'Wahnsinns'. *Forum Kritische Psychologie* 30: 6–28.
Zaumseil, M. (2006): Der 'alltägliche Umgang' mit Schizophrenie in Zentraljava. In: E. Wohlfahrt, and M. Zaumseil (eds), *Transkulturelle Psychiatrie – interkulturelle Psychotherapie. Interdisziplinäre Theorie und Praxis*, 331–360. Berlin: Springer.

29
ABSENCE OF A PRESENCE
Text, pedagogy and social anthropology in Northeast India

William N. Singh

The validity of a particular knowledge depends on territories, facts and social systems: thus knowledge has certain borders. Trees defy gravity by rising up to the sky. Like trees, social scientists need to rise above with a view to examining different cultures and interpreting different social practices: in this case, the diverse ways of living in Northeast India and their differences. This must be the hallmark of social anthropological research and pedagogy in Northeast India.

Higher education's main objective is to capture social phenomena both universal and local, revealing new forms of knowledge and making sense of such phenomena in pedagogy. Revealing mysteries and making the unfamiliar familiar to others is not just a task for ethnologists, but for all believers of science. Social scientists must question the validity of a Eurocentric understanding of social customs in order to reveal differently grounded understandings. The following will illuminate social anthropology in Northeast India from the point of view of practice and of pedagogy. It will formulate the innovations necessary to making the discipline relevant to the subjects it studies, as well as to international academic discourse.

Absence of a presence

Social anthropologists focus on different cultures and reveal different cultural codes. The interpretation of different social practices and beliefs defines social anthropology. However, the sociocultural thinking of Northeast India remains silent in mainstream academic texts. There is a fair amount of absence regarding the existing social realities of Northeast India in mainstream academia and institutions of higher learning. Northeast Indian issues are not discussed in academia, reported on by mainstream Indian media, or examined in scholarly journals. This failure to regard the social anthropological realities of Northeast India is what is meant by 'absence of a presence'. Why is local knowledge absent in mainstream texts? Why does Northeast India remain unconsidered in anthropological observations?

The term 'absence of a presence' is intended to support the visibility of social anthropology in Northeast India across the continent. It will make the inaudible audible, unnoticed values noticeable, and most importantly, counter the fickle nature of epistemology. The absence of a Northeast Indian presence urges for the creation of innovative, more grounded forms of epistemology. This 'absence of a presence' is not just a body of concepts. It is also a form of methodology in pursuing more meaningful studies of Northeast India. It looks for narratives, biographies and facts of the social realities of Northeast Indian societies. It incorporates event-based, densely contextual and spatially located forms of social facts occurring in Northeast India into the pedagogy and research of higher educational institutions.

The social history of Northeast India differs from the rest of India as much as it varies among the different parts of the region. Northeast India has brought forth diverse forms of social movements, from armed secessionist movements and new forms of violence and punishments to environmental movements and the rapid growth of Non-Government Organizations (NGOs). The growth of social problems is pandemic. Social anthropological teachings and research cannot remain confined to concepts of tradition, culture, tribe, indigeneity, etc. It must expand its horizons and engage in analysing these new forms of movement and violence. New social facts with specific historicities have arisen from the changes in social structures of Northeast Indian societies. By studying the relevant relations among facts, moral problems, and the historiography of Northeast Indian society, anthropological exercises in Northeast India can become more relevant, more concrete and more appealing. The goal is to make pedagogy and the practice of social anthropology more fruitful for the inhabitants of Northeast India, as well as contribute to the global academic discourse.

In identifying this absence of a presence, what consolidates is the need to theorize local knowledge by systematizing its existing forms in Northeast India. Indigenous knowledge is dying out due to the hegemonic nature of scientificity and universalism in knowledge systems. Western science has propounded its own forms of knowledge with certain political agendas, but in the process has threatened indigenous forms of knowledge (see Cohn 1996, also see Nandy 1983). Thus, a comprehensive examination of local knowledge is still absent in texts of higher studies in Northeast India. Practitioners of social science avoid analysing local meaning structures if they merely follow the trend towards 'universalist' knowledge. This failure to give proper treatment to particular aesthetic values or consider native points of view needs instant rectification. The absence of its own presence is, in Northeast India, characterized by excelling in receiving Eurocentric knowledge, but being crippled in the formulation of an own specific anthropological contribution.

Questioning the text

Questioning the text is pivotal for conducting good social research and pedagogy. The authority of text has never been questioned nor critically analysed in research and pedagogy in Northeast India. Thick interpretations of Northeast Indian societies, cultures, traditions, beliefs and social problems are hard to find in most anthropological texts. Anthropological practice in Northeast India is monologic in nature. Northeast social anthropology is monologic due to the lack of questioning the text.

Importing foreign theories and concepts with which to examine Northeast Indian social reality has been the trend in pedagogy and research. Social scientists in Northeast India import theories but hardly export appealing knowledge to other continents. It should not be forgotten that every important social theory has been a by-product of a specific historical social anthropology, from within a specific social context, during a specific period of time. Western epistemologies have been accepted as the norm for a macro-perspective that lends understanding to the complexities of Northeast India's social paradigm. The unquestioning acceptance of Western epistemologies has crippled the epistemological contribution of Northeast India to the international discourse. Academic endeavours within the region should be oriented towards increased presence, rather than the status quo of absence, in academic texts.

For instance, mainstream sociological and anthropological texts fail to reveal the processes of identity formation among the different tribes of Northeast India. Rituals and cultural activities are crucial to this process, and yet identity formation among tribes and its relationship to the social dynamics of Northeast India is under-observed in mainstream texts. Why have social anthropologists failed to capture this epistemologically? Anthropological practices in Northeast India need a fresh look. Anthropologists and social anthropologists should aim to produce more grounded and relative forms of new knowledge, of what Lyotard termed paralogy (see Fritzman 1990).

Beyond sociological imagination for Northeast India

Sociological imagination (Mills 1959) is a concept proposing a body of thoughts, a quality of mind used to capture information and develop meaningful reasons for achieving scientific goals. Mills's sociological imagination brings forth a dual understanding of the life of individuals and the history of society and how they shape each other. The message behind sociological imagination is to develop reasons for the lived realities of individuals and their connections to social structures. It can yield lucid summations of social problems and other forms of social practices.

However, the concept is not uncontested. First, Mills forgets to treat sociological imagination as a methodology of social studies. Second, Mills's sociological imagination misses the legacy of questioning the validity of texts. Third, Mills's sociological imagination never highlights why local knowledge remains absent in mainstream texts. This is one of the reasons why social science should think beyond sociological imagination.

Neo-sociological imagination developed out of a frustration with this exclusion of local knowledge. It is a product of the periphery. Scientifically, it is a body of epistemology and a methodology for social studies to make absence and silence visible and audible. It critically investigates universal claims of social theories and concepts and aims to highlight the essence of particular epochs. For Northeast India, neo-sociological imagination is an imperative. Social anthropology in Northeast India should create a new methodology, a methodology that will passively use meta-theories, actively use historical social anthropology and cautiously use empirical facts in the systematization of local knowledge. The task is to treat the indigenous knowledge of the peripheries scientifically. Social anthropology in Northeast India should investigate the relationship between individuals and social worlds, delineating the relationship between biography, social facts, culture, lifestyles and social structures in Northeast India.

In some cases, local values are becoming universally known (think of the tremendous increase in popularity of traditional healing practices, ancient forms of meditation or crafts made by indigenous artists), yet academia in Northeast India remains unable to analyse the scientificity of the local. Academia cannot be blind to local aesthetic values. The scientific weight of the 'local', 'particular' or 'parochial' should not be neglected by academia in favour of universal concepts and theories. Without its reference to the local, any academia is suspicious in its pedagogy and research.

Quarantine the unreliable

The beginning of the twenty-first century is characterized by the presence of multiple forms of social facts and social realities that vary from one place to another. The very idea of dissimilarity is embedded and revealed in the various social facts and social realities. Dissimilarity simply means the existence of multiple forms of social structures such as culture, beliefs, life-worlds and forms of identity. What is really frustrating in such an era of heterogeneity is the absence of grounded forms of knowledge in higher educational practices in Northeast India. Attempts to formulate new epistemologies and produce more grounded forms of knowledge are lacking.

It is time for the academia of Northeast India to realize that 'ready-made' forms of knowledge do not necessarily apply to certain remote corners of the globe. The reliability of universal forms of knowledge must be questioned, and it must be admitted that universal knowledge or grand theories are sometimes inappropriate for analysing particular social issues and social facts.

One need only examine how social theories have emerged. For instance, social theories like hegemony and civil society (Gramsci 1947), the Protestant ethic and the growth of capitalism (Weber 1904) or the medium as message (McLuhan 1964) were bodies of knowledge reflecting social issues of specific times, in specific historical environments, at specific geographical places. The twenty-first century is the moment for academics to question the universality of such social theories. It is time to deconstruct grand theories and point out their biases. Intellectuals should question and re-question the content of social theories and discard what appears unreliable.

Neo-sociological imagination in Northeast India

Mills regarded sociological imagination as a self-reflexive methodological tool for establishing intelligible relations between history, social structures and personal biographies in order to take responsible positions vis-à-vis the problems of a specific time (Mills 1959: 5). He wanted to cope with the problems of a world in which new social movements were emerging everywhere, authoritarianism and tradition were being irreversibly challenged and political instability and social conflict were becoming a general trend.

Only shortly after Mills postulated these ideals, however, postmodern thinking put the notion of universal truth under scrutiny, questioning its theretofore 'universal' appeal. The existence of multiple forms of truth made modern science no longer an adequate model of reality. The postmodern attitude aspires to produce more knowledge and more information. Lyotard defines postmodernism as a past of the present; a reflective reaction to the present; a withdrawal from and a critique of the real. It rejects nostalgia for the past and attempts to present the un-presentable (see Fritzman 1990).

Modernity is contested and the notion of multiple modernities challenges the European notion of modernity. Social scientists have questioned some of the basic backbones of modernity: universalism and enlightenment, demarcated historical phases of development and the coherent structure of human experience have been rejected in contemporary times. In fact, the very idea of the 'local' or 'indigeneity' arises from criticisms of modernity. Neo-sociological imagination welcomes the blind spots of modernity, i.e. the social issues and social facts of the present times occurring in places like Northeast India. New dimensions of social facts erupting at the present time are changing the social structures of Northeast Indian societies. Academics must come up with a more reliable body of ideas to understand such complexity. This is what neo-sociological imagination investigates. The sole aim is to make participation meaningful and produce a better outcome for all. Hannah Arendt argued for new forms of sociological imagination in thinking about, understanding and even judging the new century. The pedagogy of social anthropology in Northeast India would be much more meaningful if these issues were reflected in its syllabi.

At the present time, the revival of indigeneity is a social fact. For example, in India we have seen the rise of alternative schooling systems, where Vedic knowledge is reintroduced and has become part of school pedagogy. Yoga as a form of physical knowledge has become a global phenomenon. The Veda and yoga originated in India, yet, have been in absentia for quite some time. Their resurgence represents a kind of globalization from below (see Hall 1996). These ancient and local forms of knowledge have bounced back to capture the front pages again. The return of indigeneity is also a re-membering (see Bhabha 1994) of indigenous knowledge and one of the main goals of neo-sociological imagination.

Indigeneity in Northeast India is a cultural product in tune with environmental and social formations. These co-relationships exist outside of mainstream texts, and thus often remain invisible. Cultural relativism and the indigeneity of knowledge remain unreflected in mainstream social anthropology and anthropological texts in Northeast India. The concern here is to make mainstream texts more inclusive by reflecting the forms of indigenous knowledge and cultural practices of Northeast India.

Methodically and ideologically, it is not easy to promote local epistemologies. In neo-sociological imagination, social scientists should not just read social structures through mainstream texts. As mentioned above, the critical reflection of texts is pivotal. Neo-sociological imagination inspires social researchers in Northeast India to think beyond the limits of the text. There are many forms of social issues and social problems that do not find entrance into sociological and anthropological texts in Northeast India. Not rectifying this negligence in pedagogy and textual prescriptions is indeed a white-collar crime.

The neo-sociological imagination urges any social observer not to blindly accept a given body of knowledge. Thinking beyond the limits of the text is an essential ingredient of neo-sociological imagination. Highlighting absences and the silent aspects of texts is a prime motive of neo-sociological imagination. It attempts to systematically gather available forms of local and indigenous forms of knowledge, cultural elements and rituals.

Neo-sociological imagination demands a more sophisticated use of empirical methods. The principle of neo-sociological imagination is to passively use universal theories, actively use historicity with cultural specifics, and cautiously use facts. Ultimately, the whole business of sociological research and training should focus on lending local dispositions representation in texts. Indigenous knowledge may lead to reliable epistemologies that will ultimately transform the practice of social science in Northeast India.

Text and pedagogy of social anthropology in Northeast India

Social anthropological pedagogy and research in Northeast India remains immature and un-grounded. The tools of social anthropology, the art of social anthropology must expand beyond the notion of 'ours' or 'one's own', to seriously study the 'Other' societies 'out there'. Social anthropologists should attempt to theorize a more grounded form of knowledge by studying other communities and other cultural groups inhabiting Northeast India.

How densely described are Northeast Indian societies, cultures, traditions, beliefs and social problems in sociological texts? The task at present times is not to import alien theories and alien concepts into South Asian social reality (see Oommen 1998). Alien concepts and alien theories have already been directly applied, without any second thoughts, to Northeast India's social realities. These epistemologies and ontologies are pre-packaged forms of knowledge. They do not necessarily provide the correct frame of reference for understanding specific local complexities.

Modernity in Northeast India is opposed in its form to Western notions of modernity. What can be called 'Northeast Indian modernity' can be conceptualized as a continuation of tradition. As a continuation, this modernity is not just a binary opposite of tradition. Northeast Indian modernity is an offshoot of structural shifts happening in the political-juridical realm and in the transformation of authority. It is intriguing for two simple reasons. First, Northeast Indian societies have never moved away from their traditional ethos. These societies have respect for and keep in contact with traditional cultures. Traditional social structures and social practices still influence every individual process of socialization. Second, Northeast Indian societies have never become modern societies in the Western sense, simply because the forms and structures of modern society have never fully developed in Northeast Indian societies.

Western-oriented modernity is simply incommensurable when talking of modernity in Northeast India.

Core aspects of (Western) modernity theory – universalization, rationality, industrializing spirit, mass consumption and mass production – simply do not exist in Northeast India. Nevertheless, these concepts remain a backbone of modernity theory as it is taught in higher educational institutions in Northeast India. Topics like class, caste, status, power, alienation, strike and protest, totalitarianism etc. appear in the recommended syllabi. The historicity of these terms has been dismissed. Such technical understandings of sociological idioms and sociological phrases have never been questioned. How relevant are they to the Northeast Indian context? This should be a main question of social science and classroom pedagogy. Invoking neo-sociological imagination will make social science more meaningful in Northeast India. Scholars from Northeast India should admit that many sociological theoretical concepts do not have a counterpart in the social realities of present Northeast India.

A suitable ethnography for Northeast India

The ethnographic practices of Northeast India should not rely on Western ideas as a starting point in conceptualizing social phenomena. Western knowledge has to be countered and questioned if its notions fit and how reliable and valid its concepts are. Re-examining methodologies of Western origin should become an important ingredient when practicing social anthropology in Northeast India.

To begin with, ethnological research is hardly possible without reference to history. To understand unique social events we need historiography (see Thompson 1994; Hobsbawm 1997). Historiography is concerned with the recovery of meaningful worlds and the interplay of the collective and the subjective. Northeast India is an amalgam of multiethnic groups. Many of these tribes have been recognized as 'scheduled tribes', but not as ethnic groups, by the Indian Constitution. In the Indian Constitution, Northeast India is defined not in terms of sociological concepts, but by political terminologies such as scheduled areas, scheduled tribes, reservation/policy and improvement of living conditions. The 'scheduled tribes' of Northeast India have never been defined in terms of possessing differing religions, traditions or cultures from the rest of India. However, Indian anthropology still largely confines itself to concepts of caste, ethnicity, religion and discrimination. How can it examine the political influence on the constitution of social life without making room for new vocabularies and knowledge?

Post-colonial scholars espoused a new trait of ethnography emerging in the post-colonial world, commonly known as indigenous ethnography (see Fahim 1982). Indigenous ethnographers study their own cultures. The study of one's own culture is a definitional expansion of anthropology. It is an attack on colonial understandings of 'other' cultures. When we analyse our own culture, we call forth an innovative methodology for a different path of theorizing our own cultures. When ethnographers study their own cultures, this offers new aspects and depths of understanding. Indigenous anthropological accounts are empowered and restricted in unique ways. Indigenous ethnography emerges due to an ideological shift and a new approach to historiography. It repositions anthropology in respect to its object of study.

In ethnographic fieldwork, one must always look and welcome innovations that don't fall in line with traditional and conventional procedures. Ethnography is instrumental in the creation of and knowledge about social phenomena. Innovative procedures such as looking for the historicity of ideas or specific cultural items, as well as searching for the relevance of ideas of Western origin, should be constantly negotiated while conducting ethnographic field work. Ethnography serves to make familiar the unfamiliar, the invisible visible and the inaudible audible.

'We the Tikopia' (Firth 1936) envisaged that cultural anthropology should not be a jumble of slogans and labels or a factory of impressionistic short-cuts but a science of social studies. Firth stressed the importance of lengthy personal contact with real people, not just for days or weeks but for years. Firth also stressed the importance of an 'us' and an exotic 'them' as both a major obstacle and crucial factor in understanding 'the Other'.

Martyn Hammersley stressed the importance of participant observation and in-depth interviewing as an essential component in ethnography or in qualitative social research. Hammersley opined a belief that there may be multiple, contradictory truths and that finding one kind of truth is the hallmark of anthropological field work. Ethnography produces accurate representations of phenomena that are largely independent of the researcher and of the research process (Hammersley 2008: 243). Ethnography is concerned with societies other than the one we live in. In order to construe the gestures of others, their worlds and their words, we have to situate them within systems of signs and relations of power and meaning (Lévi-Strauss 1963: 17). Social practices always have a meaning in relation to a particular society. Ethnography involves an effort to search for cultural codes and symbols and the meanings they signify. Ethnography is always linked with problems of epistemology (Aijmer 1988: 424). Ethnography is historically contingent and culturally configured. Informant accounts and observations remain a basic ingredient for the making of ethnographic texts. Ethnography should view people's lives from the 'bottom up' (Cohn 1987: 39).

Concluding remarks

One topic worth exploring in Northeast India is the notion of 'tribe'. A sociological exercise on tribe would be productive, as it confronts the colonial definition of tribe. It will be a mine-field of knowledge: not just for social anthropology, but for other disciplines as well. If studied appropriately, it will be one of the most acknowledged contributions to social anthropology to come from Northeast India.

As mentioned, while excellent in receiving universal knowledge, social anthropology in Northeast India remains crippled in contributing towards international discussions. Postulating an 'absence of a presence' strives to diagnose this deficit of active receiver and passive contributor. Social issues in Northeast India are not discussed in mainstream texts, syllabi or pedagogy. Social anthropology in Northeast India should be more reflective of local realities. Local terms and idioms from Northeast India should find their place in scientific discourse.

Engaging in social science requires a change of mindset. Reflexivity is key. Inter-disciplinary understanding is pivotal in bringing local forms of knowledge into mainstream epistemology. Social issues and particular social facts must be studied from the various perspectives of different disciplines. We must pursue an exploratory framework for understanding social life in Northeast India. Post-foundational studies suggested theorizing or doing research from a socially situated point of view, as social interests and values also shape our ideas. Social understandings are part of shaping social life (see Alexander and Seidman 2010). In other words, post-foundationalism is not a rejection of theories but a defence of more complex, multidimensional arguments.

Social science should promote localism rather than promoting universalism. The scientificity and authenticity of local terms, if properly treated, should be a part of syllabi and pedagogy. Local terms and idioms should make their entry into the texts and pedagogy of social anthropology. New theories and epistemologies can be produced with a bottom-up approach to analysing social facts and social issues.

References

Aijmer, G. (1988): Rhetoric and the Authority of Ethnography: Post-Modernism and the Social Reproduction of Text. In: Current Anthropology 29 (2): 424–445.

Alexander, J.C., and Seidman, S. (2010): The New Social Theory Reader, 2nd ed. New York.

Bhabha, H.K. (1994): Location of Culture. London.

Cohn, B.S. (1987): An Anthropologist among the Historian and Other Essays. Oxford.

Cohn, B. S. (1996): Colonialism and Its Forms of Knowledge. Princeton, NJ.
Fahim, H. (1982): Indigenous Anthropology in Non-Western Countries. Durham.
Firth, R. (1936): We the Tikopia. London.
Fritzman, J. M. (1990): Lyotard's Paralogy and Rorty's Pluralism. In: Educational Theory 40 (3): 371–380.
Gramsci, A. (1947): Selections from the Prison Notebooks. Hyderabad 2010 (Reprint).
Hall, S. (1996): Formation of Modernity. London.
Hammersley, M. (2008): Participant Observation and Depth Interviewing. In C. Seale (ed.), Social Research Methods: A Reader, 290–294. New York.
Hobsbawm, E. J. (1997): On History. New York.
Lévi-Strauss, J. C. (1963): Structural Anthropology. New York.
McLuhan, M. (1964): Understanding Media: The Extension of Man. Toronto.
Mills, C. W. (1959): The Sociological Imagination. London.
Nandy, A. (1983): The Intimate Enemy. New Delhi.
Oommen, T. K. (1998): Alien Concept and the South Asian Reality. New Delhi.
Thompson, E. P. (1994): Making History: Writings on History and Culture. New York.
Weber, M. (1904): Protestant Ethics and the Spirit of Capitalism. London 2002.

30
DISPOSITIONS AS PROPERTIES
Irrelevance of functional characterization

S. K. Arun Murthi

I have been working with the essentialist thesis which holds dispositions as properties. What is a disposition? In science one often comes across reference to such properties as solubility, fragility, conductivity, ductility and malleability that are said to be possessed by certain kinds of objects. These terms clearly indicate that they are dispositional terms meaning that they indicate the behaviour of a thing under certain circumstances, i.e. the way it is disposed to behave. Hence they are called disposition terms. These dispositional predicates seem to denote dispositional properties. In fact, some philosophers grant the status of properties to dispositions. Mumford, Molanar, Ellis and Bird hold the view that dispositions are properties. In my thesis I have critically examined whether dispositions deserve the status of properties. In particular I had considered in detail the view of Mumford and Molnar's view that makes use of the idea of functional characterization and manifestation of dispositions in a significant way. In examining these views, I had argued how this idea of functional characterization is something that is not relevant to dispositions. During that time I had met Prof. Holm Tetens of Free University of Berlin and had the opportunity to discuss my research problem with him.[1] During the course of the discussion he referred to one of his papers, 'Teleology and the Concept' (1989), where he had differentiated between a teleologically relevant event and a causal event. I draw upon Tetens's work and the concept of information associated with teleology that further substantiates my argument against functional characterization of dispositions. I would first like to turn to the philosophical position that analyses the nature of such dispositional properties as real and occurrent and the problems in such an analysis. Later I discuss and draw upon Tetens's work to substantiate my views on functional characterization.

Dispositions as properties

What exactly are these dispositional properties? Ellis is very much anxious to emphasize the ontological independence and the genuineness of dispositional properties in his analysis of dispositions. Dispositions are the behaviour of things in certain circumstances and such a description is different from identifying the cause of such a behaviour. But, when one talks of dispositional property one is talking of a causal power that gives rise to such a behaviour and this is different from the behaviour itself. He thus makes this difference between dispositions and dispositional properties (Ellis 2002: 76). For an essentialist like Ellis, dispositional properties are there to explain the manifest behavioural dispositions. Ellis's idea of giving the status of property to dispositions fundamentally rests on the premise that such properties perform an explanatory role. But such an assumption is contentious and Mumford brings to fore these objections to such a claim and attempts to counter such objections (1998). There is the usual charge that such an explanation is a *virtus dormitiva* type explanation. But Ellis dismisses such a charge on the ground that there are many possible causal explanations of such manifest behaviour and attributing a dispositional property happens to be one of them. Dispositions of a thing are linked to a natural kind of process in which these dispositions are involved. The important aspect of Ellis's essentialism that one has to bear is his emphasis that the natural kinds of processes are something that is designated and identified but not defined in terms of the behaviour they display. The description in terms of behaviour only serves the purpose of securing reference to the kind of process and should not be construed as definitions of such a natural kind process.

It is appropriate to examine the serious objection to the property view of dispositions and Mumford's response to it. He brings up the objection in the context of the causal relevance of dispositions. He holds the view that dispositions are causally relevant and it is this that allows him to give a property status to dispositions. What is significant in this context is that he conveniently runs certain issues in parallel in his effort to grant the property status to dispositions. These issues are that of causal efficacy, explanation and functional characterization. I will now elucidate how he runs these issues in parallel. He begins his work on dispositions with a certain commonplace intuition of dispositions. According to this, dispositions are possessed by things and such possession is what is meant by the attribution of dispositions and refers to such attributions as disposition ascriptions. It should be realized here that such a characterization of attribution results from our way of speaking. Such a way of speaking leads to intuitions of something being possessed and such intuitions are sometimes faulty and not promising and therefore cannot be taken as a basis of ontological commitments. He regards such attributions 'as unproblematic' and then poses a rhetorical question: 'What is it that is being ascribed? The most natural answer is that it is properties' (Mumford 1998: 3). This is not any argument in granting the property status to dispositions and he works on intuitions as I have mentioned above. Having granted the property status he makes effort to show that these play a definite causal role and therefore have an explanatory value as dispositional explanations. In setting out his argument he points to the manifest difference in behaviour of two substances and attributes this difference to some causally relevant property. This causally relevant property, he argues, can be described in terms of dispositions by characterizing such properties functionally. It is in this sense that he runs issues of causal efficacy, explanation and functional characterization in parallel in his bid to legitimize dispositional properties. He refers to this argument of his as argument from behavioural difference. Before I take up his argument from functional difference I would like to discuss the notion of attribution with respect to dispositions and the following point: in what sense can the dispositions be associated with the idea of causation and explanation?

That the possession of disposition is only a manner of speaking can be understood if one unpacks the sense of 'attribution'.[2] Let us take the case of solubility. If one attributes solubility to something then such an attribution is limited to saying the following: that it is true of something that, whenever it is placed in a particular liquid it dissolves. The question of it (solubility) being causally efficacious and also a property – both these coming together in a package, as Mumford claims – is to give something more to a disposition. Now how does Mumford make a case for giving something more to a disposition? He claims that dispositions have an explanatory role and it is only in this sense that it makes sense for dispositions to be attributed. But then, how does disposition come to have an explanatory role? He appeals to the two features of being causally efficacious and being properties which confers the explanatory role to dispositions. But such an appeal is misconceived, because what supports the contention of casual explanatory role is an intuitive appeal to everyday talk. In fact, Michael Fara does draw upon such an appeal to support the causal explanatory role of dispositions (2009). But it should be noted that its explanatory value is derived because of the attention drawn to a causal relation which is captured in the form of regularity. Such a law referred to as a causal law 'unites situations and phenomena' of the same kind (O'Shaughnessy 1970: 3). As O'Shaughnessy rightly argues, all that is there to explanation in such cases is the attention being drawn to the known regular concomitance between the situation and phenomena and such a causation is a superficial one. The explanations that the dispositions *seem* to provide are thus non-causal explanations and are introduced as such, and not anything more, and in so arguing approaches the problem of dispositions by dividing them into based and unbased dispositions.[3] In both these cases he argues that there is no causal role for dispositions and as such dispositions fall outside the causal schema.

In passing it would be interesting to note Prior, Pargetter and Jackson's (1982) argument of why dispositions are not causally explanatory. They endorse that all dispositions have a causal basis in the form of property or property complex and they refer to this claim as 'The Causal Thesis'. In addition they also hold the 'Distinctness Thesis' where they argue that dispositions such as fragility are distinct from the causal base. The causal base is itself sufficient as antecedent operative condition for the manifestation like breaking to occur. The disposition, fragility, is not the cause or part of the cause of such breaking, the manifestation. If the casual base is doing all the work then there is nothing left for the disposition to do. Therefore dispositions cannot be invoked for causal explanatory purposes. However, I have one small concern in this chapter. They are not explicit about the status of dispositions in terms of whether they are properties or predicates.[4]

I would now turn to show how the argument from behavioural difference is a flawed one. In this whole argument from behavioural difference Mumford is more anxious to establish the causal relevance of dispositions. He is interested in this because if dispositions are held to be causally impotent, then according to causal criterion of property existence, the existence of dispositions as real properties gets threatened. Dispositions are classed into the ontological category of properties. Now if dispositions are not causes then they are not genuine properties. This conclusion hinges on the premise that if anything is a property then they should figure as legitimate causes in an explanation. There are a series of objections to the view that dispositions are causally efficacious and Mumford sets out to counter these. It is important for him to do so as otherwise it becomes easy to counter his claim that dispositions are properties.

Causal relevance of dispositions is established by invoking the idea of functional characterization. Functional characterization is nothing but identifying a property in terms of its effects. But, according to Mumford, disposition ascriptions are nothing but functional characterization of property P. In brief, the argument runs as follows. There is some property P that is causally relevant for this behaviour difference. Such a property can be functionally characterized. Such a functional characterization is what disposition ascriptions are. Therefore dispositions are causally relevant. Since dispositions are causally relevant, they are genuine and real properties. He runs so many issues in parallel that it is difficult to see how circularity looms large in his argument. I try to unpack it in the following simple steps.

1. Dispositions have an explanatory role and it is by an appeal to such a role that dispositions gain legitimacy. Dispositional explanations are a brand of causal explanations. How? Because dispositions have causal roles and therefore are causally relevant and so they have a property status (Mumford 1998: 11–17). The explanatory value is derived because they are causes.
2. Causal role relevance is set out in the argument from behavioural difference (ibid.: 119f.).
3. Behavioural difference claims that if property P is characterized functionally then it is a disposition, and therefore, causally relevant. A functional role is played in the form of a cause, and therefore, dispositional explanation gains sanctity. He reiterates this again under varieties of functionalism (ibid.: 204) where dispositional explanation gains legitimacy by the functional role that is being played in the form of a cause when disposition is ascribed. (Invoking functionalism for the analysis of dispositions would also be inappropriate. I will also consider why it is so shortly).
4. But this argument is countered by two triviality objections (actually one) because it is the contention of opponents of realism about dispositions that dispositions are just a posit, and therefore, are not causes (ibid.: 120, 134).
5. And how is the objection handled: by dismissing Rylean behaviourism and invoking functionalism, the very thing that was countered in the argument from behavioural difference (135) in (4) above.

The steps reveal the circularity in the argument. Moreover, he is already assuming the existence of a dispositional property, the very thing he is arguing for to establish. Such an argument, therefore, is open to the charge of triviality of dispositional explanations – such explanations being a *virtus dormitiva* type of explanation. Mumford here differentiates between two kinds of triviality and proceeds to counter them. I claim that such a differentiation is not required in my following arguments.

I will turn to these charges of triviality now. First let me focus on the charge of *virtus dormitiva* type of explanation. *Virtus dormitiva* type of explanation is seen to be an unsatisfactory explanation. An illustration of such an explanation comes from Molière's play (hence the term *virtus dormitiva* also come from this play) where it is asked 'Why does this drug put everyone to sleep?' An explanation is given which runs as follows 'the soporific power of the drug is the cause of the sleep'. Such an explanation is said to be *virtus dormitiva* because 'soporific' means sleep inducing and nothing seems to be added in terms of causal information other than giving some synonymous term. I must add that Mumford refers to another objection which looks similar to this but he insists that it is different, which he refers to a triviality objection (1998: 133–136). Triviality objection views dispositional explanations as no good explanations as they do not give any further information that is not already had. Such triviality arises because the dispositional terms like soluble, fragile, etc. mean nothing more than what happens in certain circumstances, say, it dissolves when put in water, breaks when dropped etc. Mumford opines that such a conception of disposition is only Rylean that is given as follows:

[Df_R] x is $D =_{df}$ if x is F-ed, then x will G

Such a Rylean understanding, according to him, is incomplete. It is his claim that disposition ascriptions are better characterized functionally. Mumford argues that there is some property which makes for the behavioural difference and it is this property that makes the dispositional ascription come true. It is in this sense that there is a causal role that is attributed, and such an added role can be represented as follows:

[Df_m] x is $D =_{df} x$ has some property P (and P is a cause of x G-ing if x is F-ed in conditions C_i).

It is Mumford's contention that what one is doing is invoking a property to explain the dissolution or the breaking of a glass and there is nothing trivial about it. It appears that important for Mumford is that one is able to complete the activity of explanation by postulating a property. Though Ellis has not gone into the details of presenting a defence of dispositions as properties, as Mumford has done, one can obviously judge that such an argument is also implicit in his elucidation. He stresses that such properties are designated or identified and not defined and reference is secured by such dispositional descriptions. But he (Mumford) has not substantiated this claim and I have shown problems with such functionalist arguments. Only when one accepts such a characterization can one hold that there is some property responsible for the dissolution of water. But if one does not accept the functionalist characterization then the difference which he makes between the two types of trivial objections is not noticeable but boils down only to *virtus dormitiva* kind.

Mumford acknowledges *virtus dormitiva* but justifies its use. Its justification lies in the fact that when opium is administered, such a dispositional ascription rules out the possibility of other explanations. Ellis also makes a similar point. But one does not require a disposition as a property for that. It is the opium *itself* which makes one sleep. We do not require a power ascription to indicate that the responsibility lies with the opium itself. That this is the case is revealed in Mumford himself when he attempts to justify the non-triviality of the explanation by comparing it with Hutchison's uncombable hair syndrome. The problem of unruly hair in some children is attributed to a condition called uncombable hair syndrome. A syndrome does not indicate a cause. It is just a group of symptoms that characterizes a particular disorder and there is no particular organic cause that is attributed. This is the same as the Rylean characterization of dispositions along behaviourist lines. Such a characterization is also betrayed by Mumford himself when he says, 'Hutchison takes uncombable hair syndrome to be akin to a *virtus dormitiva* but thinks it not useless as an explanation of unruly hair, for it assigns a responsibility for the unruly hair to the hair itself.' Assigning the responsibility to *hair itself* is not to make an ontological commitment to a dispositional property as Mumford seems to be arguing.

What is significant to note is that the *virtus dormitiva* explanation suggests something more than that, it is an empty explanation. It is that disposition is essentially a predicate term that does not need to have a corresponding property. The implication is that conditional analysis of these predicate terms exhausts its meaning and there is nothing more that needs to be attributed to it. Mumford questions the reasonableness of this *virtus dormitiva* objection as follows. Such an analysis leads one to say that it makes no difference to the world if something gains a disposition and loses it the next minute and again gains it in the following minute and thus it makes no difference whether it possesses ten dispositional properties or ten thousand. But then in the first place, I would say that the question of gaining or losing something in the form of dispositions is itself not reasonable. In this, one is assuming beforehand that dispositions are properties, the very thing that needs to be established. Therefore, if one does not presume a property account of disposition there is nothing unreasonable about the Rylean explanation that Mumford has mentioned; i.e. that the conditional was true at one time and not true at another (1998: 27).

Functional characterization of dispositions

Dispositions are closely associated with the conditionals they entail, and thus it has been claimed that what distinguishes dispositions is that they entail such conditionals. Mellor (1974) argues that one can also associate a categorical property with a conditional. In trying to establish the categorical-disposition distinction Mumford gives a more precise relation between dispositions and its corresponding conditional. Dispositions occupy a functional role in the form of causes and a conceptual connection is established between dispositions and the conditional. How is this conceptual connection between disposition and the conditional established? Mumford contends that the functional role is best expressed in the conditional form. But the point of contention is whether a functional characterization is apt. Where is functional characterization possible? How is functional role arrived at in the case of dispositions? In such cases I claim that one assumes that there is a property which is fulfilling a functional role, and one comes to understand of such a role after observing the regular sequence of events. We presuppose such a property because, as per Mumford, that is the best way to account for the behavioural difference. But why is this difference only to be accounted in terms of disposition but not in terms of any structural mechanism? This question is important because, in science, when one is asked 'why salt dissolves in water', the answer that 'it is because of solubility' is one that is not acceptable.

How far is functional characterization legitimate and relevant? This needs to be examined. Functional characterization is more relevant in cases of devices where a device is specifically meant to do something. In such cases it is appropriate to functionally characterize a device. When something is devised to play a specific role then functional characterization becomes relevant. Mumford himself brings the device of thermometer and thermostat into picture in his elucidations. Thermometer is a device that can be functionally characterized because it is designed to satisfy a certain functional requirement. But one cannot, along the same lines, construe that property is a device by which a functional requirement is satisfied. In the case of dispositions one has to bear in mind that such a property is only postulated but not functionally characterized. But Mumford seems to be postulating as well as functionally characterizing dispositions. He is construing the property along the lines of designed device which it is not. For a functional essence to be made explicit we need a thing to do something, more specifically a thing that is designed keeping the functional essence in view. One can then have different structural mechanisms in which such a functional essence is realized. Thermometer is one such example and so is the device carburettor. But in the case of dispositional property one is postulating a property that functions like a device and then functionally characterizing in the way the behavioural interaction unfolds. In other words one is postulating as well as characterizing. In the case of a device nothing is postulated. There is a device which is concretely designed to display a particular behaviour. But in the case of dispositions a particular behaviour like salt dissolving is already there for us to observe and we then postulate a device like property to be doing this act. It is for this reason that functional characterization of such dispositions seems to be inappropriate. Mumford starts with the claim that disposition ascription is a functional characterization of a property but does not see to what extent the functional characterization is appropriate. Why does one wish to characterize it functionally? It is because this is the best way, for Mumford, to give a property status to dispositional terms. Our commonplace way of speaking of disposition attributions gives a property sense to dispositions. Mumford also has taken such a commonplace attribution and in his enterprise is anxious to secure it metaphysically. But it should be realized that such a way of speaking does not allow us to construe it as a property in the ontological sense.

The idea of property being characterized functionally is difficult to accept. If something has been designed to function in a particular way, say like the gun in Molnar's example, then it is taken for granted that this implies that it has the capacity to fire (2006). But from that it is not possible to say that any property can be characterized functionally. Cummins grants that all functions are capacities but not all capacities are functions. But even when he grants that functions are capacities it should be noted that these functions are not properties. For example, the capacity of the gun to fire is not to be construed as a property of the gun. Though one can loosely make such an assertion it should just be taken as a *façon de parler*. There is no ontological commitment we make to such a property as the property of firing that exists in the gun. There are some other properties of the components of the gun which in fact are used in its design with the purpose of firing. The very activity of design involves some very systematic organization of properties to make it deliver a particular function. The deliverance of this function of the artefact cannot be ontologically construed as a property of the artefact. The capacity to function, therefore, is an idea that needs to be dissociated from the notion of property, power and disposition, contra Mumford and Molnar. I reject Mumford's claim of a property being characterized functionally.

I would now like to consider the appropriateness of accounting for dispositions along functionalist lines. Can dispositions be accounted along functionalist lines? Mumford says yes. Take the case of disposition like solubility. A thing is soluble in virtue of a property whose function it is to dissolve. A functional essence is attributed to the property. But the point to be noted is only after the event is observed that one attributes a functional essence. We come to know of such a property only through event sequences. Moreover it is in the sense of postulation that such a property is conceived. Let us take the case of objects instead of properties. Mumford also attributes functional essence to objects (1998: 196). He gives the example of thermostat. It is important to realize that thermostat is designed to play the triggering switch role when the temperature reaches a certain pre-set limit. Such a function is kept in mind in the design itself. The very use of the object is for that purpose. Functional essences do make some sense in such cases.[5] But then in such a case as a thermostat one does not observe a sequence of events where a switch is triggered as soon as a pre-set temperature is reached and then see the device along functionalist lines. Such seems to be the case with dispositional terms when we account it along functionalist lines. Such an observation has been made by Cummins in a different form. He claims that something can have the power to do something but that may not be its function. It is not its function because it has not been designed keeping that purpose in mind. Functionalist essence is significant only when one has a design purpose. Mumford responds to Cummins's charge by objecting to the latter's usage of the term function to be too narrow. But he has failed to understand the point that Cummins is attempting to drive at – the importance of purposive design as part of the usage of term function. It is this idea of purposive design that is missing in ascriptions of dispositions that makes them inappropriate to be accounted along functionalist lines. The idea of functional design is different and something that cannot be appropriately invoked in the analysis of dispositions or powers.[6] Both Molnar and Mellor have invoked this idea of functional design in their illustrations of how powers function as real properties.[7] However, closely associated with the idea of dispositions and powers is that of *manifestation* of these dispositions or powers to which I now turn my attention.

Dispositions and manifestation

Mumford, in the context of considering the examples of dispositions, refers to their key feature. It is that for every disposition there is a corresponding manifestation but a disposition can be present without manifesting itself. The disposition of fragility (the example that he takes) manifests itself in the form of breakage. For example, a thing made of glass is fragile in the sense that its possession of fragility manifests in the breaking of the object if dropped suitably. But, Mumford argues, the disposition ascription may be true even if the object never breaks in its entire life history. In other words, the fragility of an object is always present even if the breakage is not manifested. Since the actual manifestation of the breakage is not demanded for the ascription of fragility or any other disposition philosophers have drawn upon the notion of conditionals in explaining the dispositions and have debated on what exactly is the nature of the conditional.[8] The realist about disposition holds that these are 'ontologically independent of their manifestations' (Molnar 2006: 57). In fact Molnar considers independence as one of the five basic features of powers.[9] He further argues that these are actual properties. Mumford, continuing his realist defence of such dispositional properties, rejects the claim that the actualization of dispositions lies in its manifestation.[10] He bases his rejection on the fact that 'we understand dispositions to be actual whenever they are ascribed' (Mumford 1998: 33f.). But such an ascription is just our manner of speaking, and as I have already mentioned, does not carry much ontological significance. He himself makes this explicit when he says that 'the ordinary use and understanding of disposition ascriptions is based on realist assumptions' (ibid.: 51).[11]

It is the empiricist claim that dispositions are to be understood as a set of complex events followed by another set of observable events. This is the reductive account of dispositions on the lines of Humean account of causal relations. Such an account rejects the idea of dispositions as properties that describe reality. All that matters is the experience of certain regular sequence of events. It is such an understanding that leads to the conditional analysis of disposition ascriptions. Mumford gives a detailed argument for rejecting this way of understanding dispositions. Molnar asserts that powers as properties exits without manifesting and rules out that a conditional analysis of powers can be given.

However, in my view, the question of manifestation arises because of the realist interpretation of dispositions. They ascribe something more to dispositions than it deserves and by granting a property status make dispositions causally efficacious. On the other hand, if disposition ascriptions are treated as nothing more than the possibilities of a certain kind of behaviour in certain kind of circumstances, then, the issue of manifestation does not surface. It is just a predicate whose meaning is exhausted by the conditional analysis. I have already shown the problems of disposition that manifests in the form of *virtus dormitiva* kind of explanation. Such a predicative sense of disposition is reflected in the view that dispositions are not causally explanatory. Such a view can be presented as follows: If the disposition 'conceptually necessitates the occurrence of manifestation' then there is nothing causally explanatory about it (Fara 2009). This is the lesson that can be drawn from the *virtus dormitiva* explanation. But Molnar argues briefly that the powers are not possibilities but are actual properties.

It is here that he uses the idea of functionalism and design. He formulates a possibilist analysis of powers as follows:

At time t x has the power to Φ, if it is possible that x Φ's at t

He breaks this analysis into two components:

(A) If at time t x has the power to Φ, then it is possible that x Φ's at t.

And

(B) If it is possible that x Φ's at t, then x has the power to Φ at t.

According to Molnar, the restricted sense of possibility indicates the initial conditions that need to be present for x to Φ at t. But he has already taken the power as independent of initial conditions, and therefore, one that does not entail the initial conditions. Here, he takes the illustration of the gun. As a matter of precaution if the bullets have been removed (i.e. the initial conditions are absent) from the gun to prevent the possibility of firing, the power of the gun to fire is not lost. In other words, though the possibility of firing is not there, the power of the gun to fire still remains. Therefore, according to him, the conditional (A) turns out to be false. However, I do not accept this argument because the idea of design of a gun is conflated with that of power. As I have mentioned, Mumford also invokes inappropriately the idea functionalism and design with that of dispositions. The gun is designed to function in such a way as to fire bullets. Such a functional design is different from power property. In the case of functionalism something is pre-designed to function in a specific way. It is my claim that one cannot have a functionalist understanding of dispositions. For something to function as F it is designed to accomplish that purpose. A gun is something that is designed to fire bullets. It is not something it is naturally disposed to do. There is no element of design in powers and dispositions. Therefore one cannot ascribe any disposition or power to the gun as Molnar has done.

Now let me come to Molnar's possibilist analysis. In the use of the word 'possible' in the definiens in the restricted sense he interprets possible to include the initial conditions. There is no reason why one should prefer to incorporate the sense of initial conditions into the use of possible. He has taken this line of argument because earlier he has claimed that the 'having of a power by its bearer is usually independent of the occurrence of stimulus' (2006: 84). What Molnar and earlier Mumford have done already, is to grant the status of causally efficacious property to the disposition or

DISPOSITIONS AS PROPERTIES

powers and to reject the idea that disposition ascriptions merely indicate possible events. How is the truth of a statement containing dispositional terms accounted? The truth of the dispositional terms lies in the truth of the subjunctive conditional 'if x then y', where x indicates the conditions or circumstances and y indicates the events that follow these conditions. This is all there is to dispositions. Such is the contention of the anti-realists of dispositions – e.g. Hume, Ryle and Dummett. But the realist goes one step further in asking what makes the conditional true and is tempted to argue from this that it is the disposition as property with the right casual power. My claim is that the leap which they make in terms of granting the disposition the status of causally efficacious property on this basis is not a legitimate one. I make this claim because dispositional explanations are basically *virtus dormitiva*, and therefore, anything that is a consequence of such an explanation is also not legitimate. Moreover, the realist about dispositions does not adequately address the charge of *virtus dormitiva* explanation and has the tendency to play down the charge. Ignoring the fact that the cause is to be sought in some form of mechanism based on the underlying state – those which science would be precisely looking for – and maintaining that dispositions are causes they take dispositions to be actual properties.[12]

Molnar has argued on the actuality of dispositions based on the premise that a disposition is a cause; a premise I claim that has not been sufficiently argued. He says, 'What is not actual cannot be a cause or any part of a cause. Merely possible events are not actual, and that makes them causally impotent. This suffices to show that powers are not to be equated with mere possibilities. The claim that powers are causally potent has strong initial plausibility' (Molnar 2006: 101). Further he argues for the dispositional theory of causation in which he makes two very important points. First, that causation is something that is intrinsic to the system of relata. Second, the essence of causation is the generative behaviour of objects that is governed by properties and further claims that causation is a natural kind. One can easily see through the circularity inherent in such an argument in the following manner. 'Powers are actual because they are causal. When Molnar says they are actual he is committing their actuality as properties. In fact he explicitly mentions that "powers are actual properties"' (2006: 58).

They are causal because the essence of causality lies in their being governed by properties.

Information and teleology

Tetens (1989) has emphasized the fundamental importance of information in modern science in the same way as energy is important in the conceptual framework of causal process explanation. In understanding the nature of information one generally associates it with linguistic meaning. Tetens claims that such an association is a misconceived one and proposes his concept of information in the context of science and technology as one that is 'applied to the adaptive or goal-directed behaviour of organisms and machines' (1989: 231).

The importance of information in modern science lies in its application to instruments, machines and systems which are goal-directed. To understand the theories of such systems we require a different conceptual framework and not the causal notions of 'force', 'momentum' and 'energy'. One such important notion to understand goal-directed behaviour is that of information. Systems which are goal-directed are referred to as 'teleological systems' by Tetens. Instruments and machines like thermostat, cooling systems, carburettor etc. are typical examples of such systems. What distinguishes these systems is that the changes in the environment do not actually cause it to adapt any states but they provide an occasion to reach a particular goal. Such is the contention of Tetens. In particular I draw upon this idea of a teleologically relevant event to substantiate my thesis. What is this teleologically relevant event? Consider a system S which is in a certain physical state. Let us take the example of a thermostat. A thermostat is a device for the purpose of maintaining a constant temperature, i.e. its goal is directed towards maintaining a constant temperature. There are a number of interconnected sub-units of this system like a temperature sensing unit, a control device which actuates the valve that controls the flow of hot water etc. Physically, the system is in a particular state at a particular time t_1. When a particular event in the environment E occurs like a change in temperature the goal of the system is such as to maintain a constant temperature. But the physical states of the system at time t_1 make it causally impossible for it to maintain that goal of constant temperature. Such an event E is said to be a teleologically relevant event. Such an event 'does not imply that system S is actually capable of adapting its states of behaviour to that event with regard to a given goal T' (1989: 233). In other words, the device is not disposed to a particular behaviour. When Mumford and Molnar invoke the idea of functional characterization to establish a case of dispositional properties, they are, in my opinion, invoking the idea of a power or capacity of a teleological system. But functional characterization is an idea that can be applied only to such goal-directed systems. This is because, as Tetens rightly mentions, the system is endowed with a capacity to adapt its behaviour. It is by design that a system is endowed with such a capacity. It is the design which makes the goals achievable. One cannot use the idea of functional characterization in the case of dispositional properties because these dispositional properties are not goal-directed systems but are causal powers.

Part of my argument against granting the status of properties to dispositions is directed against Mumford's use of the idea of functional characterization in establishing the property status to dispositions. I have shown in my thesis how this idea is irrelevant in the context of disposition and further in this chapter I have attempted to substantiate my claim by drawing upon the work of Tetens on the concept of information.

Notes

1 I visited Free University of Berlin for the Passage to India programme from October to December 2009.
2 Ellis is at pains to emphasize that powers, capacities and propensities that are dispositional in character are real occurrent properties and the scientific essentialists believe them 'not just in a manner of speaking' (2001: 49).
3 A based disposition is one that has a basis in the categorical state of affairs and an unbased or baseless disposition is one where one is not immediately able to identify this state of affairs.
4 Of course, they clearly mention that they remain neutral to metaphysical issues like realism of properties and also that they do not discuss the metaphysics of dispositions.
5 It is for this reason that functionalism is closely associated with the idea of multiple realizability.
6 Dispositions are the causal powers and Molnar uses the term as powers to refer to dispositions as real properties (2006). I will be using these two terms interchangeably.
7 Though they have not used the term functionalism or design these ideas are very much present in their illustrations.
8 Mellor has rejected the assumption that the conditional is always of the counterfactual kind (1974).
9 The other features are directedness, actuality, intrinsicality and objectivity.
10 He was responding to such a position held by Robinson.
11 Manner of speaking gives ontological status to something and examples of such confusions are not lacking in other traditions of philosophy.
12 It is basically the Quinean idea that science in the process of revealing the mechanism demystifies the disposition ascription (Mumford 1998: 61).

References

Ellis, B. (2002): *The Philosophy of Nature: A Guide to the New Essentialism*. Montreal, Kingston: McGill-Queen's University Press.

Fara, M. (2009): Dispositions. *Stanford Encyclopedia of Philosophy* (Summer 2009 Edition), Edward N. Zalta (ed.). http://plato.stanford.edu/archives/sum2009/entries/dispositions/.

Mellor, D.H. (1974): In defense of dispositions. *The Philosophical Review* 83: 157–181.
Molnar, G. (2006): *Powers: A Study in Metaphysics*. Oxford: Oxford University Press.
Mumford, S. (1998): *Dispositions*. Oxford: Oxford University Press.
O'Shaughnessy, B. (1970): The powerlessness of dispositions. *Analysis* 31: 1–15.
Prior, E.W., Pargetter, R., and Jackson, F. (1982): Three theses about dispositions. *American Philosophical Quarterly* 19 (3): 251–257.
Tetens, H. (1989): Teleology and the concept of information. *International Studies in the Philosophy of Science* 3: 230–237.

INDEX

adolescents 13, 317, 403–8, 410–11, 413–14
adulthood 135–6, 144–5, 331
agriculture 418–19, 426, 448, 455–6
ahiṃsā 26, 59–75, 80, 86–90, 92, 99–100, 102–4, 108–11; authentic 85, 87, 90
AIE (Alternative and Innovative Education) 339
alterity 1–2, 4, 7, 11–16, 21, 24–6, 28, 257–8; explorations in 1–31; and heterological thinking 11–15
Alternative and Innovative Education (AIE) 339
alternative school 28, 277–8, 286, 289, 293–6
ancient Indian Hindu asceticism 117–19, 121, 131
animal homes 61, 74
animals 27, 59–62, 64–8, 70–1, 73–4, 170–2, 175–82, 228, 230, 337, 381, 394–5; sacrifices 66, 68, 73
anthropology 7, 60, 195, 264, 332, 404, 488
archaeology 194–5, 301, 315
asceticism 27, 48, 115–29, 158; concept of 121–7; cross cultural definitions of 116–17
ascetic reformism 125–7
asrama system 119, 125, 128, 131
authenticity 80, 85–6, 88, 92, 153, 489
authority, cultural 315–16
auto-rickshaw drivers, photographs by 226–49

basic education 95–6, 101, 104–5, 110, 112–13
beef 59, 63–4, 66, 68, 73
belief system 39, 116, 121, 197
Berlin Zoo 27, 170–1, 174, 176, 178–82
boarding schools 263, 318–19, 321, 323, 325
body posture 282, 285–6, 294
Brahmanic Hinduism 38, 40, 42, 47–8
Buddhism 66, 122, 126, 143, 145–6, 253, 380, 406
Buddhist philosophy 142–3

carriers, educational 394–6
caste membership 449, 451
caste system 128–9, 438
children 20–1, 23, 95, 103, 106–10, 133–40, 144–6, 257–8, 286–7, 319–21, 336–42, 368–70, 390–1, 396–7, 427–8; development 318–20; education of 29, 101, 330, 340–1; school-aged 342
climate change 30, 454–65
collective focus 384–5
communality 198–9, 205
communication 15, 20, 22–3, 223, 289, 300, 306, 393, 410; rituals of 23–4
communion 81–2, 89–90
Communist Party of India (CPI) 199–204, 206–9, 211–13
compassion 82, 133, 138–9, 145
conception, educational 109
conflicts, cultural 124, 437–8
conscientization 418–31

INDEX

contact, cultural 11, 16, 124
contemporary societies 97, 216
CPI (Communist Party of India) 199–204, 206–9, 211–13
cultural differences 9, 12, 16, 30, 469
cultural diversity 1–2, 5–9, 11–17, 29–31, 253–6; vs. one-world mentality 5–7
cultural exchange 16, 218, 411
cultural history 193, 205, 207, 306
cultural identity 8, 16, 31, 405–6, 414
cultural norms 441–52
cultural others 412–14
cultures 1, 3–9, 11–14, 17–19, 21–2, 24, 26–7, 134, 173–5, 178, 256–8, 369, 405–7, 480–4, 486–8; : capital 256–8, 437–8; concepts 75, 257; development 2, 15, 125, 406; dominant 5, 164; foreign 2, 11, 13–14, 21, 187, 252; identity formation 403–4, 406; linguistic alterity 251–8; national 4–5, 8, 207–8; non-school 251; phenomena 9, 26; plurality 406–7, 414–15; school 282, 294–5

dharma 26, 38, 40–3, 62, 64–5, 67, 80, 120, 206; gender-inclusive 37, 39, 50–1
differentiation 15–16
disabilities, invisible 362–3
disabled students allowance (DSA) 358
dispositional properties 491–7, 501, 504–5
disposition ascriptions 492, 494, 496, 499–501, 503
dispositions: functional characterization of 491, 497–500; idea of 500–1; information and teleology 503–5; and manifestation 500–3
diversity 2–4, 7–10, 12, 29, 31, 59–60, 253, 312, 317, 319, 350, 354, 369, 473, 475–6; cultural 1–2, 5–9, 11–17, 29–31, 253–6
divine feminine 37–52
drivers, auto-rickshaw 28, 226–8, 240, 250
DSA (disabled students allowance) 358

economic development 330, 341, 418, 455
education 8–9, 16–20, 22, 26–9, 94–8, 101–14, 259, 301–8, 319–20, 338–42, 369–71, 373–4, 389–97, 428–30, 464–5; colonial influences 97–8; compulsory 105, 338; concepts 95, 103, 107, 251, 258, 289, 292, 305, 370; Gandhi's ideas on 94–110; general 105, 363, 374, 392; and human development 16–17; ideas 95, 97–8, 101, 104, 109, 111, 293, 296; indigenous tools, perspective 368–77; institutions 104, 109, 301, 326, 348, 359, 392; intercultural 8, 108; migration and 338–41; non-formal 94, 110; philosophy of 94, 110–11; physical 102, 281; practices 29, 95, 109, 301–2, 307; private 396; privilege of 463–4; processes 339, 342; progressive 95, 109; quality 107, 368; secondary 319; social conflicts and 389–97; spiritual 27, 102, 107; sugarcane migration, impact 330–42; system 2, 20, 27, 29, 101, 106, 282, 296, 301, 319, 348, 389, 392, 437
educational experiences 97, 348–55, 357, 363–4; positive 360, 363–4; of students 347, 350, 354, 362–4
educational plan 103, 105
Education Guarantee Scheme (EGS) 339
EGS (Education Guarantee Scheme) 339
elementary education 105–7, 316, 341, 390–1; progress and challenges in 105–7; universalization of 105, 110, 112
emotions 25, 30, 102, 150, 311, 315, 458–9
employment 333–7, 422, 424
empowerment 20, 30, 352, 418, 420, 422–4, 426, 430–1; approach 424, 427, 430; process of 431; women's 420, 425
entrepreneurs 30, 441, 477
entrepreneurship 441–52; social 477–8
ethnography 303, 315, 332, 487–8

INDEX

Freie Universität Berlin (FUB) 349–51, 354, 359–61, 364
FUB *see* Freie Universität Berlin
functional characterization 491–4, 498–9, 504

GAD *see* Gender and Development
gender 40, 46, 71, 301, 332, 384, 419–21
Gender and Development (GAD) 419, 421–3
generosity 133, 138–9, 142, 145
globalisation 1, 4–9, 12, 14, 29–31, 74, 108, 139, 141, 320, 389, 403–5, 407–14, 442, 449; cultural 406, 411; distrust of 411–12, 414; dynamics of 1, 4, 13; from ethical perspectives 408–11; process 6–7, 11, 29; socialisation and 403–15; theoretical concept of 409–10
global warming 454–65
goal-directed behaviour 504
goddesses 38, 40, 47–52, 167–8
government schools 106, 257, 396; system 396

HDI (Human Development Index) 426
HDR (Human Development Report) 332, 419, 421
health promotion, diversity and 468–78
higher education 326, 347, 349–52, 354, 357, 360–1, 363–4, 392, 394, 480; disabilities in 354, 362–4; institutions 348–50, 352, 354, 358–9, 392; institutions, disabilities in 348–50, 362, 364–5; students with disabilities 347–65
high school students 321–3
himsa, science and routinization 83–5
Hindu culture 47, 50–2
Hinduism 3, 37, 40, 44, 50, 52, 59–71, 73–4, 111, 123, 151, 164, 253–4, 406; vegetarianism in 64–6, 71, 73
Hindu women 37, 40, 49, 51
holistic approach 102–3, 105, 109, 370, 424
HRD *see* Human Resource Development
human beings, ideal 96, 99–101, 103, 108–9

Human Development Concept (HDC) 419
Human Development Report (HDR) 332, 419, 421
Human Resource Development (HRD) 112, 419
hybridity 15–16

ideal human being 99–101
ideal teacher 103–4
IEA (International Energy Agency) 455
inclusive education 29, 368–70, 373, 375–7
independence, political 85–6, 98
India: asceticism 115–17, 121, 127, 129, 131; auto-rickshaw drivers 226, 241; civilization 198; culture 4, 29, 70, 97, 187–9, 194, 406, 434; economy 341, 437, 448, 456; education system 97, 317; languages 217, 254; middleclass 30, 434, 436–8, 475; middle-class 405, 437, 439; migration in 334; philosophy 146, 380, 385; population 254, 403, 405, 436; risk mentality 443, 447, 451–2; school in 28, 326; schools 2, 28, 277, 296, 303
Indian People's Theatre Association's Central Squad (IPTA CS) 27, 197–212
innovative behaviour 441–3
inquiry learning 22–3
interculturality: national culture and 4
intercultural learning 22
internal migration 330, 333–4, 342
interviewee 305, 307, 413, 435, 444–51
interviews 163, 168, 201, 210, 213–14, 278, 292, 304–5, 307, 430, 434–5, 443–5, 447–9, 451–2, 472
Inyoka, Nyota 187–94
IPCC (Intergovernmental Panel on Climate Change) 454, 456

Jainism 66–7, 122, 126, 253, 406

Kali's daughters 37–52
Khanna, Madhu 38
knowledge 384; discursive 301, 304,

509

INDEX

306, 308–9; implicit 407–8, 411, 414; indigenous 481, 483, 485–6; local 458, 481, 483; social 407–8
Kochi-muziris-biennale 221–3

languages 4–5, 20, 22, 28, 81, 153–6, 198–9, 202, 224, 252–9, 277, 305–7, 314–16, 406, 413
language teaching 5, 306–8
learning 1–2, 7, 13, 16–24, 28, 31, 107, 289–90, 293, 295, 350, 369, 371, 373–5, 377; inquiry 22–3; intercultural 9, 21–3, 31; mimetic 21–2, 256–8; multimodality of 20; for peace 17–18; rituals of 23–4; social 95; for sustainable development 18–20
linguistic alterity: culture 251–8
Linnaeus, Carolus 171–2

Manusmṛti 67–9
MDGs *see* Millennium Development Goals
mental health, social dimensions of 468–73
metaphysical presuppositions 134, 141, 144
middleclass 434–9; history 436–7
migrant children 335, 339–42; education of 331, 340, 342
migration 332–3, 342; internal and seasonal 333–4; national census and national sample survey 334–5; theoretical framework of 331–2
Millennium Development Goals (MDGs) 338, 420
mimetic learning 1, 20–2, 256–8, 291
modern education 137, 142–3
modernity 12, 79, 81–3, 85, 93, 134, 142–4, 300, 302, 484–7
moral education 108
morality 41, 81–2, 116
movement: cultural 203, 208; religious 125–6; women's 211, 425, 427
MPSHY (Mahatma Phule Sikshan Hami Yojna) 340–1
multimodality: of learning 20

Nai Talim 104–5
national culture: interculturality and 4
national education 104, 111
National Institute of Advanced Studies (NIAS) 250, 305, 307, 315
National Institute of Open Schooling (NIOS) 296
National Sample Survey (NSS) 29, 331, 334–5
neo-sociological imagination 484–6
NIAS *see* National Institute of Advanced Studies
Ninasam 218–21
NIOS (National Institute of Open Schooling) 296
non-governmental organisation (NGOs) 340–1, 421, 427–8, 477, 481
non-violence 60, 62–3, 68–70, 73–4, 80, 87–90, 92, 94, 99–100, 102, 104, 109–11, 134, 145, 219
norms, cultural 28, 441, 443, 452
NSS *see* National Sample Survey

one-world mentality *vs.* cultural diversity 5–7

Pad.ma, internet database 216–18
peace: education 108; learning for 17–18
pedagogy 22, 316, 370, 379, 382–3, 480–3, 485–6, 489; perception and 379–80; tacit logics 383
peer groups 319, 361–3
perception 12–13, 20, 28–9, 39, 52, 74, 222, 225, 252, 256, 301, 312–14, 379–88, 457–9, 462–4; and inference 380–3; pedagogy and 379–80
personality, non-violent 101, 103, 107, 109–10
perspectives: anthropological 7, 404; cultural 393, 412
photographic records 189–90, 194
photographs preferred 229, 232–3, 236, 239, 241, 250
photography 131, 187, 190, 194–6, 264–5
photomontage: montaging contexts 192–3; montaging movement 191–2; montaging pictures 190–1

510

INDEX

policies, educational 348, 369–70, 374, 392
political dimensions 396, 422, 424–5
Political Thought of Mahatma Gandhi 93, 112
poverty alleviation policies 441–52
practices, positive 468–9, 473, 477
primary schools (PS) 106, 257, 302–3, 314, 369, 391
problems, social 252, 481–3, 485–6
processes: decision-making 421–4; educational 252, 257, 319, 374; pedagogical 379
processionary becomings 135–7, 144
production, cultural 217, 223, 393
programme, educational 105, 109, 368
property status 492–3, 495, 499, 501, 505
PS *see* primary schools
Public Report of Basic Education in India (PROBE) 105
pupils 28–9, 263–8, 270, 272, 278–97, 305–9, 311–14, 389; individual 282, 285, 295
pupil–teacher ratio, high 105–6

quality education process 340
questioning the text 482

realization 8, 18, 20, 79, 81, 86–92, 99–100, 105, 118, 447
religion 3–4, 26, 60, 63, 66, 70, 96, 99, 130–2, 150, 153, 156–7, 193–4, 252–4, 487; concepts 26, 59, 72
renunciation 44, 89, 100, 118–19, 121–3, 131
research, sociocultural 407
research interests 386
resources, financial 355, 358, 361
Right to Education Act (RTE) 3, 105–6, 112–13, 331, 338, 340–2, 370
risk cultures 30, 442
risk response 458–9
risk-taking 441–52; abilities 449–50; behaviour 441–3, 447, 449, 451
ritual elements 282, 289, 294–6
ritualizations 2, 23–4

rituals 15, 20–1, 23–5, 44, 47, 265–6, 281–2, 293–6, 316, 319, 371, 374, 376, 482, 486
role models 49, 51, 257, 439, 463–5
RTE *see* Right to Education Act

sacred cow 26, 59–75; Hinduism and 61–5
sacrifice 46, 63, 66, 68, 73, 104, 126, 163–4, 167
sadhus 127–8
Sakhar Shalas 29, 331, 340–2
samnyasa upanishads 121–3
Sarva Shiksha Abhiyan (SSA) 105, 112, 339–40
sarvodaya 26, 98–9, 103–4, 109
SAS (Sri Aurobindo Society) 304–7
satyagraha 97, 99, 108, 110–11
schizophrenia 30, 468–9, 471–3
school community 296, 369, 376
school culture 22, 277, 283, 285–6, 294, 296–7, 301; official 283, 294; respective 295
school environment 28, 317–18, 321, 323, 326; impact of 318
schools 28–30, 103, 263, 266–9, 277–83, 287–96, 302–3, 305, 307–12, 317–26, 338–42, 376, 389–91, 414, 427–8; environment, impact of 317–26; ethnographical research 277–97; governmental 340, 342, 396; philosophical 173, 386–7; private 265, 307, 376, 396; pupils, discipline 263–75; rituals 23, 31; summer 255, 259, 468, 476; system 28, 277, 296, 317, 339
school textbooks 315–16
science 80, 83–4, 89–90, 92–3, 143, 172–3, 259, 264, 288, 290, 454, 456, 488, 491, 503–4
seasonal migration 29, 330–1, 333–4, 336, 338–42
sectors, educational 396–7
self-conception 6, 306–7, 387
self-confidence 209, 431
self-development 26, 302, 434–5
self-education 28, 261, 304
Self Employed Women's Association (SEWA) 425

511

INDEX

self-governance 86, 199
self-image 383–4
self-knowledge 11, 26, 80, 85, 89–90
self-reform 26, 80, 85, 89–90
self-responsibility 292
self-transformation 90, 98, 104, 109
separateness 26, 80–3, 85, 87
SEWA (Self Employed Women's Association) 425
social anthropology 480–9
socialisation 22, 42, 318–19, 403–5, 414, 486; of adolescents 405–7; factors of 318–20; : globalisation and 403–15; processes 404, 414
social justice 17–20, 31, 420, 468, 476
social norms 441–52
social practices 301, 316, 470–1, 480, 483, 486, 488
social sciences 25, 30, 114, 136, 251, 255–6, 259, 281, 288, 312–13, 429, 481, 483, 486–7, 489
social structures 17, 23, 40, 42, 44, 133, 135, 137, 144, 216, 393, 408, 418, 427, 483–5
social studies 103, 483, 488
societal development 1, 5, 301
society healthy 133–5, 144, 375
sociocultural context 404, 406
sociological texts 486
Sri Aurobindo Society (SAS) 304–7
Stree Mukti Sanghatana (SMS) 30, 427–30
student integration 348, 363
students: disabled 29; educated 462–3; empowerment of 349; female 314, 474; graduate 476; international 413; self-immolations of 392; young Indian 320
students with disabilities: findings of study 352–63; policy, implications for 364–5; research design and methodology 350–2
subculture 295–6
sugarcane cutters, Maharashtra 335–8
support services 348–50, 353–5, 361, 363–4
sustainability, learning for 19–20

sustainable development, learning for 18–20
Sustainable Development Goals (SDGs) 1
swadeshi 85–9
swaraj 26, 80, 85–9, 91, 98, 104, 109, 198
Syrian Christian Society 147–67
systems, writing 253–5

Tantra 38, 44–6, 50–2
Tantric goddesses 37–52
Tantric philosophy 39
tantrika 48
Tata Institute of Social Sciences (TISS) 94, 111, 114, 429–30, 468
teacher–student ratios, high 391
teaching 19, 22, 24, 98–9, 101, 103–7, 109–10, 151, 277, 289, 291–2, 301–3, 305–8, 311, 313
texts, anthropological 482, 485
Tibetan–Buddhist child monks 133–45
TISS see Tata Institute of Social Sciences
transgression 15–16
treasure of life, hard work and 300–14
tribes 4, 63, 115, 481–2, 487, 489; scheduled 336, 487

UNDP (United Nations Development Programme) 419, 426
United Nations Development Programme (UNDP) 419, 426
Upanishads 27, 65–6, 119, 122–3, 126

values, cultural 403, 437, 442, 447
vegetarianism 73–5

Woman and Development (WAD) model 421–3
womanhood
Woman in Development (WID) model 421–3
women 39–40, 43–4, 51; and development 425; empowerment of 420; help 30, 418; ritual roles of 50; situation of 425, 427
work 104–6, 153–4, 187–9, 200–3, 208–11, 217, 219–22, 224–5, 336–8, 358–9, 362–4, 426–30, 447–8,

450–2, 468–71; cultural 200, 208
World Bank 389, 405, 421, 426
worship 41, 50–1, 66, 69–70, 127, 162, 191

yoga 27, 100, 116–17, 119–21, 123, 128, 283–5, 485

zoos 170–82; history of 170–1